MYTH, LE...
FOLKLORE SERIES

Northern Mythology
*from Pagan Faith to Local Legends*

This frontispiece, representing the scene described in
the note on p. 101, is from a copy in Canciani,
Leges Barbarorum. The original is in a
manuscript of Snorri's Edda.

# NORTHERN MYTHOLOGY

## from Pagan Faith to Local Legends

Compiled from original and other sources by
**Benjamin Thorpe**

With an Introduction by
JACQUELINE SIMPSON

**WORDSWORTH EDITIONS**
*in association with*
**THE FOLKLORE SOCIETY**

Where there is anachronistic use of language or punctuation
likely to be misunderstood by the general reader, some small
changes have been made to the original text of this book.

This edition published 2001 by Wordsworth Editions Limited
Cumberland House, Crib Street, Ware, Hertfordshire SG12 9ET
in association with FLS Books, The Folklore Society,
c/o The Warburg Institute, Woburn Square, London WC1H 0AB

Editor FLS Books: Jennifer Chandler

ISBN 1 84022 501 7

Typeset by Antony Gray
Printed and bound in Great Britain by
Mackays of Chatham plc, Chatham, Kent

This exciting new series is made possible by a unique partnership between Wordsworth Editions and The Folklore Society.

Among the major assets of The Folklore Society is its unparalleled collection of books, in the making since 1878. The library and archives have, over the years, formed an invaluable specialist resource. Now, Wordsworth Editions, which is committed to opening up whole areas of culture through good-looking, good-value books and intelligent commentary, make these riches widely available.

Individual introductions by acknowledged experts place each work in historical context and provide commentaries from the perspective of modern scholarship

PROFESSOR W. F. H. NICOLAISEN
*President, The Folklore Society*

# Introduction

Readers who bought Benjamin Thorpe's *Northern Mythology* in 1851 would have known that this was the work of an eminent scholar of Anglo-Saxon literature, law and history, the editor and translator of many important texts; his major edition of *Beowulf*, on which he had been working for twenty years, was approaching completion (it appeared in 1855). In *Northern Mythology*, he was turning aside briefly from his own field in order to bring before the English public the most up-to-date findings of some leading contemporary Continental writers on the myths and folklore of the northern Germanic nations – that is, the four Scandinavian countries, Germany itself, Holland, and the Flemish-speaking part of Belgium.

Modern readers, however, are likely to be puzzled by Thorpe's choice and presentation of material. For the first two hundred pages or so of Volume I, he alternates between recounting the chief myths of Northern paganism, and giving a commentary on the etymology of the names of all gods and goddesses, giants, elves, dwarfs, animals, objects and places mentioned in them. Here Thorpe, like all subsequent students of Nordic myth, draws his material from two major medieval sources. The first is a collection of twenty-nine anonymous Icelandic poems about gods and heroes that Thorpe calls *Saemund's Edda* (following a mistaken theory as to the identity of the compiler), but which is more correctly called the *Poetic Edda* or the *Elder Edda*; some of these poems were composed before the conversion of Iceland (in AD 999), though the manuscript preserving them was written down only in the thirteenth century. The second source is a systematic retelling of the myths and hero-legends written *c.*1270 by a learned Icelander named Snorri Sturluson, which is correspondingly known as Snorri's *Edda*, *Prose Edda*, or *Younger Edda*. Thorpe occasionally refers to a third work, the *Gesta Danorum*, a history of Denmark written in Latin *c.*1205 by the cleric Saxo Grammaticus, some sections of which contain elaborated and partly distorted versions of myths.

In the final section of Volume I ('Epitome of German Mythology'), and throughout Volumes II and III, Thorpe turns to a very different and far more recent form of evidence, which he terms 'popular traditions and superstitions' – he either did not know, or preferred not to use, the new English word 'folklore', coined only three years before his book appeared. Drawing on material collected and published by scholars in Scandinavia and on the Continent, he translates and comments upon numerous brief but vivid rural legends dealing with encounters between humans and supernatural beings of one sort or another: forest elves, the fairies of fields and farms, changelings, mountain giants, merfolk, the Wild Hunt, the sleeping king beneath the mountain, buried treasures and their magic keepers, sunken towns, dragons, werewolves, witches, magicians, and much else All this is simply presented, and very entertaining; it may also be relatively unfamiliar, for whereas there have been many scholarly studies of the Nordic myths, and popular retellings are legion, only a handful of books on Scandinavian and Germanic folklore have appeared in English. For reasons to be discussed below, folklore from these areas has been undervalued in twentieth-century Britain: a chance to rediscover it is most welcome.

No modern writer, however, would simply set ancient myths and recent folklore alongside one another in this way, and one might well ask what Thorpe's purpose was, and what binds the two elements together. In his Preface to the original edition, he does say that he had at first envisaged only Volume I, but that someone whose judgement he valued had persuaded him to pursue the topic down to more recent times. His contemporaries would have understood the taken-for-granted assumptions which underlay that decision. To relate myth to folklore was to follow the trail blazed by *Deutsche Mythologie*, a highly respected book published in 1835 by Jacob Grimm (the elder and more scholarly of the famous Brothers Grimm). In that work, Grimm had used current beliefs and tales from rural folklore as evidence from which to build up a picture of the long-lost myths of Germany (which does not have such detailed ancient sources as the two Icelandic *Eddas*); he had argued that most of the supernatural elements in folk tradition were lightly Christianised survivals of paganism. But Grimm had limited his discussion to German-speaking countries (and England), setting Scandinavia aside as linguistically and culturally somewhat separate. By bringing folklore within the scope of his *Northern Mythology*, Thorpe was doing for Scandinavia what Grimm had done for Germany; at the same time, he was giving English readers selections from several important collections that had recently appeared.

The influence of Grimm also lies behind the extensive discussions of etymologies in the first part of Thorpe's book, which are likely to seem irrelevant to modern readers. Nowadays, it is archaeology, not etymology, to which we turn for additional insight into early religion. But in Thorpe's time, archaeology barely existed as a scientific undertaking, whereas comparative philology was at the cutting edge of scholarship; links between the various families of European languages (and Sanskrit) were being firmly established by Jacob Grimm and others, and these relationships were seen as crucial to understanding racial and cultural affinities. It had also been shown shown that a deity's name often expressed his or her essential nature (an obvious instance is Thor, whose name is a contraction of *thunor*, 'thunder'), so the consideration of names was an important aspect of this study. Indeed, Thorpe's original plan for the first volume had been merely to translate a linguistic commentary on mythical names that had recently been published by a Danish scholar, N. M. Petersen, but since Petersen's conciseness 'not unfrequently impaired the interest of the narrative', he decided to give the myths in full. So we can struggle bravely through the thorny thickets, confident that in a page or two narrative will resume.

As regards interpretation, Thorpe's guiding principle (shared by most if not all of his contemporaries) is that myths express awed admiration of the physical phenomena of nature; they are about earth and sky, the seasons, mountains, seas, storms, fire, and so forth. But he warns that the principle should not be rigidly applied: for instance, Valkyries who carry the slain up to Valhalla are a poetic image for the glory of death in battle, not personifications of meteors (p. 95). He sees some limited value in the theory, common among medieval writers including Snorri, that early national heroes may have been viewed by later generations as gods, and their wars and exploits turned into myths, but it holds little interest for him. Instead, he sees mythology as a meditation on nature and life, involving philosophical and ethical ideas, and expressed in terms of grandeur and poetic beauty. He tends to stress those elements which come closest to the doctrines of 'higher' religions, e.g. Odin as 'All-Father', and the renewal and reconciliation that follow after the destruction of the world; he even claims to see traces of a belief in 'a higher Being, the Ineffable, the Almighty' whose will set the process of creation in motion (pp. 106). This is in line with a once widespread theory that polytheism is a secondary development in the history of religion, having been preceded by an era of 'primitive monotheism'; in applying it to Nordic religion, he has to rely on a very strained interpretation of a single phrase that would no longer be thought acceptable.

Thorpe's Victorian high-mindedness made him ill at ease with the humour in the myths, which he regarded as an ignorant distortion: 'trivial and almost puerile matter, such as we may imagine the old religious lore to have become, when moulded into the later popular belief' (p. 102). Faced with embarrassing jokes, he bowdlerised them; thus the tug-of-war in which Loki ties his own penis to a goat's beard is referred to simply as 'ludicrous antics with a goat' (p. 42), and Loki's many sexual insults to other gods and goddesses are toned down The fact that Frey's statue at Uppsala had a huge phallus cannot be suppressed, but it remains discreetly concealed in the original Latin of Adam of Bremen's account, and confined to a footnote (p. 28). Sexuality, so central to many current interpretations of paganism, is barely mentioned in Thorpe's.

The folk legends that are given in Volumes II and III are chosen for their supernatural content, on the assumption that this reflects a continuity of belief from pagan times. The introductory essay to Volume II argues that folkloric giants, elves, dwarfs, and water-spirits are personified powers of nature, just as their mythological counterparts had been a thousand years earlier, and are direct descendants of the latter. This may well be true; it is accepted that the introduction of Christianity had much less impact on beliefs about these intermediate beings, non-human yet not divine, than it had on the cults of the gods. But there are also many things in folk legend that are not to be found in mythical texts – the changeling, for example, or the water horse, or the will-of-the-wisp. However, in selecting the stories, Thorpe casts his net far more widely than a strict parallelism would require; comparison with modern collections of folk legends from various countries shows that he included almost all the typical story-patterns involving an encounter with the supernatural, whether or not they have demonstrable pagan precedents. In addition, there are interesting sections on folk cures, plant lore, weather lore, rhymed charms, omens, taboos, actions bringing good or bad luck, and so forth, and even some on seasonal customs. These two volumes thus form a very valuable introduction to several categories of Germanic and Nordic folklore that are not easily available to English readers.

From its beginnings, the study of folklore has often been linked to nationalistic sentiment; it was a central tenet of Romanticism that the peasantry, by their closeness to nature and their poetic response to it, embodied the true 'national soul' or 'racial soul'. As a corollary, differences between the folklore of one ethnic group and another were often greatly exaggerated in the nineteenth century; this remained the case among popular writers throughout the twentieth, even though comparative re-search has proved that much folklore is shared internationally, with only minor regional variations. In Britain, Victorians were well aware that our folklore must come from diverse sources, in view of the complex early history of this nation: some stressed the Celtic contribution, and others the Germanic elements brought by the Anglo-Saxons and reinforced, in some areas, by Scandinavian settlers. It was recognised that Celtic regions such as Ireland, Wales and the Scottish Highlands were particularly rich in folklore, and collectors tended to concentrate their efforts there, but nobody would have denied that Anglo-Saxons had had their folklore, too, without needing to borrow from Celts. But in the twentieth century, the balance has been upset by excessive reverence for a glamorised, idealised 'Celtic tradition', and a corresponding widespread neglect of Germanic and Nordic lore. There is, of course, a socio-political explanation for this: after two World Wars, and especially after the gross exploitation of myth and heroic imagery by the Nazis, Germanic folklore carries a good many unwelcome associations. But the time is ripe now for a reassessment, and Thorpe's book is an excellent starting point for setting British traditions in a Continental European context.

One of the great pleasures of reading folklore is to recognise familiar beliefs and stories as they reappear, in slightly varying form, from one country to another. We are, indeed, better equipped to do so than Thorpe was, back in 1852. At that period, the vast majority of British traditions were still uncollected and unprinted, so although he could observe that 'many of the traditions and superstitions of England and Scotland have their counterparts in Scandinavia and the north of Germany', he could cite only a few scattered parallels to prove the point, for instance, the legend of Wayland's Smithy (p. 311). A generation or two later, however, folklore had become an important field of study in Britain, and though much energy was devoted to theoretical discussion, collection and publication of data was undertaken, too. Surveys of specific English regions were produced, which have been of lasting value: S. O. Addy's *Household Tales with Other Traditional Remains* (1895), Charlotte Burne's *Shropshire Folk-Lore* (1883), William Henderson's *Folk-Lore of the Northern Counties of England and the Borders* (1866), and Ella Leather's *The Folk-Lore of Herefordshire* (1912) are among the best-known examples of the genre. There was a further crop of English regional studies in the later twentieth century, adding recent fieldwork to information from older sources; examples are Enid Porter's *Cambridgeshire Customs and Folklore* (1969), Jacqueline Simpson's *The Folklore of Sussex* (1973), Kingsley Palmer's *Oral Folktales of Wessex* (1973), and Roy Palmer's *The Folklore of Leicester and Rutland* (1985). A very valuable work is Katharine Briggs, A *Dictionary of British Folk-Tales in the English Language* (4 vols., 1970–1), which reprints a wealth of material from earlier books; the two volumes of Part B are devoted to local legends, thematically arranged. A smaller sample, but with useful commentary, is in Jennifer Westwood, *Albion: A Guide to Legendary Britain* (1985). There is thus ample material available for comparison with the Scandinavian and German tales Thorpe translated, while the *Dictionary of Superstitions* by Iona Opie and Moira Tatem (1989) provides a firmly documented basis for comparing superstitious beliefs.

Much of what Thorpe has to say in Volume I, though by no means inaccurate, is now seen to be a somewhat limited and dated mid-Victorian approach to the study of mythology. But the material assembled in Volumes II and III is still of interest and relevance today.

JACQUELINE SIMPSON, MA, D.Lit
*Secretary, The Folklore Society*

## ABBREVIATIONS AND REFERENCES

Thorpe refers to the *Elder* (*Poetic*) *Edda* and the *Younger* (*Prose*) *Edda* as 'Saemund's Edda' and 'Snorri's Edda' respectively. *Gylfaginning* and *Skáldskaparmál* are sections within the latter, and *Ynglingasaga* is another work by Snorri, about early kings of Norway, which contains mythological matter. He often cites poems in the *Elder Edda* by their individual titles, the most important being *Grímnismál*, which describes the origin of the world, Valhalla, and the homes and treasures of the gods; *Lokaglepsa* (now called *Lokasenna*), an exchange of insults between Loki and various gods and goddesses: *Vafprúodismál*, a contest in mythological knowledge between Odin and a giant; and *Völuspa*, describing the creation, destruction and rebirth of the world. The stanza numbering he gives may not always match those in modern editions.

There are frequent references (often abbreviated) to:

Afzelius, A.A., *Swenska Folkets Sago-Häfder* (11 volumes, of which the first appeared in 1844).

Asbjørnsen, P. Chr., *Norske Huldreeventyr og Folkesagn*, 1845–8.

Faye, Andreas, *Norske Folke-Sagn*, Christiana, 1844.

Grimm, Jacob, *Deutsche Mythologie*, 1835 (2nd ed. 1844); usually as 'Grimm D.M.'.

Grimm, Jacob and Wilhelm, *Kinder- und Hausmärchen*, 1st ed. 1812–15; usually as 'Grimm K. and H. M.' This is the work known in English as *Grimms' Fairytales*.

Grimm, Jacob and Wilhelm, *Deutsche Sagen*, Berlin 1816–18; usually as 'Grimm D.S.'.

Keightley, T., *The Fairy Mythology*, London 1828.

Keyser, R., *Nordmaendenes Religionsforfatning i Hedendommen*, 1847.

Kuhn and Schwartz, *Norddeutsche Sagen, Märchen und Gebräuche*, Leipzig, 1848.

Magnusen, Finn, *Priscae Veterum Borealium Mythologiae Lexicon*. 1828; usually as 'Lex Myth'.

Mullenhof, *Sagen, Märchen, und Lieder der Herzogthümer Schleswig, Holstein und Lauenburg*, Kiel, 1845.

Müller, W., *Geschichte und Systeme der altdeutschen Religion*, 1844.

Petersen, N. M., *Nordisk Mythologi*, Copenhagen 1849.

Saxo Grammaticus, *Gesta Danorum* (1202).

Thiele, J. M., *Danske Folkesagn*, Copenhagen, 1818–23.

Wolf, P., *Niederländische Sagen*, Leipzig, 1843.

## FURTHER READING IN ENGLISH

### Mythology and Heroic Legends

Davidson, H. R. E., *Scandinavian Mythology*, 1982.

Davidson, H. R. E., *Viking and Norse Mythology*, 1996.

Faulkes, A., *Snorri Sturluson: Edda*, London, 1987.

Finch, R. G., *The Saga of the Volsungs*, Edinburgh and London, 1965.

Page, R. I., *Norse Myths*, London, 1990.

Saxo Grammaticus, *Gesta Danorum*, transl. Peter Fisher and H. R. E. Davidson, London, 1979.

Stallybrass, J. S., *Teutonic Mythology* (4 vols.), London, 1880–1900: reprint New York, Dover eds. 1966. A translation of the fourth edition of Jacob Grimm's *Deutsche Mythologie*.

Turville-Petre, E. O. G., *Myth and Religion of the North*, London, 1964.

### Folk Legends

Christiansen, R. Th., *Folktales of Norway*, London, 1964.

Kvideland, R., and Sehmsdorf, H. K., *Scandinavian Folk Belief and Legend*, Minneapolis and Oxford, 1988.

Lindow, J., *Swedish Legends and Folktales*, Berkeley and London, 1978.

Simpson, J., *Icelandic Folktales and Legends*, London, 1972.

Simpson, J., *Scandinavian Folktales*, London, 1980.

Simpson, J., *The Danish Legends of E. T. Kristensen* (forthcoming).

Ward, D., ed. and transl., *The German Legends of the Brothers Grimm* (2 vols.), London, 1981. A translation of the Grimms' *Deutsche Sagen* with full commentary.

West. J., *Faroese Folktales and Legends*, Lerwick, 1980.

# Contents

# NORTHERN MYTHOLOGY
## VOLUME I

*Northern Mythology and Illustrations*

TO THE RIGHT HONOURABLE FRANCIS,

EARL OF ELLESMERE, VISCOUNT BRACKLEY,

A TRIBUTE OF RESPECT FROM THE EDITOR

# Preface

Northern literature, more particularly that branch of it which is connected with the early times and antiquities of Scandinavia and the north of Germany, having of late become an object of increasing interest in many parts of Europe, the idea seemed to me not unreasonable that a work, comprehensive yet not too voluminous, exhibiting the ancient mythology and principal mythologic traditions of those countries, might be found both useful and entertaining not only to the lover of Northern lore at home and to the English traveller over those interesting lands, but also to the English antiquary, on account of the intimate connection subsisting between the heathenism of the Germanic nations of the Continent and those of his own Saxon forefathers, manifest traces of which are to be found in the works of our earliest chroniclers and poets. It was under this impression that the present work was undertaken.

The first, or purely mythologic, part was originally intended to consist of a mere translation of the 'Asalaere' of Professor N. M. Petersen of Copenhagen, but on comparing the several myths[1] as given in that work with the text of the two *Eddas*, it appearing that the conciseness observed

1 I use the term *myth* rather in the sense of *legend* or *fable* than in the signification now more usually attached to it, that of supposing each divinity a personification of the powers of nature, a theory which assumes a degree of mental culture to have existed among the early settlers in the North wholly incompatible with all we know concerning them. As equally applicable here, I will venture to repeat my own words used on a former similar occasion: 'In these meagre traditions exist, I firmly believe, faint traces of persons that once had being and of actions that once took place; but that they generally require a *mythic* interpretation, is to me more than questionable.' (Lappenberg's *England*, i, p. 98.)

Much more consistent with probability I consider the view taken by the Revd A. Faye, but to which he does not seem to adhere (see Introduction to vol. ii, p. xii), which is the converse of the theory before-mentioned, viz. 'that unacquaintance with nature and her powers, combined with the innate desire of finding a reason for and explaining the various natural phenomena, that must daily and hourly attract the attention of mankind, has led them to seek the causes of these phenomena in the power of beings who, as they supposed, had produced them:

*continued*

by Professor Petersen, and which he, no doubt, found necessary to his object,[1] not infrequently impaired the interest of the narrative, I resolved, while following the plan of the 'Asalaere', to have recourse to the Eddas themselves, and exhibit the several fables or myths unabridged, in all their fullness, as they appear in those authorities.

The interpretation of these myths, forming the second part of the first volume, is, with slight exceptions, from the work of Professor Petersen, though considerably abridged, particularly as regards the etymological portion, which, if given at length, could hardly have failed of being tedious to the majority of readers in this country, and the more so as much of it is necessarily based on conjecture; an objection from which, I fear, that which is here given will be pronounced not wholly free. With this deduction, Prof. Petersen's illustrations, as contained in the 'Asalaere', and in his more recent valuable work on the same subject,[2] have in general been adopted, as bearing, at least in my judgement, a nearer resemblance to probability than any others with which I am acquainted; though manifesting, perhaps, too strong a tendency to the mythic theory, from which I have already ventured to express my dissent. A small, though estimable work, by Professor Keyser of Christiania, has also been frequently and not unprofitably consulted.[3]

That many of the Northern myths are after all densely obscure is a lamentable fact; they were probably not much less so to the Northern pagans themselves, whose forefathers, it may reasonably be supposed, brought with them no great stock of recondite lore from the mountains of central Asia to their present settlements in Scandinavia. Some portion of their obscurity may, however, be perhaps ascribed to the form in which they have been preserved; as even in Saemund's Edda, their oldest source, they appear in a garb which affords some ground for the conjecture that the integrity of the myth has been occasionally sacrificed to the structure and finish of the poem; while in the later Edda of Snorri their corruption is,

---

Like 'the poor Indian, whose untutor'd mind
Sees God in clouds or hears him in the wind.'

'. . . These phenomena were too numerous and various to allow the ascribing of them to a single being, and therefore a number of supernatural beings were imagined, whose dangerous influence and pernicious wrath it was sought to avert by sacrifices and other means.'

1　The 'Asalaere' forms a part only of the work Danmarks Historie i Hedenhold, 3 vols, small 8vo.

2　N. M. Petersen, Nordisk Mythologi, Forlaesninger, Köbenhavn, 1849, 8vo.

3　R. Keyser, Noldmaendenes Religionsforfatning i Hedendommen, Christiania, 1847, 12mo.

in several instances, glaringly evident, some of them there appearing in a guise closely bordering on the ludicrous;[1] a circumstance, perhaps, ascribable, at least in part, to the zeal and sagacity of the Christian missionaries and early converts, who not unwisely considered ridicule one of the most efficacious methods of extirpating the heathenism that still lingered among the great mass of the people.

But the myths of the Odinic faith were doomed to undergo a yet greater debasement; their next and final degradation being into a middle-age fiction or a nursery tale, in which new dress they are hardly recognisable. A few instances of such metamorphoses will be found in the course of the work, and more are to be met with in the popular tales of Scandinavia, Germany, the Netherlands and Italy.[2]

But besides these, and apparently of equal if not higher antiquity, there are many traditions and superstitions which cannot be connected with what we know of the Odinic faith. These, it may not unreasonably be conjectured, are relics of the mythology of the Fins and other primitive inhabitants of Scandinavia, who were driven northwards or into the mountain-recesses by Odin and his followers, and in whom and in their posterity we are to look for the giants (jotnar, jaetter, jutuler, etc.), the dwarfs and the elves, with whom the superstition of later times peopled the woods, the hills, the rivers and mountain-caverns of the North.

Thus far I have spoken solely of the mythology and early traditions of the three northern kingdoms, and with these it was originally my intention to close the work, but at the suggestion of one, whose judgement I hold in no light estimation, I was induced to continue my labour by adding to it a selection of the principal later popular traditions and superstitions of Scandinavia, North Germany and the Netherlands; and thus present to the reader a view of Germanic mythology and popular belief from the north of Norway to Belgium, and from the earliest times down to the present. To many – should my book, unlike its predecessors, fortunately fall into the hands of many – this will, perhaps, be regarded as not the least interesting part of it, from the circumstance of its supplying matter for comparison with the popular superstitions and usages of our own country, to not a few of which those here recorded will be found closely to correspond. To the

---

1   See Thor's visit to Utgarda-Loki (p. 50), and Loki's pranks to make Skadi laugh (p. 40).
2   See Andreas Faye, *Norske Folke-Sagn*, Christianna, 1844; J. M. Thiele, *Danske Folkesagn*, Copenhagen, 1818–23; A. A. Afzelius, *Svenska Folkets Sago-Häfder*, 1844; Jacob and Wilhelm Grimm, *Kinder- und Hausmärchen*, 1812–15, henceforward K. and H. M., Wolf's *Niederländische Sagen*, Leipzig, 1843; the Pentamerone of Basli, etc., etc.

ethnographer the subject cannot be one of indifference, when even the general reader cannot fail of being struck by the strong similarity and often perfect identity of the traditions and superstitions current in countries far remote from each other and without any known link of connection. That many of the traditions and superstitions of England and Scotland have their counterparts in Scandinavia and the north of Germany, can easily be accounted for by the original identity of, and subsequent intercourse, as friends or foes, between the several nations; but when we meet with a tradition in the far North, and a similar one not only in the south of Germany, but in the south of France, and even in Naples, according to what theory of the migration of peoples are we to explain the phenomenon? One inference may, however, be drawn with tolerable certainty, viz. the great antiquity of many of these legends, some of which are, indeed, traceable to Hebrew and Hindu sources.[1]

By way of introduction to the matter contained in the third volume, I have given in the Appendix at the end of this volume, a brief sketch, chiefly from the work of William Müller,[2] of the old German mythology, so far as it appears unconnected with the Scandinavian.

From the great number of traditions contained in the works indicated in their respective places, I have chiefly selected those that seemed to spring from the old mythology, or at least from *an* old mythology, as many of the supernatural beings, of whom we read in the traditions even of the three northern kingdoms, are not to be found in the Odinic system, and probably never had a place in it; but, as we have already said, were the divinities of those earlier races, who, it may be supposed, by intermarriages with their Gothic conquerors and a gradual return to their ancient home, contributed in no small degree to form the great mass of the people. Hence the introduction among and adoption by the later population of these alien objects of veneration or dread.

To facilitate the use of the *Northern Mythology* as much as possible to the general reader, the passages quoted from the *Eddas* and Sagas are rendered literally into English. Of the poetical extracts the versions are alliterative, in humble imitation of the originals.

---

1   Of the German popular superstitions, some may be traced to the Greek and Roman writers: that of the *Bilsen-schnitters*, for instance (see p. 178), is to be found in Apuleius, and the same is probably the case with others. The inference seems to be, that such are not genuine German superstitions, but that the South is their native soil, whence they have been transplanted to Germany or, at least, enrolled as German among the superstitions of that country.
2   Wilhelm Müller, *Geschichte und Systeme der altdeutschen Religion*, Göttingen, 1844, 8vo, in which a great part of Grimm's *Deutsche Mythologie* is given in an abridged form.

With respect to the orthography adopted in the *Mythology*, it may be observed that, in the proper names of most frequent occurrence, the Old Norsk termination *r* (*n*) of the nominative masculine (sometimes feminine), is, in conformity with common custom, usually omitted; and d is generally written instead of the old þ and ð (*th, dh*): as Frey for Freyr, Odin for Odinn, Brynhild for Brynhildr. The Swedish (anciently also Danish) å and its Danish equivalent *aa* are pronounced like *a* in *warm*, or *oa* in *broad*. The pronounciation nearly resembles the German, *j* being pronounced as the English *y*, and *g* being always hard before *i* and *e*, as in *give, get*, and other English words of Anglo-Saxon origin.

BENJAMIN THORPE

# Introduction

To everyone who looks back on his past life, it presents itself rather through the beautifying glass of fancy, than in the faithful mirror of memory; and this is more particularly the case the further this retrospection penetrates into the past, the more it loses itself in obscure images without any definite outline, the more it approaches to the earliest remembrances of childhood, and, in general, the more we strive to give to that which is dark and half obliterated renewed life in our minds. Then does a single incident, which in reality was probably of a very ordinary character, expand itself into a wonderful event, the heart beats, and a longing after they lost peace, the vanished happiness, creates a dream, a state which, independent of man, has no existence, yet has its home deep in his breast. Among nations in the mass the same feeling prevails; they also draw a picture of their infancy in glittering colours; the fewer traditions they have, the more they embellish them; the less trustworthy those traditions are, the more they sparkle in the brilliancy which fancy has lent them, the more the vainglory of the people will continue to cherish, to ennoble and diffuse them from generation to generation, through succeeding ages. Man's ambition is twofold: he will not only live in the minds of posterity; he will also have lived in ages long gone by; he looks not only inwards, but backwards also and no people on earth is indifferent to the fancied honour of being able to trace its origin to the gods, and of being ruled by an ancient race.

He who devotes himself to delineate the state of a people in its earliest times, takes on himself a task of difficulty. He shares with all his predecessors the same feeling, by which the departed attracts, even, perhaps, because it is no more, the very darkness dazzles, because it is so black: they who should guide him are probably blind themselves, and of those who wandered before him, many have, no doubt, taken devious paths.

Every inquiry into the internal condition of a nation must necessarily turn on three points: the land, the people, and the state, but these three are so variously interwoven with each other, that their investigation must resolve itself into several subordinate sections: it must set out with religion, as the element which pervades all, and is itself pervaded by all. We begin, therefore, our undertaking with a most difficult inquiry, a view of the whole mythology of the North, which we shall consider in three sections: 1 the mythic matter; 2 the several ways in which it has been attempted to explain it; 3 an attempt at explanation derived from the matter itself, and founded on the original sources.

# Section One

A view of the mythology of the North begins with the creation. In the beginning of time a world existed in the north called Niflheim (Niflheimr), in the middle of which was a well called Hvergelmir, from which flowed twelve rivers.[1] In the south part there was another world, Muspellheim, (Muspellzheimr),[2] a light and hot, a flaming and radiant world, the boundary of which was guarded by Surt (Surtr) with a flaming sword. Cold and heat contended with each other. From Niflheim flowed the poisonous cold streams called Elivâgar,[3] which became hardened into ice, so that one layer of ice was piled on another in Ginnunga-gap,[4] or the abyss of abysses, which faced the north; but from the south issued heat from Muspellheim, and the sparks glittered so that the south part of Ginnunga-gap was as light as the purest air. The heat met the ice, which melted and dripped; the drops then, through his power who sent forth the heat, received life, and a human form was produced called Ymir,[5] the progenitor of the Frost-giants (Hrímthursar), who by the Frost-giants is also called Aurgelmir, that is, *the ancient mass or chaos*. He was not a god, but was evil, together with all his race. As yet there was neither sand nor sea nor cool waves, neither earth nor grass nor vaulted heaven, but only Ginnunga-gap, *the abyss of abysses*. Ymir was nourished from four streams of milk, which flowed from the udder of the cow Audhumla, a being that came into existence by the power of Surt. From Ymir there came forth offspring while he slept: for having

---

1   Their names are Svavl, Gunnthra, Fiörm, Fimbul, Thul, Slidh, Hridh Sylg, Ylg, Vídh, Leipt, Giöll, which last is nearest to the barred gates of Hel.
2   The word Muspell has disappeared from all the Germanic tongues except the Old-Saxon and the Old High German, where it signifies *fire* at the destruction of the world. See 'Heliand' *passim*, and the fragment on the day of judgement, 'Muspilli', both edited by Schmeller.
3   From el, *a storm*, and vágr (pl. vágar), *river*, *wave*.
4   From ginn, *wide*, *expanded*, occurring only in composition.
5   Ym from ymia, *to make a noise*, *rush*, *roar*. He who sent forth the heat is not Surt, who is only the guardian of Muspellheim, but a supreme ineffable being.

fallen into a sweat, from under his left arm there grew a man and a woman, and one of his feet begat a son by the other. At this time, before heaven and earth existed, the Universal Father (Al-födr) was among the Hrimthursar, or Frost-giants.

The cow Audhumla licked the frost-covered stones that were salt, and the first day, towards evening, there came forth from them a man's hair, the second day a head, the third day an entire man. He was called Buri (the producing); he was comely of countenance, tall and powerful. His son, Bör (the produced), was married to Bestla (or Belsta), a daughter of the giant Bölthorn, and they had three sons, Odin (Odinn), Vili and Ve. These brothers were gods, and created heaven and earth.

Bör's sons slew the giant Ymir, and there ran so much blood from his wound that all the frost-giants were drowned in it, except the giant Bergelmir (whose father was Thrudgelmir (Thrúdgelmir), and whose grandfather was Aurgelmir), who escaped with his wife on a chest (lúdr), and continued the race of the frost-giants. But Bör's sons carried the body of Ymir into the middle of Ginnunga-gap, and formed of it the earth, of his blood the seas and waters, of his bones the mountains, of his teeth and grinders and those bones that were broken they made stones and pebbles; from the blood that flowed from his wounds they made the great impassable ocean, in which they fixed the earth, around which it lies in a circle; of his skull they formed the heaven, and set it up over the earth with four regions, and under each corner placed a dwarf, the names of whom were Austri, Vestri, Northri, Suthri; of his brain they formed the heavy clouds, of his hair the vegetable creation, and of his eyebrows a wall of defence against the giants round Midgard (Midgardr), the middlemost part of the earth, the dwelling-place of the sons of men. They then took the sparks and glowing cinders that were cast out of Muspellheim, and set them in heaven, both above and below, to illumine heaven and earth. They also assigned places for the lightning and fiery meteors, some in heaven, and some unconfined under heaven, and appointed them a course. Hence, 'as it is said in old philosophy', arose the division of years and days. Thus Bör's sons raised up the heavenly discs, and the sun shone on the cold stones, so that the earth was decked with green herbs. The sun from the south followed the moon, and cast her[1] right arm round the heavenly horses' door (the east); but she knew not where her dwelling lay, the moon knew not his power, nor did the stars know where they had a station. Then the holy gods consulted together, and gave to every light its place, and a name to the new moon (Nyi), and to the waning moon (Nithi), and gave names to the morning and the midday,

---

1   In the Germanic tongues, the sun is feminine, the moon masculine.

to the forenoon (undern) and the evening, that the children of men, sons of time, might reckon the years thereafter.

Night (Nótt) and Day (Dagr) were of opposite races. Night, of giant race, was dark, like her father, the giant Nörvi (or Narfi). She was first married to Naglfari, and had by him a son named Aud (Audr) secondly to Anar (or Onar); their daughter was Earth (Iörd); lastly to Delling, who was of the race of the Aesir, and their son was Day, who was fair, bright and beautiful, through his paternal descent. All-father took Night and Day, and gave them two horses and two cars, and placed them in heaven, that they might ride successively, in twenty-four hours' time, round the earth. Night rides first with her horse which is named Hrîmfaxi, that bedews the earth each morn with the drops from his bit. He is also called Fiörsvartnir.[1] The horse belonging to Day is called Skinfaxi, from whose shining mane light beams forth over heaven and earth. He is also called Glad (Gladr) and Drösul. The moon and the sun are brother and sister; they are the children of Mundilföri, who, on account of their beauty, called his son Mâni, and his daughter Sôl; for which presumption the gods in their anger took brother and sister and placed them in heaven, and appointed Sôl to drive the horses that draw the chariot of the sun, which the gods had formed, to give light to the world, of the sparks from Muspellheim. Sôl was married to a man named Glen (Glenur, Glanur), and has to her car the horses Arvakur (the watchful), and Alsvith (the rapid), under whose shoulders the gods placed an ice-cold breeze to cool them. Svalin (the cooling) is the name of a shield that stands before the sun, which would else set waves and mountains on fire. Mâni directs the course of the moon, and regulates Nyi and Nithi. He once took up two children from the earth, Bil and Hiuki (Hviki), as they were going from the well of Byrgir, bearing on their shoulders the bucket Saeg, and the pole Simul. Their father was Vidfinn; they follow Mâni, as may be observed from the earth. There are also two wolves to be mentioned, one of which, named Sköll, follows the sun, and which she fears will swallow her; the other called Hati, the son of Hrodvitnir, runs before the sun, and strives to seize on the moon,[2] and so in the end it will be. The mother of these wolves is a giantess, who dwells in a wood to the east of Midgard, called Jarnvid (Járnvidr), in which those female demons (tröllkonur) dwell called Jarnvids (Járnvidjur). She brought forth many sons, who are giants, and all in the form of wolves. One of this

---

1    Finn Magnusen considers Fiörsvartnir as the name of a second horse belonging to Night, and so of Glad. Finn Magnusen, *Priscae Veterum Borealium Mythologiae Lexicon*, 1828, *sub voce*.

2    That wolves follow the sun and moon is a widespread popular superstition. In Swedish solvarg (sun-wolf) signifies a parhelion. Petersen, op. cit., p. 76.

race, named Managarm, is said to be the most powerful; he will be sated
with the lives of all dying persons; he will swallow up the moon, and
thereby besprinkle both heaven and air with blood. Then will the sun lose
its brightness, and the winds rage and howl in all directions, as it is said:

> Eastward sat the crone
> in the iron wood,
> and there brought forth
> Fenrir's offspring.
> Of these shall be
> one worse than all,
> the moon's devourer
> in a demon's guise,
> Fill'd shall he be
> with the fated's lives,
> the gods' abode
> with the red blood shall stain.
> Then shall the summer's
> sun be darken'd,
> all weather turn to storm.

The father of Winter (Vetur) was called Vindsval, of Summer (Sumar),
Svasud (Svasudr). Both shall reign every year until the gods pass away. At
the end of heaven sits the giant Hraesvelg, in an eagle's garb (arna ham).[1]
From the motion of his wings comes the wind which passes over men.

Thus the first created beings were Ymir and his race, the giants; next
were the gods, who created heaven and earth; for not until these were in
existence, and ready as places of abode for living beings, were the dwarfs
and human race created.[2]

The mighty gods, or Aesir,[3] assembled on Ida's plain (Idavöllr) in the
middle of their city Asgard. There they first erected a court (hof), wherein

---

1   The Shetlanders of the present day are said by Scott, in his *Pirate*, to adjure the
wind under the form of an eagle.
2   Both giants and dwarfs shun the light. If surprised by the breaking forth of day,
they become changed to stone. In the Alvismál, Ving-Thor amuses the dwarf Alvis with
various questions till daylight, and then coolly says to him, 'With great artifices, I tell
thee, thou hast been deceived; thou art surprised here, dwarf! by daylight: the sun now
shines in the hall.' In the Helga Kvitha Hadinga Skatha also, Atli says to the giantess
(nicker) Hrîmgerd: 'It is now day, Hrîmgerd! But Atli hath detained thee to thy life's
perdition. It will appear a laughable harbour mark, where thou standest as a stone-
image.' Saemund's *Edda*, pp. 51, 115.
3   Aesir, pl. of As.

were seats for all the twelve, and a high seat for All-father; also a lofty burgh or hall (havrgr) for the goddesses, called Vingolf. They then constructed a smithy, made hammers, tongs, anvils and, in fine, all other requisite implements. There they worked in metal, stone and wood, and so extensively in the metal called gold that all their household gear was formed of it, whence that age was called the Golden Age. This lasted until it was corrupted by the women that came from Jötunheim, or the giants' world, as it is said:

> The Aesir met
> on Ida's plain,
> altars and temples
> upraised high,
> furnaces constructed,
> forged precious things,
> fashion'd tongs,
> and fabricated tools.
> At dice they played
> in their dwelling joyful;
> rich too they were
> in ruddy gold,
> until thither three
> Thurs-maidens came
> all-powerful
> from Jötunheim.

Then the gods sitting on their thrones held counsel. They considered how the dwarfs had been quickened in the mould down in the earth, like maggots in a dead body:[1] for the dwarfs had been first created,[2] and received life in the carcase of Ymir, and were then maggots; but now, by the decree of the gods, they received human understanding and human bodies, though they dwell in the earth and in stones.[3] Modsognir (Módsognir) was

---

1  For hold, *body*, *dead carcase*, some MSS read blothi, *blood*.

2  According to Snorri's *Edda*, the dwarfs were created after mankind, while in the other *Edda* it is the reverse.

3  In the German tales, the dwarfs are described as deformed and diminutive, coarsely clad and of dusky hue: 'a little black man'; 'a little grey man.' They are sometimes described of the height of a child of four years; sometimes as two spans high, a thumb high (hence Tom Thumb). The old Danish ballad of Eline af Villenskov mentions a 'trold' not bigger than an ant. *Danske Viser*, i, p. 176. Dvergmál (the speech of the dwarfs) is the Old Norse expression for the echo in the mountains. Grimm, J., *Deutsche Mythologie*, op. cit., p. 421.

the chief, the second Durin, as it is said in the Völuspá: 'The holy gods deliberated who should create the race of dwarfs, from Ymir's blood and livid (blue) bones.' The dwarfs of Lofar's race betook themselves from the Rocky Hall (Salar-Steinn) over the earth-field's regions (Aurvángur) to Jora's plains (Jóruvellir).[1] Their several names bear allusion to the subordinate powers of nature in the mineral and vegetable kingdoms, and express the operating power which penetrates the soil, the veins of stone, the sap of plants; also the cold and heat, the light and the colours which are thereby produced.

Men came into existence when three mighty, benevolent gods, Odin, Hoenir and Lodur,[2] left the assembly to make an excursion. On the earth they found Ask and Embla (ash and elm?), with little power and without destiny: spirit they had not, nor sense, nor blood, nor power of motion, nor fair colour. Odin gave them spirit (breath), Hoenir sense, Lodur blood and fair colour. Somewhat less circumstantially, though illustratively, it is related in Snorri's *Edda*, that Bör's sons (Odin, Vili and Ve) walking on the seashore found two trees, which they took up, and created men of them. The first gave them spirit and life; the second, understanding and power of motion; the third, aspect, speech, hearing and sight. The man they called Ask, the woman Embla. From this pair the whole human race is descended, to whom a dwelling was assigned in Midgard.

## Earth and Heaven

The earth is flat and round; about it is the deep ocean. Outermost of all, around the shore, is the giants' abode, Jötunheim or Utgard, against whose attacks the gods raised a bulwark within, around Midgard, formed of Ymir's eyebrows. In the middle of the world, and on the highest spot, dwell the Aesir, in Asgard, where All-father Odin established rulers, who with himself should preside over the burgh and the destinies of men. There is the largest and noblest of all dwellings, Gladsheim (Gladsheimr), and another, roofed with silver, called Valaskiálf, which Odin, in the beginning of time,

---

1   In the later popular belief, the dwarfs are generally called the subterraneans, the brown men in the moor, etc. They make themselves invisible by a hat or hood. The women spin and weave, the men are smiths. In Norway, rock-crystal is called dwarf-stone (dvaergsten). Certain stones are in Denmark called dwarf-hammers (dvaerghamre). They borrow things and seek advice from people, and beg aid for their wives when in labour, all which services they reward. But they also lame cattle, are thievish and will carry off damsels. There have been instances of dwarf females having married and had children by men. Petersen, op. cit., p. 109.

2   Connected with Ger. lodern, *to flame, blaze.*

curiously constructed, and from the throne in which (Hlidskiálf) he looks out over all worlds, and learns the doings of all creatures. 'At the world's southern end there is a hall, the fairest of all and brighter than the sun, which is called Gimli. That will stand when both heaven and earth are past away, and good and upright men will inhabit that place to all eternity. It is, moreover, said that there is another heaven to the south, above this, which is called Andlang, and a third still higher called Vidblain (Vidbláinn), in which last we believe this hall to be; but we believe that only the Light Elves now inhabit those places.' In another hall, as we have already seen, is the abode of the goddesses, which men call Vingolf. Between the giants and the gods flows the river Ifing, on which ice never comes. From Midgard to Asgard leads the bridge Bifröst (the quaking space), known to mortals as the rainbow: it has three colours. The most sacred place or seat of the gods is by the ash Yggdrasil, where they daily sit in judgement. Yggdrasil is the largest and best of trees; its branches spread themselves over the whole world, and tower up above the heavens. It has three roots which reach far and wide. Under one of them is the abode of Hel, the goddess of the dead; under the second dwell the frost-giants; under the third, human beings. Or, according to the prose *Edda*, the first root reaches to the Aesir; the second to the frost-giants, where was formerly Ginnunga-gap, while the third stands over Niflheim, under which is Hvergelmir. This root is constantly gnawed from beneath by the serpent Nidhögg (Nidhöggr). Under the second root is Mimir's well, in which wisdom and genius are concealed. Mimir, the owner of the well, is full of wisdom, because he drinks every morning of the well from the horn Giöll (Giallar-horn). All-father once came, and craved a draught from the well, but got it not before he had given an eye as a pledge; whence it is said that Mimir drinks mead every morning from Valfather's pledge. Under the root which reaches to the Aesir's abode is the sacred fountain of Urd (Urdr), where the gods sit in judgement. Everyday the Aesir ride thither over Bifröst, which is likewise called the Aesir-bridge (Asbrú). The names of the Aesir's horses are as follow: Sleipnir, which is the best, and belongs to Odin, has eight legs, Glad (Gladr), Gyllir, Gler, Skeidbrimir, Silfrintop (Silfrintoppr), Sinir, Gils, Falhofnir, Gulltop (Gulltoppr), Lettfeti. Baldur's horse was burnt with him, and Thor walks to the meeting, and wades through the rivers Körmt and Örmt, and the two Kerlaugs, else the Aesir's bridge would be in a blaze, and the sacred water boil. By the well of Urd there stands, under the ash-tree, a fair hall, from which go three maidens, Urd, Verdandi, and Skulld[1] (past time, present time, and future time). They are called Norns (Nornir); they grave on the

---

1  Skulld the youngest of the Norns, is also a Valkyria.

tablet (shield), determine the life, and fix the destiny of the children of men. But besides these there are other Norns, viz. those that are present at the birth of every child, to determine its destiny. These are of the race of the gods, while some others are of elf-race, and others of the dwarf-kin, or daughters of Dvalin. The good Norns and those of good descent allot good fortune and when men fall into misfortunes, it is to be ascribed to the evil Norns. Mention occurs of the dogs of the Norns.

In the branches of the tree Yggdrasil sits an eagle that knows many things. Between his eyes sits the hawk Vedurfölnir. The squirrel Ratatösk runs up and down the tree, and bears rancorous words between the eagle and the serpent Nidhögg. Four harts run among the boughs and bite its buds; their names are, Dain, Dvalin, Dunneyr and Durathror. In Hvergelmir, under Yggdrasil, there are so many serpents, besides Nidhögg, that no tongue may tell them, as it is said:

> Yggdrasil's ash
> evil suffers
> more than men know of:
> at the side it moulders,
> a hart gnaws it above,
> Nidhögg beneath tears it.
> Under Yggdrasil lie
> unnumber'd snakes,
> more than mindless
> men can conceive.

Those Norns that dwell by the well of Urd take water every day from the spring, which, with the mud that lies about it, they pour over the ash, that its branches may not rot and perish. This water is so sacred, that everything that enters it becomes as white as the film of an eggshell, as it is said in the Völuspá:

> An ash I know
> Yggdrasil named,
> A branchy tree, bedew'd
> With brightest water.
> Thence come the dews
> into the dales that fall:
> ever stands it flourishing
> o'er Urda's fountain.

The dew that falls from its branches on the earth is by men called honeydew, and is the food of bees. Two birds are fed in the well of Urd, called swans, and from them descend the birds of that species.

# War

'It was the first warfare in the world when they (men) pierced Gullveig through with a spear, and burned her in the High one's (Odin's) hall. Thrice they burned her, thrice she was born anew: again and again, but she still lives. When she comes to a house, they call her Heidi (the bright, the welcome), and regard her as a propitious "vala" or prophetess. She can tame wolves, understands witchcraft (seidr), and delights wicked women. Hereupon the gods consulted together, whether they should punish this misdeed, or accept a blood-fine; when Odin cast forth a spear among the people (mankind), and now began war and slaughter in the world. The Aesir-burgh's defences were broken down. The Vanir anticipated war, and hastened over the field. The Valkyriur (choosers of those doomed to fall) came from afar, ready to ride to the gods' people: Skulld with the shield, Skögul, Gunn, Hild, Göndul, and Geir-Skögul. These were Odin's maidens, the Valkyriur ready to ride over the earth, whom he sends to every battlefield, there to choose those that shall fall, and decide the victory. Surrounded by lightnings, with bloody corselets and radiant spears, they ride through the air and on the ocean. When their horses shake their manes, dew falls in the deep valleys and hail in the high forests.'

The Aesir and the Vanir made peace, and reciprocally gave hostages. The Vanir gave to the Aesir Niörd the Rich, whom the wise powers had created in Vanaheim, together with his children, Frey and Freyia. The Aesir, on their part, gave Hoenir, and sent him with Mirmir, for whom in return they received Kvasir, the most prudent among the Vanir. Hoenir was raised to the chieftainship over the Vanir; but in all assemblies where good counsel was required, Mimir was obliged to whisper to Hoenir everything he should say; and in his absence, Hoenir constantly answered, 'Yes, consult now ye others.' The Vanir hereupon, thinking themselves deceived, slew Mimir, and sent his head to the Aesir, which Odin so prepared with herbs and incantations, that it spoke to him, and told him many hidden things.

# The Gods

There are twelve principal Aesir, besides All-father (Al-födr) or Odin, who has his own throne.

The highest among the gods is Odin.[1] He is called All-father, because he

---

1 In Norway, Thor was regarded as the principal deity. In the great temple at Upsala, his image occupied the second place. (Might it not have been the centre?) Among the Swedes, the worship of Frey seems chiefly to have been followed. The Danes, Gothlanders and Saxons appear to have been addicted to the worship of Odin (Woden). Grimm, J., *Deutsche Mythologie*, op. cit., p. 146. In the *Sagas*, Thor is usually named before Odin. Ibid., p. 147. Associated with Hâr and Jafnhâr, Odin appears

is the father of all, gods and men; also Valfather, because all the free that
fall in battle belong to him. They are received into Valhall and Vingolf, and
are called Einheriar. But in the old Asgard he had twelve names, and has
besides many others,[1] every people having given him a peculiar one.[2] In
other words, his agency in heaven and earth is so great and manifold, that
it is expressed by so many various names: as examples may be cited, Alda-
gautr[3] and Alda-födr, *creator* and *father of men*; Vera-tyr, *god of men*;
Val-födr, *father of the slain*, because those that fell in battle came to him;
Sig-födr or Seier-födr, *father of victory*; Herian, *devastator*; Sid-hat (Sid-
höttr), *broad-hat*; Sid-skegg (Sid-skeggr), *ample-beard*; Hângagud, Hânga-
tyr, *god or lord of the hanged*, because the hanged were thought to belong to
him.[4] Other names assumed by Odin are:

**1 Gangrad**   (Gangrádr, Gagnrádr), under which he paid a visit to the
giant Vafthrudnir, the object and particulars of which form the subject of
the eddaic poem, Vafdrudnismál, and are as follow:

Odin imparts to his wife Frigg that he is seized with a strong desire to
visit the all-wise giant Vafthrudnir, for the purpose of contending with him
in the wisdom of ancient times. Frigg endeavours to dissuade him from the
journey, in the belief that no one is able to contend with Vafthrudnir. Odin
then reminds her of his numerous wanderings and trials, and persists in
his resolve to see the habitation of the giant; whereupon Frigg wishes him
a pleasant journey and safe return, and prays that his sagacity may prove
sufficient in his trial of words. Odin then departs, and arrives at the hall of
the giant, in the guise of a traveller, and under the name of Gangrad. Here
he greets the giant, and tells him the object of his coming. Vafthrudnir
answers rather angrily, and gives him to understand that if he prove the
less wise of the two, he shall not leave the hall alive. Odin then informs his
antagonist that, after a long journey, he is come thirsty (after wisdom?) to
his mansion, and in need of a good reception, whereupon the giant desires
him to sit, and the contest begins. The giant then proposes that their

---

under the denomination of Thrithi (Third). *Snorra Edda*, p. 3. In the *Grimnismál* he
assigns to himself all the three names. *Edda Saem.*, p 46.
1   His other names were Herran or Herian, Nikar or Hnikar, Nikuz or Hnikud,
Fiölnir, Oski, Omi, Biflidi or Biflindi, Svidor, Svidrir, Vidrir, Jalg or Jálkr. He is also
called Drauga dróttin, *lord of spectres*.
2   Odin could change his form: his body would lie as dead or asleep, while he, as a
bird or beast, fish or serpent, would in an instant pass into other lands.
3   From alda (of men), and gauta (creator, caster), from gjota, gaut, *to cast* (*metal*).
Professor Munch, cited by Petersen.
4   Connected probably with the myth of his having hung nine nights on a tree.

contest shall be head for head, and all goes on smoothly, each answering the other's questions satisfactorily, until Gangrad asks what Odin whispered in the ear of Baldur before the latter was laid on the pile. Startled, the giant now exclaims: 'No one knows what thou, in the beginning of time, didst whisper to thy son. With death on my lips have I interpreted the wisdom of old and the fate of the gods; with Odin have I contended, with the wise speaker: ever art thou wisest of all!'

The questions are entirely of a cosmogonic or mythologic nature, as may be seen by the numerous quotations from the poem in the course of this section of the present work.

**2 Grimnir**  Why Odin assumed this appellation will be seen in the following story, being the prose introduction to the eddaic poem, *Grimnismál*.

'King Hrödung (Hrödungr) had two sons, one named Agnar, the other Geirröd (Geirrödr). Agnar was ten, and Geirröd eight years old. They once rowed out in a boat, with hook and line, to catch small fish, but the wind drove them out to sea. In the darkness of the night they were wrecked on the seashore, and went on land, where they met with a small farmer, with whom they passed the winter. The farmer's wife brought up Agnar, but the farmer himself took charge of Geirröd, and gave him good advice. In the spring the farmer gave them a vessel, and he and his wife accompanied them down to the shore, where the farmer had a long conversation alone with Geirröd. A favourable wind soon bore them to their father's dwelling. Geirröd, who was foremost in the boat, sprang on shore, and pushed the boat out to sea, saying, "Go hence in the power of the evil spirits" (smyl). He then went home to his paternal habitation, where he was received with welcome, and his father being dead, was made king, and attained to considerable reputation.

'Odin and Frigg were sitting in Hlidskialf, and looking over the whole world, when Odin said, "Seest thou thy foster son Agnar, how he passes his time in dalliance with a giantess in a cave, while Geirröd, my foster-son, is a king ruling over the land?" Frigg answered, "He is so inhospitable that he tortures his guests, when he thinks they are too numerous." Odin said that this was the greatest of falsehoods. They then laid a wager, and Odin resolved on a visit to Geirröd. Frigg now sent her confidential attendant, Fulla, to Geirröd, to advise him to be on his guard, lest the wizard that had arrived in his country should cause his destruction, adding, as a token whereby to know him, that no dog, however fierce, would attack him. That King Geirröd was not hospitable was mere idle talk; he nevertheless caused the man to be seized that the dogs would not assail. He was clad in a grey fur, and called himself Grimnir, but would give no further account of himself, although questioned. To extort a confession, the king had him tortured, by placing him between two fires, where he sat during eight days. Geirröd had a son of ten years, named Agnar after his uncle. This youth went to Grimnir and gave him a hornful of drink, saying that his father had acted unjustly in causing an innocent person to be tortured. The fire had by this time approached so near that Grimnir's fur was singed.' He then sang the mytho-cosmogonic song called *Grimnismál*, in which he enumerates and describes the habitations of the twelve chief Aesir, of which further notice will be found hereafter. The remainder of the poem consists of mythological matter, the substance of which is to be found interspersed throughout the present work. The end of the story is as follows:

'King Geirröd was sitting with his sword half-drawn across his knees, when he heard that it was Odin that was come, whereupon he rose for the purpose of removing him from the fire, when his sword slipt from his hand, in endeavouring to recover which, he fell forwards, and was pierced through with the weapon. Odin then vanished, and Agnar reigned in his father's stead.'

**3 Vegtam** (viator indefessus)   Under this denomination, Odin goes to consult the spirit of a 'vala' that lies buried near the gate of Hel's abode, respecting the fate of Baldur. The substance of this poem is given in the present work.[1]

**4 Hâr, Jafnhâr, Thrithi** (High, Even-high, Third) under which denomin– ation he appears in Snorri's *Edda* as a sort of northern trinity. In *Grimnismál* he assigns all these names to himself.

He was called *Hrafna-gud*, (the ravens' god), because he has two ravens, Hugin and Munin, which he sends forth over the wide world to get intelligence: when they return, they sit on his shoulders, and tell him all they have seen and heard. But he is anxious on account of Hugin, fearing he will not return, and still more so for Munin. As creator of heaven and earth, Odin rules and orders all things: he gives victory and riches, eloquence and understanding, the skaldic or poetic art, manliness and fair wind.

Odin's abode is, as we have said, named Gladsheim (Gladsheimr), with its hall Valhall (Valhöll) radiant with gold, where he daily receives those that fall in arms. The hall's ceiling is formed of spears, it is roofed with shields, and the benches are strewn with coats of mail; before the west door hangs a wolf; and over him an eagle hovers. It is surrounded by a

---

1   There is a beautiful paraphrase of it by Gray, under the title of 'The Descent of Odin'.

roaring river called Thund,[1] and before it is a paling or lattice named Valgrind. It has five hundred and forty gates, through each of which eight hundred men can go abreast. Without the gates of Valhall is the wood Glasir, where the leaves are of red gold. They who from the battlefield come to Odin are called Einheriar, or chosen heroes; their occupation consists in arming themselves, in going out into the court, to fight with and slay each other, but at breakfast-time they ride home to Valhall, perfectly sound, drink beer with the Aesir, and recruit themselves with the flesh of the hog Saehrimnir; for this hog, although boiled every day by the cook Andhrimnir, in the kettle Eldhrimnir, is whole again in the evening. The mead which they drink flows from the udder of the goat Heidrun (Heithrún), that feeds on the leaves of the tree Lerad (Leradr), which stands over Odin's hall. With this mead a drinking-vessel is filled of such capacity that all the Einheriar have wherewith to satisfy themselves. Here they are waited upon by the Valkyriur, who present the mead and have charge of everything belonging to the table. The branches of the tree Lerad are eaten also by the hart Eikthyrnir, from whose horns drops fall into Hvergelmir, of which many rivers are formed, some of which flow through the domains of the gods, others in the neighbourhood of men, and fall from thence to Hel. Odin takes no food, but gives that which is set before him at table to his wolves, Geri and Freki; Odin lives solely on wine. His attendant is his son Hermod (Hermódr), whom he sends on his messages.

**Thor** or **Asa-Thor**, a son of Odin and the earth (Fiörgvin, *the vivifying*; Hlódyn, the *warming*),[2] is the strongest of all the gods.[3] He rules over the

---

1    This interpretation I believe to be borne out by the context of *Grimnismál*, Str. 21, which has manifestly been misunderstood, viz. –

| thytr thund, | *Thund roars,* | árstraumr thikir | *the strong streams seem* |
| unir thiódvitnis | *Thiodvitnir's fish* | ofer mikill | *over great* |
| fiskr flódi í | *plays in the river* | valglaumi at vada | *for the band of the fallen to wade.* |

Thund, *the roaring* (like Odin's name thundr), I take for the name of the river that surrounds Valhall. Valglaumr, as Rask observes, is the company of 'valr', or fallen, that have to pass over the river to come to Valhall. What is meant by Thiodvitnir's fish is unknown. – P.

2    The goddess Hlódyn seems also to have been known to the Germans. Near Birten, on the Lower Rhine, the following inscription was found, now preserved at Bonn: DEAE: HLUDANAE SACRUM C. TIBERIUS VERUS. Thorlacius, with great probability (*Antiq. Bor. Spec.*, iii), identifies Hludana with the Hlódyn of the North, and certainly Hludana was neither a Roman nor a Celtic divinity though Schreiber (*Die Feen in Europa*, p. 63) refers the name to the town of Lüddingen, not far from Birten. Grimm, J., *Deutsche Mythologie*, op. cit., p. 235. Müller, op. cit., p. 88.

3    Thor is described sometimes as an old man, though usually as a tall, slender,

realm of Thrudvang (Thrudvángur) or Thrudheim (Thrudheimr), and his
mansion is named Bilskirnir, in which there are five hundred and forty
floors. It is the largest house ever seen by men. He is also called Hlorridi
(the Fire-driver or rider), Ving Thor, &c., and sometimes Auku-Thor, Öku-
Thor (Car-Thor), because he drives in a chariot with two he-goats,
Tanngniost and Tanngrisnir. He is the constant enemy of the giants and
trolls. He possesses three precious things: 1. the hammer Miölnir, which
the frost- and mountain-giants know but too well, when he swings it in the
air; 2. his belt of power (Megingjardar), when girded with which his
strength is doubled; 3. his iron gloves, which he requires when he grasps
the haft of Miölnir. As the jarls (men of rank, whence our *earls*) that fall in
battle belong to Odin, in like manner Thor has the race of thralls. Thor's
sons are Magni and Modi (Módi). By his wife Sif he has a daughter named
Thrud (Thrúdr). He is foster-father to Vingnir and Hlora. On his travels he
is attended by Thialfi and Röskva.[1]

**Baldur** is Odin's second son (by Frigg); he is the best and is praised by all.
He is so fair of aspect, and so bright, that light issues from him and there is
a plant, that of all plants is the whitest, which is compared to Baldur's
brow.[2] Hence an idea may be formed of his beauty both of hair and person.
He is the wisest, and most eloquent, and most amiable of the Aesir, and is
so gifted by nature that no one may pervert his judgements. His abode is in

---

comely young man with a red beard; on his head there is a crown of twelve stars
(Steph., *Notae in Sax.*, p. 139). When he waxes wroth, he blows in his red beard, and
thunder resounds among the clouds. And St Olaf the king – to whom, on the
suppression of heathenism in the North, much of Thor's character was transferred by
the missionaries, for the purpose, no doubt, of reconciling their converts to the new
faith – is celebrated as resembling his prototype even to the hue of his beard, as we
learn from the troll-wife's address to him, when he caused a rock, that had obstructed
his course, to part in two: 'Saint Olaf with thy beard so red,
                    Why sailest thou through my cellar wall?'
1   The aconite (wolfsbane, monkshood) is in Norway called Thorhjalm (Thori galea),
Thorhat (Thori pileus); Swed. Dan. stormhat. May not its denomination of wolfsbane
bear allusion to Thor's combat with the wolf? It is also called Tyrihjalm (Tyris galea).
See Grimm, J., *Deutsche Mythologie*, op. cit., p 1145.
2   In Denmark, Baldur's brow is the *anthemis cotula*; in Iceland, the *matricaria
maritima inodora* in Sweden, a plant called *hvitatoja* (white eye) or *hvitapiga* (white
lass). In Skania, the *anthemis cotula* bears the name of *balsensbro*. On the right-hand
side of the road leading from Copenhagen to Roeskilde there is a well called Baldur's
Brönd, which he is said to have opened after a battle with Hödur, to refresh his men
suffering from heat and fatigue. The tradition among the country people is that it was
produced by a stroke of the hoof of Baldur's horse. See Saxo Grammaticus, *Gesta
Danorum*, 1202, p. 120, and Bp. Müller's note; also Thiele, op. cit., i, 5.

heaven, in the place called Breidablik, into which nothing impure may enter.[1]

1  A short poem, in Old High German, of the ninth or tenth century, discovered a few years since at Merseburg by Dr Waitz, and published by Dr J. Grimm, has for subject the horse of Phol, whom Grimm, with great probability, takes to be identical with Baldur. As the anecdote it contains does not appear in either *Edda*, though the tradition, as will presently be seen, has been, and probably still is, current not only in the North and the Netherlands, but also in this island, I do not hesitate in giving the entire poem together with its more modern paraphrases.

| | |
|---|---|
| Phol endi Wôdan | *Phol and Woden* |
| vuorun zi holza: | *went to the wood;* |
| du wart demo Balderes volon | *then was of Balder's colt* |
| sîn vuoz birenkit; | *his foot wrenched;* |
| thu biguoleìl Sinthgunt, | *then Sinthgunt charm'd it,* |
| Sunnâ era suister; | *and Sunna her sister;* |
| thu biguolen Frûâ, | *then Frua charm'd it,* |
| Vollâ era suister | *and Volla her sister;* |
| thu biguolen Wôdan, | *then Woden charm'd it,* |
| so he wola conda, | *as he well could,* |
| sôse bénrenki, | *as well the bone-wrench,* |
| sôse bluotrenki, | *as the blood-wrench,* |
| sôse lidirenki; | *as the joint-wrench;* |
| | |
| bên zi bêna, | *bone to bone,* |
| bluot zi bluoda, | *blood to blood,* |
| lid zi geliden, | *joint to joint,* |
| sôse gelîmida sîn. | *as if they were glued together.* |

Under the following Christianised form it appeals in Norway:

| | |
|---|---|
| Jesus reed sig til Heede, | *Jesus rode to the heath,* |
| der reed han syndt (sönder) sit Folebeen. | *There he rode the leg of his colt in two.* |
| Jesus stigede af og laegte det; | *Jesus dismounted and heal'd it;* |
| Jesus lagde Marv i Marv, | *Jesus laid marrow to marrow,* |
| Ben i Ben, Kjöd i Kjöd; | *Bone to bone, flesh to flesh;* |
| Jesus lagde derpaa et Blad, | *Jesus laid thereon a leaf,* |
| At det skulde blive i samme stad. | *That it might remain in the same place.* |

In P. Chr. Asbjørnsen, *Norske Huldreeventyr og Folkesagn*, 1845–8, i, p. 45, an old Norwegian crone applies the veterinary remedy to a young man's sprained ankle, in the following formula muttered over a glass of brandy:

| | |
|---|---|
| Jeg red mig engang igjennem et Led, | *I once was riding through a gate,* |
| Saa fik min sorte Fole Vred; | *When my black colt got a sprain;* |
| Saa satte jeg Kjöd mod Kjöd og | *So I set flesh to flesh and blood* |
| Blod mod Blod, | *to blood,* |
| Saa blev min sorte Fole god. | *So my black colt got well.* |

From Norway, the horse-remedy most probably found its way to Shetland, where, 'when a person has received a sprain, it is customary to apply to an individual practised in casting the "wresting thread". This is a thread spun from black wool, on which are

The third As is **Niörd** (Njördr). He dwells in Noatûn. He rules the course of the wind, stills the ocean, and quenches fire. He is invoked by seafarers and fishermen, and is the patron of temples and altars. He is so rich that he can give wealth and superfluity to those that invoke him. Niörd, as we have already said, was born and bred in Vanaheim.[1]

Frey (Freyr), a son of Niörd and his sister,[2] was also bred in Vanaheim. He is beloved of all, and is one of the most renowned of the Aesir. He presides over rain, and sunshine, and the fruits of the earth. He is to be invoked for good seasons and peace. He also presides over the wealth of men. He is the god of the year, and giver of cattle, and loosens the bonds of the captive. In the beginning of time, Alfheim was given to him by the gods as tooth-money. He reigns over the Light-elves (Liósálfar), who are more beauteous than the sun, while the Black or Dark-elves (Döckálfar), who are blacker than pitch, dwell in the bowels of the earth.[3] He is the foe and

---

cast nine knots, and tied round a sprained leg or arm. During the time the operator is putting the thread round the affected limb, he says, but in such a tone of voice as not to be heard by the bystanders, nor even by the person operated upon:

| 'The Lord rade, | Set joint to joint, |
| And the foal slade; | Bone to bone, |
| He lighted, | And sinew to sinew. |
| And he righted; | Heal in the Holy Ghost's name! |

In Sweden against the horse distemper, 'flog', we find

| Oden står på borget, | Odin stands on the mountain, |
| han spörger efter sin fole, | He inquires after his colt, |
| floget har han fått. | He has got the 'flog'. |
| Spotta i din hand och i hans mun, | Spit in thy hand and eke in his mouth, |
| han skall få bot i samma stund. | He shall be cured in the same hour. |

See Jacob Grimm, *Ueber zwei entdeckte Gedichte aus der Zeit des Deutschen Heidenthums*, Berlin, 1842, 4to and Grimm, J., *Deutsche Mythologie*, op. cit., p. 1181; also Robert Chambers, *Popular Rhymes, &c. of Scotland*, p. 37, Edinburgh, 1842. A similar formula is known in the Netherlands, but which Grimm was unable to give. An attempt by the present editor to procure it from Belgium has, he regrets to say, also proved unsuccessful.

1 An aquatic plant (*spongia marina*) bears his name, viz. Niardar vöttr (Niörd's glove), which is also consecrated both to Freyia and the Virgin Mary. This plant, as well as some kinds of orchis, in consequence of the hand-shaped form of their roots, are called Mary's hand, our Lady's hand, God's hand (Dan. Gudshaand). Grimm, J., *Deutsche Mythologie*, op. cit., p. 198.

2 Adam of Bremen (*De Situ Daniae*), who calls him Fricco, thus speaks of the worship of Frey in Upsala: 'Fricco, pacem voluptatemque largiens mortalibus; cujus etiam simulacrum fingunt ingenti priapo; si nuptiae celebrandae sunt, immolant Fricconi.'

3 The Elves (Alfar) of later times seem a sort of middle being between the Light and

slayer of Beli; is owner of the ship Skidbladnir, and rides in a chariot drawn

Dark Elves. They are fair and lively, but also bad and mischievous In some parts of Norway, the peasants describe them as diminutive, naked boys with hats on. Traces of their dance are sometimes to be seen on the wet grass, especially on the banks of rivers. Their exhalation is injurious, and is called *alfgust* or *elfblaest*, causing a swelling which is easily contracted by too nearly approaching places where they have spat, &c. They have a predilection for certain spots, but particularly for large trees, which on that account the owners do not venture to meddle with, but look on them as something sacred, on which the weal or woe of the place depends. Certain diseases among their cattle are attributed to the Alfs, and are, therefore, called alf-ild (elf-fire) or alfskud (elf-shot) The Dark Elves (Döck-álfar) are often confounded with the Dwarfs, with whom they indeed seem identical, though they are distinguished in Odin's Ravens' Song. The Norwegians also make a distinction between Dwarfs and Alfs, believing the former to live solitary and in quiet, while the latter love music and dancing. Faye, op. cit., p. 48.

The fairies (elves) of Scotland are precisely identical with the above. They are described as 'a diminutive race of beings, of a mixed or rather dubious nature, capricious in their dispositions, and mischievous in their resentment. They inhabit the interior of green hills, chiefly those of a conical form, in Gaelic termed *Sighan*, on which they lead their dances by moonlight; impressing upon the surface the marks of circles, which sometimes appear yellow and blasted, sometimes of a deep green hue and within which it is dangerous to sleep, or to be found after sunset. Cattle, which are suddenly seized with the cramp, or some similar disorder, are said to be *elf-shot*.' Scott's *Minstrelsy of the Scottish Border*, 1821, ii, p. 162.

Of the Swedish elves, Arndt gives us the following sketch: 'Of giants and dwarfs, of the alp, of dragons that keep watch over treasures, they have the usual stories nor are the kindly elves forgotten. How often has my postillion, when he observed a circular mark in the dewy grass, exclaimed: "See! there the elves have been dancing!" These elf-dances play a great part in the spinning room. To those who at midnight happen to enter one of these circles, the elves become visible, and may then play all kinds of pranks with them; though, in general, they are little, merry, harmless beings, both male and female. They often sit in small stones that are followed out in a circular form, and which are called älfquarnar (elf-querns or -millstones). Their voice is said to be soft like the air. If a loud cry is heard in the forest, it is that of the Skogsrå (see Vol. ii), or spirit of the wood, which should be answered only by a "He!" when it can do no harm.' *Reise durch Schweden*, iii, p. 16.

The elf-shot was known in this country in very remote times, as appears from the Anglo-Saxon incantation printed in Grimm, J., *Deutsche Mythologie*, op. cit., p. 1192 and in the Appendix to Kemble's *Saxons in England* (i, p. 530 sq.): 'Gif hit wáere ésagescot, odde hit waeere ylfa gescot.' *If it were an aesir-shot or an elve's-shot*. On this subject Grimm says: 'It is a very old belief, that dangerous arrows were shot by the elves from the air. . . . . . The thunderbolt is also called *elf-shot*, and in Scotland, a hard, sharp, wedge-shaped stone is known by the name of *elf-arrow, elf-flint, elf-bolt*, which it is supposed has been sent by the spirits.' Grimm, J., *Deutsche Mythologie*, op. cit., p. 429. See also the old Danish ballad 'Elveskud', in which the elf-king's daughter strikes Sir Oluf between the shoulders, and causes his death. *Danske Viser*, i, p. 237; or the English translation in Jameson's *Ballads*, i, p. 219.

The wives of the elves are called 'elliser'. They are to be seen only in fine weather, and then in the 'elf-marshes', particularly in spots where someone has met his death in by the hog Gullinbursti (Goldbristle), or Slidrugtanni.[1] Frey's attendant is named Skirnir; he has also Beyggvir and his wife Beyla in his service. The Swedes were chiefly devoted to his worship.[2]

Here may also be noticed the three sons of Forniot (the old Jute), viz. Oegir or Hler[3] (Hlèr), the god of the ocean; Logi[4] (flame or fire), and Kari (wind). Oegir's wife is Rân; they have nine daughters, whose names denote waves. His servants were Fimafeng (dextre, celeriter acquirens), who was slain by Loki, and Eldir. Rân takes in her net those that perish at sea. These divinities seem to have belonged to an older mythology, most probably that of the Fins.[5]

**Ty** or **Tyr** is the boldest and stoutest of the Aesir. It is he who gives victory in war, and should be invoked by warriors. It is a proverbial saying that a man who surpasses others in valour is as bold as Ty. He is also so wise that it is usual to say of a very sagacious man, he is as wise as Ty. He is, however, not considered as a settler of quarrels among people. Odin is his father,[6] but on his mother's side he is of giant race.[7]

---

an unfortunate manner. They sometimes scatter the hay about, sometimes dance. In front they appear as beautiful women, but behind are deformed and ugly or, as they are described, 'as hollow as a dough-trough'. Thiele, op. cit., i, pp. 22, 167; ii, p. 213.

The hole in wood, where a knot has been, is called in Scotland an *elfbore*. A similar superstition prevails in Denmark and Norway.

From Afzelius we learn that elf-altars still exist in Sweden, at which offerings are made for the sick. The elves are slender and delicate, the young females are particularly beautiful. When, on a summer evening, the wanderer lies down to rest by an elf-mound (älfwehög), he hears the tones of their harp and their lively song. When an elf damsel wishes to unite herself with the human race, she flies with the sunbeam through some opening, as a knot-hole in the wainscot, etc. etc. Afzelius, op. cit., ii, pp. 150, 155.

1 In the North, a hog was offered to Frey as a sacrifice of atonement; and in Sweden, until comparatively recent times, cakes in the form of a hog were baked every Christmas Eve. Grimm, J., *Deutsche Mythologie*, op. cit., p. 45. In Denmark, even to the present day, the lower classes have roast pork for dinner on that day.

2 See some further remarks on the worship of Frey in Kemble's *Saxons in England*, i, p. 355.

3 Oegir and Hler were, no doubt, anciently considered as two, the former ruling over the stormy, the latter over the tranquil ocean. In Saxo, op. cit., p. 81, we also find two dukes in Jutland, Eyr and Ler.

4 On account of his lofty stature, Logi was called Hâlogi (High Logi). From him the most northern part of Norway has its name of Hâlogaland or Helgeland. He was father to Thorgerd Hölgabrud and Yrpa, concerning whom see hereafter.

5 Forniot was known to the Anglo-Saxons, as appears from the name given by them to a plant: Forneotes folme (Forniot's hand).

6 In the Hymiskvida, he speaks of himself as a son of the giant Hymir. See hereafter.

7 The daphne mezereon (spurge laurel) bears his name—Tyvidr (Dan Tysved). The viola Martis is in Scotland called Tysfiola.

**Bragi** is another of the Aesir. He is famed for wisdom and eloquence, and is profoundly skilled in the art of poetry, which from him is denominated bragr, and those who distinguish themselves above others in eloquence are called bragr-men, and bragr-women. He is upbraided by Loki for not being sufficiently warlike and doughty in battle. He has a long beard, and is a son of Odin.

**Heimdall**, though regarded as a Van, is nevertheless called a son of Odin. He is also called the White or Bright God, and is a great and holy god. In the beginning of time he was born, on the boundary of the earth, of nine giant maidens, who were sisters, and was nourished with the strength of the earth, and the cold sea. The nine maidens were named, Gialp, Greip, Elgia, Angeia, Ulfrun, Aurgiafa, Sindur, Atla, and Jarnsaxa. He drinks mead in his bright hall, Himinbiörg, by Bifröst, at the bridge head (brúarspordr), where the rainbow reaches heaven. There he sits, as the watchman of the gods, at the end of heaven, to guard the bridge from the mountain-giants, where he is often wetted through with rain, or, as Loki expresses it, gets a wet back. He needs less sleep than a bird, hears the grass grow on the ground and the wool on the sheep, and sees, as well by night as by day, for a hundred miles around him. His horn Giöll (Giallarhorn) is hidden under the sacred tree Yggdrasil, but when he blows it, its sound is heard through all worlds. Heimdall's horse is named Gulltopp (Gold-mane). He is himself also called Hallinskeidi (Descending), and Gullintanni (Golden-tooth), because his teeth are of gold. The head is called Heimdall's sword, because he was pierced through with a man's head.[1] He contended with Loki for the Brisinga-men, Freyia's ornament.

**Höd** (Hödur) is another of the Aesir, and is said to be a a son of Odin. He is blind, but exceedingly strong. The gods may well wish never to hear his name pronounced, for his deed[2] will be long remembered both by gods and men.

**Vidar** is called the silent god. He is the son of Odin and the giantess Grid (Gridr). He has a very thick shoe, that has been forming, from the beginning of time, of the thin shreds that are cut from shoes in shaping the toes or heels: therefore should everyone cast away such shreds, who cares about rendering aid to the Aesir.[3] In other places, mention is made of his *iron* shoes, and in the Skálda he is called eiganda iarnskoss (owner of the iron shoe): he is the strongest of the gods after Thor, and affords them aid

---

1   The myth to which this refers is lost.
2   His slaying of Baldur.
3   The reason will appear hereafter.

in many difficulties. His abode, Landvidi (Landvithi), is thickly overgrown with brushwood and high grass.

**Vali** is a son of Odin and Rind. He is stout in battle, and an excellent archer.

**Ull (Ullr)** is the son of Sif and stepson of Thor. He is a good archer, and runs so rapidly on snowshoes, that no one is a match for him. He is comely of aspect, and warlike in habit and manners. It is good to invoke him in single combats. His dwelling is Ydal (Ydalir).

**Forseti**, a son of Baldur and Nanna,[1] Nef's (Nep's) daughter, dwells in the heavenly mansion called Glitnir, which is supported on gold, and roofed with silver. He settles all quarrels, and neither gods nor men know any better judgements than his.

**Loki** (*Asa-Loki* or Lopt) is reckoned among the Aesir, and is styled the traducer of the gods, and a scandal to gods and men. His father is the giant Farbauti; his mother is Laufey (leafy-isle), or Nâl (needle), and his brothers are Byleist and Helblindi.[2] He is comely of aspect, but evil-minded, and very capricious. He is distinguished above others for guile and artifice, and has often brought the Aesir into perilous plights, from which however he has extricated them by his cunning. His wife is named Sigyn, and their sons Nari or Narvi, and Vali or Ali. But Loki has also other children by Angurboda, a giantess from Jötunheim, viz. the Wolf Fenrir, the Jormungand or Midgard's

1　The inhabitants of Heligoland were especially devoted to the worship of Forseti, from whom the isle itself bore the name of Fosetisland, *i.e.* Forseti's land. It was held so sacred by the natives, and by mariners and pirates, that no one dared to touch any animal that grazed on it, nor even to draw water from the well unless in silence. Hence no doubt its appellation of Heilig (holy) land. Alcuin, in his *Vita S. Willibrordi*, gives an interesting account of the saint's actions on the isle, on which he had been cast by a storm. The entire extract, as well as another from Adam of Bremen, 'De Situ Daniae', may be seen in Grimm, J., *Deutsche Mythologie*, op. cit., pp. 210, 211.

2　In Jutland, the plant *polytrichum commune* is called *Loki's oats*. When there is a certain trembling or waving motion in the air, which be wilders and dazzles the sight, the Jutish peasants say that *Loki is sowing his oats*.—Blicher's *Noveller*, V, p. 77. Another plant, the *rhinanthus crista galli*, or yellow rattle, is called Loki's purse. In the middle age, the idea of the devil was applied to Loki, who sows weeds among the good seed. In the Thellemark in Norway he once took a child on his back, and on setting it down, said, 'So shalt thou sit till thou art a year old.' Whence it comes that children have a hollow on each side of the hip, and cannot walk before the expiration of a year. When the fire makes a whining noise, it is said that Lokje (Loki) is beating his children.—Faye, op. cit., p. 6. In Iceland the fiery, sulphurous ignis fatuus is called Lokabrenua (Lokii incendium). Loka daun is the Icelandic name of a fiery vapour. Grimm, J., *Deutsche Mythologie*, op. cit., pp. 221, 868.

Serpent, and Hel, the goddess of the dead. In the beginning of time, Odin and Loki were foster-brothers; they had mingled blood together, on which account Odin would never hold a feast unless Loki were present. But Loki was afterwards, for eight years, down on earth, in the form of a cow, and as a woman, and there bore children. Burnt up in his innermost sense (seared up in mind), Loki found a half-burnt heart of a woman; then he became false and wicked, and thence came all unhappiness on earth.

We meet also with the names of Meili, a son of Odin and brother of Thor; Nep or Nef (Nepr, Nefir), a son of Odin, and father of Nanna; also Hildolf, a son of Odin.

**The Goddesses** The chief goddess is **Frigg**,[1] the wife of Odin. From them descend the race of Aesir. Her habitation is Fensalir. She knows the destiny of men, although she is silent thereon. During Odin's absence, she married his brothers Vili and Ve.[2] She is called Fiörgyn's daughter, Nanna's stepmother, Earth's, and Rind's and Gunnlöd's, and Gerd's rival. She possesses a feathergarb, or falcon's plumage. She is the goddess of marriage.

In equal veneration is **Freyia** held, the daughter of Niörd and sister of Frey. From her descent she is called Vana-dis, or goddess of the Vanir. She dwells in Folkvang, her hall is called Sessrymnir (roomy-seated) and when she rides to battle, one half of the slain belong to her, the other to Odin; hence her appellation of Valfreyia. She delights in love songs, and is to be prayed to in love matters. When she rides, her chariot is drawn by two cats. She owns the ornament called Brising, or Brisinga-men.[3] Like Frigg, she possesses a falcon's plumage, and, like Frey, a hog named Gullinbursti, or

---

1    Whether the sixth day of the week is named after her, or after the goddess Freyia, is very doubtful.

2    The story is thus told by Snorri. 'Odin had two brothers, one named Ve the other Vilir, and these governed the realm in his absence. Once, when Odin had travelled far away, and had been so long absent that the Aesir despaired of his return, his brothers took on themselves to divide his possessions; but of his wife, Frigg, they both took possession. Odin, however, returning shortly after, took back his wife.' – Ynglingasaga, 3. For this unlucky affair, she was afterwards jeeringly reproached by Loki: 'Thegi thú, Frigg! Thú ert Fjörgyns maer, ok hefir ae vergjörn verid; er thá Véa oc Vilja léztu thér Vithris kvaen! bátha î bathm um-tekit.' – *Lokaglepsa*, 26. Saxo (op. cit., p. 42) tells sad tales of Frigg, how she stripped her husband's statue of its gold, and demolished it, how she violated her conjugal fidelity, till Odin, provoked by the twofold injury, went into voluntary exile.

3    In the *Saga Olafs Tryggvasonar* (Vol. ii, Ch. 17, edited by Skalholt and reprinted in Rask's edition of *Snorra Edda*, p. 354), there is rather an awkward story of the manner in which Freyia became possessed of her ornament. Freyia, we are there told, was a mistress of Odin. Not far from the palace dwelt four dwarfs, whose names were Alfrig, Dvalin, Berling and Grer: they were skilful smiths. Looking one day into their stony dwelling, Freyia saw them at work on a beautiful golden necklace or collar, which she

Hildisvini (the swine of war), which the dwarfs Dain and Nabbi made for her, and whose golden bristles illumine the thickest darkness. After her name, women of condition are called Fru (*Danish* Frue, *German* Frau). Freyia was married to Od (Odr), and they had a daughter named Hnos, after whose name all precious things are called *hnosir*. Od forsook her, and went far away: she weeps for his absence, and her tears are red gold. She travelled among unknown people in search of him.[1] Freyia has many names, because she assumed a new one among each people that she visited in her journeyings: hence she is called Mardöll, Hörn, Gefn, and Syr.

Of **Nanna**, the wife of Baldur, mention will be made hereafter.

**Idun** (Ithunn, Ithúdr), the wife of Bragi, and daughter of Ivald, keeps in her casket the apples of which the gods must eat, when they begin to grow old: they then again become young; and this process will continue till the destruction of the gods, or Ragnaröck. Her dwelling is in Brunnakr.

---

offered to buy, but which they refused to part with, except on conditions quite incompatible with the fidelity she owed to Odin, but to which she, nevertheless, was tempted to accede. Thus the ornament became hers. By some means, this transaction came to the knowledge of Loki, who told it to Odin. Odin commanded him to get possession of the ornament. This was no easy task, for no one could enter Freyia's bower without her consent. He went away whimpering, but most were glad on seeing him in such tribulation. When he came to the locked bower, he could nowhere find an entrance, and it being cold weather he began to shiver. He then transformed himself to a fly, and tried every opening, but in vain; there was nowhere air enough to enable him to get through (Loki requires air). At length he found a hole in the roof, but not bigger than the prick of a needle: through this he slipped. On his entrance, he looked around to see if anyone was awake, but all were buried in sleep. He peeped in at Freyia's bed, and saw that she had the ornament round her neck, but that the lock was on the side she lay on. He then transformed himself to a flea, placed himself on Freyia's cheek, and stung her so that she woke, but only turned herself round and slept again. He then laid aside his assumed form (ham), cautiously took the ornament, unlocked the bower, and took his prize to Odin. In the morning, on waking, Freyia seeing the door open without having been forced, and that her ornament is gone, instantly understands the whole affair. Having dressed herself, she repairs to Odin's hall, and upbraids him with having stolen her ornament, and insists on its restoration, which she finally obtains.

This story, though probably based on some lost poem, is subsequent to the time of Christianity and of little value. Compare the Brisinga-men of Freyia with the ὅρμος and κεστὸς of Venus. In Beowulf (v. 2394 *sq.*) allusion is made to the 'Brósinga-men', as belonging to Hermanric, but the legend concerning it is no longer extant. See Kemble's edition, Vol. ii, Appendix.

1    Some traces of the myth of Freyia (under the name of Syr) and Od are to be found in the story of Syritha and Othar, given by Saxo (p. 330, *sq.*), though in almost every particular widely differing from the little that has been transmitted to us of that myth. The flower Freyju hâr (*supercilium Veneris*) owes its northern appellation to the goddess.

**Sif**, Thor's wife, mother of Ull and Thrud, has a noble head of hair.[1] Loki says there is but one who had unlawful intercourse with her, and that was the wily Loki.

**Saga** dwells in Söckquabeck, over which the cool waves murmur. There she and Odin joyfully drink each day from golden cups.

**Gefion**[2] is a virgin, and is served by those that die virgins. She knows the decrees of fate as well as Odin himself. Loki upbraids her with being infatuated with the fair youth that gave her a necklace, and with yielding to his embraces.

**Eir** is the best leech. **Fulla** is a maiden with dishevelled hair and a golden band round her head.[3] She bears Frigg's casket, has charge of her foot-covering, and knows her secret council. **Gna** rides through the air and over the sea, on Frigg's messages, on the horse Hofvarpnir. Once, as she was riding, some Vanir saw her in the air, one of whom said,

> What flies there?
> what goes there?
> Or is borne in air?

She answered,

> I fly not,
> though I go,
> and am borne in air,
> on Hôfvarpnir,
> that Hamskerpir
> got by Gardarôfa.

---

1    See more about Sif's hair at p. 37. A plant (*polytrichum aureum*) bears the name of Sifjar haddr (Sitae peplum).
2    Of Gefion, and the obligation under which the Danes lie to her, there is the following tradition. A king named Gylfi once reigned over the lands now called Sweden. Of him it is related that he gave a wandering woman, who had diverted him by her song, as much land as four oxen could plough in a day and a night. This *woman was of the race of the Aesir*, and named Gefiun. She took four oxen from the north, from Jötunheim, who were her own sons by a Jötun, and set them before the plough, which penetrated so deeply that it loosened a part of the land, which the oxen drew out to sea westwards, until they stopped in a certain sound, where Gefiun fixed the land, and gave it the name of Saelund. Where the land was ploughed up, a lake formed itself, called in Sweden Laugr, now the Mälar lake. And the bays and creeks in the lake correspond to the promontories of Seeland – *Snorra Edda*, p. 1; Thiele, op. cit., i, 1. The above is not contained in the Upsala MS. of Snorri's *Edda*, which is the oldest copy known.
3    Höfudband Fullu (Fulla's headband) is a periphrasis for gold.

**Hlin** guards those whom Frigg is desirous of freeing from peril. **Siöfn** inclines the mind of both sexes to love: from her name a lover is called *siafni*. **Lofn** is kind and good to those that invoke her: she has permission from All-father or Frigg to unite those who love each other, whatever hindrances or difficulties may stand in the way. From her name is derived the word lof (praise, leave), because she is greatly praised by men. **Vör** hears the oaths and vows of lovers, and punishes those who break them. She is wise, and hears of everything, so that nothing can be hidden from her. **Syn** guards the door of the hall, and locks it against those that may not enter. She is appointed as the defender in courts of those causes which it is endeavoured to defeat by falsehood. **Snotra** is sagacious and of elegant manners. From her name a man or woman of sagacity is said to be *snotr*. **Sôl** and **Bil**[1] are also reckoned among the goddesses; also **Earth**, the mother of Thor, and **Rind**, the mother of Vali.

**Of Odin's horse Sleipnir.** Odin had a horse named Sleipnir, that was the most excellent of horses. The following account is given of his origin. In the beginning of time, when the gods had founded Midgard and Valhall, there came a builder from Jötunheim, who promised to construct for them, in three half-years, so strong a fastness, that neither the mountain-giants nor the frost-giants should be able to take it, even though they were to come over Midgard, if in recompense they would give him Freyia together with the sun and moon. The gods acquiesced in his demand, provided he completed the work in one winter, but if on the first day of summer aught were wanting, or if he availed himself of anyone's assistance, the bargain should be void. The builder hereupon prayed that be might be allowed to use his horse Svadilföri (Svathilföri), to which the Aesir, by the advice of Loki, assented. He began his work on the first day of winter, and during the night his horse dragged the stones. The Aesir were amazed at the immense size of the stones brought by the horse, which performed more work by half than the builder himself; but there were witnesses to the bargain, and many oaths taken for the giant would not have deemed it safe to be among the Aesir without such security, especially if Thor should return, who was then absent in the eastern parts, on an expedition against the trolls (demons). When the winter drew near to a close, the fortification was far advanced, and was so high and strong that it was secure from assault. When three days only were wanting to summer, the gateway was all that remained to be completed. Hereupon the gods assembled, and deliberated, and inquired whence the counsel came, to give Freyia in marriage in Jötunheim, and spoil air and heaven by taking away the sun and moon and giving them to

1   See p. 15.

a giant. It was agreed that such advice could come from no one but Loki, the son of Laufey, the author of so much mischief, whom they accordingly threatened with an ignominious death, if he did not devise some means of annulling the contract. Loki was now terrified, and swore that the builder should get no payment. In the evening, when the latter was gone with his horse to fetch stones, a mare came running out of the wood to the horse, and neighed: the horse hereupon became restive, broke his rein, and ran after the mare into the wood, and the giant after the horse; and they ran during the whole night. When the builder saw that the work could not be finished in the time, he assumed his giant mood; but when the Aesir found that he was a mountain-giant, they, regardless of their oaths, called Thor to their aid, who raising his hammer Miölnir, paid him therewith, instead of the sun and moon, not even allowing him to return and build in Jötunheim; for at the first blow he crushed the giant's skull, and sent him to Niflheim. Loki, in his guise of a mare, had conceived by Svadilföri, and sometime after brought forth a gray colt with eight legs:[1] that was Sleipnir, Odin's horse, on which he rides over land and sea.

**Of the ship Skidbladnir**[2] (Skithblathnir) This ship was constructed in the beginning of time, by the dwarfs, sons of Ivaldi,[3] who made a present of it to Frey. It is the best and most curiously constructed of all ships, though Naglfar, belonging to Muspell, is the largest. But respecting this famous ship there is another story. Loki, out of mischief, once cut all Sif's hair off. When this came to the knowledge of Thor, he threatened to crush every bone in him, if he did not get the svartelves to make her a head of hair of gold, that should grow like natural hair. Loki thereupon went to the sons of Ivaldi, who made the hair for him, together with the ship Skidbladnir, and the spear possessed by Odin, Gungnir.

Loki afterwards wagered his head with the dwarf Brock that the latter's brother Sindri (Aeitri) was unable to make three such precious things. They then went to the smithy. Sindri laid a swine's skin on the fire, and desired Brock to blow until he took it from the forge. But while he was gone out, and Brock stood blowing, there came a gadfly,[4] which settled on his hand and stung him. Brock, nevertheless, went on blowing until his brother returned and took what was forged from the fire. It was a hog with

1  In Inga Bardar's *Saga*, ch. 20, Sleipnir has four legs only. Runes were inscribed on his teeth or rein.
2  From skid, *a thin plank*, and blad, a *leaf*, &c.
3  This lvaldi, the parent of certain dwarfs, is not to be confounded with the elf Ivald, the father of Idun.
4  That is, Loki under the form of a gadfly.

golden bristles. The smith then put gold into the fire, and desiring his brother to blow without intermission until he returned, went away. The gadfly came again, fixed itself on his neck, and stung him twice as sorely as before; but Brock continued blowing until the smith came back, and took from the fire the gold ring called Draupnir. The third time Sindri put iron into the fire, and exhorted his brother to blow without ceasing, for else all would be spoiled. The gadfly now took his post over Brock's eye, and stung his eyebrow and as the blood trickled down so that he could not see, he raised his hand in haste, thereby causing the bellows for a moment to stand still, while he drove away the gadfly. At this moment, the smith returned, and said that what was in the fire had been nearly spoiled. On taking it forth, it proved to be a hammer. Sindri entrusted these things to his brother, saying, he could now go to Asgard and get the wager decided. Sindri and Loki now appearing, each with his treasures, the Aesir took their places on their judgement-seats, and it was agreed that whatever Odin, Thor, and Frey might decide should be valid.

Loki made a present to Odin of the spear Gungnir, to Thor of the hair for Sif, to Frey of Skidbladnir, and, at the same time, explained the virtues of these presents: how the spear never failed to strike whatever it was aimed at; how the hair would grow rapidly as soon as it was placed on Sif's head; and that Skidbladnir would always have a fair wind, when the sails were set, and was withal so capacious that it could contain all the gods with their weapons and armour, but, at the same time, contrived so ingeniously, and of so many pieces, that it might be folded up like a cloth and put into one's pocket.

Now came Brock forwards with his wonderful handiworks. To Odin he gave the ring, saying that every ninth night eight rings equally precious would drop from it. To Frey he gave the hog, adding that it could run more swiftly than any horse, on air and sea, and that even in the darkest night a sufficiency of light would shine from its bristles. To Thor he gave the hammer, and said that he might strike with it with all his might whatever object came before him, without receiving any hurt; however far he might cast it, he should never lose it, but that it would always return to his hand, and, whenever he wished, it would become so small that he might put it in his pocket: its only defect was that the haft was rather short.[1]

The judgement was that the hammer was the best work of all, as they would find in it a powerful defence against the frost-giants; and that the dwarf had, consequently, won the wager. Loki offered ransom for his head, but the dwarf rejected it. 'Well, take me then,' said Loki; but when the

---

1   Owing to the interruption caused by the gadfly.

dwarf would lay hands on him, he was already far away for he had on shoes with which he could run both on air and water. The dwarf then begged of Thor to take him, and he did so; but when he was about to cut his head off, Loki told him that the head was his, but not the neck. The dwarf then took a thong and a knife, and would pierce holes in Loki's lips, in order to sew his mouth up; but the knife would not cut. 'It were well,' said he, 'if I now had my brother's awl,' and the instant he named it, it was there. The awl did its duty, and with the thong, which was called Vartari, the dwarf stitched up the lips of Loki.

**Origin of the Skaldic or Poetic Art.** When the Aesir made peace with the Vanir, in token of amity, they mingled their saliva in a vessel. Of the contents of this vessel the gods created the man Kvasir. He was so wise that no one could ask him a question that he was unable to answer and he travelled far and wide to impart his knowledge to mankind. Being invited to a feast by the dwarfs Fialar and Galar, they took him aside, under the pretext of a secret communication, and slew him. His blood they let run into two vessels, named Sôn and Bodn, and into the kettle Odhraerir (Odhraerir). With the blood they mingled honey, and thus composed the mead which makes everyone that partakes of it a skald or a wise man. To the Aesir they said that Kvasir was drowned in his own wisdom.

These dwarfs afterwards invited to them a giant named Gilling, and his wife, and rowed out with him to sea, but when they were some distance from land, they ran on a rock, and upset the boat, and Gilling, who could not swim, was drowned. Having set the boat right, they returned home. On relating to Gilling's wife what had befallen her husband, she was inconsolable, and wept bitterly. Fialar then asked her whether it would alleviate her sorrow to look on the sea where her husband had perished. She answered in the affirmative, when he desired his brother Galar to go up over the door, and as she was going out, to let a millstone fall on her head, as he could not endure her lamentations. The brother did as he was desired. When Suttung, the son of Gilling, was informed of what had taken place, he set out, seized the dwarfs, took them out to sea, and placed them on a rock that at high tide was under water. They prayed for their lives, and offered to give him, as blood-fine, the precious mead, which he accepted. Suttung then took the mead home, deposited it in the mountain Hnitbiörg, under the custody of his daughter Gunnlöd. Hence it is that poetry is called Kvasir's blood, the drink of the dwarfs, Odhraerir's, or Sôn's, or Bodn's liquor, or the dwarfs' passage-supply (because it supplied the means of saving their lives from the rock), or Suttung's mead, or Hnitbiörg's water.

Odin being very desirous to obtain this mead, left home, and came to a place where nine thralls were cutting hay. He asked them whether he should whet their scythes. They thanked him for his offer, and taking a whetstone from his belt, he sharpened them so that they cut much better, and they wished to buy the stone. Odin then threw it up in the air, when in struggling to seize it, each turned his scythe on the neck of another. Odin sought shelter for the night at a giant's named Baugi, a brother of Suttung, who complained bitterly of the loss he had sustained, saying that his nine thralls had killed each other, and that he knew not whence he was to get labourers. Odin, who now called himself Bölverk, offered to perform the work of nine men, on condition of receiving in reward a drink of Suttung's mead. Baugi told him that he had no power over the mead, and added that Suttung wished to have it all to himself; but that he would go with Bölverk, and endeavour to get it. During summer he performed the work of nine men for Baugi, and when winter came, demanded his reward. They thereupon went to Suttung, whom Baugi informed of the agreement, but Suttung would not part with a drop of the mead. Bölverk then proposed that they should try some stratagem, if they could not otherwise get at the mead, to which proposal Baugi assented. Bölverk then produced the auger named Rati, and requested Baugi, if the auger were sharp enough, to bore into the mountain. Baugi did so, and said that the mountain was penetrated, but when Bölverk blew into the hole, the dust made by the auger flew towards him, and he found that Baugi was deceiving him, and desired him to bore again. He bored, and when Bölverk again blew, the dust flew inwards. Bölverk now, assuming the form of a worm, crept in. Baugi made a stab after him with the auger, but missed him. Bölverk then went to the place where Gunnlöd was, with whom he stayed three nights, and obtained her permission to drink thrice of the mead. At the first draught he emptied Odhraerir; at the second, Bodn; and at the third, Sôn, and thus drank up all the mead. Then assuming an eagle's garb, he flew away with all possible speed. But Suttung, who saw the eagle's flight, also took his eagle's plumage, and flew after him. When the Aesir saw Odin flying towards them, they set out vessels in the court, and on entering Asgard, he spat the mead into the vessels. But Suttung was then so close at his heels, that he nearly overtook him, thereby causing some of the mead to go in another direction; but this not being noticed, everyone partook of it that would. This is called the poetasters' portion. Odin gave Suttung's mead to the Aesir, and to those who can compose good verses; therefore is the skaldic art called Odin's booty, Odin's find, and his drink, and his gift, and the drink of the Aesir.

**Of the abduction and restoration of Idun.** On this subject there are two compositions, one in Saemund's *Edda* (Hrafna-galdur Odins, or Odin's Ravens' Song), further mention of which, on account of its obscurity, and consequent lack of interest to the general reader, is here omitted; the other is in Snorri's *Edda*, and is as follows.

The Aesir, Odin, Loki and Hoenir, once set out from home, and took their way over mountains and desert places, where they suffered from want of food, but on descending into a valley, they perceived a herd of oxen, one of which they slaughtered for the purpose of boiling it. When they thought it was done enough they looked at it, but it was not boiled through. Sometime after, they looked at it again, and still it was not done. While talking the matter over, and wondering what could be its cause, they heard a voice above them, in the branches of an oak, and looking up, perceived an eagle of no small dimensions, which said to them, 'If ye will give me a bellyful of the ox, it shall soon be boiled.' They promised that they would; whereupon the eagle descended from the tree, placed himself on the boiled carcase, and forthwith snatched up, for his part, one of the thighs and both shoulders. Seeing this, Loki waxed wroth, and seizing a huge pole, thrust it with all his might at the eagle, which nevertheless effected its escape, and flew up, with one end of the pole hanging in its body, and the hand of Loki fast to the other. As the eagle flew, Loki's feet were dragged over stones, hillocks and trees, and he thought his arm would be torn from his shoulder. He screamed and prayed for mercy, but was told by the eagle that he should not be loosed until he had sworn to bring Idun with her apples out of Asgard. Loki having sworn, was released accordingly, and with his companions returned to Asgard.

On a certain time, he told Idun, that in a wood just without Asgard he had found some splendid apples, and so enticed her out, bidding her to take her own with her, for the sake of comparing them. Then came the giant Thiassi in his eagle's plumage (for he was the eagle), seized Idun, and flew with her to his home. But it fared badly with the Aesir while Idun was absent; they quickly grew grey and old. Thereupon they held a meeting, and inquired one of another, who had seen her last, when it was found that she went out of Asgard with Loki. Loki was now seized, and brought to the meeting, and threatened with torments and death, if he did not bring Idun back from Jötunheim. Terrified at their threats, he engaged to bring her back provided Freyia would lend him her falcon's plumage; having obtained which, he flew northwards to Jötunheim, and reached the abode of the giant, where he found Idun alone, Thiassi being gone out to sea. Loki transformed her into a nut, took her in his talons, and hastily flew away. Thiassi on his return home missing her, took his eagle's plumage and flew after Loki, and had nearly caught him; but the Aesir seeing the falcon with the nut in his talons, and the eagle closely following, went to the wall of the city, carrying with them loads of chips, to which, as soon as the falcon entered and had glided down within the wall, they set fire; so that the eagle, unable to check his rapid flight, burned his wings, and being thus disabled was slain by the Aesir. Of Thiassi we are besides told that his father's name was Ölvaldi, who possessed much gold. His sons, Thiassi, Idi, and Gang, shared the inheritance among them, by each in his turn taking a mouthful.

**Of Niörd** (Niörthr) **and Skadi** (Skathi). Skadi, the daughter of Thiassi, took helm and corselet, and went fully armed to Asgard, to avenge the death of her father. The Aesir offered her peace and compensation, and granted her permission to choose herself a husband among them, though under the condition that she should see their feet only. She accordingly went round among them, saw a pair of handsome feet, and said, 'This one I choose; few blemishes are to be found in Baldur.' She had, nevertheless, made a mistake, for the feet belonged to Niörd of Noatûn. Another article of peace was that one of the Aesir should cause her to laugh, a task successfully performed by Loki, who played some ludicrous antics with a goat. It is further related that Odin (or Thor) took Thiassi's eyes, cast them up to the heavens, and formed of them two stars. Niörd married Skadi, but dissension soon sprang up between them for Skadi would dwell among the mountains, in her father's abode, Thrymheim, while Niörd liked to be near the sea. At length it was agreed that they should stay alternately nine days in Thrymheim, and three in Noatûn.[1] But when Niörd returned from the mountains to his Noatûn, he said:

> Loathsome are the hills;
> long seem'd to me
> nine nights only.
> The noise of wolves
> sounded ill, compared
> with the swan's song.

But Skadi answered,

> Sleep I got not
> by the sea-waves,
> for wail of birds
> from the wood coming;
> the sea-mew me each morn
> with its scream waked.[2]

---

1  Or, according to another MS., 'and *another nine* in Noatûn'.
2  See in Saxo, op. cit., p. 53, the Song of Hading and Regnild, beginning:

She then went up into the mountain, and abode in Thrymheim, where she runs on snowskates, and shoots wild beasts with her bow; hence she is called Öndurgud or Öndurdis (the goddess of snowskates). 'From her habitation and fields ever come cold (pernicious) counsels to Loki,' who had been foremost in causing her father's death.

**Of Frey and Gerd** (Gerthr). Frey had one day seated himself in Hlidskialf, and was looking over all the worlds, when on turning to Jötunheim, he there cast his eyes on Gerd, a beautiful maiden, the daughter of Gymir and Aurboda, relations of Thiassi, as she was going from her father's hall to her maiden-bower. On raising her arms to open the door, both air and water gave such a reflection that the whole world was illumined. Frey descended from Hlidskialf with a heart full of love and care, went home, spoke not, drank not, slept not, nor did anyone venture to speak to him. This penalty Frey brought on himself, for having presumed to sit in Odin's sacred seat. On seeing him in this state, Niörd, his father, sent for Skirnir, Frey's attendant, and bade him go to his son and inquire what had so disturbed his temper. Skirnir went accordingly, and asked his master, why he sat all day alone in the great halls. 'How,' answered Frey, 'shall I describe my affliction to thee? The elves' illuminator (the sun) shines every day, but never to my pleasure.' 'Confide to me thy sorrow,' said Skirnir; 'at the beginning of time we lived young together, and we ought to have confidence in each other.' Frey now recounted to him how he had seen, in Gymir's mansion, the maid with the bright arms; that he loved her more fervently than a youth loves in the spring of his days but that neither Aesir nor Alfar would permit them to come together. 'Give me but thy swift courser,' said Skirnir, 'which can bear me through murky flames, and thy sword, which fells of itself the giant race, when he is stout who wields it.' Then rode Skirnir, and said to the horse: 'Dark it is without, it is time for us to go over hoar mountains, amid giant folk; we shall both return, or that mighty giant will take us both.' And Skirnir rode to Jötunheim, to Gymir's mansion, where he found fierce dogs chained at the gate of the enclosure. He rode up to a herdsman who was sitting on a hillock, and asked him how he could pass by Gymir's dogs and get speech of the young maiden. 'Art

> Hading loq.   Quid moror in latebris opacis,
>                  Collibus implicitus scruposis, etc.

> To which Regnild answers,

>           Me canorus angit ales immorantem littori
>           Et soporis indigentem garriendo concitat, etc.

The whole story of Hading and Regnild bears a striking resemblance to the myth of Niörd and Skadi.

thou doomed to death, or art thou a spectre? Never wilt thou get speech of Gymir's good daughter.' To this answer of the herdsman Skirnir replied, 'There is a better choice than to sob for him who voluntarily meets death; my life was decreed to one day only, and my days determined by fate.' But Gerd hears the stranger and says, 'What noise of noises do I hear in our halls? The earth shakes with it, and all Gymir's courts tremble.' Her waiting-maid answers, 'Here is a man without descended from his horse, which he lets graze.' 'Bid him,' said Gerd, 'enter our hall and drink the bright mead, though I fear that my brother's slayer stands without.' On his entrance Gerd says, 'Which of the Alfar's, or of the Aesir's or the wise Vanir's sons art thou? Why comest thou alone over raging flames[1] to see our halls?' Skirnir then declares his errand. For a long time she withstood his prayer, that she would dwell with Frey. He promised her eleven golden apples, in reward for her love, but she would not accept them. He promised to give her the ring Draupnir, which had been laid on the pile with Odin's young son Baldur, but she declined it, saying that she lacked not gold in her father's house. He threatened to strike off her head with the bright sword that he held in his hand, under which even the old giant her father must sink; to strike her with the taming wand; that she should go where the sons of men would never see her more; should pass her life on the eagle's mount, turned from the world towards Hel, and food should be more loathsome to her than Midgard's serpent[2] to the sons of men; that when she comes out she should be a spectacle at which Hrîmnir and all beings would stare, a monster set forth for mockery and scorn. 'Sit,' said he, 'and I will announce to thee a dire flood of bitterness, and double misery. Terrors shall beset thee all the day in the giants' dwellings; each day shalt thou wander about without joy; weeping shall be thy lot, instead of pastime, and tears shall accompany thy pain. With a three-headed giant thou shalt drag out thy life, or die a maiden; from morn to morn thy mind shall be in alarm, and thou shalt be as the thistle that withers on the house-top.' Then swinging over her his magic wand, he pronounced the malediction, 'Wroth with thee is Odin! Wroth with thee is the Aesir's prince! Frey shall shun thee, thou evil maiden! when thou art stricken by the vengeance of the gods. Hear it giants! Hear it, frost-giants, and sons of Suttung,[3] and ye, friends of the Aesir![4] how I forbid and hinder thee from

---

1　See the account of Brynhild's bower in the story of the Völsungs hereafter. Such fiery fences round a 'borg' seem to have been not infrequent.
2　Of this monster hereafter.
3　The dwarfs.
4　The elves.

man's society! Hrîmgrimnir the giant is named that shall possess thee below in the barred dwelling of the dead, where misery's thralls shall give thee only goats' water to drink. I cut for thee *Thurs*,[1] and three letters, *feebleness, frenzy* and *impatience*. I will cut them off[2] as I have cut them on: do thou only choose.' 'Be thou greeted, youth!' said Gerd, 'and in welcome take the icy cup filled with old mead; although I never thought to feel well-disposed towards a man of the Vanir's race.' She then promised to be with the son of Niörd in nine days, in the warm wood of Barri. Skirnir rode home, and announced the happy result of his journey; but full of desire, Frey exclaimed, 'One night is long, long are two; how shall I endure three? Oftentimes a month seems to me shorter than the half of such nights of desire.'

Frey having thus parted with his sword, was unarmed when he fought with Beli,[3] whom he slew with a stag's horn, although he could have killed him with his hand: but the time will come when the loss of his sword will cost him more dearly, when Muspell's sons go forth to battle.

**Of Loki's Offspring.** By Angurboda (Angrbotha), a giantess of Jötunheim, Loki had three children, viz, the wolf Fenrir, the Midgard's serpent or Jormungand, and Hel, the goddess of death. When the Aesir discovered that these three were being bred up in Jötunheim, and called to mind the predictions, that they would prove a source of great calamity to them, there being much evil to expect from them on the mother's side, and still more on the father's, All-father sent the gods to fetch the children. When they came, he cast the serpent into the deep ocean which surrounds all lands; but there it grew and became so great that it encircles the whole world, and bites its own tail. From hence it heaves itself up with violence towards heaven, rises up on land, causes the air to tremble, and sends snow, and stormy winds, and pattering rain over the earth. Hel he cast down into Niflheim, and gave her authority over nine worlds, that she might assign their places to those who are sent to her, namely, all those that die of sickness or age. Her abode of vast extent is surrounded by a high enclosure with large gates. Her hall is called Eliudnir (nimbos sive procellas late accipiens); her dish, Hungr (hunger); her knife, Sullt (starvation); her serving-man, Ganglâti (slowly moving); her woman-servant, Ganglöt (the same, but feminine); her threshold, Fallanda forat (perilous precipice); her bed, Kör (the bed of sickness); her curtains or hangings, Blikianda böl

---

1  The name of one of the letters of the runic alphabet.
2  'I will cut them off,' that is, 'I will, be erasing the runes, dissolve the spell,' in the case of Gerd's compliance.
3  The myth of Frey and Beli is lost.

(splendid misery). She is half black, half flesh-coloured, and therefore easily recognised, and very fierce and grim of aspect. The wolf was bred up among the Aesir; but only Ty had the courage to give him food. When the gods saw how much he increased daily, and as all the predictions declared that he was destined to be their destruction, they resolved on having a very strong chain made for him, called Laeding (Laethingr), which they took to the wolf, that he might prove his strength on it. The wolf to whom the chain did not appear over strong, let them do as they would; but the moment he stretched himself it broke, and he was again loose. They then made another chain half as strong again, called Dromi. This likewise the wolf was to try, they assuring him that he would be renowned for his strength, if so strong a bond could not confine him. The wolf saw plainly that this chain was exceedingly strong, but at the same time felt that his power was greatly increased since he broke the bond Laeding. It likewise occurred to him, that if he would become famous, he must expose himself to some risk. He therefore allowed them to fasten him with the chain. When the Aesir had chained him, the wolf shook himself, kicked, and dashed it on the earth, so that the fragments flew far away. Thus did he free himself from Dromi. It is since become a proverb, 'to get loose from Laeding', or, 'to burst out of Dromi', when anything is to be done with great exertion.

The Aesir being now fearful that they would be unable to bind the wolf, sent Skirnir, Frey's messenger, to some dwarfs in Svart-Alfheim, and caused them to make the chain Gleipnir, which was composed of six materials, viz. the sound of a cat's footsteps, a woman's beard, the roots of a mountain, a bear's sinews, a fish's breath, and a bird's spittle. This chain was as soft and supple as a silken cord, though of exceedingly great strength. The gods then, taking the wolf with them, went to the isle of Lyngvi, in the lake Amsvartnir. There they showed him the bond, asking him whether he could snap it asunder, as it was somewhat stronger than, judging from its thickness, it appeared to be. They then handed it from one to another, and tried to break it, but in vain: 'But the wolf,' said they, 'could easily break it in pieces.' The wolf answered, 'It does not seem to me that any great honour is to be gained by breaking so slender a thread, but as some cunning and deception may have been employed in making it appear so slight, it shall never come on my feet.' The Aesir said that he might easily break a silken cord, having already snapped asunder such strong bonds of iron, and adding, 'Even if thou canst not break it, thou hast nothing to fear from us, for we shall instantly release thee.' The wolf answered, 'If ye bind me so fast that I cannot free myself again, I am well convinced that I shall wait long to be released by you. I am, therefore, not at all desirous to let the cord be fastened on me. But rather than that ye shall accuse me of want of courage, let one of you place his hand in my mouth as a pledge that there is no guile in the case.' The gods now looked at one another, but not one would put forth his hand At length Ty stretched forth his right hand, and placed it within the jaws of the wolf. The wolf now began to struggle, and the more he strove to get loose, the more tightly did the bond bind him. Hereat they all set up a laugh, except Ty, who lost his hand for his rashness. When the Aesir saw that the wolf was effectually bound, they took the end of the chain, called Gelgia, which was fastened to the bond, and drew it through a huge rock named Giöll, which they secured far down in the earth, and beat down still lower with a fragment of rock named Thviti. In his yawning jaws they stuck a sword, the hilt of which was driven into his lower jaw, while the point penetrated the upper one. He howls dreadfully, and the foam that issues from his mouth forms the river called Von; whence he is also called Vanargand (Vanarganndr). There will he lie till Ragnaröck.

Of Thor and his journeys there were many stories, of which the following are preserved.

**Thor in the house of Geirröd (Geirröthr).**[1] Loki for his amusement had one day flown out in Frigg's falcon-plumage, and came to the mansion of Geirröd, where seeing a spacious hall, and prompted by curiosity, he perched himself, and peeped in at a window. Geirröd having caught a glimpse of him, ordered one of his people to catch and bring the bird to him; but the man to whom the order was given found difficulty in clambering up along the high wall, and Loki, who sat chuckling over the difficulties the man had to encounter, fancied he could fly away before he had surmounted them. So when at length the man made a grasp at him, Loki flapped his wings, in order to fly away; but his feet having got entangled in something, he was caught and brought to the giant, who as soon as he looked at his eyes suspected that he was a man, and commanded him to speak; but Loki was silent. The giant then locked him up in a chest, where he had to undergo a fast of three months' duration. At length the giant took him out, and again ordered him to speak, when Loki told him who he was; and, to save his life, promised on oath that he would bring Thor thither, without either hammer or belt of power. Loki persuaded Thor to undertake the journey. On their way they stopped at the giantess Grid's (Grithr), the mother of Vidar the Silent, who advised Thor to be on his guard against Geirröd, who was a crafty knave, with whom it was not desirable to have any intercourse. She at the same time lent him a belt of power, an iron glove, and her staff named Gridarvöll. Pursuing their

1 See a distorted version of this story in Saxo, op. cit., pp. 420–8.

journey, they came to the river Vimur, the greatest of all rivers, to cross which Thor girded himself with the belt, and supported himself against the stream on Grid's staff, while Loki took fast hold of the belt. On reaching the middle of the stream, they found it so greatly increased that the water washed over Thor's shoulders; when, on looking up towards a part of the river between two steep rocks, he perceived Gialp, one of Geirröd's daughters, standing with a foot on each bank, and found that it was she who had caused the river to rise; whereupon, seizing a heavy stone, he cast it at her, saying, 'The river must be stopped at its spring.' At the same time wading towards the shore, he took hold of some sorb-bushes, and so got to land. Hence the proverb: 'The sorb is Thor's salvation.' When he came to Geirröd's, a lodging was assigned him in a chamber where there was only one chair; sitting on which, he found that the seat rose with him up to the roof, whereupon, placing Grid's staff against the rafters, and pressing against it with all his might, a loud crash was heard, accompanied by an appalling cry. Geirröd's daughters, Gialp and Greip, were under the seat, and Thor had broken their backs. After this Geirröd invited Thor into his hall to play. Along one side of the hall were huge fires, from which, as Thor came just opposite to Geirröd, the latter, with a pair of tongs, snatched a red-hot iron wedge, and hurled it at Thor, who catching it with his iron glove cast it back. Geirröd took refuge behind an iron pillar, but Thor had hurled the wedge with such force, that it passed through the pillar, through Geirröd, through the wall, and deep into the earth without.[1]

**The hammer fetched.** Ving-Thor awoke and missed his hammer; his beard shook, and his head trembled with rage. He made known his loss to Loki, and they went to Freyia's fair abode, to borrow her falcon-plumage. In this Loki flew to Jötunheim, and found the giant chieftain, Thrym, sitting on an eminence without his dwelling, plaiting a collar of gold for his dog, and smoothing the manes of his horses. 'How fares it with the Aesir,' said he, 'and how with the Alfar? Why comest thou alone to the giants' land?' 'Ill fares it with the Aesir, ill with the Alfar. Hast thou hidden Hlorridi's hammer?' answered Loki. 'Yes,' replied Thrym, 'I have hidden it nine miles underground, and no one shall get it back, unless he brings me Freyia for a bride.' Loki then flew back in his rustling plumage, with the

---

1   According to the popular belief, the lightning is accompanied by a black bolt or projectile, which penetrates as far as the highest church steeple is long into the earth, but rises towards the surface every time it thunders, and at the expiration of seven years again makes its appearance on the earth. Every house in which such a stone is preserved is secure from the effects of thunderstorms, on the approach of which it begins to sweat. Grimm, J., *Deutsche Mythologie*, op. cit., pp. 163–5. The same idea seems expressed by the myth that the hammer always returns to Thor's hand. See p. 38.

giant's message, and informed Thor where the hammer was, and of the condition on which alone it could be recovered. On this they both went to the lovely Freyia, to whom they communicated the affair, and Loki said, 'Adorn thyself then with a bridal veil, and we two will go together to Jötunheim.' But Freyia snorted with anger, so that the hall trembled under her, and her necklace, the Brisinga-men, snapped asunder, and she said, 'I must, indeed, be very fond of men's society, if I went with thee to Jötunheim.' All the Aesir now held a meeting, and all the goddesses went to their rendezvous, to consult how the hammer should be recovered. Then said Heimdall the Wise, who as a Van saw well into the future, 'Let us bind a bridal veil on Thor, and decorate him with the Brisinga-men; let keys jingle at his side, female attire fall about his knees, precious stones adorn his breast, and an elegant headdress his head.' But Thor, the mighty god, answered, 'The Aesir would jeer me, if I allowed myself to be dressed out in a bridal veil.' Loki then presented to them that the giants would take up their abode in Asgard, if Thor did not fetch back his hammer. So they bound a bridal veil on Thor, and decorated him with the famed Brisinga-men, let keys jingle at his side, female attire fall about his knees, set precious stones on his breast, and an elegant headdress on his head. Loki accompanied him as a waiting-maid. The goats ran, the mountains burst, the earth stood in a blaze, when Odin's son drove to Jötunheim. Then said the giant chief, 'Stand up, giants! Lay cushions on the benches, and lead to me Freyia as a bride. Let gold-horned cows and coal-black oxen be brought in multitudes to my dwelling. Of ornaments I have enough, enough of treasures;[1] Freyia alone was wanting to my happiness.'

Early in the evening the giants assembled, and the festivity began. Thor alone devoured an ox, eight salmon, and all the dainties that are offered to ladies; to which, by way of slaking his thirst, he added three huge vessels of mead. In amazement, Thrym exclaimed, 'Never did I see a bride eat so voraciously, or drink so much mead.' But the prudent waiting-maid said, 'For eight nights and days Freyia has eaten nothing, so fervently did she long after Jötunheim.' The giant then raised her veil, and bent forwards, with the intention of kissing his bride, but starting back in terror, rushed through the hall, exclaiming, 'Why has Freyia so piercing a look? Her eyes burn like fire.' But the wily waiting-maid answered, 'For eight nights and days Freyia has had no sleep, so fervently did she long after Jötunheim.'

---

1    Indians, Greeks and Scandinavians have been accustomed to adorn the horns of cows with gilding. It has been remarked that even in recent times the practice is not quite obsolete in the North: the ox that was given to the people at the coronation of Christian VII having had gilded horns. F. Magnusen, *Den Aeldre Edda*, ii, p. 124.

Then came in the giant's unlucky sister, to ask for a bridal gift, and said, 'Give me the rings of red gold from thy hand, if thou wilt gain my love and favour.' Thrym then said, 'Bring now the hammer in, to consecrate the bridge; lay Miölnir in the maiden's lap, and unite us in the name of Vör.' But the heart of Hlorridi, the stalwart god, laughed in his breast, when he felt the hammer in his hand. First he slew Thrym, then the whole giant tribe; and the giant's sister got gashes for skillings, and hammer-strokes for ruddy rings. And thus did Odin's son get his hammer again.

**Of Thor and Utgarda-Loki.**[1] Once on a time Thor drove out in his chariot with the goats, together with Asa-Loki, and in the evening they came to a countryman's house. The goats were killed and boiled, and Thor invited the countryman and his wife, his son Thialfi, and his daughter Röskva to partake of the repast; and desired them to throw the bones into the goatskins, which he had laid by the side of the hearth. But Thialfi broke a thigh-bone, in order to get at the marrow. Thor remained there during the night, rose at dawn, raised Miölnir on high, consecrated the goatskins with it, and the goats sprang up, but one was lame of a hind-leg. He called to the countryman, who was ready to sink on seeing the angry brow of the god and his knuckles white with clenching the haft of Miölnir. Both the man and his family sued for pardon, and offered to give all they possessed, in compensation for the misfortune. Thor seeing them thus terrified, mitigated his anger, and contented himself with taking Thialfi and Röskva as his servants, who attended him ever after. Leaving the goats behind, he resolved on proceeding eastward to Jötunheim, in the direction of the sea, which he crossed, accompanied by Loki, Thialfi, and Röskva. After travelling a short distance they came to a vast forest, in which they journeyed the whole day till dark; Thialfi, who of all men was swiftest of foot, bearing Thor's wallet, though provisions to fill it were not easily to be had. Looking now on all sides for a place wherein to pass the night, they found a very spacious house, with a door at one end as broad as the house itself. They entered, and betook themselves to rest; but at midnight the earth shook under them, and the house trembled. Thor arose and called to his companions. Groping their way, they found a chamber on the right, which they entered, but Thor set himself in the doorway with hammer in hand. Those within were much terrified, for they heard a great din and crash. At dawn Thor went out, and saw a man of gigantic stature lying close by in the forest: he was sleeping, and snored loudly. Thor, who could now understand whence the noise during the night proceeded, buckled his belt of power about him, by which his divine might was increased. At this

1   See a distorted version of this story in Saxo, op. cit., pp. 429, *sq.*

moment the man awoke, and stood up. It is said that Thor did not venture to strike him with his hammer, but merely asked him his name. He was called Skrymir or Skrymnir. 'I need not,' said he, 'inquire thy name, for I know thou art Asa-Thor; but what hast thou done with my glove?' At the same moment stooping down and taking up his glove. Thor then saw that the house in which they had passed the night was the glove, and the chamber its thumb. Skrymir then asked whether he might accompany them; Thor answered in the affirmative. Skrymir then untied his wallet, and began eating his breakfast, while Thor and his companions did the same, though in another place. He then proposed that they should lay their provisions together, to which Thor also assented. Skrymir then put all the provisions into one bag, took it on his back, and walked stoutly on before them. Late in the evening Skrymir sought a resting-place for them under a large oak, saying that he would lie down and sleep. 'But,' added he, 'do you take the wallet, and prepare your supper.' Skrymir immediately began to sleep, and snored lustily. Thor now took the wallet to open it, and, incredible as it may seem, could not untie a single knot, nor make one strap looser than it was before. Seeing that all his exertions were fruitless, Thor grew angry, and grasping Miölnir with both hands, and advancing one foot, struck Skrymir, where he was lying, a blow on the head, At this Skrymir awoke, and asked whether a leaf had fallen on his head, whether they had supped and were ready for bed. Thor answered that they were then going to sleep. They went then under another oak. At midnight Thor heard Skrymir snoring so that it resounded like thunder through the forest. He arose and approached him, clenching his hammer with all his might, and struck him on the crown of the head, so that the hammer's head sank deep into his skull. Skrymir on this awoke, saying, 'What is that? Did an acorn fall on my head? How goes it with thee, Thor?' But Thor stepped quickly back, saying he was just awake; that as it was only midnight, they might sleep a while longer. He now thought that if he could only succeed in giving him a third blow, it was not probable he would ever see the light again; and lay watching until Skrymir had again fallen asleep. Towards daybreak, perceiving that the giant slept soundly, he arose, raised Miölnir with all his might, and struck Skrymir a blow on the temple, so that the hammer sank up to the haft. But Skrymir, raising himself and stroking his chin, said, 'Are there any birds above me in the tree? It seemed as I woke that a feather fell from the boughs on my head. Art thou awake, Thor? It is now time to get up and dress yourselves, though you are not far from the city called Utgard (Utgarthr). I have heard you chatting together, and saying that I was a man of no small stature; but you will see men still taller, when you come to Utgard. I will give you a piece of good advice: do not make too much of yourselves, for the followers of Utgarda-Loki will not feel inclined to endure big words from such mannikins. If you will take my advice, you will turn back, and that will, I think, be much better for you; but if you are resolved on proceeding, keep in an eastward direction. My course lies northwards to the mountains yonder. Then swinging his wallet across his shoulders, Skrymir left them, and took the path leading into the forest; and it has never been heard that the Aesir wished ever to meet with him again.

Thor and his companions travelled till the hour of noon, when they saw before them a city, on a vast plain, so high that they had to bend back their necks in order to see to the top of it. The entrance was protected by a barred gate, which was locked. Thor endeavoured to open it, and failed; but being desirous to enter, they crept through the bars, and so gained admission. Before them was a spacious hall with open door, into which they passed, where, on two benches, sat a company of men, most of them very gigantic. They then went before the king, Utgarda-Loki, and greeted him; but he, just glancing at them, said with a contemptuous smile, 'It is wearying to ask of travellers the particulars of a long journey, but is my surmise correct that this little fellow is Auku-Thor? Though, perhaps, you are taller than you appear to be. What feats can you and your followers perform? For no one is suffered here, who in one or other art or talent does not excel others.' Then said Loki, who entered last, 'One feat I can exhibit, and which I am willing to perform forthwith, and that is that I can devour my food as expeditiously as any one.' Utgarda-Loki answered, 'That is certainly a notable feat, provided thou art able to perform it, and that we will put to the proof.' He then called a man from the bench, by name Logi (flame), and commanded him to try his power with Loki. A trough full of meat was then placed on the floor, at one end of which Loki seated himself, and Logi at the other. Each ate to the best of his ability, and they met in the middle of the trough. Loki had eaten all the meat from the bones, while Logi had swallowed down meat, and bones, and the trough into the bargain. All were, therefore, unanimous that Loki was the loser at this game. Utgarda-Loki then asked at what game that young man could play? Thialfi answered that he would try a race with anyone that Utgarda-Loki might select. Utgarda-Loki said that that was a goodly craft, but added that he must be very swift-footed if he hoped to win at that game. He then rose and went out. Without on the plain there was a noble race-ground. Utgarda-Loki called to a young man named Hugi (thought), and ordered him to run a race with Thialfi. In the first run Hugi was so greatly ahead, that when he had reached the goal, he turned and came to meet Thialfi. 'Thou must step out better than that,' said Utgarda-Loki, 'if thou wilt win; though I must allow that no one has ever come here before more swift-footed than thou.' They now tried a second race. When Hugi was at the goal and turned round, there was a long bowshot between him and Thialfi. 'Thou art certainly a good runner,' said Utgarda-Loki, 'but thou wilt not, I think, gain the victory though that will be seen when thou hast tried the third course.' They now ran the third time, and when Hugi had already reached the goal, Thialfi had not arrived at the middle of the course. All were now unanimous that these trials were quite sufficient.

Utgarda-Loki now inquired of Thor what the performances were which he wished to exhibit before them, and which might justify the general report as to his great prowess. Thor answered that he would undertake to drink with any of his men. With this proposal Utgarda-Loki was content, and returning to the hall, ordered his cup-bearer to bring the horn of atonement, or punishment, out of which his men were wont to drink, saying, 'When anyone empties this horn at one draught, we call it well drunk; some empty it in two, but no one is so great a milksop that he cannot manage it in three.' Thor looked at the horn, which did not appear to him particularly capacious, though it seemed rather long. Being very thirsty, he applied it to his mouth and took a long pull, thinking there would be no occasion for him to have recourse to it more than once; but on setting the horn down to see how much of the liquor had vanished, he found there was nearly as much in it as before. 'Thou hast drunk some, but no great deal,' said Utgarda-Loki. 'I could not have believed it, had it been told me, that Asa-Thor was unable to drink more. I am sensible, however, that thou wilt drink it all at the second draught.' Instead of answering, Thor set the horn to his mouth, resolved on taking a greater draught than before, but could not raise the tip of the horn so high as he wished, and on taking it from his mouth, it seemed to him that he had imbibed still less than at the first pull, though now the horn was easy to carry without spilling. Utgarda-Loki then said, 'How now, Thor, hast thou not left more than thou canst conveniently quaff off in one draught? It appears to me that if thou art to empty the horn at the third pull, thou hast left for that the greatest portion. But thou wilt not be thought so great a man here with us as thou art said to be among the Aesir, if thou dost not distinguish thyself more at other games than, as it seems to me, thou art likely to do at this.' At this speech Thor waxed angry, raised the horn to his mouth and drank a third time with all his might, and as long as he was able; but when he looked into the horn, he saw that a part only of its contents had disappeared. He then put the horn aside and would have no more. 'It is now pretty plain,' said Utgarda-Loki, 'that thou art not quite so mighty as we thought thee. Art thou inclined to try any other feats, for it is evident thou wilt not gain much at this.' Thor answered, 'I am willing to try another: though I wonder whether among the Aesir such draughts would be called little. But what feat hast thou now to propose?' Utgarda-Loki answered, 'It is what my youngsters here do and make nothing of; it is merely to lift my cat from the ground. I should not, however, have proposed such a feat to Asa-Thor, had I not seen that thou art by no means the man I imagined thee to be.' A huge grey cat then came walking forth. Thor approaching it, took it under the belly and lifted it; but the cat arched its back, and when Thor had raised it as high as he could, one foot only was off the ground, but further than this Thor could make nothing at that sport. 'It is just as I foresaw it would be,' said Utgarda-Loki; 'the cat is very large, and Thor is short and little compared with those present.' 'Little as I am,' replied Thor, 'I now challenge anyone who likes to come forth and try a hug with me, now that I am angry.' 'There is no one here,' said Utgarda-Loki, 'who will not think it child's play to wrestle with thee; but call in the old crone Elli (age), my foster-mother. She has laid many a man on his mother earth, that did not appear weaker than Asa-Thor.' The crone came in, and the game began; but the more he squeezed her in his arms the firmer she stood. She now endeavoured to trip him up; Thor soon began to totter, and a hard struggle ensued. It had not, however, lasted long before Thor sank on one knee. Utgarda-Loki now approached, and bade them cease, adding that Thor need not challenge any more of his people, and that night was drawing near. He then caused Thor and his companions to be seated, and they stayed the night over as welcome guests.

The next morning at daybreak the guests arose, and having dressed themselves, prepared for departure. Utgarda-Loki then came, and ordered a table to be set forth. There was no lack of hospitality with regard either to meat or drink. Having finished their repast, they betook themselves to their journey. Utgarda-Loki accompanied them out of the city, and at parting inquired of Thor how he thought his visit had come off, and whether he had met with any mightier men than himself? Thor answered, that he could not but acknowledge that their mutual intercourse had greatly redounded to his discredit; 'And I know,' added he, 'that you will call me a very insignificant person, which vexes me exceedingly.'

Utgarda-Loki answered, 'Now that thou art out of the city, I will tell thee the real state of the case, which, if I live and have power, thou never again shalt enter nor shouldst thou have entered it this time, had I previously known that thou hadst so great strength in thee, and wouldst have so nearly brought us to the verge of destruction. By magic alone I have deluded thee. When we first met in the forest, and thou wouldst unfasten the wallet, I had secured it with iron wire, which thou wast unable to undo. Thou didst then strike me thrice with thy hammer. The first blow was the least, and yet it would have caused my death, had it fallen on me. Thou sawest in my hall a rock with four square hollows in it, one of which was deeper than the others: these were the dints of thy hammer. I slipped the rock under the strokes without thy perceiving it. In like manner the sports were contrived, at which you contended with my people. With respect to the first, at which Loki proved his prowess, it was thus: Loki was certainly very hungry and ate voraciously, but he who was called Logi was fire, which consumed both meat and trough. The Hugi, with whom Thialfi strove in running, was my thought, with which it was impossible for him to contend. When thou didst drink from the horn with, as it seemed, so little effect, thou didst in sooth perform a miracle, such as I never imagined possible. The other end of the horn was out in the ocean, which thou didst not observe. When thou comest to the sea, thou wilt see how much it is diminished by thy draughts, which have caused what will now be called the ebb.' Furthermore he said, 'No less a feat does it seem to me when thou didst lift the cat and, the sooth to say, all were terrified when they saw thee raise one of its feet from the ground. For it was not a cat, as thou didst imagine; it was in fact the Midgard's serpent, which encircles the whole world. It had barely length enough for its head and tail to touch, in its circle round the earth, and thou didst raise it so high that it almost reached heaven. Thy wrestling with Elli was also a great miracle for there never has been one, nor ever will be, if he be so old as to await Elli, that she will not cast to the earth. We must now part, and it will be best for both that thou dost not pay me a second visit. I can again protect my city by other spells, so that thou wilt never be able to effect aught against me.'

On hearing these words, Thor raised his hammer, but when about to hurl it, Utgarda-Loki was no longer to be seen and on turning towards the city, with the intention of destroying it, he saw a spacious and fair plain, but no city.

**Of Thor and the Midgard's serpent.** Shortly after his journey to Jötunheim, Thor, in the guise of a youth, departed from Midgard, and came one evening to a giant's named Hymir, where he passed the night. At dawn the giant rose, dressed himself, and made ready to row out to sea and fish. Thor also rose, dressed himself in haste, and begged of Hymir that he might accompany him. But Hymir answered, that he would be of little or no use to him, as he was so diminutive and young. 'And,' added he, 'thou wilt die of cold, if I row out as far and stay as long as I am wont to do.' Thor told him that he could row well, and that it was far from certain which of the two would first desire to reach land again. He was, moreover, so angry with the giant, that he almost longed to give him a taste of the hammer; he, however, suppressed his wrath, intending to prove his strength in some other way. He then asked Hymir what they should have for a bait, and received for answer, that he might provide one for himself; whereupon Thor, seeing a herd of oxen belonging to Hymir, wrung off the head of the largest, named Himinbriot, and took it with him down to the sea. Hymir had already launched his boat. Thor stepped on board, placed himself abaft, and rowed so that Hymir was compelled to acknowledge that they were making a rapid course. Hymir at the same time rowed at the prow and it was not long ere he said they were now come to the place where he was accustomed to catch flatfish. But Thor was desirous of going still farther out, and they rowed a good way farther. Hymir then said, they were now come so far that it would be dangerous to remain there, on account of the Midgard's serpent, but Thor answered that he would row a while longer, and he did so. Then laying his oars aside, he attached a very strong hook to an equally strong line, fixed the ox's head on, as a bait, and cast it out. It must be confessed that Thor here tricked the Midgard's serpent no less than Utgarda-Loki had deceived him, when with his hand he undertook to lift the cat. Midgard's serpent gaped at the bait, and so got the hook into his jaw, of which he was no sooner sensible than he struggled so that Thor's hands were dashed on the side of the boat. Thor now waxed angry, assumed his divine strength, and resisted with such firmness, that his legs went through the boat, and he rested on the bottom of the sea. He then hauled the serpent up to the boat's edge. Dreadful it was to behold, how Thor cast his fiery looks on the serpent, and how the serpent glared on him and spat forth venom. Hymir changed colour and grew pale with terror when he saw the serpent, and the water streaming into the boat; and as Thor was swinging his hammer, the giant in his trepidation drew forth his knife, and cut the line, and the serpent sank down into the ocean. Thor hurled his hammer after it, and, it is said, struck off its head; but it lives there still. He then applied his fists to the giant's head, so that he fell backwards overboard. Thor waded to land.

In an older story, this myth is combined with another, which is as follows. The gods visited the giant Oegir, the god of the sea, but he was in want of a kettle to brew beer in for them, and not one among them knew how to procure one, until Ty said to Thor that his father Hymir, who dwelt to the east of Elivâgar, at the end of heaven, had a very capacious kettle, a mile deep. Thereupon Thor and Ty went to Hymir's dwelling, where the first person they met with was Ty's grandmother, a horrible giantess with nine hundred heads: but afterwards there came forth another woman radiant with gold and light-browed. This was Ty's mother, who proffered them drink, and wished to hide them under the kettles in the hall, on account of Hymir, who often received his guests with grudge, and was given to anger. Hymir returned late from the chase, and came into the hall: the icebergs resounded with his steps, and a hard-frozen wood stood on his cheek. The woman announced to him that his son, whose coming they had long wished for, was arrived, but accompanied by their declared enemy, and that they were standing concealed behind a pillar in the hall. At a glance from the giant the pillar burst asunder, and the crossbeam was snapped in two, so that eight kettles fell down, of which one only was so firmly fabricated that it remained whole. Both guests now came forth, and Hymir eyed Thor with a suspicious look; he anticipated no good when he saw the giants' enemy standing on his floor. In the meanwhile three oxen were cooked, of which Thor alone ate two. At Thor's inordinate voracity Hymir naturally felt alarmed, and very plainly told him, that the three must another evening be content with living on what they could catch: so the next day they rowed out to fish, Thor providing the bait, as we have seen in the foregoing narrative. They rowed to the spot where Hymir was accustomed to catch whales, but Thor rowed out still farther. Hymir caught two whales at one haul, but the Midgard's serpent took Thor's bait. Having drawn the venomous monster up to the boat's edge, he struck its mountain-high head with his hammer; whereupon the rocks burst, it thundered through the caverns, old mother earth all shrank, even the fishes sought the bottom of the ocean; but the serpent sank back into the sea. Ill at ease and silent, Hymir returned home, and Thor carried the boat, together with the water it had shipped, bucket and oars, on his shoulders, back to the hall. The giant continued in his sullen mood, and said to Thor, that though he could row well, he had not strength enough to break his cup. Thor took the cup in his hand, and cast it against an upright stone, but the stone was shattered in pieces; he dashed it against the pillars of the hall, but the cup was entire when brought back to Hymir. The beautiful woman then whispered good advice in Thor's ear: 'Cast it against Hymir's own forehead, which is harder than any cup.' Thor then raising himself on his knee assumed his divine strength, and hurled the vessel against the giant's forehead. The old man's forehead remained sound as before, but the wine-cup was shivered in pieces. 'Well done,' exclaimed Hymir, 'thou must now try whether thou canst carry the beer-vessel out of my hall.' Ty made attempts to lift it, but the kettle remained stationary. Thor then grasped it by the rim, his feet stamped through the floor of the hall, he lifted the kettle on his head, and its rings rang at his feet. He then started off with the kettle, and they journeyed long before he looked back, when he saw a host of many-headed giants swarming forth from the caverns with Hymir. Lifting then the kettle from his head, he swung Miölnir, and crushed all the mountain-giants. Thus did the stout Thor bring to the assembly of the gods Hymir's kettle; so that they can now hold their feast with Oegir at flax-harvest.[1]

1   The last line of this poem is very obscure; the meaning may be, that Oegir had now got a kettle, in which he could prepare warm beer for the gods.

There was a feast also given by Oegir to the gods, at which Loki ridiculed and reviled all the principal guests and which forms the subject of an entire eddaic poem. On the above occasion, Oegir's hall was lighted with shining gold.

**Of Thor and the Giant Hrungnir.** Odin once upon a time riding on his horse Sleipnir to Jötunheim, came to the giant Hrungnir's. Hrungnir asked who he was with a golden helmet, who rode through air and water? 'Thine must,' added he, 'be a most powerful and excellent horse.' Odin answered that he would pledge his head that his horse's match was not to be found in Jötunheim. Hrungnir was, however, of opinion that his horse Gullfaxi (golden-mane) was far superior; and springing on it in anger, he rode after Odin, with the intention of paying him for his presumptuous words. Odin galloped at full speed, but Hrungnir followed him with such giant impetuosity, that before he was aware of it, he found himself within the barred enclosure of the Aesir. On reaching the gate of their hall, the Aesir invited him in to drink, and set before him the cups out of which Thor was wont to quaff. He drank of them all, became intoxicated, and threatened to take Valhall and carry it to Jötunheim, to sack Asgard and slay all the gods, except Freyia and Sif, whom he would take home with him. Freyia alone ventured to fill for him, and it appeared that he was well disposed to drink all the Aesir's beer. The Aesir, who wished to hear no more of his idle vaunt, called for Thor, who came, raised his hammer, and asked who gave that insolent giant permission to be in Valhall, and why Freyia was filling for him, as at a festival of the Aesir? Hrungnir, looking not very benignantly on Thor, answered that he came on the invitation of Odin, and was under his protection. Thor replied that he should repent the invitation before his departure. Hrungnir then said that Thor would gain but little honour in slaying him there, where he was without weapons; he would show more valour by meeting him in single combat on the frontier of the country at Griotuna-gard. 'It was,' added he, 'a great folly of me that I left my shield and stone club at home. Had I my arms with me, we would instantly engage in combat: but as it is otherwise, I proclaim thee a coward, if thou slayest me unarmed.' Thor, who had never before been challenged by anyone, would on no account decline the meeting. When Hrungnir returned to Jötunheim, the giants, to whom it was of vital importance which of the two should gain the victory, made a man of clay nine miles high, and three in breadth; but they could find no fitting heart for him, till they took one from a mare, which did not, however, remain steady when Thor came. Hrungnir's heart was of hard stone, and triangular, like the magic sign called Hrungnir's heart. His head was likewise of stone, as was also his shield, and this he held before him, when he stood at Griotuna-gard, waiting for Thor, while his weapon, a formidable whetstone, or stone club, rested on his shoulder. At his side stood the man of clay, who was named Möckurkalfi, who was excessively terrified at the sight of Thor. Thor went to the combat attended by Thialfi, who running to the spot where Hrungnir was standing, exclaimed, 'Thou art standing very heedlessly, giant! Thou holdest the shield before thee, but Thor has observed thee, and will go down into the earth, that he may attack thee from beneath.' On receiving this information, Hrungnir placed the shield under his feet, stood upon it, and grasped his club with both hands. He then saw lightning, and heard a loud crash of thunder, and was sensible of Thor's divine power; who was advancing in all his strength, and had cast his hammer from a distance. Hrungnir raising his club with both hands, hurled it against the hammer: the two met in the air, and the club was dashed in pieces, of which one portion fell on the earth, whence come all the whetstone mountains; while another fragment struck Thor on the head, causing him to fall on the earth. But Miölnir struck Hrungnir on the head, and crushed his skull: he fell forwards over Thor, so that his foot lay on Thor's neck. Thialfi fought with Möckurkalfi, who fell with little honour. Thialfi then went to Thor, and endeavoured to take Hrungnir's foot from his neck, but was unable to move it. All the Aesir came, when they heard that Thor had fallen, but they were equally powerless. At length came Magni, a son of Thor and Jarnsaxa, who, although he was only three days old,[1] cast Hrungnir's foot from his father's neck, and got from Thor in reward the horse Gullfaxi , which Odin took amiss, saying that so good a horse ought not to have been given to a giantess's son, but rather to himself. Thor went home to Thrudvang, but the stone remained fixed in his forehead. Then came a Vala (Völva) or prophetess, named Groa, the wife of Örvandil (Örvald), who sang incantations (galldrar) over him, so that the stone was loosed. In recompense, Thor would gladden her with the tidings that he had come from the north over Elivâgar, and in an iron basket, had borne Örvandil from Jötunheim; in token of which he related to her how one of Örvandil's toes had protruded from the basket, and got frostbitten, and that he (Thor) had broken it off and cast it up to heaven, and formed of it the star called Örvandil's toe. When Thor further informed her that Örvandil would soon return home, she was so overjoyed that she forgot to continue her incantations, so that the stone was not extracted, but still remains in Thor's forehead.[2] No one should, therefore, cast a whetstone across the floor, for then the stone in Thor's head is moved.

---

1   Vali, in like manner, when only one day old, avenged the death of Baldur on Höd. See hereafter.

2   It may here be observed that the Lapps represent Thor with a flintstone in his forehead.

**Of Baldur's death and Loki's punishment.** The good Baldur had been troubled with sad and painful dreams that his life was in peril. The gods were exceedingly distressed, and resolved to pray for Baldur's security against all possible danger; and his mother Frigg exacted an oath from fire, water, iron, and all kinds of metal, stone, earth, trees, diseases, beasts, birds, and venomous snakes, that they would not injure her son. When the gods had thus, as they imagined, rendered all safe, they were accustomed, by way of sport, to let Baldur stand forth at their assembly, for all the Aesir to shoot at him with the bow, or to strike or throw stones at him, as nothing caused him any harm. This was considered a great honour shown to Baldur. Yet, notwithstanding these precautions, Odin, it appears, had misgivings that something wrong would take place, and that the Norns of happiness had secretly departed from them. To put an end to this painful state of anxiety, he resolved on a journey to the infernal abodes. He arose, placed the saddle on Sleipnir, and bent his way down to Niflhel (Niflheim), there to raise and interrogate a dead Vala, whose grave lay by the eastern gate of Hel's abode. Here he was met by the fierce dog of Hel, with bloody breast and jaws, which bayed and howled terrifically; but Odin rode on until he reached the Vala's grave. Turning then his face to the north, he uttered those necromantic songs which have power to wake the dead, until the Vala, raising herself reluctantly from the tomb, demanded what man it was that had thus ventured to disturb her rest. In answer, Odin told her that his name was Vegtam, son of Valtam, and at the same time inquired of her, on what occasion the benches and gilded couches, which he perceived, were being prepared. She informed him that it was in honour of Baldur, and desired to be no more questioned. Persisting in his inquiries, she goes on to tell him the whole manner of Baldur's death and the events immediately following, as they are here related; and again deprecates all further interrogation. But Odin persists, and asks who those maidens are that do not weep for Baldur, but let their towering headgear flaunt towards heaven?[1] Hereupon the Vala exclaims: 'Thou art not Vegtam, as I before believed; rather art thou Odin, chief of men.' To this Odin answers: 'No Vala art thou, nor wise woman: rather art thou mother of three giants.' To this insulting speech the Vala replies: 'Ride home, and boast of thy feat. Never shall mortal visit me again, till Loki shall have burst his chains, and Ragnaröck be come.'

---

1   Who these maidens are we are nowhere informed, though it is evident they were not visible to mortal eyes, and that by discerning them Odin betrayed his divine nature. The lost myth concerning them must have been at variance with the story of Thökt (see hereafter) who is mentioned as the only being that would not bewail the death of Baldur.

When Loki, Laufey's son, saw the sport before mentioned, he was displeased that Baldur was not hurt, and in the likeness of a woman he went to Frigg in Fensalir. Frigg inquired of her whether she knew what the Aesir were doing in their assembly. She answered that they were all shooting at Baldur, but without hurting him. Frigg then said, 'Neither weapon nor wood will hurt Baldur: I have exacted an oath from all of them.' On hearing this, the woman asked, 'Have all things, then, sworn to spare Baldur?' Frigg told her in reply that the mistletoe, a little insignificant plant, growing to the west of Valhall, was the only thing from which she had not required an oath, as it appeared to her too young to take one. Loki then departed, went and pulled up the mistletoe, and took it with him to the assembly, where all were engaged in their sport with Baldur. Höd was standing without the circle. Turning towards him, Loki asked why he did not shoot? Höd excused himself by saying that he was both blind and unarmed. 'But,' said Loki, 'thou shouldst, nevertheless, show to Baldur the same honour as the others. Take this wand, and I will direct thee to where he is standing.' Höd took the mistletoe, and cast it at Baldur: it pierced him through, and he fell dead to the earth. This was the most deplorable event that had till then happened among gods and men.

On Baldur's fall, the Aesir were struck speechless, and lost all presence of mind. One looked at another, and all breathed vengeance on the author of the misdeed; but no one durst wreak his vengeance there, the place being sacred (a place of peace). When they essayed to speak, tears burst forth, so that they could not impart their sorrow to each other. But Odin was the most afflicted by this misfortune, for he saw how much the Aesir would lose by the death of Baldur.

When they had somewhat recovered themselves, Frigg asked which of the Aesir was willing to gain her love and esteem by riding to Hel for the purpose of finding Baldur, and offering her a ransom, if she would allow him to return to Asgard. Hermod, Odin's active son and follower, undertook the journey; Sleipnir was led forth, Hermod mounted and galloped away.

The Aesir conveyed Baldur's corpse to the seashore; but his ship named Hringhorni (which was the largest of all ships), on which they were to burn the body, they were unable to get afloat; whereupon a message was sent to Jötunheim, to the giantess Hyrrockin, who came riding on a wolf, with a viper for a rein. Dismounting from her palfrey, which four doughty champions (berserkir), called by Odin to take charge of it, could hold only by casting it on the earth, she went to the prow, and sent the ship forth with such force, that fire sprang from the rollers placed under it, and the whole earth trembled. At this Thor was incensed, and seized his hammer to cleave her head; but all the other gods interceded for her. Baldur's corpse was then borne out on the ship. His wife Nanna, the daughter of Nep, grieved so intensely that her heart burst, and her body was laid on the pile with that of her beloved Baldur. The pile was then kindled: Thor was present and consecrated it with his hammer, and kicked the dwarf Litur, who was running before his feet, into the fire. At this funeral many people were present: Odin with Frigg and his ravens and the Valkyriur, Frey in his chariot drawn by the hog Gullinborsti or Slidrugtanni, Heimdall on his horse Gulltopp, Freyia with her cats besides a great multitude of frost-giants and mountain-giants. Odin laid his ring Draupnir on the pile, from which afterwards, every ninth night, there dropped eight rings of equal weight. Baldur's horse was also cast on the pile with all his housings.

Hermod, we are told, rode nine nights and days through dark and deep valleys, until he reached the river Giöll, where he crossed over the bridge, which is paved with shining gold. The maiden Modgud (Móthguthr), who guards it, inquired his name and race, and said that the day before five troops of dead had ridden over the bridge, but that it did not resound so loudly as under him alone 'Nor,' added she, 'hast thou the hue of the dead. Why then dost thou ride on the way to Hel?' Hermod answered, 'I am riding to Hel to seek Baldur: hast thou seen aught of him on this road?' She answered that Baldur had ridden over the bridge, and showed him the way that led downwards and northwards to Hel. Hermod rode on until he came to the barred enclosure which surrounds Hel's abode. Here he dismounted, tightened the saddle-girth, and having remounted, clapped spurs to his horse and cleared the enclosure. Thence he rode straight to the hall, where he saw his brother Baldur sitting in the place of honour. He remained there that night. The next morning, he besought of Hel that Baldur might ride home with him, and represented to her the grief of the Aesir for his loss. Hel answered that it would now appear whether Baldur were really so beloved as was said for if everything in the world, living and lifeless, bewailed him, he should return to the Aesir; if not, he should continue with her. Hermod rose up, Baldur followed him out of the hall, took the ring Draupnir, and sent it to Odin as a remembrance; and Nanna sent her veil with other presents to Frigg, and to Fulla her ring. Hermod returned to Asgard, and related what he had seen and heard.

Thereupon the Aesir sent messages over the whole world, praying all things to weep for Baldur, and thereby release him from Hel. And all did so: men and beasts, earth and stones, wood and all metals. But as the messengers were returning, they found in a cavern a giantess named Thökt, who, on their beseeching her to weep for Baldur, answered:

'Yes, Thökt will wail,
weep with dry tears,
for Baldur's death;
breathes he or dies,
it boots me not:
let him bide with Hel.'

Baldur's death was avenged by Odin's son Vali, who, though only one day old, unwashed and uncombed, slew Höd.

Thökt, it was supposed, was Loki, who had thus not only caused the death of Baldur, but also prevented his release from Hel. To escape from the vengeance of the gods, he concealed himself in a mountain, where he built a house with four doors, that he might see on all sides. But in the daytime he often transformed himself into a salmon, and hid himself in the waterfall called Franangur's fors. He was one day sitting in his house twisting flax and yarn, and forming meshes, like the nets of later times, with a fire burning before him, when he perceived that the Aesir were not far off; for Odin had spied out his retreat from Hlidskialf. On the approach of the Aesir, he threw the network into the fire, and sprang into the river. Kvasir, the wisest of the Aesir, was the first that entered, who, on seeing the ashes of the network on the fire, concluded that it must be for the purpose of catching fish. On mentioning this to the Aesir, they took hemp, made a net after what they had seen on the ashes, and cast it into the waterfall; Thor holding it at one end, and all the Aesir drawing it at the other. But Loki went to a distance, and placed himself between two stones, so that the net passed over him; but they were aware that something living had touched it. They then cast it out a second time, having tied to it something heavy, so that nothing could slip from under it; but Loki went on farther, and perceiving that he was near the sea, he sprang over the net up into the waterfall. The Aesir having now ascertained where he was, returned to the waterfall, and divided themselves into two parties, Thor wading in the middle of the river towards the sea. Loki had now the alternative, either, at the risk of his life, to swim out to sea, or again to leap over the net. With the greatest promptitude he tried the latter chance, when Thor grasped him, but he slipped in his hand, and it was by the tail only that Thor could secure him. To this circumstance it is owing that the salmon has so pointed a tail.

When the gods had thus captured Loki, they brought him to a cave, raised up three fragments of rock, and bored holes through them. They then took his sons, Vali (Ali) and Narfi (Nari). Vali they transformed into a wolf, and he tore his brother Narfi in pieces. With his entrails they bound Loki over the three stones, one being under his shoulders, another under his loins, the third under his hams and the bands became iron. Skadi then hung a venomous snake above his head, so that the poison might drip on his face; but his wife Sigyn stands by him, and holds a cup under the dripping venom. When the cup is full, the poison falls on his face while she empties it; and he shrinks from it, so that the whole earth trembles. Thence come earthquakes. There will he lie bound until Ragnaröck.

**Of Ragnaröck, the twilight of the gods or the destruction of the gods and the World.** Loki lay chained under the hot spring's grove. In the iron forest east of Midgard, the old giantess brought forth Fenrir's (the deep's) progeny; one of which, named Sköll, will pursue the sun to the encircling ocean; the other, Hati, Hrodvitnir's son, called also Managarm, will run before the sun, and will swallow up the moon. He will be sated with the lives of the dying. On a height will sit the giantess's watch, the dauntless Egdir (eagle), and strike his harp; over him, in the Bird-wood, will crow the light-red cock Fialar. Over the Aesir will crow the gold-combed cock that wakens heroes in Odin's hall. But a soot-red cock will crow beneath the earth in Hel's abode. Loudly will howl the dog Garm in Gnipa's cave; bonds will be burst, loose the wolf run forth; brothers will contend and slay each other, kindred tear kindred's bond asunder. It will go hard with the world. Great abominations there shall be: an axe-tide, a sword-tide; shields shall be cloven; a wind-tide, a wolf-tide, ere the world perishes: no man will then spare another. The tree of knowledge[1] (Miótvidr, Miötudr) shall be burnt, Mimir's sons shall dance to the resounding Giallar-horn, Heimdall raise high his trump and blow, Odin consult Mimir's head; Yggdrasil's ash, that ancient tree, tremble but stand; from the east Hrym shall come driving, then shall ocean swell; Jormungand (Midgard's serpent) put on his giant-mood, and plough through the billowy deep; but glad shall the eagle scream, and with its pale beak tear corpses; Naglfar shall go forth, the keel from the east shall glide, when Muspell's sons over the ocean sail; Loki will steer it; the wolf be followed by its whole monstrous progeny, led by Byleist's brother (Loki). What now befalls the Aesir? What befalls the Elves? All Jötunheim resounds; the Aesir meet in council; the dwarfs moan before their stony doors. From the south comes Surt with flickering flames; from his sword gleams the heaven-god's sun; the stone-mountains crack, the giantesses stumble, men tread the way to Hel, and heaven is riven. Then shall come Hlin's second sorrow,[2] when Odin goes with the wolf to fight, and Beli's radiant slayer against Surt. Then shall fall Frigg's dearest god. Then shall come the great victory father's son, Vidar, to fight against the deadly monster; he with his hand shall cause his sword to stand in the

---

1    Lit. The middle tree.
2    Baldur's death was the first.

giant's son's heart. Then shall the glorious son of Hlodyn, Odin's son (Thor), go against the monster (Midgard's serpent), bravely shall slay it Midgard's defender. Then shall all men their home (the world) forsake. Nine feet shall go Fiörgyn's (Earth's) son from the serpent, bowed down, who feared no evil. The sun shall be darkened, earth in ocean sink, the glittering stars vanish from heaven, smoky clouds encircle the all-nourishing tree (Yggdrasil), high flames play against heaven itself.

**Of Ragnaröck according to Snorri's *Edda*.** There will come a winter called Fimbul-winter, when snow will drift from every side, a hard frost prevail, and cutting winds; the sun will lose its power. Of these winters three will follow without an intervening summer. But before these, three other winters will come, during which there will be bloodshed throughout the world. Brothers will slay each other through covetousness, and no mercy will be found between parents and children. Then will great events take place. One wolf will swallow up the sun, to the great detriment of mankind; the other wolf will take the moon, and will also cause a great loss. The stars will vanish from heaven. Then will it also happen that the whole earth and the mountains tremble, that the trees will be loosed from the earth, and the mountains come toppling down, and all fetters and bonds be broken and snapped asunder. The wolf Fenrir will break loose, the sea will burst over the land, because Midgard's serpent writhes with giant rage, and strives to get on land. Then also will the ship called Naglfar be loosed, which is made of dead men's nails. It should, therefore, be borne in mind, that when anyone dies with uncut nails, he much increases the materials for the construction of Naglfar, which both gods and men wish finished as late as possible.[1] In this seaflood Naglfar will float: Hrym is the giant named who will steer it. The wolf Fenrir will go forth with gaping mouth: his upper jaw will touch heaven, and his nether jaw the earth: if there were room, he would gape even more widely; fire burns from his eyes and nostrils. Midgard's serpent will blow forth venom, which will infect the air and the waters. He is most terrific, and he will be by the side of the wolf. During this tumult, heaven will be cloven, and Muspell's sons ride forth: Surt will ride first, and both before and after him will be burning fire. The gleam of his good sword is brighter than the sun, but as they ride over it Bifröst will break. Muspell's sons will proceed to the plain called

---

1   Grimm suggests that by the slow process of constructing a ship, described as the largest of all ships (see p. 37), of the parings of the nails of the dead, it is simply meant to convey an idea of the great length of time that is to elapse before the end of the world, and which the implied admonition to cut and burn the nails of the dead, is intended still further to prolong. Grimm, J., *Deutsche Mythologie*, op. cit., p. 775, *note*.

Vigrid (Vígrithr): there will come also the wolf Fenrir and Midgard's serpent; there will Loki also have come, and Hrym, and with them all the frost-giants. All the friends of Hel will follow Loki, but Muspell's sons will have their own bright battle-order. Vigrid's plain is a hundred miles wide on every side.

But when these events take place, Heimdall will stand up, and blow with all his might the Giallar-horn, and rouse up every god to hold a meeting. Odin will then ride to Mimir's well, and take counsel for himself and friends. Then will the ash Yggdrasil tremble, and nothing will be free from fear in heaven and earth. The Aesir will arm, and all the Einheriar, and go forth to the plain. Odin will ride first with his golden helmet and bright corselet, and his spear Gungnir: he will encounter the wolf Fenrir. Thor will be at his side, but may not help him, as he will be fully engaged in fighting with Midgard's serpent. Frey will fight with Surt, and after a hard conflict fall. The cause of his death will be, the lack of his good sword, which he gave to Skirnir. Then will the dog Garm be loosed, which had till then been bound before Gnipa's cave: he will prove the greatest misfortune; he will fight against Ty, and they will slay each other. Thor will gain glory from [the slaying of] Midgard's serpent; thence he will walk nine feet, and then fall dead from the venom blown on him by the serpent. The wolf will swallow Odin, and so cause his death; but immediately after, Vidar will come forth, and step on the monster's nether jaw with the foot on which he will have his formidable shoe.[1] With his hand he will seize the wolf's upper jaw, and rend his mouth asunder. Thus will the wolf be slain. Loki will enter into conflict with Heimdall, and they will slay each other. After all this, Surt will hurl fire over the earth, and burn the whole world.

After the conflagration of heaven and earth and the whole universe, there will still be many dwellings, some good some bad, though it will be best to be in Gimli, in heaven: and those who are partial to good drinking will find it in the hall called Brimir, which is also in heaven [in Okólni]. That is also a good hall which stands on the Nida-fells, made of red gold, and is called Sindri. In these halls good and upright men will dwell. In Naströnd there is a large and horrible habitation, the door of which is towards the north. It is formed of the backs of serpents, like a house built of wands, but all the serpents' heads are turned into the house, and blow forth venom, so that the venom flows through the halls, in which wade perjurers and murderers, as it is said:

---

1  See page 31.

She saw a hall
from the sun far remote
on Naströnd stand;
northward are its doors;
through the roof opening
run venom-drops;
built is that hall
of backs of snakes;
men, forswearers
and murderers,
through waters foul,
wading she saw,
and who the ears beguile
of others' wives.

But in Hvergelmir it is worst; there

the serpent Nidhögg
sucks the dead bodies,
the wolf tears them.

There too the river Slid (Slithr) falls from the east through poisonous valleys, filled with mud and swords.

**Of the New World.** There will arise, a second time, an earth from ocean, in verdant beauty; waterfalls will descend, the eagle fly over that catches fish in the mountain-streams. The Aesir will meet again on Ida's plain, and of the mighty earth-encircler speak. There will they remember the great deeds of old, and the glorious gods' ancient lore. Then will they find in the grass the wondrous golden tables, which at Time's origin, the prince of gods and Fiölnir's race had possessed. Unsown fields shall then bear fruit, all evil cease. Baldur shall return; he and Höd dwell in Odin's noble hall, the heavenly god's abode. Hoenir shall there offerings receive, and two brothers' sons inhabit the spacious Vindheim. There will be a hall brighter than the sun, roofed with gold, in Gimli; there virtuous folk shall dwell, and happiness enjoy for evermore. Then will come the Mighty One to the gods' council, powerful from above, he who rules all things: he will pronounce judgements, and appease quarrels, establish peace that shall last for ever. But from beneath, from Nidafell will come flying the dusky, spotted serpent Nidhögg, bearing dead carcases on his wings.

In Snorri's *Edda* the renewal of the world is thus described. A new earth will spring up from the sea, which will be both green and fair; there will the unsown fields bring forth fruit. Vidar and Vali will be living, as if neither the sea nor Surt's fire had injured them; they will dwell on Ida's plain, where Asgard formerly stood. And thither will come the sons of Thor, Modi and Magni, and will have Miölnir with them. Next will come Baldur and Höd from Hel. They will sit and converse together, and call to remembrance their secret councils, and discourse of events long since past of Midgard's serpent and the wolf Fenrir. Then will they find in the grass the golden tables formerly belonging to the Aesir, as it is said: 'Vidar and Vali shall inhabit the house of the gods, when Surt's fire is quenched.' Modi and Magni will possess Miölnir, and labour to end strife. But in a place called Hoddmimir's holt, two persons, Lif and Lifthrasir, will lie concealed during Surt's conflagration, who will feed on morning dew. From these will come so great a progeny, that the whole earth will be peopled by them. And it will seem wonderful, that the sun will have brought forth a daughter not less fair than herself. She will journey in her mother's path, as it is said: 'A daughter shall the sun bring forth ere Fenrir destroys her. The maid shall ride on her mother's track, when the gods are dead.'

**The Saga of Völund.**[1] Völund and his brothers, Slagfin (Slagfidr) and Egil, were the sons of a king of the Fins. They ran on snowskates and hunted the beasts of the forest. They came to a place called Ulfdal, where they built themselves a house near a lake called Ulfsiar (Wolf-waters). One morning early they found on the bank of the lake three maidens sitting and spinning flax, with swan-plumages lying beside them. They were Valkyriur. Two of them, named Hladgun Svanhvit and Hervör Alvit, were daughters of a king named Hlödver; the third was Ölrun, the daughter of Kiar, king of Valland. The brothers conducted them to their dwelling, and took them to wife, Egil obtaining Ölrun, Slagfin Svanhvit, and Völund Alvit. After having lived eight years with their husbands, the Valkyriur flew away in quest of conflicts, and did not return; whereupon Egil and Slagfin set out on their snowskates in search of them, but Völund remained at home in Ulfdal. According to old tradition, Völund was of all men the most skilful. His hours of solitude were passed in making rings of gold and setting them with precious stones: these he hung on a line of bast. Thus did he while away the long hours, anxiously awaiting his fair consort's return.

Having received intelligence that Völund was alone in his dwelling, Nidud (Nithudr), king of the Niarer in Sweden, sent a party of armed men

---

1   The Saga of Völund or Veland (Völundr), though without claim for admission within the pale of the Mythology of the Aesir, yet, on account of its intimate connection with that mythology, of its high antiquity, as well as of the widespread celebrity of its hero throughout the middle age, cannot well be omitted in a work professing to be an account of the Mythology of the North. I have, therefore, added it.

thither by night, during Völund's absence at the chase, who on searching the house, found the line of rings, to the number of seven hundred, one of which they carried off. On his return, Völund proceeded to roast bear's flesh, and while the meat was at the fire, sat down on a bearskin to count his rings. Missing one, he concluded that Alvit was returned and had taken it. In anxious expectation of seeing her enter, he at length fell asleep, and on waking found that his hands and feet were fast bound with heavy chains, and that Nidud was standing by his side, who charged him with having stolen the gold from him of which the rings were made. Völund repelled the charge, declaring that while their wives were with them they had possessed many treasures. The ring Nidud gave to his daughter Bödvildi; but a sword, in the tempering and hardening of which Völund had exerted his utmost skill, Nidud took for himself.

Apprehensive of vengeance on the part of Völund, for the injuries he had inflicted on him, Nidud, at the suggestion of his queen, caused him to be hamstringed,[1] and confined on an islet called Saevarstöd. Here he fabricated all kinds of precious things for the king, who allowed no one excepting himself to visit him. One day, however, the two young sons of Nidud, heedless of the prohibition, came to Völund's habitation, and proceeding at once to the chest in which his valuables were kept, demanded the keys. Here they feasted their eyes over the many costly ornaments of gold thus brought to view, and received from Völund the promise, that if they would return on a future day, he would make them a present of the gold they had seen, at the same time enjoining them to keep their visit a secret from all. They came accordingly, and while stooping over the contents of the chest, Völund struck off their heads, and concealed their bodies in an adjacent dunghill. The upper part of their skulls he set in silver, and presented them as drinking cups to Nidud; of their eyes he formed precious stones (pearls), which he gave to Nidud's queen; of their teeth he made breast-ornaments, which he sent to Bödvildi.

Bödvildi having broken the ring given to her by her father from Völund's collection, and fearing her father's anger, took it privately to Völund, in order to have it repaired. 'I will so mend it,' said he, 'that thou shalt appear

---

1    Another and, no doubt, older tradition respecting Völund is referred to by Deor the skald (*Cod. Exon.*, p. 377), according to which Nithhád, as he is called in the A. S. poem, only bound him with a thong of sinews:

| | |
|---|---|
| Siththan hine Nidhád on | *When that on him Nithhád* |
| nede legde, | *constraint had laid,* |
| swoncre seono-bende. | *with a tough (pliant) sinew-band.* |

The hamstringing will then appear to be a later improvement on the story.

fairer to thy father, and much better to thy mother and thyself.' He then gave her beer, which so overpowered her that she fell asleep, and while in that state fell a victim to the passions of Völund. 'Now,' exclaimed he, 'are all the sufferings save one avenged that I underwent in the forest. I wish only that I had again the use of my sinews, of which Nidud's men deprived me.' Laughing he then raised himself in air, while Bödvildi in tears departed from the islet. Descending on the wall of the royal palace, Völund called aloud to Nidud, who, on inquiring what had become of his sons, was thus answered: 'First thou shalt swear to me all these oaths: By board of ship, and buckler's rim, by horse's shoulder, and edge of sword, that thou wilt not harm the wife of Völund, or cause her death, be she known to you or not, or whether or not we have offspring. Go to the smithy that thou hast built, there wilt thou see the bloodstained trunks of thy young ones. I struck off their heads, and in the prison's filth laid their carcases; their skulls I set in silver, and sent them to Nidud; of their eyes I formed precious stones, and sent them to Nidud's crafty wife; of their teeth I made breast-pearls, which I sent to Bödvildi, your only daughter, who is now pregnant.' Then laughing at the threats and maledictions of Nidud, Völund again raised himself on high. Thereupon Nidud summoned to his presence his daughter Bödvildi, who confessed to him all that had befallen her on the islet.

The foregoing Saga, from Saemund's *Edda*, differs materially in its details from the story of 'Velint', as given in the Vilkina Saga, the substance of which has been thus condensed by the late learned Dr Peter Erasmus Müller, Bishop of Seeland.[1]

While King Vilkinus, on his return from an expedition to the Baltic, lay with his fleet on the coast of Russia, he went one day up into a forest, where he met with a beautiful woman, who was a mermaid.[2] In the following year she brought forth a son, who received the name of Vadi,[3] and grew to a gigantic stature. His father, who had no great affection for him, nevertheless gave him twelve mansions in Seeland. Vadi had a son named Velint, who, in his ninth year, was placed by his father for instruction with a smith named Mimir in Hunaland, where he had much to endure from Sigurd Svend, who was also under the same master. This coming to the knowledge of his father in Seeland, he, at the expiration of

---

1　*Sagabibliothek*, Bd. ii, p. 154.
2　In the German poem of the Rabenschlacht, 964, 969, she is called Frou wâchilt.
3　In the Scôp or Scald's Tale (*Cod. Exon.*, 320, 1) we have 'Wada (weold) Haelsingum' (Wada ruled the Helsings). Memorials of this tribe are Helsingborg, Helsingör (Elsinör), Helsingfors, Helsingland, etc. Wade's boat, Guingelot, is celebrated by Chaucer.

three years, took his son away from Mimir, and placed him with two skilful dwarfs, who dwelt in the mountain of Kallova (Kullen). Two years afterwards his father went to fetch him, but perished by a mountain-slip. Velint slew the dwarfs, who, being envious of his superior skill, had sought his life. He then placed himself with his tools in a hollowed tree, having a glass window in front, and committed himself to the mercy of the waves, which bore him to the coast of Jutland, where he was well received by Nidung, who at that time ruled in Thy. Here he availed himself of the opportunity of showing how greatly he excelled in curious works the king's own smith Aemilias.

It happened on a certain time that the king went forth to war with thirty thousand horse, and had proceeded five days at the head of his army, when he discovered that he had left behind him the talisman (sigursteinn) which brought him victory. To repair his mishap, he promised to bestow his daughter and half his kingdom on him who should bring him the talisman on the following day before sunset. Velint performs the feat, but having by the way killed one of the king's men in self-defence, it affords the king a pretext for declaring him an outlaw. To wreak his vengeance, Velint disguises himself as a cook, and puts charmed herbs in the food of the princess, but she detects the treachery, and Velint is seized, hamstringed, and condemned to make ornaments in the king's court for his enemies.

At this time, by Velint's desire, his younger brother Egil came to Nidung's court. Being famed for his skill in archery, the king commanded him to shoot an apple, at a single shot, from the head of his son, a child of three years. Having performed this deed, the king, seeing that he had taken two arrows from his quiver, demanded of him for what purpose they were intended. Egil answered, 'They were designed for thee, if I had hit the child.' This bold answer was not taken amiss by the king.

Velint in the meantime was brooding over vengeance. One day the king's daughter came to his smithy, for the purpose of getting a broken ring mended; when Velint, availing himself of the opportunity, violated her. This crime was shortly after followed by the murder of the king's two youngest sons, whom he had enticed to his smithy. Their bones he set in costly golden vessels, which were placed on their father's table. Velint then made himself a plumage of feathers collected by his brother Egil, by means of which he flew up on the highest tower of the palace, from whence he declared all that he had done. Nidung on hearing this commanded Egil, under threats of death, to shoot his brother, and he actually struck him under the left arm, but where, as had been previously concerted between them, a bladder was placed filled with blood, which Nidung imagined to be the blood of Velint: he, however, flew to his father's abode in Seeland. Shortly after these events, Nidung died, and Velint was reconciled with his son Otwin, and married his sister, who had already borne him a son named Vidga.[1]

**Of Thorgerd Hörgabrud** (Thorgerdr Hörgabrúdr or Hölgabrúdr) **and Irpa**. Objects of worship among the people of Halgoland, in Norway, were Thorgerd Hörgabrud and her sister Irpa. Who these were will appear from the following extract:

The Halgolanders had their local deities, who were but rarely worshipped by the other Scandinavians. One of these was Hâlogi (high flame), or Helgi (holy), from whom the whole district, of which he was king, derived its name of Hâloga-land, or Hölga-land. He was probably identical with the Logi and Loki (fire, flame) formerly worshipped by the Fins. His daughters were Thorgerd Hörgabrud, or Hölgabrud, and Irpa, of whom the former was an object of especial veneration with Hakon Jarl, and to propitiate whom, we are informed, he sacrificed his son Erling, a child of seven years, when engaged in a doubtful battle with the pirates of Jomsborg. She consequently appeared in a raging hailstorm from the north, and the pirates imagined that they saw both her and her sister Irpa on board the jarl's ship; an arrow flew from each of her fingers, and every arrow carried a man's death. In Gudbrandsdal, she and Irpa together with Thor were worshipped in a temple, which Hakon Jarl and the chieftain Gudbrand possessed in common. In western Norway, she had also a temple most sumptuously constructed, in which the said Hakon Jarl paid her the most profound adoration. Even in Iceland, Thorgerd was worshipped in a temple at Olves-vand, and was regarded as a tutelary spirit by the chieftain Grimkell and his family. Her statue is described as having gold rings on the arms.

**The saga of the Völsungs and Giukings or Nibelungs**. In consequence of its immediate connection with the Mythology of the Aesir, it has been deemed desirable to relate the origin of the celebrated Nibelungen Hoard or Treasure, the calamities caused by which form the subject of so many compositions, both Scandinavian and German. The following condensation of the story is chiefly by the late learned Bishop Peter Erasmus Müller.[2]

---

1 The Wudga mentioned in The Scôp or Scald's Song (*Cod. Exon.*, 326), the Vidrik Verlandsön of the Danish Kjaempeviser. For the several extracts relating to these personages, from German and Northern Sources, see W. Grimm's *Deutsche Heldensage, passim*.

2 *Sagabibliothek*, Bd. ii, p. 36.

There was a man named Sigi; he was descended from the gods, and was called a son of Odin. There was another man named Skadi, who had a bold and active thrall called Bredi. Sigi went out to hunt with Bredi, but in a fit of jealousy at the greater success of the thrall, he slew him. Sigi thus became an outlaw, and, conducted by Odin, went far away, and obtained some warships, by means of which he at length became king over Hunaland. In his old age he was slain by his wife's relations, but his son, Rerir, avenged his death on them all.

Rerir became a great warrior, but had no offspring. He and his queen prayed fervently to the gods for an heir. Their prayer was heard. Odin sent his maiden (ôskmey),[1] a daughter of the giant (jötun) Hrimnir, with an apple to the king. She assumed the guise of a crow (krageham), flew to a mound, on which Rerir was sitting, and let the apple fall into his bosom. The king ate of it, and his queen forthwith became pregnant, but could not bring forth. In this state she passed six years, when a wonderfully large child was cut from her womb. He was named Völsung, and kissed his mother before her death.

Völsung married the daughter of Hrimnir, by whom he had ten sons, and a daughter named Signi. Sigmund and Signi, the eldest, were twins. Signi was married to a king of Gothland, named Siggeir. At the nuptial feast there came a tall, one-eyed old man, barefooted, wrapped in a cloak, with a broad-brimmed hat, into the hall, in the middle of which stood an oak,[2] whose roots passed under the floor, while its branches covered the roof. The old man struck a sword into the trunk of the tree, as a gift for anyone who should draw it forth. Sigmund acquired the sword, to the mortification of Siggeir, who on his departure invites Völsung to be his guest in Gothland; but on his arrival there, attacks him with an overwhelming force, slays him, and makes all his sons prisoners.

Signi begged that her brothers might not be immediately put to death. Their feet were set fast in a large tree in the forest, and every night there came a wolf and devoured one of them, until Sigmund was the only one left. Signi caused his face to be smeared with honey, and some to be laid in his mouth, so that when the wolf came, he licked the honey, and put his tongue into Sigmund's mouth, which Sigmund seized with his teeth. The wolf kicked with so much violence that the trunk of the tree burst asunder. The wolf lost his tongue, and got his death. Sigmund fled to a cave in the forest. Signi sent her two sons to bear him company; but finding they were

---

1   The same as a Valkyria, and probably so called from Oski, one of the names of Odin. See p. 22 and *note*, and Grimm, J., *Deutsche Mythologie*, op. cit., p. 390.
2   This primitive style of building speaks strongly for the antiquity of the legend.

not sufficiently stout and valiant, he killed them by the counsel of Signi; who then changed form with a trollwife, and was three days in the cave with her brother, to whom she bore a son, who was named Sinfiotli. He, when ten years old, was sent to Sigmund's cave, and was bold enough to knead a dough, without caring for the numerous snakes that were in it. Sigmund and his son then turned robbers. One day they fell in with the sons of some king, who nine days in ten, through enchantment, wore the form of wolves.[1] By putting on their wolfish garbs, Sigmund and his son became wolves, but when the time came for laying them aside, they burnt them, so that they might do no more harm. They now went to Siggeir's castle, where they concealed themselves, but were discovered through two young children of Signi. These, at the instigation of Signi, were slain by Sinfiotli, who, together with Sigmund, was immediately after overpowered by Siggeir's men, and cast into a pit, to die of hunger. Just before the pit was closed, Signi came to it, and threw into it a helmet full of pork, and Sigmund's sword, by the aid of which they worked their way out. They then set the royal castle on fire. When Signi heard what had taken place, she went out and kissed them both, then went in again, glad to die with the man with whom she had so unwillingly lived.

Sigmund, who had returned to his paternal kingdom of Hunaland, married Borghild, by whom he had a son, Helgi, of whom the Norns foretold that he should become a powerful prince. Helgi went to war, together with Sinfiotli, and slew King Hunding, whence he acquired the name of Hundingsbani, and afterwards slew several of his sons. In a forest he met with Sigrun, a daughter of King Högni, who solicited him to free her from Hodbrod, son of Granmar, to whom her father had betrothed her. Hodbrod is slain in a battle, Helgi marries Sigrun, and becomes a powerful king.

In another expedition, Sinfiotli killed a brother of Borghild, who in revenge prepared a poisonous drink, which caused his death. Sigmund bore the corpse in his arms to a narrow frith, where there was a man with a small boat, who offered to convey him across; but no sooner had Sigmund laid the corpse in the boat, than the man pushed off and vanished. After this Sigmund parted from Borghild and married Hiordis, a daughter of King Eilimi, but was attacked in his kingdom by King Lingi, who with his brothers had assembled a numerous army. Sigmund fought valiantly in the battle, until he was met by a one-eyed man, with a broad

---

1   This is the earliest trace of the werwolf superstition occurring in the traditions of the North. While Sigmund and his son slept, their wolf-skins hung close by them. In the *Leges Eccl. of Cnut*, xxvi, the werwolf is named as a known, existing being.

hat, and blue cloak, who held his spear against the sword of the king, which it shivered into fragments. Sigmund fell with almost the whole of his army. At night, Hiordis came to the field of battle, and asked Sigmund whether he could be healed, but he declined her kind offices, for his good fortune had forsaken him, since Odin had broken his sword, of which he requested Hiordis to collect the fragments, and give them to the son she bore under her heart, who should become the greatest of the Völsung race.

Hiordis was carried off by Alf, a son of King Hialprek of Denmark, who had just landed at the battle-place with a band of vikings. She had changed clothes with her attendant, who gave herself out as queen. But Alf's mother, suspecting the artifice, caused her son to ask, how towards the end of night they could know what hour it was, when they could not look on the heavens? The servant answered, that in her youth she had been in the habit of drinking mead at early morn, and therefore always woke at the same hour. But Hiordis answered, that her father had given her a gold ring, which cooled her finger by night, and that was her sign. 'Now,' said the king, 'I know which is the mistress,' and expressed his intention to marry her as soon as she had given birth to her child. After the birth of Sigurd (Sigurthr), Hiordis accordingly became the wife of Hialprek.

Sigurd grew up in Hialprek's court, under the care of Regin, who instructed him in all the branches of knowledge known at that time, as chess, runes, and many languages. He also urged him to demand his father's treasure of Hialprek. Sigurd asked a horse of the king, who allowed him to choose one; and Odin, in the guise of an old man with a long beard, aided him to find out Grani, that was of Sleipnir's race. Regin would then have him go in quest of Fafnir's gold, of which he gave him the following account.

'Hreidmar had three sons, Fafnir (Fofnir,) Ottur, and Regin. Ottur could transform himself into an otter, under which form he was in the habit of catching fish in Andvari's waterfall, so called from a dwarf of that name. He was one day sitting with his eyes shut eating a salmon, when Odin, Hoenir, and Loki chanced to pass by. On seeing the otter, Loki cast a stone at it and killed it. The Aesir then skinned the otter, and came well satisfied with their prize to Hreidmar's dwelling. There they were seized, and compelled to redeem themselves with as much gold as would both fill and cover the otter's skin. To obtain the gold, Loki borrowed Rân's[1] net, cast it into the waterfall, and caught in it the dwarf Andvari, who was accustomed to fish there under the form of a pike. The dwarf was compelled to give all his gold as the price of his liberty; but on Loki taking from him his last ring, he

1  see pp. 30.

foretold that it should prove the bane of all its possessors. With this gold the Aesir enclosed the otter's skin, but on Hreidmar perceiving a hair of the beard still uncovered, Odin threw on it the ring of Andvari. Fafnir afterwards slew his father, took all the gold, and became one of the worst of serpents, and now watched over his treasure.'

Sigurd then requested Regin to forge him a sword. He forged two, but their blades would not stand proof. Sigurd then brought him the fragments of Sigmund's sword, of which he forged one that could cleave an anvil and cut through floating wool. Armed with this weapon, Sigurd went forth, first to his maternal uncle Grip, who foretold him his destiny. He then sailed with a chosen army to avenge his father's death on the sons of Hunding. During a storm they were hailed by an old man, from a point of land, whom they took on board. He told them his name was Hnikar,[1] together with much other matter. The storm then abated, and as he stepped on shore, he vanished. Hunding's sons with a large army encountered Sigurd, but were all slain, and Sigurd returned with great honour.

Sigurd was now impatient to slay the serpent, whose lair had been pointed out to him by Regin. An old long-bearded man warned him to beware of the monster's blood. Siguld pierces Fafnir through, who, nevertheless, holds a long conversation with his slayer, in which he answers the latter's questions relative to the Norns and Aesir, but strives in vain to dissuade him from taking the gold.[2]

After the death of Fafnir, Regin, who had concealed himself, came forth, drank of Fafnir's blood, cut out his heart with the sword named Rithil, and requested Sigurd to roast it for him. As Sigurd touched the heart with his finger, a drop by chance lighted on his tongue, and he instantly understood the language of birds. He heard an eagle[3] tell its companion that Sigurd would act wisely, if he himself were to eat the serpent's heart. Another eagle said, that Regin would deceive him. A third, that he ought to slay Regin. A fourth, that he ought to take the serpent's gold, and ride to the wise Brynhild at Hindarfiall. All these feats Sigurd performs, and rides off with the treasure on Grani's back.[4]

---

1   This was Odin, one of whose numerous names was Hnikar (see p. 22), under which he appears as a marine deity.
2   On receiving the fatal wound, Fafnir demanded to know the name of his murderer, which Sigurd at first declined giving him, in the belief (as Bishop Müller supposes) then prevalent, that the words of a dying man possessed great power, when he cursed his enemy by name.
3   The word igtha signifies the female eagle, though it may also signify *swallow*, *owl*, *partridge*.
4   Among which were the famed Oegir-hiálm, which Fafnir was wont to wear while brooding over the treasure, a golden corselet, and the sword Hrotti.

Sigurd now bent his course southwards to Frakland,[1] and rode a long time, until he came to Hindarfiall, where he saw before him a light flaring up to the sky, and a shield-burgh, within which he found a damsel sleeping in complete armour, whose corselet seemed to have grown fast to her body. On Sigurd ripping up the corselet with his sword, the maiden awoke, and said that she was a Valkyria and named Brynhild,[2] that Odin had condemned her to that state of sleep by pricking her with a sleep-thorn,[3] because, contrary to his will, she had aided King Agnar (or Audbrod) in war, and slain King Hialmgunnar.

Sigurd begged her to give him some instruction, and she taught him the power of runes, and gave him lessons for his conduct in life. They engaged on oath to marry each other, and Sigurd took his departure His shield blazed with the red gold, on it was depicted a dragon, dark brown above, and bright red beneath, a memorial of the monster he had slain, which the Vaerings call Fafnir. Sigurd's hair was brown, and fell in long locks, his beard short and thick; few could look on his piercing eyes. He was so tall that, when girded with his sword Gram, which was seven spans long, he went through a ripe rye field, the knob of his sword-sheath still stood forth. When all the stoutest warriors and greatest captains are spoken of, he is mentioned the first, and his name is current in all languages.

Sigurd rode on until he came to a spacious mansion, the rich lord of which was named Heimir. He was married to a sister of Brynhild, named Bekhild (Baenkhild). Sigurd was received with pomp, and lived there a considerable time in great honour. Brynhild was also there on a visit to her relations, and employed herself with embroidering in gold the exploits of Sigurd – the slaying of the serpent and carrying off the gold.

It chanced one day that Sigurd's falcon flew and perched on the window of a high tower. On going in pursuit of it, Sigurd discovered Brynhild at her work. Hereupon he became thoughtful, and imparted to Heimir's son, Alswith, what a beautiful woman he had seen embroidering his deeds. Alswith told him that it was Brynhild, Budli's daughter; whereupon Sigurd observed, that only a few days before he had learned that she was the most beautiful woman in the world, and expressed his resolution to visit her,

---

1    That is Frankenland, the land of the Franks, Franconia.
2    According to the Brynhildar-kvida I., she was named Sigurdrífa, another name, it is said, of Brynhild. From this passage it appears that Odin received mortals of royal race into his band of Valkyriur.
3    Svefn-thorn, *spina soporifera*. A superstition not yet wholly extinct in Denmark and Iceland. It was supposed that a person could not be wakened out of this sleep as long as the thorn lay on his body or remained sticking in his clothes.

although Alswith informed him that she would never endure a husband, but that her thoughts were solely bent on warfare.[1]

She received him with great state and friendliness. When she presented to him the golden cup with wine, he seized her hand, and placed her by him, clasped her round the neck, kissed her, and said, 'No woman born is fairer than thou.' She answered, 'It is not prudent to place one's happiness in the power of women: they too often break their vows.' 'The happy day will come,' said Sigurd, 'that we may enjoy each other.' Brynhild answered that such was not the will of fate, for that she was a shield-maid. Sigurd replied, 'It were best for both that we lived together. The pain I now feel is harder to endure than sharp weapons.' Brynhild said, 'I shall go to the battlefield, and thou wilt marry Gudrun, King Giuki's daughter.' 'No king's daughter,' said Sigurd, 'shall seduce me nor am I given to fickleness. I swear to thee by the gods, that I will have thee to wife, and none other.' Brynhild also expressed herself in words to the same purpose. Sigurd expressed his gratitude, gave her Andvari's ring, swore anew, and went away to his people.

There was a king named Giuki, who dwelt south of the Rhine. He had three sons, Gunnar, Högni and Guttorm. Gudrun (Gudrún) his daughter was fairest of maidens. Her mother was the noted sorceress Grimhild. Gudrun dreamed that a most beautiful falcon came to her hand; she thereupon became thoughtful: it was said to betoken some king's son. Gudrun betook herself to the wise Brynhild, sister to the wicked king Atli, that she might hear her interpretation. Gudrun was, however, reserved towards her, and simply inquired the names of the mightiest kings and their exploits. Brynhild named Haki and Hagbard, but Gudrun thought they were too inactive in avenging their sister, who had been carried off by Sigar. Gudrun then named her own brothers, but Brynhild said that they had not yet proved themselves; but that Sigurd Fafnisbana was the flower of all heroes. Gudrun then told her that she had dreamed of a beautiful hart, of which all were in chase, but which she alone overtook, and that Brynhild killed it in her lap. Brynhild then recounted to her her whole future destiny, and Gudrun returned to Giuki's palace.

Thither shortly after came Sigurd, riding on Grani with all his treasure. Grimhild conceived such an attachment to him that she was desirous he

---

1    According to this account, Sigurd appears now to have seen Brynhild for the first time, which is completely at variance with what we have just read of their previous meeting and mutual vows. Either Sigurdrífa is a different personage from Brynhild, or the story of Sigurd's first interview with her is a fragment of some lost version of the legend, varying considerably from what is extant in the *Eddas* and the *Volsunga Saga*.

should marry her daughter; and therefore gave him a charmed potion, which caused him to forget Brynhild, to swear fellowship with Gunnar and Högni, and to marry Gudrun.[1]

When Sigurd and the sons of Giuki had traversed far and wide over the country, and performed many great feats, Grimhild persuaded her son Gunnar to woo Brynhild, Budli's daughter, who was still dwelling with Heimir in Hlindal. Her maiden-bower was encircled with glowing fire, and she would marry that man only who should ride through it. The princes rode thither, but Gunnar could not force his horse over the fire. He and Sigurd then exchanged forms, and the latter on Grani traversed the flames and made love to Brynhild as though he were Gunnar, son of Giuki. Brynhild, though sore against her will, was obliged to fulfil her engagement. For three nights they slept in the same bed, but Sigurd laid the sword Gram between them.[2] He took Andvari's ring from her hand, and gave her in return one from Fafnir's treasure. After these events, Sigurd rode back to his comrades, and resumed his own form.

Brynhild related to her foster-father, Heimir, how Gunnar had ridden through the fire and made love to her, and how certain she till then had felt that Sigurd alone, to whom she had vowed eternal constancy, could have accomplished the adventure. Then commending Aslaug, her daughter by Sigurd, to the guardianship of Heimir, she returned to her father, Budli, and the celebration of her marriage with Gunnar lasted many days. Not until it was over did Sigurd call to memory the oaths he had sworn to Brynhild, but let all pass off quietly.

It happened one day that Brynhild and Gudrun went to the Rhine to bathe. On Brynhild going further out in the water, Gudrun asked the cause. She answered, 'Neither here nor anywhere else will I stand by side of thee. My father was more powerful than thine, my husband has performed greater feats than thine, and has ridden through the glowing fire. Thy husband was King Hialprek's thrall.' Hereupon Gudrun gave her to understand that it was *her* husband that had ridden through the fire, had passed three nights with her, had taken Andvari's ring from her, which she herself then wore. At this intelligence Brynhild grew deadly pale, and uttered not a word. The following day the two queens began jarring again about their husbands' superiority, when Gudrun declared that what had been sung of Sigurd's victory over the serpent was of greater worth than all

---

1 Sigurd gave her a piece of Fafnir's heart to eat, which rendered her more obdurate than before.
2 Remains of this custom are, it is said, still to be traced in some of the Danish isles, South Jutland, Holstein and Norway. Such nights were called Prövenaetter, Probenächte, *nights of trial* or *proof*.

King Gunnar's realm. Brynhild now went and lay down as one dead. When Gunnar came to her she upbraided him with his and his mother's deceit, and attempted his life. Högni caused her to be bound, but Gunnar ordered her to be loosed. She would engage in no occupation, but filled the palace with loud lamentations. Gudrun sent Sigurd to her, to whom she poured forth all her grief, and said that she hated Gunnar, and wished Sigurd were murdered. On the latter saying it had afflicted him that she was not his wife, and that he would even then marry her, she answered that she would rather die than be faithless to Gunnar. She had sworn to marry the man that should ride over the fire: that oath she would keep sacred or die. Sigurd said, 'Sooner than thou shalt die, I will forsake Gudrun.' His sides heaved so violently that his corselet burst asunder. 'I will neither have thee nor any other man,' said Brynhild and Sigurd took his departure.

Brynhild threatened to leave Gunnar, if he did not murder Sigurd and his child. Gunnar was bewildered. Högni dissuaded him from compliance with the will of Brynhild. At length Gunnar said there was no alternative, as Sigurd had dishonoured Brynhild.[1] They would, therefore, instigate their brother Guttorm (who had not sworn brotherly fellowship with Sigurd) to do the deed. For this purpose they gave him a dish composed of wolf's and serpent's flesh after which, being urged on by Brynhild, Guttorm stabbed Sigurd while slumbering,[2] but was himself cut asunder by the sword Gram, which his victim hurled after him. Gudrun mourned over her murdered consort, but Brynhild laughed at her grief. Gunnar and Högni reproached her for her malignity, but she set before them their baseness towards Sigurd, and their deceit towards herself; nor did she suffer herself to be appeased by Gunnar's caresses, but after having given away her gold, stabbed herself. She now again foretold the fate of Gudrun, and commanded her body to be burnt by the side of Sigurd's, on the same pile, enclosed with hangings and shields, and the sword Gram between them,[3] together with those of his

1   It would seem that Brynhild had feigned the story of her own dishonour, for the purpose of instigating the Giukings to murder Sigurd, as she is afterwards made to say, 'We slept together in the same bed as if he had been my own brother. Neither of us during eight nights laid a hand on the other.' At the same time, however, we read that Brynhild, when on the eve of her marriage with Gunnar, committed Aslaug, her daughter by Sigurd, to the care of her foster-father Heimir. Aslaug was afterwards married to Ragnar Lodbrok, whence it seems not improbable that the latter story was invented for the purpose of connecting the line of Danish kings with Sigurd and Brynhild. See *Edda Saem.*, pp. 229, 203.

2   According to other narratives, Sigurd was murdered on his way to the public assembly (thing). According to the German tradition, he was slain in a forest.

3   In the prose introduction to the Helreid Brynhildar, it is said there were two piles. Brynhild's corpse was laid on the pile in a chariot hung with silken curtains. Asuitus, a prince mentioned by Saxo (op. cit., p. 244), was buried with a dog and a horse.

three-year-old son, whom she herself had murdered, and of Guttorm; on her other side, her own attendants, two at her head and two at her feet, besides two hawks. She then mounted the pile.

Gudrun mourned for the death of Sigurd; Grani, his horse, hung down his head in sorrow. Gudrun fled to the forest, and came at length to king Hialprek in Denmark, where with Thora, the daughter of Hakon, she embroidered the exploits of heroes.[1] After the death of Sigurd, Gunnar and Högni possessed themselves of his whole treasure, which was called Fafnir's inheritance. Enmity now ensued between the Giukings and Atli, who accused them of having caused the death of his sister Brynhild. As a peace-offering, it was agreed that Gudrun should be given in marriage to Atli. Grimhild, having discovered her retreat, rode thither, accompanied by her sons and a numerous retinue of Langobards, Franks and Saxons. Gudrun would not listen to them. Grimhild then gave her an oblivious potion,[2] and thereby gained her consent to a union with Atli, from which she foreboded evil. They travelled during four days on horseback, but the women were placed in carriages; then four days in a ship, and again four days by land, ere they came to Atli's residence, where the nuptials were solemnised with great splendour: but Gudrun never smiled on Atli.

One night Atli dreamed ill-boding dreams, but Gudrun interpreted them favourably. It then occurred to his remembrance that the Giukings had kept possession of all Sigurd's gold, and he therefore sent Vingi to invite them to a banquet; but Gudrun, who had noticed what had passed between him and his messenger, cut runes and sent them to her brothers, together with a gold ring, in which some wolf's hair was twined. Vingi altered the runes before he stepped on shore. He made great promises to the Giukings, if they would visit King Atli. Gunnar had but little inclination for the journey, and Högni was opposed to it; but being overcome by wine at the protracted feast given to Vingi, Gunnar was led to pledge himself to the journey

In the meantime, Kostbera, Högni's wife, had read the runes sent by Gudrun, and discovered that they had been falsified. She strove to dissuade her husband from the journey, and related to him her terrific dreams, which he interpreted in a contrary sense. Glaumvör also,

---

1   Also Danish swans, southern palaces, noble sports, kings' retainers, red shields, Sigmund's ships with gilded and sculptured prows.

2   'A drink cold and bitter . . . mingled with Urd's power, with chilling water and blood of Sôn. In that horn were characters of all kinds cut, red of hue, which I could not interpret.' Whether the norn Urd is here alluded to is extremely doubtful, and almost equally so is the allusion to Sôn, though the vessel containing the skaldic or poetic mead may be intended, for which see p. 39.

Gunnar's queen, dreamed of treachery, but Gunnar said that no one could avert his destiny. Though all would dissuade them, they, nevertheless, stept on board with Vingi, attended by a few only of their own people. They rowed so lustily that half the keel burst and their oars were broken. They then travelled a while through a gloomy forest, where they saw a powerful army, notwithstanding which they opened the gate of the fastness and rode in. Vingi now gave them to understand that they had been beguiled, whereupon they slew him with their maces.

King Atli now commanded his people to seize them in the hall. On hearing the clash of arms, Gudrun cast her mantle aside, entered the hall, and having embraced her brothers, endeavoured to mediate, but in vain. She then put on a corselet, took a sword, and shared in the conflict like the stoutest champion. The battle lasted long; Atli lost many of his warriors. At length, the two brothers alone survived of their whole party: they were overpowered and bound. Atli commanded Högni's heart to be cut out, though his counsellors would have taken that of the thrall Hialli; but as he cried out when they were about to lay hands on him, Högni said it was a game he recked little of, so the thrall for the moment escaped. Gunnar and Högni were set in chains. It was Atli's wish that Gunnar should save his life by disclosing where the gold was deposited; but he answered, 'Sooner would I see my brother Högni's bloody heart.' They then again seized on the thrall, cut out his heart, and laid it before Gunnar. 'This,' said he, 'is the heart of a coward, unlike the brave Högni's for even now it trembles, though less by half than when in its owner's breast.' They then cut out the heart of Högni, who laughed under the process. On seeing that it did not tremble, Gunnar recognised it for Högni's, and said that now he alone knew where the gold was hidden, and that the Rhine should possess it rather than his enemies wear it on their fingers. Gunnar was then confined, with his hands bound, in a yard filled with serpents. Gudrun sent him a harp, which he played with his feet, so that all the serpents were lulled to sleep save one viper, which fixed itself on him and stung him to the heart.[1]

Elated with his victory, Atli scoffed at Gudrun, but on perceiving her exasperation, he sought to appease her. She removed his doubts and suspicions by her assumed gentleness, and a sumptuous grave-ale[2] was

---

1   This was Atli's mother so transformed.
2   Old Norse Erfiöl, Dan. Arve-öl, Welsh Aruyl. A funeral feast held in honour of the dead by the heir (O. N. arfr, Ger. Erbe). It was believed that the dead were present at their grave-ale. In the *Eyrbyggiasaga* a story connected with this superstition will be found, which being too long for insertion here, the reader is referred to Sir Walter Scott's extract in the *Illustrations of Northern Antiquities*, p. 507, and in Bohn's edition of Mallet's *Northern Antiquities*, p. 536.

ordered in memory of the fallen. Gudrun now took her two young sons, who were at play, and cut their throats. When Atli inquired for his children, she answered that their skulls, set in gold and silver, had been turned into drinking cups, that in his wine he had drunk their blood, and eaten their hearts in his food. Högni's son, Niflung, thirsting to avenge his father, consulted with Gudrun and when Atli, after his repast, lay down to sleep, they slew him.[1] Gudrun then caused the palace to be surrounded with fire, and burnt all Atli's people.

Gudrun then plunged into the sea, but the waves bore her to land, and she came to the city of the great king Jonakur, who married her, and had by her three sons, Hamdir (Hamthir), Sörli, and Erp (Erpr). Svanhild, Gudrun's daughter by Sigurd, was also bred up there. The mighty king Jormunrek, having heard of Svanhild's beauty, sent his son Randve, together with his counsellor Biki, to woo her for him. She was married to him against the will of Gudrun. As they were sailing home, Biki instigated Randve to speak in terms of tenderness to Svanhild, saying it was more suitable for a young man than for the old king to possess so fair a maiden. After their arrival, Biki told the king that Svanhild was Randve's mistress whereupon the king ordered Randve to be hanged. When led to the gallows he plucked some feathers from a hawk and sent them to his father, who understanding them to signify that he had parted with his honour, commanded his son to be taken down, but Biki had so contrived that he was already dead. At Biki's instigation, Svanhild was also condemned to an ignominious death. She was placed bound at the city gate, to be trampled to death by horses. When she turned her eyes on them, they refused to tread on her; but Biki caused a sack to be drawn over her head, and thus terminated her existence.[2]

---

1   See the account of Atli's death and funeral in Jornandes, ch xxv. The relation here given accords in some measure with what we find in the Byzantine writers, viz. Marcellinus Comes writes, 'Attilam noctu mulieris manu cultroque confossum.' According to others, 'nimio vino et somno gravatus, et copioso sanguinis profluvio obundatus, inventus est mortuus in lecto, accubans mulieri, quae de ejus nece suspecta habita est.' John Malala says that a certain armour-bearer slew Attila. See *Edda Saemundar*, edit. Copenhagen, ii, p. 954.

2   According to Saxo (op. cit., p. 414), Jarmericus was a king of Denmark and Sweden. His story differs widely from that in the *Eddas* and *Volsunga Saga*. Of Svanhild (whom he calls Swavilda) he says, 'Hanc tantae fuisse pulchritudinis fama est, ut ipsis quoque jumentis horrori foret artus eximio decore praeditos sordidis lacerare vestigiis. Quo argumento rex innocentiam conjugis declarari conjectans, accedente erroris poenitentia, falso notatam festinat absolvere. Advolat interea Bicco, qui supinam jumenta diris deturbare carminibus nec nisi pronam obteri posse firmaret. Quippe eam formae suae beneficio servatam sciebat. In hunc modum collocatum reginae corpus adactus jumentorum grex crebris alte vestigiis fodit. Hic Swavildae exitus fuit.'

Gudrun urged her sons, Sörli and Hamdir, to avenge their sister, and poured forth loud lamentations over her unhappy fate. The sons departed cased in mail that no steel could penetrate, but their mother warned them to beware of stone. On the way they met their brother Erp, whom they asked what help he would afford. He answered, he would so help them as the hand helps the hand and the foot the foot At this they were dissatisfied and slew him. Shortly after Hamdir stumbled, and, supporting himself by his hand, exclaimed, 'Erp said truly I should have fallen, had I not supported myself by my hand.' They had proceeded but a few steps further when Sörli stumbled with one foot; 'I should have fallen,' said he, 'had I not stood on both.' When they came to Jörmunrek they immediately assailed him. Hamdir cut off his hands, Sörli his feet. Hamdir said, 'His head would also have been smitten off, had Erp been with us.' Against Jörmunrek's men, who now attacked them, they fought valiantly, their armour being impenetrable to steel, until an old man with one eye came and counselled the men to stone them, and thus caused their destruction.[1]

**Of Ragnar and Thora.**[2] Widespread over all the North was the story of Jarl Heraud of Gothland's youthful daughter, Thora, though more generally known by the appellation of 'Borgar-hjort' (the Hind of the Castle), which was bestowed on her because, unlike the bold Amazons (shield-maidens) of that age, she rather resembled a tender, timid hind and being at the same time exquisitely fair and amiable, her father placed her in a strong castle, instead of a maiden-bower. By some it is related that her castle was guarded by a warrior named Orm, but according to the Saga: 'Heraud once gave his daughter a dragon in a little box, in which it lay coiled up, and under it placed gold. The serpent grew, and with it the gold, so that it was found necessary to remove it out of the castle. At length it became a formidable monster, encircling the whole castle, so that no one could enter save such as gave it food.' Hereupon the jarl held a council, and promised that whosoever should slay the monster should have his daughter to wife. Ragnar, son of king Sigurd of Sweden, who won the famous battle of Bråvalla, having heard of this, caused five woollen cloaks and hose to be made, and boiled in pitch.[3] He then encountered the

---

1    In the battle of Bråvalla, the Danish king, Harald Hildetan, is said to have been slain by Odin, under the form of Harald's own general. See Gräter's *Suhm*, ii, p. 284; Saxo, op. cit., p. 390.
2    Not having either Ragnar Lodbrok's *Saga* or the *Volsunga Saga* at command, the editor has taken these traditions from Afzelius' *Sago*, op. cit. and Müller's *Sagabibliothek*.
3    His garb was singular and gave him a ferocious appearance: from his sailor's breeches, made of wild beasts' skins, he acquired the surname of *Lodbrok*, from lód (*shagginess*), and brók (*breeches*).

dragon, or, as it is also related, the *bear*, that guarded fair Borgar-hjort's dwelling, which after much peril and fatigue he overcame. Lodbrok left his spear sticking in the dragon's back, but took the shaft in his hand, with which he went up to the castle, to the beautiful Thora, whom he thus addressed:

> 'My youthful life I've ventured,
> My age of fifteen years;
> The hateful worm I've slaughter'd
> For thee, thou beauteous maid.'

He then went before the jarl, and demanded the fulfilment of his promise, proving himself the liberator of his daughter by the shaft, which he held in his hand, belonging to the spear remaining in the dragon's body. It now appeared that he was the young King Ragnar, son of Sigurd. Their marriage was solemnised in a manner befitting their rank. By his wife, Thora Borgar-hjort, Ragnar had two sons, Eric and Agnar; but he did not long enjoy his happiness: Thora died, and Ragnar, leaving his states under the government of his sons and certain wise men, again betook himself to a roving life on the ocean, that in the society of his vikings he might drown or mitigate his sorrow for the loss of one whom he had so tenderly loved.

**Of Ragnar and Aslaug**. When Heimir of Hlindal[1] was informed of the death of Sigurd and Brynhild, and that it was intended to destroy their daughter, who had been reared by him, he caused a large harp to be made, in which he concealed the child together with many jewels, and wandered forth towards the north. He gave her an onion to taste, which has the property of sustaining life for a considerable time. Heimir is described as of a gigantic, majestic figure, though his garments but ill accorded with his mien, being those of a beggar or beadsman, while his manners and the melodious tones of his harp proved him to be something widely different. Whenever he came to a lonely spot in wood or field, he would take the child out to divert itself, but if it cried within the harp, when he was in the company of others, or in any house, he would play and sing, until the little one was appeased and silent.

Heimir with his harp came late one evening to a little, lonely dwelling in Norway, called Spangarhede,[2] in which lived an old man named Aki and

---

1 See p. 77.
2 A tongue of land near Lindesnaes, where the names still exist of Krakebaek and Guldvig, which, as the people say, are so called after the king's daughter that was concealed in a golden harp. *Krakumál*, edit. Rafn, Forord, p. 1.

his wife Grima. The crone was sitting alone, and could hardly be induced to kindle a fire on the hearth, that Heimir might warm himself. Her eyes were constantly fixed on the harp, in consequence of a piece of a costly garment that protruded from it; but her suspicion rose still higher when, from under the fringes of the harper's coat, she observed, when he stretched out his arms towards the fire, a bright, gold armlet. Heimir was then shown to a chamber, where, wearied with his journey, he soon fell into a profound sleep. At night the peasant returned. Wearied with the toils of the day, he was displeased at not finding his supper ready, and bitterly complained of the poor man's lot. Hereupon the old woman said to him that in that very moment he might better his condition for the rest of his life, if he would murder the stranger, who, as she had seen, had much gold and many precious things in his harp. At first the old man shrank from the perpetration of so base a deed, but was finally induced to murder Heimir in his sleep. When on opening the harp the little Aslaug came forth, they were terrified and would no doubt have murdered her, had not her prepossessing countenance awakened their conscience; but to prevent suspicion, they clothed her, as if she had been their own, in coarse garments, and called her Kraka. Years rolled on, and Kraka grew up and was distinguished for her understanding and beauty. The greater part of her time was passed in the woods, where she tended her foster-father's cattle. Of her descent she retained a lively remembrance from what at various times had been told her by Heimir; though with her foster-parents she pretended to be dumb, never uttering a syllable.

One evening Ragnar entered the port near Spangarhede, and sent some of his crew on shore to bake bread. When they came back, it was found that the bread was burnt and spoiled. They excused themselves to the king by saying that they had been quite bewildered by a country lass, named Kraka, who was so beautiful that they could not turn their eyes away from her: they thought, indeed, that she was quite as fair as Thora Borgar-hjort. They further related much of her excellent understanding and wit. Ragnar was now desirous of testing these accounts, and sent an order that Kraka should come to him in his ship, but not alone, nor yet in company with anyone; not clad, yet not without clothing; not fasting, nor yet without having eaten. All this she accomplished, though not until she had received the king's assurance of a safe-conduct both coming and going. She came clad in a net, with her thick, flowing hair spread over her like a mantle; she was attended only by a dog, and had tasted an onion, but eaten nothing. The king was no less astonished at her wit and understanding than at her beauty. He preferred a prayer to Odin, that she might be inspired with such love for him as at once to yield to his wishes. But Kraka prized her honour too highly and spurned his suit. He tried to prevail on her with the gift of an embroidered kirtle that had belonged to his deceased queen, saying:

> 'Art thou skill'd in such?
> Wilt thou accept
> This kirtle silver-wrought?
> Well would become thee
> The garment once
> Own'd by fair Borgar-hjort.
> Her lily hands
> Wove the curious texture.
> To me, chief of heroes,
> Faithful she was till death.'

Kraka answered:

> 'I may not take
> The kirtle silver-wrought,
> Which Borgar-hjort once own'd.
> I am call'd Kraka,
> Coal-black in vadmel;[1]
> For I must ever traverse stones
> And tend the goats
> On the seashore.'

Astonished at what he heard and saw, the king would now, by promises of marriage, persuade her to stay the night with him; but as she was inexorable, he was too honourable to break the promise he had given her. Finally, however, Kraka agreed that if the king should return in the same frame of mind of making her his queen, she would be ready to accompany him. After some time the king returned, when Kraka, bidding her foster-parents farewell, accompanied him to his castle, where their marriage was solemnised with all royal pomp.

It once happened that Ragnar visited his friend, King Östen, at Upsala. In the evening Östen's young daughter went round the hall presenting mead and wine to Ragnar and his men. The king was smitten with the beauty of the young princess, and his followers represented to him how much more befitting it would be for him to possess the fair daughter of a royal house than Kraka, the daughter of a peasant. It was then agreed on by both kings that Ragnar should return home, dismiss Kraka, and come back and marry the daughter of Östen. When this came to the knowledge of Kraka, she disclosed to the king her real name of Aslaug, and that she was

---

1   A course woollen stuff made in Norway and Iceland.

the daughter of King Sigurd and Brynhild, and the last descendant of the renowned race of the Völsungs; how that Heimir, after the mournful fate of her parents, had fled with her from their enemies and concealed her in his harp, until he was murdered by Aki at Spangarhede, from which time she had borne the name of Kraka. Awakened from his dream by this narrative, and touched by her proved affection, Ragnar returned no more to Upsala. All friendship with King Östen was now at an end, and from that time Aslaug became fierce and vindictive, like all of her race.

**The Fylgia: Vardögl, Ham, Hamingia, Dîs, Vaett and Draug.** The Fylgia was a tutelar angel or attendant spirit attached either to a single individual or to a whole race. To a person at the point of death the Fylgia became visible. 'Thou must be a fated (moribundus) man, thou must have seen thy Fylgia,' said an Icelander to one labouring under an optical delusion.[1] The Fylgia sometimes appeared to another person. Hedin, we read, returning home one Yule eve, met in the forest a Troll-wife riding on a wolf, with a rein formed of serpents, who offered to bear him company. On relating the incident to his brother Helgi, the latter foresaw his own approaching end, for he knew that it was his Fylgia that had accosted his brother, under the form of a woman on a wolf. When a person was dead or near death, his Fylgia was desirous to follow his nearest relative, or one of the family. When a person's own Fylgia appeared to him bloody, it betokened a violent death.

**Ham and Hamingia.** Identical apparently with the Fylgia are the Ham (Hamr, induviae) and the Hamingia. In the Atlamál, Kostbera dreams that she saw the Ham or genius of Atli enter the house under an eagle's form, and sprinkle them all with blood. In the Vafthrudnismál and Vegtamsquitha, the Hamíngior are identical with the Norns.

Connected with the foregoing is our own superstition about a child's caul. In Germany, children born with this membrane are regarded as fortunate,[2] and the membrane itself is carefully preserved, or sewed in a girdle for the child to wear. Among the Icelanders this caul also bears the name of fylgia; they fancy that the guardian angel, or a part of the infant's soul dwells in it: the midwives, consequently, are careful not to injure it, but bury it under the threshold, over which the mother must walk. Whoever throws it away, or burns it, deprives the child of its guardian angel. Such a guardian is called Fylgia, because it is supposed to follow the individual; it is also called Forynia, from being likewise regarded as a forerunner.[3]

---

1   *Niál's Saga*, 41.
2   See the story of the 'Devil with the Three Golden Hairs' in Grimm, J. & W., *Kinder-und Hausmärchen*, op. cit., No. 29.
3   Grimm, J., *Deutsche Mythologie*, op. cit., p. 828.

Traditions of, and a belief in, beings, of which every person has one as an attendant, are universal over the greatest part of Norway, though the name and the idea vary in different localities. In some places it is called Fölgie or Fylgia, in others Vardögl, Vardygr, Vardivil or Vardöiel, and sometimes Ham or Hau.

In some districts the Vardögl is regarded as a good spirit, that always accompanies a person, and wards off from him all dangers and mishaps for which reason people are scrupulous about following a person out, or looking after him, or closing the door as soon as he is gone, lest they should prevent the Vardögl from following its master, who, in its absence, is exposed to mischances and temptations, and even to the risk of falling into the clutches of an evil spirit called the Thusbet, which also follows every mortal.

In other places, the Fölgie or Vardögl is looked upon rather as a warning attendant, who by knocking at the door or window, tapping on the wall, rattling the latch, etc., gives notice of the coming of an acquaintance, or that one is longing to come, or that a misfortune or a death[1] is at hand. When the Fölgie shows itself, it is generally in the form of an animal, whose qualities bear a resemblance to those of the individual. The dauntless has, therefore, for Fölgie a bold animal, as a wolf, a bear, an eagle, etc. the crafty, a fox, or a cat; the timid, a hare, or the like. The Vardögl will sometimes appear under a human form resembling its master, but immediately vanishes; whence it is that the same person is seen at the same time in two places. One of these forms is the Fölgie, which will sometimes also appear to the individual himself, who, in that case, is said to see his own double.[2] A still more extraordinary case is that of a lad who tumbled over his own Fylgia. In *Fornmanna Sögur* (3, 113) we are told that when Thorsten Oxefod was yet a child of seven years, he once came running into the room and fell on the floor whereat the wise old man Geiter burst into a laugh. On the boy asking what he saw so laughable in his fall, he said, 'I saw what you did not see. When you came into the room, a young white bear's cub followed you and ran before you, but on catching sight of me, he stopped, and as you came running you fell over him.' This was Thorsten's own Fylgia.

If a person is desirous of knowing what animal he has for a Vardögl, he has only to wrap a knife in a napkin, with certain ceremonies, and to hold it up while he names all the animals he knows of. As soon as he has named his Fölgie, the knife will fall out of the napkin.

---

1   Hallager, *Norsk Ordsamling*, p. 141.
2   The Icelander Thidrandi saw nine women clad in black, come riding from the north, and nine others, in light garments, from the south. They were the Fylgiur of his kindred.

Our old divines assumed, in like manner, that every person has an attendant or guardian genius. In the Jernpostil (edit. 1513, p. 142) it is said: 'The moment any man is born in the world, our Lord sends an angel to preserve his soul from the devil, and from all other evil'; appealing, for support of the proposition, to the testimony of St Jerome and St Bernard.[1]

**Dis** (plural Dîsir) is a generic name for all female, mythic beings, though usually applied to a man's attendant spirit or Fölgie. Of these some are friendly, others hostile. The tutelar or friendly Dîsir are likewise called Spâdîsir, *i.e.* prophetic Dîsir: *Scotice* spae, as in spae-wife, *a prophetess, fortune-teller*. In Norway the Dîsir appear to have been held in great veneration. In the Sagas frequent mention occurs of Dîsa blot, or offerings to the Dîsir. A part of their temples was denominated the Dîsa-sal (Dîsarsalr).[2]

**Vaett** (Vaettr, plural Vaettir) in its original signification is neither more nor less than *thing, being, wight,* though in Scandinavia (particularly Norway and Iceland) it is used to signify a sort of female tutelary genius of a country, and then is called a Land-vaett. In the Gulathing's law it is enjoined that 'omni diligentia perquirant rex et episcopus ne exerceantur errores et superstitio ethnica, uti sunt incantationes et artes magicae . . . si in Landvaettas (genios locorum) credunt quod tumulos aut cataractas inhabitent,' etc.[3] The Landvaett assumes various forms. Hallager describes the Vaett as a Troll or Nisse inhabiting mounds, which for that reason are called Vaette-houer. He resembles a young boy in grey clothes with a black hat.[4] The word is, nevertheless, feminine. In Ulfliot's law it was ordered that the head of every ship should be taken off before it came in sight of land, and that it should not sail near the land with gaping head and yawning beak, so as to frighten the Land-vaettir.

**Draug** (Draugr), a spectre. Odin is called Drauga Drott (lord of spectres) because he could raise the dead from their graves (as in the Vegtams Kvida). The apparition to a person of his Draug forebodes his death. In the *Hervarar Saga*, Draugar are spoken of as lying with the dead in their mounds. The Draug follows the person doomed whithersoever he goes, often as an insect, which in the evening sends forth a piping sound. He sometimes appears clad as a fisherman. Both the appearance of the Draug himself, as well as of his spittle (a sort of froth that is sometimes seen in boats) are omens of approaching death.

1   Faye, op. cit., p 76 *sqq.*
2   Keyser, op. cit., p. 74.
3   *Lex. Myth.*, op. cit., p. 833.
4   *Norsk Ordsamlings*, p. 145.

# Section Two

The foregoing comprises what is most essential of the contents of the *Eddas*. On turning to the later interpretations of these dark runes of the times of old, we meet with so many mutually contradicting illustrations, that it is hardly possible to extract anything like unity amid so much conflicting matter The obscure language in which the mythology of the North is expressed, the images of which it is full, the darkness in which the first mental development of every people is shrouded, and the difficulty of rendering clear the connection between their religious ideas – all this leads every attempt at illustration sometimes in one and sometimes in another direction, each of which has, moreover, several byways and many wrong ones.

With regard to the importance and value of the Northern mythology, we meet with two widely different opinions. Some have considered the old Eddaic songs and traditions as mere fabrications, composed for pastime by ignorant monks in the middle age while others have pronounced them not only ancient, but have regarded their matter as so exalted, that even ideas of Christianity are rejected in them. That Christ, for instance, is figuratively delineated in Thor, who crushes the head of the serpent; so that the Eddaic lore is an obscure sort of revelation before Revelation. The first-mentioned of these opinions, though it may have blazed up for a moment, may be now regarded as totally and for ever extinguished; for everyone who reads the *Eddas* will at once perceive that the concord which exists between their several parts, notwithstanding that they are but fragments, the grandeur and poetic beauty, of which they in so many instances bear the impress, together with the old tongue in which the songs are composed, could not have been produced by ignorant monks.

The second opinion can have arisen only out of a blind predilection for antiquity; for when we abstract the religious element which is common to all religions, and the descriptions of the destruction of the world, which are spread over the whole globe, we find in the Northern mythology not one trace of that which constitutes the essential in Christianity; and the accidental resemblance vanishes on every closer consideration. The old religion of the inhabitants of the North is in fact neither a collection of absurdities and insipid falsehoods, nor a fountain of exalted wisdom, but is the ideas of an uncultivated people, with reference to the relation between the divine and the worldly, expressed in images intelligible to the infant understanding. The present time must not expect to find in it either a revelation of new ideas, or a guide to the way of happiness; even the poet of the present will fail to discover in it a source of inspiration, except in so far as it may supply him with a fitting dress for his own poetic images. In fact, the Eddaic lore is important, chiefly because it sheds light on the study of antiquity, on the development of the human mind in general, and of that of our forefathers in particular.

With respect to the interpretation itself, the expounders of the *Eddas* are divided into two sects: one will impart to us an illustration of what the ancients themselves thought of these myths, the other will show what may be thought of them. The first will seize the sense of a given poem, the second will try to discover what may further be imagined from it. The latter we shall at once dismiss; for however beautiful and elevating their interpretations may be, and however much poetic application may be made of them, they will, nevertheless, not conduct us *to*, but *from*, antiquity, while it is precisely that which we wish, as much as possible, to become acquainted with in its whole purity. When these myths are, for example, considered not only with relation to the history of the North, but as universally historical; when we, therefore, in the Northern mythology find figurative indications of the great epochs in the history of the world and in the several myths of nations particular manifestations of their fortunes in the course of time, it is clear that this is not truth but fiction. Though such notions of the Eddaic lore may have in themselves poetic value, though they may, in an agreeable manner, set the imagination in activity and give it a store of new images, yet will the understanding not allow itself to be set aside with impunity. If, therefore, they assume the semblance of a serious interpretation, they dissolve into airy nothingness, because they lack a firm foundation. Fiction may have its liberty, but research has its restraint.

However widely the interpreters of the *Eddas* differ in their opinions from each other, and however faithless they sometimes are even to themselves, their illustrations may, nevertheless, all be referred to three classes – the historic, the physical, and the ethical: to the historic method, in as far as every nation's mythology and earliest history come in contact and melt into each other at their boundaries, and transgress each other's domain; to the physical, because all mythology has nature and her manifestations for object; to the ethical, because laws for the conduct of mankind are the final intent of all religion.

The historic mode of illustration is the most circumscribed of all. As mythology embraces not only life physically and ethically considered, but also the creation and destruction of the world, the beginning and end of time, or eternity, we consequently find in it many elements that belong not to the province of history, and every attempt to bring them within its pale must naturally prove abortive. This mode of illustration can, therefore, at best be applied only to the agency of natural beings – the gods. It is divided into two branches. It may either be assumed that real men have been regarded as gods, or that superhuman beings have been considered as persons on the earth. Of these branches, the first may be subdivided: the deified beings may be regarded as impostors and deceivers, or as benefactors of mankind.

That the gods, Odin and his friends, were mere deceivers, magicians, and wizards (trollmen); that they dazzled the eyes of the people by their arts, and thereby induced them to believe whatever they deemed conducive to their worldly objects; that religion arose among the people, not as a necessity, but was a priestly imposture – such was the opinion entertained in the Christian middle age of the ancient mythology, all heathenism being considered a work of the devil, who through his ministers, the pagan priests, enlarged the realm of falsehood upon earth – that the earliest human beings were giants of superhuman size and powers, after whom came others, less of stature, but excelling them in sagacity, who overcame them by sorcery, and gained for themselves the reputation of gods; that their successors were a mixture of both, neither so large as the giants nor so crafty as the gods, though by the infatuated people they were worshipped as gods; such was the belief in Saxo's time, who consequently sets forth the opinions just adduced, and speaks of Odin as of a being who had acquired for himself divine honours throughout Europe, and after having fixed his residence at Upsala, he and his companions were there regarded as divine beings.[1] The first class of beings was of course Ymir and his offspring, the Frost-giants; the second, Odin and his kindred; the third, the priests of the gods, who by fraud disseminated the doctrines of their predecessors, and raised themselves to the rank of gods.

That these opinions found followers in the middle age may easily be conceived, but it may well seem extraordinary that also in modern times they have had their defenders, and that, by confounding the announcement by the priest of the pretended will of the gods with the divine beings themselves, anyone could be satisfied with the persuasion, that priestly craft and deception have alone formed the entire circle of religious ideas, which are a natural necessity among every people, and one of the earliest manifestations of man's reflection on himself and on the world.

1    Saxo, op. cit., pp. 42. *sqq.*

More probable is the opinion that, not deception, but real historical events have given rise to myths; that the worship of Odin and his kin and companions in the North originated in the immigration of a sacerdotal caste; that the priest's agency has, by the people themselves, been confounded with that of the god, whose minister he was; that his undertakings and exertions for the civilisation of the people, the evidences of his superior penetration and higher knowledge, have, after his death, been clad in a mythic garb; and that thereby, partly through learning and partly from events, a series of myths has been framed, the elements of which now hardly admit of being separated from each other. Such was the opinion of Snorri and other ancient writers, according to whom the gods were a sacerdotal caste from Asia, even from Troy; Odin and his sons were earthly kings and priests; Odin died in Sweden, and was succeeded by Niörd; after the death of whose son, Frey, Freyia alone presided over the sacrifices, being the only one of the deities still living. Such a deification of human beings is not without example in history; among the Greeks we meet with many historic personages, whom admiration of their brilliant qualities and the fictions to which they have given birth, have raised to a superhuman dignity. Connected with this opinion stands the historico-geographic mode of illustration, according to which the ideas concerning mythic beings are transferred to real actions in the North, and mythic tales of the warfare between gods and giants, and of the wandering of the gods on earth, represented as memorials of a real war between those people, and of the Aesir-religion's spread, from its chief seat in Sweden, over the neighbouring countries. This idea of the ancient doctrine having been adopted by the old writers themselves, and by so eminent a historian as Snorri, it may be regarded as the property of history. But we doubt not that the reader will have already seen, that this view is partial, that it does not exhaust the myths, but, at the utmost, embraces only a few, and even does this indirectly; for, generally speaking, it does not supply us with the original signification of the myths, but imparts only a notice of their later application. To illustrate this by an example. – The inhabitants of the North knew of a real Alfheim in Norway and applied their ideas of the alfs, as pure and exalted beings, to the people of that district who were distinguished for a higher degree of civilisation than their neighbours, but did not, on that account, renounce their belief in the alfs as superhuman beings, who they well knew stood in a superhuman relation to the rest of the creation.

All beings in the Northern mythology, says Mone may be regarded as personified ideas, or, in other words, that mythology contains philosophic views of nature and life. So far the physical and ethical interpretations coincide as to their object; for nature and life stand in a constant relation of interchange with each other, the perception of which could not escape even the earliest observers. The physical mode of interpretation has then for object to indicate those powers of nature and natural phenomena, which in the myths are represented as personal beings, and to show the accordance between the mythic representation and the agency of the natural powers. This mode of illustration has been followed and developed by the greater number of interpreters, and, on the whole, none of the proposed systems has in its several parts been so borne out as this. To the Northern mythology it, moreover, presents itself so naturally, that its application is almost unavoidable; for not only have the ancient writers themselves sometimes expressly declared the natural phenomenon intended by this or that myth, as the rainbow, an earthquake, etc., but some myths, as that of the wolf Fenrir, the Midgard's serpent and others, contain so evident a representation of a natural agency, that it is hardly possible to err as to their signification. In the case, therefore, of every obscure myth, it is advisable first to ascertain whether it is or is not a natural myth, before making any attempt to explain it in some other way. But because this mode of explanation is the simplest, most natural, and most accordant with the notions of antiquity, it does not follow that it can be applied in all cases, or that it is always applied rightly. An explanation may be right in its idea, without necessarily being so in its several parts. The idea may be seized, but the application missed. But the idea itself may also be a misconception, when no real agreement is found between the myth and the natural object to which it is applied when the resemblance is, as it were, put into it, but does not of itself spring from it. An example or two may serve to explain this, to which the reader may easily add others. An interpretation fails, when it is made up of that which is only the poetic garb of the thought. The Valkyriur are, for instance, sent forth by Odin, to choose the heroes that are to fall in a battle: they hover over the conflicting bands, they mingle in the hostile ranks, they take the fallen in their embrace, and ride with them on their heavenly horses to Valhall. Here is only a beautiful poetic expression of the thought, that Valfather Odin decides the result of the battle, that his will decrees who shall fall, and that this kind of death is a blessing, through which the hero is taken into his abode: while by explaining the Valkyriur as bright aerial meteors, balls of fire, and the like, which, by the way, could not make their appearance on every battlefield, we impair all the poetic beauty, by conceiving to be physical that which is purely imaginary. When the signification of Skirnir's journey[1] is thus

---

1   See p. 43.

explained: that Frey is the sun, Gerd the northern light, her father, Gymir, the frozen ocean, and that Frey and Gerd's love produce spring or summer, we find in this explanation many and striking resemblances with the several contents of the poem; though these appeal to be purely accidental, because a principal resemblance is wanting, because for Gerd, as the northern light, it can be no very formidable threat, that she shall always continue barren, and live united with a Frost-giant, which is, in fact, her constant lot and Frey's fructifying embrace – for without fruit it cannot be, whatever we may take Frey to be, since it takes place in the wood of buds – has on a being like the northern light no effect, which is, and continues to be, unfruitful. The explanation must, therefore, of itself pass over to the fruitfulness of the earth, effected by the summer sun, but thereby, at the same time, abandons its first direction. Here the idea, which really forms the groundwork of the poem, is in fact comprehended, viz. the earth rendered fertile by Frey; but when put aside by other similitudes, it is almost lost in another idea – the beauty of the northern light.

If, with some commentators, we take the god Vidar for the silent departure of the year, and, consequently, of the winter also; the time when Thor wanders to Geirröd,[1] for the autumn or beginning of winter and Grid, the mother of Vidar, who dwells on the way to Geirröd, for the autumn or end of summer, in opposition to her son; and when we find that she must be a giantess, seeing that her son closes the winter; if we assume all this, a series of ideas is set up which have no natural connection with the myths. Vidar, it is true, is silent, but what is the silent departure of the year? In the North it is wont to be noisy enough. And how can the silent departure of the year be said to destroy Fenrir, and to survive the gods, as it is said of Vidar?[2] How can the mother be in opposition to the son? And how can her nature be determined by the son's? If Grid is the end of summer, she might, perhaps, be said to bring forth winter, but not the close of winter; nor, because Vidar closes the winter, must his mother be a giantess, but rather the converse; if his mother is a giantess, he might be winter, and a giant himself. By this interpretation, contradiction seems heaped on contradiction .

Among the extraordinary directions which the physical mode of interpretation has taken, must be noticed that which may be called the chemical. It consists in showing the accordance between the myths and the later systems of chemistry. It explains, for instance, the three equal divinities by the three natural substances, sulphur, quicksilver, and salt; Odin, Vili, and Ve,[3] as the three laws of nature, gravity, motion, and affinity. It takes the

1    Page 47.
2    Pages 66, 68.
3    Page 14.

rivers that flow from Hvergelmir[1] to denote destructive kinds of gas in the bowels of the earth; the horses of the gods, on which they ride over Bifröst, for vibrations in the air; Sleipnir among others for the vibrations of light: Valfather Odin for elective affinity, in the chemical acceptation. According to this system, Thor is not the thunderstorm, but its profounder cause, electricity. By his name of Auku-Thor (derived from auka, *to eke*, *augment*) is signified an accumulation of electricity; his belt must then bear allusion to the electric condenser; his iron gloves are conductors. The myth of Thor's journey to Griotunagard[2] bears allusion to the diffusion of terrestrial magnetism in the vegetable kingdom, while Hrungnir is petrifaction, Freyia and Sif are carbon and oxygen, Thor's son, Magni, is the magnet, and Möckurkalfi the magnetic needle. In the story of the Origin of Poetry,[3] Kvasir is saccharine matter, Fialar and Galar, who slay him, putrefaction and fermentation, by which saccharine matter is decomposed; Odhraerir is tension, Sôn vibration, Bodn echo, Gilling dregs that are precipitated; his wife, who is crushed by a millstone, tartar, Suttung spirituous drink, and Gunnlöd carbonic acid. Many of the illustrations according to this system might be adduced as examples that the idea is there, but that the application has failed, and no wonder, as it gives credit to antiquity for a knowledge of nature, which it neither had nor could have.

In this mode of explanation is comprised that which may be termed the astronomical, as far as its object is to show that the knowledge the ancients had of the sun, the stars, and the division of the year, was applied mythically, and constituted a part of the learning of their priests. Traces of this mode are to be found in almost all mythologies, as the contemplation of the heavenly bodies must find its application in life, in determining the courses of the year, in distinguishing particular days, and, by certain significant signs, in fixing the fugacious with time in the memory. Herewith may the arithmetic of the ancients be brought in connection, and the explanation will then, at the same time, be mathematical. Both these methods of illustration are, however, in the Northern mythology of but limited application, and entirely fail in the case of myths that have another origin and object. It has already been remarked by others, that among our forefathers we find very little, next, indeed, to nothing, about the sun, moon, and stars. Sôl,[4] that is the damsel who drives the horses of the sun, is, it is true, named as a goddess, but only incidentally, and without mythic action. The sun itself was no god, but only a disk of fire issuing from

1   Pages 13, 25.
2   Page 58.
3   Page 39.
4   Page 15.

Muspellheim, the region of eternal light, drawn by two horses and guided by the damsel Sôl; in its most exalted character appearing only as Odin's eye; but of any adoration paid to it, not a trace appears in the whole mythology. Bil[1] is also mentioned as a goddess, but she is one of the moon's spots, not the moon itself: of her worship not a trace is to be found. The stars came forth as sparks from Muspellheim,[2] and were fixed on and under heaven; an idea so childish, that it could not possibly have occurred to anyone who thought of worshipping such spangles as gods. Two are mentioned as formed of earthly matter, viz. Thiassi's eyes,[3] and Örvandil's toe[4] (probably the two principal stars in the head of the bull, and the polar star, or one of the stars in the great bear); but their origin from giants must at once have prevented all adoration of them. With these exceptions, stars are neither spoken of nor even named in any myth. Where so little attention was paid to the heavenly bodies and their motions, it cannot be supposed that any idea existed of a complete solar year with its twelve months; nor do the two passages in the *Eddas*, where mention clearly occurs of the division of time, give any cause for supposing it, as they name only the parts of the day and night, according to which the year may be calculated, without, by any more precise data, bringing it in connection with the sun and moon. Of the moon they observed two principal changes, Nyi and Nithi, which implies an observation of its course. Of the sun, on the contrary, we find nothing, except in connection with the day. This leads to the supposition, that the oldest year among the inhabitants of the North, as among other nations, was a lunar year, which is corroborated by the Vafthrudnismal, where, after having made mention of day and night, in the same strophe it adds, that the gods created Nyi and Nithi for the calculation of the year; nor is there any historic information to the contrary. On the other hand, the earliest mention of a regular computation by the solar year of 364 days, or 12 months, is from the years 950 to 970, that is, at the utmost, only fifty years older than the introduction of Christianity. The Icelanders, therefore, who at that time adopted a similar computation, cannot have brought such accurate knowledge with them when they emigrated from Norway, where, it can hardly be assumed such a calculation was in use at the time of Harald Hârfagr,[5] much less before his time. Hence some doubt may be entertained whether the twelve mansions of the Aesir have reference to the year determined by the course of the sun. As, however, some distinguished

1    Page 15.
2    Page 13.
3    Page 42.
4    Page 59.
5    In whose reign the colonisation of Iceland commenced, an. 874.

commentators have adopted this view, a short sketch of the system adopted by the late Professor Finn Magnusen[1] is here given, as most in accordance with the *Grinmismál*.

| | MANSION | DIVINITY | MONTH |
|---|---|---|---|
| I | Ydal | Ull | November |
| II | Alfheim | Frey | December |
| III | Valaskialf | Vali | January |
| IV | Söckquabeck | Saga | February |
| V | Gladsheim | Hropt | March |
| VI | Thrymheim | Skadi | April |
| VII | Breidablik | Baldur | May |
| VIII | Himinbiörg | Heimdall | June |
| IX | Folkvang | Freyia | July |
| X | Glitnir | Forseti | August |
| XI | Noatûn | Niörd | September |
| XII | Landvidi | Vidar | October |

Here congruity certainly prevails in many parts: winter precedes summer, and begins with Ull just at the time when the ancients began to reckon their winter Ull can very well inhabit the humid dales (Ydalir[2]) in November; Frey, in December, may have got Alfheim for a tooth-gift;[3] Vali, who renews the year,[4] presides in January; Odin with Saga may here in February repeat the records of warlike feats performed, and the like.[5] Notwithstanding all which, it appears to me, that to these systems it may be objected, that there is no other ground for assuming that the mansions of the gods stand in any fixed order with respect to each other, than because they are so enumerated in the *Grimnismál*; for the same poem enumerates also the horses of the Aesir, the several names of Odin, etc., etc., and may, therefore, be considered a sort of catalogue or nomenclature of mythic objects. Nor is there any more reason for excluding Thor than for excluding Heimdall, the god of the rainbow, both being connected with the aerial phenomena, and have no reference to the annual course of the sun; and, in general, it is clear, as far as I can perceive, that neither Vidar, nor Niörd, the god of the wind and ocean, nor Frey and Freyia, the divinities of earth's fertility, nor Saga, the muse of history, as these beings are represented in the *Eddas*, either have reference to, or stand in

---

1 See commentary in *Den Aeldre Edda*, i, pp. 148, *seq*.
2 Page 32.
3 Page 28.
4 Pages 32, 68.
5 Page 35.

connection with the course of the sun, or with the division of the year.

With respect to the arithmetic of the Scandinavians, we find here, as among all ancient people, a frequent recurrence of certain sacred numbers, as 3, 7, 9, 4, 8;[1] but to this their whole arithmetic seems limited; and if a solitary instance occurs of something that may have a more recondite allusion, as, for instance, the 540 gates of Valhall,[2] from each of which 800 Einheriar could ride abreast, such matter can, at the utmost, only be regarded as remnants of older traditions, whose original connection is lost. By multiplying 540 by 2300, we get a number identical with an Indian period; but is not this identity purely accidental? It is impossible to conceive what connection can subsist between an Indian period of time and the doors of Valhall and the number of Einheriar.

Every religion of Antiquity embraces not only the strictly religious elements, such as belief in the supernatural, and the influence of this belief on the actions of men, but, in general, all that knowledge which is now called science. The priests engrossed all the learning. Knowledge of nature, of language, of man's whole intellectual being and culture, of the historic origin of the state, and of the chief races, was clad in a poetic, often a mythic, garb, propagated by song and oral tradition, and, at a later period, among the most cultivated of the people, particularly certain families, by writing. These disseminated, among the great mass of the community, whatever seemed to them most appropriate to the time and place. Such is the matter still extant in the *Eddas*, even as they now lie before us, after having passed through the middle age. The later interpreters are, therefore, unquestionably right in seeking in these remains not only traditions of the origin and destruction of the world, of the relation of man to the Divinity, but also the outlines of the natural and historic knowledge possessed by Antiquity. We have of course, in the foregoing sketch, omitted all that might seem to have a historic signification, and communicated that alone which may be regarded as purely mythic.

This mythic matter is comprised in two ancient monuments, the *Elder* and the *Younger Edda*, called usually, after their supposed compilers, Saemund's Edda, and Snorri's *Edda*. The first-mentioned contains songs that are older than Christianity in the North, and have been orally transmitted and finally committed to writing in the middle age. They have, for the most part, reached us as fragments only, and several chasms have,

---

1   For the predilection entertained by the Saxons for the number 8, see Lappenberg's 'England under the Anglo-Saxon Kings', i, 77.
2   Page 24.

at a later period, with greater or less felicity, been filled up by prosaic introductions or insertions. The other *Edda* consists of tales founded on, and often filled up with, verses from the *Elder*, but which have been written down after the time of paganism, preserved, as memorials of the past, by individual scholars of the time, and to which, here and there, are added illustrations of some part of the subject.[1] To all this are appended

1   The following is the introduction to the matter contained in the portion of the *Prose*, or Snorri's, *Edda*, which is entitled 'Gylfaginning', or *Delusion1 of Gylfi*:

King Gylfi (see p. 34, note 6) was a wise man and of great knowledge. He wondered much that the Aesir folk were so wise that everything went as they willed. He considered whether it might proceed from their nature, or be caused by the divine powers whom they worshipped. He undertook a journey to Asgard, and travelled in disguise, having assumed the likeness of an aged man and was thus concealed. But the Aesir were too wise in possessing foreknowledge, and knew of his journey ere he came, and received him with illusions. So when he came into the city, he perceived a hall so lofty that he could hardly see over it. Its roof was covered with gilded shields, like a shingle roof.

Gylfi saw a man at the hall gates playing with small swords, of which he had seven at a time in the air. This man inquired his name. His name, he said, was Gangleri, that he had come a tedious way, and requested a night's lodging. He then asked to whom the hall belonged. The man answered that it was their king's: 'But I will attend you to see him, you can then yourself ask him his name.' Thereupon the man turned into the hall followed by Gangleri, and instantly the gate was closed at their heels. He there saw many apartments and many people some at games, some drinking, some fighting with weapons. He then looked about, and saw many things that seemed to him incredible: whereupon he said to himself –

Every gate,    for 'tis hard to know
ere thou goest forward,  where foes sit
shalt thou inspect;   in the dwelling.

*Hávamál*, Str. 1.

Here he saw three thrones, one above another, and a man sitting on each. He then asked what the name of each chieftain might he. His conductor answered, that he who sat on the lowest throne was a king and named Hâr (High); that the next was named Jafnhâr (Equally high); and that the highest of all was called Thrithi (Third). Hâr then asked the comer what further business he had; adding, that he was entitled to meat and drink, like all in Hava-hall. He answered, that he would first inquire whether any sagacious man were there. Hâr told him that he would not come off whole, unless he proved himself the wiser:

but stand forth
while thou mak'st inquiry:
'tis for him to sit who answers.

Gangleri then began his speech.

The questions and answers that follow constitute what is called Snorri's, or the *Prose*, or the *Younger Edda*.

fragments of divers sorts of mythic learning, intended for the use of later skalds, as an illustration of, and guide to, the use of poetic expressions. Hence it will be manifest that the older of these collections is the most important, though to the understanding, arranging and completing of it, considerable help is found in the younger, and the interpretation of the one is not practicable without constantly comparing it with the other. Where the myths in the *Elder Edda* are at all detailed and complete, they are full of poetry and spirit, but they often consist in dark allusions only, a defect which the *Younger* cannot supply, for here we too often meet with trivial and almost puerile matter; such as we may imagine the old religious lore to have become, when moulded into the later popular belief. It follows, therefore, that several myths now appear as poor, insipid fictions, which, in their original state, were probably beautiful both in form and substance. In both *Eddas*, the language is often obscure, and the conception deficient in clearness; it appears, moreover, that several myths are lost,[1] so that a complete exposition of the Northern Mythology is no longer to be obtained.

All illustration of Northern mythology must proceed from the *Eddas*, and the most faithful is, without doubt, that which illustrates them from each other. It may in the meanwhile be asked whether their matter has its original home in the North, or is of foreign growth? For myths may either have originated among the Northern people themselves, and gradually in course of time have developed themselves among their descendants as a production of the intellectual and political life of the people; or they may have found entrance from without, have been forced on the people of the North at the conquest of their countries, and with the suppression of their own ideas; or, lastly, they may consist of a compound of native and foreign matter. This question has been the subject of strict and comprehensive investigation. To the faith of the ancient Finnish race is with great probability referred the myth of Forniot's three sons, Hler (sea), Logi (fire), Kari (wind);[2] also that of Thor, as the god of thunder, and a comparison with the belief still prevalent among the Lapps will tend to confirm this opinion. This, however, constitutes a very inconsiderable part of the Aesir-

---

1    Instances of lost myths are, 'How Idun embraced her brother's murderer', *Loka-glepsa*, Str. 17; 'Odin's sojourn in Samsö,' ibid., Str. 24; 'How Loki begat a son with Ty's wife', ibid., Str. 40; Myths concerning Heimdall's head, and his contest with Loki for the Brisinga-men, *Skaldskap.*, 8 (see p. 29); a myth concerning the giant Vagnhöfdi, Saxo, edit. Stephanii, p. 9; edit. Müller, pp. 34, 36, 45; and of Jötnaheiti, in *Snorra-Edda*, p. 211; of the giant Thrivaldi slain by Thor, and other of his feats, *Skaldskap.*, 4; and *Harbardslj.*, Str. 29, 35, 37, etc.
2    Page 30.

mythology, and cannot have contributed much to its development. On the other hand, everything shows that it had its original home in the South and the East; thither point tradition, resemblance to the mythology of the Germanic and even more southern nations, and language. An inquiry into this opinion of its origin, which traces it to the banks of the Ganges, may be instituted in two ways: either by tracing a similitude between its several myths and those of other nations, or by considering as a whole the spirit of the one mythology compared with that of the other. A comparison of the several myths, which has with great learning been made by Finn Magnusen, leads to the result, that between the Northern on the one side, and the Indian, Persian and other kindred mythologies on the other, are found many striking resemblances, particularly with reference to the creation of the world, the transmigration of souls, regeneration, etc. while, on the contrary, they rather diverge from each other, on a comparison together of their respective spirits. The Oriental is contemplative, the Northern is one of pure action; according to the first, the gods are to be reconciled by works of atonement, according to the second, by battle. The one was a natural consequence of the warmth of the East, the other of the Northern cold. It seems, therefore, probable, that the earliest elements of the Northern mythology were brought from Asia through divers other nations to the North, where they became developed and formed after a peculiar fashion. The rugged, wild, grand nature of the country supplied those great and lofty images, drawn from icebergs and rocks; and the ever active course of life, in which men were there engaged, transformed the sluggish half-slumbering gods of the East, absorbed in contemplation, into beings that rode on the wings of the storm and, in the raging battle, gathered men to them, to reward them in another world with combats and death, from which they rose again to life, and with the aliments known to the natives of the North as the most nutritive, and by which they were strengthened to begin the combat anew.[1] Every closer consideration of Northern life, of the people's constant warfare with nature and with foes, renders it easily conceivable, that Odin, however Buddhistic he may originally have been, must under a Northern sky be transformed into a Valfather;[2] that the Northern man, to whom death was an everyday matter, must have a Valhall, and that the idea of a state of happiness without battle, of quiet without disquiet, must be for ever excluded. After all, in explaining the *Eddas*, it does not seem necessary to resort to other mythologies, though a comparison with them is always valuable, and

1   Page 24.
2   Page 22.

highly interesting, when it shows an analogy between them and the myths of the North.

To arrive at a satisfactory explanation of the Northern myths, it is necessary to commence with the signification of the mythic names. Verbal illustration must precede every other; when that fails, the rest is almost always defective. The names of the gods are, as Grimm observes, in themselves significant, bearing an allusion to their nature.[1] But in this investigation, difficulties sometimes arise, as it is generally the oldest words of a language that form the groundwork, and all etymology is, moreover, exposed to much caprice. The illustration of myths will also be greatly prejudiced, if we yield to a blind guess among forms of like sound. Every verbal illustration must, therefore, be conformable to the laws of transition between the Northern and its kindred tongues; a rule, by the way, easier to give than to follow.

To explain a myth is to show what can have given occasion to the image on which it hinges, and to express, in unemblematic language, the thought which serves as a basis for the image. Here explanation may usually stop; for to follow the figurative picture through all its parts is not necessary, that being a process which will naturally be undertaken by every poetic mind, and the object of explanation is not to excite the fancy, but to lead it to the point whence it may begin its flight. In the myth of Frey and Gerd's love, for instance, the thought forms the basis, that the god of fecundity longs to spread his blessing over the barren earth, and to wake in the seed its slumbering efficacy. To show this is to explain the myth. But this thought is expressed by a picture of all the desires and sufferings of love, of the blessing of fruitfulness, as the effect of love in the youthful heart whereby the myth becomes a beautiful poem. To develop this poetic beauty is not the object of illustration; it can escape no one who has a feeling for poetry. And to follow all the possible resemblances between the effect of fruitfulness in the earth, and the effect of love in the heart, would be as uninteresting as tasteless.

---

1　　Grimm, J., *Deutsche Mythologie*, op. cit., p. 201.

## Section Three

Every illustration of the *Eddas* has something individual; it depends on the idea we have formed to ourselves of Antiquity. That which I shall here attempt has not for object either to disparage any foregoing one, or to render it superfluous. Availing myself of the labours of my predecessors, I shall endeavour to represent the principal Northern myths in their most natural connection, and thereby furnish my readers with a view of Northern mythology, by which the mental culture and life of the people may the more easily be conceived.

**Creation.** Before heaven and earth, gods and men existed, there were cold and heat, mist and flame, which are represented as two worlds, Niflheim and Muspellheim. Over the hovering mist and the world of fire no rulers are named, Surt being only the guardian of the latter. Between both worlds there was nothing except Ginunga-gap, a boundless abyss, empty space; but by the contact of ice and heat, there was formed, through the power of the Almighty, the first, unorganic foundation of heaven and earth – matter. This was called Ymir, and is represented under the form of a huge giant. Offspring came forth from under his arm, and his feet procreated with each other; for the unorganised mass was increased by life not inward but from without. He was nourished by the dripping rime from the constant melting of the ice, represented under the figure of a cow, the symbol of nourishment and preservation; or, in other words, matter constantly added to itself, and spread itself into a monstrous unorganic race, the Frost-giants, or the vast groups of snow-mountains and icebergs.

**Illustration.** Before the world itself, in the beginning, its foundation existed: a creation from nothing was incomprehensible. The existing things were cold and heat, ice and light. Towards the north lay Niflheim, towards the south Muspellheim. Niflheim (from nifl, Ger. nebel, Lat. nebula, Gr. νοφέλη) signifies the home, or world of mist. Here was Hvergelmir (from hver, *a large kettle*, *spring*, and gelmir, from gialla, *stridere*, comp. Ohg.

galm, *stridor*, *sonitus*,[1]) the bubbling, roaring kettle, or spring, whence the ice-streams flow forth. They are called Elivâgar (from el, *storm, rain, sleet*, and vagr (vogr), *wave, stream*). The word eitr, which is applied to these and similar icy streams, signifies poison, but originally the most intense cold. The Swedes still say 'etter-kallt', equivalcnt to our *piercing cold*. The first twelve rivers which run from Hvergelmir, some of which occur also as rivers proceeding from Eikthyrnir's horn in Valhall,[2] signify the misty exhalations, before the creation of the world, like the clouds afterwards. Muspellheim, it may be supposed, betokened (in contradistinction to Niflheim) the *world of light, warmth, fire*; but the origin of the word is unknown.[3] Over this world Surt (the *swart*, connected with svart, *niger*[4] ruled, a god who reveals himself in the burning fire, and whose sword is flames. In its signification of *swart, browned by fire*, the name resembles Kris'na (*the black, violet*), one of the names of the lndian deity Vishnu. Surt is not an evil being; he comes forth, it is true, at the end of the world, which he burns, but it is the corrupt, fallen world, after which a state of bliss will begin. Nor is he black of hue: on the contrary, he and his followers, Muspell's sons, forrn a bright, shining band. Surt, in my opinion, is not the same as he whose power sends forth the heat, for then Surt's name, not this periphrasis, would have been used. It is not he who causes the hot and cold worlds to come in contact and operate on each other, whereby the world's foundation came into being: it is a higher being, the Ineffable, the Almighty, without whose will the worlds of mist and of light would have remained for ever, each within its bounds. But He willed, His power manifested itself, and creation began. Between both worlds was Ginnunga-gap (the abyss of abysses), from ginn, denoting something great, widely extended, whence is formed ginnúngr, *a wide expanse*, here used in the genitive plural. This appellation, as well as Elivâgar, was by the geographers applied to the Frozen ocean, one of the many proofs that mythic names have obtained a historic application.

Ymir (from ómr, ymr, at ymja) signifies *the noisy, whistling, blustering*; it is the primeval chaos. In Aurgelmir (Örgelmir), his other name, aur signifies *matter, the oldest material substance*, also *mud, clay*. This grew and became consistent, strong, firm; in other words, he brought forth Thrudgelmir, who increased in size till he became a perfect mountain, Bergelmir.[5] Authhumla (derived from audr, *desert*, Ger. öde, and hum, *darkness, dusk*, with the

---

1   Grimm, J., *Deutsche Mythologie*, op. cit., p.530.
2   Page 25.
3   Page 13, note 2.
4   Grimm, J., *Deutsche Mythologie*, op. cit., p. 769
5   It should therefore be written Berggelmir.

derivative termination la) shows that the matter increased by the streams that ran through the desert darkness. The cow is found in almost all cosmogonies. Hrîmthurs (from hrím, *rime, rime frost*, and thurs, thuss, *giant*) signifies plainly enough the icebergs, and their senseless being.

The Universal Father (Alfödr) was among the Frost-giants.[1] That is, the creative power began to operate in the unorganic, elementary mass. The cow, or nourishing power, licked the salt stones, and thereby produced an internal motion, so that life sprang up. It began with the hair, the first growing plant; then the head, the abode, of thought, came forth; and lastly, the entire human creature. Vegetable, intellectual, and animal life came into activity, the strictly so-called creation began, the first intelligent being existed. It had power through its internal virtue, it increased itself of itself: Buri, *the bringer forth*, produced Bör, *the brought forth*. Bör married Bestla, or Belsta, a daughter of the giant Bölthorn; the higher mental power began to operate in the better part of the miserable material, which was thereby ennobled, and the creative powers, the Aesir, came forth: they were good gods, opposed to monsters, to the wicked giants. The Aesir are represented as three brothers, that is, three directions of the same agency, Odin, Vili, and Ve, or Mind, Will, and Holiness. These sons of Bör slew Ymir or Chaos, and formed of him heaven and earth. But a part of the material escaped from their quickening power, the highest mountain peaks remained untouched by the inundation produced; the sea gradually subsided, and around the inhabited earth high icebergs were formed, the family of Bergelmir. From the world of light came the bright heavenly bodies, but they wandered about without object or aim. The gods placed them in order and fixed their course: night and day, winter and summer, took each its turn; days and years might be reckoned. The most central part of the earth, or Midgard, was appointed for the future human race; the Aesir fixed their abode in Asgard, the highest part of the world. This was the first period of creation: they rested.

**Illustration.** The word *salt*, Lat. sal, salum, Gr. σάλος, ἅλς, is referred to the Sanskrit zal, *to put oneself in motion* (Lat. salire). It is the expression for the moving, animating, recreative power. Buri denotes *forth-bringing, origin, source*: it is referred to the Sansk. b'ú, *to be*, also *to consider, think*, with many derivatives. Börr, Burr, or Bors, is the *brought forth, born*, Sansk. b'áras, Goth. baurs, Lat. por, puer. It also forms an adjective bor-inn, *born*, from bera, *to bear, bring forth*, from the past tense of which, bar, is derived barn, *a child*, A. S. bearn, Scottish bairn: burr also ( A. S. byre) is used by the skalds for *son*. By Bölthorn (from *trouble, evil, bale*, and thorn, *thorn*) is

1    Page 14.

expressed the bad quality of matter, as opposed to the gods. Of Bestla, or
Belsta, the etymon is uncertain, as is also the signification of the myth. The
names Odin, Vili, and Ve will be noticed hereafter. The general denomination of these gods is As, plural Aesir; Goth. ans, A. S. ós, plural és
(analogously with Ger. Gans, A. S. gós, gés, *goose*, *geese*). Jornandes calls
them Anses. The root is the Sansk. as, *to be*, *exist*, and is the same as the
Lat. termination ens.[1] The boat in which Bergelmir escaped is called lúdr,
signifying a *lute*, *drum*, also a sort of sack or case used in the ancient mills;
its meaning here cannot, however, be doubtful, as it evidently corresponds
to Noah's ark: its radical signification may lie in its hollowed-out form.

With the creation of the gods this world begins. There was a state before
it, and a state will follow it. In the state before it the raw elements existed,
but it was a rough, unformed life: mind was yet lacking in the giant's body.
With Odin and the Aesir the intellectual life began to operate on the raw
masses, and the world in its present state came into existence.

Day and night were opposed to each other; light came from above,
darkness from beneath. Night was before day, winter before summer. Light
existed before the sun. The moon preceded, the sun followed.

**Illustration.** Here are several denominations, the significations of which
are of little importance, and also very doubtful. The three husbands of
Night, it is supposed, bear allusion to the three divisions of the night
(eyktir). The similarity of the name of her first husband, Naglfari, to
Naglfar, that of the ship formed of the nails of the dead, that is to appear at
Ragnaröck,[2] is remarkable, though probably purely accidental. And, the
name of their son, denotes *void*, *desert*. Annar, her second husband's
name, signifies merely *second*, *other*. Onar, as he is also called, has been
compared with the Gr. ὄναρ, a *dream*. Delling (Dögling), her third
husband's name, may be a diminutive of dagr, *day*, and signify *dawn*.[3]

Hrîmfaxi, the name of the horse of night, signifies *rime* or *frosty-mane*.
His other appellation, Fiörsvartnir, may be rendered *life-obscurer*. Skinfaxi,
the name of the horse of day, denotes *shining-mane*; his other name, Glad,
*brightness*. Mundilföri has been derived from O. Nor. möndull, *an axis*; a
derivation, if to be relied on, which seems to indicate a knowledge of the

---

1   The Aesir are the creators, sustainers and regulators of the world, the spirits of
thought and life that pervade and animate all dead nature, and seek to subject it to the
spiritual will. They assemble daily to hold council on the world's destinies. The human
form and manner of being are ascribed to them, but in a higher and nobler manner;
they hear and see more acutely, they go from place to place with inconceivable speed.
Petersen, op. cit., p. 116.
2   Page 65.
3   Page 15.

motion of the heavens round the earth. The spots in the moon, which are here alluded to, require but little illustration.[1] Here they are children carrying water in a bucket, a superstition still preserved in the popular belief of the Swedes.[2] Other nations see in it a man with a dog, some a man with a bundle of brushwood, for having stolen which on a Sunday he was condemned to figure in the moon,[3] etc.

Glen, the husband of the sun, is the Kymric word for *sun*. Her horses are Arvakr, *the vigilant*, and Alsvith, *the all-burning*, *all-rapid*. The sun is feminine and the moon masculine, because day is mild and friendly, night raw and stern; while in the south, day is burning and night the most pleasant. The father of Winter, Vindsval, denotes *windy*, *cold*. The father of Summer is Svasud, or *mild*, *soft*. Hraesvelg, the name of the north wind, represented as an eagle, signifies *corpse-devourer*.[4]

**Dwarfs and Men**. The gods assembled on Ida's plain,[5] etc. The maidens from Jötunheim, were, without doubt, the maidens of fate or destiny, who craved the creation of the beings that should be subjected to them. Now, therefore, follows the creation of dwarfs and men. The subordinate powers of nature were generated in the earth; men were created from trees. This is the gradual development of organic life. The nature of the three gods who

---

1   Page 15.
2   Ling's *Eddornas Sinnebildslära*, i, 78.
3   Lady Cynthia is thus described by Chaucer (*Testam. of Cresseide*, 260–3):

> Her gite was gray and ful of spottis blake,
> And on her brest a chorle paintid ful even,
> Bering a bushe of thornis on his bake,
> Whiche for his theft might clime no ner the heven.

In Ritson's *Ancient Songs* (ed. 1790, p. 35) there is one on the 'Mon in the Mone'.

Shakespeare also mentions him and his bush:

> Steph.   I was the man in the moon, when time was.
> Cal.     I have seen thee in her, and I do adore thee;
>          My mistress showed me thee, and thy dog and thy bush.
>
> *Tempest*, ii, 2

Again:

> Quince.   . . . One must come in with a bush of thorns and a lantern, and say, he comes to disfigure, or to present, the person of moonshine.
>
> *Midsummer Night's Dream*, iii, 1

For Oriental and other traditions connected with the man in the moon, see Grimm, J., *Deutsche Mythologie*, op. cit., p. 679.
4   Grimm calls attention to the apparent connection between the Lat. *aquilo* and *aquila*, the Gr. ἄνεμος and ἀετὸς, from the root ἄω, ἄημι, etc.
5   Page 17.

were active in the creation of man is particularly marked by their respective donations to the trees, that is, to organic nature in its first development, whereby man is distinguished from the vegetable.

**Illustration.** Idavöllr, or Ida's plain (whether derived from id, *action*, or from the dwarf's name, Idi, *gold*, and signifying either *the plain of action*, or *of gold*) denotes a heavenly, bright abode. The occupations of the Aesir are an imitation of those of men. To forge metals was one of the most honourable employments of a freeman; equally so was the game of tables. To play at tables signifies simply to lead a life of enjoyment and happiness. Hence, on the other hand, the son says to his mother Groa, 'Thou didst set an odious play-board before me, thou who didst embrace my father'; that is, 'Thou didst prepare for me an unhappy life.' With respect to the three maidens from Jötunheim, opinions have been much divided. The most natural interpretation seems to me, that they were the three Norns, the goddesses of fate. When these came, the attention of the gods became directed to that which should yet come to pass, and their hitherto useless energies acquired a definite object. The Norns, who had been reared among the giants, must also come before the beings were created who, during the whole course of their existence, were to be subjected to them. It is, moreover, said that mankind lay like senseless trees without fate and destiny (örlögslausir), but that they now got fate (örlög). Askr is the ash tree; what tree is meant by embla is doubtful.

The Northern Mythology, like almost every other, presents us with three equally powerful gods. In the *Gylfa-ginning* they are called Hâr, the *High*; Jafnhâr; the *Equally High*; and thridi, the *Third*. The first and last of these are also surnames of Odin; it might otherwise seem probable, that here, where they are opposed to King Gylfi, and the scene lies in Sweden, the three chief gods worshipped at Upsala, Odin, Thor, and Frey, were intended. At the creation of the world, the three active deities are Odin, Vili, and Ve, who are brothers; at the creation of mankind, they are Odin, Hoenir, and Lodur, who are not brothers. These beings, therefore, denote several kinds of the divine agency, but are not the same. Odin's name shall be further considered hereafter; here we will merely observe that it bears allusion to mind or thought, and breathing it is the quickening, creating power. Vili, or Vilir, is the O. Nor expression for *will*, which, if referred to the Sansk. vél, or véll, Gr. εἰλέω, Lat. volo, velle (volvo), would denote the power that sets matter in motion. Among the dwarfs also the name of Vili occurs. Ve signifies in the O. Nor. tongue, *a place of assembly*, with the idea of holiness and peace, and is the root of at vígja, *to consecrate* (Goth. veihs, Ohg. wîh, *sacred*; Goth. vaihts, *a thing, the created, consecrated*; O. Nor. vaettr, *thing*, opp. to óvaettr, *a monster*). It expresses therefore *consecration*, that is, *separation from the evil, hurtful or disturbing*. Hence, at the creation of the world, Ve operates so far as the divine power obstructs the opposing evil matter, that would not yield to Thought and Will. Thus explained, Odin, Vili and Ve accurately correspond to the Indian trinity, Trimurti, and the three chief Indian gods, Brahma, Vishnu, and Siva, the creating, reserving, and judging powers, or omnipotence, goodness, and justice. As Frigg is said to be married to Odin, Vili, and Ve,[1] so is the primeval mother of the Indians, Parasiakti, represented as the wife of the three first-created gods. According to Finn Magnusen, Vili is *light*, and Ve *fire*, whereby it is, at the same time, assumed that Vili is the same with Hoenir, and Ve with Lodur. At the creation of man, Odin gave önd, Hoenir ódr, Lodur lá and litu godu. Önd signifies *spirit* or *breath*, the intellectual or physical life; ódr signifies *sense, mind*; önd and ódr are to each other as *anima* and *mens* (ódr from vada, *vadere*; mens from meare); ódr is then the outward and inward sense, or *perception*. Lá is *water; fluid*; litr, *colour*, whereby allusion is made to the circulation of the blood and the vital warmth thereby produced. Here then are expressed the three actions of animal life: *to breathe, to perceive, to move from within*. The derivation of Hoenir is unknown. He is called Odin's friend, and associate, and fellow-traveller, with reference to the close connection between perception and mind. He is also called the rapid As, and Long-foot, in allusion to the far-reaching activity of perception in space; in other words, Hoenir operates in space as Odin does in time. He is also called Aur-konúngr,[2] king of matter. Lodr (Lödr) is, without doubt, related to lá, *blood*, litr, *colour*, A. S. wlite, and expresses the motion of the fluid with its consequences, vital warmth and colour.

The beings different from men are – besides the giants the oldest of all, and the Aesir, who created heaven and earth, and preserve all things – the Elves and Vans (Alfar and Vanir).[3] The Elves are the subordinate powers of nature; some of them, the Light-elves (Liósálfar) are airy, light beings, hovering over, and, as it were, protecting the earth: in other words, they are the powers that operate on all that thrives in air, in plants, in rivers and on the earth's surface. Others, Dark-elves (Döckálfar, Svartálfar), dwell in the bowels of the earth, and are nearly related to, if not identical with, the Dwarfs, or powers that work in stones, earth, metals: they are skilful workers in metal.[4] The whole transition from the hard, dark stone, through the glittering metals, to the germinating powers in the earth, which

1    Page 33, and note.
2    From aur, *argilla, lutum*. Finn Magnusen (*Lex. Myth.*, op. cit., p. 464) would read ör-konúngr, *sagittarum rex*, from ör, *sagitta, telum*.
3    Pages 28, 21.
4    Page 37.

develop themselves in the fairest, coloured, fruitful forms – the plants – seems represented by the gradual transition through Dwarfs (stones), Swart-elves (metals), Dark-elves (earth and mould), Light-elves (plants). Between the Aesir and the Elves are the Vanir. Their creation is nowhere spoken of; they are the powers of the sea and air; as active beings they appear only in their relation to the Aesir and Elves, that is, to heaven and earth. They made war against and concluded peace with the Aesir, and one of them, Frey, obtained the sovereignty over the Light-elves.[1] The Vanir rule in the sea and air, encircling the whole earth in a higher and remoter sphere. The Light-elves rule in the rivers and air, surrounding the inhabited earth in a lower and more contracted sphere.

**Illustration.** Besides the before-mentioned appellation of thurs (Goth. thaursus, *dry*; thaursjan, *to thirst*), the giants are also called jötunn, plural jötnar (A. S. eoten, Lat. edo, edonis), from at eta, *to eat*, thus signifying *the voracious, greedy*.[2] These beings use stones and fragments of rock as weapons, and, within the mountains, iron bars also. Among the common people the belief is still lively, how mountains, islands, etc. have arisen through their wanderings, how they hurled vast stones and rocks, and how they fled before the husbandmen. The giants dwell in large caverns, in rocks and mountains, and are intelligent and wise, for all nature has proceeded from them; voracious, large, powerful, proud, insolent:[3] were it not for Thor, they would get the mastery, but he stands between them and heaven, and strikes them down when they approach too near. Like nature, which is still or agitated, the giant at rest is blunt and good-humoured; but when excited, savage and deceitful. This latter state is called jötun-módr (giant-mood) in contradistinction to ás-módr (As-mood). The giantesses are sometimes described as large, ugly, and misshapen, like the giants; sometimes as exceedingly beautiful, exciting desire among the gods, who

---

1   Page 28.
2   Ic mesan maeg · meahtlicor · and efan eteh · ealdum thyrre (thyrse), *I can feast and also eat more heartily than an old giant*. Cod. Exon., p. 425, 1. 26–9.
3   They are represented as having many hands and heads: Staerkodder had six arms; in Skirnis-for a three-headed Thurs is mentioned. Of their relative magnitude to man an idea may be formed from the following. 'At the entrance of the Black Forest on the Hünenkoppe, there dwelt a giantess (hünin) with her daughter. The latter having found a husbandman in the act of ploughing, put him and his plough and his oxen into her apron, and carried the "little fellow with his kittens" to her mother, who angrily bade her take them back to the place whence she had taken them, adding, "They belong to a race that can inflict great injury to the giants." ' See Grimm, J., *Deutsche Mythologie*, op. cit., p. 506, where other examples are given: see also the story of Thor's journey to Jötunheim.

long to unite with them in marriage. Such a one was Gerd.[1] Of these the gygr (plural gygjur) is represented as inhabiting mountain-caves, and guarding the descent through them to the nether world. Thus it is related that Brynhild, after her death, when on the way to Hel, came to a giantess, who thus addressed her: 'Thou shalt not pass through my courts upheld by stone.'[2] Such a giantess was Saxo's Harthgrepa[3] (O. Nor. Hardgreip) . Thor also came to the giantess Grid, the mother of Vidar, on his way to Geirröd, or the Iron-king. Vidar, as we shall see hereafter, ruled in a wood above ground, the giantess dwelt at the entrance of the cavern, Geirröd in its depth. It will now appear what is meant by the class of giantesses called Járnvidjur (sing. Járnvidja). These dwelt in the Járnvidr (Iron wood), where Fenrir's offspring were brought forth, the wolves that will swallow the sun and moon,[3] and cause calamity above, as the wolf Fenrir in the deep. Jarnsaxa, one of Heimdall's mothers, was of this number.[4] The lord of this impenetrable forest was Vidar. In all this dead inert nature seems to be depicted, but at the same time, how it is subjected to the higher power of the gods, who, as soon as they came into existence, began and ever continue to operate on it. And in general, it must be remarked, that the giants are not merely beings dwelling in Utgard, or on the edge of the earth, but are all nature, in opposition to the gods.

**The Vanir**. Their name is to be traced in the adjective vanr, *empty*, *vanus*; though they rule also in the water. In all the Gothic and Slavonian tongues a relationship is found between the denominations of wind and water and weather. That the Vanir ruled over the sea appears manifestly from Niörd; that they ruled in the air may be inferred from their seeing Gna riding in the air.[5]

**The Elves and Dwarfs** are not clearly distinguished from each other. The Light-elves border on the Vanir, the Dark- or Swart-elves on the dwarfs. According to the popular belief, the elves (elle-folk) dwell by rivers, in marshes, and on hills; they are a quiet, peaceful race. The etymon of the word dvergr (durgr), *dwarf*, is unknown, but their habitation in stones, down in the earth, and their occupation in smith's work, remove all doubt as to their nature. They were created from the earth, or Ymir's body.[6] The name of their chief Módsognir signifies *the strength-* or *sap-sucker;* the

1 Page 43.
2 Page 36, ed. Müller, *Skáldskap*. p. 210.
3 Page 15–16.
4 Page 31.
5 Page 35.
6 Page 17.

second, Durin, *the slumbering*, from dúr, *slumber*. From Lofar, *the graceful, comely* (?) descend those of the race of Dvalin (*torpor*). It was this family that wandered from their rocky halls, where they lay in a torpid state (í dvala), over the clayfield, to Jóra's plains. If the word Jóra be here taken in its usual acceptation of *conflict*, then by jóru-vellir will be meant *fields of contest, men's habitations*; but, at all events, the contest shows that the development of nature is here intended, from the lifeless stone, through the fertile earth, to the plant and tree so that these beings seem to have presided over the transition from inorganic to organic nature. To this interpretation their names, as far as we can explain them, are particularly favourable: Móinn, *earth-dweller* Draupnir, *the dripper*, or *former of drops* Glói, *the glowing, glittering, giver of colour*; Hliódálfr, *the elf* of *sound*. The dwarfs work in the service of the gods, and their productions are emblems of the different agencies of nature. Of these the sons of Ivaldi are particularly named, who made the artificial hair of Sif, the ship Skidbladnir for Frey, and the spear Gungnir for Odin; while Sindri and Brock made Frey's hog with golden bristles, the ring Draupnir and the hammer Miölnir.[1] Thus they wrought both in the vegetable kingdom and in metals. Odin, it is said, cut or engraved runes for the Aesir, Dvalin for the elves, Dain for the dwarfs. That the elves and dwarfs are blended together, appears not only from this passage, where Dvalin, a dwarf, is named as the teacher of the elves, but from the list of names in the Völuspá. Without the earth, we meet with the dwarfs Northri, Suthri, Austri, and Vestri, the four cardinal points of the compass; also Nyi and Nithi, the increasing and waning moon, mere ideas, which are referred to the dwarfs as representing the subordinate powers.[2]

**There are nine worlds**, and as beings inhabiting them, the following are named: Aesir, Vanir, Men, Elves, Dwarfs, Jötuns, Halir, or inhabitants of Helheim. These nine worlds are,

1  Muspellheim, the farthest towards the south, inhabited by Surt and Muspell's sons: it is the highest heaven, with light, warmth and fire, and older than either heaven or earth;
2  Asgard or Godheim, the world of the Aesir or gods, heaven;
3  Vanaheim, or the abode of the Vanir;
4  Midgard or Manheim, the world of men, the middlemost inhabited part of the earth;
5  Alfheim, or Liós-álfheim, inhabited by the elves;

1  Pages 37–8.
2  Page 14. It is singular, what Keyser remarks, that the *Eddas* omit all mention of the creation of animals.

6  Svart-álfheim, inhabited by swart-elves and dwarfs;
7  Jötunheim, or Utgard, inhabited by jötuns or giants, the utter-
   most boundary of the earth;
8  Helheim, inhabited by those dead who go to Hel, the world of
   spectres;
9  Niflheim, the world of mist, the farthest north, and the
   nethermost, uninhabited, older than heaven and earth.[1]

**Illustration.** The nine worlds mentioned in the Alvísmal must not be confounded with the nine over which the gods gave dominion to Hel, which are identical with the nine worlds below Niflheim, where the Halir or subjects of Hel wander about.[2] She acquired the dominion over a portion of Niflheim, and that she had nine worlds to rule over, means simply that her realm was boundless. Some explain the nine worlds thus:

1  Muspellheim, the abode of Muspell's sons;
2  Alfheim, of the Light-elves;
3  Godheim, of the Aesir;
4  Vanaheim, of the Vanir;
5  Vindheim, of souls;
6  Manheim, of men;
7  Jötunheim, of giants;
8  Myrkheim, of dwarfs;
9  Niflheim, of spectres.

But Vindheim is the same as Vanaheim, and is not inhabited by souls, who go either to Valhall or to Hel. Others place Alfheim, or Liós-álfheim, either, as here, after Muspellheim, or even above it. This collocation is founded on *Gylfaginning* 17, where, in speaking of the heavenly dwellings, after mention made of Gimli, it is said that there is a heaven, Andláng, above Gimli, and above that another Vidbláin (wide-blue); 'and we believe that the Light-elves alone now inhabit those places.' But the text of Snorri seems to have been here made up by additions at different times; for the state of things there alluded to is evidently what is to take place after Ragnaröck; as not until then will either good men inhabit Gimli, or the elves Andláng and Vidbláin. Not until after Ragnaröck, will men, elves, and giants, the beings who till then had dwelt on earth, come to their heavenly abodes. This is, moreover, clear from the circumstance, that not till the conclusion of the chapter above-mentioned of *Gylfaginning*, is there any mention of the heavens, Andláng and Vidbláin, but previously the abode of the Light-elves in Alfheim is spoken of.

1  Page 13.
2  Page 45.

**Heaven and Earth.** The ideas of these are formed in accordance with their seeming figure. Outermost was the ocean, on which Utgard bordered. In the middle of the earth was Midgard. Above all Asgard raised its head, first on earth, but afterwards, it would seem, transferred to heaven. This scheme is a perfect image of the *Thing*, or popular assembly, around the king's exalted seat. He was immediately encircled by his priests and officials as Odin by the Aesir. Without them stood the people or free men; outermost of all was the circle of thralls. In like manner, the holy offering-tree, with its three branches and its sacred spring, whence oracles were issued, was transferred to heaven. By one of Yggdrasil's roots are the spring and dwelling of the Norns,[1] like the priestesses or Valas on earth. There the will of the fates is to be learned, to which even the gods themselves are subjected; by another of its roots is Mimir's spring, where is the wisdom of the deep; by the third root are serpents, herein also resembling the earthly tree, by which serpents were fed. Between the giants and the gods there is a river named Ifing, which never freezes,[2] that is, the atmosphere: but from the abode of men a bridge leads up to the latter, herein again resembling the earthly temples, built probably on an isle, and accessible only over a sacred bridge. The guardian of the bridge was Heimdall, who from the river Giöll, the horizon, raised his Giallar-horn, which is kept under the tree Yggdrasil.[3] But there was another guardian, Mimir, at the descent into the nether world, at the junction of heaven and sea, in the north, as the abode of night, and the region where the inhabitants of the North found the country surrounded by the sea. The spring of the Norns is that of superhuman wisdom, Mimir's that of sublunary. Odin must possess both. With his one eye, the sun, he saw all that passed in heaven and on earth; but the secrets of the deep he must learn, either by sinking, as the sun, into the sea, or by getting possession of Mimir's head, as the seat of subterranean wisdom.

**Illustration.** Ifing – The name of this river seems derived from the verb at ífa, which now signifies *to doubt*, though the primitive idea has probably been *to totter*, *to move from place to place*; Ifing will then signify that which is in constant motion, like the air, which also never freezes. Bifröst is the rainbow, from at bifa, *to tremble*, *swing*, and röst, *a measure of length*, *mile*. Yggdrasil has never been satisfactorily explained.[4] But at all events, the

1    Page 19.
2    Page 19.
3    Page 31.
4    The ash Yggdrasil is an emblem of all living nature. The name is obscure, but may be explained. Ygg's, i.e. Odin's, horse, seat, or chariot, from Ygg, a name of Odin, and

sacred tree of the North is, no doubt, identical with the 'robur Jovis', or sacred oak of Geismar, destroyed by Boniface,[1] and the Irminsul of the Saxons,[2] the *Columna universalis*, the terrestrial tree of offerings, an emblem of the whole world, as far as it is under divine influence. The giant-powers and the children of death are not overshadowed by it. But the gods, as well as mortals, must have their offering-tree, and one naturally of far greater magnitude. The animals described as living in the tree, bear, without doubt, all allusion to real symbols on the terrestrial one; but unfortunately nothing worthy to be called a description or this tree has reached our time. There was on it a sort of weathercock, which is, perhaps, alluded to by the hawk Vedurfölnir. As from the ash Yggdrasil three roots issue in different directions, so from the *Irminsul* proceeded three or four great highways. According to the old scholiast on Adam of Bremen, such a tree – which was green both summer and winter – stood near the ancient temple at Upsala; near which was the sacred spring, into which the offerings were sunk. Ratatösk is a name of very doubtful etymon. Finn Magnusen would derive it from at rata, *vagari*, and tauta, *susurrare*, therefore (an animal) going up and down, whispering tales of strife between the serpent and the eagle. The names of the four harts are also, the names of dwarfs, viz. Dáin, *swooning*; Dvalin, *torpid*; Duneyr, *the noisy, maker of din*? Durathrór, *the door-breaker*? Nidhögg (of very doubtful etymon) is *the gnawing serpent*. The whole tree and its inmates are significant, but an allegorical interpretation of them is no longer possible. The myth is both Indian and Lamaic. It is the tree of life, which gathers around it all higher creatures in one worship, as the earthly offering-tree assembled all followers of the same faith under its over-shadowing branches.

---

drasill or drösull, from draga, *to bear*, &c. Living nature is regarded as moved and ruled by the divine power, which has its seat in it as the soul in the body. The word thus explained is in perfect accordance with the old skaldic notions, and the myth seems a poetic allegory throughout. The image accords with their cosmogony. In the tree's top sits an eagle, the emblem of spirit or life; at its root in Hvergelmir lies Nidhögg, the serpent of darkness and death; but the squirrel Ratatösk runs up and down the trunk, carrying rancorous words between the eagle and the serpent; i.e. contending powers move in nature, and false malice steals with its calumny through human life, and disturbs its peace. The fundamental idea seems to be the great strife that pervades worldly life, the strife between spirit and matter, good and evil, life and death. Keyser, op. cit., pp. 24, 25.

1 Grimm, J., *Deutsche Mythologie*, op. cit., pp. 62, 63, from Willibaldi *Vita Bonifacii*.
2 Grimm, J., *Deutsche Mythologie*, op. cit., p. 106, who gives the following passage from Ruodolf of Fulda: 'Truncum ligni non parvae magnitudinis in altum erectum sub divo colebant, patria eum lingua *Irminsul* appellantes, quod Latine dicitur *universalis* columna, quasi sustinens omnia.'

The goddesses of fate are called Norns. The word Norn does not occur in any kindred dialect. They decide the fate of the hero, while they twist or spin the threads of destiny, and the extent of his dominion, by fastening and stretching it from one quarter of the earth to another; and herein they resemble the spinning Μοῖραι or Parcae, only that the Northern picture is more comprehensive. Their functions are *to point out*, *show*, and *to determine*; they show or make known that which was destined from the beginning, and determine that which shall take place in time. Of the Fylgiur and Hamingiur, sorts of guardian angels, that accompany every mortal from the cradle to the grave, we have already spoken.[1] Nearly allied to, and almost identical with the Norns, are the Valkyriur. They are also called Valmeyiar (battle-maids), Skialdmeyiar (shield-maids), Hialmmeyiar (helm-maids), and Ôskmeyiar, from their attendance on Odin, one of whose names is Ôski. They spin and weave like the Norns. In *Niálssaga*[2] we read that Darrad (Dörrudr) looking through a chasm in a rock, saw women singing and weaving, with human heads for weights, entrails for woof and warp, swords for bobbins, and arrows for comb. In their appalling song, they designated themselves Valkyriur, and announced that their web was that of the looker-on, Darrad. At last, they tore their work in fragments, mounted their horses, and six rode southwards, and six northwards.[3]

The origin of the name of Mimir is unknown, and the myth concerning him differs in the several sources. According to the *Ynglinga-saga*, he was slain by the Vanir, but of his fate no traces are to be found in either *Edda*. There was a tree apparently connected with Mimir, called Miótvidr, which is usually rendered by *Middle tree*, and is considered identical with Yggdrasil; but Mimir dwelt under Yggdrasil's root. In the *Völuspá*, the context evidently shows that the nether world is spoken of; here Miótvidr appears manifestly to signify the tree of knowledge.[4] In the obscure *Fiölsvinnsmal*, Mímameidr (Mimir's tree) is spoken of, which spreads itself round all lands, is not injured by fire or iron, but few only know from what roots it springs; neither then is this Yggdrasil, whose roots are known. In the following strophes it appears that it went deep down to the nethermost region of earth. Here mention is also made of Thrymgiöll, *a gate or lattice*, made by Sôlblindi's (Night's) three sons. The meaning of all which seems

---

1   Pages 88–9
2   Cap. 158.
3   On this Grimm (p. 397) not inaptly observes: 'So at least may be understood the words "vindum vindum vef Darradar", though the story may have its origin in a "vef darradar" (tela jaculi). Comp. A. S. darrod, a *dart*.' The story has been beautifully versified by Gray.
4   Page 64.

to be, that, besides the heavenly tree, Yggdrasil, there was a tree under the earth, whose roots were lost in the abyss, and whose top spread itself in the horizon around all lands, on the limit of the upper and nether worlds; and it was on this tree that Odin hung for nine nights, of whose roots no one had knowledge. The rivers Giöll and Leipt flow near to men, and thence to Hel. Giöll (Ger. Gall = Schall) signifies sound; it probably means the horizon, and has reference to the popular belief of the sun's sound, when it goes down,[1] and when it rises, or when day breaks forth. Leipt – the name of the other river – signifies *lightning, flash*. Both words may then denote the glittering stripe of the horizon. Mimir is also called Hoddmimir,[2] which has been rendered *Circle-Mimir* or *Sphere-Mimir*, as alluding to the circle of the horizon. Awaiting the regeneration of mankind, the original matter of the new human race will be preserved in Hoddmimir's holt or wood.[3] This explanation is confirmed by the Sólarljód, where it is said, 'in full horns they drank the pure mead from the ring- (circle-) god's fountain'. According to a popular belief in Germany, Denmark and England, a golden cup, or hidden treasure lies where the rainbow apparently touches the horizon. This seems a remnant of the belief in Mimir's spring, in which wisdom's golden treasure was concealed.[4]

War burst forth in the world when men pierced Gullveig (gold) through with their spears, and burnt her in the high one's hall.[5] That is, when they

1 'The skreik of day'. *Hunter's Hallamshire Glossary* Our 'break of day.' (?) See Grimm's remarks on the A. S. word wóma (daeg-wóma, daegréd-wóma) in 'Andreas und Elene,' p. xxx. and Grimm, J., *Deutsche Mythologie*, op. cit., pp. 131, 132.

2 It is far from certain that Mímir and Hoddmímir are identical.

3 Page 68.

4 The name Mimir signifies *having knowledge*, and seems identical with A. S. meomer, Lat. memor. The giants, who are older than the Aesir, saw further into the darkness of the past. They had witnessed the creation of the Aesir and of the world, and foresaw their destruction. On both points, the Aesir must seek knowledge from them, a thought repeatedly expressed in the old mythic poems, but nowhere more clearly than in the *Völuspá*, in which a Vala or prophetess, reared among the giants, is represented rising from the deep to unveil time past and future to gods and men. It is then this wisdom of the deep that Mimir keeps in his well. The heavenly god Odin himself must fetch it thence, and this takes place in the night, when the sun, heaven's eye, is descended behind the brink of the disc of earth into the giants' world. Then Odin explores the secrets of the deep, and his eye is there pledged for the drink he obtains from the fount of knowledge. But in the brightness of dawn, when the sun again ascends from the giants' world, then does the guardian of the fount drink from a golden horn the pure mead that flows over Odin's pledge. Heaven and the nether world communicate mutually their wisdom to each other. Through a literal interpretation of the foregoing myth, Odin is represented as one-eyed. Keyser, op. cit., pp. 25, 26.

5 Page 21.

hammered and forged gold, and bestowed on it a certain value, then the idea of property arose, a distinction between *mine* and *thine*, and Heidi (Heithi, from heidr, *honour, dignity*) or riches awakened desire.

Odin is Allfather, the universal ruler over all, his nature is, therefore, manifold. He is the world's creator, the father of time, the lord of gods and men, and of all nature, the god of heaven, the king of the year, the god of war, and giver of victory. He operates through heaven and earth, but, at the same time, allies himself with the giants and powers of the deep, as the spirit that operates throughout the material world. And from all these relations his sons proceed, who are a part of his essence. He is heaven; his eye, the sun, looks out over all on earth, and at night beholds all in the deep. He has connection with Earth, and becomes the father of Thor, the thunder. He who quickens all nature has intercourse with the giant powers, and begets the unperishing Vidar.[1] As god of time and king of the year, he with Frigg[2] begets Baldur,[3] the bright summer. Höd also, the dark nights of winter, who slays Baldur,[4] and Vali,[5] the forthcoming new year, who avenges him, are likewise his children. As lord of the intellectual world he is father of Bragi,[6] the god of eloquence and poetry. As god of war, or father of hosts (Heriafödr), he begets Hermod,[7] the spirit, who goes on his messages; sends Ty,[8] the god of valour and honour into the heat of battle; and his maidens, the Valkyriur choose the heroes that shall be his guests in Valhall, the hall of the chosen. He is the heavenly image of earthly kings, surrounded by his men, the Aesir, with his skald, Bragi, and his supreme judge, Forseti.[9] As ruler of heaven, he dwells in Valaskiálf,[10] and sits on a throne in Hlidskiálf.[11] As the Einheriar's prince, he dwells in Gladsheim,[12] and gathers them around him in Valhall. As king of mind, he daily visits Saga, the goddess of history, in her abode, Söckquabeck;[13] and this, his mental dominion, is further indicated by his ravens, Hugin and Munin[14] (thought and memory). Odin is described as a tall, one-eyed old man, with a long beard, a broad-brimmed hat, a wide, blue or variegated, rough cloak, with a spear (Gungnir) in his hand, and the ring Draupnir on his arm. On his shoulders sit his two ravens, his two wolves lie at his feet, and Charles's wain rolls above his head. He sits on a high seat (as he was represented at Upsala), whence he sees over the whole world.

| | | |
|---|---|---|
| 1  Pages 31, 67–8. | 6  Page 31. | 11  Page 19. |
| 2  Page 33. | 7  Page 25. | 12  Page 18. |
| 3  Page 26. | 8  Page 30. | 13  Page 35. |
| 4  Pages 31, 61. | 9  Page 32 | 14  Page 24. |
| 5  Page 63. | 10  Page 18. | |

The following account of his appearing to King Olaf Tryggvason is particularly interesting.

'The first evening that King Olaf kept Easter at Ögvaldsnaes, there came an old man, of very shrewd discourse, one-eyed, of sombre look, and with a broad-brimmed hat. He entered into conversation with the king, who found great pleasure in talking with him, for he could give information of all countries both ancient and modern. The king asked him about Ögvald, after whom the naze and the dwelling were called, and the old man told him about Ögvald and the cow that he worshipped, seasoning his narrative with old proverbs. Having thus sat until late in the night, the bishop reminded the king that it was time to retire to rest. But when Olaf was undressed and had lain down in bed, the old guest came again and sat on the footstool, and again conversed long with him; for the longer he spoke the longer did Olaf wish to hear him. The bishop then again reminded the king that it was time to sleep. Unwilling as he was, for he was very loth to end their conversation, he nevertheless laid his head on the pillow, and the guest departed. Scarcely however was the king awake, before his first thought was his guest, whom he ordered to be called, but he was nowhere to be found. It now was made known that while preparations were making for the feast, there came an elderly man, whom no one knew, to the cook, and said they were cooking some bad meat, and that it was not fitting to set such on the king's table on so great a festival; and thereupon gave him two thick, fat sides of an ox, which he cooked with the other meat. The king commanded them to burn the whole together, to cast the ashes into the sea, and prepare some other food; for it was now manifest to him that the guest was the false Odin, in whom the heathens had so long believed, and whose tricks he now saw.'[1]

**Illustration.** The name Odin (Odinn, Ohg. Wuotan) has been satisfactorily interpreted. It is derived from vada, *to go*, Lat. vadere, pret. ód, or strictly, vód; whence the double participle ódinn and ódr, *the impetuous disposition or mind*. Hence it denotes *the all-pervading, spiritual godhead*. In accordance with this interpretation are the words of Adam of Bremen: 'Wodan, id est fortior' (furor?). In the Grisons, Wut signifies *idol*. The Wüthendes Heer (Wild Hunt) of the Germans is ascribed to Odin. To the god of war the name is also appropriate, as at vada uppá signifies to attack in battle. He pervades not only the living, but the dead. Nine songs of power (fimbul-liód) he learned from Bölthorn, Bestla's father; obtained possession of Mimir's head, and embraced Gunnlöd; he is likewise the

---

1    Saga Olafs Tryggv. quoted by Petersen, op. cit., p. 161.

lord of spectres (drauga drottinn). It is also said, that by the aid of certain incantations, sung by the dwarf Thiodreyrir, the Aesir acquired power or strength (afl), the elves fame, advancement, prosperity (frami), Hróptatr or Odin thought, reflection (hyggia). Odin's oldest habitation was Valaskiálf, which he built for himself in the beginning of time.[1] The signification of this word is extremely doubtful. Grimm is inclined to consider the first part of the compound as identical with Val in Valhall, Valkyria, and bearing an allusion to Odin's own name of Valfadir; skiálf (which signifies *tremor*) he regards as expressing the trembling motion of the air, like the first syllable of Bifröst.[2] Another derivation is from the verb at vaela, *to build with art*, whence comes the participle valr, *artificially built*, *round*, *vaulted*. This interpretation is, moreover, corroborated by a passage in the *Grimnismál*.[3] Skiálf may also be interpreted *bench*, *seat*, *shelf*. His throne in Valaskiálf was Hlidskiálf (from lid, *door*, *window*, *lid* ) and skiálf as above. As god of war, Odin's abode was in Gladsheim (the home of gladness and splendour). There is his hall Valhall (from valr, *the fallen in battle*), of kindred origin with the first syllable in Valkyria; *a chooser* (feminine) *of the fallen*. Here we meet with the goat Heidrun (from heidr, *clear*, *serene*, and renna, *to run*, *flow*), that is, *the clear*, *heavenly air*, whence mead comes, like honeydew, from Yggdrasil's top. By the goat may possibly be typified the whiteness and abundance of sustenance. The tree Laerad (that which produces lae or calm) signifies the higher region of the air, where the winds do not rage. Under the emblem of Eikthyrnir, *the oak-thorned stag* (from eik, *oak*, and thorn, *thorn*), are represented the branches of the tree, that project like the antlers of a stag. From its horn flow many rivers, which are enumerated in the *Grimnismál*, of which some flow near the gods, others near men, and thence to Hel. Of those that flow near the gods, some are designated *the deep*, *the wide*, *the striving*, *the loud-sounding*, etc. Of those that take their course by men, *the friendly*, *way-knowing*, *folk-griping*, *useful*, *fertilising*, *rushing*, *swelling*, *roaring*, etc. All these names, as well as the whole context, which begins with the upper air, and ends with the before-mentioned Giöll and Leipt, show that by these rivers nothing more is meant than the higher and lower clouds. Through some of these, too, the Thunder-god must pass on his way to the place of meeting under Yggdrasil, as he could not go over the rainbow without setting it on fire. These are named Körmt and Örmt,

1    Page 18.
2    Grimm, J., *Deutsche Mythologie*, op. cit., p. 778, note.
3    Str. 6.      Valaskiálf heitir,        *Valaskiálf it is called,*
                  er vaelti sèr            *which for himself constructed*
                  Ass í árdaga.            *Odin in days of yore.*

and the two Kerlaugar, names which cannot be explained. The foregoing may serve as examples of the old enigmatic, periphrastic way of expressing very simple things, and, I believe, no deeper signification is to be sought for. The chosen heroes were called Einheriar (from einn, *one, chosen, single*, and heri, *lord, hero*), also Odin's Ôskasynir; Odin himself, as god of war, being named Ôski, *the granter of wishes*.[1] The number of the Valkyriur is sometimes three, sometimes nine, also thirteen, and twenty-seven, sometimes an indefinite number. The youngest Norn, Skulld, was one of them. They crave, and long after war. They are white maidens that ride through the air, from the manes of whose horses dew falls in the valleys, and hail on the high woods. Their names have reference sometimes to war, sometimes to clouds, rain and wind: as Hild and Gunn, *war*; Svafa, *the hovering, impending*; Kara, *wind*; Göll, the same word as the river Giöll; Sigurdrífa and Sigrún, from sígr, *victory*, and drífa, *to drive*. They are also called Ôskmeyiar. Odin's spear, Gungnir (from at gúngna, *to shake, brandish*), is a symbol of his warlike might. His horse Sleipnir (from sleipr, *smooth, gliding*) is described as having eight legs, whereby it is meant merely to express his great speed, as Odin's horse is mentioned elsewhere as four-footed. Like his shield, Odin's horse was white, in allusion probably to the clearness of heaven. In the myth of Sleipnir's birth, Svadilföri is the winter's cold (according at least to Finn Magnusen), from svad, *a heap of melting snow*, therefore *that which brings sleet and snowstorms*; and the simplest interpretation of a part of the myth is, perhaps, the following. Loki (fire, heat), who was probably desirous of resting a while, persuaded the Aesir to allow the stranger architect (Winter) to raise a fortress of ice, which he began with his assistant, the horse Svadilföri, that is, *the intense cold*. But while he was still engaged on the work, the gods saw that the beauty of life, Freyia, would be lost to them, and the sun and moon hidden in the foul giant's eternal fog. Whereupon they caused Loki to connect himself with Svadilföri, from which union was born the gray colt, Sleipnir (the wind), which demolished the ice-mansion, and soon increased in growth, so that the god of the year (Odin) could mount his steed, the cooling wind of summer.[2] That the wind is betokened is apparent from the popular belief in Mecklenburg, that on Wednesday (Woden's day) no flax is weeded, that Woden's horse may not trample on the seed; nor may any flax remain on the distaff during the twelve days of Christmas, lest Woden's horse ride through and tangle it, and that in Skania and Bleking, after the harvest, a

1   Page 22, note 1. Grimm, J., *Deutsche Mythologie*, op. cit., p. 126.
2   See a similar tradition from Courland, of the giant Kinte, and his white mare, Frost, in Grimm, p. 516.

gift was left on the field for Odins's horse.[1] It was also on this horse that
Odin conveyed Hading across the sea, wrapping him in his mantle, so
that he could see nothing.[2] It is on the same white horse that he rides as
the Wild Huntsman.[3] In the later sagas (as in that of Hrólfr Kraki), we
already find it believed of Odin, that he was an evil and perfidious being,
who mingled in the tumult of battle, and caused the fall of warriors. In
the middle age, this belief became more and more prevalent. To the
singular method, by which, according to Saxo, one might 'praesentem
cognoscere Martem,'[4] a corresponding tradition exists even in the heart

---

1    Grimm, p. 140. In Lower Saxony also it is customary to leave a bunch of grain on
the field for Woden s horse. In the Isle of Möen a sheaf of oats was left for his horse, that
he might not by night trample on the seed. Woden occasionally rides also in a chariot.
Petersen, op. cit., p. 173. Grimm, p. 138.

In Öland, Högrum parish, there lie great stones called Odin's flisor (Odini lamellae),
concerning which the story goes, that Odin being about to feed his horse, took the bit
from his mouth, and laid it on a huge block of stone, which by the weight of the bit was
split into two parts, that were afterwards set up as a memorial. According to another
version of the story, Odin, when about to fight with an enemy, being at a loss where to
tie his horse, ran to this stone, drove his sword through it, and tied his horse through
the hole. The horse, however, broke loose, the stone sprang asunder and rolled away,
making a swamp called Högrumsträsk, so deep that although several poles have been
bound together, they have not sufficed to fathom it. Geijer's *Schw. Gesch.*, i, 110. Abr.
Ahlquist, *Ölands Historia*, i, 37; ii, 212, quoted by Grimm, J., *Deutsche Mythologie*, op.
cit., p. 141.

A small waterfowl (tringa minima, inquieta, lacustris et natans) is to the Danes and
Icelanders known by the name of Odinshani, Odin's fugl. In an Old High-German gloss
mention occurs of an Utinswaluwe (Odin's swallow). Ibid. p. 145.

2    Saxo, op. cit., p. 40.

3    Grimm, J., *Deutsche Mythologie*, op. cit., p. 880

4    Saxo, op. cit., p. 106. Grimm, J., *Deutsche Mythologie*, op. cit., p. 891. Biarco being
unable to perceive Odin on his white horse, giving aid in a battle to the Swedes, says
to Ruta:

> Et nunc ille ubi sit, qui vulgo dicitur Othin
> Armipotens, uno semper contentus ocello?
> Dic mihi, Ruta, precor, usquam si conspicis illum?

To which she answers:

> Adde oculum propius, et nostras prospice chelas,
> Ante sacraturus victrici lumina signo,
> Si vis praesentem tuto cognoscere Martem.

Whereupon Biarco replies:

> Quantumcunque albo clypeo sit tectus et altum (l. album)
> Flectat equum, Lethra nequaquam sospes abibit;
> Fas est belligerum bello prosternere divum.

Petersen, op. cit., cites Orvar Odd's *Saga* (c. 29) for a similar instance.

of Germany. We are told, that as some people were one day walking on the Odenberg, they heard a beating of drums, but saw nothing; whereupon a wise man bade them, one after another, look through the ring which he formed by setting his arm akimbo. They did so, and immediately perceived a multitude of warriors engaged in military exercises, going into and coming out of the Odenberg.[1] Many authors have identified the Odin of the North with the Indian Buddha; of their original identity there can hardly exist a doubt, though the myths relating to each have naturally taken widely different directions. What I have seen hitherto in opposition to this opinion seems to me to favour, if not confirm it. Schlegel repudiates it because Buddha signifies *the Wise*, and is an adjectival form from bud', *to think* but Odinn is a similar form from vada, so that the verbal identity can hardly be greater; the form ódr, *ingenium, anima sensitiva*, agreeing with ódinn, shows also that the signification of both words is one and the same.

The other gods also, as princes, had their horses, though the authorities do not state which belonged to each in particular, and their names bear a close resemblance to each other. They may be rendered the *Shining*, the *Golden*, the *Precious stone*, the *Rays shedding on the way*, *Silver-mane*,[2] *Sinew-strong*, the *Ray*, the *Pale of head*, *Gold-mane*[2] and *Light-foot*. Gold-mane was Heimdall's, in allusion to the radiant colours of the rainbow.

War was too weighty an affair not to have, besides the universal ruler Odin, its appropriate deity. This was Ty,[3] who, at the same time, was god of courage and honour. He is a son of Odin, but his mother was of giant race, light-browed and radiant with gold.[4] No one equals him in daring; in the midst of the battle's rage, he fearlessly stretches forth his hand decked with the martial gauntlet. He is the Mars of the Northern nations.

**Illustration.** Tyr is the general appellation of a distinguished divinity, though particularly of the god of military prowess and honour (from tyr, tír, *honour*). His name is found in Old Norse Tígsdagr, Danish Tirsdag, Anglo Saxon Tiwesdaeg, Dies Martis, *Tuesday*; also in Tíghraustr, valiant as Ty. The strength of beer, too, is described as blandinn megin-tíri, *medicata magna virtute*. Loki upbraids him with his inability ever to bear a shield, or to use two hands, and further informs him that his wife had a son by him (Loki), and that Ty did not get a rag or a farthing as damages.

---

1  Grimm, p. 891.
2  Gulltoppr, Silfrintoppr horses were called, whose manes (toppr, Ger. zopf) were entwined with gold or silver. Grimm, p. 623.
3  Page 30.
4  Page 56.

That Odin is his father and the beautiful giantess his mother, may signify that she is the ennobled giant-spirit which through Odin connects itself with the Aesir-race.[1]

Odin's wife was Frigg (the earth). She occurs but rarely under the general appellation of earth, but often under other denominations, according to the several points of view from which she is considered. The supreme among all the goddesses is Frigg, the fertile summer-earth, who more than all others bewails her noble son Baldur's (the summer's) death. Her attendants are Fulla (plenty), a pleasing emblem of the luxuriant aspect of the blooming fields; Hlin, (the mild protecting warmth); and Gna, who as the gentle breeze rides on her swift courser, bearing to every land the produce of the fruitful earth.[2] Under another form, the earth appears as Rind, the hard-frozen winter earth, with whom Odin begets Vali, the bright, winter days, with clear, hard frost, which passes over to spring. Frigg's rivals are Gerd and Gunnlöd: the first may be regarded as the germinating spring earth, which in seed-time is embraced by Frey; the latter is the autumnal earth, which is embraced by Odin, and gives him Suttung's mead,[3] at the time when the labours of summer and warfare are over, when the harvest songs resound in the field, and the shout of warriors in the hall. But neither of these two are strictly earth's divinities. As mother of Thor, the thunder, the earth is called Fiörgyn (Fiörgvin) (Goth. Fairguni,[4] *mountain*) and Hlódyn, another name for mountain, which when begrown with grass, is represented as Thor's wife, Sif.[5]

**Illustration.** The general name of the earth is iörd. Frigg or Frygg is related to the Lat. *Fruges*, the root of which is found in the participle *fructus*, Ger. *Frucht*, Dan; *Frugt* it therefore denotes the fruitful earth. Her dwelling is called Fensalir, the lower and humid parts of the earth; for as the divinity of the fertile earth, she does not rule over the high, barren mountains. Fulla, *the full*, *abundant*, the *luxuriant cornfield*, is opposed to Sif, the grass-grown mountain. Hlín or Hlyn (from hly, at hlúa, at hlyna, *calescere*), *the mild*, *refreshing warmth*. The danger from which she protects

---

1  Besides numerous names of places, the name of Ty (Tyr) appears also in the following names of plants: O. Nor. Tysfiola, *viola Martis*; Tyrhialm, *aconitum*, *monk's hood*, Dan. Troldhat; O. Nor. Tyvidr, Dan. Tyved, Tysved, *daphne mezereon*, *spurge laurel*. Grimm, p. 180.

2  In Sweden, Fyen and some other places, the constellation Orion is called by the common people Frigg's rok (distaff). The *orchis odoratissima* is called Friggjar-gras and hjona-gras (marriage grass).

3  Pages 39, *sqq*.

4  Grimm, pp. 156, 610, and Pref. to 1st edit. p. xvi.

5  See p. 25 for other interpretations of Fiörgyn and Hlódyn.

is cold. That her name denotes a property of earth, appears from the circumstance, that Frigg herself is also called Hlín.[1] By Gna, and its derivative at gnaefa (to be borne on high) is expressed *motion on high, in the air*; as is also apparent from the name of her horse, Hófvarpnir (the hoof-caster), and that of its sire, Hamskerpnir (skin-drier), or Hattstrykir (hatsweeper), and of its dam, Gardrófa (house, or fencebreaker). The word rindr is still used in Iceland to denote barren land. It is the English *rind*. Rind betokens the frost-hardened surface of the earth. Of her son Vali's birth the *Eddas* supply no details: it is merely said, she gave birth to him í vestur sölum (in the halls of the West), for which a various reading has í vetur sölum (in the halls of winter), which suits remarkably well with Rind. In Saxo[2] we find the chief features of a myth which has there assumed an almost historic colouring, but evidently belongs to our category. It is a description of Odin's love for Rinda, and forms a counterpart to the myths of Odin and Gunnlöd,[3] Frey and Gerd.[4] – 'Rostiophus[5] Phinnicus having foretold to Odin, that by Rinda the daughter of the king of the Rutheni,[6] he would have a son, who should avenge the death of Baldur; Odin conceal-ing his face with his hat, enters into that king's service, and being made general of his army, gains a great victory; and shortly after, by his single arm, puts the whole army of the enemy to flight with immense slaughter. Relying on his achievements, he solicits a kiss from Rinda, in place of which he receives a blow, which does not, however, divert him from his purpose. In the following year, disguised in a foreign garb, he again seeks the king, under the name of Roster the smith, and receives from him a considerable quantity of gold, to be wrought into female ornaments. Of this, besides other things, he fabricates a bracelet and several rings of exquisite beauty, which, in the hope of gaining her love, he presents to Rinda, but by whom he is repulsed even more ignominiously than before. He then comes as a young warrior, but on demanding a kiss, receives a blow which lays him flat on his face. On this he touches her with a piece of bark, on which certain incantations were inscribed, whereby she is rendered as one frantic. He then appears in the guise of a woman, under the name of Vecha, and is appointed to the office of Rinda's waiting-maid. Availing himself of her malady, he prescribes a potion, but which, on

1 Page 64.
2 Pages 126, sq. ed. Müller.
3 Page 39.
4 Page 43.
5 Hrossthióf was one of the Frost-giant Hrímnir's children; it is therefore clear that with him it is the middle of winter.
6 The Russians.

account of her violence, he declares cannot be administered, unless she is bound. Deceived by the female attire of the leech, the king orders her to be bound forthwith, when Odin, taking advantage of her helplessness, becomes by her the father of a son,' whose name is, not Vali, but Bo (Bous), but who, nevertheless, is identical with Vali, being the avenger of Baldur. The signification of the myth is evident enough, particularly when compared with those allied with it. Rinda is the hard-frozen earth, that repulses Odin; the ornaments which he proffers her, are the glories of spring and summer; as a warrior, he represents war to her as the most important occupation of summer. But by his four appearances are not meant, as some have imagined, the four seasons, but merely the hard winter and its transition to spring. Fiörgynn occurs once as a masculine, viz. as the father of Frigg,[1] but elsewhere always as a feminine (Fiörgyn) and mother of Thor. Hlódyn, which also denotes the earth as the mother of Thor, is rightly referred to hlód, hearth, which is derived from at hlada, *to heap up*, *load*,[2] pret. hlód. But Hlódyn does not denote the deity of the hearth, who could not in any way be mother of Thor; while if we only enlarge the idea, it will be clear that the word signifies *a mountain*, that which is piled up. In like manner, we shall presently see that another name for mountain, Hrugnir (Hrungnir), comes from at hrúga, *to heap up*, *to lay stratum upon stratum*. Both Fiörgyn, then, and Hlóydn fundamentally signify the same, viz. *a mountain*; but the idea is viewed under different aspects, sometimes as the compact mass, sometimes as a pile of strata upon strata.

Thor is the god of thunder; he dwells in Thrudheim, *the dense gloom of clouds*,[3] and sends forth, from time to time, the gleaming lightning from his hall, Bilskirnir. His other names and attributes, as well as those of his attendants, bear allusion to the rapid course of the thunderstorm, terrific sounds, pernicious lightnings, together with the furious winds and deluging rains which accompany them. His crushing hammer denotes the lightning; with that he visits rocks and sea, and nothing withstands its might. His strength is especially expressed by his belt, the crash of thunder by his chariot. We often find Loki (fire) in his train, and even as his hand-maiden[4] for the fire of the clouds is akin to earthly fire, but the latter fights more with craft, the former with force. Thor receives slaves, partly, perhaps, as the divinity particularly worshipped by the Fins, before the

1  Skáldskap. 19.
2  Grimm, J., *Deutsche Mythologie*, op. cit., p. 235.
3  Keyser, op. cit., (p. 34) delives Thrudheim from thrudr, *i.e.* throttr, *strenth*, *endurance*.
4  Page 49.

spread of the Asreligion in the North, partly because slaves could not follow their masters to Valhall, but must occupy an inferior place. According to old Finnish usage, bridegroom and bride are consecrated, while the father strikes fire with flint and steel; fire-apparatus is also given to the dead By the Fins, Thor was worshipped as the chief god, and a portion of his worship passed into the As-religion.

As Thor is the thunderstorm, so are his journeys its divers manifestations. As the god of clouds, he is scarcely ever at home with the Aesir, but visits the giants – the rocks and mountains – and it is only when the gods call on him, that he is at hand. Sometimes we find him in conflict with Midgard's serpent,[1] which he strikes to the bottom of the ocean, or raises in the air; he hurls the roaring waves against the cliffs that project from the deep, and forms whirlpools in the rocky halls; sometimes he is contending with the giant (mountain) Hrungnir,[2] the crown of whose head pierces the clouds, and who threatens to storm the heavens. Thor cleaves his jagged summit, while Thialfi,[3] his swift follower, overcomes the weak clay hill by the mountain's side. He also visits the metal-king, Geirröd,[4] passes through the mountain streams into the clefts, and splits their stones and ores. In vain will the giant Thrym,[5] groaning in his impotence, imitate the Thunderer; in vain he hopes that the goddess of fruitfulness will be his; he gets neither her nor the Thunderer's might, who despises the powerless matter's presumptuous and bootless attempt. The thunderbolt returns to the hand of the Thunderer. In winter, only Thor loses a part of his resistless might: his hammer rests not, but its force is deadened with Skrymir on the ice-rocks.[6]

**Illustration.** Thórr, as Grimm observes, seems contracted from Thonar, whence the modern Germ. Donner, *thunder*. Hereto belong also the Lat. tonus, tonare, tonitru. Thrudheim, or Thrudvang, where he dwells, is from thrúdr, *strong*, strictly, *closely packed together*. Bilskirnir is from bil, *an interval (of time or space)*, and skír, *clear, bright*; skírnir, *that which illumines, glitters in the air*. The masses, like strata, lying one over another, are represented as the several storeys of the dwelling. The rolling thunder is expressed by Thor's chariot, reid (Lat. rheda); whence also the thunder-crash is called reidar-thruma (the rattling of the chariot). The names of the goats, Tanngniost and Tanngrisnir, have also a reference to sound; the first

---

1  Page 55.
2  Page 58.
3  From thiálf *severe labour*.
4  Page 47.
5  Page 48.
6  Page 51.

from gnist, *gnash*. Thor's chariot is drawn by goats, probably because those animals inhabit the highest mountain-tops; whether they were accounted sacred to Thor, is unknown. The Ossetes, in the Caucasus, a half Christian race, sacrifice a black goat to Elias, and hang the skin on a pole, when anyone is killed by lightning.[1] The rapid course and warmth are expressed in Ving-Thor, or the Winged Thor, and in his foster-children, Vingnir and Hlora, male and female; the latter is akin to hlaer, hlyr, *warm*, *lukewarm*, and with at hlóa, *to glow*. From hlóa or hlóra Thor's name of Hloridi, or Hlorridi, is most readily derived, the latter part of which is formed from reid, *a chariot*, as Hallinskeidi[2] is from skeid. Auku-Thor, or Öku-Thor, is by the ancient writers referred to aka, *to drive*, though it is probably no other than Thor's Finnish name, Ukko-Taran. The thunderbolt and the lightning are denoted by the hammer Miölnir, *the crusher*, *bruiser*, from at mala (mölva, melia), *to crush*. It is also called thrudhamar, signifying, according to Finn Magnusen, *malleus compactus*. Megingiàrdar, from megin, *strength*, is literally *the girth*, *or belt*, *of power*. Thor is also called Veor (Vör), and Midgard's Veor, the signification of which is extremely doubtful. As followers of Thor are named Thialfi and Röskva, brother and sister, consequently kindred ideas. Röskva signifies *the quick*, *active*, and her brother, who ran a race with Hugi[3] (thought), is also a good runner. Thialfi may not improbably denote the rushing thundershower, which will well suit his conflict with, and easy conquest of, the clay-giant Möckurkalfi;[4] for it is undoubtedly either the wind that blows him down, or the rain that washes him away. The father of Thialfi and Röskva is in Snorri's *Edda* called a peasant, but in Saemund's *Edda*, he is designated a hravnbui[5] (sea-dweller), a name well suited to the character just assigned to his son.

The stories of Thor's journeys are chiefly found in Snorri's *Edda*, though allusions to many of them occur in that of Saemund. Their mythic import is unquestionable. The giant Hymir (from hum or humr, *the sea*, Gr. κῦμα)[6] is manifestly, both from his name and from the matter of the poem, a sea-giant; he represents the cliffs which stretch themselves out from the land

---

1　Grimm, J., *Deutsche Mythologie*, op. cit., p. 159.
2　Page 31.
3　Page 52.
4　Page 59.
5　Hravn (Hrön) is the Anglo-Saxon hrón, signifying the ocean. In this sense, hrón-rád (the sea-road) is used in Caedmon (pp. 13, 19), and in the *Legend of St Andrew* (v. 740) hrón-fixas (sea-fishes), but where it is written 'horn-fixas'. So *Beowulf*, v. 19, ofer hrón-ráde (over the sea-road).
6　Olafsen's *Nord. Digtek.* p. 23. Njála, Ind., Skáldskap. 61.

into the vast unfathomable deep, where lies the Midgard's serpent. The drinking cup is smashed against his forehead, viz. the cliffs' projecting summits.[1] The kettle signifies the whirlpool among the rocks. Hrungnir, or Hrugnir (from at hrúga, *to heap up*) is the mountain formed by stratum upon stratum, whose head penetrates the clouds, and contends with heaven.

The following popular tradition from the Upper Thellemark is both interesting in itself and will serve as a further illustration of the story of Thor and Hrungnir.

At the upper end of the long Totak water in the Upper Thellemark is a very remarkable and imposing assemblage of stones which, seen from the water, resembles a town with its gables and towers; of its origin the peasants relate the following story:

'On the plain now covered by the stones, there were formerly two dwellings, and, as some say, a church, whence the largest stone, which rises amid the others like a church roof, is to this day called the church-stone. In these two dwellings, two weddings were once held, at which, according to the old Norwegian fashion, the horn with foaming beer was in constant circulation among the guests. It occurred to the god Thor that he would drive down and visit his old friends the Thellemarkers. He went first to the one wedding, was invited in, presented with strong beer, the bridegroom himself taking up the cask, drinking to Thor and then handing him the barrel. The god was pleased both with the drink itself and with the liberal manner in which it was given, and went greatly gratified to the other wedding party, to taste their wedding beer. There he was treated nearly in the same manner, but a want of respect was manifested in their not pledging him in a general bowl. The god, perhaps a little affected by the deep draught he had taken at the other wedding, became furiously wroth, dashed the bowl on the ground, and went away swinging his hammer. He then took the bridal pair that had presented him with the cask, together with their guests, and set them on a hill, to be witness of and to secure them from the destruction he in his revenge had destined for those who by their niggardliness had offended Asgard's most powerful god. With his 'tungum-hamri'[2] he then struck the mountain with such force that it toppled down and buried under it the other bridal pair with their habitation. But in his anger, the god let his hammer slip from his hand, which flew down with the rocky fragments and was lost among them.[3]

---

1  Page 57.
2  Heavy hammer.
3  It did not then return to his hand. See p. 38.

Thor had therefore to go down and seek after it, and began casting the fragments aside and turning and tugging them until he found his hammer. Hence it was that a tolerably good path was formed through the stony heap, which to this day bears the name of Thor's way.'[1]

Hrungnir's mountain-nature is also well expressed in the beginning of the narrative: the only beings for whom he entertains a regard, are the goddess of beauty herself, Freyia – whom the giants constantly desire – and Sif, who might clothe the mountains' naked sides with grass. His abode is named Griotunagard (from griót, *stone*, and tún, *enclosure*, English *town*). It lies on the boundary between heaven and earth. The description of the giant himself portrays plainly enough a mountain with its summits; nor does it require illustration that Thor cleaves his skull and the mass of rock, which he holds before him as a shield, with a thunderbolt.

Like his father, Odin, Thor also manifested himself to King Olaf Tryggvason. As the latter was once sailing along the coast, a man hailed him from a projecting cliff, requesting to be taken on board, whereupon the king ordered the ship to steer to the spot and the man entered. He was of lofty stature, youthful, comely, and had a red beard. Scarcely had he entered the vessel when he began to practise all sorts of jokes and tricks upon the crew, at which they were much amused. They were, he said, a set of miserable fellows, wholly unworthy to accompany so renowned a king or to sail in so fine a ship. They asked him whether he could relate something to them, old or new? He said there were few questions they could ask him which he could not resolve. They now conducted him to the king, praising his vast knowledge, when the latter expressed the wish to hear one or other old history. 'I will begin then,' said the man, 'with relating how the land by which we are now sailing was in old times inhabited by giants, but that such a general destruction befell those people, that they all perished at once, except two women. Thereupon men from the east countries began to inhabit the country, but those giant women so troubled and plagued them that there was no living there until they thought of calling on this Red-beard to help them; whereupon I straightway seized my hammer and slew the two women; since which time the people of the country have continued to call on me for aid, until thou, king, hast so destroyed all my old friends that it were well worthy of revenge. At the same moment, regarding the king with a bitter smile, he darted overboard with the swiftness of an arrow.' In this wonderful story we see expressed Thor's hostility to the giants, and their extirpation

1    Faye, op. cit., p. 1.

through him or, in other words, how by his operation he prepares and facilitates the culture of the earth among mankind.[1]

Thor had a daughter named Thrud[2] (prúdr), and Hrungnir is called Thrud's thief or abductor (thrúdar thiófr); also an allusion to a mountain, which attracts the clouds; Thrud, agreeably with what has been already said, being the dense thundercloud. Möckurkalfi (from mökkr, *a collection of thick mist or clouds*, and kálfr, the usual expression for any small thing with reference to a greater, as a calf to a cow, though usually applied to a little island lying close to a larger) is a giant of clay, not, like Hrungnir, of stone, and, therefore, denotes the lower earthy mountain. Thor's son, Modi,[3] signifies *the courageous*; his other son, Magni,[3] *the strong*, may be compared with Odin's son Vali, whose name has the same signification. Both perform mighty deeds immediately after their birth; whence it would seem, as Professor Finn Magnusen is inclined to suppose, that Magni denotes a god of spring. A similar allusion is contained in the name of Groa, signifying *causing to*, or *letting, grow*. By the star Örvandil's toe[4] is probably meant the small and scarcely visible star over the middle star in the pole of the wain. The frozen toe was, no doubt, the great toe, and is identical with the Dümeke or Hans Dümken (thumbkin) of the northern Germans, which is regarded as the driver of the carriage.[5] The rest of the myth seems inexplicable. Geirröd, who also in the *Grimnismal* appears as a giant,[6] is lord of the ores in the bowels of the earth. His name, as well as that of Grid (Gridr), the giantess at the entrance of the mountain,[7] Jarnsaxa[8] and the like, have reference to metals, and have afterwards passed into names of weapons, as grid, *an axe*;[9] geir (A. S. gar), *a dart*. Grídarvöllr, *Grid's staff*,[7] is also a metal rod. Thrym[10] (the drummer, thunderer) from at thruma, *to thunder, make a thundering noise*, is a fitting name for the giant who would rival the thunderer Thor, and fancied that the goddess of fertility and beauty would fall to his lot. Skrymir, or Skrymnir (from skrum, *show, brag, feint*) designates the crafty, false giant who by his magic deceives Thor. He is supposed to denote winter, a symbol of which is, moreover, his woollen

1   Saga Olafs Tryggvasonar, ii, p. 182.
2   Pages 26, 35.
3   Page 26.
4   Page 59.
5   Grimm, J., *Deutsche Mythologie*, op. cit., p. 688.
6   See Saxo, op. cit., p. 420, for the account of Thorkill-Adelfar's perilous and marvellous journey to visit the giant Geruth (Geirröd).
7   Page 47.
8   Page 31.
9   Egils *Saga*, p. 443.
10  Page 48, and note.

glove.[1] The myth about Utgarda-Loki is probably a later addition, its object being apparently to represent the weakness of the Aesir-gods, in comparison with the Finnish divinity.[2]

Thor's wife is Sif. Loki (fire) destroyed her lovely locks, but the dwarfs, sons of Ivaldi,[3] who work in the earth, made her a new head of hair, the germinating, bright-green grass. Her (but not Thor's) son is Ull (winter), which proceeds from the mountains to the humid valleys. He is Baldur's (the summer's) brother, the deity of the skate or snowshoe, of the chase, the bow and the shield (which is called his ship), and runs in snowshoes out over the ocean.

**Illustration.** As Frigg has reference to the cultivated earth, so Thor's wife, Sif, denotes the mountains that surround it, but which are uncultivated. Siva, the corresponding deity of the Slavs and Wends, is, on the contrary, represented with an abundance of beautiful hair and crowned with a wreath of flowers, holding a golden apple in one hand, and a bunch of grapes and a green leaf in the other.[4] Here she represented the cultivated earth with its produce, while in the North she retains only her golden hair, and is limited to be the goddess of grass only; while Frigg and Frey preside over the earth's fruitfulness. This appears, too, from the circumstance that Ull is her son. Haddr Sifjar (Sif's head of hair) is a periphrasis for gold. In Saxo[5] there is a fragment of a myth of Oller (Uller), which is there treated historically. Odin is driven from Byzantium (Asgard) by Oller, who tyrannises over Odin's subjects: the latter returns, wins back his dominion by gifts, and Oller is forced to flee to Sweden, where, as it were in a new world, he endeavoured to establish himself, but was slain by the Danes. This story has justly been regarded as a myth of the good dispenser of light, who is expelled by winter, but returns again to his dominion. Saxo in his recital makes mention of a bone, on which Oller could cross the sea, which Finn Magnusen[6] has well explained to be skates, which in the earliest times were made of the bones of horses or oxen.[7]

---

1    Page 51. Magnusen, op. cit., pp. 494, 630.
2    It may rather, perhaps, be regarded as a burlesque on the old religion, composed at a period when common sense began to operate among the followers of the Odinic faith.
3    Page 37.
4    See a representation of her in Arnkiel, *Cimbrische Heyden-Religion*, i, p. 120; also in *Vulpii Handwörterbuch der deutschen Völker*, etc., 1826, Tab. III, fig. 1. See also Magnusen, op. cit., p. 681.
5    Pages 99, 100.
6    Magnusen, op. cit., p. 765.
7    And so in Iceland, even at the present day. The words of Saxo are: 'Fama est, illum adeo praestigiarum usu calluisse, ut ad trajicienda maria osse, quod diris

Loki is fire. In the beginning of time he was, as Lodur,[1] the mild, beneficent warmth, united with All-father; but afterwards, like a fallen angel, having descended on earth, he became crafty, devastating and evil, like the desolating flame. There he was born in the foliage, and had the wind for his father.[2] His brothers are devastation and ruin. At one time he flutters, like a bird, up along a wall, beats with his wings and peeps in at a window, but his heavy feet cling to the earth;[3] sometimes he flies, whirled by the storm-wind, over stock and stone, floating between heaven and earth; but while, as Lopt, he is traversing the free air, he, nevertheless, suffers himself to be shut up and tamed by hunger;[4] the humid grass can bind his mouth, and yet his heart is not consumed. It became so when he wrought and begat children in the bowels of the earth, with giantesses and jarnvidiur, i.e. the metals and combustible parts of the earth. There he begat with Angurboda (the announcer of sorrow),[5] the wolf Fenrir, Midgard's serpent and Hel. The ravenous wolf, (subterranean fire) would have destroyed the world, if the powerful gods had not chained it in the mountain-cavern; but even there the foam issues from its open jaws as a dense vapour, and sparkling smoke. The foul, pernicious Loki was by the gods thrust down into the earth and confined in its caverns; there he yet works, though men notice it only when he moves, for then the earth trembles. The bonds yet hold him, but when they are loosed the gods will lose their sway over the world. Then will Loki come forth with his son

---

carminibus obsignavisset, navigii loco uteretur, nec eo segnius quam remigio praejecta aquarum obstacula superaret.' (p. 100) That such was also the custom in our own country in the twelfth century, appears from a curious passage in Fitzstephen's *Description of London*, of which the following is a translation: 'When that great pool, which washes the northern wall of the city is frozen, numerous bodies of young men go out to sport on the ice. These gaining an accelerated motion by running, with their feet placed at a distance from each other, and one side put forwards, glide along a considerable space. Others make themselves seats of ice like great millstones, when one sitting is drawn by many running before, holding each other's hands. During this rapid motion they sometimes all fall on their faces. Others, more skilled in sporting on the ice fit to their feet and bind under their heels the bones, i.e. the leg-bones, of animals, and holding in their hands poles with iron points, which they occasionally strike on the ice, are borne away with a speed like that of a bird flying, or an arrow from a bow.' The great pool above alluded to afterwards gave place and name to *Moor-fields*.

1   Page 18.
2   Page 32.
3   Page 47.
4   Page 41.
5   Page 32.

Fenrir, whose under jaw is on earth, while his upper jaw reaches heaven,[1] and fills all the air with flame. The fire confined in the earth will also cause commotion in the sea; then will the great serpent move itself in the deep, threaten the land and raise itself to heaven. The raging fire will cause death and desolation around it, etc. etc.

**Illustration.** The root of the word Loki is found in many languages, as Sanskrit lóc (lótsj), *to shine*; Lat. luceo, lux (lucs); Kymr. llug, *fire*; O. Nor. logi, *flame*, etc. He is a mixed being, good and evil, but as terrestrial fire, particularly the latter. He is the cause of almost all evil, wherefore some connect his name with the Gr. λοχάω, O. Nor. lokka, *to entice*.[2] His other name, Loptr, from lopt, *air*, Ger. Luft, signifies *the aerial*. In the *Völuspá* the wolf Fenrir is called Hvedrung's son; in like manner Hel is called Hvedrung's daughter, the signification of which is extremely doubtful. As the terrestrial fire, he has Farbauti for his father, from far, *a ship*, and bauta, *to beat*, therefore *the ship-beater*, an appropriate periphrasis for the wind. For his mother he has Laufey (leafy isle) or Nál, needle (*i.e.* the leaflet of the fir[3]); for his brothers, Byleist, from bu, a *habitation*, and lesta, *to lay waste;* or from bylr, *storm*, and aestr, *raging*; and Helblindi,[4] which is also one of Odin's names. But Loki also does some good: it is he who has almost always to procure what is wanting; he causes the implements and ornaments to be made for the gods, both by the sons of Ivaldi,[5] who work in wood, as well as by those who forge.[5] It is fire that sets all things in activity. Loki visits the metal king, Geirröd, who causes him to be confined and nearly starved: both types are in themselves sufficiently clear. Thiassi flies with Loki, who hangs fast by the pole:[6] this is evidently fire, which by the storm is borne through the air. Thiassi has been explained as identical with Thiarsi, from thiarr, *violent, impetuous*. His windy nature is manifest enough, partly as being the father of Skadi,[7] and partly from appearing in the form of an eagle, like Hraesvelg.[8] It is the storm in the hollows of the

1    Pages 64, 66.
2    Asaloki forms a contrast to all the other gods. He is the evil principle in all its varieties. As sensuality he runs through the veins of men; in nature he is the pernicious in the air, the fire, the water; in the lap of earth as the volcanic fire, in the ocean's depth as a fierce serpent, in the nether world as the pallid death. Hence he is not bound to any individual nature; like Odin he pervades all nature. Petersen, op. cit., p. 355.
3    Trees with acicular leaflets, like the fir, cedar, yew and the like, are called needle-trees.
4    Page 32.
5    Page 37.
6    Page 41.
7    Page 42.
8    Page 16.

mountains that rushes out, and bears along with it the burning trunks of trees through the air. Snorri's *Edda*[1] gives two brothers to Thiassi, Idi (Ithi, *brightness, splendour*) and Gang (Gángr, *the gold diffused in the innermost recesses of the mountain*). In the story of Sindri, who forges, and Brock, who stirs the fire, and afterwards closes up Loki's mouth,[2] Sindri denotes the smith, from sindr, the *red-hot sparks that spring from under the hammer*. The name of Brock might also be explained, if we knew how they anciently nourished and quelled the fire in their smithies. It has been interpreted, *dry sedge from marshy places*, but was this in use? By closing up Loki's mouth is signified, that he quenched the fire. In the name of the band Vartari, there is evidently a play on the word vör, *lip*; the other part, tari, is not intelligible. From the whole context, however, it would seem that the allusion is to a fitting mode of preserving fire, of quelling it, when becoming too fierce, and finally, when the forging is over, of quenching it. When Loki came into the abyss he became particularly evil (kyndugr). This word (from at kynda, to *kindle*, Lat. candeo, cendo, Sansk. cand (tsjand), and hugr, *mind* is an excellent example of the transition of physical ideas to moral. He is represented as a cow and as a woman, both emblems of bringing forth; and he there gave birth to his terrific offspring. The gods were at length compelled to confine him. He abides as a salmon in Franangur's fors[3] (from fránn, *glistening*). With this may be compared the Finnish myth, according to which, fire produced by the gods falls in little balls into the sea, is swallowed by a salmon, and afterwards found in the captured fish.[4] The glistening appearance of a salmon, its red flesh and quick motion, might easily induce the ancients to say there was fire in it. Loki assumed that shape to be as effectually hidden from the gods as possible, and appeared in fire's most innocent form; but they were too well acquainted with his guile. His son Vali, or Ali (the strong), was by the gods transformed into a wolf, and tore his brother Nari or Narvi (the binding); and Loki was bound with his bowels. Skadi hung a serpent above his head.[5] Eitr, as we have already seen, was the most intense cold; the serpent, consequently, is the cold stream that flows from the mountains into the deep. The name of Loki's wife, Sigyn, is plainly from at siga (A. S. sigan), *to sink, fall, glide down*, consequently a *watercourse*. It is said that Loki lies under Hvera-lund (the wood or forest of hot-springs), and that his wife, Sigyn, sits 'not right glad' with him. Sigyn denotes the warm subterranean springs, which receive the

1   Page 42.
2   Page 39.
3   Page 63.
4   Grimm, J., *Deutsche Mythologie*, op. cit., p. 577, note.
5   Pages 32–3, 63–4.

cold stream that comes from Skadi; but when the warm springs, swollen with the mountain-streams, rush violently down upon the fire, then the earth trembles. In Saxo[1] we find traces of this myth, though, according to him, it is Utgarda-Loki that lies bound in a cavern. Angurboda, the mother of Loki's children, denotes *the boder of sorrow* (from ángur, *sorrow*). Fenrir (the inhabitant of the abyss or deep), or Fenrisulf (the howling wolf of the deep), is another form of the subterranean fire – the volcanic. The bands by which he is bound (Laeding, Drómi, Gleipnir) have allusion to strength and pliability. The holm or islet of Lyngvi, which is overgrown with ling or heath, and surrounded by the black lake Amsvartnir, is the fire-spouting mountain. The river Van, or Von, is the ascending smoke. In a Skaldic poem cited by Finn Magnusen,[2] several names occur belonging to this place, among others, Víl and Von, two rivers flowing from the mouth of the wolf (signifying, *howl*, *lament*, and *vapour*), whose lips are named Giólnar (from gióla, *a gust of wind*), consequently the craters of a volcano. Two rivers, Vid and Van are named in the *Grimnismal*, evidently in allusion to vapour and clouds. The World's Serpent (Midgardsormr), or the Terrestrial Serpent, or Wolf (Jórmungandr), is the deep ocean. That it is excited by subterranean fire, and thereby becomes baneful, is quite intelligible; but it is by a bold transition that the ancients made fire (Loki) the father of Hel or Death, with whom there is only cold. The dominion, however, over cold she did not obtain until the gods sent her to Niflheim.[3] On the way to her abode lay the dog Garm,[4] which bays before Gnipa-llellir,[5] a being that both in name and signification (from gerr, *voracious*) answers to Cerberus.[6] This dog seems to have guarded the descent to Hel through the earth; as those taking the way by the Giallar-bru met with the maiden Modgud,[7] of whom more when we speak of Baldur.

Baldur the good, with the light or bright brows, is, as almost all have admitted, the warm summer, the season of activity, joy and light. On his life depend the activity and joy of the gods; his death brings sorrow to all, to gods and men, and to all nature. One being only, the evil Loki, the terrestrial fire, loses nothing by Baldur's death, and is, therefore, represented as the cause of it, and as hindering Baldur's release from Hel. Baldur, the light, is slain by the darkness, Höd; the bale-fires blaze at his

---

1  Pages 431, 433.
2  Magnusen, op. cit., p. 340.
3  Page 45.
4  Page 64.
5  Page 66. Magnusen, op. cit., p. 398.
6  Magnusen, op. cit., p. 111.
7  Page 62.

death; he journeys to Hel, and there is no hope of his return. His mother, the fruitful earth, mourns, and all beings shed tears, all nature is filled with weeping, like the days of autumn. Darkness prevails almost as much by day as by night; but the earth stiffens, and Rind brings forth a son, the powerful Vali, so that darkness is again dispelled by pure, clear days. Baldur's wife, Nanna, is the busy activity of summer, its unwearied, light occupations.[1] Their son, Forseti (the fore-sitter, president, in the assembly), holds spring, summer, and autumn meetings (guilds), as the maintainer of justice.[2] War, the principal employment of summer, was reserved for Odin himself, as the highest god.

**Illustration.** Baldur is referred to the Lithuanian baltas, *white*; Slavic bel or biel; bielbog, *the white*, or *bright god*. Beauty and goodness are the fundamental ideas contained in the name. Baldur's abode is Breidablik (*the broad glance*). The clear, white light is also indicated by the plant sacred to him, Baldur's brá.[3] Nanna, the name of Baldur's wife, has received various interpretations, among which the least improbable is, perhaps, to derive it from at nenna, *to have a mind, feel inclined*; both nenna and the adjective nenninn, signify *a sedulous worker, one indefatigably active*; hence Nanna would denote the active, summer life. Very appropriately, therefore, is the name of Nönna applied to Idun, and that Odin's active maidens, the Valkyriur, are called nönnur herjans (maidens of Odin). Nanna's father is named Nef or Nep, but by Saxo he is called Gevar (Gefr); one of these must be erroneous. Nef has not been interpreted, but Gefr is simply *giver*; the father gives, and the daughter operates. Saxo relates how Gevar was treacherously burnt alive by night (nocturno igni) by his jarl (satrapa) Gunno, but that Hotherus (Höd) caused Gunno to be cast on a burning pile;[4] an allusion possibly to the piles kindled at

---

1   There is much, as Keyser remarks, to object to in this interpretation of the myth of Baldur, but more particularly the circumstance of Baldur continuing with Hel until the dissolution of the world, while Summer returns annually. The whole story of Baldur and of his bright abode Breidablik, where nothing impure enters, points him out as the god of innocence. His name signifies *the strong*, and alludes to mental strength combined with spotless innocence. The blind Höd will then represent bodily strength with its blind earthly strivings, who, instigated by sin – Loki – unconsciously destroys innocence, and with it die both the desire and activity for good—Nanna. The homicide is avenged by quick-waking reflection – Höd is slain by Vali: but pure innocence has vanished from this world to return no more, though all nature bewails its loss. Only in the regenerated world will it again predominate. Keyser, op. cit., pp. 45, 46.

2   Page 32.

3   Page 26, note 2.

4   Page 100.

midsummer, or at the end of summer, wherein also lies a myth, viz. how the avocations of summer are interrupted by war (Gunno, gynni, signifying *a warrior*), which, in its turn, is at a stand during the dark winter. Höd (Hödr, *gen.* Hadar) in many compounds, signifies (like the A. S. heatho) war, or battle;[1] whence it would seem that the idea of war prevails where we might expect to find blindness, or darkness the prominent one. The name of Vali is also of doubtful signification; it may be a derivative of at vala, and the masculine of völva (vala) a prophetess, *Scot* spae-wife, or it may signify *the strong*; but, at all events, Vali is the new year, which begins with brighter days. In the old Swedish runic calendar, Yule-day is denoted by a child in swaddling clothes with a radiant crown, and the 25th January, among the modern Norwegians, by Paul the archer, or Paul with the bow (qu. Vali?). In the Danish runic calendars, the same day is noted by a sword, in the Norwegian by a bow, and in the Swedish by a sword and a bow, in remembrance of the arms of Vali.[2] Although Christian ideas may have been mixed up with the first-mentioned of these hieroglyphics, the pagan Vali seems, nevertheless, to be the fundamental one, who was only one day old when he slew Höd, and had a bow for his attribute. The ancient Scandinavians admitted only two seasons, summer and winter. Neither spring not autumn appear as distinct beings, but as transitions; Vali may, therefore, be regarded as the transition of the year to spring. The mistletoe shoots forth towards the end of June, flowers in May, and is green all the winter. The Romans were acquainted with it, and among the Gauls, the chief druid, on a certain day in spring, ascended the oak on which it grew, and cut it off with a golden knife,[3] that it might not injure Baldur, or that the summer might come without hindrance: a proof of the widespread veneration for Baldur, and also a confirmation of the just interpretation of the myth. The giantess Thökt, whose form Loki assumed,[4] has been well illustrated by Finn Magnusen, by a saying still current in Iceland: '*All things would weep (release by weeping) Baldur from Hel, except coal.*'[5] The name of the giantess he explains by *tecta, operta*; it will then be derived from at thekja, Lat. tego, *to deck, cover*, whence the adjective thaktr, fem. thökt, Lat. tego, and signify *the covered (fire)*. Coal knows no other tears than dry sparks; it suffers no detriment from the death of summer, and has no joy in it. Hyrrokin, *the whirling, smoking fire* (from hyrr, *fire*, and roka, *whirlwind*), may have allusion to the manner in

---

1   Grimm, J., *Deutsche Mythologie*, op. cit., p. 204.
2   Specimen Cal. Gentil. ad calcem *Lex. Mythol.*, pp. 1052, 1060.
3   Plinii H. N., xvi, 95.
4   Page 62–3.
5   Allir hlutir gráta Balldur úr Helju, nema kol. Magnusen, op. cit., p. 297.

which they anciently eased the motion of their ships along the rollers. Litur (Litr) *colour*, whom Thor kicks into the fire, indicates the hue of the flaming fire which dies with the light.[1] The presence of all beings at the funeral pile of summer, in which all, more or less, had had pleasure, is perfectly intelligible; nor is Thor (thunder) inactive on the occasion. The funeral is princely, according to the custom of the North. The watch at the Giallar-bru, Modgud, signifies *the contentious, quarrelsome*. The Giallar-bru is, from what has been said, opposed to the rainbow, and Modgud here, instead of Mimir, to Heimdall. Forseti, as has already been observed, denotes a president; his abode is Glitnir (from at glita, *to shine, glitter*), *the shining, glittering*, and betokens the solemnity, sanctity and purity of justice.

**Bragi and Idun (Idunn Ithudr).**[2] Bragi is a son of Odin and husband of Idun, the originator of poetry and eloquence, the most exquisite skald; hug-runes (mind-runes) are inscribed on his tongue; he is celebrated for his gentleness, but more particularly for eloquence and wise utterance. After him poetry is called bragr; and after him men and women distinguished for wisdom of speech are called bragr-men or bragr-women. He is described as having an ample beard, whence persons with a similar appendage are called Skeggbragi (from skegg, *beard*). His wife, Idun, keeps in her casket the apples of which the gods bite when they are growing old; they then again become young, and so it will go on until Ragnaröck. On hearing this relation of Hâr, Gangleri observed: 'It is a very serious charge which the gods have committed to Idun's care'; but Hâr answered, laughing at the same time, 'It was once near upon bringing with it a great misfortune.' (In what it consisted is nowhere said.) For the story of her being carried off by Thiassi see page 00. In the Loka-glepsa, Bragi offers a horse and a sword to Loki, if he will desist from raising strife, who in return upbraids him with being, of all the Aesir and Alfar present, the most fearful in battle and the greatest avoider of shot. Idun beseeches her husband to keep peace with Loki, and declares that she will utter no contemptuous words to him, but will only appease her husband, who is somewhat heated by drink. But Loki, who appears very regardless of her gentleness, tells her that she is the most wanton of women, since she threw her nicely washed arms around her brother's slayer.

At guilds the Bragarfull, or Bragi-cup was drunk. A troll-wife told Hedin that he should pay for his contempt of her at the Bragi-cup. It was the

---

1 Page 62.
2 Connected with id, *activity*; idinn, *active*. Keyser, op. cit., p. 39.

custom at the funeral feast of kings and jarls, that the heir should sit on a lower seat in front of the high seat, until the Bragarfull was brought in, that he should then rise to receive it, make a vow and drink the contents of the cup. He was then led to his father's high seat. At an offering-guild the chief signed with the figure of Thor's hammer both the cup and the meat. First was drunk Odin's cup, for victory and power to the king; then Niörd's cup and Frey's, for a good year and peace; after which it was the custom with many to drink a Bragarfull.[1] The peculiarity of this cup was, that it was the cup of vows, that on drinking it a vow was made to perform some great and arduous deed, that might be made a subject for the song of the skald.

From the foregoing, Bragi's essence seems sufficiently manifest, that of Idun is involved in obscurity. One myth concerning her we have already seen (page 44), the other is contained in Odin's Ravens' Song, where she is represented as having sunk down from Yggdrasil's ash to the lower world. Odin then sends her a wolf's guise, and despatches Heimdall, accompanied by Bragi and Lopt, to ascertain from her what she had been able to discover respecting the duration and destruction of the nether world and of heaven; when, instead of answering, she bursts forth into tears, etc. The whole is wrapped in dense obscurity, and all that can be gathered seems to be, 'that she is the goddess that presides over the fresh young verdure, and herein to be compared with Proserpine, the blooming daughter of Ceres. She dwells in well-watered fields (Brunnakr), and keeps in a casket the apples which preserve the gods in eternal youth. When the green vegetation vanishes from the earth, she falls, through Loki, as it is mythically expressed, into the power of Thiassi, but by whom she is again liberated in the spring. Or she sinks down from Yggdrasil, and dwells mute and weeping in the nether world.'[2]

Saga is the goddess of history and narration. Her name is from at saga, segja, *to narrate*, that of her abode, Söckqvabek[3] (from sökk, sokkvi, *abyss*, *gulf*; at sökkva, *to sink*, *swallow*), in allusion to the abundant and flowing stream of narrative. Söckqvabek signifies literally *the sinking*, *brook*.

As king of mind, Odin procured for mankind the drink of poesy.[4] The story on this subject has not reached us in its most ancient form. It describes in the usual periphrastic manner of Antiquity, the preparation of the inspiring beverage, must, mead, or beer, which, as long as it belongs to dwarfs and giants, is still earthly, only with Odin does it become inspiring. As god of war, he operates in summer, and then seeks his reward; but the

1    Full signifies *cup*.
2    Müller, op. cit., p. 281.
3    Page 35.
4    Page 39.

gift of poesy is not easily acquired: Gunmöd long withstands his embraces; but having partaken of the drink, he rises with an eagle's flight on the wings of inspiration

**Illustration.** The difficulty of this myth lies chiefly in the beginning; though it is sufficiently obvious that it relates to the preparation of the drink.[1] Kvasir is produced from the saliva of the Aesir and Vanir. The Vanir, the spirits of air and water, supplied the watery part, the Aesir the inspiring. This also appears from the story of Geirhild, to whom, when brewing, Odin gave his saliva for barm, and the beer proved of the most excellent kind. Kvasir then is fruit, and his blood must or wort. He died in his own wisdom, and in himself was vapid. The dwarfs that slew him and squeezed out his blood, would consequently be those who stood at the must-press. Fialar's drink sweetened with honey is then the poetic drink, must. But the myth does not end here; it passes on to the preparation of a species of beer, for which it must be assumed that must was also employed. The name Gilling may be referred to at gilja, *to separate*, and in Norse, gil is the vessel into which the beer passes.[2] He enters a boat or vessel, which is upset in the great ocean, or brewers' vat; here the barm is meant; and the wife who is crushed by the millstone, when she is going to look at the sea where her husband was drowned, is the malt, or something similar, that is ground. All this would probably be evident, if only we knew how the ancients prepared their mungat,[3] whether it was a sort of beer mixed with must and honey. Suttung (probably for Suptung) seems akin to the English *sup*, an allusion to the drinking tendency of the giant race; while his daughter, Gunnlöd, represents the beverage itself. Her name is compounded of gunnr (A. S. guth) *war*, and lada, *to invite*; therefore *that which invites to war or battle*; the liquor which also inspires the skald to overcome all obstacles in his art. The vessel Odhraerir (that which moves the mind) expresses the effects of the drink. The same may possibly be the case with the two others, Bodn (invitation) and Sôn (redemption, or reconciliation). Odin now comes forth as Bölverk (from böl, *calamity, hardship, bale*, and virka, *to work*), *one who performs deeds of hardship*. When he causes the reapers to kill one another with their scythes, he represents the god of war; when he enters the service of Baugi, he resembles the reaper who, when the labours of summer are over, is rewarded with song. The giant Baugi signifies *the bowed*, but why Bölverk enters his service cannot be explained. The auger or borer, Rati, is derived from at rata, *to*

---

1  See Magnusen, op. cit., p. 542.
2  Hallager, *sub voce*.
3  A sort of beer; 'cerevisia secundaria'. Biörn Haldorsen, *sub voce*.

*find the way*. Hnitbiörg signifies a group of close, impenetrable mountains. This myth, though not wholly devoid of beauty, is, in the form in which it appears in the *Prose Edda*, as insipid as most of the far-fetched periphrases of the old Northern poetry. It has more than once, in later times, served as the subject of *comic* fiction.

Vidar[1] is the son of Odin and of the giantess Grid, who dwells in a mountain-cave, and guards the descent to the giant-chieftain's abode in the interior of the mountain.[2] The name of his habitation, Landvidi (the wide, boundless land), marks him for lord of the thick, impervious woods which, through Odin's power, rear their summits on the huge inaccessible mountains, where axe never sounded, where man's footsteps never trod, where human voice was never heard. Rightly, therefore, is he named the Silent. Vidar is the imperishability of nature, her incorruptible power. Who has ever wandered, or even imagined himself a wanderer, through such forests, in a length of many miles, in a boundless expanse, without a path, without a goal, amid their monstrous shadows, their sacred gloom without being filled with deep reverence for the sublime greatness of nature above all human agency, without feeling the grandeur of the idea which forms the basis of Vidar's essence? This great nature was familiar to Antiquity, which dwelt, as it were, in her lap; and we must feel veneration for the ancients, who neglected not to conceive and ennoble the idea of her infinite creative power, even without any view to man. The blooming fields they glorified in Fulla, the whole cultivated earth in Frigg, the grass-grown mountain in Sif; the boundless woods must also have their divinity. Around the dwellings of men Frey and his elves hold sway. He is mild and beneficent, he loves the earth and its swelling seed; but Vidar is silent and still; after Thor he is the strongest; he moves not among men, he is rarely named among the gods, but he survives the destruction of the world, of the gods, and of mankind. With Earth Odin begat Thor; with Frigg, Baldur; with Rind, Vali; but with a giantess, Vidar, the connection between the eternal creative power of matter and spirit. These gods and these men shall pass away, but neither the creative power in nature, Vidar, nor in man, Hoenir, shall ever have an end.

---

1 Finn Magnusen rejects the story of Vidar's shoe made of shreds of leather (p. 31) as a nursery tale. For the same reason he might, I fear, have rejected a vast deal more. Keyser derives his name from at vinna, *to conquer*, in allusion to his victory in the last conflict with the gods (p. 66), and thinks he may be an emblem of the regenerative power which is supposed to be in the earth. Therefore he is a son of Odin and a giantess, of spirit and matter; therefore his habitation is Landvidi, *the wide earth*; therefore he is the silent, inactive god in the world's present state. Not until its destruction does he come forth in his strength overcoming the powers of darkness and destruction, and finally dwells in the regenerated world. Keyser, op. cit., pp. 39, 40.

2 Pages 31, 47.

**Illustration.** The name of Vidar is formed from vidr, *a wood, forest*. His abode, Landvidi, is thus described:

> Begrown with branches
> and with high grass
> is Vidar's dwelling.

His leathern or iron shoe has been already described, and in the Sagas leather is mentioned as a protection against fire. Hence we find him unscathed presenting the drinking-horn to Loki at Oegir's banquet; nor does the wolf Fenrir harm him, but he seizes it and rends its jaws asunder. All this pronounces him lord of the iron wood.

According to Finn Magnusen's interpretation of this myth, Vidar is neither more nor less than the phenomenon *typhon*, or the waterspout. That this illustration has not met with general approval, will occasion but little surprise. Geijer considers it an excellent example of the *lucus a non lucendo*,[1] while Rask approved of it as the best he had seen. But Vidar is not one-footed like the waterspout, nor is it easy to imagine the latter an inhabitant of Landvidi, 'begrown with branches and with high grass'. In general, as well as in this instance, I have merely endeavoured to represent, as clearly as I could, what I believed to have found in the *Eddas*, without any wish to give greater weight to my own opinions than to those of others, or than they deserved.

When the Aesir had entered into a league with the Vanir,[2] or gods of the air, and received them into their community,[3] fertility and abundance prevailed over the earth. Father Niörd is the universal nourishing power in air and water;[4] he rules over the wind and the sea, at least over that portion of it which is nearest to and encircles the earth, and, consequently, over navigation and fishing. As god of the ocean and the wind, he appears very manifestly in his marriage with Skadi,[5] who would dwell in the mountains of Thrymheim. This myth requires no elaborate explanation, as everyone will readily perceive that it represents the alternations of the mild sea-breezes and the rough gales from the mountains.

1   *Svearikes Häfder*, i, 348.
2   According to some, the myth of the war between the Aesir and Vanir signifies that the light of heaven broke through the dense clouds that originally enveloped the earth, in order to produce fertility, which is supposed to be an effect of the combined powers of heaven and the cloudy atmosphere. Others interpret it as a contest between the fire-worshippers and the water-worshippers, which was ended by the blending of the two religions. Keyser, op. cit., pp. 35, 36.
3   Page 21.
4   Page 28.
5   Page 42.

**Illustration** The origin of the word Niördr is uncertain; it has been
referred to the verb at naera (to nourish). He is supposed to be identical
with the German goddess Nerthus, the Gothic form of which, Nairthus,[1]
may be either masculine or feminine.[2] Niörd's habitation is Noatûn, *the
place of ships*, i.e. *the sea*, from nór, nós (ναῦς, navis) *ship*, and tún, *an
enclosed place, house and land*. Skaidi signifies *the hurtful*. Her habitation,
Thrymheim, is from thrymr, *noise, uproar*, and bears allusion to the stormy
winds.

Far more conspicuous than Niörd are his children, Frey[3] and Freyia,[4]
who spread the fructifying power of the air over the earth, and bring
abundance around and into the dwellings of men. Frey gives fruitfulness to
the earth, Freyia to human beings. Frey rules over the Light-elves, and their
united influence brings good years and prosperity. In the most spirited of
the Eddaic poems, Skirnir's Journey,[5] is described Frey's longing to impart
his blessings to the earth. Earth, with the seed deposited in it, as Gerd,
resists his embraces. His messenger, Skirnir, who impels the seed forth
into the light, vainly promises her the harvest's golden fruit, and a ring
dripping with abundance. From her giant nature, not yet quickened by the
divine spirit, she has no idea of the benefits that will accrue to her through
Frey's love; Skirnir must impress on her mind how, without Frey's
embraces, she will to all eternity be the bride of the frost-giant Hrîmnir,
and never feel the joys of conception. She yields herself up to Frey, and
they embrace when the buds burst in the woods.

Freyia's abode is Folkvang; she has her dwelling amid the habitations of
people, and fills them with abundance. Her hall is Sessrymnir, *the roomy-
seated*. But her influence is also pernicious; seeing that as many fall
through the frantic power of love as before the sword of the god of war. Her
chariot is drawn by cats, an emblem of fondness and passion. She longs
constantly after Od, *the intoxicating pleasure of love*, and by him has a
daughter, Hnos, *the highest enjoyment*. Her tears and ornaments are of gold;
for she is beautiful and fascinating even in her grief. She travels far and
wide, and assumes many names and forms among the children of men,[6] as
various as are her operations on their minds: for one is the sacred joy of

---

1  The identity of the names seems unquestionable; but how is the account here
given of Niörd as 'the universal nourishing power in air and water', and 'as god of the
ocean and the wind', etc. to be reconciled with what Tacitus says of Nerthus:
'Nerthum, id est Terram matrem, colunt'?
2  Grimm, J., *Deutsche Mythologie*, op. cit., p. 197.
3  Page 28.
4  Page 33.
5  Page 43.
6  Pages 33, *sqq.*

marriage, whose fruit is a numerous offspring; for another, only the impure pleasure of the senses.

The nature of Frey and Freyia seems quite comprehensible, if we confine ourselves to the accounts in the *Eddas*, and not mingle with them the ideas of other nations. As god of the year, Frey presides over sunshine and rain, without which no seed would germinate. Frey and Freyia denote, in the Scandinavian and kindred tongues, *master* and *mistress*. Frey is particularly represented as lord of men; and Snorri remarks that from Freyia highborn women are called freyior (frúr), Danish Fruer; Ger. Frauen. The word freyr (the feminine of which is freya) denotes either *the fructifying*, or *the mild*, *joyous*; Ger. froh. Both these interpretations spring from a common root, which is to be found in many tongues, having reference to earthly fertility, enjoyment, joy, etc.; comp. Lat. fruor, frumentum.

Frey obtained dominion over the Light-elves in the beginning of time, i.e. of the year (í árdögum). Skirnir (from skírr, *pure*, *clear*) *is the clarifier*, *that which brings the pure, clear air*. Gerd (Gerdr) is from gera, *to do*, *make*, as in akrgerd, *agriculture*. As she dwells in the mansion of Gymir, the allusion may possibly be to the word gard, *enclosure*, *court*, *garth*. When represented as Frigg's rival, the allusion is perhaps to the earth prepared by the plough; but when, in Skirnir's journey, she is described as a beautiful girl, with bright, shining arms, the image is without doubt borrowed from the seed, the bright, yellow corn, so beneficial to man. She is of giant race, of earth, and as yet dead, but, nevertheless, fair and fertile. Her resemblance to Ceres is evident: *Geres*, quod *gerit* fruges;[1] O. N. gera, gerdi; Latin gero, gessi. Barri, or Barey, is *the wood or isle of germs or buds*, from bar, *bud*, *the eye in a tree*, *the winged seed*. When the god of fruitfulness embraces the seed, it shoots forth; and that takes place with the aid of Skirnir. Gerd's father, Gymir (Geymir), denotes *one who keeps*, *lays by*. Her mother's name, Aurboda, alludes to the material, earthly substance that is not yet developed. Frey parted with his sword. This seems to indicate that he lost his fertilising power: he gave it to Skirnir, but whether the latter retained it, or what became of it, does not appear from the myth. He does not require it in his combat with Beli.[2] The myth respecting Beli is not complete, and, therefore, obscure. It may, however, be noticed that the interpreters take him for Gerd's brother, of whom she says that she is fearful Skirnir will be her brother's destroyer. We may here also observe, that in the *Lokaglepsa* two attendants are attributed to Frey, Beyggvir and his wife Beyla. Of Beyggvir Loki says, that he is a little, pert being that is always hanging at the ear of Frey, and makes a rattling under or by the

1 Varro de L. L., v, 64.
2 Pages, 45, 64, 72–3.

hand-mill; that he can never distribute meat to men, and that he hid himself in the bed-straw when men contended. Of Beyla he says, that she is full of evil, and that an uglier monster never came among the Aesir, nor a dirtier slut. Professor Petersen considers it evident that by Beyggvir the refuse of the mill, as chaff, etc. is signified, and that Beyla is the manure which softens and develops the seed that is put in the earth. Professor F. Magnusen supposes Beyggvir and his wife to be two little parhelia attendant upon Frey, the solar divinity. Frey's ship, Skidbladnir,[1] belonged according to some to Odin, or, in general, to all the gods. Frey obtained it in days of old (í ardögum), *i.e.* in the early part of the year, when navigation commences. His hog, Gullinbursti, *gold-bristled*, is probably an emblem of the earth's fertility. With the ship of Frey is no doubt connected the custom, formerly prevailing in some parts of Germany, of carrying about a ship and a plough, in the beginning of spring;[2] both the one and the other with reference to Frey, as the god of agriculture and prosperity. Freyia is the chief of the Valkyriur, and like them a chooser of the slain.

**Oegir and Rân.** As Niörd is the mild sea of the coast, so is Oegir the wild, raging, more distant ocean, which is, nevertheless, in contact with the agency of the Aesir; hence the double nature of Oegir; he is a giant, and yet has friendly intercourse with the Aesir. In Mimir, Oegir and Niörd we thus have the entire ocean from its origin to its last development, where like a benevolent divinity it attaches itself to the Aesir, that is, to men. Oegir and Hler are usually considered as one and the same deity. Oegir visits the Aesir in Asgard, where Bragi relates to him those narratives in Snorri's *Edda*, which are called Bragaraedur, or discourses of Bragi. The Aesir returned his visit, on which occasion they remark that his brewing kettle is not large enough, and Thor accompanied by Ty fetches, as we have seen, a more capacious one from the giant Hymir. After Baldur's death, the Aesir visit him a second time, when Loki comes and vents all his spleen on them. Here we learn that he has two serving-men, Fimafeng (Funafeng) and Eldir; that bright gold was used in his hall instead of fire, and that Oegir himself handed the beer round. Oegir's, or Rân's, or their daughters' fire is a skaldic periphrasis for gold.

**Illustration.** The whole myth is simple and intelligible. Oegir is the stormy ocean, from óga, *to dread, shudder at*. His wife's name, Rân, signifies *plunder, robbery*. It is a common expression in the North that the ocean brews and boils, which serves to illustrate Oegir's kettles; the frothy drink also bears itself round, and there is plenty of it. Equally common is

---

1    Page 38.
2    Grimm, J., *Deutsche Mythologie*, op. cit., p. 242.

the idea of the ocean's surge, which in its most violent motion becomes phosphorescent. Seafaring men have much to relate of the shining of the sea, which is ascribed to insects. Oegir's servants are, therefore, good stokers. Eldir is from ellda, *to make a fire*, and Fimafeng is *the rapid, agile*. (Funafengr is probably from funi, *fire*). His daughters' names, as we have already remarked, denote waves.[1] With Oegir is associated an idea of the terrific; hence the Oegishiálmr belonging to Fafnir, at which all living beings were terrified.[2]

The attributes of Heimdall, as far as they are not descriptive of the vigilant guardian, are derived from the rainbow. He is a Van, because the rainbow appears in the sky. He is, at the same time, Odin's son, as being superhuman. His mothers, the nine giantesses, are the aqueous, earthy, and, on account of their brightness, the metallic parts of which the rainbow was thought to consist. Here there is no allusion to the number of the colours of the rainbow, which are given as three, but to their appearance. He is called Golden-tooth, because of the beauty of the rainbow, and Descending (Hallinskeidi), because of its curved figure.[3]

**Illustration.** Heimthallr is derived from heimr, *the world*, and thallr or dallr, *a tree which sends forth shoots and branches*. This word is the same with thollr, *a long pole*; the name Heimthallr will therefore signify the pole or post of the world. The rainbow also, when incomplete, is still by the Northern nations called a Veirstolpe (Veirstötte), literally a *weather-post*; and the Slavonic word for the rainbow, duga, signifies strictly *the stave of a cask*.[4] The ancients must therefore have had in view the rainbow's rarely perfect figure; but when it appeared in its full beauty, like a broad bridge, it is easy to conceive why they called it Bifröst, or *the trembling, swinging way*, leading from earth to heaven.[5] Its curved figure gave occasion also for regarding it as a horn, one end of which was at Giöll (the horizon), the other at Himinbiörg (the heavenly mountains, i.e. the clouds), whence Heimdall raised his Giallar-horn, as it is said,

> Eally up Bifröst
> ran Ulfrun's son,
> the mighty horn-blower
> of Himinbiörg.

1   Page 30.
2   Page 46 note 2.
3   Page 31.
4   Grimm, J., *Deutsche Mythologie*, op. cit., p. 695.
5   It was believed that at the place where the rainbow rises, a golden dish or a treasure was hidden, and that gold money falls from the rainbow.

By nine, the number of Heimdall's mothers, nothing more seems implied than its well-known sanctity among almost all the people of antiquity. The number of Oegir's daughters is also nine.[1] Heimdall descended among mankind under the name of Rig,[2] whence the whole human race are called children of Heimdall. In the contest between Heimdall and Loki for the Brisinga-men,[3] the idea seems to lie that fire and the rainbow vie with each other in displaying the most beautiful colours.

From the foregoing attempt to illustrate the mythology of the Scandinavian nations, it appears that their gods were neither more nor less than figurative representations of the agency of nature and mankind. Nothing is there without signification, yet there is nothing that lies without the pale of our forefathers' experience, or that is incompatible with the manner in which Antiquity was wont to conceive it. Heaven and earth are the two great leading ideas which comprise the others; between both are sea and air. Thunder and the rainbow are the two most prominent natural phenomena, which first and most impressively must excite the attention of mankind. The Northman was encompassed with bare ice-mountains, nearer to him were high hills and boundless forests, but immediately around his dwelling was the fertile field. Plenty and contentment at home, and the bloody game of war abroad, were his earthly desires. What wonder then, if he imagined all around him to be animated by divine beings, which he represented with all the sagacity he possessed? But this conception of physical images was not without application to his intellectual and moral nature. This connection was so close, that it is inseparable even in language, and everywhere we meet with proofs that Antiquity also raised itself to this higher conception. Odin is not only lord over the whole physical world, but is king also of the intellectual. Heimdall is not only the rainbow, but is, at the same time, the benignant announcer of the divine care. Thor is not only

---

1   Page 30.
2   This forms the subject of the Eddaic poem *Rigsmál*. Heimdall, one of the Aesir, wanders in green ways along the sea-strand. He calls himself Rig (Rígr); he is strong, active and honourable. In a hut he finds a great-grandfather and a great-grandmother (ái and edda), with whom he stays three nights. Nine months after, the old woman gives birth to the swarthy thrall, from whom the race of thralls descends. Rig wanders further and finds in a house a grandfather and a grandmother (afi and amma). Nine months after, the grandmother gives birth to a boy, the progenitor of the peasant race. Rig proceeds still further, and finds in a hall a father and mother, and nine months after, the mother brings forth Jarl (earl). Jarl marries Erna, a daughter of Hersir (baron), and the youngest of their sons is the young Konr (Konr úngr, *contr*, konúngr, *king*). The last-mentioned are objects of Rig's especial care; he is solicitous not only with regard to their birth, but for their instruction and culture, thus affording a striking example of the aristocratic spirit that prevailed in the North from the remotest period.
3   Page 31.

the thunder, but also courage and strength. Vidar is not only lord of the boundless forests, but is incorruptibility itself. Baldur is not alone the god of summer, but is also all goodness and piety. Ty is not only war, but is also honour and glory. Frey and Freyia are not alone givers of fruitfulness, but, at the same time, the germinating, blooming and beatifying, the boundless love in the breast of man. Nor is Loki the god of fire alone, but is also the origin of all evil and the father of lies. Hence proceeds the multitude of names and epithets (always significant, though we may not always be able to explain them) that are applied to the gods; they express their natures from different points of view, and describe their characters. Loki, for instance, is *active, shrewd of speech, cunning, inventive, sagacious, false, wicked*; Baldur is *white (bright), good*; Heimdall *holy, white*; Thor is *large, strong, not remarkably clever*, but *good-nattered with all his strength*, etc. etc. In describing Odin, *the old, venerable, long-bearded, one-eyed being*, in all his might, wisdom, goodness, austerity and ferocity; in all his manifestations in heaven and on earth, the Old Norse language employed all its riches, a far greater store than can now be furnished from the combined stores of its descendants.

**The destruction and renewal of the world**. A people that raised their thoughts to beings higher than heaven and earth, must naturally, at the same time, believe in the cessation of that heaven and earth. Before the gods existed there were higher powers, from whose breath all creation drew life. These could annihilate their own work, though its nobler part might not pass away, which is as imperishable as themselves. To these ideas leads also the consideration of nature herself. The circumvolution on a small scale is repeated on a larger; the darkness of night and the light of day are a reduced repetition of the interchange of winter and summer, and both amplified are prefigurations of the destruction and renewal of all nature. This time or age is brought forth like every other, and must, therefore, like every other, pass away; but as the year is renewed, in like manner shall time also be renewed. In the myth of Baldur's death with its conclusion, the birth of Vali, the idea of Ragnaröck is so evident, that the one cannot well be conceived without drawing with it the presence of the other. The death of summer is a presage of the downfall of the gods, which begins with the great, severe winter (fimbul-vetr). All nature is described as agitated by the storms of autumn, snow drifts, frost prevails, fire struggles in its bonds, and the earth is filled with conflict. The powers of darkness unite with the super-celestial spirits, and fire and water desolate the world. The sun and moon were also created, and they shall be swallowed by the pursuing wolves. But a new earth shoots forth, a new human race appears, a new sun beams in the heaven. Of the moon there is no more mention, for there will be no more night. The noblest of the gods return to their pristine innocence and joy. The nature that had until then prevailed is perished with Odin, but Vidar and Vali live, imperishable nature survives and blooms like the ever-youthful year. Baldur and Höd live peaceably together, there is no longer strife between summer and winter, light and darkness. Thor no more thunders, but his strength and courage pervade nature as Modi and Magni. Freyia with her sensual pleasure is no more, but Hoenir, the unperishing sensitive faculty, continues to operate in the new human race. Earth's former creatures live now in heaven. As individual heroes could be renewed and regenerated here on earth, so were chosen bands of warriors assembled in Valhall, for the purpose of continuing, while the earthly age lasted, the best of earthly occupations; but even in life there was something higher than warfare – peace; battle itself shall, therefore, cease with the great battle of nature, and all the gods be assembled in Gimli, the abode of peace and innocence. Over this a new heaven will be spread, where the benignant and protecting elves will watch over mankind as of old in earthly life. Even dwarfs and giants shall all live in peace. The Mighty One shall come from above and sit in judgement; there shall be an eternal separation between good and evil, which had previously been confounded. An everlasting reward shall await the good, everlasting torment the evil. Beyond this no eye may see.

**Illustration.** Ragnaröck, *the darkness* or *twilight of the gods* (from regin, *gen. pl.* ragna, *deus, potestas,* and röckr, *twilight, darkness*). That wolves pursued and would swallow up the sun and moon, is a general figure to express the eclipse of the heavenly bodies. The solar wolf has also been explained to be a parhelion.[1] Egdir, the eagle, and Fialar, and the other two cocks,[2] do not strictly belong to Ragnaröck, but to the previous state of the world. What they signify is extremely obscure, or, rather, unknown. Who the two brothers are, whose sons shall inhabit Vindheim,[3] is quite uncertain: some suppose them to be Thor and Baldur. Gimli is the clear, bright heaven; Vidblain and Andlang, the spacious blue heaven the boundless aether; Okólnir, the warm (literally *the uncold*). Cold had hitherto been the lot of the giants, but now they also shall share in the warmth; to this also the name Brímir alludes, from brími, fire. Náströnd is from ná, *a corpse,* therefore *the strand of corpses*. Slid (Slidr) signifies *the sluggish* or *pernicious*; Nidhögg, the serpent of darkness, or envy. The idea of all nature awaiting a deliverance from the existing state of things, and a renewal or exaltation of its blunted powers, is deeply impressed on the human mind; it is also Oriental, but manifests itself among several nations under various forms, though essentially the same.

1    Magnusen, op. cit., p. 414, note.
2    Page 64.
3    Page 67.

# Appendix

## The Grottasavngr or Mill-song

As belonging to the province of Northern mythology, it has been deemed desirable to add an account of the celebrated Gróttasavngr, or Mill-song, which is to be found in every manuscript of Saemund's *Edda*, except the parchment one in the Royal Library at Copenhagen.

King Frodi (Fróthi) paid a visit to King Fiölnir in Sweden, and there bought two female slaves, called Fenia and Menia, who were both large and strong. At that time, there were found in Denmark two millstones so large that no one was able to drag them. These millstones had the property that they produced whatever the grinder wished for. The mill was called Grótti. Hengikiaptr (hanging jaw) was the name of him who gave the mill to Frodi. King Frodi caused the slaves to be led to the millstones, and ordered them to grind gold, and peace, and prosperity to Frodi, giving them no longer rest or sleep than while the cuckoo was silent or a song might be sung. It is said that they then sang the song called Gróttasavngr, and before they left off, that they ground an army against Frodi; so that in the same night there came a sea-king called Mysing, who slew Frodi, and took great spoil. Mysing took with him the mill Grótti, together with Fenia and Menia, and ordered them to grind salt. At midnight they asked Mysing whether he had salt enough? He bade them go on grinding. They had ground but a little more when the ship sank. There was afterwards a whirlpool in the ocean, where the water falls into the eye of the millstone, and thence the sea became salt.

Professor Petersen[1] considers the myth to signify the cultivation of the land during peace, and the prosperity consequent thereupon, that prosperity begets desire, and desire war. The grinding of salt is a later adoption, as in the latter part of the song it is said that one of the stones had been split asunder in grinding for Frodi.

1  *Nordisk Mythologie*, op. cit., p. 221.

# The three solemn Pagan festivals[1]

Three great festivals were celebrated every year in the time of heathenism, when sacrifices were made to the gods. The first was held at the new year, which was reckoned from the 'mother-night', so called because the new year sprang, as it were, out of her lap. The month, which began then with the first new moon, was called Yule-month (Jule-tungel), and, from the sacrifice, Thorablot,[2] which was then chiefly celebrated. This season, even to the present day, is called Thorsmånad. Kings and jarls, not only in Sweden, but also in Denmark and Norway, held at this time their great sacrificial meetings or guilds. Rich landholders then made ready their Yule-beer for friends and kindred; but the poorer, who had no wealthy relatives, assembled in feastings, to which they all contributed, and drank hop-öl (social beer). On these occasions offerings were made to the gods for a prosperous year, both to Odin for success in war, and to Frey for a good harvest. Animals of various kinds were slaughtered, but the principal victim was a hog, which was especially sacred to Frey, because the swine is supposed to have first taught mankind to plough the earth. This was led forth well fattened and adorned and it was a custom to make vows over the sacred hog, and pledge themselves to some great enterprise, to be achieved before the next Yule-meeting (Jula-môt). Feastings, bodily exercises, and Yule-games occupied the whole of this month, whence it was denominated skämte-månad (the merry month).

Midwinter sacrifice was the second grand festival, and took place on the first new moon after Yule-month, to the honour of Göa or Goa. This goddess was believed to preside over the fertility of the earth, and to be a daughter of Thor. Hence in many places, when thunder is heard, the people still say, *Goa is passing*. After her the month of February is called Göje-månad. At a later period, this sacrifice acquired the appellation of Disa-blot, when the celebrated Queen Disa, whose memory is still preserved in the traditions of the Swedish people, had not only partaken in, but almost superseded, the worship of Frigg and Goa at this festival. The story of Queen Disa is usually related as follows:

When King Frey, or, according to other accounts, a King Sigtrud, far back in the times of heathenism, ruled in the North, the population, during a long peace, had so greatly increased, that one year, on the coming of winter, the crops of the preceding autumn were already consumed. The king therefore summoned all the commonalty to an assembly, for the

---

1  Afzelius, op. cit., i, 15.
2  So called, it is supposed, from Thorri, an ancient king or deity of the Fins and Lapps, of the race of Forniot, and blót, *sacrifice*. See *Snorra-Edda*, ed. Rask, p. 358.

purpose of finding a remedy for the impending evil, when it was decreed, that all the old, the sickly, the deformed, and the idle should be slain and offered to Odin. When one of the king's councillors, named Siustin, returned from the assembly to his dwelling in Uppland, his daughter, Disa, inquired of him what had there taken place; and as she was in all respects wise and judicious, he recounted to her what had been resolved on. On hearing it she said she could have given better counsel, and wondered that among so many men there was found so little wisdom. These words reached at length the ears of the king, who was angry at her boldness and conceit, and declared he would soon put her to her wit's end. He promised to take her to his counsel, but on condition that she should come to him not on foot nor on horseback, not driving nor sailing, not clad nor unclad, not in a year nor a month, not by day nor by night, not in the moon's increase nor wane. Disa, in her perplexity at this order, prayed to the goddess Frigg for counsel, and then went to the king in the following manner. She harnessed two young men to a sledge, by the side of which she caused a goat to be led; she held one leg in the sledge and placed the other on the goat, and was herself clad in a net. Thus she came to the king neither walking nor riding, nor driving, nor sailing, neither clad nor unclad. She came neither in a current year nor month, but on the third day before Yule, one of the days of the solstice, which were not reckoned as belonging to the year itself, but as a complement, and in like manner might be said not to belong to any month. She came neither in the increase nor in the wane, but just at the full moon; neither by day nor by night, but in the twilight. The king wondered at such sagacity, ordered her to be brought before him, and found so great delight in her conversation, beauty and understanding, that he made her his queen. Following her advice, he then divided the people into two portions, one of which, according to lot, he furnished with arms, hunting gear, and as much seed-corn as would suffice for one sowing, and sent them to the uninhabited regions of the north, there to establish a colony and cultivate the land. Much other good counsel this queen gave for the benefit of the country, for which she was loved and honoured both by king and people; and so highly was she prized for her wisdom, that many difficult disputes were referred to her judgement at the midwinter sacrifice, which soon acquired the name of Disa-blot, and Disa-ting, of which the great winter fair at Upsala is a memorial.

The above saga has been variously interpreted. According to some, Disa will represent to the king the importance and necessity of agriculture; she herself, neither clad nor unclad, represents the earth in early spring, when grass here and there is beginning to shoot forth, but does not yet deck the fields with green; the trees begin with their swelling buds to show signs of foliage, but still lack their beauteous, leafy summer clothing. Then it is not good to travel, neither in a carriage nor a sledge; then is it best for the husbandman to watch the season, to be observant of the changes and influences of the sun and moon, of the weather, of old signs and tokens, a knowledge of which is a useful heritage from his forefathers' experience.

The third great yearly festival was held at the beginning of spring, for prosperity and victory by land and sea, though more especially for the naval expeditions or 'vikingafärder', in which almost every freeborn, warlike man now prepared to participate. At this festival Odin was chiefly invoked.

## The quicken tree or mountain ash[1]

According to a superstition derived from the time of heathenism, the quicken-tree or mountain-ash[2] possesses great occult virtues. A staff of it is believed to be a preservative against sorcery. In ancient times, the people made a part of their ships of it, supposing it to be good against the storms raised by Rân. The superstition originated in the aid it afforded to Thor.[3]

## Of places of worship[4]

Spacious and magnificent temples, in honour of the gods, were erected in many parts of the Scandinavian countries, besides which there were stone-groups or altars for sacrificial purposes. Such a pagan altar was called a *horg*, whence the priestesses attending it were denominated *horgabrudar*. By every horg or temple there was a sacred grove, or a solitary tree, on which the offerings were suspended. Such trees were supposed to possess great virtue in the cure of diseases. Hence it is that even now some trees are regarded with a superstitious veneration, particularly the lime, and those in which 'elf-holes', or openings formed by two branches that have grown together are found. These are often cut down for superstitious purposes. Women, who have difficult labours, are drawn through them, and have thereby not infrequently lost their lives and superstitious persons may be often seen carrying sickly children to a forest, for the purpose of dragging them through such holes.

By every sacred grove there was a well or fountain, in which the offerings were washed.

---

1  Afzelius, op. cit.,i, 21.
2  The *Sorbus aucuparia*, the Rowan of the Scottish Highlanders.
3  When fording a river on the way to Geirröd's house; see above, p. 48.
4  Afzelius, op. cit., i, 18, 20.

# Of soothsayimg and sorcery[1]

Besides the regular priests, the Northern nations had also their wise men and women, or soothsayers. The principal kinds of witchcraft were seid (seidr) and galder (galdr); though there seems also to have been a third species, as the prophetesses (völur), prophets (vitkar), and seid-workers (seid-berendr) are distinguished from each other, and spring from different origins. Galder is a derivation of at gala, *to sing*,[2] and consisted in producing supernatural effects by means of certain songs, or by cutting certain runes. This in itself may not have been criminal, as there was also a species called meingaldr (from mein, *harm*, etc.), by which something evil was brought forth. Groa sang over the stone that was lodged in Thor's forehead, Oddrun over Borgny when the latter could not bring forth. A particular kind of galder was valgalder, by which the dead were waked and made to converse, that the will of fate might be known from their mouth. This is ascribed to Odin, who sat under one hanged and compelled him to speak, or went down to the nether world, waked the dead Vala, and made her prophesy. We also find that Hardgrepe cut songs on wood, and caused them to be laid under a corpse's tongue, which compelled it to rise and sing.[3] Hild by her song waked Högni and Hedin's fallen warriors, that they might continually renew the combat.[4] As examples of such songs may be mentioned that by which Hervör woke Angantyr, and the so-called Busla's prayer and Serpa's verse.[5]

Seid, according to some, consisted in a kind of boiling (from at sioda, *to boil*) although in the original authorities there is nothing that evidently alludes to that process.[6] The Aesir learned it from Freyia;[7] it was regarded as unseemly for men, and was usually practised by women only: we nevertheless meet with seid-men. Both seid and galder were practised by Odin himself. The seid-woman occupied an elevated seat with four pillars. All changes in nature, such as quenching fire, stilling the sea, turning the wind, waking the dead, seem to have been mostly effected by galder; while by means of seid the fate of individuals was ascertained and control over futurity acquired; by seid death, misfortune and disease could be caused to others, intellect and strength taken from one and given to another, storms raised, etc. etc. On account of its wickedness, it was held unworthy

---

1   From Petersen, *Danmarks Historie* and Keyser, op. cit.
2   Like our *enchant*.
3   Saxo, p. 38, edit. Müller.
4   Ibid. p. 242.
5   Saga Herrauds ok Bosa, cap. 5.
6   Grimm, J., *Deutsche Mythologie*, op. cit., p. 988.
7   Ynglingas. c. 4.

of a man to practise seid, and the seid-man was prosecuted and burned as an atrocious trollman. The seid-women received money to make men hard, so that iron could not wound them.

The most remarkable class of seid-women were the so-called Valas, or Völvas. We find them present at the birth of children, when they seem to represent the Norns. They acquired their knowledge either by means of seid, during the night, while all others in the house were sleeping, and uttered their oracles in the morning; or they received sudden inspirations during the singing of certain songs appropriated to the purpose, without which the sorcery could not perfectly succeed. These seid-women are common over all the North. They were invited by the master of a family, and appeared in a peculiar costume, sometimes with a considerable number of followers, e.g. with fifteen young men and fifteen girls. For their soothsaying, they received money, gold rings and other precious things. Sometimes it was necessary to compel them to prophesy. An old description of such a Vala, who went from guild to guild telling fortunes, will give the best idea of these women and their proceedings:

Thorbiörg during the winter attended the guilds, at the invitation of those who desired to know their fate or the quality of the coming year. Everything was prepared in the most sumptuous manner for her reception. There was an elevated seat, on which lay a cushion stuffed with feathers. A man was sent to meet her. She came in the evening, dressed in a blue mantle fastened with thongs, and set with stones down to the lap; round her neck she had a necklace of glass beads, on her head a hood of black lambskin lined with white catskin; in her hand a staff, the head of which was mounted with brass and ornamented with stones; round her body she wore a girdle of dry wood (knöske), from which hung a bag containing her conjuring apparatus; on her feet were rough calfskin shoes with long ties and tin buttons; on her hands catskin gloves, white and hairy within. All bade her welcome with a reverent salutation; the master himself conducted her by the hand to her seat. She undertook no prophecy on the first day, but would first pass a night there. In the evening of the following day, she ascended her elevated seat, caused the women to place themselves round her, and desired them to sing certain songs, which they did in a strong, clear voice. She then prophesied of the coming year, and afterwards all that would advanced and asked her such questions as they thought proper, to which they received plain answers.[1]

---

1  The saga of Erik the Red. The scene described is set in the Norse colony on Greenland.

Besides galder and seid, there were no doubt other kinds of sorcery. It was believed, for instance, that the Fins in particular possessed the art of raising storms and of deceiving the sight of their enemies, so that the stones they cast in their way appeared to them as lofty mountains, and a snowball as a great river. These arts may therefore be regarded as more ancient than the Aesir-lore. The Danish sea-commander, Odde, could without a ship traverse the ocean, by magic spells raise a storm against his enemies, and so deceive their eyesight, that the swords of the Danes appeared to them as emitting rays and glittering as if on fire. Gudrun so beguiled the vision of Jarmerik's warriors that they turned their weapons against each other. Others, like Gunholm and Hildiger, could by magic songs blunt the edge of swords. The trollman and the witch could, like Harthgrebe, assume various forms, make themselves little or big, ugly or handsome; also invest themselves with the likeness of a whale or other animal, as the trollman sent by Harald Blâtand to Iceland, and the troll-wife who, in order to kill King Frodi, transformed herself to a sea-cow, and her sons to calves. With viands prepared from snakes or serpents, a person procured strength, wisdom and success in war for any favourite individual. By oblivious potions and philtres lovers were made to forget their old love and contract a new one. That which Grimhild gave to Gudrun consisted of a strong drink, ice-cold water and blood: and with this drink were mingled many potent (evil) things, as the juice of all kinds of trees, acorns, soot, entrails of victims, and boiled swine's liver, which has the virtue of extinguishing hatred. In the horn containing it runes were sculptured.

Trollmen, it was believed, could derive much aid from certain animals: thus the art of interpreting the voice of birds is spoken of as a source of great discoveries. The crow was in this respect a bird of considerable importance, and that such was also the case with the raven is evident from Odin's Hugin and Munin. The cat is also mentioned as a special favourite among trollmen. The skilful Icelandic magician, Thorolf Skegge, is said to have had no less than twenty large black cats, that valiantly defended their master when attacked, and gave eighteen men enough to do.

Of the 'hamhlaup', or power of assuming various forms, we have an example in Odin himself, who could change his appearance (hamr), and as a bird, a fish or other animal transport himself to distant lands; also in the falcon-plumage (valshamr, fiathrhamr) of the goddesses, which they could lend to others, and in the swan-plumage of the Valkyriur. It was likewise believed that men could by magic be changed to the form of wolves, which they could lay aside only at certain times. Of some it was believed that by putting on a magical hat or hood (dularkufl, hulidshjálmr), they could render themselves invisible to, or not to be recognised by, others[1] or by certain arts alter the whole aspect of the surrounding country. Of all this many instances occur in the Sagas. The witch Liot would change the aspect of the country in the sight of others, by placing one foot over her head, walking backwards, and protruding her head between her legs but the process failed, as they saw her before she saw them. Svan, when desirous of concealing another, wrapped a goatskin round his head, and said: 'There will be fog, and bugbears, and great wonders for all who seek after thee.' A man became 'freskr', i.e. capable of seeing the concealed trollman by looking under another's arm placed a-kimbo on the left side. Even to the glance or look of the eye, an extraordinary effect was ascribed, sometimes harmless, as Svanhild's when the horses were about to trample on her, or as Sigurd's, whose sharp glance held the most savage dogs at bay; sometimes pernicious. The effect of either might be neutralised by drawing a bag over the head, by which process the trollman lost his power. It is told of one, that he saw through a hole in the bag, and with a glance destroyed a whole field of grass. Hence the common saying of one having *an evil eye*. Troll-wives and noxious demons (uvaettir) are described, as Hyrrockin, riding on wolves with snakes or serpents for a rein. Such ridings generally took place by night, and the heroes pursued and slew these beings of the dark. In an old narrative of such a ride the circumstance appears that the troll rode on a staff; but of assemblies of witches on mountains, as on the Blåkulla in Sweden, Troms in Norway, Hekla in Iceland, the Blocksberg in the north of Germany, of which we read so much in the legends of the middle age, we find absolutely nothing: this superstition must have arisen at or after the introduction of Christianity.

A peculiar kind of magic was that called 'sitting out' (útiseta, at sitja úti), which consisted in sitting out at night, and by certain magical proceedings, which are no longer known, though oftenest with 'galder', summoning forth trolls, or raising the dead, for the purpose of interrogating them.

In the more fabulous Sagas mention occurs of a variety of superstitions, such as of a wooden image endowed with life, by means of 'galder', and sent to Iceland, by which Thorleif Jarlaskiáld was slain; the raising of charmed weather, by shaking a weather-bag (vedrbelgr), from which storms proceeded; the belief that certain men every ninth night became women; that a man, by a kind of grass placed under a woman's head, might excite her love; that persons could by magic be fixed to the spot where they stood, without the power of stirring from it; that there are

---

1   This was effected by a kind of powder resembling ashes, which the operator sprinkled over and around the person it was intended to conceal.

mantles, woven by elves, whereby women's fidelity and maidens' chastity may be tested, etc. etc. Some of these superstitions may have prevailed in the North, though many of them are no doubt mere later fictions.

Garments also could be charmed, either for the protection of the wearer, or to cause injury or death. Of the chieftain Thorir Hund it is said, that he caused several frocks of reindeer skin to be made by the Fins, that were so charmed that no weapon could cut or pierce them; and in the battle of Stiklastad one of these frocks protected him against the sword of St Olaf, when that king struck him across the shoulders. Harald Hákonson, jarl of the Orkneys, died, we are told, in consequence of a charmed garment, that had been wrought by his own mother and her sister, but intended for his half-brother, Pâl Jarl. Swords were sometimes so enchanted, that success in battle attended those that bore them, and the wounds made by them could be healed only by being spread over with 'life-stone' (lífsteinn). That such swords might have their full effect, much was to be attended to: the famous sword Sköfnung, for instance, that was taken from Hrolf Kraki's sepulchral mound, might not be drawn in the presence of women, or so that the sun shone on the hilt, otherwise it lost somewhat of its virtue.

The most efficient and solemn mode of wishing evil to another was that called 'níd' (enmity), which consisted in setting up a nith-stake (at reisa níd). The process is thus described by Saxo, who relates how such a nid-stake was raised against Eric the Eloquent: – The head of a horse, that had been sacrificed to the gods, was set on a stake, the jaws being held distended by wooden pins. And this is confirmed by the Sagas. When Egil Skallagrimsson would 'nída' King Eric Blodöxe and Queen Gunnhild in Norway, he took a hazel-stake, ascended a mountain-peak that looked towards the interior of the country, and set a horse's head on the stake, while he uttered the following malediction: 'Here raise I a nith-stake, and turn this "nith" against King Eric and Queen Gunnhild – at the same time turning the head towards the country. And I turn this "nith" against the "land-vaettir" that abide in this land, so that they may wander about, without finding house or habitation, until they shall have driven King Eric and Queen Gunnhild from the country.'[1] He then drove the stake fast down in a cleft of the mountain, and cut runes on it containing the same malediction.[1] In perfect accordance with this is the law of Ulfliot,[2] that no

---

1   Gunnhild had at a banquet caused a poisoned drink to be presented to Egil, who having cause for suspicion, scratched runes on the horn with his knife, wounded himself in the palm, and smeared the runes with blood, when the horn burst asunder and the liquor was spilt. Hence his enmity.
2   The first lawgiver of Iceland. He lived in the tenth century.

one might sail towards the land with a yawning head at the stem, in order not to terrify the land-vaettir, or guardian deities. In other narratives we find that a human head of wood was set in the breast of the slaughtered horse. Another species of nith was performed with runes, which in some way or other must be conveyed to the enemy or his property: for this purpose, the operator cut runes on wood, smeared them with his blood, uttered 'galder' over them, and walked round them against the sun, then cast them into the sea, with the wish that they might be drifted to the object against whom the nith was directed.

But as misfortune and lasting calamity could be caused to others by imprecations, so could one individual, by good wishes, impart to others good fortune and happiness; and the belief was general, that the father's luck could continue to operate on the life of the son, and of generous, kind relatives on that of succeeding generations, and that the king or a chieftain could communicate his good fortune to others. Thus it is related of Odin, that to render his men successful in battle, he laid his hands on them and blessed them; of Olaf Tryggvason, that to Halfred and others he gave his good luck; of Höskuld Dalakolssenn in Iceland, that just before his death he gave his son a ring together with his own and his kindred's good fortune; and Svend Tveskiaeg, who formed a commercial connection with Van-helds-Roe, communicated to him a share of his prosperity.

## Epitome of German[1] Mythology

To the Germans no *Edda* has been transmitted, nor has any writer of former times sought to collect the remains of German heathenism. On the contrary, the early writers of Germany having, in the Roman school, been alienated from all reminiscences of their paternal country, have striven, not to preserve, but to extirpate every trace of their ancient faith.[2] Much, therefore of the old German mythology being thus irretrievably lost, I turn to the sources which remain, and which consist partly in written documents, partly in the never-stationary stream of living traditions and customs. The first, although they may reach far back, yet appear fragmentary and lacerated, while the existing popular tradition hangs on threads which finally connect it with Antiquity.[3]

---

1   It is to be observed that the word *German* is here used in its modern signification, to the exclusion of the Scandinavian nations; when meaning to include the whole race, I have generally adopted the term *Germanic*.
2   Grimm, J., *Deutsche Mythologie*, op. cit., Preface, p. viii.
3   Ibid. p. x.

The principal sources of German mythology are, therefore,

    I   Popular narratives;
    II   Superstitions and ancient customs, in which traces of heathen myths, religious ideas and forms of worship are to be found.

Popular narratives branch into three classes:

    I   Heroic Traditions (Heldensagen)
    II   Popular Traditions (Volkssagen)
    III   Popular Tales (Märchen).

That they all in common – though traceable only in Christian times – have preserved much of heathenism, is confirmed by the circumstance that in them many beings make their appearance who incontestably belong to heathenism, viz. those subordinate beings the dwarfs, water-sprites, etc., who are wanting in no religion which, like the German, has developed conceptions of personal divinities.[1]

The principal sources of German **heroic traditions** are a series of poems, which have been transmitted from the eighth, tenth, but chiefly from the twelfth down to the fifteenth century. These poems are founded, as has been satisfactorily proved, on popular songs, collected, arranged and formed into one whole, for the most part by professed singers. The heroes, who constitute the chief personages in the narrative, were probably once gods or heroes, whose deep-rooted myths have been transmitted through Christian times in an altered and obscured form. With the great German heroic tradition – the story of Siegfried and the Nibelunge, this assumption is the more surely founded, as the story, even in heathen times, was spread abroad in Northern song.[2]

If in the Heroic Traditions the mythic matter, particularly that which forms the pith of the narrative, is frequently concealed, in the **popular traditions** (Volkssagen) it is often more obvious. By the last-mentioned title; we designate those narratives which, in great number and remarkable mutual accordance, are spread over all Germany, and which tell of rocks, mountains, lakes and other prominent objects. The collecting of those still preserved among the common people has, since the publication of the *Deutsche Sagen* by the Brothers Grimm, made considerable progress. Of such narratives many, it is true, belong not to our province, some being mere obscured historic reminiscences, others owing their origin to ety-mologic interpretations, or even to sculpture and carvings, which the people have endeavoured to explain in their own fashion; while others have demonstrably sprung up in Christian times, or are the fruits of

---

1   W. Müller, op. cit., p. 12.
2   Ibid.

literature. Nevertheless, a considerable number remain, which descend from ancient times, and German mythology has still to hope for much emolument from the Popular Traditions, since those with which we are already acquainted offer a plentiful harvest of mythic matter, without which our knowledge of German heathenism would be considerably more defective than it is.[1]

**The popular tale** (Volksmärchen), which usually knows neither names of persons or places, nor times, contains, as far as our object is concerned, chiefly myths that have been rent from their original connection and exhibited in an altered fanciful form. Through lively imagination, through the mingling together of originally unconnected narratives, through adaptation to the various times in which they have been reproduced and to the several tastes of listening youth, through transmission from one people to another, the mythic elements of the Popular Tales are so disguised and distorted, that their chief substance is, as far as mythology is concerned, to us almost unintelligible.[2]

But Popular Traditions and Popular Tales are, after all, for the most part, but dependent sources, which can derive any considerable value only by connection with more trustworthy narratives. A yet more dependent source is the **superstitions** still to be found in the country among the great mass of the people, a considerable portion of which has, in my opinion, no connection with German mythology; although in recent times there is manifestly a disposition to regard every collection of popular superstitions, notions and usages as a contribution to it.[3]

Among the superstitions are to be reckoned the charms or spells and forms of adjuration, which are to be uttered frequently, with particular ceremonies and usages, for the healing of a disease or the averting of a danger, and which are partly still preserved among the common people, and partly to be found in manuscripts.[4] They are for the most part in rime and rhythmical, and usually conclude with an invocation of God, Christ and the saints. Their beginning is frequently epic, the middle contains the potent words for the object of the spell. That many of these forms descend from heathen times is evident from the circumstance that downright heathen beings are invoked in them.[5]

---

1   Müller, op. cit., p. 14.
2   Ibid. p. 15.
3   Müller, op. cit., p. 16.
4   Many such conjurations and spells are given by Grimm, J., *Deutsche Mythologie*, op. cit., pp. cxxvi–clix and in Mone's *Anzeiger*, also in *Altdeutsche Blätter*, Bd. ii, etc.
5   As Erce and Fasolt. See Grimm, J., *Deutsche Mythologie*, op. cit., pp. cxxx–cxxxii. Müller, op. cit., p. 21.

Another source is open to us in **German manners and customs**. As every people is wont to adhere tenaciously to its old customs, even when their object is no longer known, so has many a custom been preserved, or only recently fallen into desuetude, the origin of which dates from the time of heathenism, although its connection therewith may either be forgotten or so mixed up with Christian ideas as to be hardly recognisable. This observation is particularly applicable to the popular diversions and processions, which take place at certain seasons in various parts of the country. These, though frequently falling on Christian festivals, yet stand in no necessary connection with them; for which reason many may, no doubt, be regarded as remnants of pagan usages and festivals. And that such is actually the case appears evident from the circumstance, that some of these festivals, *e.g.* the kindling of fires, were at the time of the conversion forbidden as heathenish, and are also to be found in the heathenism of other nations. But we know not with what divinities these customs were connected, nor in whose honour these festivals were instituted. Of some only may the original object and probable signification be divined; but for the most part they can be considered only in their detached and incoherent state. It may also be added, that Slavish and Keltic customs may have got mingled with the German.[1]

---

1    Müller, op. cit., p. 22. Upon this subject Grimm, J., *Deutsche Mythologie*, op. cit., (Vorrede, p. xxxii) remarks:

'Jewish and Christian doctrine began to insinuate itself into the heathen belief, heathen fancies and superstitions to press into, and, as it were, take refuge in every place not occupied by the new faith. Christian matter sometimes appears disguised in a heathen form, and heathen matter in a Christian.' See a striking instance of this in the old Thuringian pagan spell at p. 27n.

'As the goddess Ostara (Eastre) became changed into an idea of time, so was Hellia (Hel) into an idea of place. The belief of Antiquity in elves and giants became changed into that of angels and devils, but the old traditions remained. Woden, Thor, Ty, were invested with the nature of pernicious, diabolical beings, and the tradition of their solemn yearly processions was changed into that of a wild, frantic troop, from which the people shrank with dread, as they had formerly rushed forth to share in it.'

'A circumstance yet more striking is, that to the Virgin Mary are transferred a number of pleasing traditions of Hold and Frouwa, the Norns and Valkyriur. How delightful are these stories of Mary, and what could any other poesy have to compare with them! With the kindly heathen characteristics are associated for us a feeling of the higher sanctity which surrounds this woman. Flowers and plants are named after Mary, images of Mary are borne in procession and placed in the forest-trees, in exact conformity with the heathen worship; Mary is the divine mother, the spinner, and appears as a helpful virgin to all who invoke her But Mary stands not alone. In the Greek and the Latin churches a numerous host of saints sprang up around her, occupying the place of the gods of the second and third classes, the heroes and wise women of heathenism. [*continued overleaf*

While the Scandinavian religion may, even as it has been transmitted to us, be regarded as a connected whole, the isolated fragments of German mythology can be considered only as the damaged ruins of a structure, for the restoration of which the plan is wholly wanting. But this plan we in great measure possess in the Northern Mythology, seeing that many of these German ruins are in perfect accordance with it. Hence we may confidently conclude that the German religion, had it been handed down to us in equal integrity with the Northern, would, on the whole, have exhibited the same system, and may, therefore, have recourse to the latter, as the only means left us of assigning a place to each of its isolated fragments.[1]

Although the similitude of language and manners speaks forcibly in favour of a close resemblance between the German and Northern mythologies, yet the assumption of a perfect identity of both religions is, on that account, by no means admissible; seeing that the only original authorities for German heathenism, the Merseburg poems,[2] in the little information supplied by them, show some remarkable deviations from the religious system of the North.[3]

The question here naturally presents itself, by what course of events did the Odinic worship become spread over the larger portion of Germany and the Netherlands? By Paulus Diaconus (*De Gestis Langobard*, i, 8) we are informed that **Wodan** was worshipped as a god by all the Germanic nations. And Jonas of Bobbio ('Vita St Columbani', in *Act. Bened.*, sec. 2, p. 26) makes mention of a vessel filled with beer, as an offering to Wodan, among the Suevi (Alamanni) on the Lake of Constance.[4] Hence it is

---

and filling the heart, because they mediate between it and a higher, severer Godhead. Among the saints also, both male and female, there were many classes, and the several cases in which they are helpful are distributed among them like offices and occupations . . . For the hero who slew the dragon, Michael or George was substituted, and the heathen Siegberg was transferred over to Michael; as in France out of *Mons Martis* a Mons martyrum (Montmartre) was formed. It is worthy of remark that the Osseten out of *dies Martis* (Mardi) make a George's day, and out of *dies Veneris* (Vendredi) a Mary's day. Instead of Odin and Freyia, at *minne* drinking, St John and St Gertrud were substituted.'

1 Müller, op. cit., p. 34.
2 See page 27n.
3 Müller, op. cit., p. 35
4 Sunt etenim inibi vicinae nationes Suevorum, quo cum moraretur et inter habitatores illius loci progrederetur, reperit eos sacrificium profallum *litare* velle, vasque magnum, quod vulgo *cupam* vocant, quod viginti et sex modios amplius minusve capiebat, *cerevisia* plenum, in medio habebant positum. Ad quod vir Dei accessit et sciscitatur quid de illo fieri vellent? Illi aiunt: deo suo Wodano, quem Mercurium vocant alii, se velle *litare*.

reasonable to conclude that his worship prevailed especially among those tribes which, according to their own traditions and other historic notices, wandered from north to south.[1] Whether Wodan was regarded as a chief divinity by all the German tribes is uncertain, no traces of his worship existing among the Bavarians; and the name of the fourth day of the week after him being found chiefly in the north of Germany, but in no High German dialect.[2]

The following is Snorri's account of Odin's course from the Tanais to his final settlement in Sweden:

'The country to the east of the Tanais (Tanaqvisl) in Asia was called Asaheim; but the chief city (borg) in the country was called Asgard. In this city there was a chief named Odin (Wodan), and there was a great place of sacrifice (offersted), etc.[3]

'At that time, the Roman generals were marching over the world and reducing all nations to subjection; but Odin being foreknowing and possessed of magical skill, knew that his posterity should occupy the northern half of the world. He then set his brothers Ve and Vili over Asgard, but himself, with all the *diar*[4] and a vast multitude of people, wandered forth, first westwards to Gardariki,[5] and afterwards southwards to Saxland.[6] He had many sons *and after having reduced under his subjection an extensive kingdom in Saxland*, he placed his sons to defend the country. He afterwards proceeded northwards to the sea, and took up his abode in an island which is called Odins-ey in Fyen.[7] But when Odin learned that there were good tracts of land to the east in Gylfi's kingdom, he proceeded thither, and Gylfi concluded a treaty with him . . . Odin made his place of residence by the Mälar lake, at the place now called Sigtuna. There he erected a vast temple.

The worship of **Thunaer** or **Donar**, the Northern Thor, among the

---

1  Grimm, J., *Deutsche Mythologie*, op. cit., p. 49. Müller, pp. 80, 85.
2  Müller, op. cit., p. 86. In the Westphalian dialect, Wednesday is called *Godenstag, Gaumstag, Gunstag*; in Nether Rhenish, *Gudenstag*; in middle age Netherlandish or Dutch, *Woensdach*; in New Netherl., *Woensdag*; in Flemish, *Goensdag*; in Old Frisic, *Wernsdei*; in New Fris., *Wânsdey*; in Nor. Fris., *Winsdei*; in Anglo-Sax., *Wodenes-* and *Wodnesdaeg*; in Old Nor., *Odinsdagr*.
3  *Yuglingasaga*, c 2.
4  The *diar* were the twelve chief priests.
5  The Great and Little Russia of after-times.
6  Strictly the Saxons' land; but by the Northern writers the name is applied to the whole of Germany, from the Alps in the south to the Rhine in the west.
7  A singular inaccuracy, Odense (Odins ey or rather Odins ve) being the chief town of Fyen.

Germans appears certain only from the Low German formula of renuncia-tion[1] and the name of the fifth day of the week.[2]

The god **Zio**, who is identical with the Northern Ty (Tyr), is nowhere directly named but as he has given his name to the third day of the week, his right to a place in the list is established.[3] His name seems to be preserved in some local appellations in the south of Germany.

**Baldur** appears in the Merseburg poem under the name of **Phol**.[4]

The Frisic god **Fosite** is, according to all probability, the Scandinavian Forseti.[5] Of him it is related that a temple was erected to him in Heligoland, which formerly bore the name of Fositesland. On the island there was a spring, from which no one might draw water except in silence. No one might touch any of the animals sacred to the god, that fed on the island, nor anything else found there. St Wilibrord baptised three Frisians in the spring, and slaughtered three of the animals for himself and his companions, but had nearly paid with his life for the profanation of the sanctuary, a crime which, according to the belief of the heathen, must be followed by madness or speedy death.[6] At a later period as we are informed by Adam of Bremen, the island was regarded as sacred by pirates.[7]

Besides the above-named five gods, mention also occurs of three goddesses, viz. **Frigg**, the wife of Wodan, who is spoken of by Paulus Diaconus (i. 8) under the name of *Frea*.[8] In the Merseburg poem, where she is called *Frua* or *Friia*, she appears as a sister of **Volla**, the Northern *Fulla*.[9] The sixth day of the week is named either after her or after the Northern goddess Freyia,[10] but who in Germany was probably called

---

1   Ec forsacho allum dioboles uuercum and uuordum *thunaer* ende *uuoden* ende *saxnote* ende allêm them unholdum the hira genotas sint. *I renounce all the works and words of the devil*, Thunaer *and* Woden *and* Saxnôt *and all those fiends that are their associates.* Massmann, *Abschwörungsformeln*, No. 1.
2   Ohg. *Donares tac*, Toniris tac; Mhg. *Donrestac*; Mnl. *Donresdach*; Nnl. *Donderdag*; O. Fris. *Thunresdei*, *Tornsdei*; N. Fris. *Tongersdei*; Nor. Fris. *Türsdei*; A. Sax. *Thunres daeg*; O. Nor. *thorsdagre*; modern English Thursday.
3   Ohg. *Cies dac*, earlier perhaps *Ziuwes tac*, later Swab. *Ziestac* (For other forms see Grimm, J., *Deutsche Mythologie*, op. cit., p. 113.) The modern German *Dienstag* is a corruption of *Diestag*. Mnl. *Disendach*; Nnl. *Dingsdach*; O. Fris. *Tysdei*; N. Fris. *Tyesdey*; Nor. Fris. *Tirsdei*; A. Sax. *Tiwes daeg*; O. Nor. *Tysdagr* .
4   See p. 27.
5   See p. 32.
6   Alcuini *Vita S. Wilibrordi* cited by Grimm, J., *Deutsche Mythologie*, op. cit., p. 210.
7   *De Situ Daniae*, p. 132. Müller, op. cit., p. 88.
8   See Grimm, J., *Deutsche Mythologie*, op. cit., p. 276.
9   See pp. 27n, 35.
10  The names of the sixth day of the week waver: Ohg. *Fria dag*, *Frîje tag*; Mhg. *Frîtac*, *Vriegtag*; Mnl. *Vrîdach*; O. Fris. *Frigendei*, *Fredei*; N. Fris. *Frêd*; A. Sax. *Frige daeg*; O. Nor. *Friadagr*, *Freyjudagr*; Sw. Dan. *Fredag*.

*Frouwa*; and the goddess **Hludana**, whom Thorlacius identifies with Hlodyn.[1]

Of the god **Saxnôt** nothing occurs beyond the mention of his name in the renunciation, which we have just seen. In the genealogy of the kings of Essex, a Seaxneât appears as a son of Woden.[2]

As the common ancestor of the German nation, Tacitus, on the authority of ancient poems[3] places the hero or god Tuisco, who sprang from the earth; whose son Mannus had three sons, after whom are named the three tribes, viz. the Ingaevones, nearest to the ocean; the Herminones, in the middle parts; and the Istaevones.[4]

After all it is, perhaps, from the several prohibitions, contained in the decrees of councils or declared by the laws, that we derive the greater part of our knowledge of German heathenism. Of these sources one of the most important is the 'Indiculus Superstitionum et Paganarium', at the end of a Capitulary of Carloman (AD 743), contained in the Vatican manuscript No. 577, which is a catalogue of the heathen practices that were forbidden at the council of Lestines (Liptinae), in the diocese of Cambrai.[5] In the manuscript this catalogue is preceded by the formula of renunciation already given.

1   *See page* 21. Müller, op. cit., p. 88.
2   Lappenberg's *England* by Thorpe, i, p. 288. Müller, op. cit., p. 89.
3   Celebrant carminibus antiquis, quod unum apud illos memoriae et annalium genus est, Tuisconem deum terra editum, etc.
4   *Germania*, c. 2
5   Although the *Indiculus* has been frequently printed, we venture to give it a place here, on account of its importance for German Mythology.

### INDICULUS SUPERSTITIONUM ET PAGANIARUM.

i De Sacrilegio ad Sepulchra Mortuorum.   ii De Sacrilegio super Defunctos, id est *Dadsisas*.   iii De Spurcalibus in Februario.   iv De Casulis, id est Fanis.   v De Sacrilegiis per Ecclesias.   vi De Sacris Silvarum, quae *Nimidas* vocant.   vii De his quae faciunt super petras.   viii De Sacris *Mercurii* vel *Jovis* ( *Wodan* or *Thor*).   ix De Sacrificio quod fit alicui Sanctorum.   x De Phylacteriis et Ligaturis.   xi De Fontibus Sacrificiorum.   xii De Incantationibus.   xiii De Auguriis vel avium vel equorum, vel bovum stercore, vel sternutatione.   xiv De Divinis vel Sortilegis.   xv De Igne fricato de ligno, id est *nod fyr*.   xvi De Cerebro Animalium.   xvii De Observatione pagana in foco vel in inchoatione rei alicuius.   xviii De Incertis Locis, quae colunt pro Sacris.   xix De Petendo quod boni vocant Sanctae Mariae.   xx De Feriis, quae faciunt *Jovi* vel *Mercurio*.   xxi De Lunae defectione, quod dicunt *Vinceluna*.   xxii De Tempestatibus et Cornibus et Cocleis.   xxiii De Sulcis circa Villas.   xxiv De Pagano Cursu, quem *Frias* (*Yrias*, Grim) nominant, scissis pannis vel calceis.   xxv De eo quod sibi sanctos fingunt quoslibet mortuos.   xxvi De Simulacro de consparsa farina.   xxvii De Simulacris de pannis factis.   xxviii De Simulacro quod per campos portant.   xxix De Ligneis Pedibus vel Manibus pagano ritu.   xxx De eo quod credunt, quia Feminae lunam commendent, quod possint corda hominum tollere juxta paganos.

From the popular traditions and tales of Germany a sufficiently clear idea of the nature of the giants and dwarfs of Teutonic fiction may be obtained. As in the Northern belief the giants inhabit the mountains, so does German tradition assign them dwellings in mountains and caverns. Isolated mounts, sand-hills or islands have been formed by the heaps of earth which giant-maidens have let fall out of their aprons when constructing a dam or a causeway.[1] Scattered fragments of rock are from structures undertaken by them in ancient times and of the huge masses of stone lying about the country, for the presence of which the common people cannot otherwise account, it is said that they were cast by giants, or that they had shaken them out of their shoes like grains of sand.[2] Impressions of their fingers or other members are frequently to be seen on such stones. Other traditions tell of giants that have been turned into stone, and certain rocks have received the appellation of *giants' clubs*.[3] Moors and sloughs have been caused by the blood that sprang from a giant's wound, as from Ymir's.[4]

In Germany, too, traces exist of the turbulent elements being considered as giants. A formula is preserved in which Fasolt is conjured to avert a storm; in another, Mermeut, who rules over the storm, is invoked,[5] Fasolt is the giant who figures so often in German middle age poetry;[6] he was the brother of Ecke, who was himself a divinity of floods and waves.[7] Of Mermeut nothing further is known.

In the German popular tales the devil is frequently made to step into the place of the giants. Like them he has his abode in rocks,[8] hurls huge stones, in which the impression of his fingers or other members is often to be seen,[9] causes moors and swamps to come forth, or has his habitation in them,[10] and raises the whirlwind.[11] According to a universal tradition,

1    See p. 491.
2    See p. 495.
3    A rock near Bonn is called Fasolt's Keule (club).
4    See page 13.
5    Ich peut dir, Fasolt, dass du das wetter verfirst (wegführest), mir und meinen nachpauren ân schaden. Grimm, J., *Deutsche Mythologie*, op. cit., p. cxxxii. Müller, op. cit., p. 317, *sqq*.
6    See the passages in which mention of him occurs in W Grimm, *Deutsche Heldensage*.
7    See Grimm, J., *Deutsche Mythologie*, op. cit., pp. 218, 602. Müller, op. cit., pp. 310, 319.
8    Grimm, J. & W., *Kinder- und Hausmärchen*, op. cit., No. 125.
9    Grimm, J. & W., *Deutsche Sagen*, No. 191–198, 200–205. Wolf, *Niederl. Sagen*, No. 178, etc.
10    Grimm, J. & W., *Deutsche Sagen*, No. 202; Harrys, *Sagen, Märchen und Legenden Niedersachsens*, i, No. 11.
11 Stöpke, or Stepke, is in Lower Saxony an appellation of the devil and of the whirlwind, from which proceed the fogs that pass over the land. The devil sits in the

compacts are frequently made with the devil, by which he is bound to complete a building, as a church, a house, a barn, a causeway, a bridge or the like within a certain short period; but by some artifice, through which the soul of the person, for whom he is doing the work, is saved, the completion of the undertaking is prevented. The cock, for instance, is made to crow because, like the giants and dwarfs, who shun the light of the sun, the devil also loses his power at the break of day.[1] In being thus deceived and outwitted, he bears a striking resemblance to the giants, who, though possessing prodigious strength, yet know not how to profit by it, and therefore in their conflicts with gods and heroes always prove the inferior.[2]

While in the giant-traditions and tales of Germany a great degree of uniformity appears, the belief in dwarfs displays considerable vivacity and variety; though no other branch of German popular story exhibits such a mixture with the ideas of the neighbouring Kelts and Slavs. This intermingling of German and foreign elements appears particularly striking on comparing the German and Keltic elf-stories, between which will be found a strong similitude, which is hardly to be explained by the assumption of an original resemblance independent of all intercommunication.[3]

Tradition assigns to the dwarfs of Germany, as the *Eddas* to those of the North, the interior of the earth, particularly rocky caverns, for a dwelling. There they live together as a regular people, dig for ore, employ themselves in smith's work, and collect treasures. Their activity is of a peaceful, quiet character, whence they are distinguished as *the still folk* (*the good people*, *the guid neighbours*) and because it is practised in secret, they are said to have a *tarncap*, or *tarnmantle*,[4] or *mistmantle*, by which they can make themselves invisible. For the same reason they are particularly active at night.[5]

---

whirlwind and rushes howling and raging through the air. Märk., *Sagen*, p. 377. The whirlwind is also ascribed to witches. If a knife be cast into it, the witch will be wounded and become visible. *Schreibers Taschenbuch*, 1839, p. 323. Comp. Grimm, Abergl., pp. 522, 554; *Mones Anzeiger*, pp. 8, 278. See also vol. iii, p. 23. The spirits that raise storms and hail may be appeased by shaking out a flour-sack and saying: 'Siehe da, Wind, koch ein Mus für dein Kind!' (See there, Wind, boil a pap for thy child!); or by throwing a tablecloth out of the window. Grimm, *Abergl.*, p. 282. Like the Wild Huntsman, the devil on Ash Wednesday hunts the *wood-wives*. Ibid. pp. 469, 914. See p. 472, note 1.

1   See p. 16, note 2.
2   Müller, op. cit., p. 317.
3   Müller, op. cit., p. 327.
4   From Old Saxon dernian, A. S. dyrnan, *to conceal*. With the dwarfs, the sun rises at midnight. Grimm, J., *Deutsche Mythologie*, op. cit., p. 435.
5   Müller, op. cit., p. 335.

The dwarfs in general are, as we have seen, the personification of the hidden creative powers, on whose efficacy the regular changes in nature depend. This idea naturally suggests itself both from the names borne by the dwarfs in the *Eddas*, and from the myths connected with them. These names denote for the most part either activity in general, or individual natural phenomena, as the phases of the moon, wind, etc.[1]

The activity of the dwarfs, which popular tradition symbolically signifies by smith's work, must be understood as elemental or cosmical. It applies particularly to the thriving of the fruits of the earth. We consequently frequently find the dwarfs busied in helping men in their agricultural labours, in getting in the harvest, making hay and the like, which is merely a debasement of the idea that, through their efficacy, they promote the growth and maturity of the fruits of the earth. Tradition seems to err in representing the dwarfs as thievish on such occasions, as stealing the produce from the fields, or collecting the thrashed-out corn for themselves; unless such stories are meant to signify that evil befalls men, if they offend those beneficent beings, and thereby cause them to suspend their efficacy, or exert it to their prejudice.[2]

The same elemental powers which operate on the fruits of the earth also exercise an influence on the wellbeing of living creatures. Well-known and widespread is the tradition that the dwarfs have the power, by their touch, their breathing, and even by their look, to cause sickness or death to man and beast. That which they cause when they are offended they must also be able to remedy. Apollo, who sends the pestilence, is at the same time the healing god. Hence to the dwarfs likewise is ascribed a knowledge of the salutary virtues of stones and plants. In the popular tales we find them saving from sickness and death; and while they can inflict injury on the cattle, they often also take them under their care. The care of deserted and unprotected children is also ascribed to them, and in heroic tradition they appear as instructors.[3] At the same time, it cannot be denied that tradition much more frequently tells a widely different tale, representing them as kidnapping the children of human mothers and substituting their own changelings, 'dickkopfs' or 'kielkropfs'. These beings are deformed, never thrive, and, in spite of their voracity, are always lean, and are, moreover, mischievous. But that this tradition is a misrepresentation, or at least a part only, of the original one, is evident from the circumstance, that when the changeling is taken back the mother finds her own child again safe and sound, sweetly smiling, and as it were

1   Müller, op. cit., p. 332.
2   Müller, op. cit., p. 336.
3   Of this description was Regin, the instructor of Sigurd.

waking out of a deep sleep. It had, consequently, found itself very comfortable while under the care of the dwarfs, as they themselves also declare, that the children they steal find better treatment with them than with their own parents. By stripping this belief of its mythic garb, we should probably find the sense to be, that the dwarfs take charge of the recovery and health of sick and weakly children.[1]

Hence it may also be regarded as a perversion of the ancient belief, when it is related that women are frequently summoned to render assistance to dwarf-wives in labour; although the existence of such traditions may be considered as a testimony of the intimate and friendly relation in which they stand to mankind. But if we reverse the story and assume that dwarf-wives are present at the birth of a human child, we gain an appendage to the Eddaic faith – that the Norns, who appeared at the birth of children, were of the race of dwarfs. In the traditions it is, moreover, expressly declared that the dwarfs take care of the continuation and prosperity of families. Presents made by them have the effect of causing a race to increase, while the loss of such is followed by the decline of the family;[2] for this indicates a lack of respect towards these beneficent beings, which induces them to withdraw their protection. The anger of the dwarfs, in any way roused, is avenged by the extinction of the offender's race.[3]

We have here made an attempt, out of the numerous traditions of dwarfs, to set forth, in a prominent point of view, those characteristics which exhibit their nobler nature in the supposition that Christianity may also have vilified these beings as it has the higher divinities. At the same time, it is not improbable that the nature of the dwarfs even in heathen times, may have had in it something of the mischievous and provoking, which they often display in the traditions.[4]

Among the wicked tricks of the dwarfs, one in particular deserves notice – that they lay snares for young females and detain them in their habitations, herein resembling the giants, who, according to the *Eddas*, strive to get possession of the goddesses. If services are to be rendered by them, a pledge must be exacted from them,[5] or they must be compelled by force; but if once overcome, they prove faithful servants and stand by the heroes in their conflicts with the giants, whose natural enemies they seem to be, though they are sometimes in alliance with them.[6]

---

1  Müller, op. cit., p. 337.
2  See p. 465,
3  See p. 397, and Müller, op. cit., p. 339.
4  Müller, op. cit., p 341.
5  Arndt's *Märche*, i, p 152.
6  Müller, op. cit., p. 342.

Popular tradition designates the dwarfs as heathens, inasmuch as it allows them to have power only over unbaptised children. It gives us further to understand that this belief is of ancient date, when it informs us that the dwarfs no longer possess their old habitations. They have emigrated, driven away by the sound of church bells, which to them, as heathenish beings, was hateful, or because people were malicious and annoyed them, that is, no longer entertained the same respect for them as in the time of heathenism. But that this faith was harmless, and could without prejudice exist simultaneously with Christianity, appears from the tradition which ascribes to the dwarfs Christian sentiments and the hope of salvation.[1]

The Northern conception of the Norns is rendered more complete by numerous passages in the Anglo-Saxon and Old-Saxon writers. In Anglo-Saxon poetry, Wyrd manifestly occupies the place of Urd (Urdr), the eldest Norn, as the goddess of fate, who attends human beings when at the point of death; and from the *Codex Exoniensis*[2] we learn that the influence of the Norns in the guiding of fate is metaphorically expressed as the weaving of a web as the μοῖραι and parcae are described as spinners. Thus too, does the poet of the Heliand personify **Wurth**, whom, as a goddess of death, he in like manner makes an attendant on man in his last hour.[3]

We find not only in Germany traditions of **wise women**, who, mistresses of fate, are present at the birth of a child, but of the Keltic fairies it is also related that they hover about mortals as guardian spirits – appearing either three or seven or thirteen together – nurse and tend newborn children, foretell their destiny, and bestow gifts on them, but among which one of

---

1   Dwarfs go to church. Grimm, J. & W. , *Deutsche Sagen*, No. 23, 32. Kobolds are Christians, sing spiritual songs, and hope to be saved. Ibid., i, pp. 112, 113. Müller, op. cit., p. 342.

2

| Met haet Wyrd gewaef | That *Wyrd* wove for me.   *Cod. Exon.*, p. 355, 1. |
| Wyrd oft nered | *Wyrd* oft preserves |
| unfaegne eorl, | an undoom'd man, |
| thonne his ellen deáh. | when his valour avails.   *Beowulf*, 1139. |
| Him waes Wyrd | To him was *Wyrd* |
| ungemete neáh. | exceedingly near.   Ibid., 4836. |
| Thiu uurd is at handum. | The *Wurd* is at hand.   Heliand, p. 146, 2. |
| Thiu uurth a nahida thuo, | The *Wurth* then drew |
| mari maht godes. | the great might of God.   Ibid., p. 163, 16. |

In an Old High German gloss also we find *wurt*, fatum.   Graff, i,. p. 992.

The English and Scots have preserved the word the longest, as in the *weird sisters* of Macbeth and Gawen Douglas's *Virgil*; the *weird elves* in Warner's *Albion's England*; the *weird lady of the woods* in Percy's *Reliques*. See Grimm, J., *Deutsche Mythologie*, op. cit., pp. 376–8 for other instances.

3   Müller, op. cit., p. 346.

them usually mingles something evil. Hence they are invited to stand sponsors, the place of honour is assigned them at table, which is prepared with the greatest care for their sake. Like the Norns, too, they spin.[1]

Let us now endeavour to ascertain whether among the Germans there exist traces of a belief in the Valkyriur. In Anglo-Saxon, the word waelcyrige (waelcyrie) appears as an equivalent to *necis arbiter, Bellona, Alecto, Erinnys, Tisiphone*; the pl. vaelcyrian to *parcae, veneficae*; and Anglo-Saxon poets use personally the nouns Hild and Gud, words answering to the names of two Northern Valkyriur. Hildr and Gunnr (compare *hildr,* pugna; gunnr, proelium, bellum). In the first Merseburg poem, damsels, or *idisî,* are introduced, of whom 'some fastened fetters, some stopt an army, some sought after bonds'; and therefore perform functions having reference to war;[2] consequently are to be regarded as Valkyriur.[3]

We have still a superstition to notice, which in some respects seems to offer a resemblance to the belief in the Valkyriur, although in the main it contains a strange mixture of senseless, insignificant stories. We allude to the belief in witches and their nightly meetings.

The belief in magic, in evil magicians and sorceresses, who by means of certain arts are enabled to injure their fellow-creatures[4] – to raise storms,

---

1 Muller, op. cit., p. 349.
2 The following is the poem alluded to in the text, with Grimm's Latin version:

| | |
|---|---|
| Eiris sâzun idisî, | Olim sedebant nymphae, |
| sazun hera duoder, | sedebant huc atque illuc, |
| suma hapt heptidun | aliae vincula vinciebant, |
| suma heri lezidun, | aliae exercitum morabantur, |
| suma clûbôdun | aliae colligebant serta, |
| umbi cuniouuidi, | |
| insprincg haptbandun, | insultum diis complicibus, |
| inuar uîgandun. | introitum heroibus. |

the last two lines of which are particularly obscure. See Grimm, über zwei entdeckte Gedichte aus der Zeit des Deutschen Heidenthums. Berlin, 1842; also W. Wackernagels, *Altdeutsches Lesebuch,* edit. 1842. Vorrede, p. ix.; Grimm, J., *Deutsche Mythologie,* op. cit., p. 372.
3 Müller, op. cit., p. 355
4 We subjoin the principal denominations of magicians and soothsayers, as affording an insight into their several modes of operation. The more general names are: *divini, magi, harioli, vaticinatores,* etc. More special appellations are: *sortilegi (sortiarii,* χρησμόλογοι), diviners by lot; *incantatores,* enchanters; *somniorum conjectores,* interpreters of dreams; *cauculatores* and *coclearii,* diviners by offering-cups (comp. Du Fresne *sub voce,* and *Indic. Superst.,* c. 22); *haruspices,* consulters of entrails (*Capitul.,* vii, 370, Leges. Liutprandi vi, 30; comp. *Indic.* c. 16, and the divining from human sacrifices. Procop. *de B. G.,* 2, 25); *auspices* (Ammian. Marcel., 14. 9); *obligatores,* tiers of strings or ligatures (for the cure of diseases); *tempestarii,* or *immissores tempestatum,* raisers of storms.

destroy the seed in the earth, cause sickness to man and beast – is of remote antiquity. It is found in the East and among the Greeks and Romans; it was known also to the Germans and Slavs in the time of their paganism, without their having borrowed it from the Romans. In it there is nothing to be sought for beyond what appears on the surface, viz. that low degree of religious feeling, at which belief supposes effects from unknown causes to proceed from supernatural agency, as from persons by means of spells, from herbs, and even from an evil glance – a degree which can subsist simultaneously with the progressing religion, and, therefore, after the introduction of Christianity, could long prevail, and in part prevails down to the present day. Even in the time of heathenism it was, no doubt, a belief that these sorceresses on certain days and in certain places met to talk over their arts and the application of them, to boil magical herbs, and for other evil purposes. For as the sorcerer, in consequence of his occult knowledge and of his superiority over the great mass of human beings, became, as it were, isolated from them, and often harboured hostile feelings towards them, he was consequently compelled to associate with those who were possessed of similar power. It must, however, be evident that the points of contact are too few to justify our seeing the ground of German belief in witch-meetings in the old heathen sacrificial festivals and assemblies. And why should we be at the pains of seeking a historic basis for a belief that rests principally on an impure, confused deisidaimonia, which finds the supernatural where it does not exist? That mountains are particularly specified as the places of assembly, arises probably from the circumstance that they had been the offering-places of our forefathers and it was natural to assign the gatherings of the witches to known and distinguished localities.[1] Equally natural was it that the witches should

---

1    The most celebrated witch-mountain is the well-known *Brocken* (*Blocksberg*) in the Harz; others, of which mention occurs, are the *Huiberg* near Halberstadt; in Thuringia the *Horselberg* near Eisenach, or the *Inselberg* near Schmalkalde; in Hesse the *Bechelsberg* or *Bechtelsberg* near Ottrau; in Westphalia the *Köterberg* near Corvei, or the *Weckingsstein* near Minden; in Swabia, in the *Black Forest*, at *Kandel* in the Brisgau, or the *Heuberg* near Balingen; in Franconia the *Kreidenberg* near Würzburg, and the *Staffelstein* near Bamberg; in Alsace the *Bischenberg* and *Büchelberg*. The Swedish trysting-place is the *Blåkulla* (according to Ihre, a rock in the sea between Småland and Öland, literally the *Black mountain*), and the *Nasafjäll* in Norrland. The Norwegian witches also ride to the *Blaakolle*. to the *Dovrefjeld*, to the *Lyderhorn* near Bergen, to *Kiärru*, to *Vardö* and *Domen* in Finmark, to *Troms* (i.e. Trommenfjeld), a mountain in the isle of Tromsö, high up in Finmark. The Neapolitan *streghe* (*striges*) assemble *under a nut-tree* near Benevento. Italian witch-mountains are: the *Barco* di Ferrara, the *Paterno* di Bologna, *Spinato* della Mirandola, *Tossale* di Bergamo and *La Croce del Pasticcio*, of the locality of which I am ignorant. In France, the *Puy de Dôme*, near

proceed to the place of assembly through the air, in an extraordinary manner, as on he-goats, broomsticks,[1] oven-forks and other utensils.[2]

After having thus briefly noticed the gods, the giants, the dwarfs, etc., there remains for consideration a series of subordinate beings, who are confined to particular localities, having their habitation in the water, the forests and woods, the fields and in houses, and who in many ways come in contact with man.[3]

A general expression for a female demon seems to have been *minne*, the original signification of which was, no doubt, *woman*. The word is used to designate female water-sprites and wood-wives.[4]

*Holde* is a general denomination for spirits, both male and female, but occurs oftenest in composition, as *brunnenholden*, *wasserholden* (spirits of the springs and waters). There are no *bergholden* or *waldholden* (mountain-holds forest-holds), but dwarfs are called by the diminutive *holdechen*. The original meaning of the word is *bonus genius*, whence evil spirits are designated *un*holds.[5]

The name of *Bilwiz* (also written *Pilwiz*, *Pilewis*, *Bulwechs*) is attended with some obscurity. The feminine form *Bulwechsin* also occurs. It denotes a good, gentle being, and may either, with Grimm,[6] be rendered by *aequum sciens*, *aequus*, *bonus*; or with Leo by the Keltic *bilbheith*, *bilbhith* (from *bil*, good, gentle, and *bheith* or *bhith* a being). Either of these derivations would show that the name was originally an appellative, but the traditions connected with it are so obscure and varying, that they hardly distinguish any particular kind of sprite. The Bilwiz shoots like the elf, and has shaggy or matted hair.[7]

---

Clermont in Auvergne, is distinguished, Grimm, J., *Deutsche Mythologie*, op. cit., p. 1004. In Lancashire the witches assembled at Malkin Tower by the side of 'the mighty Pendle', of whom the same tradition is current relative to the transforming of a man into a horse by means of a bridle, as we find on p.360; also that of striking off a hand (see pp. 250 and 447). See Roby's *Popular Traditions of England*, vol. ii, pp. 211–53, edit. 1841.

1   On their way to the Blocksberg, Mephistopheles says to Faust:

> Verlangst du nicht nach einem Besenstiele?
> Ich wünschte mir den allerderbsten Bock.
>
> *Dost thou not long for a broomstick?*
> *I could wish for a good stout he-goat.*

2   Müller, op. cit., p. 357.
3   Ibid., p. 365.
4   Ibid., p. 366.
5   Ibid., p. 366.
6   Grimm, J., *Deutsche Mythologie*, op. cit., p 440, which see for further illustration of the subject and Müller, op. cit., p. 367.
7   Bilwitzen (bilmitzen) signifies *to tangle* or *mat the hair*. Müller, op. cit., p. 367.

In the latter ages, popular belief, losing the old nobler idea of this supernatural being, as in the case of Holla and Berchta, retained the remembrance only of the hostile side of its character. It appears, consequently, as a tormenting, terrifying, hair- and beard-tangling, grain-cutting sprite, chiefly in a female form, as a wicked sorceress or witch. The tradition belongs more particularly to the east of Germany, Bavaria, Franconia, Voigtland and Silesia. In Voigtland the belief in the *bilsen-* or *bilver-schnitters*, or reapers, is current. These are wicked men, who injure their neighbours in a most unrighteous way: they go at midnight stark naked, with a *sickle tied on their foot*, and repeating magical formulae, through the midst of a field of corn just ripe. From that part of the field which they have cut through with their sickle, all the corn will fly into their own barn. Or they go by night over the fields with little sickles tied to their great toes, and cut the straws, believing that by so doing they will gain for themselves half the produce of the field where they have cut.[1]

The *Schrat* or *Schratz* remains to be mentioned. From Old High German glosses, which translate *scratun* by pilosi, and *waltschrate* by satyrus, it appears to have been a spirit of the woods.

In the popular traditions mention occurs of a being named *Jüdel*, which disturbs children and domestic animals. When children laugh in their sleep, open their eyes and turn, it is said *the Jüdel is playing with them*. If it gets entrance into a lying-in woman's room, it does injury to the newborn child. To prevent this, a straw from the woman's bed must be placed at every door, then no Jüdel nor spirit can enter. If the Jüdel will not otherwise leave the children in quiet, something must be given it to play with. Let a new pipkin be bought, without any abatement of the price demanded; put into it some water from the child's bath, and set it on the stove. In a few days *the Jüdel will have splashed out all the water*. People also hang eggshells, the yolks of which have been blown into the child's pap and the mother's pottage, on the cradle by linen threads, that the Jüdel may play with them instead of with the child. If the cows low in the night, *the Jüdel is playing with them*.[2] But what are the *Winseln*? We are informed that *the dead must be turned with the head towards the east*, else they will be terrified by the Winseln, who wander hither from the west.[3]

Of the several kinds of spirits, which we classify according to the locality and the elements in which they have their abode, the principal are the

---

1    Müller, op. cit., p. 367.
2    Grimm, *Abergl.*, No. 62, 389, 454, from the *Chemnitzer Rockenphilosophie*.
3    Ibid., No. 545.

demons of the water or the *Nixen*.[1] Their form is represented as resembling a human being, only somewhat smaller. According to some traditions, the Nix has slit ears, and is also to be known by his feet, which he does not willingly let be seen. Other traditions give the Nix a human body terminating in a fish's tail, or a complete fish's form. They are clothed like human beings, but the water-wives may be known by the wet hem of their apron, or the wet border of their robe. Naked Nixen, or hung round with moss and sedge, are also mentioned.[2]

Like the dwarfs, the water-sprites have a great love of dancing. Hence they are seen dancing on the waves, or coming on land and joining in the dance of human beings. They are also fond of music and singing. From the depths of a lake sweetly fascinating tones sometimes ascend, oftentimes the Nixen may be heard singing. Extraordinary wisdom is also ascribed to them, which enables them to foretell the future.[3] The water-wives are said to spin. By the rising, sinking, or drying up of the water of certain springs and ponds – caused, no doubt, by the Nix – the inhabitants of the neighbourhood judge whether the seasons will be fruitful or the contrary. Honours paid to the water-spirits in a time of drought are followed by rain,[4]

---

1   The male water-sprite is called *nix*, the female *nixe*. Comp. Ohg. *nichus*, crocodilus; A. S. *nicor*, pl. *niceras*; Sw. *neck*; Dan. *nök*. Hnikärr and Hnikudr are names of Odin.
2   Müller, op. cit., p. 369.
3   That water-sprites have the gift of prophecy has been the belief of many nations. We need only remind the reader of Nereus and Proteus.
4   Gregor. Tur., *De Gloria Confess.*, cap. ii: 'Mons erat in Gabalitano territorio (Gevaudan) cognomento Helanus, lacum habens magnum, ad quem certo tempore multitudo rusticorum, quasi libamina lacui illi exhibens, linteamenta projiciebat, ac pannos, qui ad usum vestimenti virilis praebentur: nonnulli lanae vellera, plurimi etiam formas casei ac cerae vel panis, diversasque species, unusquisque juxta vires suas, quae dinumerare perlongum puto. Veniebant autem cum plaustris potum cibumque deferentes, mactantes animalia et per triduum epulantes. Quarta autem die, cum discedere deberent, anticipabat eos tempestas cum tonitruo et coruscatione valida; et in tantum imber ingens cum lapidum violentia descendebat, ut vix se quisquam eorum putaret evadere. Sic fiebat per singulos annos, et involvebatur insipiens populus in errore.' Without doubt it was believed that the storm was in consequence of the offerings made to the spirit of the lake.

The Keltic spring of Barenton, in the forest of Breziliande, may be here mentioned. If water was poured from the spring on its margin, rain was the consequence. Wace thus speaks of it:

> Aler i solent venéor
> A Berenton par grant chalor,
> Et o lor cors l'ewe puisier,
> Et li perron de suz moillier,
> Por ço soleient pluée aveir.

*Roman de Rou*, ii, p. 143.

as any violation of their sacred domain brings forth storm and tempest.[1]
They also operate beneficially on the increase of cattle. They possess flocks
and herds, which sometimes come on land and mingle with those of men
and render them prolific.[2]

Tradition also informs us that these beings exercise an influence over the
lives and health of human beings. Hence the Nixen come to the aid of
women in labour[3] while the common story, as in the case of the dwarfs,
asserts the complete reverse. The presence of Nixen at weddings brings
prosperity to the bride; and newborn children are said to come out of
ponds and springs; although it is at the same time related that the Nixen
steal children, for which they substitute changelings. There are also
traditions of *renovating springs* (Jungbrunnen), which have the virtue of
restoring the old to youth.[4]

The water-sprites are said to be both covetous and bloodthirsty. This
character is, however, more applicable to the males than to the females,
who are of a gentler nature, and even form connections with human beings,
but which usually prove unfortunate. Male water-sprites carry off young
girls and detain them in their habitations, and assail women with violence.

The water-sprite suffers no one from wantonness forcibly to enter his
dwelling, to examine it, or to diminish its extent. Piles driven in for an
aqueduct he will pull up and scatter; those who wish to measure the depth
of a lake he will threaten; he frequently will not endure fishermen, and
bold swimmers often pay for their temerity with their lives. If a service is
rendered to the water-sprite, he will pay for it no more than he owes;
though he sometimes pays munificently; and for the wares that he buys, he
will bargain and haggle, or pay with old perforated coin. He treats even his
relations with cruelty. Water-maidens, who have stayed too late at a dance,
or other water-sprites, who have intruded on his domain, he will kill
without mercy: a stream of blood that founts up from the water announces
the deed.[5] Many traditions relate that the water-sprite draws persons down

---

Even at the present day, processions are made to the spring, when the chief of the
community dips his foot crosswise into the water. It is then believed that rain will fall
before the procession reaches home. Villemarqué in *Rev. de Paris*, t. 41, pp. 47–58.

1    If stones are thrown into the Mummelsee, the serenest sky becomes troubled and
a storm arises. Grimm, J. & W. , *Deutsche Sagen,* No. 59. The belief is probably Keltish.
Similar traditions are current of other lakes, as of the Lake of Pilatus, of Camarina in
Sicily, etc.

2    See p. 347. Müller, op. cit., p. 371.

3    *Märk., Sagen,* No. 83.

4    Thus the rugged Else, Wolfdietrich's beloved, bathed in such a spring and came
forth the beautiful Sigeminne. Müller, op. cit., p. 373.

5    See p. 582.

with his net, and murders them; that the spirit of a river requires his yearly offering, etc.[1]

To the worship of water-sprites the before-cited passage from Gregory of Tours bears ample witness. The prohibitions, too, of councils against the performance of any heathen rites at springs, and particularly against burning lights at them, have, no doubt, reference to the water-sprites. In later Christian times, some traces have been preserved of offerings made to the demons of the water. Even to the present time, it is a Hessian custom to go on the second day of Easter to a cave on the Meisner,[2] and draw water from the spring that flows from it, when flowers are deposited as an offering.[3] Near Louvain are three springs, to which the people ascribe healing virtues.[4] In the North, it was a usage to cast the remnants of food into waterfalls.[5]

*Rural sprites* cannot have been so prominent in the German religion as water-sprites, as they otherwise would have acted a more conspicuous part in the traditions. The Osnabrück popular belief tells of a *Tremsemutter*, who goes among the corn and is feared by the children. In Brunswick she is called the *Kornweib* (Cornwife). When the children seek for cornflowers, they do not venture too far in the field, and tell one another about the Cornwife who steals little children. In the Altmark and Mark of Brandenburg she is called the Roggenmöhme,[6] and screaming children are silenced by saying: 'Be still, else the Roggenmöhme with her long, black teats will come and drag thee away!' Or, according to other relations, 'with her black iron teats'. By others she is called *Rockenmör*, because like Holda and Berchta she plays all sorts of tricks with those idle girls who have not spun all off from their spinning-wheels (Rocken) by Twelfth day. Children that she has laid on her black bosom easily die. In the Mark they threaten children with the *Erbsenmuhme*,[7] that they may not feast on the peas in the field. In the Netherlands the *Long Woman* is known, who goes through the cornfields and plucks the projecting ears. In the heathen times this rural or field sprite was, no doubt, a friendly being, to whose influence the growth and thriving of the corn were ascribed.[8]

---

1   Müller, p. 373.
2   A chain of hills in Electoral Hesse.
3   The Bavarian custom also of throwing a man wrapped in leaves or rushes into the water on Whit Monday may have originated in a sacrifice to appease the water-sprite.
4   See p. 630.
5   Müller, p. 376.
6   From roggen, *rye*, and muhme, *aunt, cousin*.
7   From *Erbsen*, peas.
8   Müller, op. cit., pp. 378, *sqq.* Grimm, J., *Deutsche Mythologie*, op. cit., p. 445. Adalbert Kuhn, who in the collecting of German popular traditions is indefatigable,

Spirits inhabiting the forests are mentioned in the older authorities, and at the present day people know them under the appellations of *Waldleute* (Forest-folk), *Holzleute* (Wood-folk), *Moosleute* (Moss-folk), *Wilde Leute* (Wild folk).[1] The traditions clearly distinguish the Forest-folk from the Dwarfs, by ascribing to them a larger stature, but have little more to relate concerning them than that they stand in a friendly relation to man, frequently borrow bread and household utensils, for which they make requital,[2] but are now so disgusted with the faithless world that they have retired from it. Such narratives are in close analogy with the dwarf-traditions, and it is, moreover, related of the females, that they are addicted to the ensnaring and stealing of children.[3]

On the Saale they tell of a *Buschgrossmutter* (Bush-grandmother) and her *Moosfräulein* (Moss-damsels). The Busch-grossmutter seems almost a divine being of heathenism, holding sway over the Forest-folk; as offerings were made to her. The Forest-wives readily make their appearance when the people are baking bread, and beg to have a loaf baked for them also, as large as half a millstone, which is to be left at an appointed spot. They afterwards either compensate for the bread, or bring a loaf of their own batch, for the ploughmen, which they leave in the furrow or lay on the plough, and are exceedingly angry if anyone slights it. Sometimes the Forest-wife will come with a broken wheelbarrow, and beg to have the wheel repaired. She will then, like Berchta, pay with the chips that fall, which turn to gold; or to knitters she gives a clew of thread that is never wound off. As often as anyone twists the stem of a sapling, so that the bark is loosed, a Forest-wife must die. A peasant woman, who had given the breast to a screaming forest-child, the mother rewarded with the bark on which the child lay. The woman broke off a piece and threw it in her load of wood: at home she found it was gold.[4]

---

makes us acquainted with another female being, who bears a considerable resemblance to Holda, Berchta and others of that class, and is called the *Murraue*. See more of her on pp. 539–40.

1   The appellation of *Schrat* (p. 245) is also applicable to the Forest-sprites. The Goth. skôhsl (δαιμόνιον) is by Grimm (Grimm, J., *Deutsche Mythologie*, op. cit., p. 455) compared with the O. Nor. Skôgr (forest), who thence concludes that it was originally a forest-sprite. Jornandes speaks of sylvestres homines, quos *faunos ficarios* vocant. 'Agrestes feminas, quas silvaticas vocant.' Burehard of Worms, p. 198d.

2   The wood-wives (Holzweibel) come to the woodcutters and ask for something to eat, and will also take it out of the pots, though they remunerate for what they have taken or borrowed in some other way, frequently with good advice. Sometimes they will help in the labours of the kitchen or the wash, but always express great dread of the Wild Huntsman, who persecutes them. Grimm, J., *Deutsche Mythologie*, op. cit., p. 452.

3   Müller, op. cit., p. 379

4   Grimm, J., *Deutsche Mythologie*, op. cit., p. 452.

Like the dwarfs, the Forest-wives are dissatisfied with the present state of things. In addition to the causes already mentioned, they have some particular reasons. The times, they say, are no longer good since folks count the dumplings in the pot and the loaves in the oven, or since they *piped*[1] the bread, and put cumin into it. Hence their precepts:

> Peel no tree,
> relate no dream,
> *pipe* no bread, or
> bake no cumin in bread,
> so will God help thee in thy need.

A Forest-wife, who had just tasted a new-baked loaf, ran off to the forest screaming aloud:

> They've baken for me cumin-bread,
> that on this house brings great distress!

And the prosperity of the peasant was soon on the wane, so that at length he was reduced to abject poverty.[2]

Little Forest-men, who have long worked in a mill, have been scared away by the miller's men leaving clothes and shoes for them. It would seem that by accepting clothes these beings were fearful of breaking the relation subsisting between them and men. We shall see presently that the domestic sprites act on quite a different principle.[3]

We have still a class of subordinate beings to consider, viz. the domestic sprites or *Goblins* (Kobolde). Numerous as are the traditions concerning these beings, there seems great reason to conclude that the belief in them, in its present form, did not exist in the time of heathenism; but that other ideas must have given occasion to its development. The ancient mythologic system has in fact no place for domestic sprites and goblins. Nevertheless, we believe that by tracing up through popular tradition, we shall discern forms, which at a later period were comprised under the name of Kobolds.[4]

---

1    To *pipe* the bread (das Brot pipen) is to impress the points of the fingers into the loaf, as is usual in most places. Perhaps the Forest-wives could not carry off *piped* bread. From a like cause they were, no doubt, averse to the counting. Whether the seasoning with cumin displeased them merely as being an innovation, or for some hidden cause, we know not, but the rime says:

| Kümmelbrot unser Tod! | Cumin-bread our death! |
| Kümmelbrot macht Angst und Noth! | Cumin-bread makes pain and affliction! |

2    Grimm, J., *Deutsche Mythologie*, op. cit., p. 452.
3    Ibid.
4    Müller, op. cit., p. 381. According to the Swedish popular belief, the domestic sprite had his usual abode in a tree near the house.

The domestic sprites bear a manifest resemblance to the dwarfs. Their figure and clothing are represented as perfectly similar; they evince the same love of occupation, the same kind, though sometimes evil, nature. We have already seen that the dwarfs interest themselves in the prosperity of a family, and in this respect the Kobolds may be partially considered as dwarfs, who, for the sake of taking care of the family, fix their abode in the house. In the Netherlands the dwarfs are called Kaboutermannekens, that is, *Kobolds*.[1]

The domestic sprite is satisfied with a small remuneration, as a hat, a red cloak, and party-coloured coat with tingling bells. Hat and cloak he has in common with the dwarfs.[2]

It may probably have been a belief that the deceased members of a family tarried after death in the house as guardian and succouring spirits, and as such, a veneration might have been paid them like that of the Romans to their *lares*. It has been already shown that in the heathen times the departed were highly honoured and revered, and we shall presently exemplify the belief that the dead cleave to the earthly, and feel solicitous for those they have left behind. Hence the domestic sprite may be compared to a *lar familiaris*, that participates in the fate of its family. It is, moreover, expressly declared in the traditions that domestic sprites are the souls of the dead,[3] and the White Lady who, through her active aid, occupies the place of a female domestic sprite, is regarded as the ancestress of the family, in whose dwelling she appears.[4]

When domestic sprites sometimes appear in the form of snakes, it is in connection with the belief in *genii* or spirits who preserve the life and health of certain individuals. This subject, from the lack of adequate sources, cannot be satisfactorily followed up; though so much is certain, that as, according to the Roman idea, the genius has the form of a snake,[5] so, according to the German belief, this creature was in general the symbol of the soul and of spirits. Hence it is that in the popular traditions much is related of snakes which resembles the traditions of domestic sprites. Under this head we bring the tradition, that in every house there are two snakes, a male and a female, whose life depends on that of the master or mistress of the family. They do not make their appearance until these die, and then die with them. Other traditions tell of snakes that live together

---

1   Müller, p. 382.
2   Grimm, J., *Deutsche Mythologie*, op. cit., p. 479.
3   Kobolds are the souls of persons that have been murdered in the house. Grimm, J. & W. , *Deutsche Sagen*, No. 71. A knife sticks in their back. Ibid. i, p. 224.
4   See p. 435.
5   Servius in Virgil, *Aen.* v, 85. 'Nullus locus sine genio est, qui per anguem plerumque ostenditur.'

with a child, whom they watch in the cradle, eat and drink with it. If the snake is killed, the child declines and dies shortly after. In general, snakes bring luck to the house in which they take up their abode, and milk is placed for them as for the domestic sprites.[1]

We will now give a slight outline of the externals of divine worship among the heathen Germans.

The principal places of worship were, consistently with the general character of the Germans, in the free, open nature. The expression of Tacitus was still applicable – 'lucos ac nemora consecrant'. Groves consecrated to the gods are therefore repeatedly mentioned, and heathen practices in them forbidden.[2] In Lower Saxony, even in the eleventh century, they had to be rooted up, by Bishop Unwan of Bremen, in order totally to extirpate the idolatrous worship.[3] But still more frequently, as places of heathen worship, trees and springs are mentioned, either so that it is forbidden to perform any idolatrous rites at them, or that they are directly stigmatised as objects of heathen veneration.[4] At the same time we are not justified in assuming that a sort of fetish adoration of trees and

1  Müller, op. cit., p. 383.
2  Lucos vetusta religione truces. Claud., *Cons. Stilich.*, i, 289; De sacris silvarum, quae Nimidas vocant. *Indic. Superst.*, 6; Lucorum vel fontium auguria. Bonifac., Ep. 44. ed. Würdtw.; Si quis ad lucos votum fecerit. *Capit. de Part. Saxon.* c. 21. Comp. *Capit. Francof.* a. 794, c. 41; Sylvam Sytheri, quae fuit Thegathon sacra. Pertz Monum., ii, 377. For the name of Thegathon see Grimm, J., *Deutsche Mythologie*, op. cit., p. 65.
3  *Vita Meinwerci*, c. 22; comp. Adam. Brem., c. 86.
4  Claud., *Cons. Stilich.*, i, 290: Robora numinis instar barbarici; Agathias, 28. 4. edit. Bonn., of the Alamanni: δένδρα τε γάρ τινα ἰλάσκονται καὶ ῥεῖθρα οταμῶν καὶ λόφους καὶ φάραλλας, καὶ τούτοις ὧσ ερ ὅσια δρῶντες. Gregor., Tur., ii, c. 10. of the Franks: sibi silvarum atque aquarum, avium, bestiarum et aliorum quoque elementorum finxere formas, ipsasque ut deum colere ejusque sacrificia delibare consueti. Comp. Gregor., M. *Epist.*, 7, 5: ne idolis immolent, nec cultores arborum existant. Rudolf of Fulda (Pertz, ii, 676) of the Saxons: Frondosis arboribus fontibusque venerationem exhibebant. In the *Lives of the Saints* sacred trees are particularly noticed. In the first place the oak dedicated to Jupiter, at Gheismar near Fritzlar, which St Boniface cut down, is to be mentioned: Wilibaldi, *Vita Bonifacii* (Pertz, ii, 313): Arborem quandam mirae magnitudinis, quae prisco paganorum vocabulo appellatur *robur Jovis*, in loco qui dicitur Gaesmere, servis Dei secum astantibus, succidere tentavit. 'Vita S. Amandi' (ob. AD 674), Mabillon, *Act. Bened.*, sec. 2, p. 714: arbores et ligna pro deo colere; and p. 718: ostendit ei locum, in quo praedictum idolum adorare consueverat, scilicet arborem, quae erat daemoni dedicata. Audoëni Rotomag., *Vita Eligii*, II, c. 16: Nullus Christianus ad fana, vel ad petras, vel ad fontes, vel ad arbores, aut ad cellos, vel per trivia luminaria faciat, aut vota reddere praesumat. – nec per fontes aut arbores, vel bivios diabolica phylacteria exerceantur. – fontes vel arbores, quos sacros vocant, succidite. On the *Blood Tree* of the Langobards, 'Vita S. Barbati' (ob. AD 683), *Act.* S.S. 19 Feb. p. 139: Quinetiam non longe a Beneventi moenibus devotissime sacrilegam colebant arborem. Comp. Leges Liutpr. vi, 30: Qui ad arborem, quam rustici

springs existed among them, and that their religious rites were unconnected with the idea of divine or semi-divine beings, to whom they offered
adoration; for the entire character of the testimonies cited in the note
sufficiently proves that through them the externals only of the pagan
worship have been transmitted to us, the *motives* of which the transmitters
either did not or would not know.[1]

As sacred spots, at which offerings to the gods were made, those places
were particularly used where there were trees and springs. The trees were
sacred to the gods, whose festivals were solemnised near or under them, an
instance of which is the oak sacred to Jupiter, which Boniface caused to be
felled. These trees, as we shall presently see, were, at the sacrificial feasts,
used for the purpose of hanging on them either the animals sacrificed or
their hides, whence the Langobardish Blood-Tree derives its name.[2]
Similar was the case with regard to the springs at which offerings were
made; they were also sacred to the god whose worship was there
celebrated, as is confirmed by the circumstance, that certain springs in
Germany were named after gods and were situated near their sanctuaries.[3]

---

sanguinum (*al.* sanctivam, sacrivam) vocant, atque ad fontanas adoraverit. The
prohibitions in the decrees of the councils and the laws usually join trees with springs,
or trees, springs, rocks and crossways together. Conc. Autissiod. a. 586, c. 3: ad
arbores sacrivas vel ad fontes vota exsolvere. Comp. Conc. Turon. ii, a. 566, c. 22;
*Indic. Superst.*, c. 11; Burchard of Worms, *Collect. Decret.*, x, 10 (Conc. Namnet. a. 895,
c. 8): arbores daemonibus consecratae, quas vulgus colit et in tanta veneratione habet,
ut nec ramum vel surculum audeat amputare. lbid., xix, 5 (comp. Grimm, J., *Deutsche
Mythologie*, op. cit., p. xxxvi): Venisti al aliquem locum ad orandum nisi ad ecclesiam,
i.e. vel ad fontes, vel ad lapides, vel ad bivia, et ibi aut candelam aut faculam pro
veneratione loci incendisti, aut panem aut aliquam oblationem illuc detulisti, aut ibi
comedisti? Comp. x, 2, 9. *Capitul. de Part. Sax.*, c. 21: Si quis ad fontes, aut arbores, vel
lucos votum fecerit, aut aliquid more gentilium obtulerit et ad honorem daemonum
comederit *Capit. Aquisgr.*, 1, c. 63: De arboribus, vel petris, vel fontibus, ubi aliqui
stulti luminaria accendunt, vel aliquas observationes faciunt. Comp. *Capit. Francof.*, a.
794, c. 41. *Capit.*, Lib. i, c. 62, vii, 316, 374, *Lex Wisigoth.*, lib. vi, 2, 4. Ecgb. Penit., iv,
19. *Law of North. Priests*, 54; *Leges Cnuti*, Sec. 5; *Can. Eadgari*, 16. Whether all the
passages which refer to Gaul are applicable to German heathenism is not always
certain, as trees and springs were held sacred also by the Kelts.
1    Müller, op. cit., p. 58.
2    If such be the true reading, which is very questionable (see previous note). The
word *blood* has no connection with the verb blôtan, *to sacrifice*.
3    Müller, op. cit., pp. 58–61. Near the grove of the Frisian god Fosite there was a
sacred spring. Comp. *Vita S. Remacli*, c. 12: Warchinnam rivulum accedit (the scene of
the incident was the Ardennes), invenit illic certa indicia loca illa quondam idololatriae
fuisse mancipata. Erant illic lapides Dianae, et id genus portentosis nominibus
inscripti, vel effigies eorum habentes; *fontes* etiam, hominum quidem usibus apti, sed
gentilismi erroribus polluti, atque ob id etiamnum daemonum infestationi obnoxii.

How far these were needful in sacrificial ceremonies, and in what manner they were used, we know not.[1]

But the worship of trees and springs may in reality have consisted in a veneration offered to the spirits who, according to the popular faith, had their dwelling in them; tradition having preserved many tales of beings that inhabited the woods and waters, and many traces of such veneration being still extant, of which we shall speak hereafter. It seems, however, probable that the worship of such spirits, who stood in a subordinate relation to the gods, was not so prominent and glaring that it was deemed necessary to issue such repeated prohibitions against it.[2]

This double explanation applies equally to the third locality at which heathen rites were celebrated – stones and rocks.[3] In stones, according to the popular belief, the dwarfs had their abode; but principally rugged stone altars are thereby understood, such as still exist in many parts of Germany.[4]

We are unable to say with certainty whether the before-mentioned offering-places served at the same time as burying-grounds of the dead, a supposition rendered probable by the number of urns containing ashes, which are often found on spots supposed to have been formerly conse-crated to heathen worship. But the graves of the dead, at all events, seem designated as offering-places.[5] That such offerings at graves were some-times made to the souls of the departed, who after death were venerated as higher and beneficent beings, may be assumed from the numerous prohibitions, by the Christian church, against *offering to saints*, and regarding the dead indiscriminately as holy;[6] although not all the *sacrificia mortuorum* and the heathen observances, which at a later period took place

---

1   Müller, op. cit., p. 61.

2   Ibid. p. 62.

3   See p. 185, note 4. Comp. *Indic. Superst.* c. 7. Conc. Namnet. c. 20: lapides, quos in ruinosis locis et silvestribus daemonum ludificationibus decepti venerantur, ubi et vota vovent et deferunt. Eccard, *Fran. Orient.*, i, p. 415.

4   Müller, op. cit., p. 62.

5   Burchard 19, 5: Comedisti aliquid de idolothito, i.e. de oblationibus quae in quibusdam locis *ad sepulchra* mortuorum fiunt, sel ad fontes, aut ad arbores, aut ad lapides, aut ad bivia.

6   *Indic. Superst.*, c. 9: De sacrificio quad fit alicui sanctorum; c. 25: De eo quod sibi sanctos fingunt quoslibet mortuos. Conc. Germ., a. 742. can. 5 (comp. *Capitul.*, vii, 128): ut populus Dei paganias non faciat, sed omnes spurcities gentilitatis abjiciat et respuat, sive profana sacrificia mortuorum, sive hostias immolatitias, quas stulti homines juxta ecclesias ritu pagano faciunt, sub nomine sanctorum martyrum vel confessorum.

at burials,[1] may have had reference to the dead, but may also have had the gods for object. Hence we may safely conclude that all the heathen rites, which were performed at springs, stones and other places, had a threefold reference: their object being either the gods, the subordinate elementary spirits, or the dead; but in no wise were lifeless objects of nature held in veneration by our forefathers for their own sakes alone.[2]

It now remains for consideration whether the gods were worshipped only in such places in the open air, or whether temples were erected to them. In answer to this question, we shall limit ourselves to a few general observations.[3]

In general it appears that temples, even at the period of the conversion, were, as in the time of Tacitus, but few. In the interior of Germany it is probable that none existed for, had the case been otherwise, we should hardly have been without some notice of a temple among the Saxons.[4] There is, however, little doubt that the Frisians had temples; for the words of the *Lex Frisionum*: 'Qui templum effregerit . . . immoletur diis, quorum templa violavit',[5] precludes all doubt on the subject. But with respect to the temples, of which mention is made, either on the Rhine or in Gaul (where the greater number occur), it is doubtful whether they are not rather to be considered as Keltic, which the invading Franks and

1   *Indic. Superst.*, cc. 1, 2. Burchard, 10, 34. Bonifac., Ep. 44: sacrificia mortuorum respuentes. Ep. 82: sacrilegis presbyteris, qui tauros et hircos diis paganorum immolabant, manducantes sacrificia mortuorum. *Capit.*, vi, 197: Admoneantur fideles ut ad suos mortuos non agant ea quae de paganorum ritu remanserunt. Et quando eos ad sepulturam portaverint, illum ululatum excelsum non faciant . . . et super eorum tumulos nec manducare nec bibere praesumant. Towards the middle of the ninth century the Roman synod under Leo IV forbade to the Saxons the *carmina diabolica*, quae nocturnis horis super mortuos vulgus facere solet. Comp. Wackernagel, *Das Wessobrunner Gebet*, p. 25.

2   Müller, op. cit., p. 63.

3   Grimm has collected and discussed all the authorities which make mention of temples among the German tribes. See Grimm, J., *Deutsche Mythologie*, op. cit., pp. 70–7. Muller, op. cit., p. 65.

4   The passage of the *Capitulary de Part. Saxon.*, i: 'ut ecclesiae Christi non minorem habeant honorem, sed majorem et excellentiorem quam fana (ap. Pertz vana) habuissent idolorum,' is rejected by Schaumann, *Gesch. des Niedersächs. Volks*, p. 133. Comp. Beda's account of the destruction of the Anglian temple at Godmundham in Yorkshire (*c.* AD 627), also in Lappenberg's *England*, i, pp. 151–3.

5   *Lex Frisimlum Addit. Sap.*, xii. According to the 'Vita S. Liudgeri', i, 8, treasures were kept in the Frisian temples. Comp. also '*fana* in morem gentilium circumquaque erecta' in the 'Vita S. Willehadi' (ob. AD 789) ap. Pertz, ii, 381, and the *fana* of Fosite in 'Vita S. Willebrordi' (ob. AD 739) in *Act. Bened.*, sec. 3, p. 609; Altfridi Vita S. Liudgeri ap. Pertz, ii, 410.

Burgundians appropriated to themselves; as heathenism is inclined to dedicate to its own worship places regarded by others as holy. With respect to other places, the accounts supplied by the authorities are so vague, that it cannot be pronounced with certainty whether the question is of a temple or a grove, as the 'fanum arboribus consitum', which mentioned among the Langobardi,[1] can certainly have been only a grove. The fourth chapter of the Indiculus, 'De casulis, i.e. fanis', may refer to small buildings, in which probably sacrificial utensils or sacred symbols were kept.[2]

The paucity of temples among the Germans implies also a paucity of idols among them; for the heathen temple did not, like a Christian church, serve for the reception of a holy day congregation, but was originally a mere shelter or house for the image of the god. Certainly we are not justified in totally denying the presence of images; as it is expressly stated that the Gothic king Athanric (ob. AD 382) caused a carved image to be carried about,[3] which, like Nerthus, was everywhere received with prayers and offerings. Nor are we, at the same time, justified in assuming the fact of their existence among all the German nations; and although in the authorities *idola* and *simulacra* are repeatedly mentioned, and great zeal is manifested against the folly of the heathen, in expecting aid from images of gold, silver, stone and wood; yet are these only general forms of speech directed against idolatry, and applying rather to Roman than German heathenism.[4] We have in fact no genuine or trustworthy testimony that clearly describes to us an idol in Germany proper. In no life of a saint is it related that a converter destroyed such an idol. On the contrary, all the passages, which here enter into consideration, point either to a blending of foreign worship, or, on closer examination, there is no question in them of an idol, or they are of doubtful character.[5]

The three brazen and gilt images, which St Gall found and destroyed at Bregenz on the Lake of Constance, built into the wall of a church dedicated to St Aurelia, and venerated by the people as gods, were no doubt of

1 'Vita S. Bertulfi Bobbiensis' (ob. AD 640), in *Act. Bened*. sec 2, p. 164.
2 Müller, op. cit., p. 65
3 ξόανον ἐφ' ἁρμαμάξης ἑστώς. Sozomen., *Hist. Eccles*., vi, 37.
4 Similar forms of speech are numerous: e.g. Gregor., Tur. *Hist. Franc*., ii, 29. Willibald, *Vita Bonifac*., ii, 339, ap. Pertz., *Vita Willehadi*, ibid., ii, 380. Bonifac., Ep. 6; *Vita Lebuini*, ibid. ii, 362. 'Vita S. Kiliani' in *Act. Bened*., sec. 2. p. 992. *Idola* was the usual denomination of the heathen gods. The passages, however, in the 'Vita Bonifacii' and 'Vita Willehadi', which refer to the Frisians, may appear convincing, as they had temples also.
5 Müller, op. cit., p. 65.

Roman origin,[1] like those stone images which St Columban (ob. AD 615) met with at Luxeuil in Franche Comté.[2] The statue of Diana at Treves, and the images of Mars and Mercury in the south of Gaul, of which Gregory of Tours makes mention,[3] are likewise rather Roman or Keltic than German. Not even the noted and in other respects remarkable passage of Widukind (ob. AD 615), according to which the Saxons, after their victory over the Thuringians on the Unstrut, raised an altar and worshipped a god 'nomine Martem, *effigie columnarum* imitantes Herculem, loco Solem, quem Graeci appellant Apollinem,' appears to us unquestionably to indicate a true idol. We can infer from the words of Widukind nothing more than the erection of a column similar to the Irmenseule at Eresburg, which Charles the Great destroyed. In the passages which relate to this latter[4] it is called sometimes *idolum*, sometimes *fanum*, sometimes *lucus*; but the word itself shows that Rudolf of Fulda was right in defining it 'truncum ligni non parvae magnitudinis in altum erectum', nor is his expression for it of 'universalis columna' an unfitting one.[5]

The history of the development of Greek and Roman image worship may aid us to a clearer insight into our native heathenism. The Greek representation of a god had not from the commencement the pretension of being a likeness of the god, but was only a symbol of his presence, for a sense of which the piety of ancient times required the less of externals the more deeply it was impressed with the belief of that presence.[6] An external sign of the divinity was, nevertheless, necessary for the sake of having an object on which pious veneration of the gods might manifest itself. As, therefore, both in Hellas and Italy, the antique representations of the gods, as lances, etc., were mere symbols, in like manner we may regard the swords of the Quadi and the golden snakes of the Lango bardi only as consecrated signs announcing the presence of the god. The representations of the gods next developed themselves, among the Greeks, under the form of rough stones, stone pillars and wooden poles, which were set up and regarded as images of the gods. Raised-up poles or beams were, no doubt, also among the Germans the prevailing and still symbolic species of images. The Irmenseule

---

1   Walafrid. Strab., 'Vita S. Galli', in *Act. Bened.* sec. 2, p. 233. Comp. 'Vita S. Galli' ap. Pertz, ii, 7; Ratperti Casus S. Galli, ap. Pertz, ii, 61.

2   Jonae Bobbiensis, 'Vita S. Columbani', c. 17, in *Act. Bened.*, sec. 2, pp. 12, 13.

3   *Hist. Franc.*, viii, 15. Mirac., 2, 5: grande delubrum, ubi in columna altissima simulacrum Martis Mercuriique colebatur.

4   See the passages relating to the Irmenseule in *Meibom. de Irminsula Saxonica*, in *Rer. Germ. Scriptt.*, iii, pp. 2, *sq.* Grimm, J., *Deutsche Mythologie*, op. cit., pp. 105, *sq.* Comp. also Ideler's *Einhard*, i, 156, *sq.*

5   Müller, op. cit., p. 67. Rudolf. Fuld. Transl. S. Alexandri, ap. Pertz, ii, 676.

6   O. Müller, *Handbuch der Archaeologie der Kunst*, § 66.

was such a pole: to such an image, if so it can be called, to a simple up-raised pillar, does the before-quoted passage of Widukind allude.[1]

That prayers to the gods were frequently composed in a metrical form, that religious songs and poems existed, is evident from the circumstance that the Langobardi offered to one of their gods the head of a goat, with certain ceremonies and accompanied by a song.[2] The passage which gives this account affords ground for the supposition that certain saltations took place at the sacrifices. And why should there not be religious songs at this period, when, at a still earlier, songs in honour of Hercules were sung before a battle, when Tacitus makes mention of old mytho-epic songs in which the traditions of the German people were recorded? The oldest poetry of a nation generally attaches itself closely to religion, and the numerous forms of adjurations and spells, which through tradition we have inherited from heathenism, are for the most part composed in a rhythmical garb. It may, therefore, be reasonably supposed that the popular songs were, in the first Christian centuries, so bitterly decried by the clergy because they contained many remains of heathenism, and, consequently, seemed perilous to Christianity. The stigmatising of the popular songs as *carmina diabolica*, the predicates *turpia*, *inepta*, *obscoena* applied to them give to this supposition additional strength; and the Capitularies explicitly forbid dances and songs as relics of heathenism.[3] At funerals also heathen religious songs were sung.[4]

With prayer, sacrifice, which formed the chief part of heathen worship, was inseparably connected. In general there was prayer only at the sacrifices. The principal sacrifice was a human one, the offering of which by all the Germanic races is fully proved.[5] Human beings appear chiefly to

---

1 Müller, op. cit., p. 70.

2 Gregor., *M. Dialog.*, iii, 28: Caput caprae ei (diabolo) per circuitum currentes, carmine nefando dedicantes. In the grove of sacrifice by Upsala naeniae *inhonestae* resounded. *Ad. Brem.*, p. 144, edit. Lindenbrog.

3 Capit., vi, c. 196: Illas vero balationes et saltationes, cantica turpia et luxuriosa, et illa lusa diabolica non faciat, nec in plateis nec in domibus neque in ullo loco, quia haec de paganorum consuetudine remanserunt. *Vita S. Eligii*, ii, 16: Nullas saltationes, aut choraulas, aut cantica diabolica exerceat. For the prohibitions of the ancient popular songs, the reader is referred to the collections of extracts on the subject, as Wackernagel, *Das Wessobrunner Gebet*, pp. 25–9; Hofinann, *Geschichte des Deutschen Kirchenliedes*, pp. 8-11; Massmann, *Abschwörungsformeln*.

4 Müller, op. cit., p. 74.

5 For human sacrifices among the Goths, see Jornandes, c. 5; Isidori, *Chron. Goth aera 446*; among the Heruli, Procop. *de Bello Goth.*, ii, 14; among the already converted Franks, ibid., ii, 25; the Saxons, *Sidon. Apoll.*, 8, 6, *Capit. de Part. Sax.*, 9; the Frisians, *Lex Fris. Addit. Sap.*, Tit. 12; Thuringians, *Bonifac.*, Ep. 25. Comp. Grimm, J., *Deutsche Mythologie*, op. cit., p. 39.

have served for sacrifices of atonement, and were either offered to the malign deities, or, as propitiatory, to the dead in the nether world.[1] The custom of burning the servants and horses with the corpse, must, therefore, be understood as a propitiatory sacrifice to the shade of the departed.[2]

The testimonies just cited on the subject of human sacrifices inform us at the same time that prisoners of war – as in the time of Tacitus – purchased slaves or criminals were especially chosen for sacrifice.[3] When a criminal was sacrificed, his death was at the same time the penalty of his misdeeds. He was offered to the god whom, it was believed, he had particularly offended, and his execution, decreed by the law, was reserved for the festival of that divinity. This usage, which gives an insight into the intimate connection between law and religion, and shows the punishment of death among the Germans in a peculiar light, is particularly conspicuous among the Frisians. This people put criminals chosen for sacrifice to death in various ways; they were either decapitated with a sword, or hanged on a gallows, or strangled, or drowned.[4] A more cruel punishment awaited those who had broken into and robbed the temple of a god.[5]

Of animals used for sacrifice, horses, oxen and goats are especially mentioned. The horse-sacrifice was the most considerable, and is particularly characteristic of the Germanic races. The heads were by preference offered to the gods, and were fixed or hung on trees. The hides also of the sacrificed animals were suspended on sacred trees. In the North the flesh

---

1   The great sacrifice at Lethra, described by Dietmar of Merseburg, i, 9 at which ninety-nine men, and a like number of horses, dogs and cocks were offered, was evidently a sacrifice of propitiation.
2   Müller, op. cit., p. 76. Tacitus (*Germ.*, 27) testifies only to the burning of the horse. In the North servants and hawks were burnt with the corpse. In the grave of King Childeric a human skull was found, which was supposed to have been that of his marshal. The wives of the Heruli hanged themselves at the graves of their husbands. Procop., *B.G.*, ii, 14. Among the Gauls also it was customary to burn the slaves and clients with the corpse of a man of high rank. Caesar, *B.G.*, iv, 19.
3   According to the 'Vita S. Wulframmi' (ob. AD 720) in *Act. Bened.*, sec. 3, pp. 359, 361, the individuals to be sacrificed were sometimes chosen by lot. The accounts given in this Life seem rather fabulous, but are, nevertheless, not to be rejected. S. Willibrord and his companions, when they had desecrated the sanctuary of Fosite, were subjected to the lot, and the one on whom the lot fell was executed. Alcuini, *Vita S. Willibr.*, c. 10. Among the Slavs also human sacrifices were determined by lot. Jahrb., *für Slaw. Lit.*, 1843, p. 392.
4   *Vita S. Wulframmi*, p. 360.
5   Müller, op. cit., p. 77. *Lex Frisionum, Addit. Sap.,* Tit. 12. Qui fanum effregerit et ibi aliquid de sacris tulerit, ducitur ad mare, et in sabulo, quod accessus maris operire solet, finduntur aures ejus, et castratur, et immolatur diis, quorum templa violavit.

of the sacrifices was boiled, and the doorposts of the temple were smeared with their blood.[1]

The Indiculus (cap. 26) leads to the supposition of a particular kind of offering. The *Simulacrum de consparsa farina* there mentioned appears to be the baked image of a sacrificial animal, which was offered to the gods in the stead of a real one. Similar usages are known to us among the Greeks and Romans, and in Sweden, even in recent times, it was a custom on Christmas Eve to bake cakes in the form of a hog.[2]

It was extremely difficult to prevent a relapse into heathenism, seeing that to retain a converted community in the true faith, well-instructed ecclesiastics were indispensable, and these were few in number, the clergy being but too frequently persons of profane and ungodly life. In many cases it was doubtful whether they had even received ordination.[3] Instances might therefore occur like that recorded in the *Life of St Gall*, that in an oratory dedicated to St Aurelia idols were afterwards worshipped with offerings; and we have seen that the Franks, *after their conversion*, in an irruption into Italy, still sacrificed human victims. Even when the missionaries believed their work sure, the return of the season, in which the joyous heathen festivals occurred, might in a moment call to remembrance the scarcely repressed idolatry; an interesting instance of which, from the twelfth century, we shall see presently. The priests, whose duty it was to retain the people in their Christianity, permitted themselves to sacrifice to the heathen gods, if, at the same time, they could perform the rite of baptism.[4] They were addicted to magic and soothsaying,[5] and were so infatuated with heathenism that they erected crosses on hills, and with great approbation of the people, celebrated Christian worship on heathen offering-places.[6]

---

1   Müller, op. cit., p. 79.

2   Müller, op. cit., p. 80. See pp. 263–4.

3   *Bonifac.*, Ep. 38, 46.

4   *Bonifac.*, Ep. 25: Qui a presbytero Jovi mactante et immolatitias carnes vescente baptizati sunt. Comp. Ep. 82 and Capitul. vii, 405.

5   *Statut. Bonifac.*, 33, p. 142, ed. Würdtw.: Si quis presbyter aut clericus auguria, vel divinationes, aut somnia, sive sortes, seu phylacteria, id est, scripturas, observaverit.

6   Müller, op. cit., p. 103. *Bonifac.*, Ep. 87: Pseudosacerdotes, qui sine episcopo, proprio arbitrio viventes, populares defensores habentes contra episcopos, ut sceleratos mores eorum non confringant, seorsum populum consentaneum congregant, et illud erroneum ministerium non in ecclesia catholica, sed per agrestia loca, per colles rusticorum, ubi eorum imperita stultitia celari episcopos possit, perpetrant, nec fidem catholicam paganis praedicant, nec ipsi fidem rectam habent. Of the Frankish priest Adalbert it is said, that he seduced the people, ita ut cruces statuens in campis et oratoriola, illuc faciat populum concurrere, publicasque ecclesias relinquere. Comp. Ep., 59, 67.

But the clergy were under the necessity of suffering much heathenism to remain, if they would not totally disturb and subvert the social order of life. Heathen institutions of a political nature might no more be attacked than others, which a significant and beneficial custom had made venerable and inviolable. The heathen usages connected with legal transactions must for the most part remain, if the clergy would not also subvert the law itself, or supplant it by the Roman code, according to which they themselves lived. Hence the place and time of the judicial assemblies remained unchanged in their connection with the heathen offering-places and festivals;[1] although the offerings which had formerly been associated with these meetings had altogether ceased. In like manner the old heathen ordeals maintained their ground, though in a Christian guise. Offenders must be punished, and the clergy patiently saw heathen practices accompanying the punishment, because the culprit was an unworthy Christian.[2] In matters of warfare and the heathenism still practised in the field, the clergy were equally powerless. Hence the *Christian* Franks, as we have already seen, when they invaded Italy, sacrificed men, while such cruelty in ordinary life had long been abolished among them. Thus did much heathenism find its way back during the first Christian age, or maintained its ground still longer, because it was sanctioned by law and usage. Where the converters in their blind zeal would make inroads into the social relations, the admission of Christianity met with many hindrances. The teaching of St Kilian had found great favour with the Frankish duke Gozbert, but when he censured that prince for having espoused a relation, he paid for his presumption with his life. Among the Saxons Christianity encountered such strong opposition, because with its adoption was connected the loss of their old national constitution.[3]

As the missionaries thus found themselves obliged to proceed with caution, and were unable to extirpate heathenism at one effort, they frequently accommodated themselves so far to the heathen ideas as to seek to give them a Christian turn. Many instances of such accommodations can be adduced. On places, for instance, regarded by the heathen as

---

1   Grimm, *Deutsche Rechtsalterthümer*, pp. 793, 822.
2   E.g. When criminals were hanged with wolves or dogs, which at a later period was regarded as particularly ignominious. Grimm, *Deutsche Rechtsalterthümer*, p. 685. Criminals were buried in crossways, the old heathen offering-places, and the gallows stood at the intersection. Ibid., pp. 720, 683. In general, certain customs at executions, as dragging the criminal on a cowhide, are probably regarded as the more ignominious, because they were originally heathen.
3   Müller, op. cit., p. 104.

sacred, Christian churches were constructed,[1] or, at least crosses there erected,[2] that they might no longer be used for heathen worship, and that the people might the more easily accustom themselves to regard them as holy in a Christian sense. The wood of the oak felled by Boniface was made into a pulpit, and of the gold of the Langobardish snake altar-vessels were fabricated. Christian festivals were purposely appointed on days which had been kept as holy days by the heathens; or heathenish festivals, with the retention of some of their usages, were converted into Christian ones.[3] If, on the one side, through such compromises, entrance was gained for Christianity, so on the other they hindered the rapid and complete extirpation of heathenism, and occasioned a mixture of heathenish ideas and usages with Christian ones.[4]

To these circumstances it may be ascribed that heathenism was never completely extirpated, that not only in the first centuries after the conversion, an extraordinary blending of heathenism and Christianity existed, but that even at the present day many traces of heathen notions and usages are to be found among the common people. As late as the twelfth century, the clergy in Germany were still occupied in eradicating the remains of heathenism.[5]

The missionaries saw in the heathen idols and in the adoration paid to them only a delusion of the devil, who, under their form, had seduced men to his worship, and even believed that the images of the gods and the

---

1   'Vita S. Agili Resbac.', in *Act. Bened.*, sec. 2, p. 317; 'Vita S. Amandi', ibid. p. 715; 'Vita Luidgeri' ap. Pertz, ii, p. 410; Gregor., *M. Ep. ad Mellitum* (Beda, *H.E.*, i, 30): 'Dicite ei (Augustino) quid diu mecum de causa Anglorum cogitans tractavi: videlicet, quia fana idolorum destrui in eadem gente minime debeant; sed ea quae in ipsis sunt idola destruantur; aqua benedicta fiat, in eisdem fanis aspergatur, altaria construantur reliquiae ponantur; quia si fana eadem bene constructa sunt, necesse est ut a cultu daemonum in obsequium veri Dei debeant commutari, ut, dum gens ipsa eadem fana sua non videt destrui, de corde errorem deponat, et Deum verum cognoscens et adorans, ad loca quae consuevit familiarius concurrat.'

2   Mone, *Gesch. des Heidenthums*, ii, 52. Schreiber, *die Feen in Europa*, p. 18.

3   In the letter just cited of Gregory it is further said: 'Et quia boves solent in sacrificio daemonum multos occidere, debet eis etiam in hac re aliqua sollemnitas immutari; ut die dedicationis, vel natalitiis sanctorum martyrum, quorum illic reliquae ponuntur, tabernacula sibi circa easdem ecclesias, quae ex fanis commutatae sunt, de ramis arborum faciant, et religiosis conviviis sollemnitatem celebrent; nec diabolo jam animalia immolent, sed ad laudem Dei in esu suo animalia occidant, et Donatori omnium de satietate sua gratias referant; ut dum eis aliqua exterius gaudia reservantur, ad interiora gaudia consentire facilius valeant. Nam duris mentibus simul omnia abscidere impossibile esse non dubium est; quia et is, qui summum locum ascendere nititur, gradibus vel passibus, non autem saltibus elevatur.'

4   Müller, op. cit., p. 106.

5   Ibid. p. 108.

sacred trees were possessed by the evil one. Thus they did not regard the heathen deities as so many perfect nonentities, but ascribed to them a real existence, and, to a certain degree, stood themselves in awe of them. Hence their religion was represented to the heathens as a work of the devil, and the new converts were, in the first place, required to renounce him and his service. In this manner the idea naturally impressed itself on the minds of the people that these gods were only so many devils; and if any person, in the first period of Christianity, was brought to doubt the omnipotence of the God of the Christians, and relapsed into idolatry, the majority regarded such apostasy as a submission to the devil. Hence the numerous stories of compacts with the evil one, at which the individual, who so devoted himself, must abjure his belief in God, Christ, and the Virgin Mary, precisely as the newly converted Christian renounced the devil. That the devil in such stories frequently stood in the place of a heathen god is evident from the circumstance, that offerings must be made to him in crossways, those ancient places of sacrifice.[1]

But heathenism itself entertained the belief in certain beings hostile alike to gods and men, and at the same time possessed of extraordinary powers, on account of which their aid frequently appeared desirable. We shall presently see how in the popular Tales the devil is often made to act the part which more genuine traditions assign to the giant race, and how he not infrequently occupies the place of kind, beneficent spirits.[2]

Let it not excite surprise that, in the popular stories and popular belief, Christ and the saints are frequently set in the place of old mythologic beings.[3] Many a tradition, which in one place is related of a giant or the devil, is in another told of Christ, or Mary, or of some saint. As formerly the *minne* (memory, remembrance, love) of the gods was drunk,[4] so now a cup was emptied to the memory or love of Christ and the saints, as St John's *minne*, Gertrud's *minne*. And, as of old, in conjurations and various forms of spells, the heathen deities were invoked, so, after the conversion, Christ and the saints were called on. Several religious usages which were continued became in the popular creed attached to a feast-day or to a

---

1    Müller, op. cit., p. 109. Hence the expressions 'diabolo sacrificare', 'diaboli in amorem vinum bibere.' A black hen was offered to the devil. See vol. iii, p. 256. Harrys, i, No. 55. Temme, Sagen Pommerns, No. 233.
2    Müller, op. cit., p. 110.
3    For instances see vol. iii, pp 545–6, 557, 559, 563–8.
4    Goth. man (*pl.* munum, *pret.* munda), *I think, remember*, whence Ohg. minna = minia, *amor*; miniôn = miniôn, *amare, to remember the beloved*. In O. Nor. there is man, munum, and also minni, *memoria*, minna, *recordari*. Grimm, J., *Deutsche Mythologie*, op. cit., p. 52, which see for further details.

Christian saint, although they had formerly applied to a heathen divinity.[1] In like manner, old heathen myths passed over to Christian saints,[2] some of which even in their later form sound heathenish enough, as that the soul, on the first night of its separation, comes to St Gertrud. That in the period immediately following the conversion, the heathen worship of the dead was mingled with the Christian adoration of saints, we have already seen from the foregoing; and the manner in which Clovis venerated St Martin, shows that he regarded him more as a heathen god than as a Christian saint. It will excite little or no surprise that the scarcely converted king of the Franks sent to the tomb of the saint, as to an oracle, to learn the issue of a war he had commenced against the Visigoths,[3] as similar transmutations of heathen soothsaying and drawing of lots into apparently Christian ceremonies are to be found elsewhere.[4]

We will now add two instances, one of which will show how an individual mentioned in the New Testament has so passed into popular tradition as to completely occupy the place of a heathen goddess, while the other will make it evident how heathen forms of worship can, through various modifications, gradually assume a Christian character.

Herodias is by Burchard of Worms[5] compared with Diana. The women believed that they made long journeys with her, on various animals, during the hours of the night, obeyed her as a mistress, and on certain nights were summoned to her service. According to Ratherius, bishop of Verona (ob. AD 974), it was believed that a third part of the world was delivered into her subjection.[6] The author of Reinardus informs us that she loved John the Baptist, but that her father, who disapproved of her love, caused the saint

---

1 Instances are the fires kindled on St John's day and the usages on St Martin's day. See pp. 528 and 530.

2 A striking instance of this is the second Merseburg poem with its several variants. See pp. 27n, *sq.*

3 Gregor., Tur., ii, 37.

4 Müller, op.cit., p. 110. Conc. Autissiod. a. 578, c. 3. 'Non licet ad sortilegos vel ad auguria respicere; nec ad *sortes,* quas *sanctorum* vocant, vel quas de ligno aut de pane faciunt, adspicere.' According to the *Lex Frisionum,* Tit. 14, two little staves, one of which was marked with a cross, were laid on the altar or on a relic. A priest or an innocent boy took up one of them with prayer.

5 10, 1. (from the Conc. Ancyran. a. 314): 'Illud etiam non omittendum, quod quaedam sceleratae mulieres, retro post Satanam conversae, daemonum illusionibus et phantasmatibus seductae, credunt se et profitentur nocturnis horis cum *Diana,* paganorum dea, vel cum *Herodiade* et innumera multitudine mulierum equitare super quasdam bestias, et multa terrarum spatia intempestae noctis silentio pertransire, ejusque jussionibus velut dominae obedire, et certis noctibus ad ejus servitium evocari.'

6 *Opera,* edit. Balierini, p. 20. Grimm, J., *Deutsche Mythologie,* op. cit., p. 260.

to be beheaded. The afflicted maiden had his head brought to her, but as she was covering it with tears and kisses, it raised itself in the air and blew the damsel back, so that from that time she hovers in the air. Only in the silent hours of night until cockcrowing has she rest, and sits then on oaks and hazels. Her sole consolation is, that, under the name of *Pharaildis*, a third part of the world is in subjection to her.[1]

That heathen religious usages gradually gave rise to Christian superstitions will appear from the following. It was a custom in the paganism both of Rome and Germany to carry the image or symbol of a divinity round the fields, in order to render them fertile. At a later period the image of a saint or his symbol was borne about with the same object.[2] Thus in the Albthal, according to popular belief, the carrying about of St Magnus' staff drove away the field mice. In the Freiburg territory the same staff was employed to extirpate the caterpillars.[3]

Of all the divinities, of whom mention has been already made, Wodan alone appears to have survived in the north of Germany. From the following customs it will appear that he was regarded as a god, in whose hand rested the thriving of the fruits of the field.

In Mecklenburg it was formerly a custom at the rye-harvest to leave at the end of every field a little strip of grain unmowed; this with the ears the reapers plaited together and sprinkled it. They then walked round the bunch, took of their hats, raised their scythes, and called on Wodan thrice in the following verses:

1           Lenit honor luctum, minuit *reverentia* poenam,
                *Pars hominum moestae tertia servit heroe.*
            *Quercubus et corylis a noctis parte secunda*
                *Usque nigri ad galli carmina prima sedet.*
            Nunc ea nomen habet *Pharaildis*, *Herodias* ante
                Saltria, nec subiens nec subeunda pari.

Reinardus, i, 1159–64. Müller, op. cit., p. 112; Grimm, J., *Deutsche Mythologie*, op. cit., p. 262.
2    Eccard, *Franc. Orient.*, i, p. 437
3    Müller, op. cit., p. 113. *Act. Sanct.*, ii, p. 774. 'In agrum Friburg, quod est in Brisgoia circumjectum, aliquot annis adeo copiosa saeviterque grassata erant insecta, ut vix jam herbae quid excresceret, sed omnia veluti nimiis solibus torrida ruberent. Motus diuturno hoc malo urbis ejus magistratus enixe petiit, ut adversus diros vermes afferretur sacra *cambatta*. Quae ubi allata est a quodam S. Magni coenobita, *eaque campi prataque illa lustrata*, eodem adhuc anno, qui seculi hujus fuit xi (1711), tellus laeto herbarum vigore convestiri; vermes pars migrare alio, pars emori. Ut tanti beneficii perennaret memoria, decreverere Friburgenses posthac natalem S. Magni habere sacrum et festum.' Comp. Schreiber's *Taschenbuch für Geschichte und Alterthum in Süddeutschland*, 1839, p. 329.

| | |
|---|---|
| *Wode*, hale *dynem rosse* nu voder, | *Wode, fetch now fodder for* |
| | *thy horse,* |
| nu distel unde dorn, | *now thistles and thorn,* |
| thom andren jahr beter korn! | *for another year better corn!* |

The corn thus left standing for the horse of the god was a simple offering to the bestower of the harvest. At the mansions of the nobility and gentry, it was a custom, when the rye was cut, to give *Wodel-beer*. On a *Wednesday* people avoided all work in flax or sowing linseed, lest the horse of the god, who with his dogs was often heard in the fields, might tread it down.[1]

With these customs a custom of the Mark may be compared. In the neighbourhood of the former monastery of Diesdorf, during the whole rye-harvest, a bundle of ears is left standing in every field, which is called the *Vergo-dendeel's Struus*. When all is mowed, the people, in holiday attire, proceed to the field with music, and bind this bundle round with a variegated riband, then leap over it and dance round it. Lastly the principal reaper cuts it with his scythe and throws it to the other sheaves. In like manner they go from field to field, and finally return to the village singing: 'Nun danket alle Gott', and then from farm to farm, at each of which some harvest lines are repeated. The name of this harvest festival is *Vergodendeel*, which is said to signify *remuneration for the hard harvest-work*, and is to be met with also in some of the neighbouring villages. From among the several harvest-verses we select the following:

| | |
|---|---|
| Ich sage einen ärndtekranz, | *I saw a harvest-garland,* |
| es ist aber ein Vergutentheils kranz. | *but it is a Vergutentheil's garland.* |
| Dieser kranz ist nicht von disteln und dornen, | *This garland is not of thistles and thorns,* |
| sondern von reinem auserlese-nem winterkorne, | *but from clean, selected winter-corn,* |
| es sind auch viele ähren darin; | *there are also many ears therein;* |
| so mannich ahr, | *so many ears* |
| so mannich gut jahr, | *so many good years,* |
| so mannich körn | *so many corns,* |
| so mannich wispeln auf den wirth seinen börn (boden)[3] | *so many wispels[2] for the master's granary.* |

---

1  Müller, op. cit., p. 115.
2  A wispel = 24 bushels.
3  Müller, op. cit., p. 116. Kuhn, *Märk. Sagen*, p. vi, and p. 339.

As the resemblance between this custom and the Mecklenburg one is obvious, the 'Vergodendeels struus' may without hesitation be explained by *Fro Goden deels struus*, i.e. the *strauss* or wisp, which Fro (Lord) Wodan gets for his share.[1] Hence a similar harvest custom in Lower Saxony, at which *Fru Gaue* is invoked, may likewise refer to Wodan. When the reapers mow the rye, they leave some straws standing, twine flowers among them, and, after the completion of their labour, assemble round the wisp thus left standing, take hold of the ears and cry:

| | |
|---|---|
| *Fru Gaue*, haltet ju fauer, | *Fru Gaue, hold your fodder,* |
| düt jar up den wagen, | *this year on the wagon,* |
| dat andar jar up der kare. | *the next year on the cart.* |

It will excite but little surprise that in the uncertainty of later popular tradition this appellation[2] has afterwards been attributed to a female divinity.

The names of the other gods have passed out of the memory of the people. Of the worship of Donar (Thor) there is, perhaps, still a faint trace in the custom, that in Mecklenburg the country people formerly thought it wrong to perform certain work on a *Thursday*, as hopping, etc.[3]

Of the goddesses, Wodan's wife, Frigg, was, till comparatively recent times, still living in the popular traditions of Lower Saxony, under the name of *Fru Frecke*,[4] but now seems defunct. In the neighbourhood of Dent in Yorkshire the country people, at certain seasons, particularly in autumn, have a procession, and perform old dances, one of which they call the giants' dance. The principal giant they call *Woden*, and his wife *Frigga*. The chief feature of the spectacle is, that two swords are swung round the neck of a boy and struck together without hurting him.[5]

But in the popular traditions of the Germans the memory still lives of several female divinities, who do not appear in the Northern system. Goddesses can longer maintain themselves in the people's remembrance, because they have an importance for the contracted domestic circle. But their character, through length of time and Christianity, is so degraded,

---

1   We must here bear in mind the dialectic form *Gwodan* (*Goden*). On the Elbe, Wodan is still called *Fru Wod*. Lisch, Meklenb. Jahrb. 2, 133.
2   Goth. Frauja, *dominus*, whence the modern feminines Frau, Fru, *domina*, lady. The masculine is no longer extant.
3   Müller, op. cit., p. 116.
4   Eccard, *de Orig. Germ.*, p. 398: 'Celebratur in plebe Saxonica *Fru Frecke*, cui eadem munia tribuuntur, quae Superiores Saxones Holdae suae adscribunt.'
5   Grimm, J., *Deutsche Mythologie*, op. cit., p. 280, from a communication by Kemble. Müller, op. cit., p. 121.

that they usually appear more as terrific, spectral beings than as goddesses. Whether their names even are correct, or have sprung out of mere secondary names or epithets, whether several, who appear under various names, were not originally identical, a supposition rendered probable by a striking resemblance in the traditions, can no longer be decided. We can here only simply repeat what popular tradition relates of them.[1]

**Frau Holda**, or Holle, still survives in Thuringian and Hessian, as well as in Markish and Frankish tradition and story. The name of this goddess signifies either *the kind* (holde) or *the dark, obscure*.[2] She is represented as a being that directs the aerial phenomena, imparts fruitfulness to the earth, presides over rural labours and spinning. She appears likewise as a divinity connected with water, as she dwells in wells and ponds, and particularly in the 'Hollenteich' (so called from her) in the Meissner. From her well children come, and women, who descend into it, become healthy and fruitful. But she also takes persons drowned to her, and is so far a goddess of the nether world, a circumstance that is alluded to in the tradition that she has her abode in mountains,[3] in which, as we shall see, the souls of the departed dwell. On account of these manifold and important functions, Holda, in the time of heathenism, must, no doubt, have been a divinity of high rank. Other traditions concerning her are more obscure and difficult to explain. Burchard of Worms (p. 194[a]) mentions, as a popular belief, that some women believed that on certain nights they rode with her on all kinds of animals, and belonged to her train, according to which she completely occupies the place of Diana and Herodias and it is still a popular belief in Thuringia, that the witches ride with *the Holle* to the Horselberg, and that, like Wodan, she leads the Wild Host. It is also said that she has bristling, matted hair.

This goddess had apparently two chief festivals, one in the twelve nights of Christmas, during which she makes her tour; the other at Shrovetide, when she returns.[4]

**Frau Berchta** is particularly at home among the Upper German races, in Austria, Bavaria, Swabia, Alsace, Switzerland, also in some districts of Thuringia and Franconia. She is even more degraded in popular story than Holda. She also appears in the twelve nights as a female with shaggy hair,

---

1 Müller, op. cit., p. 121.
2 The word is connected either with hold, *propitious, kind*, O. Nor. hollr, or with O. Nor. hulda, *obscurity, darkness*. Grimm, J., *Deutsche Mythologie*, op. cit., p. 249.
3 E.g. in the Horselberg near Eisenach. See p. 243.
4 Müller, op. cit., p. 122. For the Norwegian Huldra, or Hulla, see pp. 228, 233 and 237.

to inspect the spinners, when fish and porridge (Brei)[1] are to be eaten in honour of her, and all the distaffs must be spun off. She is also the queen of the 'Heimchen' (little elementary spirits), who by watering the fields rendered the soil fertile, while she ploughed beneath the surface, and so far has claims to the character of an earth-goddess and promoter of the fertility of the land.[2] To those who mend her chariot she gives the chips by way of payment, which prove to be gold.[3]

Between Berchta and Holle there is unquestionably a considerable resemblance, although their identity is extremely doubtful, as they apparently belong to different German races. The name of Berchta (Berhta, Perahta, Bettha) signifies *resplendent*, *shining*, with which the Welsh substantive berth, *perfection*, *beauty*, and the adjective berth, *beautiful*, *rich*, may be compared. As this goddess appears only in the south of Germany, it is a question whether she did not pass from the Kelts to the German races. We will not decide in the affirmative, though it is worthy of remark that the name enters also into French heroic lore. Bertha with *the great foot*, or with *the goose's foot*, was, according to tradition, the daughter Flore and Blancheflor, the wife of Pepin and mother of Charles the Great. In France, too, the phrase *the time when Bertha span* is used to express days long since gone by. It was also customary to swear by the spinning-wheel of the *reine pedauque*.[4]

In German tradition the name of Berchta is given to the so-called White Lady, who appears in many houses, when a member of the family is about to die, and, as we have seen, is thought to be the ancestress of the race. She is sometimes seen at night tending and nursing the children, in which character she resembles the Keltic fairy. In other and more widespread traditions, the White Lady is an enchanted or spellbound damsel, who usually every seventh year appears near some mountain or castle, points out treasures, and awaits her release.[5] Sometimes she is seen combing her long locks or drying flax-knots. Some pretend that, like Huldra, she is

---

1   Of those who have eaten other food than her festival-dishes she rips open the bodies, takes out the forbidden viands, stuffs them with chaff, and sews them up again with a ploughshare and an iron chain. Grimm, J. & W., *Deutsche Sagen*, No. 268; *Abergl.*, No. 525.

2   Müller, op. cit., p. 124.

3   Grimm, J., *Deutsche Mythologie*, op. cit., p. 252.

4   'Au temps que la reine Berthe filait'; in Italian, 'nel tempo ove Berta filava', or, 'non è piu il tempo che Berta filava'. Comp. *Altdeutsche Wälder*, 3, 47, 48. Roman de Berte as Grans Pies, edit. P. Paris, pref. pp. iii, iv. She is elsewhere called Frau 'Precht mit der langen nas'. See Grimm, J., *Deutsche Mythologie*, op. cit., pp. 250–60.

5   She is also called Bertha. See in Harrys, i, No. 3, 'Die schöne Bertha von Schweckhäuserberge'.

disfigured by a tail. She wears a white robe, or is clad half in white half in black; her feet are concealed by yellow or green shoes. In her hand she usually carries a bunch of keys, sometimes flowers, or a golden spinning-wheel. These traditions evidently point to a goddess that possesses influence over life and death, and presides over domestic economy; although the glimmering shed on her through the medium of popular tradition does not enable us to ascertain more of her nature.[1]

In the traditions of the Altmark there lives another goddess – **Frau Harke**, of whom it is related, that in the twelve nights of Christmas she passes through the country, and if by Twelfth-day the maids have not spun off all the flax, she either scratches them or befouls the spinning-wheel. Stories concerning her must formerly have been more numerous. Gobelinus Persona relates, that Frau Hera in the Twelfths flies through the air and bestows abundance.[2] As this account points to an earth-goddess, there seems no doubt that the *Erce*,[3] invoked as mother of earth in an Anglo-Saxon spell for the fertilising of the land, is identical with her.[4]

In German popular story other names are mentioned of female beings, but who are enveloped in even greater obscurity than the before-mentioned. The **Werre**, who is at home in Voigtland, inspects, like Frau Holle, the spinners on Christmas Eve, and, if all the distaffs are not spun off, befouls the flax. Like Berchta, she rips up the bodies of those who have not eaten porridge. The **Stempe** tramples on those children who on New Year's day will not eat. The **Sträggele** appears in Lucerne the Wednesday before Christmas, and teases the maids, if they have not spun their daily task.[5] **Wanne Thekla** is in the Netherlands the queen of the elves and witches.[6] This tradition is probably of Keltic origin, which may likewise be the case with the following one. **Domina Abundia**, or **Dame Habonde**, who is mentioned by Guilielmus Alvernus, bishop of Paris (ob. AD 1248),[7]

---

1   Müller, op. cit., p. 126.
2   Cosmodrom. Act. vi, Meibom. Scriptt. Rer. Germ. i, p. 235: 'Inter, festum Nativitatis Christi ad festum Epiphaniae Domini, domina *Hera* volat per aëra. Dicebant vulgares praedicto tempore: *Vrowe Hera*, seu corrupto nomine *Vro Here de vlughet*, et credebant illam sibi conferre rerum temporalium abundantiam.'
3   Thorpe, *Analecta Anglo-Saxonica*, p. 116, 2nd edit. Grimm, J., *Deutsche Mythologie*, op. cit., p. cxxix.

| Erce, Erce, Erce, | *Erce, Erce, Erce,* |
|---|---|
| eordan módor, etc. | *mother of earth, etc.* |

4   Müller, op. cit., p. 127.
5   Grimm, J., *Deutsche Mythologie*, op. cit., pp. 251, 255; Grimm, J. & W., *Deutsche Sagen*, p. 269.
6   See p. 626.
7   *Opera*, Paris, 1674, i, 1036, 1066, 1068.

and who also figures in the *Roman de la Rose*,[1] is said, on certain nights, accompanied by other women, who are likewise styled *Dominae*, and all clad in white,[2] to enter houses and partake of the viands placed for them. Their appearance in a house is a sign of good luck and prosperity. In these white-clad females we at once recognise the Keltic fairies. The name Habundia has no connection with the Latin *abundantia*, from which Guilielmus Alvernus would derive it.[3]

Together with Habundia Guilielmus Alvernus places **Satia**, whose name he derives from *satietas*. The goddess **Bensozia**, whom Augerius episcopus Conseranus mentions as a being with whom, as with Herodias, Diana and Holda, the women were believed to ride at night, may be identical with her, and her name be only a fuller form of Satia.[4]

The foregoing are the principal memorials of heathen divinities that have been preserved in Christian times. Together with them we find traces of that living conception of nature, which is perceptible among the Germans from the remotest period. The sun and moon were always regarded as personal beings, they were addressed as *Frau* and *Herr* (Domina and Dominus),[5] and enjoyed a degree of veneration with genuflexions and other acts of adoration.[6] To certain animals, as cats, the idea of something ghostly and magical was attached; to others, as the cuckoo, was ascribed the gift of prophecy while others, as snakes, had influence on the happiness of men, or are accounted sacred and inviolable. Trees, also, even to a much later period, were regarded as animated beings, on which account they were addressed by the title of *Frau* or it was believed that personal beings dwelt in them, to whom a certain reverence was due.[7]

Of processions and festivals, which have pretensions to a heathen origin, we can give only a brief notice.

---

1   Edit. Méon, vv. 18622, *sqq.*
2   Nymphae albae, dominae bonae, dominae nocturnae. Wolf, *Niederl. Sagen.*, No. 231.
3   Müller, op. cit., p. 129.
4   Ibid., p. 130.
5   In Germanic tongues, the sun is feminine and the moon masculine.
6   *Vita Eligii*, ii, 16: Nullus dominos solem aut lunam vocet. *Nic. Magni de Gawe de Superstitionibus* (written in 1415: comp. Grimm, J., *Deutsche Mythologie*, op. cit., p. xliv): Itaque hodie inveniuntur homines . . . qui cum novilunium primo viderint, flexis genibus adorant, vel deposito capucio vel pileo inclinato capite honorant alloquendo et suscipiendo. Immo etiam plures jejunant ipso die novilunii. See also Grimm, J., *Deutsche Mythologie*, op. cit., p. 668, and *Abergl.*, No. 112: 'If a woman at going to bed salutes the stars of heaven, neither vulture nor hawk will take a chicken from her.'
7   See pp. 345 and 570. Müller, op. cit., p. 130.

As, according to Tacitus, the goddess Nerthus was drawn in a carriage in a festive procession, through the several districts, so in Christian times, particularly during the spring, we meet with customs, a leading feature of which consists of a tour or procession. Such festive processions are either through a town, or a village, or through several localities, or round the fields of a community, or about the *mark* or boundary. On these occasions a symbol was frequently carried about, either an animal having reference to some divinity, or else some utensil. A procession may here be cited which, in the year 1133, took place after a complete heathenish fashion, notwithstanding the strenuous opposition of the clergy. In the forest near Inda,[1] a ship was constructed, and furnished beneath with wheels; this was drawn by weavers (compelled to the task), harnessed before it, through Aix-la-Chapelle, Maestricht, Tongres, Looz and other localities, was everywhere received with great joy, and attended by a multitude singing and dancing. The celebration lasted for twelve days. Whosoever, excepting the weavers who drew the ship – an office they regarded as ignominious – touched the same, must give a pledge, or otherwise redeem himself.[2] This custom maintained itself to a much later period in Germany, as by a protocol of the council of Ulm, dated on the eve of St Nicholas, 1330, the procession with a plough or a ship is prohibited. A connection between the above custom and the worship of the Isis of Tacitus, whose symbol was a ship, seems in a high degree probable; it had, at least, reference to a goddess, as, according to the original narrative, the women took part in it with bacchanalian wantonness.[3]

Mention also occurs of a procession with a plough, about Shrovetide, in other parts of Germany, viz. on the Rhine, in Upper Saxony and Franconia, with the remarkable addition, that young unmarried women were either placed on the plough, or were compelled to draw it.[4]

Another procession, called *the driving*, or *carrying*, *out of Death* (winter), took place formerly about Midlent, usually on the Sunday *Laetare* (the fourth in Lent), and sometimes on the Sunday *Oculi* (the third in Lent), in Franconia and Thuringia, also in Meissen, Voigtland, Lusatia and Silesia.

1   Inden in the territory of Jälich, afterwards Cornelimünster.
2   See a circumstantial account of this custom in Grimm, J., *Deutsche Mythologie*, op. cit., pp. 237, *sqq*.
3   Müller, op. cit., p. 133. *Rodolfi Chron. Abbatiae S. Trudonis*, lib. ix, 'Sub fugitiva adhuc luce diei imminente luna, matronarum catervae abjecto femineo pudore audientes strepitum hujus vanitatis, sparsis capillis de stratis suis exiliebant, aliae seminudae, aliae simplice tantum clamide circumdutae, chorosque ducentibus circa navim impudenter irrumpendo se admiscebant.'
4   Müller, op. cit., p. 134.

Children carried a figure of straw or wood, or a doll in a box, or stuck on a pole, through the place, singing all the time, then cast the figure into the water or burnt it. In its stead a fir-tree was brought back to the place. If the procession met any cattle on their return they beat them with sticks, believing that they thereby rendered them fruitful.[1]

In other places, the beginning of the beautiful season is represented as the entrance of a benignant divinity into the country. In Thuringia, on the third day of Whitsuntide, a young peasant, called the *green man*, or *lettuce-king*, is in the forest enveloped in green boughs, placed on a horse, and amid rejoicings conducted into the village, where all the people are assembled. The Schulze (Bailiff or Mayor) must then guess thrice who is concealed under the green covering. If he does not guess, he must forfeit a quantity of beer; and even if he does guess, he must, nevertheless, give it. Of the same class is the procession of the Maigraf (Count of the May), (called also the *King of the* May, or *King of Flowers*), which formerly, usually on the first of May, took place with great rejoicings, not only in Lower Germany, but in Denmark[2] and Sweden. Attended by a considerable company, and adorned with flowers and garlands, the Count of the May paraded through the several districts, where he was received by the young girls, who danced round him, one of whom he chose for *Queen of the May*.[3]

We shall conclude this sketch of the festive processions with a short notice of some other heathen customs.

It is a widespread custom in Germany to kindle bonfires on certain days, viz. at Easter and St John's (Midsummer) day, less usually at Christmas and Michaelmas. In Lower Germany the Easter-fires are the most usual, which are generally lit on hills; while in the south of Germany the St John's fires are the commonest, and were formerly kindled in the marketplaces, or before the gates of the town. The ceremonies connected with these fires are more and more forgotten. In former times old and young, high and low regarded the kindling of them as a great festival. These customs had apparently an agrarian object, as it is still believed that so far as the flame of the Easter-fire spreads its light will the earth be fertile and the corn thrive for that year. These fires, too, were, according to the old belief, beneficial for the preservation of life and health to those who came in contact with the flame. On which account the people danced round the St John's fire, or sprang over it, and drove their domestic animals through it. The coal and ashes of the Easter-fire were carefully collected and preserved as a remedy for diseases of the cattle. For a similar reason it was a custom to drive the

---

1   Müller, op. cit., p. 135.
2   See 417–18.
3   Müller, op. cit., p. 139.

cattle when sick over particular fires called *need-fires* (Notfeuer), which, with certain ceremonies, were kindled by friction;[1] on which account the St John's fire is strictly to be regarded as a need-fire kindled at a fixed period. Fire is the sacred, purifying and propitiating element, which takes away all imperfections.[2]

A similar salutiferous power is, according to the still existing popular belief, possessed by water, particularly when drawn in silence on certain holiday nights, as St John's or Christmas, from certain springs that were formerly sacred to some divinity. To wash in such water imparts health and beauty for the whole year.[3]

On Death, and the condition of souls after death, a few words are necessary. Even in Christian ideas of hell, the remains of pagan belief are here and there discernible. Among these may be reckoned that the devil has his habitation in the north,[4] as in the Scandinavian belief the nether world lies in the north. According to some traditions, the entrance to hell leads through long, subterranean passages, to a gate; in the innermost space lies the devil fast bound, as Utgarthilocus is chained in the lower world.[5] According to another tradition, the emperor Charles, when conducted to hell by an angel, passed through deep dells full of fiery springs, as, according to the Scandinavian belief, the way to Hel's abode led through deep valleys, in the midst of which is the spring Hvergelmir.[6] The popular tales also relate how a water must be passed before arriving at Hell.[7]

According to all appearance, the idea was very general in the popular

1   *Indic. Superst.*, c. 15. De igne fricato de ligno.
2   Müller, op. cit., p. 141. For details relating to these fires, see Grimm, J., *Deutsche Mythologie*, op. cit., pp. 570–94. Particularly worthy of notice is the employment of a cartwheel, by the turning of which the need-fire is kindled. In some places, at the Easter-fire, a burning wheel is rolled down a hill. In the Mark, a cartwheel is set on fire and danced round. A wheel, too, is hung over the doors of the houses for the thriving of the cattle. *Märk. Sagen*, p. 362. Comp. Grimm, J., *Deutsche Mythologie*, op. cit. *Abergl.*, No. 307: 'Whoever puts a wheel over his doorway has luck in his house.' This custom of kindling sacred fires on certain days prevails throughout almost the whole of Europe, and was known to Antiquity, particularly in Italy. The Kelts kindled such fires, on the first of May, to the god Beal (thence even now called *bealtine*), and on the first of November to the god Sighe. *Leo, Malb. Gl.*, i, 33. But whether the need-fire is of Keltic origin remains a doubt. 'The fires lighted by the [Scottish] Highlanders on the first of May, in compliance with a custom derived from the pagan times, are termed the *Beltane-Tree*. It is a festival celebrated with various superstitious rites, both in the north of Scotland and in Wales.' Scott's *Minstrelsy*, iii, p. 324.
3   Müller, op. cit., p. 143.
4   Caedmon, p. 3, l. 8.
5   Saxo, op. cit., p. 431, edit. Müller.
6   See pp. 19, 20.
7   Grimm, J. & W., *Kinder- und Hausmärchen*, op. cit., No. 29. Müller, op. cit., p. 389.

belief of Scandinavia, that the souls of the departed dwelt in the interior of mountains. This idea at least very frequently presents itself in the Icelandic Sagas, and must have been widespread, as it is retained even in Germany to the present day. Of some German mountains it is believed that they are the abodes of the damned. One of these is the Horselberg near Eisenach, which is the habitation of Frau Holle; another is the fabulous Venusberg, in which the Tanhäuser sojourns, and before which the trusty Eckhalt sits as a warning guardian.[1] Of other mountains it is also related that heroes of ancient times have been carried into them. Thus the emperor Frederic Barbarossa sits in the Kyfhäuser at a stone table; his beard has already grown twice round the table; when it has grown thrice round he will awake,[2] The emperor Charles sits in the Odenberg, or in the Unterberg,[3] and an emperor not named, in the Guckenberg near Fränkishgemünden.[4]

Almost all the descriptions of the sojourn of souls after death have this in common, that the nether world was thought to be in the bowels of the earth, that is, in the interior of mountains or at the bottom of waters, and that its aspect was that of a spacious habitation, in which a divine being received the departed. That it was, at the same time, also a belief that the dead in their graves, in a certain manner, continued to live, that they were contented or sad, and heard the voices of those who called – a subject to which we shall presently return – is strictly in contradiction to the other ideas; but, in the first place, heathenism easily tolerated such inconsistencies, and, secondly, the depth of the grave became confounded with the nether world in the bowels of the earth. Thus while, on the one hand, it was thought that the dead preserved their old bodily aspect, and appeared just as when they sojourned on earth, although the freshness of life had departed, on the other hand there is no lack of passages, according to which a particular form is ascribed to the soul when separated from its body.[5]

---

1    The relationship of the traditions of Frau Venus and Holda is indubitable. The Venusberg is considered by some as identical with the Horselberg, in which Frau Holle holds her court. Before the Venusberg – according to the preface to the Heldenbuch – sits the trusty Eckhard, and warns people; as he also rides and warns before the Wild Hunt. Grimm, J. & W., *Deutsche Sagen,* No. 7. The tradition of the Venusberg first appears in monuments of the fourteenth century.

2    Grimm, J. & W., *Deutsche Sagen,* Nos. 23, 296. Comp. Bechstein, *Thür. Sagenschatz,* 49–54. See also vol. iii. pp. 101, *sqq.* According to another tradition, the emperor Frederic sits in a rocky cavern near Kaiserslautern.

3    Grimm, J. & W., *Deutsche Sagen,* Nos. 26, 28. *Mones Anzeiger,* 4. 409. Of Wedekind also it is said that he sits in a mountain, called Die Babilonie, in Westphalia, until his time comes. Redecker, *Westf. Sagen,* No. 21. Similar traditions are in Grimm, J. & W. , *Deutsche Sagen,*  Nos. 106, 207, and in *Mones Anzeiger,* 5, 174.

4    Müller, op. cit., p. 396

5    Müller, op. cit., p. 401.

As mountains, according to the heathen popular belief, were supposed to be the sojourns of the dead, so it was imagined that in the bottom of wells and ponds there was a place for the reception of departed souls But this belief had special reference to the souls of the drowned, who came to the dwelling of the Nix, or of the sea-goddess Rân. The depths of the water were, however, at the same time, conceived in a more general sense, as the nether world itself. For which reasons persons who otherwise, according to the popular traditions, are conveyed away into mountains, are also supposed to be dwelling in wells and ponds;[1] and the numerous tales current throughout the whole of Germany of towns and castles that have been sunk in the water, and are sometimes to be discerned at the bottom, are probably connected with this idea. It is particularly worthy of notice that beautiful gardens have been imagined to exist under the water.[2] Yet more widespread is the tradition that green meadows exist under water, in which souls have their abode.[3] In an old German poem in it is said that these meadows are closed against suicides,[4] according to which they would appear to be a detached portion of the nether world.[5]

The soul was supposed to bear the form of a bird. Even in Saemund's *Edda* it is said, that in the nether world singed birds fly that had been souls,[6] and in the popular tales similar ideas occur frequently. The ghost of the murdered mother comes swimming in the form of a duck, or the soul sits in the form of a bird on the grave; the young murdered brother mounts up as a little bird, and the girl, when thrown into the water, rises in the air as a white duck.[7] The frequent conjurations into swans, doves and ravens[1]

---

1 Thus the emperor Charles is said to sojourn in a well at Nuremberg.Grimm, J. & W. , *Deutsche Sagen,* No. 22.
2 Thus Frau Holla has a garden under her pool or well, from which she distributes all kinds of fruits. Grimm, J. & W., *Deutsche Sagen,* No. 4. Comp. 13, 291, and Grimm, J. & W., *Kinder- und Hausmärchen,* op. cit., No. 24.
3 Grimm, J. & W., *Kinder- und Hausmärchen,* op. cit., No. 61. Wolf, *Niederl. Sagen,* No. 506.
4 Flore, 19b.
5 Müller, op. cit., p. 399.
6

| Frá thví er at segja, | Of that is to be told, |
|---|---|
| hvat ek fyrst um sá, | what I first observed, |
| thá ek var í kvölheima kominn: | when I had come into the land of torment: |
| svidnir fuglar, | singed birds, |
| er sálir váru, | that had been souls, |
| flugu svá margir sem my. | flew as many as gnats. |

Sólarljod, Str. 53.
It is however to be remarked that the Sólarljód is a Christian poem, though composed at a period when heathenism still prevailed in the North.
7 Grimm, J. & W., *Kinder- und Hausmärchen,* op. cit., Nos. 11, 13, 21, 47, 96, 135.

originate in the same ideas: these birds are the souls of the murdered, a belief which the popular tale ingeniously softening, represents merely as a transformation. With this belief the superstition must be placed in connection, that, when a person dies, the windows should be opened, that the departing soul may fly out.[2]

From the popular traditions we also learn that the soul has the form of a snake. It is related that out of the mouth of a sleeping person a snake creeps and goes a long, distance, and that what it sees or suffers on its way, the sleeper dreams of.[3] If it is prevented from returning, the person dies. According to other traditions and tales, it would seem that the soul was thought to have the form of a flower, as a lily or a white rose.[4]

These ideas may be regarded as the relics of a belief in the transmigration of souls, according to which the soul, after its separation from the body, passes into that of an animal, or even an inanimate object. More symbolic is the belief that the soul appears as a light. Hence the popular superstition that the *ignes fatui*, which appear by night in swampy places, are the souls

---

1    Grimm, J. & W., *Kinder- und Hausmärchen*, op. cit.,  Nos. 9, 25, 49, 93,193, pp. 103, 221.

2    Müller, op. cit., p. 402; Grimm, J., *Deutsche Mythologie*, op. cit., *Abergl.* Nos. 191, 664; Kuhn, *Märk. Sagen*, p. 367.

3    When the grave of Charles Martel was opened, a large snake was found in it; such at least is the story, which, moreover, tells us that having exhausted his treasures, he gave the tenth, which was the due of the clergy, to his knights to enable them to live. The story of the snake was told by St Eucherius, bishop of Orleans. See Wolf, *Niederl. Sagen*, No. 68. Other traditions tell that the soul proceeds from the mouth of a sleeping person in the form of a butterfly, a weasel or mouse. Grimm, J. & W., *Deutsche Sagen*, Nos. 247, 255; Grimm, J., *Deutsche Mythologie*, op. cit.,  pp. 789, 1036. Goethe alludes to a similar superstition in Faust:

> Ach! mitten im Gesange sprang          *Ah! in the midst of her song*
> Ein rothes Mäuschen ihr aus dem Munde.   *A red mousekin sprang out of her mouth.*

4    Seep. 631. Grimm, J. & W., *Kinder- und Hausmärchen*, op. cit., Nos. 9, 85. The popular tales tell also of persons transformed into lilies or other flowers. Grimm, J. & W., *Kinder- und Hausmärchen*, op. cit., Nos. 56, 76. On the chair of those that will soon die a white rose or lily appears. Grimm, J. & W., *Deutsche Sagen*, Nos. 263, 264; Harrys, i, p. 76. From the grave of one unjustly executed white lilies spring as a token of his innocence; from that of a maiden, three lilies, which no one save her lover may gather; from the mounds of lovers flowery shrubs spring, which entwine together. Also in the Swedish ballads lilies and limes grow out of graves. In the Scottish ballad of Fair Margaret and Sweet William it is said:

> Out of her breast there sprang a *rose*,
> And out of his a *briar*;
> They grew till they grew unto the church top,
> And there they tied in a true lovers' knot.

See also the story of Axel and Valdborg pp. 258–60, where the trees are the *ash*.

of the dead. Men, who during life have fraudulently removed landmarks, must, after death, wander about as *ignes fatui*, or in a fiery form.[1]

According to a well-known popular tale, there is a subterranean cavern, in which innumerable lights burn: these are the life-tapers of mortals. When a light is burnt out, the life of the person to whom it belonged is at an end, and he is the property of Death.[2]

How do the souls of the departed arrive at their destined abode? German tradition assigns the office of receiving the souls of mortals at their death to dwarfs. Middle High German poems, and also the belief still existing among the people, regard Death as a person, under various names, who when their hour arrives, conducts mortals away by the hand, on a level road, dances with them,[3] sets them on his horse, receives them in his train, invites them to his dwelling, lays them in chains, or – which is probably a later idea – fights with them, and with spear, dart, sword or scythe, slays them.[4]

In some parts of Germany it is a custom to place a piece of money in the mouth of a corpse,[5] probably to pay the passage-money, or defray the expenses of the journey.[6]

As the dead in the nether world continue their former course of life,[7] it naturally follows that they are not wholly estranged from earthly life. No oblivious draught has been given them, but the remembrance of their earthly doings cleaves to them. Hence they gladly see again the places frequented by them while on earth; but they are particularly disquieted

1   Müller, op. cit., p. 404. See instances of this superstition *passim*.
2   See Grimm, J. & W., *Kinder- und Hausmärchen*, op. cit., No. 44. Müller, op. cit., p. 404. The same idea is contained in the popular superstitions. On Christmas Eve the light may not be extinguished, else someone will die. Grimm, *Abergl.*, Nos. 421, 468. In the Albthal, On a wedding-day, during the service, a triple twisted taper is borne by each of the bridal party: the person whose taper is first burnt out will be the first to die. Schreiber's *Taschenbuch*, 1839, p. 325.
3   According to the preface to the Heldenbuch, a dwarf fetches Dietrich of Bern with the words: 'Thou shalt go with me, thy kingdom is no more in this world.' According to Christian ideas, angels or devils receive the departed souls, an office particularly assigned to Michael.
4   The dance of death cannot, however, be traced further back than the fifteenth century. Müller, op. cit., p. 405.
5   Grimm, J., *Deutsche Mythologie*, op. cit., *Abergl.* No. 207. *Märk. Sagen*, Nos. 19, 30.
6   Müller, op. cit., p. 408.
7   Many of the German popular stories make the dead to appear as they were in life and to follow the same pursuits. In ruined castles, knights in their ancient costume hold tournaments and sit at the joyous feast; the priest reads mass, the wild huntsman and the robber continue their handiwork after death. Grimm, J. & W. , *Deutsche Sagen*, Nos. 527, 828; *Niederl. Sagen*, Nos. 422, 424, 425; *Mones Anzeiger*, 4, 307; Harrys, i, No. 51 et alibi.

when anything still attaches them to earthly life. A buried treasure allows them no rest until it is raised;[1] an unfinished work, an unfulfilled promise forces them back to the upper world.[2]

In like manner the dead attach themselves to their kindred and friends. Hence the belief is very general that they will return to their home and visit them, and that they sympathise with their lot.[3] Thus a mother returns to the upper world to tend her forsaken children,[4] or children at their parents' grave find aid, who, as higher powers, grant them what they wish.[5] Slain warriors also rise again to help their comrades to victory.[6] But it disturbs the repose of the dead when they are too much wept for and mourned after. Every tear falls into their coffin and torments them; in which case they will rise up and implore those they have left behind to cease their lamentation.[7]

---

1   Grimm, *Abergl.*, No. 606, comp. 207, 588.
2   Müller, op. cit., p. 410.
3   In the neighbourhood of Courtrai it is a custom, when conveying a corpse to the churchyard, to repeat a Pater noster at every crossway, that the dead, when he wishes to return home, may be able to find the way. *Niederl. Sagen*, No. 317. The dead usually reappear on the ninth day. Grimm, *Abergl.*, No. 856. According to the *Eyrb. Saga*, c. 54, the dead come to their funeral feast.
4   For a mother that has died in childbirth the bed is to be made during six weeks, that she may lie in it when she comes to give her child the breast. *Niederl. Sagen*, No. 326.
5   Grimm, J. & W., *Kinder- und Hausmärchen*, op. cit., No. 21. Comp. *Hervarar Saga* and *Udvalgte Danske Viser*, i, p. 253.
6   Grimm, J. & W., *Deutsche Sagen,* No. 327. Comp. Wunderhorn, i, 73, 74. The dead also wreak vengeance. *Niederl. Sagen*, No. 312. It is an old belief that if a person is murdered on Allhallows' day, he can have no rest in the grave until he has taken revenge on his murderer. Ibid., No. 323.
7   Müller, op. cit., p. 412. Grimm, J. & W., *Kinder- und Hausmärchen*, op. cit., No. 109. This belief is feelingly expressed in the old Danish ballad of Aage and Else:

> Hver en Gang Du glaedes,                    *Every time thou'rt joyful,*
>     Og i Din Hu er glad,                        *And in thy mind art glad,*
> Da er min Grav forinden                      *Then is my grave within*
>     Omhaengt med Rosens Blad.                    *Hung round with roses' leaves.*
>
> Hver Gang Du Dig graemmer,                   *Every time thou grievest,*
>     Og i Din Hu er mod,                         *And in thy mind art sad,*
> Da er min Kiste forinden                     *Then is within my coffin*
>     Som fuld med levret Blod.                    *As if full of clotted blood.*

                                            Udvalgte Danske Viser, i, p. 211.

**NORTHERN MYTHOLOGY
VOLUME II**

*Popular Traditions and Superstitions of
Scandinavia*

# Introduction[1]

Amid the lofty *Fjelds*[2] of Norway the gigantic Jutul has fixed his home, of whose fingers and feet traces may be seen in the hard stone, and whom fragments of rock and ponderous grave-stones serve for weapons; in the lower ridges the wily Troll and the beautiful Huldra have their dwelling; in mounds and by lofty trees the countless swarms of Elves have their haunt, while beneath the earth the small but long-armed and skilful dwarfs exercise their handicrafts. In the evening twilight Thusser and Vaettir still wander about, and the merry, wanton Nisser frisk and dance by moonlight. In the rivers and lakes lurks the fell Nök, and through the air flies the Aasgaardsreia's frantic crew, announcing bloodshed and war, while a guardian, warning Fölgie attends each mortal on his earthly career. Thus speaks tradition, and that this belief is of long-standing in the North may be concluded from the testimony of Procopius: – 'The Thulites worship many gods and spirits, in heaven, in air, on earth, in the sea, and some even that are said to inhabit the waters of springs and rivers. They constantly make to them all kinds of offerings.'[3]

The question that naturally first presents itself to us, on hearing these wondrous stories, is: What can have given birth to, and indelibly imprinted and quickened in the imagination of the people a superstition, which is the more remarkable, as similar opinions are found among the majority of the people in the north of Europe?

It is probable that unacquaintance with nature and her powers, combined with the innate desire of finding a reason for and explaining the various natural phenomena, that must daily and hourly attract the attention of mankind, has led them to see the causes of these phenomena in the power of the beings who, as they supposed, had produced them, and afterwards frequented and busied themselves with and in their own

---

1   From Faye's *Norske Folke-Sagn*, Christiania, 1844.
2   I have preserved the native orthography of this word (signifying a far outstretched stony mountain), to prevent confusion with the English word *field*. It is our north of England *fell*.
3   Geijer, *Svea Rikes Häfder*, p. 87.

productions. These phenomena were too numerous and various to allow the ascribing of them to a single being, and therefore a number of supernatural beings were imagined, whose dangerous influence and pernicious wrath it was sought to avert by sacrifices and other means.

The hollow thundering that is at times heard among the mountains, the smoke and fire that ascend from some of them, the destruction often caused by a sudden earth-slip or earthquake, all of which in our times are easily explained from natural causes, might to the rugged peasant, wholly unacquainted with nature and her hidden powers, appear as supernatural, and as the operations of Jutuls, Giants, and similar mighty, evil beings, that were supposed to dwell in the mountains, and of whose huge feet and fingers a lively imagination easily found marks in the hard rocks. Fear and superstition gradually invested these imaginary beings with all sorts of terrific forms,[1] and people fancied they saw these direst foes of man transformed into stone all over the country.

Crystals and other natural productions were found, which could not have been made by human hands; a voice, a sound, was sometimes heard where least expected, either an echo, or arising from other natural causes, and which could now be easily accounted for; footsteps of men were seen where no one had ever chanced to meet a human being; among many comely children there was a deformed one, which either by its ugliness or its excessive stupidity was distinguished from the others. All these things, it was said, must have a cause, and from ignorance of nature, joined to superstition and a lively imagination, the idea suggested itself of conjuring up beings, to whom all these phenomena might be ascribed, and who, according to the places of sojourn assigned them, were called Forest-trolls, Huldres, Mountain-trolls, Vaettir, Elves, Dwarfs, Nisser, Mares, etc.

The sea's smooth surface, its hidden, unfathomable depth, the raging of the storm, and the foamy billows of the troubled ocean, make a deep and often a wonderful impression on the human mind. This state of feeling, together with the extraordinary creatures of the ocean that are sometimes caught, and the terrific marine monsters that are sometimes seen, must supply the ignorant fisherman, in his sequestered home, with such abundant food for his invention or fancy, that it is almost a wonder there are not even more stories of mermen, mermaids, and other creations of the deep.

---

1    In Orvarodd's *Saga*, ch. 15, a giant is thus described: He was quite black except his eyes and teeth, which were white; his nose was large and hooked; his hair, which hung down over all his breast, was as coarse as fish's gills, and his eyes were like two pools of water.

The monotonous roar of the waterfalls, the squalls and whirlpools that render our fords and rivers so dangerous, and in which many persons annually perish, together with the circumstance, that in several fresh waters, when a thaw is at hand, the ice splits through the middle with a fearful crash, leaving an open strip, have given occasion to superstition to imagine the depths of the water inhabited by malignant sprites, that yearly at least require a human being for a sacrifice, and which, under the names of Nöks, Grims and Quaernknurrer, are sufficiently known.

When it suggested itself to the imagination to people the mountains, the earth and the water with supernatural beings, it could not be long before it must also give inhabitants to the boundless space above our heads. In the countless stars, in the extraordinary figures often assumed by the clouds and the mist, in the balls of fire and the blazing northern lights, in the pealing thunder and the wind howling through the narrow mountain-valleys, the uninstructed might easily see and hear the passing of the gods, the Aasgaardreia's wild course, the Troll-wives' ride, and thence draw omens of impending misfortune. The lightning oftenest strikes downward among the high mountains, what then can be more reasonable than the belief that the god who reveals himself in thunder and lightning, the mighty Thor, is chastising the demons of earth, who dwell in the places that have been struck by the lightning?

Wicked, and injurious to man were the greater number of these supernatural beings, who may strictly be regarded as personified powers of nature, and as there hangs a degree of obscurity over their whole being, the night was supposed to be the season of their activity, when imagination and fear are most disposed to create all kinds of terrific images.

Although personified powers of nature are to be regarded as the primary elements of mythic tradition, it would, nevertheless, be a great error to suppose that every individual myth or tradition of supernatural beings can be explained on that principle. The explanation would in such case often be not only far-fetched but false; for, in the first place, many a myth, or some particular part of it, is mere poetic embellishment, and, secondly, it often contains an obscure tradition of the country's earliest history. An almost inscrutable blending of various traditions is a peculiar characteristic of a myth. In the representations of the gods and other beings, their wars and other relations, lies the oldest history of a people in the guise of a myth. That it must be dark and fabulous is a consequence both of its antiquity and the rudeness in which most nations live in their earliest infancy, when it never occurs to them, nor in fact have they the means, to transmit to after-ages accounts of their transactions. Consequently the earliest history of every people consists of traditions, which in the course of time may have been subjected to various changes. Through the mist that envelops the primitive history of the North, the historic inquirer thinks that he discerns a struggle between the primitive inhabitants and a more civilised invading people; and in our popular traditions of Jutuls, Trolls, Elves and Dwarfs, are sought traces of these elder and more rugged people, the conquest and expulsion of whom, as dark monuments of times long gone by, is alluded to and eternised in the old skaldic songs and sagas.

That these primitive inhabitants consisted of one and the same people it is not necessary to assume. On the contrary, the great difference found in the sagas between the huge Jutul, who plays with fragments of rock, and the little wily dwarfs, who conceal themselves in the earth and its caverns, seems to indicate that they were as different as could well be, although in particular places they may have lived together, and combined in opposition to and as common enemies of the invading Goths. In some places it would seem as if the intruding conquerors had mingled with the older inhabitants, settled among them and formed intermarriages with them. 'In ancient times,' a Thellemark saga relates, 'the Thusser were so numerous that Christians could not inhabit Norway, nor Norway be colonised, before they formed intermarriages.' And in our old sagas mention frequently occurs of historic personages, who, on the father's or mother's side, descended from giants, or were 'half-trolls'.

In other places it would appear that it was only after an obstinate struggle that the original inhabitants were driven from the plains and valleys to the wooded and mountainous regions, where caves were their dwelling-places, the chase afforded them sustenance, and the skins of beasts covering. That they continued to stand in a hostile relation to their conquerors, and that, whenever an opportunity presented itself, they attacked, plundered and murdered the intruders, in the tracts nearest to their hiding-places, and then disappeared with their booty, is in the highest degree probable. Their sudden attacks and disappearance, the bloody traces they left behind them, their vast strength, savage aspect and garb, together with the darkness, under cover of which they chose to visit their enemies' stores or to attack them, must give to these people a terrific, demonlike colouring in the eyes of the peaceful inhabitants of the valley. The less often they showed themselves the more wonderful were the stories told of them; and so formidable did they at length appear, dressed out in all the terrors of imagination and superstition, that, according to the general opinion, it required powers greater than human to contend with them. It was, therefore, a fitting task for the Thunder-god himself, who sometimes crushed them with his bolt, or for his earthly representative, who in the old skaldic poem is described as the overthrower of the altars of the Forniotish gods, the mountain folk's, the fjeld-wolves', the sons of the rock's and the giants' terror and destroyer.[1]

In the Norse Sagas we read not only of the mighty Jutuls, Giants (Riser) and Mountain-trolls, but also, and even more frequently, of Thusser and Dwarfs. The tradition of a former dwarf-race may probably in part be ascribed to an obscure reminiscence that the Lapps once, during Norway's savage state, inhabited tracts whence they have been driven away. If the diminutive Lapps were not formidable to the invading Goths in battle, they might, nevertheless, through their acquaintance with the secrets of nature, their cunning and their dexterity, be dangerous neighbours, who could drive off the cattle, change children (whence probably the numerous stories about changelings), steal household utensils and provisions, give persons stupefying drinks, entice them into their caves with songs, presents, etc., traits which supply us with the key to many a tradition of the subterraneans.

These views are confirmed by the testimony of history. Adam of Bremen, who lived in the eleventh century, relates from oral information given him by the Danish king Svend Estrithson, that in Sweden 'there was a people who were in the habit of suddenly descending from the mountains in sledges, laying all around waste, unless most vigorously opposed, and then retiring'. 'In Norway,' he says in another place, 'I have heard there are wild women and men, who dwell in the forests, and seldom make their appearance; they use the skins of wild beasts for clothing, and their speech is more like the growling of animals than the talk of human beings, so that they are hardly intelligible to their neighbours.'

At the first glance it must appear wonderful, that after Christianity has been established in the North for eight hundred years, there should still be so many remains of heathen superstitions there. On closer consideration, however, the enigma may be solved. The first Christian teachers, finding the old ideas too deep-rooted, and, as it were, too fast interwoven with the physical condition of the country, its ancient history and poetry, to be immediately eradicated, strove to render the heathen superstition less offensive by giving it a Christian colouring. The heathen festivals, which had formerly been held in honour of the gods of Valhall, were now transferred to Christian saints, and in St Olaf the Norse clergy were so fortunate as to get a saint of such high repute for his wonderful strength, that they could well place to his account the marvellous deeds that had been previously ascribed to the mighty Thor and the gods of Valhall. These latter, who were sometimes regarded by the Christians as mere human

---

1   *Comp. Thorsdrapa*, pp. 16–22, and Thiodolf hin Hvinerske's poem *Höstlanga*, also Geijer's *Svea Rikes Häfder*, p. 276.

beings, and at others as evil spirits, were at length almost totally forgotten by the people, as it was but seldom that any visible sign appeared before them which could tend to retain them in remembrance; while belief in the other supernatural beings, that were attached to the surrounding nature, could not be so easily eradicated. As giants and other beings of that class had never been objects of adoration, but of hatred and aversion, they were allowed to retain their old denominations and character, and even served to confirm the Christian doctrine of the devil and his angels, among whom the giants and other supernatural beings were reckoned.

The Lutheran reformation, instead of checking this superstition as it had done many other errors, let it remain unheeded; the belief in the devil and his angels (the common name for the supernatural beings), together with their influence, both on mankind and all nature, seems rather to have acquired new life. Persecutions for witchcraft, and assignments to the fiend belonged to the order of the day.

It was, it is true, considered an impiety to have any concern with the subterraneans and other such 'petty devils'; but to the untutored and superstitious people it was a necessity to have some beings of whom they could ask counsel; and as the reformed clergy had made an end of the Catholic saints and relics, superstition was driven to betake itself secretly to its old heathen friends, the subterraneans, the Nisser, and the like, whose favour it was sought to gain, or whose enmity it was hoped to avert by offerings at hollow trees, in woods, or under vast, venerable stones, on a Thursday evening, or the eve of a holy day.

The more expanded ideas which began to prevail towards the end of the last century, and the increase of knowledge, which has manifested itself in so many ways in these latter times, have greatly contributed to diminish the belief in these supernatural beings. In many parts such traditions are already sunk into oblivion, in some they are regarded as pleasant stories, or are related merely to frighten children; while in other places, among the less enlightened and more superstitious peasantry, many are still to be found who are convinced of the existence of these mythic beings, who played so important a part in the imagination of their fathers. They themselves or, more usually, an aunt, a father or mother, have seen the underground folk and their dogs and cattle, heard their sweet music, known persons that have been taken into the fjelds, or had their infants changed for those of the subterraneans.[1] The places where such beings

---

1    We ought not in fact greatly to wonder that the belief in the subterranean people still finds followers among the uninstructed peasantry, when we read, that it is scarcely a hundred years since learned men disputed whether the subterraneans were created

were supposed to have their resort are in some parts still looked upon as sacred. No superstitious peasant, who has a regard for his health and property, dares venture to meddle with a Vaettir-mound, a Butree or Thunbede, which is frequented by the invisible folk; but, on the contrary, that they may not, in their anger, pass their dwelling and take the luck of

---

by God, whether they were preadamites, whether they can hold intercourse with mankind, etc. Herman Ruge, clergyman of Slidre in 1754, in his *Rational Thoughts on various curious matters*, was of opinion 'that the subterraneans formed, as it were, the boundary between brutes and human beings!' The said clergyman, Ruge, who has dedicated a whole chapter of his book to the subject of changelings, informs us (as an ancient method to be applied with regard to such children), that if a mother has been so unfortunate as to have her child changed, she must take the changeling on three successive Thursday evenings and whip it unmercifully with rods on a heap of sweepings; for then the subterranean mother, taking pity on her infant, will come and restore the genuine child and take back her own. The belief in changelings is universal also out of Norway. As many persons will, no doubt, be gratified to know what the great German reformer, Martin Luther, thought and said with regard to changelings, we will give an extract or two from his *Table Talk*:

> Changelings (Wechselbälge) and Kielkropfs Satan lays in the place of the genuine children, that people may be tormented with them. He often carries off young maidens into the water, has intercourse with them, and keeps them with him until they have been delivered; then lays such children in cradles, takes the genuine children out, and carries them away. But such changelings, it is said, do not live more than eighteen or twenty years.
>
> In the year 1541 Dr Luther mentioned this subject at table, adding, that he had told the Prince of Anhalt that such changelings should be drowned. On being asked why he had so advised? he answered, that it was his firm belief that such changelings were only a lump of flesh, a *massa carnis,* as there was no soul in them, for such the devil could easily make, as well as he can destroy men, who have body, reason and soul, when he possesses them bodily, so that they neither hear nor see nor feel anything; he makes them dumb, deaf and blind; the devil is therefore in such changelings as their soul.
>
> Eight years ago there was a changeling in Dessau, which I, Dr Martin Luther, have both seen and touched; it was twelve years old and had all its senses, so that people thought it was a proper child; but that mattered little; for it only ate, and that as much as any four ploughmen or thrashers, and when anyone touched it it screamed; when things in the house went wrong, so that any damage took place, it laughed and was merry; but if things went well, it cried. Thereupon I said to the Prince of Anhalt: 'If I were prince or ruler here, I would have this child thrown into the water, into the Moldau that flows by Dessau, and would run the risk of being a homicide'. But the Elector of Saxony, who was then at Dessau, and the Prince of Anhalt would not follow my advice. I then said: 'They ought to cause a Pater noster to be said in the church, that God would take the devil away from them'. That was done daily at Dessau, and the said changeling died two years after. See Dobeneck, I, p. 168.

the house with them, the people wait upon them on holy day eves with cakes, sweet porridge and other offerings.[1]

An example or two will serve to show how deeply imprinted is the belief in the subterraneans, in many places, even at the present day. 'At Lurö in the Northlands,' the Revd G. Faye writes to me, 'an incredible degree of superstition prevails, particularly with regard to the subterraneans, who have their sojourn in certain places, how they take in persons and make away with them; they are even said to have a church somewhere here in the parish, of which one of my parishioners, a great ghost-seer, is, as I am told, the priest. It is, moreover, said that in the neighbourhood of the parsonage there dwelt a subterranean, who had a pleasure-boat, whom people that were *synsk* often saw sailing on the lake. I have repeatedly endeavoured to talk them out of this superstition; but before me they will never confess that they entertain such belief; because, as I afterwards learned, they think it is to the priest's advantage to suppress all belief in the subterraneans: "For," say they, "he is as sensible of it as we are; he has read it in the sixth book of Moses, which does not, it is true, stand in the Bible, but which the priests keep to themselves." ' That the Sönderfjeld Norwegians stand on about the same level with regard to belief in the subterraneans will appear from the following traditions, but to which I will add a passage from my college days.

In company with some University friends, I undertook, in the summer of 1824, a foot-journey to the Riukanfoss and Gaustafjeld. As a guide on the Gausta, we took an active peasant from Vestfiorddal, a man singularly well-informed for his station, but who was, nevertheless, thoroughly convinced of the existence of the subterraneans. 'I once myself,' said he, 'saw in the fjeld a man who suddenly sank down in the earth before my eyes, and it is well known,' added he, 'that one of the subterraneans, who in outward appearance perfectly resembled one of us, courted a girl who rejected him, although he promised her a house, chattels and as much silver plate as she desired.' On our objecting that either his imagination must have played him a trick, and the courtship have been a mere idle invention on the part of the girl; or that some person for a joke had imposed upon her, by giving himself out for a subterranean, he continued: 'But it is known for certain, that a man, who one day went into the forest, came suddenly upon a

---

1 'In Moland, in the Upper Thellemark,' writes Pastor Buch, 'they paid adoration to the Thusser, under the name of *Vetir*, by offering to them some of their best meat and drink, upon up-raised mounds, particularly buttermilk, or wort when they brewed. Such a libation was called a *saup*, i.e. a sup or gulp. Those who had not such Vetir-mounds poured out a little cup of drink on the hearth. The friendship of these beings was very useful to the peasant both for his cattle and general welfare.'

mansion with its appurtenances, the inmates of which, on his coming, instantly abandoned it. The man, who from fear of troll-craft did not venture to take up his abode in the mansion, announced the incident to the authorities, who took possession of the place in the king's name, which to this day, in remembrance of the event, bears the name of *Findland*.' As we still continued incredulous, and suggested that the persons mentioned might have been culprits, who on the man's coming betook themselves to flight, through fear of being discovered, our guide came forth with his last and weightiest argument: 'But it stands in the Bible, that every knee, both of those who are in heaven and on earth, and *under* the earth, shall bow before the Lord. And who then are those under the earth, if they are not the subterraneans?' Thus may even passages in the Bible itself, when misunderstood, serve to confirm superstition!

Having thus endeavoured to explain how the belief in these supernatural beings originated, and by some examples shown that in certain parts of the country it is still the popular belief, it only remains to lay before the reader a slight sketch of the similar ideas and kindred superstitions existing in the other Northern countries. In this sketch we shall confine ourselves chiefly to the subterraneans, who, according to both the old mythology and the popular traditions, are divided into several classes, as Thusser, Vaettir, Dwarfs, Elves, etc. In the old mythology the dwarfs – under which denomination seem to be comprised several of the species which now constitute the subterraneans – play an important part. They came forth, as we have already seen, as maggots in the rotten carcase of the giant Ymir, and at the behest of the gods received human form and understanding, and had habitations assigned them in the earth and in stones.

From these we may consider the subterraneans in all the Northern countries to derive their origin. We will first direct our attention to Iceland. As in Norway, the subterraneans here also dwell in hills and mounds, they are neat and clean, comely and flighty, readily hold converse with Christians, by whom they formerly had children. These they strove to exchange for the children of Christians before they were baptised, that their own might enjoy the benefit of baptism. Such substituted children were called *Umskiptingar,* and are usually stupid and weakly. The subterraneans have beautiful cattle, which, like themselves, are invisible, though they sometimes let themselves be seen in the bright sunshine, which they lack in their dwellings, and in which they therefore from time to time recreate themselves. On New Year's night they sometimes change their habitations, at which time it was formerly a custom in Iceland to leave well-provided tables standing, and the doors open, in order to gain the goodwill both of the comers and goers. According to old traditions, the subterraneans of Iceland were governed by two chieftains, who are changeable every second year, when, accompanied by some of their subjects, they sailed to Norway, to appear before the king of the whole race, who had his residence there, to renew their oath of fealty, and render an account of their administration, which, if found good and just, was continued to them; but in the contrary case they were instantly deposed; justice and equity being in high estimation among these elves.[1]

In the Farö isles, the subterraneans are, as in some parts of Norway, called Huldefolk, and resemble the Norse Vaettir, being described as full-grown, clad in grey, with black hats. Their large, fat cattle graze, though invisible, among those of the inhabitants; a sight of them is, however, sometimes obtained, as also of their dogs. They are fond of Christian females and of their children, which they exchange for their own.

In Sweden, the people have nearly the same ideas with regard to the subterraneans. Of their origin they have a singular tradition, viz, that they are fallen angels, and that when God cast down from heaven the adherents of Lucifer, they did not all fall into hell, but that some fell on the earth, others into the sea. Those that fell in the woods and forests became *Wood-trolls* (Skovtroll, Skogsnufvor); those that fell in the green fields and groves, *Vaettir* or *Lysgubbar;* those that were cast into the sea or waters became *Nächer;* those that fell among houses, *Tomtegubbar,* and those in trees, *Elfvar*.

In Denmark, we meet with the same ideas as in the rest of Scandinavia, though, in consequence of the nature of the country, somewhat modified. The subterraneans there dwell in mounds, in which they often have merrymakings; they brew, bake, steal beer from the peasants, if they neglect to mark the casks with a cross, punish tattlers with blindness, cannot endure the sound of bells, thunder, drums or water, are jealous, and can transform themselves into cats. Steel, as needles, keys, scissors and the like, either laid in the cradle or crosswise over the door, will, as in Sweden, prevent them from exchanging children; but if such an exchange is accomplished, there is no other remedy than to ill-treat the changeling.

The subterraneans or dwarfs of Germany resemble their Scandinavian brethren, and are officious, good-humoured and patient; they wear a *mist-mantle* or cap (Nebelkappe), which renders them invisible. They also exchange children; and if the changeling is ill-treated, its mother brings back the stolen child. The black dwarfs of Rügen bear a near resemblance to the Norwegian dwarfs; they are ugly of aspect, but are able smiths, particularly in steel, are unsocial, seldom leave their hills and mounds, and are no lovers of music. The white dwarfs, on the contrary, who in summer

1   Finni Johannaei, *Hist. Eccles. Islandiae,* ii, p. 368; Pref. to *Hist. Hrolfi Krakii;* F. Magnusen; *Eddalaere,* iii, p. 308.

sport among the trees and dance on the grass, resemble the Danish, Swedish and Norwegian elves. With the brown dwarfs of Rügen, who are eighteen inches high, wear glass shoes, have delicate hands and feet, are skilful smiths, but roguish, there are none to be compared.

In Pomerania, there was formerly a number of earth-sprites or dwarfs, who eagerly exchanged their own ugly offspring for comely, human children. They also fell in love with handsome girls and courted them. By day they crawled about in the form of toads and other reptiles, but at night they appeared in their own form, and danced merrily by moonlight. The people called them *Uellerkens*. Like the Nisser, they often lived in cellars. The German subterraneans differ from those of Scandinavia, in having adopted the true faith, and in sometimes wandering abroad.

# Popular Traditions of Norway

## Thurser, Vaetter, Dwarfs, etc.

In Norway the subterranean people – under which denomination are comprised Thurser (Thusser), Vaetter and Dwarfs, and sometimes Huldres, Nisser and Elves – are exceedingly numerous. The Thusser or Trolls, who are as large as men, inhabit the mountain-ridges and hills. In former days they were in such multitudes that no Christians could dwell in Norway, until they formed marriages with them. Like ourselves, they have houses, churches, chattels, and beautiful cattle, which graze in the night, and are watched by female keepers and black dogs. The Thusser are well formed, but of a pale or blue colour. When the sun is set and the twilight (Thus-mörk) begins, they are in full activity; then it is dangerous for persons, more particularly young females, for whom they have an especial liking, to pass by the places where they resort, where most delightful music is to be heard; and many are the instances, particularly in former days, of young maidens having been conveyed by them into the mountains and hills. They are also partial to little children, and formerly would often exchange them for their own, which were neither so handsome nor so thriving. But a cross made on the child, or steel in any shape laid in its cradle, is an effectual preventive of all such exchanges.[1]

With respect to these supernatural beings, the belief current in the North is, that when our Lord cast down the fallen angels, some fell to hell, while those who had not sinned so deeply were dispersed in the air, and under the earth, and in the waters.[2]

*A similar belief with regard to fairies prevails in Ireland. Keightley, F.M., p. 363.*

---

1 Faye, op. cit., p. 20.
2 Asbjörnsen, *Norske Huldreeventyr og Folkesagn*, i, 29.

## Huldra or Hulla

Over the whole of Norway the tradition is current of a supernatural being
that dwells in the forests and mountains, called Huldra or Hulla. She
appears like a beautiful woman, and is usually clad in a blue petticoat and
a white snood; but unfortunately has a long tail, like a cow's, which she
anxiously strives to conceal, when she is among people. She is fond of
cattle, particularly brindled,[1] of which she possesses a beautiful and
thriving stock. They are without horns. She was once at a merrymaking,
where everyone was desirous of dancing with the handsome, strange
damsel; but in the midst of the mirth, a young man, who had just begun a
dance with her, happened to cast his eye on her tail. Immediately guessing
whom he had got for a partner, he was not a little terrified; but collecting
himself, and unwilling to betray her, he merely said to her, when the dance
was over, 'Fair maid, you will lose your garter.' She instantly vanished, but
afterwards rewarded the silent and considerate youth with beautiful
presents and a good breed of cattle.[2]

The idea entertained of this being is not everywhere the same, but varies
considerably in different parts of Norway. In some places she is described
as a handsome female, when seen in front, but is hollow behind, or else
blue;[3] while in others she is known by the name of *Skogsnerte,* and is said
to be blue, but clad in a green petticoat, and probably corresponds to the
Swedish *Skogsnufvor.*[4] Her song – a sound often heard among the mountains – is said to be hollow and mournful,[5] differing therein from the
music of the subterranean beings, which is described by ear-witnesses as
cheerful and fascinating. But she is not everywhere regarded as a solitary
wood-nymph: Huldremen and Huldre-folk are also spoken of, who live
together in the mountains, and are almost identical with the subterranean
people. In Hardanger the Huldre-people are always clad in green, but their
cattle are blue, and may be taken when a grown-up person casts his belt
over them. They give abundance of milk. The Huldres take possession of
the forsaken pasture-spots in the mountains, and invite people into their
mounds, where delightful music is to be heard.[6]

1  In the original *brandede,* the meaning of which is doubtful.
2  Faye, op. cit., p. 39.
3  Hallager, *Norsk Ordsamling,* p. 48, *voce* Huldre.
4  *Linnaei Gotländske Resa,* p. 312.
5  'Huldre dwells in the mountains and in the valley; hers are all the riches, splendour
and beauty of the North; but hers is also its deep melancholy; to this her music and her
song bear witness, which cannot be heard without a feeling of sadness and tears.'
*Norske Huldreeventyr,* I, p. iv.
6  Faye, op. cit., p. 42.

*The belief in Huldra is very ancient. We read that as far back as the year 1205, the queen of Magnus Lagabaeter, when detained by an adverse wind at Bergen, having heard that the Icelander Sturli Thordsen was an excellent storyteller, desired him to relate to her the Saga of the giantess Huldra. Her name appears to be derived from the Old Norsk hollr, findus, propitius.*[1]

## Jutuls and Mountain-giants

The Jutul is large and strong, and has his dwelling in the highest mountains, where riches and costly treasures are to be found in abundance. He is of evil disposition, hates churches and the sound of bells, and is greedy after Christian blood. When a storm is at hand, or a whirlwind howls among the rocks, he shakes himself in the mountain, so that the pots and kettles resound, in which his wife Gyvri or Giögra prepares their food. All over the country traditions and traces of these monstrous beings are to be found. Marks of their footsteps are often to be seen in the mountains.

Of all the supernatural beings of the North, none bear so evident a mark of high antiquity as the gigantic Jutuls. The traditions concerning them rise always to the monstrous, and harmonise with the cloud-capped mountains among which they dwell.

On comparing the traditions of the vulgar with the old mythology, we find a great accordance between them, and at once recognise in the Jutuls and Röser (giants) the Jötuns and Risar, the foes of gods and men, who in Thor, the mighty god of thunder, found a dangerous enemy. The Jötuns in the Northern mythology are considered as chaotic beings, ruling over the dark and cold regions of the earth, shunning the light of day, and by the sun's rays (as we have already seen) becoming changed to stone.[2]

In Old Norse a giantess was called *gyfr* or *gygr*, a word to be recognised in the Gyvri and Giögra of the vulgar.

Besides Jutuls or Jötuns, we meet with Riser and Biergriser (giants and mountain-giants), who dwelt in mountain-caves, and are supposed to be the earliest inhabitants of the North. In the Sagas they are often called Trolls, which may be considered a common denomination for all noxious, supernatural beings.

1  *Sagabihl.*, i, 367; Grimm, J., *Deutsche Mythologie*, op. cit., p. 249.
2  Faye, op. cit., p. 7.

## The Jutul on Hestmandöe[1]

On Hestmandöe in the Nordlands there is a mountain, which at a distance resembles a horseman with a large cloak over him. This mountain was once a Jutul, who dwelt on the spot. Twelve miles to the south, on Leköe in Nummedal, there lived at the same time a maiden to whom he made love; but the haughty damsel, who was skilled in all kinds of magic, not only rejected him, but turned all his messengers to stone, who are still to be seen as rocks round the northern part of the isle. Exasperated at such conduct, the Jutul bent his bow, to take instantaneous vengeance. The mighty arrow flew and passed clean through the lofty mountain called Torgehat, where is still to be seen the large hole made by the arrow through the hard rock.[2] 'That straw stands in the way,' exclaimed the Jutul. Being somewhat checked in its flight, by forcing its way through the Torgehat, the arrow did not quite reach its destination, but fell at the feet of the maiden on the north side of Leköe, where it yet lies in the form of a huge, long stone. By their mutual magic they were both changed to stone, and shall so remain, looking on each other until doomsday.

Even at the present time a Nordlander seldom sails by without taking his hat off to the maid of Leköe.[3]

## The Jutul's Bridge

In Spirillen, at low water, a sort of stone bridge is to be seen, about the eighth of a mile in length. It owes its origin to a Jutul that dwelt on the Elsrudkolle. This Jutul courted a Huldra on the Engerkolle, which lies on the opposite side of the water. That he might visit her without getting wet, which sorely grieved his beloved, he resolved to construct a bridge, but burst in pieces, when the sun rose and surprised him at his work.[4]

## The Girl at the Saeter[5]

A land proprietor in Norway was betrothed to a very pretty young woman, who, although a farmer's daughter, went out with the cattle to their summer pasture, where she employed herself in weaving a piece of drill. Being, however, unable to finish her work by the time when the cattle

1 Horseman's isle.
2 That the size of the hole is considerable, may be inferred from its height, which is estimated at 600 feet.
3 Faye, op. cit., p. 13.
4 Faye, op. cit., p. 15, and see p. 000 of this volume, note 3.
5 The Saetere are grassy spots among the mountains of Norway, to which the cattle are sent for summer pasture. They are frequently a considerable distance from the dwelling.

should return home, she resolved to stay behind till she had accomplished her task: but no sooner had her lover received intelligence of her design, than he set out for the pasture, justly thinking it hazardous to leave the damsel alone exposed to the attempts of Huldres and other subterranean beings. He reached the spot in the nick of time, for he found the cattle-house surrounded by black horses ready saddled. Suspecting, therefore, that there was something wrong in the wind, he stole into the pasture, and peeping through a little window in the hut, saw his intended sitting in a bridal dress with a golden crown on her head, and by her side an old red-eyed Huldreman. Seizing his pistol, which he had wisely loaded with a silver bullet,[1] he fired over the head of the girl, before the witchery could be dissolved, rushed into the hut, seized her, placed her behind him on his horse, and rode off, followed by the whole company of Trolls. One of these held out to him a well-filled golden horn, to retard his flight: he took the horn, but cast the liquor it contained behind his horse, and galloped off with both horn and girl. At length he reached a steep mountain near his dwelling, in which some subterranean folk had their abode, who were on terms of hostility with his pursuers, and who cried to him, 'Ride on the rough, and not on the smooth.' He followed their advice, and rode through a rye-field, where the Trolls were unable to follow him, but in their exasperation cried after him, 'The red cock shall crow over thy dwelling.'[2] And behold! his house stood in a blaze.[3]

## Gurri Kunnan[4]

At Osterraad there dwelt formerly a rich and powerful man, who had a daughter named Aslaug, the fairest damsel far and near. She had, as may be easily imagined, many a gallant suitor, but she preferred to every other a young man who had been fostered with her in her father's mansion, notwithstanding that he was of low extraction. As they could not hope that the proud father would consent to their union, they fled secretly, and

1 Great in the good days of yore was the efficacy of a silver bullet, or a silver button, when fired at a witch, or wizard, or the like. See *Anecdotes and Traditions*, by Thoms, Camd. Publ., pp. 111, 112, and the note.
2 The symbol of a red cock for fire is of remote antiquity (See *Völuspá*, pp. 34, 35). 'I will set a red cock on your roof,' is the incendiary's threat in Germany, where fire is compared to a cock flying from house to house. Grimm, J., *Deutsche Mythologie*, op. cit., p. 568.
3 Faye, op. cit., p. 25.
4 T. Keightley, *The Fairy Mythology*, London, 1828, p. 130 gives a more elaborate version of this story from an oral tradition communicated to Dr Grimm, and inserted in Hauff's *Märchenalmanach* for 1827. The simpler form, in which it here appears, I take to be the older.

sought concealment and shelter in a deep cave, which is to be seen at this day not far from Osterraad. By chance the enraged father, in the following spring, got intelligence of the place where his daughter was concealed, and instantly proceeded thither, for the purpose of punishing the audacious seducer; but just as he reached the cave there fell down such a quantity of stones and rubbish, that the entrance was completely closed, so that the fugitives were not to be taken. When the first danger was over, the loving pair succeeded, though with difficulty, in working their way out from amid the fallen stones. They then took a boat, that was lying near the shore, and through many perils succeeded in reaching the uninhabited group of islands called Tarven, which at that time served as a retreat for Trolls. The chief among these, the Huldre, Gurri Kunnan, received them kindly, and allowed them to stay in her habitation, though on condition that they should never make the sign of the cross, which she could not endure. One Yule-eve, when Gurri, with a countless number of Trolls, were assembled at a festivity, the wonder-struck Aslaug forgot her promise and crossed herself, at the same time pronouncing the name of Jesus. On a sudden all the witchery vanished, and of the whole parade a huge copper kettle alone remained, which for time out of mind has since been kept in the largest isle of the group, the now inhabited Hunsöe.[1]

This Gurri was the daughter of a giant, who dwelt on the isle of Kunnan off Helgeland. Being very beautiful, she had many suitors, who fought for the possession of the fair giantess, and round about Kunnan[2] is to be seen a cluster of rocks formed of the stones they hurled at each other. All were, however, forced to cede to the giant Anfind, who married the beautiful Gurri, and lived happily with her, until her father was slain, together with the powerful 'Sout', by the mighty 'Gout', who came from the east, when the whole family was driven from Kunnan, and Anfind with his wife sought shelter with Fröi, who gave them Tarven for a residence. Here they lived in peace until St Olaf came to the island, who, with the sign of the cross and the name of Jesus, not only quelled the storm that the giant had raised, but turned the giant himself into a hard block of stone.

*The above is the story on which the beautiful poem of 'Gurri Kunnan' is founded. Its author, Professor Steenblock, kindly communicated the tradition to me, as he had heard it in his youth. A prose paraphrase of the poem is given in the* Mythologie der Feen und

---

1    The other isles are used merely for the grazing of cattle, in consequence of the superstition that no one can inhabit them, on account of the Trolls and other devilish beings. The copper kettle, as I have been assured, is still preserved by the inhabitants of the isle.

2    Kunnen is a promontory on the north side of Helgeland.

*Elfen, by Prof. Wolff, i, 234. This in many respects interesting story seems to point to a remote antiquity, when the original inhabitants of the North were forced to retire before the invading Goths (the 'Gout' of the tradition), who, by means of their greater civilisation and superior skill, destroyed or expelled their adversaries.*[1]

## The Bridal Crown

In Nummedal there once lived a young girl so beautiful that a Thuss fell in love with her; but notwithstanding that he promised her a sumptuous mansion, abundance of cattle, and in short whatever she could desire, if she would betroth herself to him, she continued faithful to her old lover. When the Thuss found that nothing was to be done by gentle means, he carried her off. Accompanied by a numerous body of Thusser, he was already on his road with his prey to the subterranean people's church, there to be married to her, when her lover was so fortunate as to get traces of their route. Having overtaken the bridal party, he shot with steel over his betrothed's head, when the whole witchery vanished, and he not alone recovered the maiden, but got a splendid silver crown, which the Thuss had placed on her head. The crown still exists in the 'dal', and as it is supposed to bring good luck to every bride that wears it, it is let out at almost every wedding of the better class.

---

It is not long beyond the memory of man since a young man in Nummedal, when passing by a forsaken saeter-hut, saw in it a gay Huldre-wedding party. Through a window he was witness to all that passed among the mountain-folk; but his attention was chiefly directed to the bride, by her beauty and elegant attire, especially by a massive, glittering silver crown that she wore. The young man continued gazing on her till he contracted a violent passion for her, and soon resolved on depriving the wedding party of their mirth, and the bridegroom of his rich and lovely bride. Quickly he drew forth his knife, and as quickly flew the shining steel through the window and over the head of the bride. The company vanished in the twinkling of an eye, the maiden alone remaining spellbound by the steel. The pair came soon to an understanding; the Huldre bride accompanied him to the village and then to the altar, after having been baptised. But her magnificent bridal attire was insufficient to withdraw attention from an ugly cow's tail, which, however, after a time, gradually disappeared. They lived long and happy together, and of her rich wedding ornaments, the fame of which is yet preserved, there is still to be seen at Maerabru the costly silver crown.

---

1   Faye, op. cit., p. 10. Henceforth when no authority is given, the traditions are generally from Faye.

## The Bishop's Cattle

One summer, a long time ago, the bishop of Drontheim sent his cattle to the mountains to graze. They were the finest cattle in all Norway; and the bishop, when he sent them away, strictly enjoined those who were to watch them, not, on any account, to suffer them, for one moment, to be out of sight, as the mountains thereabouts swarmed with subterranean people, who, however, had no power over any animal, as long as it was under a human eye. The cattle were then sent up to the mountains. One day, while the animals were grazing, and the keepers sitting in various places with their eyes directed towards them, there appeared suddenly, on the highest point of the mountain, an elk of an extraordinary size. At this apparition, the eyes of the three keepers were drawn off from the cattle, and for an instant fixed on the elk; but when they again looked down into the valley, they saw their beautiful large cattle transformed to a set of diminutive mice, running along the mountain's side, and before the keepers could approach them, they all vanished through a crevice in the earth. Thus did the bishop of Drontheim get rid of his three hundred head of cattle.

*Conway, in his* Journey through Norway, *p. 240, relates this story, and adds: 'This tradition is universally credited in the mountainous parts.' A woman, who was watching cattle on a hill, was more fortunate; she saw her cattle suddenly vanish, but while she was bewailing her loss, she heard a voice from the mountain, desiring her to hasten home, and lo! there she found not only her own cows, but also a new one, which, although it never calved, yet had a greater abundance of milk than the others.*

## The Midwife

There was once a man and his wife that had an only daughter. Suddenly she disappeared, and notwithstanding that her parents – who took the loss of their dear child sorely to heart – sought for her in every direction, they could not discover the faintest trace of her. A considerable time had elapsed, when late one evening there came a stranger to the house and asked the woman, who was at home alone, whether she would visit her daughter, who abode in the neighbourhood, and was in labour, and required her aid. The mother, who was both glad and grieved at this unexpected intelligence, instantly made herself ready, and by means of a thread, which the stranger gave her, was in one moment with her daughter, who gave birth to a lively, well-formed child. Before it was dressed, the man gave her a liquid, desiring her to rub it over the infant's body, at the same time cautioning her not to let any of it come in contact with herself. But her eye beginning to itch, she inadvertently rubbed it, and thus got some of the liquid in her eye. When her help was no longer required, the man – who was her daughter's husband and a Troll – told her she might depart, when by means of the thread she found herself in a few seconds again at home. The following day, while at work with her husband in the field, she on a sudden saw her daughter with her subterranean spouse walking close at her side. On her addressing them, her son-in-law asked her with astonishment, whether she really could see them? 'Yes, surely, I can see you with my right eye,' said the woman; but at the same instant the Troll touched her eye, and from that time she saw no more with it.

*The superstition of anointing the eyes, and being thereby enabled to see what would else be invisible, appears to have been generally current among the inhabitants of western Europe, both Keltic and Germanic. Instances of its prevalence in Denmark we shall see hereafter; of its existence in other countries, our own included, we give the following proofs.*

*Mrs Bray* (Letters to Southey) *relates a story of the* sage femme *of Tavistock, who was one night summoned to a fairy labour, and who, on receiving an ointment to rub the child's eyes with (thinking, no doubt, that what was good for the baby must be equally so for herself), applied a little of it to one of her own eyes, when lo! all things around her suddenly appeared in their true form, all delusion was dissipated. On the next market day she saw the old fellow who had conveyed her, pilfering from the stalls in the market, and accosted him. 'What,' exclaimed he, 'do you see me today?' 'See you! to be sure I do, and I see you are busy too.' 'And pray with which eye do you see all this?' 'With my right.' 'Take that for meddling with what did not belong to you: you shall see me no more.' He then struck her eye, and from that hour till the day of her death she was blind of that eye.*[1]

*A similar story is related of a cottager and his wife at Nether Whitton.*

*The author of* Round about our Coal fire (quoted by Brand, Pop. Antiq.) *says, 'The moment anyone saw them (the fairies), and took notice of them, they were struck blind of an eye.'*[2]

*Ritson* (Fairy Tales) *relates that a woman who had been in their (the fairies') society, challenged one of the guests, whom she espied in the market selling fairy-butter. This freedom was deeply resented, and cost her the eye she first saw him with.*[3]

*In a Scottish tradition it is related that a fairy left a child to be suckled with a young woman of Nithsdale, and rubbed her eyes with a wonderful salve, by virtue of which she could discern the otherwise invisible fairy folk. Some of the salve she contrived to secure. Happening one day to meet the fairy lady, she attempted to shake hands with her. 'What ee d'ye see me wi?' whispered she. 'Wi them baith,' said the woman. The fairy breathed on her eyes, and the salve lost its efficacy.*[4]

---

1  Keightley, op, cit., p. 301.
2  Ibid., p. 298.
3  Keightley, op, cit., p. 309.
4  Cromek's *Remains of Nithsdale and Galloway Song*, quoted by Keightley, p. 353.

*Mr Keightley relates (F.M., p. 417), from a communication made to him by a lady in North Wales, of a gipsy, that desired the narrator, who wished to see fairies, to meet her by moonlight on the top of Craig y Dinis. She there washed his eyes with the contents of a phial which she had, and he instantly saw thousands of fairies, all in white, dancing to the sound of numerous harps.*

*Gervase of Tilbury, who lived in the twelfth century (I quote from Dobeneck, i, 45), speaks of certain water-sprites in the south of France called Drakes. These assume a human form and appear in the public market. They are said to inhabit the caverns of rivers, and to allure women and children while bathing, under the form of gold rings and cups, striving to obtain which they are suddenly dragged down to the bottom. This oftenest happens to women giving suck, whom the Drakes seize to suckle their own unblest offspring. These, after seven years thus passed, sometimes return rewarded to our hemisphere. They relate that with the Drakes and their wives they dwelt in spacious palaces in the caverns and banks of the rivers . . . On men thus seized the Drakes are said to feed. One day a Drake having given a woman in his service some eel-pasty, she happened to draw her fingers, greasy with the fat, over one eye and one side of her face, and thereby acquired a most clear and sharp power of vision under water. Having completed the third year of her servitude, and being returned home, she one morning early met the Drake in the market-place of Beaucaire, whom she accosted, and inquired after her mistress and nursling. 'With which eye did you recognise me?' asked the Drake. She pointed to the eye she had greased with the fat of the pasty. Having ascertained this, the Drake thrust his finger into that eye, and thus continued thenceforth unseen and unknown by all.*

*A story somewhat similar is told of a Countess Ranzau.*

## The Öiestad Horn

Near the river Nid in Nedenaes there is a mansion called Neersteen, in which there once dwelt a man named Siur, who was both powerful and rich; for besides Neersteen he owned six other mansions, and a considerable salmon fishery in the Nid; but what was more than all these, he had a daughter, who was the fairest maid of all the surrounding neighbourhood. She was courted by a Westland man named Ring, but the wealthy Siur rejected him for a son-in-law, although his daughter was fondly attached to him. The lover, however, was not disheartened, so while the father one St John's day was at matins in Öiestad church, Ring came to the mansion and found his lass, although her father had taken the precaution of locking her up in one of the presses – which, according to the custom of the time, were made at the foot of the bed – a corner of her apron having protruded and betrayed her. They now fled, and Siur, the instant he was apprised of their elopement, mounted his horse and went in pursuit of them. On the way he was stopped by a Troll, who came out of a mount, and bade him welcome, at the same time presenting to him a full drinking-horn. Instead of emptying it, he cast its contents behind him, but some drops that fell on the horse's loins instantly singed the hair off. Siur, who had from the first suspected mischief, put spurs to his horse, and galloped away with the horn in his hand and the Troll whining after him. He was now in a most serious dilemma, from which he was unexpectedly rescued by another Troll, who was on terms of hostility with the former one, who called to him when he had just reached a large field: 'Ride through the rye and not through the wheat.' Following this counsel he got the start of his pursuer, who could not proceed so rapidly through the tall rye. The danger was not, however, completely over until he came near the mansion of Bringsvaer, when the cock crew and the Troll vanished. Slur now continued his pursuit without further delays, and overtook the fugitives on a hill where they had stopped to take a few moments rest. When the men got sight of each other, they immediately drew their knives, and a contest ensued, the result of which was, that Siur stabbed Ring in the belly, who instantly gave up the ghost.

In expiation of this homicide, Siur was compelled to make heavy compensation. The horn, which he kept, was preserved in the family down to our times. Of the daughter's fate tradition makes no mention.

*The (or rather a) horn, which had long been an heirloom in Siur's family, has lately been presented by Shipmaster Berge to the public library and museum of Arendal school, where it now is. It is very handsome, and has on its three silver-gilt rings the following inscription, in monkish characters: potum servorum benedic deus alme [tuorum reliqvam unus, benede le un]? casper, melchior, baltazar.*

*A similar occurrence to the above took place many years ago near Hahauger in Hallingdal, where one Christmas Eve a subterranean woman presented drink in a horn to a man named Gudbrand Goelberg, which he threw over his shoulder and rode off with the horn; but down to the ninth generation, his posterity, as a penalty, were afflicted with some bodily blemish or defect, as the Troll had threatened. This horn, which was long preserved at Halsteensgaard in Aal, contained nearly three quarts, and was encircled by a strong gilt copper ring about three inches broad, on which, in monkish characters, stood melchior, baltazar, caspar. In the middle was a small, gilt copper plate, in which an oval crystal was set.*

## Huldre Marriage

It is related that an active young fellow in Nordland, by laying the barrel of his rifle over a Huldre in a forest, got her into his power and made her his wife. They lived happily together and had a child; but on a sudden, as the child was one evening playing by the fireplace, where the Huldre was sitting and spinning, while the man was at his work, something of her savage

nature came over her, during which she said to her husband, alluding to the
child, that it would make a capital roast for supper. The man was horrified,
and the woman, who was conscious that she had grievously committed
herself, changed her tone, and begged her words might be forgotten. But
they were not: the man bore them in remembrance; the horrid sounds rung
incessantly in his ears; he perceived in them a proof of his now no longer
blooming wife's real nature, and their domestic peace was at an end. From
being a good man he became morose, frequently upbraided his wife with
her diabolical proposal, cursed the hour when he resolved on marrying her,
beat and ill-used her. Thus it continued for a season. The woman suffered
and repented. One day she went to the smithy, to see with a friendly eye her
husband at his work; but he began as before, and on its coming to blows,
she, by way of proving her superior strength, seized an iron bar and twisted
it round her husband as if it had been a wire. The husband was now forced
to submission and to promise domestic peace.

## The Nisse or Niss

This is a supernatural being, nearly resembling our Goblin, the Scottish
Brownie, the German Kobold, and the Kaboutermanneken of the Netherlands. In the good old times they were infinitely more numerous than they
are in our days. They are not larger than small children, are clothed in grey,
and wear a red, pointed cap. Their habitation is usually in barns and
stables, where they help to tend the cattle and horses, for which they show
the same partiality as for men. There are many instances of the Nisse
having drawn the hay from the cribs of the other horses to that of the one
for which he entertains a predilection. He is fond of pranks, will sometimes
let all the cows loose in the cow-house, plague the milkmaids, either by
blowing out the light, or by holding the hay so fast that the poor girls
cannot draw out a particle; then, while they are tugging with all their
might, he will suddenly let go his hold, so that they fall at full length on the
ground. This delights the Nisse exceedingly, and causes him to set up a
horse-laugh. If he feels attached to the master of the house, he will do all he
can for his benefit. Instances, indeed, are not wanting of his having
endeavoured to abstract hay and other things from his neighbours, for the
use of his master; whence contention and conflicts sometimes take place
between the Nisser of the two houses, so that the hay and straw may be
seen flying about in all directions. As they are obliging to those they favour,
but spiteful and vindictive when anyone slights or makes game of them, it
is not surprising that their goodwill is deemed worth the gaining. On
Christmas Eve, therefore, and on Thursday evenings, in many places, they
set sweet porridge, cakes, beer, etc. for the Nisse, which he gladly

consumes, provided they are to his taste; for he is sometimes dainty. Ridicule and contempt he cannot endure, and as he is strong, notwithstanding his diminutive size, his opponent often comes off second best. A peasant, who one winter evening met a Nisse on the road, and in an authoritative tone ordered him to get out of the way, found himself, before he knew a word of the matter, pitched over the hedge into a field of snow. With a girl also, who one Christmas Eve brought him food accompanied with mockery, he danced such a dance, that she was found, on the following morning, lying dead in the barn.

They love the moonlight, and in winter may sometimes be seen amusing themselves in little sledges, or in leaping over the fences. Although they are lively, yet they do not at all times like noise and bustle, particularly on Christmas Eve, or a Thursday evening. In general the Nisse is liked, and is, therefore, in many places called *good fellow*.

Of all the beings that live in the imagination of the Norwegian peasantry, the Nisse is that of whose existence they are the most thoroughly convinced. Though belonging to the dwarf-race, he nevertheless differs from the dwarfs by his sprightliness and well-proportioned figure, as well as by his sojourn in houses and barns, for which his predilection is so strong, that he cannot endure a removal; for he will then forsake the family, and take their good luck with him. It is this partiality to old tofts that has obtained for him the names of Toft-vaette, Tomtevaette,[1] and Gardbo.

Neither in the *Eddas* nor the Sagas is there any mention of the Nisse. Akin to him are, the Niägriusar of the Faeröe isles, who are described as diminutive, with red caps, and bringers of luck; also the Swedish Tomtegubbe.

They frequently dwell in the high trees that are planted round the house, on which account care should be taken not to fell them, particularly the more ancient ones. Many a one has paid for his disregard herein by an incurable disease.[2]

## The Werwolf

That there were persons who could assume the form of a wolf or a bear (Huse-björn), and again resume their own, is a belief as widespread as it is ancient. This property is either imparted by Trollmen, or those possessing it are themselves Trolls. In the *Volsunga Saga* we have very early traces of this superstition.

---

1   Toft and tomt are synonymous, and signify the space on which a messuage has stood.
2   Arndt, iii, 15.

## The Mara (Qvaeldrytterinde)

The Mara (Eng. *mare*, in *nightmare*) belongs to the same family with the Vardögl, Draug, etc. In appearance she resembles a most beautiful woman, but in acts the most malignant Troll. She passes through locked doors, assails persons sleeping by setting herself across them, and tormenting them so that it is horrible. The person afflicted by such a nightly visit is said to be Mare-ridden, and is often nearly suffocated. She is not satisfied with tormenting persons, but will ride both sheep and horses. In the Thellemark she is called *Muro,* and there, as in other places, they have many methods of getting rid of her; one of the most effectual is to wrap a knife in a cloth, and, in a manner prescribed, let it turn three times round the body, while uttering certain rimes.

*Like other supernatural beings, the Mara can enter by the smallest hole, but, like them, she must also make her exit by the way through which she entered, even though every door and window should be open (Thiele, II, 282). Hence Mephistopheles, in answer to Faust's inquiry* why he did not depart through the window? *says –*

> 's ist ein Gesetz der Teufel und Gespenster,
> wo sie hereingeschüpft, da müssen sie hinaus.

See also Holberg's Uden Hoved og Hale, Act 1, Sc. 4.

   The Ynglingasaga, cxvi. has a story of a King Vanlandi in Upsala, who was trodden to death by a Mara. When his men held his head, she trod on and almost crushed his legs; and when they held his feet, she so pressed his head as to cause his death.

## Ghosts

The belief that the souls of the departed find pleasure in revisiting the places where they have experienced joy or sorrow and pain, is universal among almost every people. Hence the current opinion, that the soul of a murdered person willingly hovers around the spot where his body is buried, and makes its appearance, for the purpose of calling forth vengeance on the murderer. The eye of superstition sees them sometimes as white spectres in the churchyard, where they stop horses, terrify people, and make a disturbance; sometimes as executed criminals, who in the moonlight wander round the place of execution, with their head under their arm. Sometimes they pinch people while asleep both black and blue, and such marks are called ghost-spots (Dödningepletter), or ghost pinches (Dödningeknib). Such spectres cannot find peace in the grave, in consequence of the crimes either of themselves or of others, before they are asked what it is they want; after which they do not appear again. Bullets, gunpowder, and weapons are wasted on them; but at the sight of a cross and from exorcisms they must retire. Under this head may be included the so-called *Udburrer* or *Udbore,* who in some districts cry like children in the woods, and entice people to them, and in other places, have their abode in steep mountains, and retired spots near the sea, and are supposed to derive their origin from murdered children.

*The Danish word for ghost is Gjenganger, or Gjenfaerd, answering exactly to the French revenant. The belief in ghosts was deeply impressed on the minds of the heathen Northmen; a belief closely connected with their ideas of the state after death. The soul, they believed, returned to the place whence it sprang, while the body and the grosser life bound to it passed to the abode of Hel or Death. Herewith was naturally combined the belief that the soul of the departed might, from its heavenly home, revisit the earth, there at night-time to unite itself in the grave-mound with the corporeal shadow released from Hel. Thus the dead could show themselves in the opened grave-mounds in the same form which they had in life. See Völsungakv., I, Str. 37, 38, in Edda Saem.*

*In the Eyrbyggiasaga is a story of an ejectment of a whole troop of ghosts from a house by judicial process.*

## The Nök

The Norwegian Nök (O. Nor. Nikr, Sw. Neck) generally has its abode in rivers and lakes, sometimes also in friths (Fiorde). It requires a human sacrifice every year; for which reason one person at least is annually missing in the vicinity of every river or water that is inhabited by a Nök. When any person is drowned the Nök is often heard to cry in a hollow, unearthly voice: 'Saet over!' (Cross over). The Nök can transform himself into all kinds of things. Sometimes he will appear like half a boat in the water, at others like a half horse on the bank, sometimes like gold and other valuables. If a person touches any of these things, the Nök instantly gets power over him. He is particularly greedy after little children. He is, however, dangerous only after sunset. On approaching any water, it is not amiss to say: 'Nyk! Nyk! Naal I Vatn! Jomfru Maria kastet Staal I Vatn! Du saek, aik flyt!' ('Nyk! Nyk! needle in water! The Virgin Mary cast steel into water! Thou sink, I float!') This formula requires some explanation, which will be found hereafter in what is related of the Swedish Neck.

The Nök is known in many places under the name of the Söetrold (water-sprite), which is said to abide always in the water, and to have many heads. If persons are in danger of shipwreck, they must promise him a son or a daughter for their deliverance; for which he, on the other hand, bestows on them riches and good fortune as much as they desire. He frequently changes his form, and takes his name from the place where he has his abode. In one place in Norway, whenever it is stormy, or a tempest is gathering, he appears in the form of a large horse, plashing with his monstrous hoofs in the water, which he causes almost constantly to be in violent motion. In the same water, another being, called the Vigtrold, has its habitation, which shouts terrifically when any danger is at hand.

Although the Nök is a dangerous being, he nevertheless sometimes meets with his master. In the waterfall of Sund, as the story goes, there dwelt for a long time a Nök, who caused the loss of many persons, when they rowed up or down the fall. The priest, who apprehended danger from this Nök, took with him on his passage four stout men, whom he ordered to row with all their might up the fall. They made the attempt twice, but at each time glided back. In making the third attempt, it was observed that, at the upper part of the fall, the priest, dashing his hand into the water, drew up a black creature resembling a little dog. He then ordered the men to row farther up, at the same time placing the animal firmly between his feet, and keeping a constant silence. Having now reached the stone-mound at Tvet, he conjured the Nök into it. From that time no one has perished in the fall.

*In Iceland, where the Nök is called* Hnikur, *he appears like a handsome grey horse, though with his hoofs turned backwards, and strives to tempt people to mount him, when he will gallop off with them into the water. Some efforts to tame him have been partially successful, and he has been made to work, though for a short time only.*

*In the Faroe islands the* Nikar *has his abode in fresh waters or lakes, where he will drag people down and drown them.*

*In Scotland the Nök is sometimes represented by Shellycoat, who is covered with seaweed and mussel-shells; sometimes by the Kelpie who, at least in the Highlands, appears in a horse's shape. In the Orkneys he appears either as a little horse, or as a man under the name of Tangie.*[1] *In Shetland he is called Shoopiltee, and appears as a handsome little horse, tempting persons to mount him, when he runs with his rider into the sea. In the Scottish islands they make him an offering, in the shape of a cup of good beer.*[2]

*Grimm (Deutsche Mythologie, op. cit., p. 4 79) interprets the name of Shellycoat by the German Schellenrock (Bell-coat), supposing him so named from his coat being hung with bells; and cites the instance of a Puck, who for thirty years served in the kitchen and stable of a Mecklenburg monastery. He appeared always well-disposed, and only stipulated for tunicam de diversis coloribus et tintinnabulis plenam.*

*The Norwegian Nök and the Kelpie of Scotland are identical beings. When one of the Grahams of Morphie was building the old castle, he secured the assistance of the water-kelpie or river-horse, by the accredited means of throwing a pair of branks (a sort of*

---

1   In Ben's *Description of Orkney* (1599) he is thus described: 'Indutus est algis marinis toto corpore, similis est pullo equino convoluto pilis, membrum habet simile equino, et testiculos magnos.' Hibbert, p. 504.
2   See Hibbert, pp. 5, 26.

*yoke) over his head. When released from his labour, and about to return to the water, he said:*

> 'Sair back and sair banes,
> Drivin the Laird o' Morphie's stanes!
> The Laird o' Morphie'll never thrive
> As lang 's the kelpie is alive!'[1]

## The Grim or Fossegrim

Closely allied to the Nök is the musical Grim or Fossegrim of Norway, a being whose sojourn is by waterfalls and mill-works. He generally plays in still and dark evenings, to entice persons to him, and teach those to play on the violin or other stringed instrument, who, on a Thursday evening, offer to him, with averted face, a white kid, which is to be cast into a waterfall running northwards. If the offering is lean, the learner's progress will extend only to the tuning of the violin; but if it is fat, the Fossegrim will grasp the player's right hand, and move it backwards and forwards until the blood springs out at the end of every finger. The pupil is then fully instructed, and can play so incomparably that the very trees will dance and the waterfalls stop their course.

## The Rore-trold

In the Rorevand in Nedenaes, a lake enclosed within steep mountains, and much exposed to squalls of wind, a Troll, called the Rore-trold, has his abode. He appears under various forms, sometimes as a horse, sometimes as a load of hay, sometimes as a huge serpent, and sometimes as a number of persons. In the winter, and when the ice is thickest, there may be seen, on one night, a long, broad chasm, with fragments of ice lying in it, all which is the work of the Rore-trold.

## The Brunmîgi

Another somewhat noxious Troll is the Brunmîgi, who is supposed to dwell near and infest springs. His name (from Brunn, *fons,* and mîga, *mingere)* sufficiently indicates his nature.

---

1 Chambers' *Pop. Rh.*, p. 35.

## The Qvaernknurre

This being seems in many respects identical with the Fossegrim. In Gierrestad it was formerly the custom to place a soft loaf, a cup of beer, or something of the kind, by the millstone, that the Qvaernknurre might increase the flour in the sacks. For some time he took up his abode in Sandager waterfall, where a man had a mill. As often as the man began to grind corn the mill stopped. Knowing that it was the Qvaernknurre that caused this annoyance, he took with him one evening, when he was about to grind, some pitch in a pot, under which he made a fire. As soon as he had set the mill in motion it stopped as usual. He then thrust downwards with a pole, in the hope of driving away the Qvaernknurre, but in vain. At last he opened the door to see, when lo! there stood the Qvaernknurre with extended jaws, and of such magnitude that while its lower lip rested on the threshold, its upper one touched the top of the doorway. It said to the man: 'Hast thou ever seen such great gaping?' Instantly seizing the boiling pitch-pot, the man dashed it into his mouth, with the words: 'Hast thou ever tasted such hot boiling?' With a howl the Qvaernknurre vanished, and was never again seen.

*A being nearly resembling the Qvaernknurre is the Urisk of the Scottish Highlands, which is described as a rough hairy sprite that sets mills at work in the night, when there is nothing to grind. He is sent howling away by a panful of hot ashes thrown into his lap while he is sleeping.*[1]

## The Finngalkn

This monster is often named, though not accurately described, in the later romantic Sagas. According to these it has a human head with enormous teeth, a beast's body and a large heavy tail, terrific claws and a sword in every claw.[2]

## Gertrud's Bird

In Norway the red-crested, black woodpecker is known under the name of Gertrud's Bird. Its origin is as follows: 'When our Lord, accompanied by St Peter, was wandering on earth, they came to a woman who was occupied in baking; her name was Gertrud, and on her head she wore a red hood. Weary and hungry from their long journeying, our Lord begged for a cake.

---

1   Keightley, op, cit., p. 396, from the *Quarterly Review*, 1825.
2   Keyser, *Normaendenes Religionsforfatning*, p. 163. See *Snorra-Edda*, edited by Bask, p. 342.

She took a little dough and set it on to bake, and it grew so large that it filled the whole pan. Thinking it too much for alms, she took a smaller quantity of dough, and again began to bake, but this cake also swelled up to the same size as the first; she then took still less dough, and when the cake had become as large as the preceding ones, Gertrud said: 'You must go without alms, for all my bakings are too large for you.' Then was our Lord wroth, and said: 'Because thou givest me nothing, thou shalt for a punishment become a little bird, shalt seek thy dry food between the wood and the bark, and drink only when it rains.' Hardly were these words spoken, when the woman was transformed to the *Gertrud's bird,* and flew away through the kitchen chimney; and at this day she is seen with a red hood and black body, because she was blackened by the soot of the chimney. She constantly pecks the bark of trees for sustenance, and whistles against rain; for she always thirsts and hopes to drink.'[1]

## Aasgaardsreia (Wild Hunt)

This band consists of spirits who have not done so much good as to deserve heaven, nor so much evil as to be sent to hell. It consists of drunkards, brawlers, singers of slanderous songs, crafty deceivers, and those that for the sake of lucre have perjured themselves. Their punishment is to ride about till the end of the world. At the head of the troop rides Guro-Rysse or Reisa-Rova with her long tail, by which she is distinguished from the rest. After her follows a multitude of both sexes. If seen in front, they appear tall and comely, both riders and horses; but behind, nothing is to be seen but Guro's long tail. The horses, which are coal-black, and have eyes that glow in the dark hike fire, are guided with red-hot rods and iron reins, which, together with the screaming of the riders, cause such a terrific noise that it may be heard at a vast distance. They ride as easily over water as over land, their horses' hoofs scarcely touching the surface of the water. Wherever they cast a saddle on a roof, there a person must soon die; and where they understand there will be fighting and murder in a drinking bout, there they enter, and set themselves on the ledge above the door. They conduct themselves quietly as long as nothing is going forwards, but set up a horse-laugh and make a loud rattling with their iron rods, when the fighting is begun and murder committed. The troop rides about chiefly at Christmas, when the great drinking bouts are held. When a person hears the troop coming, he should get out of the way or fall down on his face, and appear to be asleep; for there are instances of men having been caught

---

1    Asbjörnsen og Möe, No. 2; Grimm, J., *Deutsche Mythologie*, op. cit., p. 639.

up by them, and either carried back to the place whence they were taken, or found half stupified at a distance from it. A good man who takes this precaution has nothing more to apprehend than that each of the troop will spit on him. When all are passed by, he must spit in his turn; otherwise be would receive injury therefrom.

*This remarkable tradition, the title even of which points to heathenism, is known, at least by name, over the greater part of the diocese of Christiansand, but it is found most complete in the Upper Thellemark, where I myself have heard it; where it is called the Aaske-Rei or Asanerfoerd, which cannot be seen but only heard. It devours the Fladbröd (thin cakes), butter, etc., that have been prepared for Christmas, unless they be crossed previously to being put away. In one district of Norway, if anyone, on hearing the troop, does not throw himself down, his soul must accompany it, while his body remains lying. When the soul returns to the body, the latter is quite enfeebled, and remains so ever after. In some places this noisy troop is called Aaskereia, in others Hoskelreia. Sometimes they ride with a rushing noise through the air; sometimes they are to be met by night, on the roads, riding on black horses with glowing eyes. On Christmas Eve, and the three nights of Christmas, they are the most riotous, and the countryman who has neglected the precaution of placing a bar before his horses, or a cross over his door, may be certain of finding them the next morning dripping wet and almost broken-winded; for the Hoskelreia will have used them, and they are not the people to treat them gently.*

## The Merman (Marmennill) and Mermaid (Margygr)

Sailors and fishermen, when the weather is calm, sometimes see Mermen and Mermaids rise from the bosom of the tranquil deep. The Mermen are of a dusky hue, with a long beard, black hair, and from the waist upwards resemble a man, but downwards are like a fish. The Mermaids are beautiful upwards, but downwards, like the Mermen, have a fish's form. Their children are called Marmaeler. These are sometimes caught by fishermen, who take them home, that they may gain from them a knowledge of future events; for both they, as well as the Mermen and Mermaids, can see into futurity. It is now rare to hear a Mermaid speak or sing. Mariners are not pleased at the sight of them, as they forbode a storm.

It is dangerous to hurt them. A sailor once enticed a Mermaid so near, that she laid her hand on the gunwale of the vessel, which he struck off. For his barbarity he was overtaken by a storm, in which he nearly perished. St Olaf, on one of his piratical expeditions, fell in with a Mermaid, who by her sweet song was wont to lull mariners to sleep, and then drag them down. If, in diving under water, they turn towards a ship, it betokens misfortune; if they turn from the ship, it is a good sign.[1]

1   Keyser, op. cit., p. 162.

*Belief in Mermen and Mermaids is as old as it is general. According to Gervase of*
*Tilbury, we had Mermaids in our seas, and they are mentioned in the Icelandic Sagas.*
*See Dobeneck, I, pp. 38 sqq., also for an account of the German Water-nix. In Ireland*
*they are called* Merrows, *and legends are told of them similar to those of other countries.*

## The Sea-snake

In fresh waters and rivers, as well as along the coasts of Norway, enormous
snakes are said to exist, but varying with regard both to their appearance
and magnitude. According to the general belief, they are brought forth on
the land, and have their first abode in forests and mounds of stone,
whence, when they grow large, they betake themselves to the great lakes or
inland seas, or to the ocean, where they grow to a tremendous size. They
seldom make their appearance, and when they do, are regarded as
forerunners of important events. In most of the lakes and rivers of any
considerable magnitude, these monsters have, in former times, on one or
other extraordinary occasion, been seen to rise from the water's depth. In
the fresh waters none have been seen within the memory of man, but they
sometimes, when there is a dead calm, appear in the fiords or firths.
Sometime after the Black Death[1] there came, according to tradition, two
large snakes from the Foksöe, by the town down to the 'loug' (bath), where
one, it is said, is still to be found; but the other attempted, about two
hundred years since, to go down to the river's mouth, where it perished in
the fall and was driven across in the vicinity of Drontheim, where it became
putrid, and emitted such a stench that no one could approach the place.

In the Lundevand, on Lister, there is a Sea-Snake that appears only
before a king's death or some great revolution, Some assert that they have
seen it.

In Bollarnvatn also, in Bahuus,[2] there was formerly a Sea-Snake, whose
body was as thick as a calf's of a year old, and whose tail was about six ells
in length. It destroyed the fish, and had its abode in a little isle called
Svanviksöe. It never showed itself, except when some calamity was at
hand. But of all the snakes inhabiting the waters of the North, none are so
celebrated as those that were and are to be found in Miös. In an old
writing[3] we are told of a tremendous snake, that seemed to approach from

---

1   AD 1350. Two-thirds of the people of Norway are said to have perished. It visited
England two years earlier.
2   This tradition belongs strictly to those of Sweden, but is left here, in order not to
divide the several accounts of the Sea-Snake.
3   Beskrivelse over hammer.

the island, and to go from thence to the 'King's land', but instantly vanished. In like manner, many large snakes appeared day after day in Miös, which twisted themselves into a variety of curves, and cast the water to a considerable height. At length the first-mentioned enormous snake made its appearance a second time, and darted with rapidity up on a rock. Its eyes were as large as the bottom of a barrel, and it had a long mane that hung far down its neck. As it could not get off the rock, but lay and beat its head against it, one of the bishop's servants, who was a daring fellow, took a steel bow, and shot so many arrows into its eye, that the water round about was coloured green from the outflowing humour. This snake, which displayed a variety of colours, was appalling to look upon. It died of the wounds it had received, and sent forth such a stench, that the people thereabouts, by the bishop's order, united for the purpose of burning it, which was done. Its skeleton lay for many years on the shore. A grown-up youth could hardly carry the smallest portion of its backbone. It is also said that there is a Sea-Snake, which winds itself round the great bell from Hammer, which was sunk during the seven years' war in the Akersvig, and when the water is clear may still be discerned. All attempts to raise it have been in vain, though it was once lifted to the water's surface.

That this Miös snake was not a thing to be played with, will appear from an account of the year 1656, given in Pontoppidan's *Natural History of Norway*, 2, p. 65. Such a water-snake made a land trip from Miös to Spirillen, and is probably the same with the one that was wont to appear in that lake against evil and perilous times. 'It was in appearance like a huge mast, whatever stood in its way it overthrew, even trees and huts. With its loud hissing and horrid roaring it terrified all the people round about.'

That in calm weather such enormous Sea-Snakes sometimes appear on the coast of Norway, can hardly be denied, as credible persons, even in our own time, declare that they have seen them;[1] to whose testimony may be added that of Hibbert, who says: 'The existence of the Sea-Snake, a monster fifty-five feet long, is placed beyond a doubt by the animal, that was thrown on shore in Orkney, the vertebrae of which are to be seen in the Edinburgh Museum.'[2]

The writer, who among us has most amply treated of the Sea-Snake, is Eric Pontoppidan, in his *Natural History of Norway*, in which two representations of Sea-Snakes are given. According to his testimony, founded on the accounts of Bergen and Nordland mariners, as well as of other eye-

1    Compare the Vestlandske Tidende No. 22, and Sorenskriver Blom's, also Bishop Neumann's paa trovaerdige Folks Beretninger grundede Vidnesbyrd, Budstikken 6te Aargang 159 and 578.
2    Description of Shetland, p. 565.

witnesses, these monsters live in the depths of the ocean, except in July and August, when in calm weather they come up to the surface; but sink again the moment the wind begins to ruffle the watery mirror. According to the testimony of Commander de Ferrys in 1746, given before a court, 'the Sea-Snake seen by him in the vicinity of Molda, had a head resembling in shape that of a horse, which it held about an ell above the water, of a greyish hue, the snout quite black, very large black eyes, and a long white mane, which hung from its neck into the sea. Seven or eight coils of its body, which was very thick, were also seen: according to conjecture, there was a fathom between the coils.'[1] According to the testimony of the priest Tuchsen of Heröe, and of some neighbouring priests, these Sea-Snakes were as thick as a double hogshead (Oxehoved), had large nostrils and blue eyes, which at a distance resembled a couple of bright pewter plates. On the neck there was a mane, which from afar appeared like seaweed.

## Dragons

Traditions of Dragons that fly through the air by night and spit forth fire, are very general, and holes in the earth and the mountains are yet shown over all the country, whence they have been seen issuing like a glowing fire, when war or other public calamity was at hand. When they return to their habitations – where they brood over vast treasures and precious things, which, according to some traditions, they have collected in the bottom of the sea – the sound may be heard of the great iron doors, which close after them. As they are fierce and spit pernicious fire, it is dangerous to contend with them. Under Agers church, which stands on four golden pillars, a dragon broods over immense riches. It has been seen, even within the memory of persons living, or a short time before the last war, issuing from a hole near the church. From the Dragon's Hole on Storöe in Aadal, from the Dragon's Hill on Rasvog, and numerous other places, firedrakes with long tails were to be seen issuing in former times, and sometimes even in our days. That they are not invincible appears from an old tradition, which tells of a priest, named Anders Madsen, who is said to have lived about 1631, that shot a dragon which brooded over silver in the so-called Dragon Mount near the Tvedevand.

*The important part played by dragons, firedrakes and the like in the old songs, legends and romances, where the killing of a dragon forms one of a hero's earliest proofs of valour, has probably given birth to the innumerable traditions concerning these monsters; an accidental electric fire, a fire-ball or the like, being enough to keep the belief alive.*

---

1   Pontoppidan, 2, 321.

## The Severed Hand [1]

There was a miller whose mill was burnt down on two successive Whitsun-eves. In the third year, just before Whitsuntide, he had a tailor in his house to make holy day clothes.

'I wonder how it will go with the mill this time; whether it will be burnt again tonight,' said the miller.

'You need not fear that,' said the tailor, 'give me the key, and I will keep watch in it.'

This seemed to the miller both good and highly acceptable; and when it drew towards evening the tailor got the key and went to the mill, which was still empty, having but just been rebuilt. So placing himself in the middle of the floor, he chalked round him a large circle, on the outside of which he wrote the Paternoster; and thus fortified, would not have feared if the arch-enemy himself had made his appearance. In the dead of the night the door suddenly flew open, and there came in such a multitude of black cats, that the place literally swarmed. But a short time had elapsed when they set a large earthen pot in the chimney, and lighted a fire under it, so that it began frying and hissing in the pot as if it were full of boiling pitch and tar.

'Oho,' thought the tailor, 'is that what you are after?' And scarcely had he given utterance to the thought when one of the cats put its paw behind the pot and tried to upset it.

'Whisht cat, you'll burn yourself!' cried the tailor.

'Whisht cat, you'll burn yourself! the tailor says,' said the cat to the other cats, and all ran from the chimney, and began hopping and dancing round the circle; but in the meanwhile the cat again sneaked to the chimney and endeavoured to upset the pot.

'Whisht cat, you'll burn yourself!' cried the tailor, and drove it from the chimney.

'Whisht cat, you'll burn yourself, the tailor says,' said the cat to the other cats, and all began dancing and hopping again, but in a moment the same cat was away trying a third time to overturn the pot.

'Whisht cat, you'll burn yourself!' cried the tailor in a rage, and so terrified them that they tumbled one over another, and then began to jump and dance as before.

They then formed a circle without the tailor's circle, and began dancing round it with an ever-increasing velocity, till at length it seemed to the tailor that everything was whirling round before him. All this while the cats were staring at him with their large, fierce eyes, as if they would swallow him.

1   Asbjörnsen, op. cit., i, pp. 11–14.

While they were in the thick of it, the cat that had tried to upset the pot, put her paw within the circle, as if she felt inclined to seize hold of the tailor, but who seeing her design, drew out his knife and stood on his guard. After a few moments the cat again put her paw within the ring, when the tailor in one instant chopped it off; and all the cats took to their heels, screaming and howling, as speedily as they could, and left the tailor in quiet possession of the field.

The tailor then lay down in the circle till long after the sun had been shining in upon him. He then rose, locked the mill-door and proceeded to the miller's house.

When he entered the room the miller and his wife were still in bed, it being Whit-Sunday.

'Good-morning,' said the tailor, giving the miller his hand. 'Good-morning,' said the miller in return, and was both glad and surprised to see the tailor again.

'Good-morning, mother,' said he, holding out his hand to the miller's wife.

'Good-morning,' said she, but appeared pale and sorrowful, and kept her hand under the bedclothes, but at last offered him her left hand. The tailor now saw how matters stood; but what afterwards took place is not said.

*The North-German story, Die Katzenmühle, closely resembles the above, but is much simpler. The Norwegian one is probably embellished by the author, from whose work it is extracted.*

## Of St Olaf

St Olaf was the Norwegian people's hero, and yet lives in their remembrance, while few only and imperfect traditions are occasionally to be met with of his equally valiant predecessors and successors. Let us, therefore, consider this man, in order more easily to comprehend the causes of his great celebrity.

Olaf was born in 995; his father, Harald Graenske, was of the race of Harald Hárfager, and his mother, Ásta, the daughter of Gudbrand, from the Uplands. In his third year he was baptised, King Olaf Tryggvason standing godfather to him. In his youth he sailed on piratical expeditions, in which he acquired great experience and fitness for warfare. Supported by powerful relations and friends, as well as by his own sagacity and military skill, he gained possession of his paternal kingdom, over which he reigned for fifteen years with great vigour and reputation. His exertions were chiefly directed to the complete establishment of the Christian faith in Norway, which, after the death of Olaf Tryggvason, had greatly declined; but the violence with which he proceeded, together with his ambition and severity, rendered him so hateful, that he found it advisable to flee from the country to Gardarike,[1] from his discontented subjects, who were, moreover, instigated and supported by the ambitious Dano-English king, Cnut the Great. Olaf, who in the school of adversity had begun to act the saint, was on the eve of starting for Jerusalem, when Olaf Tryggvason, in a dream, bade him return to Norway. He obeyed the behest and marched with an army into the country, where, in an obstinate battle at Stiklastad in Vaerdal, he was defeated and slain by his revolted subjects, on 29th July 1030.

Shortly after the death of Olaf, the fame of his sanctity and the miracles said to have attended his corpse formed a topic of conversation among the people, who found them the more credible, as they were highly dissatisfied with what they had got in exchange for him. Olaf's body, which had been buried in a sandbank at Stiklastad, was taken up, and being found, after the expiration of a year, unchanged, with the hair and nails grown, Grimkell, Olaf's court-bishop, declared him a holy person, and the commonalty thereupon determined that Olaf was a true saint. His body was by his son, King Magnus the Good, laid in a costly shrine, and placed by the high altar in the church of St Clement at Nidaros (Drontheim), where, as well as afterwards in the magnificent Christchurch (the present cathedral), it is said to have wrought numerous miracles. St Olaf's festival, the 29th July, was by law commanded to be celebrated throughout the country as the chief solemnity, and churches to his honour were erected not only in Norway, but in Denmark, Sweden, Russia, England, and even by his countrymen at Constantinople. Pilgrims journeyed in crowds to St Olaf's shrine, and legends of cripples who had there recovered the use of their limbs, and of other miracles soon became numberless.

St Olaf's shrine of silver, inlaid with gold and precious stones, a single one of which cost Archbishop Walkendorf twenty lasts of butter,[2] was on solemn occasions, such as the Saint's yearly festival, or the election of a king, borne in procession by sixty men, and was an abundant source of revenue to the clergy and the cathedral. The last archbishop, Olaf Engelbretson, carried it with him to his strong castle of Steinviksholm, where, after his flight, it fell into the hands of the Danish commander, Christopher Hvitfeld, who sent St Olaf's shrine of silver gilt, weighing about 3200 ounces, together with another silver shrine, in which the Saint's shirts were preserved, and many other valuables, to the Danish treasury.

When the Swedes in 1564 had taken possession of Drontheim, they found nothing remaining of St Olaf's treasures, except his helmet, spurs,

1    Russia, in its then restricted signification.
2    Equal to about forty tons.

and the wooden chest that had contained his body.[1] The helmet and spurs they took with them to Sweden, where they are still preserved in the church of St Nicholas at Stockholm; but the chest they left behind in a church, after having drawn out the silver nails, which had been left by the Danes. After the expulsion of the Swedes, St Olaf's body and chest were, with great solemnity, carried back to the cathedral, where, a contemporary bears witness, that the body was found entire in a grave of masonry in 1567, and 'his blood is seen to this day in a barn, and can never be washed out by water or human hands'. In the following year, St Olaf's body was by a royal ordinance covered with earth.

St Olaf's sanctity is no more thought of, even his last resting-place is forgotten, but his name still lives, as is proved by the numerous traditions still fresh in the memory of the Norwegian people. Throughout the land are to be found traces of St Olaf's deeds and miraculous power. Fountains sprang forth when he thirsted, and acquired salutary virtue when he drank; rocks were rent at his bidding, and sounds (sunde) were formed at his nod; churches were raised, and Trolls found in St Olaf a foe as formidable as they had formerly had in the mighty Thor, whose red beard even was inherited by St Olaf. In many places Trolls are still shown, who at St Olaf's command were turned into stone.

Out of Norway also St Olaf lived long in popular tradition. In Denmark and in Sweden are many places where traditions are yet current of St Olaf and the Trolls he turned into stone. Thus, as he was one day riding by Dalby church in Värmeland, he was addressed by a Troll-wife in these words:

> 'Kong Olaf med dit pipuga Skägg![2]
> Du seglar för när min Badstuguväg.'

> *King Olaf with thy pointed beard!*
> *Thou sailest too near my bathroom wall.*

To which he answered

> 'Du Tröll med din Råck och Ten
> Skal bli I Sten,
> Och aldrig mer göra Skeppare Men.'

> *Thou Troll-wife with thy rock and wheel*
> *Shall turn to stone,*
> *And never more do shipman harm.*

---

1   This was, without doubt, one of the cases in which his silver shrine was preserved. What became of his armour, battle-axe, spear, and the banner given him by an angel, while he slept on the place where he was martyred, is not known.
2   The same probably as Sw. Pipskägg (Grimm, J., *Deutsche Mythologie*, op. cit., p. 517), the little pointed beard on the under lip.

In the Shetland isles, we learn from Hibbert, the inhabitants, as late as the eighteenth century, maintained that they had their ancient, but now lost, law-book from 'St Olla', of whom they relate wonderful things in their songs, which they call 'Vissacks'. A Faröe tradition ascribes it to St Olaf, that they have now no woods on the islands. St Olaf having inquired of some of the inhabitants whether they had any woods at home, they suspecting that he made the inquiry with the view to taxing them, answered in the negative. 'Be it so,' said the king, and at the same time the Faröe woods sank into the earth.

If it be asked what can be the origin of many of these wondrous traditions, we answer, that it must be sought for in the same ignorance of nature and its effects, together with the desire of finding a reason for everything that seems uncommon, which has given birth to so many traditions of supernatural beings. What heathenism attributed to the gods of Valhall and to the mighty Thor, the cunning Catholic ecclesiastics, with their earliest converts, no doubt transferred to the powerful suppresser of the Asa-faith, St Olaf, whose axe supplanted Thor's Miölnir, and whose steed, renowned in tradition, the goats of the Thunder-god.[1] Olaf's own renown, the tales of pious pilgrims and monkish legends have gradually combined to make of St Olaf a hero, whom the superstitious and ignorant multitude believed capable of performing the most impossible things.

## Of St Olaf and the First Church in Norway

In Norrland there is the following tradition respecting the first church erected in Norway.[2]

As St Olaf was one day wandering among the woods and mountains, deeply meditating how, without laying heavy burthens on his people, he could accomplish the construction of a church he had planned in his

---

1  The numerous representations, which in the days of Catholicism were no doubt to be found in many of the churches dedicated to St Olaf, are now for the most part destroyed; but from the notices which we have of them, the hero was generally represented with a battle-axe in his hand, and treading on a Troll or a dragon. In Ladvig church there is a remarkable processional banner, on which is the figure of St Olaf, in complete armour, treading on a dragon. In St Mary's church at Lübeck, I have seen an old, but very good painting, the principal figure in which is St Olaf completely armed, with his battle-axe in his hand and a royal mantle over his shoulders. With one foot he is treading on a dragon, but which has a human head. In the Kollmann chapel, in the same church, there is likewise an ancient picture of 'St Olaus'. Even in London there are two or three churches dedicated to St Olave.

2  For other versions of this story, see 'Danish Traditions', p. 309 and 'Swedish Traditions', p. 263, both in this volume.

mind, of such magnitude that its like should hardly be found, he met a man of gigantic size, who asked him what he was pondering over. 'I may well be pondering,' answered the king, 'having made a vow to build a church for magnitude and magnificence without its like in the whole world.' The Troll thereupon undertook by a certain fixed time to complete such a structure, but only on condition that, if the work should be finished at the time appointed, St Olaf would engage to give him, in remuneration for his labour, the sun and moon, or St Olaf himself. The king agreed to the condition, but fancied he could form such a vast plan for the edifice, that the giant would find it impossible to finish the work by the time agreed on. The church was to be so spacious that seven priests might preach in it at the same time without hearing or disturbing one another. The pillars and ornaments, both within and without, were to be of the hardest flint; besides which many other and equally difficult conditions were included in the bargain. But within a much shorter time than the period agreed on, St Olaf saw the church finished, with the exception of the spire, which was still to be erected. Seeing this, the Saint went out again among the woods and mountains, in deep tribulation, thinking of his unfortunate engagement; when suddenly he heard a child crying in the mountain, and a giantess comforting it with the following song:

> 'Vys! vyss! sonen min!
> I morgon kommer Vind och Väder, fader din,
> Och bar med sig Sol och Mane,
> Eller sjelfver Sanct Olof.'

> *Hush! hush! my son!*
> *Tomorrow comes Wind and Tempest, thy father,*
> *And has with him sun and moon,*
> *Or St Olaf himself.*

Now the king was overjoyed, because Trolls, as we are told, always lose their power when a Christian man calls them by their name. On his return he saw the giant standing on the top of the tower, in the act of placing the spire, and called to him:

> 'Vind och Väder,
> Du har satt spiran sneder!'

> *Wind and Tempest,*
> *Thou hast set the spire awry!*

From the summit of the church the Troll now fell with a terrific smash, and was shivered in fragments, all which were mere flints. According to another version the giant's name was Slätt, and St Olaf cried out:

'Slätt! sätt spiran rätt!'

*Slätt! set the spire straight!*

According to another, he is called Bläster, and St Olaf calls to him:-

Bläster! sätt spiran väster!'

*Bläster! set the spire westward!*

The same tradition is also current in Norway itself, where the giant is called Skalle, and the magnificent cathedral of Nidaros (Drontheim) is the church erected by him.[1] A similar tradition respecting the name of the Troll is found also in Germany.[2]


## St Olaf at Vaaler

When travelling over the country, for the purpose of introducing the Christian faith, St Olaf came to a place on the east bank of the Glommen, which, together with its church and the whole parish, acquired the name of Vaaler in the following manner: In the above-named place, St Olaf held an assize, at which, after some hesitation, it was decided that the God whom the king worshipped should also be worshipped by the people, and that Odin's religion should give place to that of Christ. It was further decided, on the king's proposal, that a church should be erected there, as at other places, where the new faith had been adopted. With respect, however, to the spot where it should be built, a great difference of opinion arose; whereupon, as the tradition informs us, St Olaf bent his bow, sent forth an arrow, and declared that on the spot where it fell the church should stand. The king was standing at the time by the fountain that still bears the name of St Olaf's, and the arrow fell in a *Vaal*,[3] where a wooden church was afterwards built, which, together with the house and parish, was by St Olaf named Vaaler. This church, at which the sick and dying were wont to make offerings, existed till the year 1805, when a new one was erected, in the vestment-chest of which there is an elaborate iron wire clasp, called St Olaf's clasp, which, according to tradition, was placed in the old church by the king himself, and is said to have belonged to the halter of his horse. This horse the king was accustomed to water in the crystal spring, which is never dry in summer nor frozen in winter, and also bears St Olaf's name. Miraculous powers were formerly ascribed to it. The

---

1   Afzelius, *Swenska Folkets Sago-Hädfer*, in 11 volumes from 1844, iii, 97, 98; Grimm, J., *Deutsche Mythologie*, op. cit., pp. 515, 516.
2   Grimm, J. & W., *Kinder- und Hausmärchen*, op. cit., No. 55.
3   A Vaal is a quantity of trunks and roots of trees, piled in a heap for fuel.

sick placed money or anything of silver in it, for the recovery of their health; and great misfortune was supposed to await the person who should make free with these sacred deposits. Only a few years ago, it was customary for the people, on the first day of every celebration, to strive who should first arrive at the fountain, and it was regarded as something to boast of by him who was the first to water his horse at St Olaf's well.

## St Olaf at Ringerige

When St Olaf was journeying from place to place, for the purpose of introducing the Christian faith and erecting churches in the place of the heathen temples, he found much opposition and hindrance not only from his refractory pagan subjects, but also from the numerous Trolls, Jutuls and Giantesses inhabiting the mountains round about. The Trolls could not endure St Olaf, partly because, by using the sign of the cross, he did them much harm, and partly because he founded so many churches, the sound of whose bells disturbed their quiet. But notwithstanding their frequent efforts, they could effect nothing against the holy king, who, on the other hand, turned them at once to stone. Such petrified Trolls are still to be seen in all parts of the country. Thus, when St Olaf was on one of his progresses, a fierce giantess suddenly sprang from a steep rock, crying aloud:

> 'St Olaf med det brede skjaeg!
> Du rider saa naer min Kjeldervaeg!'

> *St Olaf with the broad beard!*
> *Thou ridest so near my cellar wall!*

St Olaf instantly answered

> 'Stat du der i Stok og Steen,
> Til jeg kommer her tilbars igjen.'

> *Stand thou there in stock and stone,*
> *Till I come hither back again.*

The petrified giantess is yet to be seen there.

When St Olaf came to Steen, where his mother at that time dwelt, he resolved on building a church there. With this resolution a giantess (gyvri) that lived in the mountain (which is two thousand feet high, and after her was called Gyrihauge) was highly displeased; and, although she might, from the above-mentioned example, have known that St Olaf was not a person to be trifled with, she determined to try her strength, and challenged him to a competition. 'Before thou art ready with thy church,' said she, 'I shall have laid a stone bridge across Steen's fiord.' Olaf accepted the challenge, and before she was half ready with her bridge, the sweet tones of the bells were heard from St Olaf's already finished church. In her rage the Troll hurled the stones, which she had destined for the completion of the bridge, from Gyrihauge, straight across the fiord, at the church; but as none of them hit the mark, she was so exasperated that she tore off one of her legs and cast it at the churchtower. Some say that it carried the tower along with it, others that she aimed too high. But be that as it may, the leg sank down in a swamp behind the church, where it causes a foul stench even to this day. The swamp is still called by the country folk Giögraput, and the stones which she cast at the church were not long since to be seen in the neighbouring fields. The bridge begun by the giantess is now completed, and at Steen are still to be seen the ruins of St Olaf's church, which deserve to be preserved more carefully than they now are. Formerly service was performed on every St John's day, but about a hundred and fifty years ago the building was struck by lightning.

## Axel Thordsen and Fair Valdborg

In the land of Norway there lived in former days a maiden so fair, that she was universally denominated the Fair Valdborg. Her father, Sir Immer, died in her tender infancy, and her mother, the Lady Julli, rested also in the dark earth before her daughter was grown up. Being of noble race she had powerful relatives all over the country, but the choicest of them all was Axel Thordsen, who chose her for his bride, while she was yet a child, and was betrothed to her, previous to his departure from the country to visit foreign courts, among which he took service under the emperor Henry.

His young bride was, in the meanwhile, placed in a cloister, that she might learn to sew, and there she remained for eleven years, when Queen Malfred received the fair maiden into her court, where she was held in high honour; for Malfred and the Lady Julli had been intimate acquaintances and often played at tables together. Axel was, in the meantime, beginning to feel a longing after his betrothed, and having been informed by a pilgrim of Valdborg's race, that she was the most beauteous maiden in the whole land, and that her powerful kindred had destined her for the king's son, Hagen, he obtained leave of absence from the emperor, and hastened back to his native country. Thirty attendants followed him, but when he reached his mother's mansion, he rode alone. At the gate he was met by his fair sister, the Lady Helfred, who advised him to disguise himself as a messenger, at the same time giving him a letter to Valdborg, whom he found, attending the queen, just coming from vespers. In the letter, which was filled with expressions of love, lay five gold rings, on which roses and lilies were embossed. On reading the letter, she plighted to him her faith anew, and adhered to her oath, although eleven knights made love to her, besides Hagen, the king's son, who was the twelfth. The young prince was sunk in despair and weary in spirit, when fair Valdborg would not be moved, and his mother, Queen Malfred, answered his complaint with: 'By force thou canst not gain her.' He nevertheless recovered hope, when he by chance met his confessor, the black friar Knud, who gave him the unexpected consolation, that Axel could not be united to Valdborg, because they were cousins german, and one woman had held them both over the font.

Hagen now addressed himself to Valdborg's three maternal uncles, who were jarls of high degree, and of them demanded her in marriage. Joyfully they gave their consent, but Valdborg said: 'Axel is my dearest friend, I will never deceive him.' Hagen then caused letters to be written and the archbishop summoned, together with seventy ecclesiastics, and declared that the two lovers should be cited before the archbishop.

With beating hearts the loving pair attended before the archbishop in St Mary's church, where the black friar Knud stepped forth, and with the pedigree in hand, showed that they could not be joined in wedlock, as they were cousins on the mother's side, and were besides godchildren of the same sponsor. They then went up to the altar, where a handkerchief was delivered to them, which was then cut in two between them, and a part retained by each. Thus were they parted for ever. The gold ring was then taken off Valdborg's finger and the bracelet from her arm, both of which were returned to Axel, who casting them on the altar, made a present of them to St Olaf, at the same time swearing, that for the remainder of his life he would be the friend of Valdborg.

At this oath Hagen waxed wroth, and stepping forth swore, that Axel should on the following day make oath on sword and holy writ, that Valdborg was a virgin for him. Not only did the two lovers swear on the mass-book, but eleven jarls of the same race, with gilded swords and yellow locks, attended to swear with the fair maiden, with whom Hagen offered to share his throne whenever he became king; but she declared to the sorrowful Axel that she would never forget him, but would pass her days in solitude.

Thus stood matters for a considerable time. Axel and his beloved never entered into any amusements and never were seen to laugh. At length a war broke out, and Hagen, who had now become king, summoned all his men to the field. He made Axel his general, and the bold knight, in whose shield of white and azure stood two red hearts, was ever at hand wherever his country's honour or his own required him. The conflict was obstinate. Axel slew King Amund's sons and many of the nobles of Upland. But King

Hagen fell, mortally wounded, from his horse, requesting, at his last moments, Axel to avenge his death, to receive the kingdom of Norway, and take to wife the beloved of them both. Axel now again rushed into the thickest of the fight, slaughtering the enemy until his sword broke, and he had received seven mortal wounds. His last words were of his betrothed.

Valdborg divided all she possessed of value among her relations, and retired to the convent of St Mary, where she was consecrated a nun by Archbishop Aage.

*The foregoing notice of the story of Axel and Valdborg is abridged from the beautiful old Danish ballad of 'Axel Thordsen og Skjön Valdborg', of which we know neither the name of its author nor the time of its composition. It is printed in the* Udvalgte Danske Viser *(Bd. III, pp. 257 sqq.), and a German translation by W. C. Grimm is given in his* Altdänische Heldenlieder, *pp. 357 sqq. It has been dramatised by Oehlenschlaeger.*

*If the ballad, has any historic worth beyond the circumstance that it affords an accurate picture of Norwegian costume in the middle age, and that in it may be seen, as in a mirror, the spirit and manners of the time, it seems most probable that its scene was in Romsdal and the neighbouring Söndmör. At the mansion of Houe in Söndmör, tradition tells of a battle fought there, in which both Axel Thordsen and the king's son, Hagen, were slain; and on the little isle of Gidske, by the church, there is a marble slab, shaped like a coffin lid, about six feet long and in the widest part scarcely an ell broad, on which are some illegible runic characters, which has always been known as Fair Valdborg's grave. On the other side of the quire, tradition further says, Axel Thordsen lies buried, but without a memorial. By each grave an ash was planted, both of which grew to an equal height, and when they had risen above the roof of the church, they inclined towards each other, and entwined their boughs together. Axel's tree yet stands flourishing, but Valdborg's is dead.*

## The Signe-kjaerring or Witch

To ascertain under what disease a sickly child was labouring, recourse was – and, perhaps, is – had to a *signe-kjaerring*,[1] who employed for that purpose the process of *melting* or *casting*. This was done by melting lead taken from church windows after sunset, into water drawn from a stream running from the north. Over the vessel containing the water there was laid a barley cake, having in it a hole made with a darning needle, through which the molten lead was slowly poured into the water. This operation was usually performed in the case of rickets, in order to discover under which of the nine species of that disease – for such was the number of its

---

1   From at signe, i.e. *to exorcise*, and Kjaerring (Nor. for Kjaerling) *an old crone*; an undoubted descendant of the Vala of the heathen times.

varieties – the child was suffering. According to the form assumed by the lead in the water, the species was determined; if, for instance, it resembled a man with two large horns, it was the troldsvek (troll-rickets); if a mermaid, the vassvek (water-rickets).

While pouring the lead the sorceress muttered the following spell:

> I charm for guile, and I charm for rickets;
> I charm it hence, and I charm it away;
> I charm it out, and I charm it in;
> I charm in weather, and I charm in wind;
> I charm in the south, and I charm in the east;
> I charm in the north, and I charm in the west;
> I charm in the earth, and I charm in water;
> I charm in the mountain, I charm in the sand;
> I charm it down in an alder-root;
> I charm it into a colt's foot;
> I charm it into the fire of hell;
> I charm it into a north-running stream;
> There shall it eat, and there shall consume,
> Till harm for the babe there shall be none.[1]

---

1  Asbjörnsen, op. cit., ii, pp. 158, *sqq.*

# Popular Traditions of Sweden[1]

## Christmas or Yule Pastimes

Many Christmas customs and pastimes derive their origin from the sacrifices, which, in the days of heathenism, were appointed, in order to render the gods propitious. The sacrifices consecrated to Odin, which sometimes consisted of human beings, were celebrated with games and dancing. In Gothland, where most memorials of Odin are to be met with, a game still exists in some places, which represents such a sacrificial dance. It is performed, amid many nimble springs and changes of motion, by young men disguised, with their faces blackened or coloured. One of these represents the victim, everything required for the sacrifice is brought forth, which is apparently carried into effect to the sound of music or of song. Sometimes the person selected as the victim sits clad in skin on a stool, holding a wisp of straw in his mouth, which, cut sharp at the ends and standing out from his ears, is intended to resemble a swine's bristles; he is thus supposed to represent the sacrifice made at Yule to Frey, and which consisted of a hog. In many places a loaf or cake is baked, which is called the Yule-hog (Julgalt), and is kept till the spring, when it is given to the cattle with which the labours of spring are to be executed; all in commemoration of the pagan sacrifices at midwinter or Yule for a good year. Even the name of Yule (O. Nor. Jol, Dan. Sw. Jul) is derived from the circular motion of the sun;[2] the first half-year *till* Yule with decreasing days, the second *from* Yule with increasing days; whence the time when both these halves meet is called the 'Jula-môt'. This was the ancient new year: it began with the longest night of winter, which was called the *Modernatt* (Mother night). The new year's wish of old was, 'a good Jula-môt'.

*The hog of propitiation (sônargöltr) offered to Frey was a solemn sacrifice in the Nort, and in Sweden, down to modern times, the custom has been preserved of baking, on*

---

1    From Afzelius, *Svenska Folkets Sago-Häfder*, unless otherwise expressed.
2    From O. Nor. hjol, Dan. Sw. hjul (wheel). See Grimm, J., *Deutsche Mythologie*, op. cit., p. 664.

*every Christmas Eve, a loaf or cake in the form of a hog. Verelius, in his remarks on the*
*Hervararsaga (p. 139) relates that the Swedish peasants dry the baked Yule-hog, and*
*preserve it till the spring; then having pounded a part of it in the vessel out of which the*
*seed is to be scattered, they give it mixed with barley to the plough-horses, leaving the*
*other part to be eaten by the servants that hold the plough, in the hope of having a*
*plentiful harvest.*[1]

## Modern Traditions of Odin

In Gothland, and particularly in Småland, many traditions and stories of
Odin the Old still live in the mouths of the people. In Bleking it was
formerly the custom to leave a sheaf on the field for Odin's horses. In
Kråktorps gård in Småland, a barrow was opened about a century ago, in
which Odin was said to have been buried, and which, after the introduction of Christianity, was called Helvetesbacke (Hell's mount). In it was
found a vault, from which when opened there burst forth a wondrous fire,
like a flash of lightning. A coffin of flints also and a lamp were found at the
same time. Of a priest, named Peter Dagson, who dwelt near Troienborg, it
is related, that when the rye he had sown there sprang up, Odin came
riding from the hills every evening, of stature so lofty that he towered above
the buildings in the farmyard, and with spear in hand. Stopping before the
entrance, he hindered everyone, during the whole night, from going in or
out. And this took place every night until the rye was cut.

A story is also current of a golden ship, which is said to be sunk in
Runemad, near the Nyckelberg, in which, according to the tradition, Odin
fetched the slain from the battle of Bråvalla to Valhall. Kettils-ås, it is said,
derives its name from one Kettil Runske, who stole Odin's runic staves
(runekaflar), with which he bound his dogs and bull, and at length even
the mermaid herself who came to Odin's help. Many such traditions have
been and may still be found in those parts; all of which, it may well be
conceived, are not regarded as articles of faith; it is, nevertheless, a
pleasure for the countryman, when, walking over his fields, he comes to a
mount, a water, a pile of stones, to know what old traditions were current
concerning them, and have given names to villages and dwellings.

It is worthy of remark that one of our (Swedish) handsomest birds of
passage, the black heron (*Ardea nigra*, Linn.) was in ancient times called
Odin's swallow.

1   Ibid., pp. 45, 1188.

## Modern Traditions of Thor

Thor, as well as Odin the Old, came to the North with some immigration, which in remote times took place from Asia and Asgard. Here he had to contend with the land's earliest inhabitants, who from their dwelling in mountain-caverns and dens, as well as from their gigantic stature and ferocity, were called Jättar (Giants), Trolls and Bergsboar (mountain-dwellers). Hence have all the traditions about giants and the like their origin. Those smooth, wedge-shaped stones, which are sometimes found in the earth, are called Thorwiggar, i.e. Thor's wedges: these, it is said, have been hurled by Thor at some Troll. In many places where the meadows border on the mountains, stories were once rife of the terror felt by the Trolls when it thundered, and how they then, in various shapes, though most frequently as large balls or clews, would come rolling down the mountain, seeking shelter among the mowers who, well aware of their danger, always held them back with their scythes; on which occasions it has often happened that the thunder has struck and shivered the scythe, when the Troll with a piteous piping sound would again return to the mountain.

Aërolites are found in many places and are memorials of Thor. Although not always of great magnitude, they are, nevertheless, so heavy that there is now scarcely any man who can lift them. These, it is said, Thor handled like playthings. Of the aërolite at Linneryd in Småland it is related, that Thor, as he was once passing by with his attendant, met a giant whom he asked to what place he was going. 'To Valhall,' answered he, 'to fight with Thor, who with his lightning has burnt my cattle-house.' 'It is hardly advisable for thee to measure strength with him,' answered Thor, 'for I cannot imagine that thou art the man to lift this little stone up on the large one here.' At this the giant waxed wroth, and grasped the stone with all his might, but was unable to raise it from the earth, so wonderfully had Thor charmed it. Thor's follower then made the attempt, and lifted the stone as though it had been a glove. The giant now aimed a blow at Thor which brought him on his knees; but Thor with his hammer struck the giant dead. He lies buried under the great stone heap hard by.

Thor was worshipped in Gothland above and more than the other gods. The Thorbagge (*scarabaeus stercorarius*) was sacred to him. Relative to this beetle a superstition still exists, which has been transmitted from father to son, that if anyone in his path finds a Thorbagge lying helpless on its back, and turns it on its feet, he expiates seven sins; because Thor in the time of heathenism was regarded as a mediator with a higher power, or All-father. On the introduction of Christianity, the priests strove to terrify the people from the worship of their old divinities, pronouncing both them and their adherents to be evil spirits and belonging to hell. On the poor Thorbagge the name was now bestowed of Thordjefvul or Thordyfvel (Thor-devil), by which it is still known in Sweden proper. No one now thinks of Thor, when he finds the helpless creature lying on its back; but the good-natured countryman seldom passes it without setting it on its feet, and thinking of his sins' atonement.

That the remembrance of and veneration for Thor were long retained in Norway and in Bohuslän, appears from many traditions. Of some sailors from Bohuslän, about a hundred years since, it is related, that while out in a Dutch ship from Amsterdam, on the whale fishery near Greenland, being driven out of their known course, they observed for many nights the light of a fire from an island or shore, at which some of the sailors, and among them one of the men from Bohuslän, were seized with a desire to visit the place and see what people were there. They therefore took the ship's boat and rowed to the spot. Having landed and approached the fire, they found sitting by it an old man warming himself, who immediately asked them whence they came. 'From Holland,' answered the man from Bohuslän. 'But from what place art thou thyself?' inquired the old man. 'From Säfve on Hisingen,' answered the sailor. 'Art thou acquainted with Thorsby?' 'Yes, well.' 'Dost thou know where the Ulfveberg is?' 'Yes, I have often passed it, because there is a direct way from Gothenborg to Marstrand across Hisingen through Thorsby.' 'Do the great stones and the earth-mounds still stand in their places?' 'Yes, all but one stone which is ready to fall.' 'Tell me further,' said the old heathen, 'dost thou know where Glosshed's altar is, and whether it is still safe and sound?' On the sailor answering that it was not, the old man said: 'Wilt thou desire the people in Thorsby and Thores-bracka not to destroy the stones and mounds under the Ulfveberg, and above all things to keep the altar at Glosshed safe and whole, so shalt thou have a good wind to the place for which thou art bound.' All this the sailor promised to perform on his return home. On asking the old man his name, and why he so anxiously inquired about such objects, he answered the sailor, 'My name is Thorer Brack, and my habitation is there; but I am now a fugitive. In the great mound by the Ulfvesberg my whole race lies buried, and at Glosshed's altar we performed our worship to the gods.' They then parted from the old man and had a fair wind home.

## Of Rocking Stones and Thundering Stones

With Rocking Stones, like those in England and elsewhere, and with Thundering Stones, or such as when passed over give forth a dull, hollow sound, much sorcery is practised, because they are regarded as a resort for Elves and Trolls.

## Superstitious Usage in Case of Theft

The following barbarous superstition is still practised in an enlightened Christian age.

If a person is robbed, he goes to a so-called cunning man, who engages to strike out the eye of the thief. The following is the process. The Trollman cuts a human figure on a young tree, mutters certain dire spells to obtain the devil's aid, and then drives some sharp instrument into the eye of the figure. It was also a practice to shoot with an arrow or bullet at one of the members of the figure, by which pain and sore are, it is believed, inflicted on the corresponding member of the living person.

## Finnish Superstition

With the foregoing may be classed the Finnish superstition of producing the image of an absent person in a vessel of water and aiming a shot at it, and thereby wounding or slaying a hated enemy at many hundred miles distance. Even on a neighbour's cattle this degrading superstition has been practised. Apoplexy and other sudden diseases have hence acquired the name of *shots, Troll-shots*.

A young Swede had, during his wanderings in Finland, engaged himself to a handsome Finnish girl, but after his return home, had quite forgotten both his love and his promise to return to his betrothed. A Lapp skilled in the magic of his country coming one day to him, it occurred to the young man to inquire of him how it fared with his betrothed in Finland. 'That you shall see yourself,' answered the Lapp, who having, while muttering divers spells, filled a bucket with water, bade him come and look into it. There, we are told, the young man saw the well-known country round the cottage of his betrothed, and his heart beat violently on perceiving her pale and in tears stepping out at the door, followed by her father, with an angry countenance and holding a gun in his hand. The old Fin now approached a pail filled with water, looked in the direction whence the young man had been expected, shook his head, and cocked the gun, while the daughter stood wringing her hands. 'Now,' said the Lapp, 'he will shoot you, if you do not prevent it by shooting him. Make haste and take aim with your gun.' The Fin, having levelled his piece, went to the pail. 'Shoot now,' said the Lapp, 'or you are a dead man.' He fired accordingly, and the Fin fell lifeless on the earth. Conscience sometime after prompted the young Swede to revisit the scene of his perfidy, where he learned that the old man had died of apoplexy on the very day that the Lapp had displayed his magical skill.[1]

1  For more on this curious subject, see Grimm, J., *Deutsche Mythologie*, op. cit., p. 1045 *sq*. and note.

## Of Giants and Dwarfs

According to the testimony of several Sagas and other writings, there dwelt
in Sweden, in remote times, a gigantic, wild, cruel race called Jotens
(Jotnar), and the country they inhabited, about the Gulf of Finland and
thence northwards, was named Jotunaland, or Jättehem. But when a more
enlightened people from Asia, who knew the God of the whole universe,
and worshipped him under the name of All-father, entered Sweden across
its eastern boundary, there arose, between them and the Jotnar or Jätte-folk
a war which lasted for many centuries. And as David slew the presumptuous giant Goliah, so did the new Asiatic settlers in the North, through skill
and superior understanding, overcome the earlier, savage inhabitants of the
country, who withdrew more and more into the deepest forests, and took
up their abode in mountain-caves and dens. From these times are derived
all our popular traditions of Mountain-trolls, Giants, and Mountain-
dwellers. They are described as possessing vast stores of gold and other
valuables, as bad, but credulous. Their women are described as ugly.

A distinct species of Berg- or Mountain-troll were the Dwarfs. These were
good mechanics and cunning, their wives and daughters are spoken of as
very beautiful. This Dwarf-race seems to spring from a people that
migrated from the eastern countries at a later period, as they were
acquainted with runes, which they used in sorcery, accompanied by the
harp, as we read in the old ballad of Sir Tynne:

> That was Ulfva, the little dwarf's daughter,
> To her maiden thus she spoke:
> Thou shalt fetch my harp of gold;
> Sir Tynne will I cause to love me.
> Ye manage well the runes . . . [1]

A similar art of enchanting and bewitching the Lapplanders are supposed to possess even at the present day, and with some probability it may
be conjectured that the Asiatic people, who in the Sagas are mentioned
under the name of Dwarfs, was no other than an immigration of oriental
Lapps, and the origin of the race among us which still bears that name:
also that the Fins descend from the giants, and are thus the oldest of the
races that now inhabit Sweden. These peoples had no unanimity, no
general government and laws, and were therefore so easily conquered by
the combined Aesir-race, who led by their *drotts* or *kings,* in two separate
invasions (the Swedes and Goths) arrived in the North.

---

1    The old Danish ballad of 'Herr Tönne', or 'Runernes Magt', is only a variety of the
Swedish one. It is printed in the *Danske Viser,* i, p. 281.

At a period when self-defence was the first duty of man and victory his greatest happiness, and even Gimle itself, or heaven, was to be gained by valour and a good sword, it was natural that well-tempered, efficient weapons should be regarded as one of the most precious possessions. A good armourer was said to be instructed by the Elves or Dwarfs. A well-hardened, good and elastic sword was usually regarded as of Dwarf workmanship. Other precious things also, particularly armlets of gold, set with jewels or of beautiful colours, were called sometimes Elfin-ornaments[1] and sometimes Dwarf-ornaments. In the smith's art the Giants and the Mountain-dwellers were considered as eminently skilful, and among the mountains are sometimes found smaller rocks detached from the larger ones, which by the common people are called Giants' anvils, on which it is supposed the Giants executed their works.

## King Eric's Dream

It was long believed by the people that King Eric was a great magician (Trollkarl) and conversant in hidden knowledge, also that he gained from Odin information concerning things that were hidden from other men. After his victory at Fyriswall, he had no more enemies to contend with him the tranquil possession of his dominions. He saw Christianity spread itself more and more in every direction, and felt conscious that he was the last heathen king in the North. He therefore made a sacrifice to Odin, that he might learn from him how many Christian kings after him should sit on the throne of Sweden. In a dream he received for answer, that he must burst King Sverker's rock, in which he would find a tablet that would elucidate all that he wished to know concerning his successors. This instruction he followed; but who this Sverker was and where his rock was, our chronicles tell us not. When the rock in question was split, there was found in it a stone tablet set round with golden plates and precious stones. On the one side was represented an oblong, quadrangular table, around which were thrice nine crowns distinguished by the names of kings; on the other side was a triangular table or plate with thrice seven crowns. All these crowns were distinguished by colours, to indicate the race of the several princes, as blue for the Swedes, green for the Norse, red for the Danes, and yellow for the Germans. This tablet, we are told, was long preserved among the treasures of the kingdom in the state treasury, until Archbishop Gustaf Trolle in the war time carried it with him to Denmark, and, after the precious stones were taken out, left it in the custody of a priest in Roeskilde. This priest took it with him to Söfde in Scania, and had it

---

1    In the *Völundarkvitha* Völund is called *lord of alfs, companion of alfs*.

entered in the inventory of the church there. Here it was found by Nils Hvide, bishop of Lund, who stole it. A priest in Scania, named Master Jacob, composed a lampoon in verse, charging the bishop with the theft, but was unable to prove the charge, and was therefore condemned and executed at Copenhagen. His last words at the place of execution, and which stand on his gravestone, are said to have been:

> 'Skall nu Mäster Jacob miste sitt lif,
> For hanen gal,
> San er dog Bispen en tyff,
> For stenen han stal.'

> *Though now Master Jacob shall lose his life,*
> *Ere the cock crows,*
> *Yet is the bishop a thief,*
> *For he stole the stone.*

In a book belonging to Frösunda church in Roslagen, this story of King Eric's dream is to be found, also a representation of the tablet in Sverker's rock.

## Of Björn the Swede, Ulf Jarl, and Cnut the Great

There dwelt once in Sweden a rich man, who had a young daughter of exquisite beauty. Near the town where they dwelt, there was a green and pleasant place, to which the youth of both sexes were wont to resort for amusement. It befell one day that when the damsel above mentioned was out playing with her companions, a bear came out of the forest, rushed in the midst of the terrified children, and seizing her with his forepaws, hastened with her to his den in the forest. He showed her the greatest affection, every day procured for her both game and fruits, and let her want for nothing. But the bear having killed much cattle for his own subsistence, the people assembled in a general hunt and destroyed him. The damsel was now found again, and soon after was delivered of a son who was called Björn (Bear). He grew up, became stronger than other men, and possessed great understanding. In this he seems to have taken after his forefathers, according to the old saying: 'A bear has twelve men's understanding and six men's strength.' A grandson of this Björn was Ulf Jarl in Scania, who, against her brother's will, married Estrid, the sister of Cnut the Great. It was this Ulf who aided King Cnut, when his fleet was on the point of falling into the hands of the enemy at the isle of Helge. Yet, notwithstanding this aid, Ulf could never gain the king's friendship, and was ill rewarded in the end, as we shall presently see.

King Cnut and Ulf Jarl were sitting one day after the battle of Helge playing at chess in Roeskilde. Cnut moved a pawn, but wished to put it back; at this Ulf was so irritated that he overthrew the board and was rushing from the apartment, when the king in anger called to him: 'Art thou running away, cowardly Ulf?' Ulf answered: 'Thou wouldst have run farther in the fight at Helge, had I not come: I was not called cowardly Ulf when the Swedes were beating you like dogs, till I came to your relief.' It soon appeared how unwise it is for an inferior person to speak too freely to a superior. On the morrow, the king was informed that the jarl had taken refuge in the church of St Lucius, and thereupon sent a man who slew him before the high altar. After the extinction of the house of Cnut in the male line, Svend, the son of Ulf Jarl and Estrid, ascended the Danish throne, the last of whose descendants was the celebrated Queen Margaret, *ob.* AD 1412.


## Christian-heathen Traditions of Trolls, Etc

The first light of Christianity was insufficient to dispel all the darkness of heathenism. There still remained on the public ways and in fields small oratories built over some pagan idol, for the accommodation both of travellers and of those employed in the fields. From these oratories or 'scurds', as they were called, the heathen images were indeed removed, but those of saints were set up in their place, and many a neophyte prayed sometimes to the Virgin Mary, St Peter and other saints, and at others to Thor and Freyia. The Christians, therefore, strove now with all their might to suppress among the people all faith in these heathen deities, condemning them as spirits of hell that sought the ruin of mankind. The spectres of heathenism, Trolls and Elves, together with those, in their mounds or harrows, who had died in the time of idolatry, were represented as bugbears to Christian men, so that they were always held in fear, and trembled on their way, particularly by night, for the 'evil meeting', that is, the meeting with Trolls or Elves, whence, it was said, many diseases and troubles were caused to mortals; nor was self-interest behindhand in finding remedies for all such calamities. The simple people paid dearly to monks, troll-wives and exorcising women for these remedies, consisting in superstitious mummery with incense and spells, performed in crossways, churches, and at Elf-stones. At such places strange prayers were said, mingled with the invocation and misuse of the names of Jesus and the saints. These prayers, which were for the most part composed in the monasteries, were sometimes in rime. We could adduce some that have been in use even in our time; but, as offensive to Christian ears, they had better be forgotten.

What still remains of these superstitions of Elves, Trolls and the like, either in traditions or popular belief, shall be here briefly related.

# *Of Elves*

## 1

Both in the heathen and the Christian supernatural world, Elves occupy the most conspicuous place. What we have already communicated concerning the pagan belief in Elves has been propagated by traditions, from age to age, until our times, with the addition of much Christian fable. There are still to be found elf-altars, where offerings are made for the sick. The so-called wise women – the Horgabrudar of our days – anoint with swine's fat, which was used in the pagan offerings, and read prayers, which they say are mystic; after which something metallic, that has been worn or borne by the sick person - a small coin or even a pin is sufficient – and lastly a cross (as a token that the Saviour's power is also here superstitiously invoked), are laid upon the elf-mill (älf-qvarn) or, as it is also called, elf-pot (älf-gryta). These conjuring women (signerskor), when they are called to the sick, usually begin with pouring melted lead into water, and from the forms which the fluid metal assumes, they usually pretend to judge that the disease has been caused by Elves; when having secured payment, they commence a new juggle, which they call 'striking down', or 'anointing for the Elves', at sunset on the following Thursday. Some country people will anoint the elf-mill without applying to a cunning woman; these read no prayers, but instead only sigh out: 'Lord, help me!'

Among the oldest popular traditions concerning Elves, is that which is to be read on the runic stone at Lagnö, on Aspö, in Södermanland. Within a serpentine line of runes, there sits, cut out of the rock, an Elf with outstretched legs, seizing with his hands the heads of two serpents. The runes inform us, that 'Gislög caused those characters to be executed after (in memory of) Thord; and Slodi caused true witness to be taken concerning the Elves that he saw, and something else – what was that?' These seem to have been cut with the object of bearing testimony to the Elves and other Trolls that Slodi had seen about the rock.

The traditions concerning Elves current among the people divide them into three classes: those belonging to the earth, the air and the water.

## 2 – Of the Mount-folk

Among the Elves belonging to the earth, or, perhaps more correctly, the subterranean Elves, the Mount- or Berg-folk occupy the most prominent place. It seems probable that Christian compassion for those that died in the time of heathenism, without participation in the blessings promised in the Gospel, but in heathen wise have been placed in unhallowed earth, is the foundation for the cheerless notion, that, awaiting in their green mounds the great day of universal redemption in fear and trembling, they are tormented by sensual desires, as formerly in life; that they long for the love and society of Christians, yet, when they come in contact with them, cause them injury, and if speedy rescue come not, even death itself. In stature the Elves are said to he equal to the generality of the human race, but are more slim and delicate. Their young females are described as extremely beautiful, slender as lilies, white as snow, and with sweet, enticing voices. Their time for playing and dancing is from sunset till cock-crowing; but when the cock has crowed they have no longer permission to stay above ground. Of all the spectre world it is said, that if they do not go to rest when the cock has crowed thrice, they become 'dagstånd', that is, stationary on the spot where the third cock-crowing reached their ears. It is said to be dangerous for a person to come in contact with such an invisible 'dagstånd' on his way, and many are believed to have contracted pain and sickness from that cause. If the wanderer in a summer's evening lays himself to rest by an elf-mount, he soon hears the tones of a harp with sweet singing. If he then promises them redemption, he will hear the most joyful notes resound from numerous stringed instruments; but if he says, 'Ye have no Redeemer,' then with cries and loud lament they will dash their harps in pieces; after which all is silent in the mount. In the green woods and valleys, in the meadows and on the hills, the Elves perform their nightly 'stimm', that is, play and dance, from which cause the grass grows luxuriant and of a darker green in circles; these by the people are called elf-dances, and must not be trampled on.

In nearly all the most distinguished families of Sweden are to be found jewels or ornaments connected with traditions of Trolls and Elves. Thus it is related of the State councillor Harald Stake's wife, how late one summer's evening an elf-woman came to her, who desired to borrow her bridal dress to wear at an elfin wedding. After some consideration the lady resolved on lending it to her. In a few days it was returned, but set with gold and pearls on every seam, and had hanging from it a finger-ring of the finest gold set with the most costly stones, which afterwards, together with the tradition, passed for several centuries as an heirloom in the Stake family.

Among the simple country folks, even at the present day, a bridegroom stands in dread of the envy of the Elves, to counteract which it has long been a custom to lay in the clothes on the wedding day certain strong-smelling plants, as garlic or valerian. Near gates and in crossways there is supposed to be the greatest danger. If anyone asks a bridegroom the reason of these precautions, he will answer: 'On account of envy.' And there is no one so miserable whose bride will not think herself envied on her wedding day, if by no others, at least by the Elves. Hence the tenor of most of the elfin traditions is nearly as follows.

The bride sits ready in her bridal bower, in anxious expectation and surrounded by her bridesmaids. The bridegroom saddles his grey steed, and clad in knightly attire, with his hawk perched proudly on his shoulder, he rides forth from his mother's hall, to fetch home his bride. But in the wood where he is wont to hunt with hawk and hound, an elfin maiden has noticed the comely youth, and is now on the watch for an opportunity, though for ever so short a time, to clasp him to her breast in the flowery grove; or, at least, to the sweet tones of their stringed instruments, lightly to float along with him, hand in hand, on the verdant field. As he draws near to the elf-mount, or is about to ride through the gateway of the castle, his ears are ravished with most wondrous music, and from among the fairest maidens that he there sees dancing in a ring, the Elf-king's daughter herself steps forth fairer than them all, as it is said in the lay

> The damsel held forth her snow-white hand:
> 'Come join in the merry dance with me.'

If the knight allows himself to be charmed, and touches the fascinating hand, he is conducted to Elfland, where in halls indescribably beautiful, and gardens such as he had never beheld, he wanders about, on his Elf-bride's arm, amid lilies and roses. If at length the remembrance of his mourning betrothed enters his mind, and the Elves, who do not deliberately desire evil to mankind, are moved to lead him out on his way, he sees, it is true, his former home again, but he has been absent about forty years, though to him it seemed an hour only. On his return no one knows him, he is a stranger on whom all look with wonder. The old people remember a young knight who disappeared about forty years before, when he rode forth to fetch his bride – and his bride? she has died of grief.

According to another turn of the story, the knight answers the elfin damsel's invitation to dance with her thus:

> 'I may not tread the dance with thee;
> My bride in her bower is awaiting me.'

The elves are then compelled to leave him, but pale and sick to death he returns to his mother, who anxiously addresses him:

> 'But tell me now, my dearest son,
> Why are thy cheeks so deadly pale?' –
> 'Oh well may my cheeks be deadly pale;
> For yonder I've been at the elfin dance.' –
> 'And what shall I answer, oh tell to me,

When thy fair young bride asks after thee?' –
'Oh say I have ridden to the gay green wood,
To chase the deer with hawk and hound.'
  But he will return,
  While the leaves of the forest are green.

The young bride waited two long long days,
Then rode with her maids to the bridegroom's hall.
  But he will return, etc.

And there they pour'd mead and there they pour'd wine:
'But where is my bridegroom, thy dear young son?' –
  But he will return, etc.

'Thy bridegroom's gone to the gay green wood,
To chase the deer with hawk and hound.'
  But he will return, etc.

But the bride had a presentiment that he would never return, and going to his bed, and drawing the sheet aside, there saw him lying cold and pale. At the sight her heart broke, and when morning came, three corpses were borne from the bridal hall; for his mother had also died of grief.

*In the old Danish ballad (Elveskud) the elfin lady, on Oluf's refusal to dance with her, says:*

> *'If then thou wilt not dance with me,*
> *Sickness and death shall follow thee.'*

*She then strikes him violently between the shoulders, lifts him on his horse, and desires him to ride home to his betrothed, etc.*

 *The Swedes have a similar ballad, and the Breton ballad of 'Lord Nann and the Korrigan' bears a striking resemblance to the Scandinavian.*[1]

---

1 See a translation of it in Keightley, op, cit., p. 433, and the original in Villemarqué, *Chants Populaires.*

## 3 – Elfin Gardens

In most country places traditions are current of magic gardens. The spot where such are said to exist, is pointed out by the country people, and some person is always named who has been conducted into them, has wandered about under trees of a finer verdure than any to be seen elsewhere, has tasted fruit the like of which is not to be found in any other place; seen flowers of extraordinary beauty, but afterwards, when all this has been sought for on the same spot, not a trace was to be found: all was either wild wood or plain open fields.

## 4 – Of Bergtagning (Mount-taking)

In old writings many stories are told of persons that have been 'mount-taken', that is, carried off by the Elves into their mounts. Examinations before magistrates and the clergy have taken place even in our time into cases of individuals, who have imagined themselves to have been so carried off, and who in the delirium of fever have believed that they saw elves and wood-demons, which distempered state of body has not seldom been followed by death itself.

Elfin halls or elfin rooms are grots or subterranean houses in mountains and hills, into which sometimes the wanderer enters and reposes; but when he again seeks for the place, he finds it no more. At Estorp on Mösseberg there dwelt an intelligent man, who related as truth, how in returning home one beautiful summer evening from Fahlköping, he took a wrong path, and among the rocks unexpectedly found one of these elf-halls, which he entered and seated himself on a mossy bench in a delightful coolness. On leaving it, he particularly noticed the spot, in order that he might again find so remarkable a place, but could never discover it afterwards.

Three sisters (thus relates the survivor of them) went out one beautiful summer's day to a meadow near the mansion of Boda in Bohuslän. Near the meadow there is a mountain, about which they had often played, and knew the place well. To their great astonishment, however, they found themselves at the entrance of a most beautiful grotto. It was an elf-hall, of a triangular form, with moss-covered seats around it. In the middle there stood a little fir-tree, as an ornament, on the floor. They entered, reposed themselves in the refreshing cool, took accurate notice of the place, but could never find it again.

## 5 – The Flying Elves

Mention of these occurs but rarely. They are described as extremely beautiful, with small wings on their snow-white shoulders; but whether these wings are a borrowed plumage, or belong to the body of these tender beings, has not been decided; though the first opinion seems most in accordance with the Sagas, seeing that mortal men have taken such elfin maidens to wife. Transformed to swans, in full plumage, the people say they have often seen them coming through the air, and descending into some water to bathe; but as soon as they enter the water, they assume the fairest human forms.

A young hunter once saw three such swans descend on the seashore. With astonishment he observed that they laid their plumages aside, which bore a resemblance to linen, and that, instead of swans, three damsels of dazzling whiteness were swimming in the water. He soon saw them leave the water, draw on their linen coverings, which then became changed to swans' plumage, and fly away. One of them, the youngest and fairest, had so captivated the heart of the young man, that he could rest neither by night nor day, for thinking of her lovely form. His foster-mother soon perceived that neither the chase nor the other pastimes, in which he formerly found delight, afforded him any more pleasure, and therefore resolved to discover the cause of his sorrow. From himself she soon learned the wondrous sight he had witnessed, and that he must either win the fair maiden or never again enjoy happiness. His foster-mother assured him: 'I can advise a remedy for thy affliction. Go next Thursday at sunset to the spot where thou last sawest her. The three swans will not fail to come. Observe where thy chosen damsel lays her linen; take it, and hasten with it from the shore. Soon thou wilt hear two of the swans fly away with a great noise, but the third, in search of her plumage, will in her distress come to thee; but although she beseech thee on her knees, do not give back the linen, if thou wilt have the maiden in thy power.' The young man was not backward in following this counsel. Long seemed the days till the coming of Thursday, but longer still seemed to him the hours of that day. At length the sun sank, and ere long a rustling was heard in the air, and the three swans descended on the shore. They were instantly changed to three most beauteous damsels, and having laid their linen on the grass, they hastened to the white sands, and were soon covered with the waves. From his hiding-place the young hunter had closely watched his beloved, and where she had laid her plumage, which was now fine snow-white linen. He then stole forth, carried it off and concealed it among the foliage. Shortly after he heard two of the swans flying away with a great rustling; but the third, as his foster-mother had said, came and fell before him on her snowy knees, praying him to restore her plumage. But the hunter refused, and taking her in his arms, wrapped his cloak round the tender damsel, lifted her on his good steed, and bore her to his home. His foster-mother soon made all things ready for their marriage, and they both lived happily together. Of their children it was said, that fairer never played together. But when seven years had passed, the hunter, one Thursday night, when they were going to bed, related to his wife how he had obtained possession of her; and at her request showed her the white linen, which he had till then concealed; but no sooner had she got it in her hand, than she became changed to a swan, and vanished like lightning through an open window. The husband, it is said, did not live long after that luckless day.[1]

---

The grass which, in luxuriant circles, called, as we have seen, *elf-dances,* is here and there to be observed in the fields, is said so to flourish from the dancing of the elves, and is thence called älfexing (cynosurus caeruleus). The miliary fever is said by the country people to be caused by the elf-mote, or meeting with elves, as a remedy for which the lichen called älfnäfver (lichen aphosus, or lichen caninus) is to be sought for. In old topographical works there is no lack of accounts of families, which, on the mother's side, are supposed to descend from such beings. In Småland a tradition has been credited of a well-known family, whose ancestress, a young, beautiful elfin girl, is said to have flown with the sunbeams through a knot-hole in the wall, and by the heir of the family to have been taken to wife. After having given her husband seven sons, she vanished by the way she came.

## 6 – Löfjerskor

The 'Löfjerskor' named in the old Swedish catechism seem identical with the Grove-damsels (Lundjungfrur), a species of Elves which is also called the Grove-folk (Lund-folk). The sacred groves of the heathens which, by the ecclesiastical law, it was forbidden to approach with superstitious worship, were believed, in the time of paganism, to be protected by invisible deities. If a lime or other tree, either in a forest or solitary, grew more vigorously than the other trees, it was called a *habitation-tree* (boträd), and was thought to be inhabited by an Elf (Rå, Rådande), who, though invisible, dwelt in its shade, rewarded with health and prosperity the individual that took care of the tree, and punished those who injured it.

---

1   The origin of this and other kindred tales must, no doubt, be sought for in the East. The 'Peri-wife', from the Bahar Danush, is almost identical with the above. See Keightley, op, cit., p. 20.

Thus did our heathen forefathers hold in reverence and awe such groves and trees, because they regarded them as given by the Almighty as ornaments to his noble creation, as well as to afford protection to the husbandman and cattle against the scorching heat of the midday sun. In this and in many other instances, simple Antiquity may serve us as a lesson not wantonly to destroy the life even of a shoot, which may one day become a useful, umbrageous tree, or to injure and profane a grove, into which no reflecting Christian can enter, for the purpose of enjoying its refreshing shade, without thinking of the Creator's goodness, and calling to mind how the Saviour of the world had a grove, a garden, to which he oftentimes went, with his disciples, when he would discourse with them on heavenly things and on the immortality of their souls. It was under the shade of a tree that he prayed, and there the comforting angel appeared and strengthened him. Let a Christian meditate on this, and let him have a care of all planting for the ornament and benefit of the earth; and if, when out on his way, he feels tempted to break off a growing shoot, thus let him think: 'I will not destroy a growing life, I will not spoil the embellishment of my mother-earth; it is my neighbour's property, to injure it is unjust, and all injustice is sin.'

The sanctity of the heathen groves and trees originated, it would seem, from the custom of hanging there the limbs of the human and other victims, after they had been for a time immersed in the sacred fountain. But rational Christians have had another reason for retaining the superstition, namely on account of its aid in withholding mischievous persons from violence to the woods and trees. Even at the present day the people in many places point out such groves and trees as no one may approach with an axe. These noted trees often stand alone, and have a singular aspect. Stories are in some places not wanting among the common people of persons, who by cutting a chip or branch from a 'habitation tree', have in consequence been struck with death. Such a famed pine was the 'klinta tall' in Westmanland. Old and decayed it appeared to the traveller standing on the bare rock, until a few years ago it fell down from age. A mermaid, who ruled in the neighbouring creek of the Mälar lake, was said to inhabit the mountain under the pine, and to have been that tree's 'Rå'. The country people had frequently seen snow-white cattle driven up from the lake to the meadow beneath it. The trunk and branches of the tree still lie untouched on the rock. In an old writing there is a story of a man, who was about to cut down a juniper bush in a wood, when a voice was heard from the earth, saying, 'Friend, hew me not!' But he gave another stroke, when blood flowed from the root. Terrified and sick he hastened home.[1]

---

1   Manifestly from the story of Polydorus in the *Aeneis*, iii, 21, sqq. et alibi.

In ballads and traditions stories occur of young maidens that have been transformed to trees and bushes through sorcery, but of the 'Löfjerskor' there are not many tales; nor is it easy to arrive at the origin of the name. But the 'Horgabrudar' in the groves of the heathen divinities were much consulted by the people in cases of doubt and difficulty, whence may probably be derived the superstition, in later times, of seeking help of the 'Rås' that inhabit trees, and are called Löfjerskor, in cases of sickness and trouble, against which there stands a prohibition in our ancient catechism. Loki's mother was named Löfja (Laufey); it seems, therefore, not improbable that evil Troll-wives and Löf-maids derive their name from her. The heathen, in all countries, have celebrated their idolatrous rites in groves and under trees. In the *Lives of the Saints* it is related of St Martin, how among a heathen people, who were willing to adopt Christianity, he demolished a temple, and met with no opposition; but on his proceeding to cut down a fir that stood close by, the people rushed forward, and would on no account allow the tree to be destroyed.

## 6 – The Skogsrå – The Sjörå [1]

Of the same race with the Elves already mentioned, the Skogs- or Forest-elves seem to have been originally, and have undoubtedly belonged to the time of heathenism. As the merwife for fishermen, so is the Skogsrå for hunters regarded among the unlucky objects to meet with. According to old hunting traditions, the Skogs-elf announces her approach by a peculiar, sharp, rushing whirlwind, that shakes the trunks of the trees so that they seem ready to snap asunder. If then the hunter spits and strikes fire, there is no danger, because it is mere noise, there being no power in such winds. The Skogsrå, according to the popular belief, is only of the female sex; whence comes the superstition, that it presages badly for the hunter's luck, if, on leaving home, the first person he meets is a female. He then spits and calls it käringmöte (*lit*. crone-mote). In the Sagas these forest-wives are represented as evil, wanton and foreboders of misfortune; though stories are, nevertheless, told by hunters of their having seen these beings come very friendly to their fires, who, when they have been suffered to remain in peace, have said at their departure: 'There will be excellent sport today.' On which occasions they have invariably killed an abundance of game. When the hunters are reposing in the forest at midnight, they will come to warm themselves by their fires, taking care to show their front side only, and always moving so that their backs may not be exposed to view. Those who have tales to tell of these beings, usually conclude by saying

1   Compounds of skog, *wood, forest;* sjö, *sea, lake;* and rå, *fairy, goblin.*

something like the following: 'Just as she was standing before the fire, quite proud and showing her beautiful person, I took a brand from the fire and struck her, saying: 'Go to the woods, thou odious Troll!' She then hurried away with a whining cry, and a strong wind rose, so that the very trees and stones seemed as if they would be torn up. When she turned her back she appeared as hollow as a hollow tree or a baker's trough.' If a Christian man has intercourse with a forest-woman, there will be born a pernicious being, to the sorrow and misfortune of others.

The Skogsrå is further described as a female spirit of the woods, and as a young person in elegant attire, of friendly demeanour and small figure, but – with claws instead of nails! An eye-witness of her existence relates, that once when out grouse-shooting, having just kindled a fire, and while taking his repast, she appeared before him, and kindly greeted him. To his invitation to warm herself she responded by a friendly nod. He then offered her a share of his fare, holding it, however, at the end of his axe, as he felt somewhat diffident at the sight of her talons; but she declined his offer, smiled and vanished. He now shot five grouse. If he had not offered a part of his fare to the Skogsrå, he would not have killed a single bird.

He, with seven others, was once sitting watching grouse, when a Skogsrå darted past them from a tree. Never before had they seen the birds so numerous; but they missed every one. For fourteen days their shooting seemed bewitched, until at length he was so fortunate as to see another Rå come rustling by from a tree, and to throw his knife over her, whereby the spell was broken. These little goblins milk the cows and deprive the horses of their strength, but anything of steel cast over them hinders them from doing harm. The narrator of the above[1] secured his horses with garlic and asafoetida, which must be placed concealed somewhere about the head.

The same individual relates, that being with several of his neighbours on a fishing expedition, they began to joke about the Siörå and beings of a similar kind, treating them as ridiculous fictions, when on a sudden a Siörå appeared before them, and with a loud plash plunged into the lake. They saw fish in abundance, but could not catch one.

---

1 He was Arndt's postillion during a part of his journey.

## Of Water Elves

### 1   The Mermaid

Learned men, who have given attention to the wonders of the creation, have described a water to be found in certain lakes, called spectre-water (spökvatten). It has the property, when warmed by the sun, of sending up a thick, snow-white mist, resembling at one time a human form, at another that of an animal, changing its appearance and course as it is driven by the wind. The simple people, that dwell by such lakes, bewildered by this phenomenon, relate as a fact that they have seen, innumerable times, a Mermaid sitting by the lake, combing her long locks with a golden comb, or standing on the islets, spreading out her snowy linen on the bushes, or driving before her her snow-white cattle. The Mermaid is thought to be false and deceitful, and is spoken of by the fishermen as the Skogsrä is by the hunters. They all have something to say about her, and anticipate a bad capture, storm and tempest, when she makes her appearance. It is said to be good and advisable, when the fisher sees one of these beings, not to speak of it even to his comrades, but to take his flint and steel and strike fire. From the time that Thor hurled his thunder at the Trolls, they lost, it is said, both power and courage. Hence it is, that in our country places, in every house where there is a newborn child, either fire on the hearth, or a light, must burn by day and night, until the child is christened; else it is to be feared that the Trolls may come and carry off the child, and leave one of their own in its stead. Of the Mermaids it is said that they dwell at the bottom of the ocean or of an inland sea, have castles and mansions, also domestic animals and cattle, which are called 'brand-cattle', the signification of which is far from evident.[1]

---

In West Gothland, in the district of Biärke, there is a lake with beautifully wooded shores, called Anten. On an isle in this lake there was formerly an ancient castle, remains of which are still to be seen, called Loholm, in which dwelt Sir Gunnar, a renowned knight, and ancestor of the famous family of Leionhufvud, or Lewenhaupt. Once, when out on the lake he had fallen into danger, a Mer-wife came to his aid, but exacted from him the promise, that on a certain day he should meet her again at the same place. One Thursday evening she sat expecting the knight; but he forgot his promise. She then caused the water of the lake to swell up over Loholm, until Sir Gunnar was forced to take refuge in a higher apartment; but the

---

1   Qu. Angl. *brindled*.

water reached even that. He then sought safety in the drawbridge tower; but there the billows again overtook him. He next committed himself to a boat, which sank near a large stone, called to this day Gunnar's stone; from which time Sir Gunnar, it is said, lives constantly with the Mer-wife. When fishermen or the country people row by the stone, they usually lift their hats, as a salutation to Sir Gunnar, in the belief that if they neglected to do so, they would have no success. From that time no one dwelt at Loholm, of the materials of which was built the noble castle of Gräfsnäs, on a peninsula in the same lake, with towers, ditches, and drawbridges, remains of which are still visible. From this Sir Gunnar descended Erik Abrahamsson, father-in-law of Gustavus the First.

## 2 – Fountain Maidens

Mention has been already made of the priestesses of the heathen gods, or Horgabrudar, who watched by the sacred fountains, in which the members of the victims were washed, and received gifts from the people for advice in cases of sickness, as well as on other occasions. After the country became Christian, the monks and priests took the fountains under their care, placed by them images of saints or a cross, and caused the people to make offerings to, and seek health from, the saint that was supposed to have the well under his protection. Thus did Christian superstition step into the place of pagan, and continues even to the present day. But the heathen Horgabrudar, who died without baptism or sacrament, were still in the remembrance of the people, and had become Elves, who await salvation, dwelling till doomsday under their fountains' silvery roof. In song and in story the beauty of the Fountain-maids is praised, when they have been seen by mortal man and displayed their fair forms either in the depth of a fountain, or reposing by its side on a bed of flowers. To the person who cleanses a fountain, or plants over it an umbrageous tree, the Fountain-maid will be kind and propitious; while he who profanes or sullies the fountain's salubrious stream will be followed by sickness and misfortune.

## 3 – The Neck and the Strömkarl

The Neck appears sometimes in the form of a grown man, and is particularly dangerous to haughty and pert damsels; sometimes in that of a comely youth, with his lower extremities like those of a horse; sometimes like an old man with a long beard; and occasionally as a handsome youth, with yellow locks flowing over his shoulders and a red cap, sitting in a summer evening on the surface of the water with a golden harp in his hand. If anyone wishes to learn music of him, the most welcome remuneration that can be offered to him is a black lamb, especially if the hope of his salvation – which the Neck has greatly at heart – be at the same time expressed to him. Hence when two boys once said to a Neck, 'What good do you gain by sitting here and playing? You will never enjoy eternal happiness,' he began to weep bitterly.[1]

If one of the common people has a disease, for which they cannot otherwise account, they imagine that it is caused by the spirit of the place where the disease was contracted, or was supposed to be contracted; whence the expression, which is often to be heard, 'He has met with something bad in the air, in the water, in the field.' In such case the Neck must be propitiated, which is done in the following manner: They pour a drink into a cup, and mix with it the scrapings from the wedding ring, from silver, brass, or any other metal possessed by inheritance, but so that the odd number, particularly three, be observed. With this mixture they repair to the place where they suppose the disease was contracted, and pour it out over the left shoulder. On the way they must neither turn about nor utter a sound. If there be any uncertainty as to the place, the pouring is made on the doorpost, or on an anthill.[2]

A Neck at Bohuus, in West Gothland, had transformed himself into a horse and gone on the bank to eat; but a cunning man, whose suspicions were roused, threw such a curiously contrived halter over him, that he could not get loose again. The man now kept the Neck with him all the spring, and tormented him most thoroughly, by making him plough all his fields. At length the halter accidentally slipping off, the Neck sprang like lightning into the water, dragging the harrow after him.[3]

A Neck who takes up his abode under a bridge or in a stream, is commonly called a Strömkarl. He always plays on the viol; and when any musician plays with extraordinary boldness and skill, he is said to play with the Strömkarl's touch. Near Hornborgabro, in West Gothland, a Strömkarl was once heard singing, to a pleasant melody, these words thrice repeated: 'I know – and I know – and I know – that my Redeemer liveth.' As seen by sailors, the Neck is described as an old man, sitting on a rock, wringing the water out of his large, green beard. Their appearance is said to forebode storm and tempest. Under this form they may be more correctly called Mermen. He is sometimes seen on the shore under the form of a handsome horse, but with his hoofs reversed.

A priest riding one evening over a bridge, heard the most delightful tones of a stringed instrument, and, on looking round, saw a young man, naked

---

1   Faye, op. cit., p. 54. *Svenske Folk-Visor*, iii, p. 127.
2   Arndt, iii, p. 15.
3   Faye, op. cit., p. 53.

to the waist, sitting on the surface of the water, with a red cap and yellow locks, as already described. He saw that it was the Neck, and in his zeal addressed him thus: 'Why dost thou so joyously strike thy harp? Sooner shall this dried cane that I hold in my hand grow green and flower, than thou shalt obtain salvation.' Thereupon the unhappy musician cast down his harp, and sat bitterly weeping on the water. The priest then turned his horse, and continued his course. But lo! before he had ridden far, he observed that green shoots and leaves, mingled with most beautiful flowers, had sprung from his old staff. This seemed to him a sign from heaven, directing him to preach the consoling doctrine of redemption after another fashion. He therefore hastened back to the mournful Neck, showed him the green, flowery staff, and said: 'Behold! Now my old staff is grown green and flowery like a young branch in a rose garden; so likewise may hope bloom in the hearts of all created beings; for their Redeemer liveth!' Comforted by these words, the Neck again took his harp, the joyous tones of which resounded along the shore the whole livelong night.

The Strömkarl's melody (Strömkarlslag) has eleven varieties, ten only of which may be danced, the eleventh belongs to the night-spirit and his troop; for if anyone were to cause it to be played, tables and benches, pots and cups, old men and grandmothers blind and lame, even babes in the cradle, would begin to dance.[1]

Those who are desirous of learning the Strömkarl's ten variations, must place their violin for three Thursday nights under a bridge, where there is a constantly running stream. On the third night, the Neck, or Strömkarl, will come and strike the strings of his instrument, when the learner must tune his fiddle and accompany him. If the eleventh melody is played, inanimate things, as trees and stones, will dance.

An equally wonderful composition is the Elf-king's tune, which no musician will venture to play; for having once begun it, he cannot cease from playing, unless he can play it backwards, or someone behind him cuts the strings of the violin.[2]

*The same anxiety as to their state hereafter prevails among the Daoine Ski of the Scottish Highlands, one of whom, issuing from a lake, questions a clergyman on the subject. Like the Neck, they also have melodious music.*[3]

Of the earths which gather among the foam in the still creeks, and of river waters, there is formed a loose, white, porous kind of stone, resembling

1  Arndt, iv, 241.
2  Thiele, *Danske Folksagen*, Copenhagen 1818–23, i, pp. 166, *sq.*
3  Stewart, *Superstitions of the Highlands*, quoted by Keightley, op, cit., p. 385.

picked or pulled bread: this is called 'Necke-bröd'; the masses or cakes of which are called marlekor (marekor), because the *mare* (still water) cements them together. The beautiful white or yellow flowers, that grow on the banks of lakes and rivers, and are called 'Neck-roses', are well-known memorials of the popular idea of the Neck. The poisonous root of the water hemlock (*cicuta virosa*) formerly bore the name of the Necke-root.

*In Beowulf frequent mention occurs of the Nicor (pl. Niceras)[1] Connected with the name is that of Odin, Hnikarr, in his character of a sea-god.[2]*

The following extract may serve as a commentary on what is related both of the Swedish Neck and Danish Nök. 'Husby is very pleasantly situated, and its church is said to be one of the oldest in Sweden. Here is shown St Siegfried's well, with the water of which the holy man Sigfridus, according to the tradition, baptised king Olov Skötkonung. The well is still famous, and is said on many occasions to be used nightly by the country people. Fifty years ago' (the author travelled in 1803) 'many superstitions and ceremonies were practised at wells. Almost every province had some that at certain periods of the summer were visited, and into which a piece of money, iron or any metal was cast as an offering. But this illusion is now almost extinct. Still it is, nevertheless, worth inquiring, *what* power, and *why* a power is everywhere ascribed to metal of counteracting the influence of witchcraft and of evil spirits? For no other reason than to propitiate the Neck of the well, did people throw into it anything metallic. Connected with the above is the popular belief, that, when bathing in the sea, a person should cast into it, close by him, a fire-steel, a knife, or the like, to prevent any monster from hurting him. The steel, or whatever it may be, may be taken out again. Formerly a fire-steel, or a pair of scissors, was laid on the cradle of a child, until it was christened. Even to the present day the custom exists of pouring melted silver or other metal on the spot where it is believed that a person is suffering from the work of the evil one. With such a pouring the injury is also poured out.'

Having thus propitiated, or rather neutralised the pernicious propensities of, the Neck, it was not unusual while bathing to address him scoffingly in the following words: 'Neck, Neck, Nåleputa, du är på lann, men jag är i vann' (Neck, Neck, needle-thief, thou art on land, but I am in the water). On quitting the water, the person took the steel again, saying: 'Neck, Neck, needle-thief, I am on land, and thou art in the water.'[3]

1    Ver. 838, 1144, 2854.
2    *Edda-Saem.*, pp. 46, 91, 184; *Edda-Snorra*, pp. 3, 24, 322.
3    Arndt, i, p. 259, *sq.*; iii, p. 17 *sq.*

## The Wild Hunt

In Scania the sounds like voices, that are at times heard in the air in November and December, are by the common people called Odin's hunt.[1] Grimm also connects time Wild Hunt (Wütendes Heer) with Odin (Ohg. Wuotan), the tradition of which is current over almost all Germany. In the course of time, after the introduction of Christianity, the pagan deity degenerated into a wild hunter, regarding whom almost every place where he is said to ride has its tradition.

## Mystic Animals

According to the Swedish popular belief, there are certain animals which should not at any time be spoken of by their proper names, but always with euphemisms, and kind allusions to their character. If anyone speaks slightingly to a cat, or beats her, her name must not be uttered; for she belongs to the hellish crew, and is intimate with the Bergtroll in the mountains, where she often visits. In speaking of the cuckoo, the owl, and the magpie, great caution is necessary, lest one should be ensnared, as they are birds of sorcery. Such birds, also snakes, one ought not to kill without cause, as their associates might avenge them. It is particularly sinful to tread toads to death, as they are often enchanted princesses. Many a one has become lame without fall or fracture, but as a penalty for such wantonness. In speaking of the Troll-pack or Witch-crew, one must name fire and water, and the name of the church to which one belongs; then no injury can arise. The weasel must not be so called, but the *aduine*; the fox, *blue-foot*, or *he that goes in the forest*; and the bear, *the old one* (Gubbe, Gammeln), *grandfather* (Storfar), Naskus; rats, *the long-bodied*; mice, *the small grey*; the seal, *brother Lars*; the wolf, *gold-foot* or *grey-foot*, *grey-tosse*, not *varg*, because it is said that formerly, when the now dumb animals could speak, the wolf made this announcement:

> Kallar du mig *Varg*, så blir jag dig arg,
> Men kallar du mig *af Guld*, så blir jag dig huld.
>
> *If thou callest me Varg I will be wroth with thee,*
> *But if thou callest me of gold, I will be kind to thee.*

Even inanimate things are not at all times to be called by their usual names: fire, for instance, is on some occasions not to be called *eld* or *ell* but

---

1   These sounds are by Nilsson (*Skandiv. Fauna*, ii, p. 106) ascribed to certain water-fowls on their way to the South.

*hetta* (heat); water used for brewing, not *vatn*, but *lag* or *löu*, else the beer would not be so good.[1]

The magpie – like others of the raven or crow family – is also a mystic bird, a downright witches' bird, belonging to the devil and the other hidden powers of night. When the witches, on Walpurgis Night, ride to the Blåkulle, they turn themselves into magpies. When they are moulting in summer, and become bald about the neck, the country people say they have been to the Blåkulle, and helped the evil one to get his hay in, and that the yoke has rubbed their feathers off.

*The above superstition of the wolf is very ancient and widespread, an evident trace of it existing in Anglo-Saxon and Old Norse: 'gryre sceal for greggum' (terror shall there be for the grey one).*[2]

## 1 – The Mountain-troll

The extraordinary tales of Mountain-trolls and their kidnappings that are told by credible persons, and confirmed by very singular circumstances, might afford ground for the supposition that the primitive inhabitants of Sweden, the wild mountaineers, had not altogether died out, but that in the recesses of the great mountain-forests some in recent times might have still resided. Memorials of the hostility entertained by these people against the light of Christianity are preserved in the traditions concerning the several stones or masses of rock called *giant-casts*. These are shown by the people in all country places, and are usually in such situations as to give birth to the tradition of their having been hurled from a mountain towards some church. 'The Giant', as the story goes, 'could not endure the noise of the bells from the holy edifice, and therefore cast this rock, in the hope of knocking it down, but being too strong, he hurled it far beyond the church.' Or it is said, 'The stone was too heavy, and the church too far away, so that it fell short of the mark.' In some of these stones, as in the one near Enköping, are to be seen marks as if made by the five fingers of a gigantic hand. Near the celebrated church of Warnhem lies the Himmelsberg, in which, as we are told, a giant dwelt, until the convent bells ringing for prayers drove him away. It is related that, on leaving the mountain, he inquired of a lad, that worked in the neighbourhood, in which direction Ålleberg lay, for thither he intended to take his course. The lad having directed him, he went off as in a whirlwind, and the lad now

---

1   Arndt, i, p. 49; iii, pp. 18, 19; Thiele, op. cit., iii, p. 122; Finn Magnusen, *Den Aeldre Edda*, ii, p. 9.
2   *Cod. Exon.*, p. 342; *Kraka Mál*, p. 54, edit. Rafn.

discovered, to his no small astonishment, that his forefinger, with which he had pointed out the way, had followed along with the giant. In the Description of Uppland there is a story of a mountain near Lagga church, and how a giant with his family quitted it on account of the bells, 'the sound of which he was not inclined to hear'. 'When wilt thou come again?' asked a man standing by, and witnessing their departure; whereupon the man of the mountain answered, 'When Lagga fiord is field, and Öst-tuna lake meadow.' The fiord and the lake are now like to become field and meadow; but the Troll's return seems by no means so certain.

## 2 – The Mountain-troll – Sten of Fogelkärr

In an old Description of Bohuslän the following event is related. – Sten of Fogelkärr was an excellent marksman. One day when out hunting, he came to a mountain, where he saw a young, beautiful girl sitting on a stone; and as he instantly formed the design of obtaining her, he cast his fire-steel between her and the mountain, for that purpose. He then heard a loud laugh within the mountain. It was the damsel's father, who at the same moment opened his door and said, 'Wilt thou have my daughter?' Sten answered, 'Yes,' and as she was stark naked, he wrapped her in his cloak, and so took her home with him, and had her christened. Before, however, he left the mountain, the damsel's father gave him this injunction: 'When thou celebratest thy marriage with my daughter, thou shalt send to the mountain in which I dwell twelve barrels of beer, together with bread, and the meat of four oxen; and when the bridal gifts are to be given, mine shall not be wanting.' Nobly did the man of the mountain keep his promise; for while the company was sitting at the nuptial board, and the guests, according to ancient custom, were bestowing the bridal presents, the roof was suddenly raised, and a large purse of money thrown down; at the same time was heard the old man's a voice: 'Here is my bridal gift, and when thou wilt have thy dower, drive to the mountain with four horses and take thy share.' Sten did so, and got copper kettles of various sizes, besides 'brand-cattle', descendants from which good stock were long to be found in those parts. Sten became a rich and influential man, and had many comely children by his wife; even now families exist in the neighbourhood, that profess to derive their descent from Sten of Fogelkärr and the damsel of the mountain.[1]

---

1   Grimm (*Deutsche Mythologie*, op. cit., p. 435) gives the story with some variations from Ödman's Bahuslän. The cattle are there distinguished as *white-headed* (hielmeta), O. Nor. hjálmóttr, *vertice albus, alias discolor; de pecudibus dicitur.*

## 3 – The Mountain-troll

A peasant, in a village named Fyrunga, had in like manner married a giant's daughter, with whom he had received considerable wealth; but he lived unhappily with her, beat and misused her, although she was of a meek and compliant disposition. When the giant was apprised of this, he withdrew from his son-in-law, so that he became poor. This peasant being one day about to shoe his horse, in the absence of other aid, ordered his wife to hold up the horse's feet. With astonishment he saw that she not only lifted up the horse's feet with the utmost ease, but that when a shoe did not fit, she bent it as if it had been wax instead of cold iron. Not without signs of fear the man said to her, 'As thou art so strong, why dost thou allow me to strike thee?' 'I bear in mind,' said she, 'what the black man said who united us, that I shall be obedient to thee, and I will hold to my engagement, although thou hast often broken thine; else I could have chopped thee up like cabbage.' From that moment the man became so changed through his wife's good sense and forbearance, that he ever after treated her with affection. When apprised of this change, the giant again bestowed on them all sorts of good, so that they became rich and prosperous.

## 4 – The Mountain-troll

In the district of Näs in Wärmland there is an immense stone, having in it a cavity like a room, in which the peasant children sit and play while they are out with the cattle. By some it is called Stygges stone, by others Halvar's room. In this hollow, so says the tradition, there dwelt, in the time of heathenism, a giant, who lived on the best terms possible with a farmer in the nearest grange. One day as the farmer and another man came out of the forest from their labour, they found the giant sitting outside of the stone. 'Can I barter with thee?' said the giant. 'Six she-goats and the he-goat seven I will give thee for a cow.' The farmer expressed his willingness. On the following morning when the farmer's wife entered the cowhouse, she saw to her surprise that the cow was gone and that there were seven goats in its place. The bargain proved a good one, for they were lucky with the goats. Once when they were out raking in the field they saw before them a great frog big with young. The farmer's wife had pity on the heavy creature and wound a woollen band round its body. In the evening the giant came to the farm requesting the wife to come and loose that which she had bound. The woman followed him to the stone, where she found that the frog was no other than the giant's wife, who had assumed that form. She loosed the band and delivered her. In reward for this service, they desired her to come with a bag, into which the giant poured as much silver money as she could carry. It is further related that one evening, when the people were at work in the field, there came from the giant's habitation such a quantity of cattle and goats that they were forced to leave the field. One Easter eve, the farmer was passing by, when the giant, who was sitting on his stone seat, said to him, 'Wilt thou come in and eat milk porridge with me?' 'No,' answered the other. 'If thou hast more than thou canst eat, keep it till tomorrow.' 'Thanks,' said the giant, 'had I known that before, I should now be rich.' The giant was never seen afterwards.

When the Trolls and Giants were driven away by the Christians, they took refuge out at sea, on uninhabited rocks and on desert strands, where, according to general tradition, they have in later times been seen by mariners. Some sailors belonging to Bohuslän, when once driven on a desert shore by a storm, found a giant sitting on a stone by a fire. He was old and blind, and rejoiced at hearing the Northmen, because he was himself from their country. He requested one of them to approach and give him his hand, 'That I may know,' said he, 'whether there is yet strength in the hands of the Northmen.' The old man being blind, was not sensible that they took a great boat-hook, which they heated in the fire and held out to him. He squeezed the hook as if it had been wax, shook his head and said, 'I find the Northmen now have but little strength in their hands compared with those of old.'

## The Trolls Celebrate Christmas

Of the manner in which the Trolls celebrate Christmas Eve there are traditions throughout the whole North. At that time it is not advisable for Christian men to be out. On the heaths Witches and little Trolls ride, one on a wolf, another on a broom or a shovel, to their assemblies, where they dance under their stones. These stones are then raised on pillars, under which the Trolls dance and drink. In the mount are then to be heard mirth and music, dancing and drinking. On Christmas morn, during the time between cock-crowing and daybreak, it is highly dangerous to be abroad.

One Christmas night in the year 1490, as Fru Cissela Ulftand was sitting in her mansion at Liungby in Scania, a great noise was heard proceeding from the Trolls assembled at the Magle stone, when one of the lady's boldest servants rode out to see what was going on. He found the stone raised, and the Trolls in a noisy whirl dancing under it. A beautiful female stepped forth, and presented to the guest a drinking horn and a pipe, requesting him to drink the Troll-king's health and to blow in the pipe. He took the horn and pipe, but at the same instant clapped spurs to his horse, and galloped straight, over rough and smooth, to the mansion. The Trolls followed him in a body with a wild cry of threats and prayers, but the man kept the start, and delivered both horn and pipe into the hands of his mistress. The Trolls promised prosperity and riches to Fru Cissela's race, if she would restore their pipe and horn; but she persisted in keeping them, and they are still preserved at Liungby, as memorials of the wonderful event. The horn is said to be of an unknown mixture of metals with brass ornaments, and the pipe of a horse's leg-bone. The man who stole them from the Trolls died three days after, and the horse on the second day. Liungby mansion has been twice burnt, and the Ulftand family never prospered afterwards. This tradition teaches that Christians should act justly even towards Trolls.

It is also related of some priests, who were riding before daybreak by a mount on a Christmas morning, while the Trolls were at their sports, how a Berg- or Mount-woman came out and offered them drink in metal bowls; and how they cast the drink behind them, but that some drops chanced to fall on the horses' loins and burned the hair off. The bowls they carried away with them, and such are still to be found in several churches, where, it is said, they were formerly used as chalices.[1]

This drink, which the Trolls were in the habit of offering so liberally, was believed to have the property of obliterating from the memory all the past, and of rendering the guest who partook of it contented with all he met with in the mount.


## Origin of the Noble Name of Trolle

On the wall of Voxtorp church in Småland there is a painting representing a knight named Herve Ulf, when one Christmas morning he received a drinking horn from a Troll-wife with one hand, while with his sword he struck off her head with the other, kept the horn and rode to church. In remembrance of this deed, the king commanded him to call himself Trolle, and to take a Troll without a head for his armorial bearing. Such is the origin of the noble name of Trolle. This wonderful horn was of three hundred colours, and was first preserved in the cathedral of Wexiö; but when the Danes in 1570 burned Wexiö, the horn was carried to Denmark.

It is said that the Trolls are very prolific, but that their offspring for the most part dies when it thunders; whence the saying: 'Were it not for thunder, the Trolls would destroy the world.'

1    For more on this subject see *Danish Traditions*.

## The Giant's Path

In a large cleft in the mountain of Billingen in West Gothland, called the Jättestig (Giant's Path), it is said there was formerly a way leading far into the mountain, into which a peasant once penetrated, and found a man lying asleep on a large stone. How he came there no one could tell, but every time the bell tolls for prayers in Yglunda church, he turns round and sighs. So he will continue till doomsday.

## The Tomte or Swedish Niss

Two husbandmen dwelt in a village; they had like arable land, like meadow, like wood and pasture, but the one grew richer and the other poorer from year to year. The one had a house painted red, well tarred, with boarded walls and a sound turf roof; the other's habitation was moss-clad, with bare, rotten walls and a leaky roof. Whence all this difference? Many a one will answer: 'The rich man had a *Tomte* in his house.' He appears before the master, and, if she is kind to him, before the mistress also. 'But what are they like, these propitious little beings?' In magnitude like a child of a twelvemonth old, but with an ancient and sagacious looking face under a little red cap; with a grey, coarse woollen jacket, short breeches, and shoes like those worn by peasant children. He appears at noontide, in summer and autumn, and has generally a straw or an ear of corn, which he drags slowly along, panting at every step, like one under the heaviest burden. On such an occasion the poor peasant had once laughed at a Tomte, and said, 'What difference is there whether thou bringest me that or nothing?' This vexed the little, weary collector, and he transferred himself to the other peasant's abode, who was at that time a poor new beginner. From that day prosperity withdrew itself from him who had despised the diminutive being. But the other man, who esteemed the industrious little Tomte, and took care of the smallest straw or ear, became rich, and cleanliness, order and abundance reigned in his dwelling.

---

If a stableman takes care of his horses, speaks kindly to them, feeds them at ten o'clock at night, and again at four in the morning, he has no cause to stand in fear of the Tomte. But the careless one, who maltreats the cattle, curses and swears when he enters the stable, forgets their nightly food, and sleeps till day, must take good care of himself, lest when he steps into the stable he get a buffet on the ear from the unseen but hard fist of the Tomte, that brings him to a stand on his nose.

It has been believed that the souls of those who in heathen times were slaves, and while the master and his sons were engaged in piracy, had charge of the land and buildings, and were employed in agriculture, are represented in these small, gray beings, as pursuing their former earthly labours until doomsday. There are still many Christians who believe in these Tomt-spirits, and annually make them a kind of offering, or, as they now term it, 'give them a reward'. This takes place on the day when joy was proclaimed to all the world, and salvation even to the Tomtar – Christmas morning; and consists in some small pieces of coarse, grey woollen cloth, a little tobacco, and a shovelful of earth.

Tomtar are also called Nissar. 'For the good Niss,' the country folks in Blekinge and other places are wont to say, when out at work in the fields and sitting at their repast, they lay a piece of bread, cheese, etc. under a green turf, whereby they hope to gain his goodwill.

A peasant in Scania was in the habit of placing food on the stove daily for the Tomtar or Nissar. This came to the knowledge of the priest, who thereupon searched the house, for the sake of convincing its inmates that no Nissar were to be found. 'How then does the food disappear every night?' asked the peasant. 'That I can tell you,' said the priest. 'Satan takes it all and collects it in a kettle in hell, in which kettle he hopes to boil your souls to all eternity.' From that time no more food was set out for the Nissar.

Where building and carpenters' work are going forward, it is said that the Tomtar, while the workmen are at their dinner, may be seen going about and working with small axes. When a tree is felled in the forest, it is said: 'The woodsman holds the axe, but the Tomte fells the tree.' When the horses in a stable are well tended and in fine condition, it is said: 'The groom lays the food in the crib, but it is the Tomte who makes the horse fat.'

---

A housewife when she sifted meal had long remarked that there was an uncommon weight in the tub, and that although she had frequently taken considerable quantities from it, the weight exceeded all belief. But once, when going to the storeroom, she chanced to look through the keyhole, or through a chink in the door, and beheld a little Tomte in tattered grey clothes sitting and busily sifting in the meal-tub. The woman withdrew softly, and made a new, handsome kirtle for the industrious little fellow, and hung it on the edge of the tub, at the same time placing herself so that she might see what he thought of his new garment. When he came he immediately put it on and began to sift most sedulously; but seeing that the meal dusted and damaged his new kirtle, he exclaimed, casting the sieve from him:

> 'The young spark is fine;
> He dusts himself:
> Never more will he sift.'

## Ravens – Pyslingar and Mylingar – Skrat

Ravens scream by night in the forest-swamps and wild moors. They are said to be the ghosts of murdered persons, who have been concealed there by their undetected murderers, and not had Christian burial.

In forests and wildernesses the spirits of little children that have been murdered are said to wander about wailing, within an assigned space, as long as their lives would have lasted on earth, if they had been permitted to live. As a terror for unnatural mothers that destroy their offspring, their sad cry is said to be, 'Mamma! Mamma!' When travellers by night pass such places, these beings will hang on the vehicle, when the liveliest horses will toil as if they were dragging millstones, will sweat, and at length be unable to proceed a step farther. The peasant then knows that a ghost or Pysling has attached itself to his vehicle. If he goes to the horses' heads, lifts the headstall, and looks through it towards the carriage, be will see the little pitiable being, but will get a smart blow on the ear, or fall sick. This is called *ghost-pressed* (gastkramad).

The Myling, as well as the Tomte and Skogsrå, are exposed to persecution from the wolves. Some hunters, who had one evening taken up their quarters in a barn in the forest, were waked in the middle of the night by the howling of wolves and an extraordinary noise; and on seeking the cause, they saw a Skogsrå fleeing before a number of wolves that were pursuing her. On reaching the barn she jumped up to the little window that stood open, whence she jeered the wolves standing beneath, showing them first one foot then the other, and saying, 'Paw this foot! Paw that foot! If you get both, take them.' One of the hunters, tired of her proximity, gave her a push in the back, so that she fell down among the wolves, saying, 'Take her altogether!' She was instantly devoured by the wolves. Similar stories are related of Mylingar and Tomtar.

Of the Myling it is related that it can assume the form of persons both living and dead, thereby deluding the nightly traveller; also that it can imitate the speech, laugh and singing of persons.

The Skrat[1] is a species of Myling that with a horse-laugh makes game of persons that are out at night in the forests or fields. A peasant in Westmanland had while digging found a ring that shone like gold, and would, as he said, have certainly become possessor of it, had not the Skrat, before he had well got hold of it, laughed it away. So it is said frequently to happen to treasure-diggers. He comes at midnight, chiefly in winter, out of the forests, to the public roads, and hangs on the hinder part of a sledge or other vehicle, when on a sudden it becomes so heavy, that the horses,

---

1   See Grimm, J., *Deutsche Mythologie*, op. cit., p. 447.

however good they may be, become jaded, sweat, and at length stop; then the Skrat generally runs off with a malicious laugh, and vanishes.

## The Werwolf

In a hamlet within a forest there dwelt a cottager, named Lasse, and his wife. One day he went out in the forest to fell a tree, but had forgotten to cross himself and say his Paternoster, so that some Troll or Witch (Vargamor)[1] got power over him and transformed him into a wolf. His wife mourned for him for several years; but one Christmas Eve there came a beggar woman, who appeared very poor and ragged: the good housewife gave her a kind reception, as is customary among Christians at that joyous season. At her departure the beggar woman said that the wife might very probably see her husband again, as he was not dead, but was wandering in the forest as a wolf. Towards evening the wife went to her pantry, to place in it a piece of meat for the morrow, when on turning to go out, she perceived a wolf standing, which raising itself with its paws on the pantry steps, regarded the woman with sorrowful and hungry looks. Seeing this she said, 'If I knew that thou wert my Lasse, I would give thee a bone of meat.' At that instant the wolf-skin fell off, and her husband stood before her in the clothes he had on when he went out on that unlucky morning.

*The heathen sorcery of transforming a person to the likeness of a wolf, is still believed by many to be transmitted to some wicked individuals, even to our days. Fins, Lapps and Russians are held in particular aversion on this account; and when, during the last year of the war with Russia, Calmar was unusually overrun with wolves, it was generally said that the Russians had transformed the Swedish prisoners to wolves, and sent them home to infest the country.*

## Jack O' Lantern

A flaming light moves backwards and forwards on the hearth, not unlike a lantern borne by one in search of something. It is 'Jack with the lantern', who, as many a simple person, after old traditions, will tell us, was a mover of landmarks, and is thus doomed to wander with a light in his hand.

According to the old popular belief, a man, who during life has rendered himself guilty of such a crime, is doomed to have no rest in his grave after death, but to rise every midnight, and with a lantern in his hand to proceed to the spot where the landmark had stood which he had

---

1   Old women dwelling in the forests, who not infrequently give themselves out as sorceresses, have got the name of *Vargamor* (Wolf-crones), and are believed to have the wolves of the forest under their protection and control.

fraudulently removed. On reaching the place, he is seized with the same desire which instigated him in his lifetime, when he went forth to remove his neighbour's landmark, and he says as he goes, in a harsh, hoarse voice, 'It is right! It is right! It is right!' But on his return, qualms of conscience and anguish seize him, and he then exclaims: 'It is wrong! It is wrong! It is wrong!'

## The Ram in the Getaberg

Near Ingelstad, in the district of Oxie, in Scania, there is a mount called the Getaberg, where before misfortunes and public calamities, a ram, terrible to look upon, makes its appearance. The neighbouring peasantry can tell, both with year and day, of calamities that have been so foreboded. One evening a boy passed over the mount singing a song about the ram, that was current in the neighbourhood, and by his ill-timed mirth waked the ram, which soon stuck him on his horn, and would have killed him, had not a handsome young damsel come and saved him; for when young girls come to him the ram becomes as gentle as a lamb.

## The Dragon or White Serpent

Among the fabulous beings of former days must he reckoned the Dragon, concerning which many traditions and songs are extant. In the heathen Sagas no mention is made of its colour; but in later writings we find it usually designated the White Serpent. This must not be confounded with the white Tomt-serpent (Tomtorm), which in the southern parts is numbered among good domestic sprites, and is gladly fed by the inmates of the house in which it vouchsafes to take up its abode under the flooring. The White Serpent now to be spoken of is very rarely seen, some suppose only every hundred years, and in desert places. Sorceresses were in the habit of seeking for it, and boiling it in their magical compounds, for the attainment of profound knowledge in the secrets of nature; for by insinuating itself, in the innermost parts of the earth, around the roots of rocks and mountains, among the lowest fibres of the trees and plants, it is believed to have imbibed their occult virtues, and to communicate them to the individual by whom it allows itself to be found. If anyone finds a White Serpent, he should instantly grasp it by the middle of its body, when it will leave its skin. Only to lick this is thought to strengthen the inward powers of man, so that, without previous instruction, he will know the virtues of plants, earths and stones, how to heal wounds and cure all kinds of diseases. This is called 'To become cunning'.[1]

1    Att blifva klok.

A poor little peasant boy, who had wandered out of his path, came to a small hut in the forest, in which one of these so-called cunning women and serpent-boilers dwelt. When the boy entered she was not at home; but a large kettle was standing on the fire, in which a white serpent was boiling. The boy was hungry, and seeing bread on a table, and a thick, fat scum in the kettle, which he supposed to arise from boiling meat, he dipped a piece of bread in the kettle and ate it. The old beldam, who now came in, was instantly aware of what had taken place; but feeling convinced that the boy, however he might excel others in wisdom, would not surpass her, and that he could not do any harm to her, suffered him to depart, and accompanied him until he was again in his right path, instructing him on the way how he should apply the wondrous gift he was possessed of.

Of Sven in Bragnum in West Gothland, who was so famous that he was visited by Linnaeus, the story goes, that he found a White Serpent, the skin of which he licked, whereby he became cunning (klok), so that he knew the virtues of all kinds of creeping things and plants, which he sedulously collected about Mösseberg and the meadows of Boulom, for the cure of diseases. It is remarkable that he knew beforehand that he should lose his knowledge as soon as he married; so that from the day of his marriage he never would receive a visit from a patient.

*The Swedish people ascribe the virtue of certain medicinal springs to* White Serpents. *In 1809 thousands flocked from Halland and West Gothland to the wonder-working Helsjö (a small lake near Rampegärda). It was said that some children on its banks tending cattle had in that year often seen a beautiful young female sitting on its shore, holding in her hand a white serpent, which she showed them. This water-nymph with the serpent appears only every hundred years. Bexell's Halland, quoted by Grimm* (Deutsche Mythologie, op. cit., p. 554). *See Danish traditions. According to a German story, by eating of a white serpent, a person acquires a knowledge of the language of all animals.* [1]

## The Uninvited Wedding Guests

A farmer in Bahuus was celebrating his daughter's marriage, but scarcely was the table covered and the viands brought in, before all – even before the guests had seated themselves – was eaten up. When the master came in and saw this, he said, 'Now Hue has been here and eaten up all the meat.' He then ordered other viands to be brought in, of which the company began immediately to partake; but whatever the guests might

---

1    Grimm, J. & W., *Kinder- und Hausmärchen*, op. cit., No. 17.

eat, it was evident that more vanished than was consumed by them. Near the door stood an old cavalry soldier, who knew more than the others, and who, on hearing what was being talked of at table, mounted his horse and rode to a neighbouring mount, where he knocked. On the mountain being opened, the soldier said to its inhabitant, 'Lend me thy hat; thou shalt have mine in the meantime.' Such a hat was called an *uddehat,* and made the person that wore it invisible. The old man of the mount answered, 'Thou shalt have it; but thou must promise me to return it before sunset.' No sooner said than done. The old soldier now hastened back to the wedding party, where he saw that by the side of every guest there sat two Trolls, who helped themselves from the dishes with both hands and ate to their hearts' content. Grasping his whip, he lashed the sponging intruders so smartly over the fingers, that they lost all inclination to make further havoc among the dishes, and turned them head over heels out of the apartment. Then taking off the borrowed hat, which had till then made him invisible to the company, he said, 'Till this moment the fiend has been feasting with you; but now set more meat on the table, and I will bear you company.' They did so, ate in peace, and had a quantity over. When evening approached, the old man remounted his horse and rode to the mount, where he cast down his borrowed hat and hastened away with all possible speed; and had scarcely turned his horse, before a multitude of Trolls came running, and even got hold of the horse's tail, as he rode over a bridge: but the horse was strong and active, so that the rider escaped, and the Trolls returned to whence they came.[1]

## Of Lund Cathedral [2]

The cathedral of Lund was regarded as a miracle of Gothic architecture, with respect both to its magnitude and decorations, which monuments of an early age are for the most part still preserved. The giant Finn is said to have built it, and his effigy with those of his wife and child are yet to be seen in the undercroft, concerning whom there is the following legend. The holy St Lawrence (or Lars), when walking among the mountains and forests, and

---

1  Faye, op. cit., p. 30. The old soldier's horse was more fortunate than Tam o'Shanter's Maggie, which at

> Ae spring brought off her master hale,
> But left behind her ain grey tail.

2  Lund, a famous city and university in Skania (Skåne), with a noble old cathedral. It is called the Canterbury of the North, and before the cession of the province by Denmark to Sweden in 1658 was the metropolitan see of the former kingdom. It lies nearly opposite to Copenhagen.

thinking how he could raise a spacious temple worthy of the Lord, was met by a huge giant from a mountain, who engaged to accomplish his wish, but on condition of receiving as a remuneration the sun and moon and both St Lawrence's eyes. The time, however, fixed for the completion of the work was so short, that the undertaking seemed impracticable. But the holy man soon saw the building drawing too near its completion, and the day approaching when the Troll should come and demand his reward. He now again went wandering about sad and sorrowful in the mountains and forests, when he one day suddenly heard a child crying in the mountain, and the mother, a giantess, singing to appease it:

> 'Hush, my babe, hush!
> Thy father, Finn, comes home tomorrow;
> Then shalt thou play with sun and moon,
> And with St Lars' two eyes.'

St Lawrence now knew the giant's name, and so had power over him. When the Trolls were aware of this, they both came down into the undercroft, where each seized a pillar, with the intention of throwing down the whole edifice; but St Lawrence, making the sign of the cross, cried out, 'Stand there in stone till doomsday!' They instantly became stone as they are yet to be seen; the giant embracing one pillar, and his wife, with a child on her arm, another.[1]

## The Church-grim and the Church-lamb

Heathen superstition did not fail to show itself in the construction of Christian churches. In laying the foundation, the people would retain something of their former religion, and sacrificed to their old deities, whom they could not forget, some animal, which they buried alive, either under the foundation or without the wall. The spectre of this animal is said to wander about the churchyard by night, and is called the Kyrkogrim, or Church-grim.

A tradition has also been preserved, that under the altar in the first Christian churches a lamb was usually buried, which imparted security and duration to the edifice. This is an emblem of the genuine Church-lamb, the Saviour of the world, who is the sacred cornerstone of his church and congregation. When anyone enters a church at a time when there is no service, he may chance to see a little lamb spring across the quire and

---

1    See the story of King Olaf, p. 254 and of Esbern Snare and Kallundborg church in 'Danish Traditions', pp. 309, *sq*. The original is manifestly the Eddaic story of the builder that engaged to fortify Asgard.

vanish. That is the Church-lamb. When it appears to a person in the churchyard, particularly to the grave-diggers, it is said to forebode the death of a child that shall be next laid in the earth.

## Helige Thor's Källa (Well)

From the time of heathenism there is a well in Småland, in the parish of Skatelöf, which is remarkable for a deplorable event. On the spot where the well now is, a young damsel, it is said, met her lover, and from some suspicion of his infidelity, murdered him. The god Thor caused the well to spring up from his blood. In consequence of the change that the heathen religion underwent in the minds of the people, the name of the god Thor became altered to 'Helige Thor' (Saint Thor), the festival of our Saviour's Ascension was called 'Helig Thor's-dag' (Holy Thursday), and Skatelöfs Källa was named 'Helige Thor's Källe'. From ancient documents it appears that a particular song was formerly sung in the neighbourhood of this well, when the country folks, every Holy Thursday eve, assembled there to play and make offerings.

## Of the Virgin Mary

All that is most beautiful and glorious in the creation was dedicated to the Virgin Mary, memorials of which exist even at the present day. One of the earliest and fairest flowers of spring was, and in many places still is, called *Our Lady's bunch of keys* (primula veris; common cowslip); the galium verum luteum is *Our Lady's bedstraw*;[1] a very green grass, with flowers of a more beautiful blue than those of the common flax, is *Our Lady's flax;* in low, wild places a flower called *Our Lady's hand* lifts its rose-coloured spike: it has two roots like hands, one white the other black, and when both are laid in water, the black one will sink – this is called *Satan's hand*; but the white one – called *Mary's hand* – will float. This plant the peasant shows to his children, and tells of the holy mother and of Him who overcame the powers of hell. The pretty, small green seed-vessels of the shepherd's purse (thlaspi bursa pastoris) are called *Our Lady's pincushion;* and the dew-flower (alchemilla vulgaris) with its plaited leaves, *Our Lady's mantle.*

As the Thorbagge, in the time of heathenism, was sacred to Thor, so was the ladybird (*coccinella septempunctata*) dedicated to the Virgin Mary, and

---

1 N. Poussin has painted this plant, instead of straw, under the infant Jesus in the manger, with its bright yellow flowers gilded, as it were, by the rays emanating from the child.

is to this day called *Our Lady's key-maid* (nyckelpiga). It is thought lucky when a young girl in the country sees this little creature in the spring; she then lets it creep about her hand, and says: 'She measures me for wedding gloves.' And when it spreads its little wings and flies away, she particularly notices the direction it takes, for thence her sweetheart shall one day come. This little messenger from the Virgin Mary is believed to foretell to the husbandman whether the year shall be a plentiful one or the contrary; if its spots exceed seven, bread-corn will be dear; if they are fewer than seven, there will be an abundant harvest and low prices.

## Yule-straw

It was a custom in many places to carry Yule-straw (Julhalm) into the fields, in the belief that it would be of avail in bringing forth an abundant harvest, for the sake of the Child, through whom come all grace and blessings. It is in remembrance of the Virgin Mary, who laid the Saviour of the world on hay and straw; therefore all little children may well play and rejoice in the Yule-straw, the infant Jesus having celebrated Yule on a bed of straw.

It is also said, that of the Yule-straw (as of the Yule-hog, or loaf) a part should be preserved and given to the draught horses and other cattle in the spring, to preserve them against sickness and mishaps, and to keep them together, so that they shall not be dispersed, although they should go to graze on large heaths or in forests.

In some places it is the custom to make a so-called fraternal bed (syster-säng) on the floor, in which the children and domestics sleep together on Yule-straw. On this night all the shoes must be put in one place close together, in order that all may live in harmony throughout the coming year. Great is the virtue of Yule-straw. To the nests of the fowls and geese, in which it is laid, no martens nor any witchcraft dare approach; strewn on the earth it promotes the growth of fruits and corn. If given to the cows before they are driven to their summer pasture, it secures them against distempers, and prevents them from separating.

## The Bjäraan or Bare

This was a milk-pail composed of nine kinds of stolen weaver's knots. Three drops of blood from the little finger were to be dropped into it, and the following formula uttered:

> På jorden skal tu för mig springa,
> I Blåkulla skal jag för thig brinna!

*On earth shalt thou before me spring,*
  *In Blåkulla shall I for thee burn!*

Blåkulla (the Blue mountain) is the Swedish Blocksberg, a rock between Småland and Öland.[1]

## Midsummer Eve

On St John's eve they gather and bind together all sorts of flowers and plants, which they call Midsommarsqvastar (midsummer-posies). These are hung up in every house, particularly in the stables, the cattle then cannot be bewitched. The St John's wort (hypericum) must be among the rest, as possessing extraordinary virtue. On St John's eve much may happen, and much be foreseen of importance for a person's remaining life. Some then mount, under white blankets, up on the roof, and lie down to listen and see; whatever words they then by chance may hear, or whatever face they may see, will have a meaning, which must be interpreted. Whoever, braving all risk of annoyance from witches and spirits of the night, will look more boldly into futurity, proceeds to a spot where three ways diverge, and there awaits what may happen or suggest itself as prophecy or warning. But what shall the lovesick do? The forest is lonely, and the gathering of plants in remote places, on mountains and in crossways, is too formidable. But it is to the solitary only that the divinities appear with the keys of futurity. The oppressed heart has, nevertheless, a resource. Thoughtful the sufferer goes forth, entwines wreaths of nine sorts of flowers, and lays them under his, or her, pillow. How many then are the sweet thoughts and wishes! How slowly comes the light sleep! At length it is there, and with it the desired dreams, and whatever they whisper over such flowers will prove true.

The witch-crew also may at this joyous season be constrained and seen. Witches' butter is to be found both on the corn and on flowers, and is either an exudation from the plants, or what is usually called honey-dew, and the production of some insect. This the wanton forest-sprites, or old witches are said to spread abroad. If nine kinds of wood be formed into a pile and kindled, and some of this witches' butter be cast into it; or if the fire be only beaten with nine kinds of wood, those who have justly been suspected as witches must come and discover themselves.[2]

---

1   Grimm, J., *Deutsche Mythologie*, op. cit., pp. 1004, 1044.
2   Arndt, iii, pp. 73 *sqq.*, p. 84, p. 86.

## Christmas

At Christmas it was formerly the custom to set little bowls of Yule-porridge (Julgröt) and other eatables on the barn-floor, together with a jacket, for the Tomtegubbe, in order that he might continue to bring prosperity to the house.[1]

Another old custom, but now obsolete, it was, to go on Christmas night, in the morning twilight, into a wood or forest, without uttering a word or letting a sound be heard, without looking around, without eating or drinking, or seeing any fire, or hearing a cock crow. If anyone so qualified goes on the path leading to the church as the sun is rising, he will see as many funerals as will pass that way during the ensuing year; and see how the produce will be in the meadows and pastures, and whether any fires will break out, within the same period.[2]

## The Cuckoo

When the cuckoo is first heard in spring-tide, it is a custom in Sweden to ask him, 'How many years shall I live?' or, 'When will this or that happen?' Such inquiries are comprised in the following rimes, which are uttered line by line, on every cry of the bird:

| | |
|---|---|
| *Cantat cucullus* – Göker grå, | *Gucku* – Cuckoo grey, |
| *Cantat cucullus* – Saeg mig då, | *Gucku* – Tell me now, |
| *Cantat cucullus* – Uppå qvist, | *Gucku* – Up on bough, |
| *Cantat cucullus* – Sant och vist, | *Gucku* – True and sure, |
| *Cantat cucullus* – Hur många år, | *Gucku* – How many years |
| *Cantat cucullus* – Jag leva får? *or* | *Gucku* – I have to live? *or* |
| – Jag ogift går? | – I shall unmarried go? |

As many times as he repeats his note so many years will the person live, or pass in single blessedness. But the maidens are wary and provident withal. That he may not afflict them by declaring too many years of maidenhood, they have established the rule that ten is the highest number he may lawfully cry. If he cries oftener than ten times, they say he sits on a bewitched bough (på galen qvist), and give no heed to his prediction.

Much depends on the quarter whence the note of the cuckoo is first heard. If heard from the north, the year will be one of sorrow; if from the west or east, one of prosperity; if from the south, it will be a good butter year; or a year of death, according to another account.[3]

1 Ibid., p. 84
2 Ibid., p. 86
3 Thiele, op. cit., iii, pp. 108 *sq.*; Grimm, J., *Deutsche Mythologie*, op. cit., pp. 640 *sq.*

# Swedish Popular Belief[1]

1 Be careful not to meet with sweepings in the doorway, if you wish to be married in the same year.

2 If a maiden and a youth eat of one and the same beet-root, they will fall in love with each other.

3 If on midsummer night nine kinds of flowers are laid under the head, a youth or maiden will dream of his or her sweetheart.

4 A youth may not give a knife or pins to a girl, because they sever love.

5 A girl must not look in a looking-glass after dark, nor by candlelight, lest she lose the goodwill of the other sex.

6 A bride must endeavour to see her bridegroom before he sees her; she will then have the mastery.

7 She must, for the same reason, during the marriage ceremony, place her foot before his.

8 For the same reason, she must take care to sit down first in the bridal chair.

9 For the same reason, she must, as if by accident, let her shoe slip off, or her handkerchief, or anything else fall on the floor, which the bridegroom from politeness will stoop to pick up. It will then be his lot to submit (*lit.* to bend his back) during the whole continuance of their marriage.

10 The bride must stand near to the bridegroom, that no one thenceforward may press between them.

11 In the church let them hold a riband or napkin between them, that they may live solely for each other.

13 The bride shall touch with so many fingers on her naked body, while sitting in the bridal chair, as she desires to have children.

14 That she may have an abundance of milk, let her mother meet her, when she comes home from church, with a glass of milk to drink.

15 As food in her first confinement, let her provide herself with a cake and a cheese, which she should have lying by her in the bridal bed.

16 When children are newly born, a book is to be placed under their head, that they may be quick at reading.

2 Grimm, J., *Deutsche Mythologie*, op. cit., Anhang, p. cviii.

17 When they are bathed for the first time, let money be put into the water, that they may become rich. A purse with money in it should also be sewed round their neck.

18 A part of the father's clothes should be laid on a female child, and the mother's petticoat on a male child; to find favour with the opposite sex.

19 The mother should meet the child at the door, when it is carried out to be christened; but when it is carried home after it is baptised, it should be met at the door with a loaf, that it may never want bread.

20 As long as a child remains unnamed, the fire must not be extinguished.

21 No one may pass between the fire and a sucking babe.

22 Water may not be brought in late where there is a sucking child, without throwing fire into it.

23 No one that enters a house may take a child in his hands, without previously having touched fire.

24 When a child gets teeth early, other children may be expected soon after.

25 An empty cradle must not be rocked, the child will else be given to crying and noisy.

26 If a first-born child, that is born with teeth, bites a whitlow, it will be cured.

27 A child may not read and eat at the same time, else it will get a dull memory.

28 A child should first touch a dog, but not a cat.

29 If a child plays with fire, it will with difficulty retain its water.

30 A child may not creep through a window, nor may anyone step over a child, or walk round a child that is sitting on the floor or is in a carriage; for then, it is believed, it will never grow bigger than it is.

31 If a sick person gets strange food, he becomes well.

32 If thanks are given for a remedy (medicine), it will have no effect.

33 If a person walks over graves with an open sore, it will heal either very slowly or never.

34 One must not mention before morning whether one has seen a spectre, lest one be pressed[1] and spit blood.

35 After dark one must not go by water, for fear of getting a whitlow.

---

1   Qu. by the night-mare?

36 For the same reason, or also that one may not be pressed, one should spit thrice in crossing the water after dark.

37 For the sick one ought to cause prayers to be said in three churches, one of which should be an offering-church, if there be one near. It will then speedily be decided whether the sick is to recover or die.

38 The teeth of large fish should be burnt, in order to be lucky in fishing.

39 One ought to tell no one when one goes out to fish, and not mention whether one has caught many or few.

40 Nor should any stranger see how many fish one has taken.

41 When one rows out from land to fish, one must not turn the boat against the sun.

42 Pins found in a church and made into fish-hooks catch the best.

43 If a woman passes over the rod, no fish will bite.

44 Stolen fishing tackle is lucky, but the person robbed loses his luck.

45 A light must not be held under the table, lest the guests should fall out.

46 One should not turn round when going on any business, that it may not turn out ill.

47 One must not return thanks for pins.

48 There must be no spinning on a Thursday evening, or in Passion week; for else there will be spinning in the night.

49 If a stranger comes in where a pudding (sausage) is being boiled, it will split asunder.

50 If you turn your slippers or shoes with the toes towards the bed, the mara will come in the night.

51 On Eastereve a cross should be made over the door of the cattle-house, against harm from witches.

52 When you sleep for the first time in a house, you should count the beams; then what you dream will come to pass.

53 If a person forgets something when setting out on a journey, there is good hope of his safe return; but to look behind is not a good sign.

54 When cats wash themselves, or magpies chatter near the house, they expect strangers. If a slothful housewife, or a careless servant, has not already swept the floor, it ought forthwith to be done.

55 The person that comes first home from church on Christmas Day, will be the first to die.

56 If a person walks thrice round a bed of cabbages, after having planted them, they will continue free from worms.

57 An empty sack must never be carried untied. If a pregnant woman follows it, her child will never be satisfied with food.

58 When you bathe, be careful to put steel in the water to bind the Neck, and cry, 'Neck, Neck, steel in strand, thy father was a steel-thief, thy mother was a needle-thief; so far shalt thou be hence as this cry is heard.' Then let all cry as loud as they can, 'Ho hagla'.[1]

59 On Easter Saturday, a long horn (lur) is to be blown through the window of the cattle-house: so far as the sound is heard, so far away will beasts of prey continue during that year.

60 If a person seeking cattle in the forest meets with a titmouse on his right hand, the cattle sought for will be found.

61 If swine are let out on St Lucius' day, they get vermin.

62 If the cattle, on Michaelmas eve, are driven in without noise, they will be quiet in the cattle-house the whole year.

63 All labour when completed is to be signed with the cross.

64 If a grain of corn is found under the table in sweeping on a new year's morn, there will be an abundant crop that year.

65 If a suspicious female enters the yard, to counteract the effects of witchcraft, you must either strike her so that the blood runs, or cast a firebrand after her.

66 When a bride comes from church, she must herself unharness or unsaddle the horse, that she may easily have children.

67 If a bride dances with money in her shoes, no witchery can affect her.

68 In Sweden, as well as in Norway and Finland, the belief is general that when wolves appear in great multitudes it forebodes war. The same superstition prevails also with regard to squirrels.[2]

---

1   See p. 286.
2   Afzelius, op. cit., i, p. 172.

## Popular Traditions of Denmark –
## Trolls, Barrow-folk or
## Mount-folk, Elf-folk and Dwarfs[1]

### Origin of Trolls

The people in Jutland relate, that when our Lord cast the fallen angels out of heaven, some of them fell down on the mounds or barrows and became *Barrow-folk*, or, as they are also called, *Mount-folk, Hill-folk*; others fell into the elf-moors, who were the progenitors of the *Elf-folk*; while others fell into dwellings, from whom descend the domestic sprites or *Nisser*.

---

While Eve was one day washing her children by a spring, our Lord unexpectedly appeared before her, whereat she was terrified, and concealed those of her children that were not yet washed. Our Lord asked her if all her children were there; she answered 'yes,' to avoid his anger, if he should see that they were not all washed. Then said our Lord, that what she had concealed from him should thenceforth be concealed from mankind; and at the same moment the unclean children disappeared and were concealed in the hills. From these descend all the underground folk.

*In a rabbinic tradition it is said, that after Adam had eaten of the tree of knowledge he was accursed for a hundred and thirty years. During all these years, as we are informed by Rabbi Jeremias ben Elieser, he procreated only schedim, i.e. demons and the like.*

### Elf-folk

The Elf-folk dwell in the Elf-moors. The male appears as an old man with a broad-brimmed hat; the female Elf is young and seducing in appearance, but behind she is as hollow as a dough-trough. Young men should be particularly on their guard against her, for it is difficult to withstand her, and she has besides a stringed instrument, when she touches which she infatuates every heart. The male is often to be seen by the Elf-moors

1    From *Danmark's Folkesagn* samlede by J. M. Thiele, Bk 2, Kiöbenhavn, 1843.

basking in the sunbeams; but if anyone approach him too near, he will stretch his jaws and blow on them, which causes sickness and pestilence.[1] The females are most frequently to be seen in the moonlight, when they dance their circling dance in the high grass with such lightness and grace, that they seldom get a refusal, when they offer a young man their hand. Good care must be taken to prevent cattle from grazing where the Elf-folk have been; for if an animal come on a place where they have either spat or done worse, it will be seized with grievous complaints, which can be remedied only by giving them to eat a handful of St John's wort, gathered on St John's night at twelve o'clock. It may also happen that they receive injury by mingling with the Elf-folk's cattle, which are particularly large and of a blue colour. Such are sometimes to be seen in the fields licking the dew from the grass, for it is on that they live. The peasant may, however, provide against the evils above-mentioned, if, before he lets his cattle loose, he goes to the Elf-barrow and says, 'Thou little Troll! May I graze my cows on thy mount?' If he gets no refusal, he may feel easy.

Between Terslöse and Sobierg lies Sobierg-Banke, which is the richest barrow in all Seeland; it is in fact impossible to tell the precious things to be found there. In this hill there dwells a Troll-wife, to whom there was once a grand procession from Steenlille field, when the Troll in Galtebierg took her to wife.

It often happens, in fine weather, that the passer-by sees the most beautiful copper utensils and choicest beddings lying on the mound to be aired; and on approaching still nearer, he may see the young Elflings labouring to get them all in with the utmost speed.

----

In Illerup field near Kallundborg there is a mount called Fibierg-Bakke, in which there is a vast number of Trolls, who have much property and gold there. It may be plainly seen that they have a hole in the mount through which they drag those on whom they seize. At Yule one may see how they bring out their silver and gold to sun it, at which time it is dangerous to go on the mount. But on St John's night the entire mount is set on red pillars, and then dancing and merrymaking may be seen there. At this time anyone may approach, and may also see how they drag great chests full of money backwards and forwards.

In Laanehöi on Aerö the Troll-folk may frequently be heard slamming their coffer-lids. Some harvest-people once sitting on the mount at their repast, heard, by placing their ear to the earth, that they were grinding corn in it.

----

1    That the blast of the elves is dangerous, is also a popular belief in Scotland.

That Mount-folk formerly dwelt in Gallehöi on Aerö there can hardly be entertained a doubt; for not only have people heard them slam their coffer-lids, but the smith in Lille-Rise, who in the war time kept watch there, heard every morning a clock strike five in the mount.

———

Near Östrel, between Aalborg and Thisted, there is a mount, in which there dwells an elfin smith. At night one may plainly hear that smith's work is going on there; and in the side of the mount there is a hole, by which in the morning slag and flakes of iron may be found.

———

In the neighbourhood of Sundby, on the isle of Mors, there is a mount inhabited by a Troll who is a smith. At night one may hear when he is at work. Opposite to this mount there is a sandhill, where the same smith has another workshop, whence may be heard the strokes of ponderous hammers. At midnight he often rides through the air from one workshop to the other, on a horse without a head, with hammer in hand, followed by all his apprentices and journeymen.

———

In the parish of Buur there are three large mounts. In one of them dwells a Troll who is a smith and has his workshop there. At night fire may frequently be seen issuing from the top of the mount, and, singular enough, entering again at the side; but it is by that means he keeps his iron hot. If anyone is desirous of having a piece of iron forged, he needs only to lay it on the mount, together with a silver skilling, at the same time saying what he wishes done, and the next morning the skilling will have disappeared, and the piece of work desired will lie ready and well executed.[1]

Once some of the country people of Buur determined to dig up this Troll's treasure; for which purpose they one night assembled with spades and pickaxes. After all had been informed that they must beware of uttering even a single word, however strongly they might be tempted, they set to work. But scarcely had they put a spade in the ground before all sorts of frightful sights came out of the mount. Still they dug on unconcerned in the most perfect silence, until they arrived at a spacious stone apartment. There lay the treasure before them, to wit, a large copper kettle full of gold money, close by which was an enormous black dog asleep. One of the men then taking off his coat, laid the dog gently upon it, for the purpose of carrying him away. At this moment came a great load of hay out of the mount, drawn by two cocks, which drew their load thrice round the

———

[1] The Wayland smith of Kenilworth. A similar legend is told of Weyland's Smithy on the Berkshire Downs.

mount; still no one uttered a syllable, until one of the cocks kicked out behind with such force that he broke the thick pole of the wagon, at which one of the men exclaimed, 'That was a deuce of a kick for a cock!' But scarcely had he said the words when all the men, many as they were, were projected to a considerable distance out of the mount, which was instantly closed again. On making a second experiment, it seemed to them that the whole Öster-Buur was in flames, at which sight, casting away their spades, they ran to their several homes; but on reaching the village they found all safe and quiet.

*In these goblin smiths may evidently be recognised the descendants of the dwarfs of the Eddaic mythology.*

---

At Gamtofte, not far from Assens, there is a mound in a field in which a Troll is said to have taken up his abode. Of this Troll it is related that he is very obliging when persons wish to borrow anything; on which occasion it is simply necessary to go to the mount and knock thrice on the north side, at the same time naming the things required, whether pots, pans or other domestic utensils, when they instantly get what they need, but may be reckoned as dead, if they do not return them at the time fixed.

---

On the isle of Möen[1] there is a mount called Östed-Höi. Once when Margaret Skaelvigs was passing it on her way to Elmelund castle, an old woman met her and asked, 'Whither art thou going, my child?' Margaret answered that she was on her way to Elmelund castle, to borrow a gown of Peter Munk's wife, to be married in. Then said the old woman, 'If thou wilt be here on Saturday, I will lend thee a bridal dress.' On the Saturday following Margaret went accordingly to Östed-Höi, and the woman brought her beautiful clothes of gold embroidery, ordering her to bring them back in a week; if then no one appeared to receive them, she might consider them her own property. Thus did Margaret Skaelvigs appear as a bride in clothes of gold embroidery; and when she took them back at the time appointed, no one was there to receive them, so she rightfully kept them as her own.

---

In Thyholm there is a series of lofty mounts which were formerly inhabited by the Mount-folk. A peasant once passing them on his way to Vestervig market, happened at the moment to utter complaints that he was mounted on such a sorry jade. On his way back, he saw lying precisely on the spot where he had sent forth his lamentations, four horseshoes, which he took

---

1   One of the Danish islands, lying close to the most southern point of Seeland.

home and shod his horse with them. But from that time no other horse in the neighbourhood could go with such speed as his.

Another time, some peasants, who were passing by the mounts, by way of joke prayed the Mount-folk to give them some good beer. At the moment a little Troll came out of the mount with a large silver can, which he held out to the men, one of whom had no sooner got it in his grasp, than he set spurs to his horse with the intention of keeping it. But the little man of the mount being quicker than he, soon overtook him and compelled him to give back the can.

At length these Mount-folk grew weary of their abode in Thyland, and one day departed in a body to the ferry, for the purpose of crossing the fiord. When the ferryman was to be paid, they threw something into his hat which burned through it and sank under the floor, and which must have been gold; for otherwise it would be impossible to account for the comfort which afterwards prevailed in the ferry-house.

---

A little Elf-girl once came to a man in Dunkiaer on the isle of Aerö with a peel, the handle of which was loose, begging him to fasten it, which he refused to do. Whereupon a lad, who was standing by, undertook to assist her, and in reward for his service found lying by his plate at dinner-time a dainty slice of fine bread with butter on it. The man, who well knew whence the present came, advised him not to eat it, saying it would cause his death; but the lad ate it without fear, and was well and cheerful when he rose the following morning; but the man lay stone-dead in his bed.

---

In the neighbourhood of Lynge, near Sorö, there is a mount called Bodedys, not far from which dwelt an aged peasant that had an only son, who made long voyages. For a considerable time the father had received no tidings of his son, and thinking that he had perished, mourned for his loss. One evening as he was passing by Bodedys with a full load, the mount opened and the Troll came out, who desired him to drive in. At this the man felt somewhat disconcerted, but knowing that it would not turn to his profit if he refused compliance with the will of the Troll, he turned his horses and drove into the mount. There the Troll began to deal with him, and paid him liberally for all his wares. When he had unloaded his wagon and was about to drive out, the Troll said, 'If thou canst keep thy mouth shut with regard to what has taken place, I shall look to thy advantage hereafter; and if thou wilt come again tomorrow, thou shalt find thy son here.' At the first moment the man knew not what to answer, but believing that the Troll was able to keep his promise, he felt extremely glad, and at the time fixed returned to Bodedys. There he sat waiting for a considerable time, and at length fell asleep. When he awoke his son was lying by his side, and both father and son found it no easy matter to say how all this had come to pass. The son now related how he had been in prison and there suffered great hardships; but that one night he had dreamed that a man came to him and said, 'Dost thou still hold thy father dear?' and on his answering 'Yes,' it was as if all chains and walls were broken. During this narrative, happening to raise his hand to his neck, he found that a piece of the iron chain still remained there. At this they were struck dumb with amazement, and went to Lynge, where they hung the piece of chain up in the church as a memorial.

––––––––––

Not far from Sorö is the village of Pedersborg, a little beyond which is another called Lynge. Between these two places there is a mount called Bröndhöi, which is said to be inhabited by Troll-folk. Among these there was an old jealous Troll, on whom the others had bestowed the name of Knurremurre; because through him there was often dissension and ill-feeling in the mount. It once reached the ears of this old Knurremurre that there was too close an intimacy between his young wife and a young Troll, which the old Troll took so much amiss that he threatened the life of the other, who consequently deemed it advisable to flee from the mount, and betake himself, transformed into a yellow cat, to the village of Lynge, under which form he ingratiated himself with a poor housekeeper named Platt. With him he lived a considerable time, got milk and porridge every day, and lay from morning till night in the easy-chair behind the stove. One evening Platt came home just as puss in his usual place was lapping some porridge and licking the pot. 'Well, mother,' said the man, 'I will now tell thee what happened to me on my way home. As I was passing by Bröndhöi, a Troll came out and called to me, saying, "Holla you, Platt! Tell your cat that Knurremurre is dead." ' At these words the cat rose on his hind legs, let the pot roll and said, while stealing out at the door, 'What? Is Knurremurre dead? I must then hasten home.'

## The Klint-King on the Isle of Möen

There is a Klint-king who rules over the klints (cliffs) of Möen, Stevn[1] and Rügen. He has a curious chariot, drawn by four black horses, in which he rides from one klint to another, over the sea, which then becomes agitated. On these occasions the neighing of the horses may be distinctly heard.

By the 'Queen's chair' on Möen's Klint, there are some caverns high up in the rock, where in former times dwelt the Jöde[2] of Upsala. A foolhardy

––––––––––

1   A remarkable cliff on the east side of Seeland.
2   Jöde, i.e. *Jew*, but no doubt a corruption for Jötn, *giant*. The white horse and his denomination *of Upsala* manifestly identify him with Odin.

person, it is said, once undertook to visit him in his abode, and suffered himself to be let down by a rope, but he never appeared again.

Sometimes the said Jöde of Upsala may be seen driving over the sea with his black horses; and in the last Swedish war he passed with his green hunters over the rocks, for the purpose of defending the land, which he has promised to do once more. It is said that he has now betaken himself to Stevn's Klint.

Not far from the Queen's chair there is a falling in the cliff, which is called the Orchard fall. There he had a beautiful orchard. To this Jöde, or Giant, of Upsala the peasants of Möen were, until a few years since, in the habit of giving the last sheaf, when they had housed their corn.

In Möen's Klint there are said to be two caverns, in one of which dwells 'Jon Opsal' himself, in the other his dog and white horse.

Twice already he has ridden the 'king's ride', and saved the land from danger, and he will now soon ride a third time. He will then transform all the stones on the beach to cavalry, and with them overcome the foes of the country. Sometimes he rides to Stevn's Klint, and visits the king there.

It is not long since that he came riding through Busserup, and stopped before the house of an old woman, of whom he begged a drink of water for himself and his white horse. The old woman told him she had only a sieve to give him the water in. 'It's no matter,' said he, 'only fill it.' And the sieve held the water, so that both he and his horse could drink from it.

### The Underground Folk in Bornholm[1]

In Bornholm, particularly in foggy weather, the Underground folk are sometimes to be seen on the sides of the heaths practising the use of arms. They have a captain who is called the Ellestinger, and who, as well as all the other chieftains in this army, rides on a horse that has only three legs. These troops, as far as it is possible to discern, are clad in light blue or steel-grey uniforms, and have red caps, though sometimes three-cornered hats. The sound of their drums is often to be heard, and small, round stones are sometimes found, which are said to be their bullets. Whenever any hostile power has threatened Bornholm, these subterraneans have always made their appearance, fully prepared to defend the country; so that the enemy, at such a formidable spectacle, has frequently retired with all possible speed.

Thus it happened on the 6th February in the year 1645, when two Swedish ships of war appeared off the 'Hammer', with the intention of

---

1 A small island, belonging to Denmark, in the Baltic, to the northeast of Rügen.

effecting a landing, that they saw the whole mountain covered with troops swarming forth from every side, and although there were but two companies of soldiers on the island, the enemy was led to believe that the place was so strongly defended, that it would be vain to attempt a landing, and withdrew accordingly.

———

In the parish of Ulvsborg there is a high mount, in which dwells a Troll, whom many persons have seen, when in the night he has all his bright copper utensils out in the moonlight. This Troll once came to a woman and requested her to lend him a loaf, promising to bring her another in two days; but the woman made him a present of the loaf. Then said the Troll, 'Thou shalt not have given me this for nothing; from this day forwards all shall go well with thee; and thy race shall share the benefit until the fourth generation.' And so it proved.

## The Mount Folk Borrow Beer

At Holmby near Aarhuus, as a woman was standing at her door, there came to her a little Troll with a peaked hump, who said, 'Today Store-Bierg is to be married to Lille-Bierg: if mother will be so good as lend us a cask of beer for a few days, she shall have it back equally strong and good.' Hereupon the woman followed the Troll to the brewhouse, and desired him to take whichever cask he liked best; but as there was a cross marked on all of them, the Troll was unable to take one, but only pointed and said, 'Cross off!' The woman now understood that she must first remove the cross; and when she had so done, the little Troll took the largest cask upon his hump and walked off with it. On the third day he came again, bringing with him a cask of beer equally good with that which he had borrowed. From that time prosperity prevailed in the house.

## The Elf-folk under the Hearth

In a mansion in Lille-Rise, on the isle of Aerö, the Elf-folk dwell under the stove. A little Elf-girl once came to the mistress of the house, begging the loan of a pair of scissors, to cut out her bridal dress with. When the woman heard that there was to be a wedding, she felt a wish to be present, and promised to lend her the scissors, provided she would let her see what took place at the wedding. The girl directed the woman to peep through a crack in the hearth, but at the same time cautioned her against laughing; for if she laughed the whole spectacle would vanish before her eyes.

When the wedding-day arrived the woman went to the crack and peeped in, and there saw the entire festivity, how the Elf-folk sat at table in their best clothes and enjoyed the beer and eatables. At this moment it happened that a quarrel arose between two of the guests, which proceeded so far that they both sprang on the table. There they pulled each other's hair, and at length fell into the soup-bowl, out of which they crept quite crestfallen; as the whole company laughed at the two heroes in the soup-bowl, the woman could not refrain from doing the like; when at the same moment the whole vanished.

These same Elf-folk were at one time so offended with two girls that served in the house, that they took them out of their bed and carried them to a remote apartment, where after much search they were found in a deep sleep, though it was long past noon.

## Fru Mette [1]

On the isle of Mors in Jutland there is a mansion called Overgaard, in which there once dwelt a lady named Fru Mette. To this lady a little Troll one day came, saying, 'Fru Mette of Overgaard! Wilt thou lend thy silken skirt to Fru Mette of Undergaard, to be married in?' Having lent the skirt and waited a long time in vain for its return, she went one day to the mount, and cried, 'Give me back my skirt.' At this the Troll came out and gave her the skirt quite covered with drippings of wax, and said: 'As you have demanded it, take it; but if you had waited a few days, there should have been a diamond in the place of every drop of wax.'

## The Underground Folk Fetch a Midwife

One Christmas Eve, as a woman was preparing meat for the family, an Elf-man came to her, begging her to accompany him and help his wife who was in labour. The woman having consented to accompany him, he took her on his back and descended with her into the earth through a fountain. Here the woman learned that the Elf-wife could not be delivered without the aid of a Christian woman, she being herself a Christian, but had been carried off by the Elf-man.

When the child was born, the Elf-man took it in his arms and went away with it, which, as the mother told the woman, he did for the reason, that if he could find two newly married persons, in the bridal bed, before they had repeated their Paternoster, he could, by laying the child between them, procure for it all the good fortune that was designed for the newly married pair. The wife then instructed her helper as to what she had to do when the Elf-man returned. 'First,' said she, 'you must eat nothing, if he

1 Females of the higher classes are styled *Frue* (Ger. Frau), while those of an inferior grade, as merchants' and tradesmen's wives, are called *Madame*.

asks you; for I ate, and therefore never returned. Next, if he will make you a present, and gives you the choice between something that looks like silver and something that looks like potsherds, do you choose the latter. And when he again bears you hence, seize, if you can, on a gooseberry bush, and say: Now, in the name of God, now I am on my own!'

In an hour the man returned with the child, quite angry that he had not found what he had been seeking after. He then offered the stranger woman some refection, and on her refusal to take any, said, 'They did not strike thee on the mouth who taught thee that.' He then offered her a present, but she accepted only some black potsherds; and when she again found herself on the face of the earth, she did as she had been directed. With the potsherds in her apron, she now proceeded to her dwelling, but before she entered she cast them into the ash-hole, and refused to tell her husband where she had been. But when the maidservant came running into the room, saying that something shone like silver in the ash-hole, and when she herself saw that it was pure silver, she told her husband where she had been, and they came into good circumstances through that Christmas Eve.

———

One night a Troll came to a midwife in Bingsbierg and requested her to accompany him down through a mound to help his wife. She followed him into the earth, without suffering any injury; but having afterwards divulged what she had seen in the mound, she lost her sight.

———

An Elf-wife who was in labour sent a message to a midwife, requesting her aid. Having received the child, the Elf-folk gave her an ointment to rub over its eyes; but in doing which some adhered to her fingers, so that she inadvertently anointed her own eyes with it. On her way home, she remarked that something had happened to her sight; for as she passed by a rye-field she saw that it swarmed with small Elf-folk, who went about clipping off the ears. 'What are ye doing there?' cried the woman, on seeing them steal the corn from the field; and got for answer, 'If thou canst see us, thus thou shalt be served.' They then thronged about her and put out her eyes.

## Trolls at Uglerup

In Uglerup there once dwelt a man well to do in the world, named Niels Hansen. The wealth he possessed, it was said, he acquired through the Trolls. One day, to wit, as his wife was raking hay together in the field, she caught a large fat toad between the teeth of her rake, which she gently released, saying, 'Poor thing! I see that thou needest help: I will help thee.' Sometime after, a Troll came to her by night, desiring her to accompany him into the mount where he dwelt. When, in compliance with the Troll's request, she had entered into the mount, she there found a Troll-wife lying in bed, and at the same time remarked a hideous serpent hanging down just above her head. Thereupon said the Troll-wife to her, 'As you are now frightened at the serpent that hangs over your head, so frightened was I when I stuck in your rake. But as you were kind to me, I will give you good advice. When you go from this place, my husband will offer you a quantity of gold; but, unless you cast this knife behind you when you go out, it will be nothing but coal when you reach home. And when he causes you to mount and rides away with you, be mindful to glide down from the horse, when you come over a slough; else you will never see your home again.'

While Niels Hansen's wife was thus in the mount, she went into the Troll's kitchen, where she saw her own serving-man and maid standing and grinding malt. As they did not know her, she went up to them and cut a piece out of the linen of each, which she kept. At length, the Troll made her a costly present of gold, and she did as the Troll-wife directed; and when she was riding home with him, she slipped from him, according to the instructions she had received, and before morning reached her house with all her treasure.

The next day, when the man and maid appeared before her, they both complained of pain in the arms, as if from excessive fatigue. She then told them that they should recite a prayer and make the sign of the cross before going to bed, seeing that, unknown to themselves, they had been in the mount during the night, and had there ground malt for the Trolls. At this they laughed and thought she was joking; but when she showed them the pieces of linen, they could no longer withhold their belief, seeing that the pieces corresponded with the holes. She then related to them the adventure of the night.

## The Midwife of Fuur

Many years ago there was a midwife on the isle of Fuur, who was one night waked by a violent knocking at her door. On opening it she saw a diminutive creature who begged of her to follow him to attend an Elf-wife. She yielded to his entreaties, and was missing for a long time after. At length her husband, happening one night to pass by the Elf-mount, saw that it was illuminated, that there was great parade and merrymaking within, and, on taking a more accurate survey, that among the gayest of the company was his own wife. He beckoned to her, and they conversed together for a while; and when, in spite of her caution, he called her by name, she was compelled to accompany him; but from that time he never had the least good of her: she sat constantly by the kitchen table, and was dumb ever after.

## Skotte

At Gudmandstrup there is a mount called Hiulehöi. The Troll-folk that inhabit this mount are well known in the neighbouring villages, and if any person forgets to make a cross on his beer cask, the Trolls will sneak out of Hiulehöi and steal his beer. One evening late a peasant passing by the mount, saw that it was standing on red pillars, and that beneath were music, dancing and a grand festivity. While he stood viewing the joyous spectacle, the music and dancing ceased on a sudden, and amid much lamentation he heard a Troll cry out, 'Skotte has fallen into the fire! Come and help him out!' The mount then sank and all the merrymaking was at an end.

In the meantime, the peasant's wife was at home alone, and while she was sitting spinning her flax, she was not aware that a Troll had crept in at the window of the adjoining room and was standing by the cask drawing beer into his copper kettle. At this moment the peasant entered the apartment quite bewildered at what he had seen and heard. 'Now, mother,' said he, 'now I will tell you what has just happened to me' – The Troll was all attention – 'As I passed by Hiulehöi, there was a great merrymaking; but when it was at the highest, there was an outcry in the mount that Skotte had fallen into the fire.' On hearing this, the Troll, who was still standing by the beer cask, was so startled that he let the beer run, the kettle fall, and hurried away as quickly as possible through the window. By the noise the people were soon led to discover what had been going on at the beer cask; but as they found the copper kettle, they took it as an equivalent for the spilt beer.

## King Pippe is Dead!

Between Nordborg and Sönderborg, on the isle of Als, there is a mount called Stakkelhöi, which in former days was inhabited by a multitude of the subterranean folk, who were noted for their diligent researches in the neighbouring pantries. One evening late, as a man was passing over Stakkelhöi to Hagenbierg, he heard someone in the mount exclaim, 'Now King Pippe is dead!' These words he retained in his memory. At the same time, one of the Mount-people of Stakkelhöi was paying a visit at a peasant's in Hagenbierg, for the purpose of letting some of his beer flow into a silver jug that he had brought with him. The Troll was just sitting cheek by jowl with the cask, when the aforesaid man entered the house and told the peasant how, as he was passing over Stakkelhöi, he heard a voice in the mount saying, 'Now King Pippe is dead!' At this the Troll in a fright exclaimed, 'Is King Pippe dead?' and rushed out of the house with such haste that he forgot to take his silver jug with him.

## The Troll at Maehred

At Maehred near Praestö, as a smith was one day hammering at his forge, he heard a great moaning and sobbing outside. Looking out at his door he saw a Troll driving a pregnant woman before him and crying without intermission, 'A little farther yet! A little farther yet!' At this spectacle the smith sprang forwards with a red-hot iron, which he held behind the woman, so that the Troll was forced to abandon his prey and take to flight. He then took the woman under his protection, who was shortly after delivered of two sons. Thereupon he went to her husband, in the supposition of finding him inconsolable for her loss; but on stepping into the apartment, he perceived a woman, exactly resembling the man's wife, lying in bed. He at once saw how the matter stood, seized an axe, and with it struck the witch on the head as she lay. While the man was bewailing the death of his supposed wife, the smith brought him the genuine one together with the two newborn babes.

## The Man in the Öxnebierg

At Rolfsted there is a mount called the Öxnebierg, by which there runs a rivulet, but between the mount and the rivulet there is to be seen a pathway trodden down in the corn, and which, according to the testimony of three men, who lay one night on the mount, is known to be so trodden by 'the Man in the Öxnebierg' who rides out every night on his dapple-grey horse, which he waters in the rivulet.

There was a similar path from the mount down to a spring in a garden at Baekstrup. It passed through a break in the hedge, which, how often soever it might be filled up, was always found open again on the following day. In the dwelling to which the spring belonged, the mistress was hardly ever in good health; but her husband, in consequence of advice given him, having filled up the well and dug another in another place, the woman from that time recovered her health, and the hole in the hedge was no more opened.

## The Unbidden Guests

In a house in the neighbourhood of Östrel, between Aalborg and Thisted, the master and mistress remarked that the meat at dinner always disappeared very speedily, however large the quantity might be. They consulted with their serving-man, who was a knowing fellow, as to the cause, who being aware that a neighbouring mount was inhabited by a swarm of little Trolls, hit upon the idea that some of these probably partook of the fare, and therefore resolved to keep watch. On the following day, when the dinner was nearly ready, he went to the mount, where, applying his ear, he heard a great bustle and confusion beneath, and one saying to another, 'Give me my hat, dinner is ready.' Hearing this, the man also cried out, 'Give me my hat,' and was answered, 'Here's none but old dad's.' 'That will do,' said the man, and instantly a hat was flung to him out of the mount. Having put it on his head, he saw the Trolls coming out of the mount in swarms, and running towards his master's house. He speedily followed them, and on entering the apartment saw them already seated at the table, and busily regaling themselves with a pancake, which the mistress had just served up. The man also sat down and ate with them; but in a few seconds the pancake vanished. Angry that there was no more, one of the little Trolls leaped on the table and untrussed his points over the empty dish. On seeing this, the man took up his knife and gave the shameless little wretch a slash, who uttered a loud scream and all ran away. The man now took off his hat, called his mistress and the people of the household, and asked them whether they had seen anything. They answered, that they had heard the door bang, also a scream, but seen nothing.

In the evening, when the man was going to bed, he heard the bucket in the well drawn up and down. Whereupon he put on the hat, went into the yard and saw the Trolls watering their little horses. He asked them whether they wished for a repetition of what they had experienced at dinner? But they besought him earnestly to allow them to water their horses at the well, as there was no water in the mount. This the man allowed them to do, on condition that they should never more steal the dinner.

On the following morning, the man found two gold pieces hanging to the well; and from that day the good housewife has kept her dinner secure from uninvited guests.

## Ellevilde or Elf-crazed

Not far from Ebeltoft, as a boy was watching cattle, there came to him a beautiful damsel, who asked him whether he was hungry or thirsty. But he, observing that she was particularly careful not to let him see her back, felt convinced that she was an Elf, the Elves being hollow behind. He would therefore hold no converse with her, but endeavoured to avoid her. When she remarked this, she presented her breast that he might suck her, in which there was so much fascination, that he had no more power to resist. After he had done as she bade him he was no longer master of himself, so that she found it no difficult matter to induce him to go with her. For three days he was absent. In the meantime, his parents were at home bewailing his loss; for they felt certain that he had been decoyed away. But on the fourth day the father saw him coming at a distance, and desired his wife to set a pan on the fire with bacon as speedily as possible. Immediately after the son entered and sat down without uttering a syllable. Nor did the old man speak a word, but acted as if everything was as it should be. The mother then set the meat before her son, and the father desired him to eat; but he let the food stand untouched, saying that he knew where he could get better fare. The man now grew angry, and taking up a heavy stick, again ordered him to take his food. The lad was then compelled to eat, and when he had once tasted the bacon, he devoured it greedily, and then fell into a profound sleep. He slept as many days as the fascination lasted, but never from that time recovered the use of his understanding.

## The Brudehöi or Bride Mount

Near Borbierg church, in the diocese of Ribe, there is a mount called Brudehöi, or The Bride's Mount, which name it is said to have derived from the following event.

When King Cnut the Great was engaged in building Borbierg church, there dwelt in the above-mentioned mount a vicious Troll, who every night demolished what had been erected during the day, so that the work could not proceed. Thereupon the king made an agreement with the Troll, promising him the first girl that should come to the church as a bride. The building now went on prosperously and was soon completed. There then sat the Troll, waiting in his mount till a bridal company should pass. On the first opportunity he seized the bride and dragged her into the mount. From that time the place has been held in such dread, that all bridal couples, on their way to Borbierg church, rather go a mile or more about than pass by the mount.

*In Reiersen's Description of St Bent's church at Ringsted, it is said of that structure: 'There are two entrances to the church, viz, a large gate in the north chapel, through which the people usually pass into the church; and a smaller one on the same side towards the end of the edifice, through which all children that have been christened and all corpses are brought; also all bridal pairs pass that have been united in the church; nor would it be possible to get any of these to be conveyed or pass through the large door, though from what cause no one can tell.' In Scania there is also a Bride-mount, where a Troll named Gyllebert carried off a bride, on which account no bride ever passes by it.*

# Hans Puntlaeder

In the field of Bubbelgaard in Fyen there are three mounts, which from the following event are known by the name of the 'Dandse-höie'. At Bubbelgaard there was a serving-lad named Hans, who one evening passing through the field above-mentioned, saw that one of the mounts was raised up on red pillars[1], and that there were dancing and merriment beneath. Struck with the beauty of the spectacle which he witnessed, he felt singularly attracted nearer and nearer, until the fairest of all the fair lasses approached him and gave him a kiss. From that moment, he was no more master of himself, and became so unmanageable that he tore all his clothes to tatters, until at length it was found necessary to make him a garment of sole leather (puntlaeder), which he was unable to tear asunder; for which reason he ever after went by the name of Hans Puntlaeder.

# The Aged Bride

At a marriage at Nörre-Broby near Odense, the bride during a dance left the apartment and walked without reflection towards a mount in the adjacent field, where at the same time there were dancing and merriment among the Elf-folk. On reaching the mount, she saw that it was standing on red pillars, and at the same moment an Elf came and presented to her a cup of wine. She took the cup, and having emptied it, suffered herself to join in a dance. When the dance was ended, she bethought herself of her husband and hastened home. Here it appeared to her that everything in and about the place was changed, and on entering the village, she recognised neither house nor farm, and heard nothing of the noisy mirth of the wedding. At length she found herself standing before her husband's dwelling, but on entering saw no one whom she knew, and no one who knew her. One old woman only, on hearing the bride's lamentation, exclaimed: 'Is it then you, who a hundred years ago disappeared at my grandfather's brother's wedding?' At these words the aged bride fell down and instantly expired.

# Bondevette

In Bornholm there was once a peasant named Bondevette, who, it was said, was born of a Mer-wife. His father, as it is related, going once down to the seashore, saw a Mer-wife there, with whom he had intercourse. At their parting she said to him, 'In a year thou shalt return, when thou shalt find a son here, who shall drive away the Mountain-imps and Trolls.' It befell as

---

1    In a Sleswig tradition the pillars are said to be golden. Müllenhoff, *Sagen, Märchen, und Lieder der Herzogthümer Schleswig, Holstein und Lauenburg*, Keil, 1845, No. cdii, 2.

she had said; for the man, on returning exactly a year after, found a little male child lying on the shore, which he took with him, fostered it, and called it Bondevette, because its father was a *bonde*[1] and its mother a *vette*.[2] As the child grew up he became large and strong, and also *synsk,* so that he could see what was invisible to others. When his father died, Bondevette succeeded to the farm and took to himself a wife.

Not far from his dwelling there was a mount called Korshöi. As he was one day passing by, he heard the Trolls within, who were busied in carving a piece of wood, utter the words, 'Cut it, Snef! That's almost like Bondevette's wife.' His wife was just at that time lying in, and the Trolls had made a wooden image of her, which they intended to lay in her place, when they had carried her off. And this they accomplished; for while she was lying in bed, and the women were sitting around her, the Trolls brought their wooden figure into the room, took the woman out of bed, and laid the image in her place, as if it were the woman herself. Their next object was to convey her through the window to some other Trolls, who stood without to receive her; but Bondevette, who had had an eye upon their proceedings, placed himself by the window, took his wife and concealed her in the house, unknown to the other women. He then caused the oven to be heated very hot, took the image that lay in the bed, and thrust it into the oven, where it blazed and crackled prodigiously, while the women who were sitting in the room and saw what he had done, made a woeful outcry, thinking that he had burnt his wife. But he afterwards set their minds at ease, by showing them where he had laid his own wife.

Another time, as he was passing by Korshöi, he heard the Trolls within say, 'Tomorrow Bondevette's wife brews, so we will away and steal her beer.' Whereupon he went home and ordered the brewing kettle to be filled with water, and the water to be heated to boiling. He then said to his men, 'Wherever I cast water do you strike with stout cudgels.' So when the Trolls came with their bucket and a strong iron rod to fetch the beer, Bondevette cast the boiling water over them and scalded them, while the men beat about with their cudgels, but without seeing that they were belabouring the Trolls. In this manner he drove them off with such speed that they had no time to take with them either bucket or iron rod. The latter Bondevette afterwards gave to the church; and it is the same on which the church door yet hangs.

Once, as he was passing the same mount by night, he saw how the Trolls were dancing around it. When they saw him they would drink to him, and

---

1   A countryman, peasant of free condition.
2   See p. 90.

handed him a cup; but he cast the liquor over his shoulder, some of which falling on his horse, burnt both its hide and hair. Bondevette hastened away with the cup, which he afterwards gave to the church, and which was subsequently made into a chalice and paten. It is furthermore said of him, that he continued in the same course towards the Trolls, until they at last grew tired of inhabiting Korshöi.

## The Giant's Daughter and the Ploughman

In Tröstrup Mark there is a barrow, in which a giant lies buried, of whom it is related that he had a daughter of gigantic form and power. As she was one day crossing a field, she found a man ploughing, and thinking it was some sort of plaything, she took him with his team and plough up in her pinafore, and carried them to her father, saying, 'See what I have found in the fields, while I was raking in the ground.' But her father answered, 'Let them go: they will drive us away.'[1]

## Svend Faelling

Svend Faelling was a doughty champion, born at Faelling in Jutland. For a considerable length of time he served on the farm of Aakiaer near Aarhuus, and as the roads were not secure, on account of Trolls and other subterranean beings, who bear enmity towards all Christian folk, he undertook the office of letter-carrier. As he was once passing along, there came to him the Troll from Jelshöi, requesting his aid in a battle with the Troll of Borum-Eshöi. Svend Faelling expressed his willingness, thinking himself sufficiently strong and daring. To try his strength, however, the Troll held out to him a thick iron bar, but which, strong as he was, he was unable to lift. The Troll then handed him a horn, desiring him to drink from it, and when he had drunk a little, he could lift the bar; and when he had again drunk, it was still lighter to him; but when he had emptied the horn, he was able to brandish the bar, and learned from the Troll that he had the strength of twelve men. He then made ready to proceed against the Troll of Borum-Eshöi, and was told that he would meet a black and a red bull on the way, and that he should attack the black one, and drive him with all his might from the red bull. This he did, and afterwards learned that the black bull was the Troll from Borum-Eshöi, and the red one the Troll from Jelshöi, from whom, in recompense, he received, as a perma-nent gift, the strength of twelve men, though with the condition that if he

1   See more on this subject in Grimm, J., *Deutsche Mythologie*, op. cit., pp. 505, sq.

ever divulged to anyone how he had acquired such power, he should, as a punishment, receive also the appetite of twelve.

From that time, the report of Svend Faelling's strength became widespread throughout the country, seeing that he was constantly displaying it in divers manners. It is related of him that being once offended at a milkmaid, he so threw her that she found herself sitting across the gable of a house. When this feat was reported to the proprietor of Aakiaer, he ordered Svend Faelling to be called before him, and commanded him to relate how he had acquired such vast bodily strength. But as Svend well remembered the Troll's warning, he refused until he got his master's promise that he should have as much to eat as he desired. From that day he ate and drank the portion of twelve men. At Aakiaer there is still shown a flesh pot which he emptied daily, and which is called Svend Faelling's flesh pot. At the same place there is also said to be a huge two-handed sword three ells long, which once belonged to him; also an ancient beech with a large ring in it, to which he was accustomed to tie his horse.

––––––––

According to other accounts, Svend Faelling served as a boy at the farm of Siellevskov, and it once happened, when he had ridden on a message to Ristrup, that it was evening before he reached home. As he passed by the mount called Borum-Eshöi, he observed the Elf-girls, who kept incessantly dancing round his horse. One of these approaching him, presented to him a costly drinking horn and invited him to drink. Svend took the horn, but having no great faith in what it contained, he threw it out behind him, so that it fell on his horse's back and singed the hair off. The horn he held fast, and clapping spurs to his horse, rode away with all possible speed, followed by the Elf-damsel, until he reached Trigebrand's mill, where he rode over the running water, across which the Elves cannot follow. Thereupon the Elf-damsel earnestly implored him to give her the horn back, promising him in recompense the strength of twelve men; on which assurance he returned the horn to her, and got what she promised him. But he thereby frequently found himself in difficulty, seeing that he had at the same time acquired the appetite of twelve. When he returned home in the evening of that day, the people were just having their Christmas beer; and feeling disposed to be merry at his expense, they sent him to fetch beer, saying, 'Svend! do thou go and fetch us our beer, then we will drink no more this Christmas.' Svend said nothing and went, but came back with a cask in each hand and one under each arm.

Near the village of Steenstrup there is a mount called Havbierg, on which the doughty Svend Faelling was wont to sit while washing his hands and feet in Sönderstrand, which is distant about an eighth of a mile. In Holmstrup the peasants cooked meat for him, which they brought him in huge brewing vessels. When he was dead, he was buried at Dalhöi, between Loms and Holmstrup.

*In the old Danish ballad of 'Svend Faelling's Kamp med Risen', Svend is described as going on a pilgrimage to Rome, and on his way arriving at a city called Hövdingsö, the princess of which informs him that the land is being made desolate by a giant who feeds only on women and maidens. Svend undertakes to encounter this monster, and a number of horses are led forth, that he may select one qualified to bear him in the ensuing combat. These proving either too shy or too weak, he wishes for a Jutland horse, when a miller passes by, who informs him that he has a Jutland horse that can carry fifteen skippund. This horse is so powerful and violent that he bursts every saddle-girth that is applied to him, until fifteen maidens knit a girth of silk and gold, seven ells long, a quarter of an ell thick and five spans broad, which fully answers its purpose. Svend finally kills the giant.[1]*

In Borberg church, in the diocese of Ribe, there is a remarkable gilt altar-piece with figures of alabaster, representing the history of Svend Faelling, so celebrated in the Danish chronicles, as well as that of the giant, who would have only women and maidens; also the Danish horse that could carry fifteen skippund of corn, which the miller gave to Svend Faelling to bear him in the combat; the giant's head, which Svend Faelling cut off; the damsels who wove the thick saddle-girth; the priest who absolved Svend Faelling of his sins before he went to the encounter.[2]

## Altar-cups

In Holbek amt, in Seeland, between Marup and Aagerup, there was once a large castle, the ruins of which may still be seen on the shore. At this place, tradition tells us, there are vast riches, and that a dragon under the earth broods over three kings' ransoms. The underground folk are often to be seen here, particularly on solemn occasions, when they have dancing and merrymaking on the shore.

One Christmas Eve a man in Aagerup asked his master to let him ride down to see the Trolls' merrymaking. The master allowed him to take the best horse in the stable. On reaching the spot, he sat a while on his horse witnessing the festivity, and while wondering to see the Mount-folk dance, a little Troll came to him, who invited him to dismount and partake of their mirth. Another then came springing, who took his horse's rein and held it while the man dismounted and danced with them the whole night. When the morning drew nigh, he thanked them for their hospitality and mounted his horse, when they invited him to come again on the following new year's

---

1   *Danske Viser*, fra Middelalderen, i, 150.
2   J. Hofman, *Fundgr.*, iv, 613.

night, when there would be another merrymaking. A damsel then brought him a gold cup, bidding him take a parting draught; but feeling some mistrust, he, while feigning to put the cup to his lips, cast the liquor over his shoulder, so that it fell on the horse's back, the hairs of which it singed. Applying then the spurs to his horse's sides, he rode away cup in hand over a ploughed field, followed by all the Trolls, who finding it very difficult to traverse the deep furrows, cried incessantly, 'Ride on the smooth and not on the rough!' But it was not until he approached the village that he found it necessary to ride on the level road, whereby he was exposed to great peril, as the Trolls came nearer and nearer at every moment. In his extremity, he put up a prayer, and for his safety promised to give the cup to the church. Having now reached the churchyard, he threw the cup over the wall, that that might at all events be secure. He then quickened his pace and entered the village, and just as the Trolls were about to seize the horse, it darted through the gateway of the house, and the man slammed the gate after him. He was now safe, but the Trolls were so exasperated that they fetched an enormously large stone, which they hurled with such force against the gate that four of the planks flew out. Of the house not a vestige remains, but the stone yet lies in Aagerup village. The cup was given to the church, and the man got as a reward the best farm on the estate of Ericsholm.

*It is well worthy of remark, that William of Newbridge, who lived as early as the twelfth century, relates a story of a man in Yorkshire, who returning home one night, saw a mound open, in which a number of persons were feasting, one of whom offered him a cup, the contents of which he poured out, and rode off with the cup. The cup was presented to Henry I, from whose hands it passed into those of David, king of Scotland, and was finally given by William the Lion to King Henry II. The province of Deiri, the scene of this tradition, it must be recollected was chiefly inhabited by the descendants of the Northmen.*[1]

*In Scotland it is still currently believed, that he who has courage to rush upon a fairy festival, and snatch from them their drinking cup or horn, shall find it prove to him a cornucopia of good fortune, if he can bear it in safety across a running stream. A goblet is still carefully preserved in Edenhall, Cumberland, which is supposed to have been seized at a banquet of the elves, by one of the ancient family of Musgrave; or, as others say, by one of their domestics, in the manner above described. The fairy train vanished, crying aloud,*

> *If this glass do break or fall,*
> *Farewell the luck of Edenhall!'*[2]

1   Keightley, op, cit., p. 283.
2   Scott's *Minstrelsy*, ii, p. 130.

Between North and South Kongerslev are two mounts, one of which is called Örnehöi, the other Kiaerlinghöi; both are inhabited by Troll-folk, who are at enmity with each other.

One Christmas Eve, a farmer in South Kongerslev was sitting at table talking with his man. 'Christian,' said he, 'what may the Mount-folk in Kiaerlingbierg be about?' 'What are they about?' answered the man. 'What can that concern us?' The farmer then said that it would be amusing to see the mount standing on four pillars and all the merriment beneath. To which the man replied, that if he might take the one-coloured horse that stood in the stable, he would go and bring him back the information he wished, and also a token that he had been there. The farmer allowed him to take the horse, and when he reached the spot he found the mount standing on four pillars, and great feasting and mirth beneath. For a while he sat quiet on the horse and looked on, but when just about to return, he began crying out, 'Hou! Vildt! Hou! Vildt!' which people are wont to cry when they have lost their way. As soon as the Mount-folk saw him, a little boy, with a red cap on his head, came out and offered him drink from a gold cup. He took the cup, but cast out the liquor and hastened away at full speed. Being followed by all the Trolls, he was nearly overtaken by them just as he passed by Örnebierg; but the Trolls there, seeing him pursued by those of Kiaerlingbierg, cried out, Ride off the hard, up on the fallow, and you will escape them!' This the man understood quite well, quitted the road, rode up into the ploughed field, and so escaped, the little Trolls of the mount being unable to follow him over the furrows. On reaching the farm, he made a cross at the gate, a cross on the horse, a cross on the door, and a cross on the cup, which he still held in his hand.

Now he must tell his master all he had seen and heard: first, that all the Trolls in Kiaerlinghöi are called either Vidrik or Didrik, so that during their feast it was to be heard on every side, 'Your health, Vidrik!' 'Thank you, Didrik!' 'Your health, Vidrik's wife!' 'Thank you, Didrik's sweetheart!' and the like. He further told him that they could not say a *merry feast*. At length, in proof of the truth of his story, he drew forth the costly cup that he had taken from the Trolls, which precious acquisition was highly valued in the house, and brought forth only on extraordinary occasions.

On the following Christmas Eve, a little man in tatters came to the house and begged a night's lodging of the mistress. 'Yes, certainly,' said the woman, 'come into the room and get something to live on.' She then cut him an excellent luncheon of fine bread with butter and other good things upon it, but the miserable fellow would not touch it. In the evening, when supper was brought in, the mistress invited him to sit down and partake of their meal, but still he would touch nothing. 'What if I were to offer him a drink of good beer in our beautiful cup,' thought the woman within herself; and did so accordingly; but no sooner had the beggar received it, than both he and the cup vanished from her sight, although the door continued closed.

## Trolls in the Red Stone

As a man on horseback, accompanied by his dog, was passing one evening late by the Red-stone, a projecting crag on the isle of Fuur in the Liimfiord, he saw by the moonlight the Trolls carrying their gold and silver treasures out to the little knolls thereabout, for the purpose of exposing them to the air. The man happened to have his gun with him, and having heard that, if anyone can shoot three times over them, the Trolls must go into the mound and leave their treasure behind them, he shot accordingly; but being unable to restrain his cupidity until daybreak, when he could convey the treasure home at his ease without hindrance, he put the whole into a bag and hurried away. As he was riding along between two banks, he heard something puffing and panting behind him, and on looking round, saw a little man with a long beard, on a horse not larger than a cat, but without a head, and with a diminutive black dog by his side. He easily guessed that it was the Troll of the Red-stone. 'Wilt thou let thy horse fight with mine?' said the little man. 'No, God forbid!' answered the man. 'Or thy dog with mine?' 'No, God forbid!' 'Or wilt thou thyself engage with me, little as I am?' 'No, God forbid!' At the same time the man whipped his horse and rode away as fast as he could. When be got home and was within his own doors, there seemed to be a storming and hissing without, and the whole house appeared to be in a blaze. Being well aware what sorcery was going forward, he took up the bag with the treasure and flung it out. The sorcery thereupon ceased, and a voice without cried, 'Thou hast still enough!' Next morning he found a heavy silver cup that had fallen behind a chest of drawers.

## The Troll's Glove

Near Hvidovre in Seeland there is a large mount in which a Troll dwelt, who went every night from the mount, through a neighbouring farmyard, down to the rivulet, to fetch water: his footmarks might easily be traced in the grass. One morning, as the farmer was going to his turf-field, he found on this path a glove so large that the thumb could hold a barrel of rye. When he brought it home, all were amused with it, and were unanimous that it must belong to the Troll. The following midnight, as the man lay asleep, he was awaked by a loud knocking at the window, followed by the words:

'Vante, Ven!
Giv mig min Vante igien;
Ellers ligge to af dine Heste,
De störste og de bedste,
Döde imorgen paa Mosen!'

*The glove, friend!*
*Give me my glove again;*
*Else shall lie two of thy horses*
*The largest and the best,*
*Dead tomorrow on the moor.*

Thereupon the farmer took the glove, went out of the house, and hung it on a beam-end over the window, and having made a cross on the door, again went in. In the morning the glove was away and the beam-end was found snapped off level with the wall. From that time nothing more was ever heard of the Troll; his path became grown over and was no longer to be traced.

*The idea of the gigantic glove is evidently derived from that of Skrymir, in the story of Thor and Udgarda-Loki.*

## The Troll Outwitted

A husbandman, who had a little mount on his field, resolved not to let it lie waste, and began to plough it up. At this the Troll, who dwelt in the mount, came out and demanded who it was that dared to plough on his roof. The husbandman said that he did not know it was his roof, and at the same time represented to him that it was disadvantageous for both to let such a piece of land lie uncultivated; that he was willing to plough, sow and reap every year, and that the Troll should alternately have that which in one year grew on the earth, and the man that which grew beneath, and the next year the reverse. To this the Troll agreed, and the man in the first year sowed carrots, and in the year following, corn, and gave the Troll the tops of the carrots and the roots of the corn. From that time there was a good understanding between them.

# Raginal

A farmer fell into poverty because he could not keep any cows in his stalls, the necks of all having been broken one after another. He therefore left the dwelling, which was sold to another. When the new proprietor came into the cowhouse one evening and saw that everything was in tolerable condition, he exclaimed, 'Good-evening, Raginal!' Whereupon a voice answered, 'What! Dost thou know me?' 'Yes, I have known thee for many a year!' 'If,' said the Troll, who dwelt beneath, 'thou wilt move thy cowhouse to some other place, thou shalt then become an opulent man. I have my habitation under the cows, and their dirt falls down on my table every day, so that I have been obliged to break their necks.' The man removed the cowhouse, and thrived from that time.

*That a similar superstition was known in Scotland, will appear from the following: 'The Scottish fairies, in like manner, sometimes reside in subterranean abodes, in the vicinity of human habitations, or, according to the popular phrase, under the "door-stane", or threshold; in which situation they sometimes establish an intercourse with men, by borrowing and lending, and other kindly offices. In this capacity they are termed "the good neighbours", from supplying privately the wants of their friends, and assisting them in all their transactions, while their favours are concealed. Of this the traditionary story of Sir Godfrey Macculloch forms a curious example.*

*'As this Gallovidian gentleman was taking the air on horseback, near his own house, he was suddenly accosted by a little old man, arrayed in green, and mounted upon a white palfrey. After mutual salutation, the old man gave Sir Godfrey to understand, that he resided under his habitation, and that he had great reason to complain of the direction of a drain, or common sewer, which emptied itself directly into his chamber of dais. Sir Godfrey was a good deal startled by this extraordinary complaint; but, guessing the nature of the being he had to deal with, he assured the old man, with great courtesy, that the direction of the drain should be altered; and caused it to be done accordingly. Many years afterwards, Sir Godfrey had the misfortune to kill, in a fray, a gentleman of the neighbourhood. He was apprehended, tried, and condemned. The scaffold, upon which his head was to be struck off, was erected on the Castle-hill of Edinburgh; but hardly had he reached the fatal spot, when the old man upon his white palfrey, pressed through the crowd, with the rapidity of lightning. Sir Godfrey, at his command, sprang on behind him; the "good neighbour" spurred his horse down the steep bank, and neither he nor the criminal were ever again seen.'*[1]

*A woman was returning late one night from a gossiping. A pretty little boy came up to her and said, 'Coupe yere dish-water farther frae yere door-step; it pits out our fire.'*[2]

1  Scott's *Minstrelsy*, ii, pp. 169, sq.
2  Cromek, *Nithsdale and Galloway Song*, quoted by Keightley, op, cit., p. 353.

# Gillikop

Some Jutlanders having got a little Troll into their power, thought they could not do better than make him a Christian, and therefore set him in a cart for the purpose of driving him to church and having him baptised. As he there sat peeping out, the men heard a voice in the road calling aloud, 'Where now, Gillikop?' to which the little Troll in the cart responded, 'A long way, Slangerop! I am going to a little water yonder, where I hope to become a better man.'

## The Trolls Desire to be Saved

One night as a priest was going from Hiorlunde to Rolskilde, he passed by a mount in which there were music, dancing and other merriment. At this moment some Dwarfs sprang forth from the mount, stopped the priest's vehicle, and said, 'Whither art thou going?' 'To Landemode,' answered the priest. They then asked him whether he thought they could be saved; to which he replied that he could not then inform them. They then appointed him to meet them with an answer in a year. In the meantime, it went ill with the coachman, who the next time he passed by the mount was overturned and killed on the spot. When the priest came again at the end of a year, they again asked him the same question, to which he answered, 'No! You are all damned!' Scarcely had he uttered the words before the whole mount was in a blaze.

*A similar story is told of the Nök, see p. 00. In the Irish story named 'The Priest's Supper', a fisherman, at the request of the fairies, asks a priest who had stopped at his house, whether they would be saved or not at the last day. The priest desired him to tell them to come themselves and put the question to him, but this they declined doing, and the question remained unanswered.*[1]

## The Trolls' Fear of the Cross

Near Aarhuus there dwelt a smith, who one day, on his way to church, observed a Troll sitting by the roadside on a heap of coals and busied with two straws that were accidentally lying across each other on the heap; but in spite of all his labour, being unable to get them to lie otherwise, he besought the smith, who stood looking at him, to take the straws away. But the smith, who well knew the real state of the case, took the whole heap together with the cross, paying little attention to the outcry made by the Troll. It was found afterwards, when he reached home, that what appeared like coals was a great treasure over which the Troll had no longer power.

---

1   Keightley, op, cit., p. 365.

# The Trolls' Fear of Thunder

The Mount-folk are exceedingly terrified at thunder, and therefore hasten to get into their mounts when they see a storm drawing up to windward. In consequence of this terror they cannot endure the beating of drums, which is, in their opinion, a species of thunder. A good method, therefore, to get rid of them is to drum vigorously every day in the neighbourhood of their mounts; for then they will at length pack up, and wander to a more peaceful spot.

A countryman once lived in good fellowship with a Troll, who had his mount in the countryman's field. When his wife was once lying-in, he was a little embarrassed because he could not well avoid inviting the Troll to the birthday feast, which would give him a bad reputation both with the priest and with the other townsfolk. In this state of perplexity, from which he knew not how to extricate himself, he sought counsel of his swineherd, who was a shrewd fellow, and had often helped him on other occasions. The swineherd undertook to settle the matter with the Troll, so that, without being offended, he should not only stay away, but should give a handsome present. In pursuance of his plan, taking a bag with him, he went to the mount, knocked, and was admitted. He then in the name of his master invited the Troll to honour them with his presence at the lying-in festival. The Troll thanked him and said, 'So, I shall then have to give you a gossip-gift;' at the same time opening his money chest and causing the man to hold the bag up, while he poured money into it. 'Is there enough now?' – 'Many give more, few give less,' answered the swineherd. Thereupon the Troll began again to pour into the bag, and again asked, 'Is there enough now?' The swineherd lifted the bag a little as a trial whether he could carry more, and answered, 'Most people give as much.' The Troll thereupon emptied the whole chest into the bag, and asked: 'Is there now enough?' The man finding that he had now as much as he could carry, answered, 'None give more, most people give less.' 'Well,' said the Troll, 'let us now hear who is to be there besides.' 'Ah,' said the man, 'we shall have great personages: first three priests and a bishop.' 'Umph!' growled the Troll. 'Though such high dons generally look only after what's to eat and drink; they are not likely to notice me. Now, who else?' 'Then there's the Virgin Mary.' 'Umph! umph! Still there will be a retired place for me behind the stove. Now, who next?' 'Then our Lord is to be there.' 'Umph! umph! umph! Still such exalted guests come late and make a short stay; but what music are you to have?' 'Drums,' answered the swineherd. 'Drums,' repeated the Troll, startled. 'No thank you; I remain at home. Greet thy master from me, and thank him for his invitation; but I shall not come; for once, when I went out for a little walk, the folks began to drum, and when I was hastening away and had just reached my own door, they threw a drumstick after me and broke one of my thighs. From that time I have been lame, and shall beware of such music!' With these words he helped to lift the bag on the man's shoulders, and again desired him to greet his master.

*The dread entertained by the Trolls for thunder dates from the time of paganism, Thor, the god of thunder, being the deadly foe of their race.*

## The Trolls' Hatred of Bells

In Egens Mark a multitude of the dwarf race once made their appearance. They were all clad in grey jerkins and wore red caps. With respect to their persons, they were hump-backed, and had long hooked noses. Whithersoever they came they made sad havoc among the pantries, and people found it no easy task to get rid of them, until a pious and experienced man advised that a bell should be hung in the tower of Ebeltoft church. When this was done, people saw no more of the Trolls.

*The Korrigan of Brittany have a similar abhorrence of bells.*

_____

In Dishöi a Troll had lived undisturbed for many years, because at that time there was no church in the neighbourhood. But when at length a church was built hard by, and the bells for the first time rung in the tower, the Troll in great tribulation came riding on a gold-shod horse to a peasant his neighbour, and delivered to him the keys of his treasure, as he himself must take his departure. The next day the peasant went to the mount to get the treasure: he found the door, but in his joy exclaimed, 'Now I have it!' At the same instant both door and key vanished.

_____

A peasant once observed a Troll in deep affliction sitting on a stone between Mullerup and Dalby. At first he imagined him to be a proper Christian man, and asked him to what place he was going. 'I am going out of the country,' answered the Troll, 'for no one can now stay in it for sheer ringing and tolling.'

## The Trolls Forsake Vendsyssel

It happened one evening that a stranger came to Sundby ferry and agreed with all the ferrymen, that during the whole night they should ferry over from Vendsyssel, without knowing what lading they were to have. They were told that half a mile east of Sundby they were to take in their freight. At the time appointed the stranger was on the spot, when the ferrymen, although they saw nothing, yet remarked that their boat sank more and more, whence they concluded that they had received an exceedingly heavy lading on board. In this manner the ferry boats, during the whole night, passed backwards and forwards across the water; and although they at each time took a new freight, the same stranger was always present, that all might be done according to his orders. At the approach of morning the ferrymen received the stipulated payment, and on inquiring what it was they had conveyed across, could get no information. Among the ferrymen there was, however, a shrewd fellow, who knew much more about such matters than the others. He sprang on shore, took the earth from under his right foot and put it into his cap, and having set it upon his head, he perceived that all the sandhills east of Aalborg were entirely covered with small Trolls, having red, peaked caps on their heads. From that time no dwarfs of that description have been seen in Vendsyssel.

## The Elf-folk Forsake Aerö

After that the miller in Dunkiaer had repeatedly disturbed the subterranean folk in Elleshöi, and at length even ploughed over their mount in every direction, which they could not possibly endure, they prepared to quit the country and migrate to Norway.

There came one day a little old man to a poor skipper, who had no employment, and asked him whether he would like to have charge of a vessel. The man answered that he would gladly; but when the little man led him down to the shore at Gravendal, and showed him an old wreck, the skipper objected, telling him that such a wreck could not possibly keep the sea. The little man answered, that he might make himself quite easy on that score, might hire a sailor, and meet him again in three days, when the vessel should be ready to sail. The skipper in the meanwhile found it difficult to hire a sailor, for all that he applied to turned their backs on him and laughed, as soon as they heard that he was going to sail in the old wreck at Gravendal. At length he met with a poor lad who, in the hope of getting something to eat, allowed himself to be hired.

On the third day the skipper and his helpmate were at Gravendal, where they found the bark lying at anchor and, instead of sails, hung with rags. The wind being fair they departed instantly. When on their way, the skipper being curious to see what sort of cargo he had on board, peeped down the hatchway, where he perceived the whole place swarming as with innumerable rats and mice. And now the little man taking off his hat, placed it on the head of the skipper, who thereby became so clear-sighted that he could see a multitude of small elves in travelling dresses, and withal a vast quantity of gold and silver, which they were taking with them.

On their arrival in Norway, the old man said, 'Do thou go on shore: I will unload the vessel.' The skipper did so, and when he came back the bark was empty, and on their return the little man desired him within three days to expect another freight. The skipper having fulfilled his engagement, the old man desired him to follow him and take with him two sacks. 'Now thou shalt be paid for thy labour,' said he, at the same time filling one of the sacks with shavings and the other with coals. 'Give the lad his share,' added he, and took his departure. With such payment the skipper was not over-satisfied. 'Yes!' he muttered to himself, 'we have, sure enough, got our pockets full.' When they had been sailing about an hour, the skipper said, 'Go, lad, and make us a drop of tea.' 'Yes, master,' answered the lad, 'but I have no fuel.' 'Take a handful of shavings out of the sack.' 'Master, they shine!' cried the lad. 'What shines?' asked the skipper. 'Take from the other sack.' 'Master, they shine!' cried the lad a second time. The skipper himself now looked at the sacks, and found that one was full of gold coin and the other of silver. On their return they divided their treasure and became wealthy people.

*The North German traditions of the departure of the 'little people' resemble the foregoing in every essential particular, excepting that the water they have to cross is the Eider, the Weser, or the Aller, in place of those above-mentioned.*[1]

## The Trolls Cast Stones at Churches

Before the Trolls had forsaken the country, in consequence of the constant din of the church bells, the erection of a new church was an intolerable vexation to them. Hence the numerous traditions, how during the night they destroyed the work, particularly when a church was to be raised near their habitations. Equally numerous, too, are the traditions all over the country, which tell how the Trolls hurled huge stones against the churches already built; a circumstance which affords a most satisfactory explanation of the manner in which the vast stones, which are scattered about, came into places where no human hand could have deposited them.

1   See Müllenhoff, op. cit., No. cdxxix; Kuhn and Schwartz, *Nordeutsche Sagen, Märchen und Gebräuche*, Leipzig, 1848 No. 270; Grimm, J., *Deutsche Mythologie*, op. cit., 428 *sq*. See also 'The Departure of the Fairies' in Keightley, op, cit., p. 356, from Cromek's *Nithsdale and Galloway Song*.

## The Nisse Or Niss

In a house in Jutland, a Nisse had long been accustomed, after the servant was gone to bed, to fetch his porridge from the kitchen, where it was set for him in a little wooden bowl. But one evening, on taking his porridge, he saw that the girl had forgotten to put butter in it, and in his anger at the omission went to the cowhouse and wrung the neck of the best cow. Afterwards feeling hungry, he sneaked back, deeming it advisable to put up with the despised porridge, when after he had eaten a little, he discovered that there was butter in it, but that it had sunk to the bottom. For having thus wronged the servant he was sorely grieved, and to repair the injury he had done to the good folks, he went again to the cowhouse and placed a chest full of money by the side of the dead cow.

*A similar tale is current in Holstein, with the difference only, that instead of a chest full of money, the Niss procures a cow similar in appearance to the one killed by him.*[1]

---

At a farm in Seeland, there was a Nisse who was active and cheerful at all kinds of work, provided only that he got butter in his porridge every night; for any reward beyond that he did not require. One morning, as the men were going to plough, he went to the farmer and requested him to let him drive the plough. The man thought that he was too little to drive four horses, but he answered, ' I can very well sit up in the ear of one of the horses[2] and drive with four: I have done it before now.' The man then let him have his way, and afterwards could not help confessing that he had never before had so excellent a driver. It was, moreover, highly amusing when anyone passed and could not see the driver, who sat in the horse's ear, but only heard him crying out, 'Hyp so! Hop so! Will ye go, ye old jades! Ye'll get your hides curried! That ye may swear to!' When the farmer died the Nisse would no longer remain there, but transferred himself to the manor-house, where he continued for some time in concealment. Some days after, the proprietor got a new man, who was to thrash the winter corn. The first day, when the man came into the barn, he did nothing, but merely looked at the corn; the second day he did no more than the first, until Nis towards evening said to him, 'Hear! I will come and help thee.' To this the man had nothing to object, so it was settled that Nis should every night have for his supper porridge with butter in it. On the following morning, when the man came into the barn, Nis had already thrashed a heap of corn, containing about twenty-five loads. 'Thou canst now cut up the straw by noon,' said Nis, and as he helped him, so it was done. Then said the man,

---

1   See Müllenhoff, op. cit., No. cdxxxviii.
2   See the story of 'Daumesdick,' in Grimm, J. & W., *Kinder- und Hausmärchen*, op. cit., No. 37.

' But how shall we get the chaff separated from the barley?' 'That I will soon show thee,' said Nis. 'Just go up outside on the top of the barn, and make a large hole in the roof, we shall then easily separate the chaff.' When the man had so done, the Nisse opened every door in the barn, then went up to the hole, laid himself on his face, thrust his head through the hole, and sent forth a loud scream, so that all the chaff flew about over the whole yard. This brought the proprietor out, who on seeing what had been done was highly incensed. 'I believe thou art mad, fellow!' said he. 'Dost thou let the chaff, that we should have for the cattle in the winter, fly away in that manner?' 'O! Is that all, master?' said the man. 'If you want the chaff in again, that you can soon have.' The Nisse now helped the man to gather up the chaff and carry it in again, all which was accomplished in half an hour. 'Go now in to your master,' said the Nisse, 'and tell him that the corn is thrashed, and the chaff gathered in a heap, if he will now come out and measure, that we may know how many bushels there are. But tell him, at the same time, that we must be paid for every bushel of chaff as well as for every bushel of corn; and that if he refuses, we will throw down the whole barn.' When the man had delivered this message, the master answered laughing, 'Yes, do so, if you can; but I am not so silly as to pay the same for chaff as for corn.' When the Nisse received this answer, he merely said, 'Well! If he will not, then come; we shall soon overthrow it.' Both then went and placed their backs against one of the side walls, when it instantly began to totter. Seeing this, the proprietor ran out into the yard and yielded to the demand. So the man got well paid for his trouble, and did not forget to give his due recompense to the Nisse.

———

It is difficult to get rid of a Nisse. A man dwelt in a house where a Nisse carried his jokes so far, that he resolved to quit it, and leave the Nisse by himself. Just as he was about to send off the last load of his chattels, consisting chiefly of empty tubs and the like, and had taken a last farewell of the house and, as he thought, of the Nisse also, he went by chance to the back part of the cart, where to his unutterable dismay and astonishment, he espied the Nisse seated in a tub, and ready to accompany him. The man was of course excessively vexed at finding all his labour in vain, but the Nisse burst into a hearty laugh, and popping up his head from the tub, said, 'So! we are moving today.'

*A being in many respects similar to the Niss is the Yorkshire* Boggart, *by whose pranks an honest farmer was nearly driven from his habitation. When his chattels were already in the cart, a voice from a deep upright churn cried out, 'Aye, aye, Georgey, we are flitting ye see.'*

*Such, too, is the Irish* Cluricaun. *To get rid of one, the householder had resolved on removing, and the last cart, filled with empty barrels, etc., was just moving off, when from the bunghole of one of them Wildbean cried out, 'Here, master! Here we go all together!' 'What,' said the master, 'dost thou go also?' 'Yes, to be sure, master; here we go all together!*[1]

---

In the parish of Alstrup there once lived a man who had a beautiful white mare, which for many years had descended from father to son, and was the cause that a Nisse and, consequently, good luck were attached to the farm. This Nisse had such an affection for the mare that he could not endure to see her used for labour, and every night fed her in the best manner; and as he was accustomed to bring a superabundance of corn, both thrashed and unthrashed, from a neighbour's barn, all the other cattle had benefit thereof. But the farm at length got a new proprietor, who would not believe what was told him about the mare, and sold her to a poor neighbour. When five days had elapsed, the poor peasant, who had bought the mare, began to find his condition manifestly improving, while the other's circumstances became everyday narrower, so that at length he could scarcely make shift to subsist. Had now the man that bought the mare only known how to profit by the good fortune that was come to him, his children's children would have been in affluence to this day; but seeing the great quantity of corn that was every night brought in, he felt a strong desire to see the Nisse also, and therefore concealed himself one night in the stable. At midnight he perceived the Nisse coming from his neighbour's barn, and bringing with him a sack full of grain; but the Nisse, having discovered that he was watched, was grievously vexed, and after having fed the mare tended her for the last time; then turning towards the place where the man lay watching, he bade him farewell. From that time the condition of both neighbours continued alike, seeing that each enjoyed the fruits of his own labour.

*Of the predilection entertained by the Nisser for horses there are also many Swedish traditions.*

---

Jutland once literally swarmed with Nisser. At Vosborg they found such good cheer that their abode there was characterised by their great diligence and care for the welfare of the proprietor. Every evening they got in their sweet porridge a large lump of butter, for all which they once gave a strong proof of zeal and gratitude. In a very severe winter, a remote cowhouse, in which were six calves, was so overwhelmed with snow, that for fourteen days no human being could get access to it. When the snow disappeared, it was naturally thought that the calves would be found starved to death – but quite the contrary; they were all found strong and well, the stalls were swept, and the cribs full of excellent corn. It may easily be guessed who had taken care of them.

But the Nisse is, at the same time, sure to have revenge for any injury done him. One day, when a Nisse had run up into the loft over the cowhouse, a plank gave way, so that one of his legs went through. The farmer's boy, who happened just at the moment when this happened to be in the place beneath, on seeing the Nisse's leg hanging down, snatched up a dung-fork and gave it a violent blow. At dinner, when the people were all sitting at table in the servants' hall, the boy was constantly laughing to himself, and on being questioned by the overseer, he answered, 'I've had such a bout with Nis this morning, and given him an infernal bang with my fork, as he poked his leg down through the floor of the loft.' 'Nay,' cried Nis from outside the window, 'thou didst not give one, thou gavest me three; for the fork had three prongs; but it shall be paid thee back.' On the following night, while the boy lay asleep, came Nis, seized him, and threw him over the house, but was so instantaneously on the other side that he caught him and again cast him back. This game was continued until the boy had been eight times over the house; the ninth time he let him fall into a large pool of water, and then set up a horse-laugh, so that all who were in the dwelling were waked by it.

———

In a farmhouse in Jutland, there was a Nisse, who every evening got his porridge in proper time, and therefore helped both man and maid, and saw to the master's interest in every way possible. But there once entered into the farmer's service a mischievous lad, who took every opportunity of annoying the Nisse, and one night, when all were gone to rest, and the Nisse had taken his little wooden bowl, and was about to enjoy his evening meal, he discovered that the boy had concealed the butter at the bottom, in order to make him first eat the porridge and then find the butter when the porridge was consumed. Hereupon he resolved on giving the boy like for like. Going then up into the loft where the boy and the manservant lay sleeping in the same bed, he took the coverlid off, when seeing the short lad by the side of the long carle, he said, 'Short and long unequal,' and so saying pulled the legs of the boy down, to make them even with those of the man. He then went to the head of the bed, and dragged the boy up again, uttering the same words. But as this process, in whichever way applied, did not succeed in making the boy as long as the man, he continued dragging the boy up and down until broad daylight; when feeling himself tired, he crept up and seated himself in the windowsill. At the sight of him, all the dogs in the yard – dogs bearing a great aversion to

Nisser – began to bark, at which the Nisse, who was beyond their reach, was highly amused, and thrusting forth first one diminutive leg then the other, continued to tease them, saying, 'Look at this little trotter! Look at that little trotter!' In the meanwhile the boy waked, and sneaking behind the Nisse, who was going on with his 'Look at this and look at that little trotter,' pushed him down among the dogs, crying out, 'There! Now look at him from top to toe!'

*The North Germans have a story nearly identical with the foregoing.*[1]

*The Scandinavian Niss is identical with the Scottish Brownie, who is described as 'of a somewhat grotesque figure, dwarfish in stature, but endowed with great personal strength . . . It was customary for the mistress of the house to leave out work for him . . . To have offered him wages, or even to present him with an occasional boon, would have ensured his anger, and perhaps caused him to abandon the establishment altogether. The goodman of a farmhouse in the parish of Glendevon leaving out some clothes one night for the brownie, he was heard during the night to depart, saying, in a highly offended tone,*

> 'Gie brownie coat, gie brownie sark,
> Ye'se get nae mair o' brownie's wark!'[2]

*Numerous other instances might be quoted.*

*Our own Robin Goodfellow was equally sensitive on this point. See a passage from 'The Mad Pranks and Merry Jests of Robin Goodfellow'.*[3]

*Hilton Hall, in the vale of the Wear, was in former times the resort of a Brownie or House-spirit, called the Cauld Lad. For the purpose of getting rid of him, the servants left a green cloak and hood for him by the kitchen fire and remained on the watch. They saw him come in, gaze at the new clothes, try them on, and, apparently in great delight, go jumping and frisking about the kitchen; but at the first crow of the cock he vanished, crying:*

> Here's a cloak and here's a hood!
> The Cauld Lad of Hilton will do no more good;

*and he never again returned to the kitchen.*[4]

*A similar story is told by Mrs Bray (Letters to Southey) of the Devonshire Pixies, one of whom, on receiving new clothes, exclaims*

> Pixy fine, Pixy gay,
> Pixy now will run away.

*A being closely resembling the Brownie is the Phynnodderie of the Isle of Man.*

---

1    Müllenhoff, No. cdxlvi. See also p. 295.
2    See p. 294, and Chambers, *Pop. Rh.*, p. 33.
3    Keightley, op, cit., 287, *sq.*
4    Keightley, op, cit., p. 296, from Richardson, *Local Historian's Table-book.*

## The Kirkegrim (Church-grim)

In churches also there are Nisser, one in each, called a Kirkegrim, who dwells either in the tower or wherever he can find a place of concealment. He keeps order in the church, and punishes when any scandal is perpetrated.

In Sorö church there is a large, round hole in the roof, in which dwells that church's Nisse. Of this hole it is also said, that in former times the evil one was accustomed to fly out through it, when the priest in baptising said, 'Go out, thou unclean spirit!

## The Kirkegrim and the Strand-varsel

At the time 'when the seashores were not yet consecrated,' it was dangerous to pass by night on the ways which lay along the coast, on account of the Strand-varsler by which they were infested. These were the spectres of those corpses that were driven on shore and still lay unburied. One night as a peasant was going along the strand towards Taarbek, a Strand-varsel sprang suddenly on his back and there clung fast, crying, 'Carry me to the church!' The man having no alternative, carried him the shortest way to Gientofte. On their reaching that village, and when close under the churchyard wall, the Varsel sprang quickly over it, when instantly the Kirkegrim approached, and an obstinate battle ensued between them. After having fought for a while, they both sat down to rest, when the Varsel said to the peasant, 'Did I stand up well?' The peasant answered, 'No.' The battle then commenced anew, and when they again sat down to rest the Varsel again asked, 'Did I stand up well now?' and the peasant a second time answered, 'No.' The fight then recommenced, and the Varsel for the third time said, 'Now! Have I stood up well?' and on the peasant answering, 'Yes,' 'It is well for thee,' said the Varsel, 'that thou hast answered so, for otherwise I would surely have broken thy neck.'

---

At Niveröd as a woman was going to milk her cows, she saw a corpse that had been washed up on the sand, and noticed that a large money-bag was bound round its body; and no one being near, she was tempted to take the money, to which she had as good a claim as anyone else. But the next night the Strand-varsel came to the village and made a great noise before her window, desiring her to come out and follow him. Supposing that she had no alternative, she bade her children farewell and accompanied the Varsel. When they were outside of the village, the Varsel said to her, 'Take me by the leg and draw me to the church.' But the nearest church lay three-quarters of a mile distant. When the church appeared in sight, the Varsel said, 'Let me go now; then go to the house by the church gate, and desire the people to sit up until thou comest again. When thou hast helped me over the churchyard wall, run as fast as thou canst, lest the Kirkegrim should seize thee.' She did accordingly, and scarcely had the corpse been placed over the wall, when the Kirkegrim came out after the woman and seized her by the petticoat, which being old gave way, and so she slipped into the house in safety. From that time all went well with the woman, who lived contented with her children on the money she found on the Strand-varsel.

## Hyldemoer – Elder

There dwells in the elder-tree a being called Hyldemoer (Elder-mother) or Hyldeqvinde (Elder-wife). She avenges all injuries done to the tree. Of an elder standing in a small court in the Nyboder,[1] it is related, that at dusk it often moves up and down the court, and sometimes peeps through the window at the children, when they are alone. It is not advisable to have moveables of elder. A child having been laid in a cradle made of elder wood, the Hyldemoer came and pulled it by the legs, nor would she let it have any rest until it was taken out of the cradle. A peasant once heard his children crying in the night, and on inquiring the cause, was told that someone had been there and sucked them; and their breasts were found to be swollen. The cause of the annoyance was, it is said, that the room was boarded with elder.

This wonderful medicinal tree derives its name, it is supposed, from a healing deity named Hildi, who together with her spirits or subordinate deities, has her abode under its roots. From early times the Danes have loved and honoured the elder, and planted it by walls and fences.

The elder may not be cut without permission previously asked in these words: 'Hyldemoer, Hyldemoer, allow me to cut thy branches.' The peasants, when about to cut the tree, spit thrice, in order to drive away the Vaetts and other evil beings.

## The Werwolf

A man, who from his childhood had been a Werwolf, when returning one night with his wife from a merrymaking, observed that the hour was at hand when the evil usually came upon him; giving therefore the rein to his wife, he descended from the vehicle, saying to her, 'If anyone comes to thee, only strike at it with thy apron.' He then withdrew, but immediately after, the woman, as she was sitting in the vehicle, was attacked by a Werwolf. She did as the man had enjoined her, and struck it with her apron, from which it bit a piece and ran off with it. After some time the

---

1   A quarter of Copenhagen, built for and inhabited by persons belonging to the navy.

man returned, holding in his mouth the torn fragment of his wife's apron, on seeing which she cried out in terror, 'Good Lord, man! Why thou art a Werwolf !' 'Thank thee, mother!' said he, 'but now I am free!' and from that time the evil never returned.

---

If a female at midnight stretches between four sticks the membrane that envelops the foal when it is brought forth, and creeps through it naked, she will bring forth children without pain; but all the boys will be Werwolves, and all the girls Maras. By day the Werwolf has the human form, though he may be known by the meeting of his eyebrows above the nose. At a certain time of the night, he has the form of a dog on three legs. It is only when another person tells him that he is a Werwolf, or reproaches him with being such, that a man can be freed from the affliction.

*Not only the belief in, but the name also of the Werwolf, has been transplanted to Normandy, where it is called le Warou or Warwou.*

## The Mara

A peasant had a sweetheart, who, without being herself conscious of it, was a Mara, and came every night to the man, so that he soon saw how the case was. He therefore kept watch, and having discovered that she crept in to him through a little hole in the doorpost, he made a peg which fitted the hole, and when she came on the following night, he drove in the peg, so that she was compelled to remain within. She then assumed a human form, the man took her to wife, and they had many children. When many years had passed, and they were both advanced in life, it chanced one evening that the man cast his eye on the peg, which still remained in the hole, and asked his wife in joke whether she knew how she had entered the house? On her confessing her ignorance, he informed her, made himself right merry at the story, and even drew the peg out, that she might see in what manner she had entered. The woman then peeped through the hole, but as she peeped she became on a sudden quite small, passed out through it, and from that time was never more seen.

---

There was once in Jutland a queen who was a great lover of horses; she had one in particular to which she was most attached, and which occupied her thoughts both waking and dreaming. It frequently happened, when the groom entered the stable at night, that he found this horse out of order, and thence concluded that it had been ridden by the Mara. Taking therefore a bucket of cold water, he cast it over the horse, and at the same moment saw that the queen was sitting on its back.

## Mermen and Merwives

In the neighbourhood of Assens in Fyen there once appeared an incredible number of Mermen and Merwomen on the strand. Aged fishermen relate how they often and often have seen the Merwives sitting there on large stones out in the water, with children at the breast, which they quickly cast on their backs when, terrified at the approach of man, they darted down into the water. It is further related, that in those places sea-cows and sea-bulls have been seen to land in the fields, seeking intercourse with other cattle.

In the year 1619, King Christian IV sent two of his councillors, Old Rosenspar and Christian Holck, to Norway, there to hold a diet. On their return they captured a Merman. In form this Merman resembled a man. For a long time he rolled himself backwards and forwards, but at length lay as if he were dead. On one of the bystanders saying to him, 'It must, indeed, be a wonderful God that has such human creatures also in the water,' he answered, 'Yes! If thou knewest that as well as I, then mightest thou say so. But if ye do not instantly restore me to the water, neither the ship nor yourselves shall ever reach land.' After this he would not utter a word, but was placed in the boat, and thence sprang into the water.

---

Out in Nordstrand there dwells a Merwife, who once drove her cattle up on the seashore, and let them graze the whole day on Tibirke Mark. This did not at all please the peasantry thereabouts, who for ages have been notorious for their covetousness; they therefore took measures for intercepting the cattle, whereby they succeeded in driving the Merwife with all her herd into an enclosure near the town, from which they would not allow her to escape until she had paid them for pasturage on their lands. Having assured them that she had no money to give, they required her to give them the girdle she wore round her body, which appeared very costly and shone as with precious stones. There being no alternative, she redeemed herself and cattle by giving them the girdle. But as she was driving her cattle down to the shore, she said to her large bull, 'Rake up now!' Whereupon the animal began to throw up the earth with his horns and to cast up the sand along the seacoast; and as the wind now blew from the north-west, the sand was drifted in over the country towards the village of Tibirke, so that the church was nearly buried under it. Of the costly girdle, too, they had but a short-lived gratification, for on returning home and examining it more closely, it was found to consist of worthless rushes.

---

In the diocese of Aarhuus there once dwelt two poor people who had an only daughter named Margaret, or Grethe. One day when she had been sent down to the seaside to fetch sand, and was scooping it into her apron, a Merman rose from the water. His beard was greener than the salt sea, he was of comely aspect and spoke in friendly words to the girl, saying, 'Follow me, Grethe! I will give thee as much silver as thy heart can desire.' 'That would not be amiss,' answered she, 'for we have not much of that article at home.' So she suffered herself to be enticed, and he took her by the hand, and conducted her to the bottom of the ocean, where she became mother of five children.

After a long lapse of time, and when she had nearly forgotten her Christian belief, as she was sitting one holy-day morning, rocking her youngest child in her lap, she heard the church bells ringing above her, and was seized with a strong fit of melancholy and longing after church; and as she sat and sighed with the tears rolling down her cheeks, the Merman, observing her sorrow, inquired the cause of it. She then besought him earnestly, with many expressions of affection, to allow her once more to go to church. The Merman could not withstand her affliction, but conducted her up to land, repeatedly exhorting her to return quickly to her children. In the middle of the sermon the Merman came outside of the church and cried, 'Grethe! Grethe!' She heard him plainly enough, but resolved within herself that she would stay and hear the sermon out. When the sermon was ended the Merman came a second time to the church, crying, 'Grethe! Grethe! Art thou soon coming?' But she did not obey him. He came a third time, crying, 'Grethe! Grethe! Art thou soon coming? Thy children are longing after thee.' On finding that she did not come, he began to weep bitterly, and again descended to the bottom of the sea. But from that time Grethe continued with her parents, and let the Merman himself take care of the poor little children. His wail and lamentation are often to be heard from the deep.

*The foregoing forms the subject of the old Danish ballad 'Agnete og Havmanden' (Danske Viser, I, p. 313), also of two beautiful poems by Baggesen and Oehlenschlaeger.*

*In the Farö islands the superstition is current that the seal casts off its skin every ninth night, assumes a human form, and dances and amuses itself like a human being, until it resumes its skin, and again becomes a seal. It once happened that a man passing during one of these transformations, and seeing the skin, took possession of it, when the seal, which was a female, not finding her skin to creep into, was obliged to continue in a human form, and being a comely person, the man made her his wife, had several children by her, and they lived happily together, until, after a lapse of several years, she chanced to find her hidden skin, which she could not refrain from creeping into, and so became a seal again.*

*According to the old Danish ballad, a Mermaid foretold the death of Queen Dagmar, the wife of Valdemar II, surnamed Seier, or the Victorious. And in the Chronicle of Frederick II of Denmark we read the following story: 'In the year 1576 there came late in*

*the autumn a simple old peasant from Samsö to the court, then being held at Kallundborg,*
*who related that a beautiful female had more than once come to him while working in his*
*field by the seashore, whose figure from the waist downwards resembled that of a fish, and*
*who had solemnly and strictly enjoined him to go over and announce to the king, that as*
*God had blessed his queen so that she was pregnant of a son (afterwards Christian IV),*
*who should be numbered among the greatest princes of the North, and seeing that all sorts*
*of sins were gaining ground in his kingdom, he, in honour of and in gratitude to God who*
*had so blessed him, should with all earnestness and diligence wholly extirpate such sins,*
*lest God should hereafter visit him with his anger and punishment.'*

    *Tales of Mermaids are most complete in the Shetland isles. There, it is said, that 'they*
*dwell among the fishes, in the depth of the ocean, in habitations of pearl and coral; that*
*they resemble human beings, but greatly excel them in beauty. When they wish to visit the*
*upper world, they put on the ham or garb of some fish, but woe to those who lose their ham,*
*for then are all hopes of return annihilated, and they must stay where they are. Ve-Skeries*
*(the sacred rocks) are a very favourite place with the fair children of the sea, who,*
*undisturbed by men, here lay aside their ham, inspire the air of earth, and revel in the clear*
*moonlight. As ocean's green-haired beauties are mortal, they are often, on their excur-*
*sions, exposed to dangers; examples, indeed, are not wanting of their having been taken*
*and killed by superstitious fishermen. It has also happened that earthly men have married*
*Mermaids, having taken possession of their ham, and thus got them into their power'[1] A*
*case somewhat similar is that of Völund and his brothers and the three Valkyriur.*

## Changelings

A man and his wife were sorely troubled with a changeling that had been
left with them by the subterranean folk, who had carried off their genuine
child, that had not been baptised in time. This changeling conducted
himself in a most extraordinary way. When no one was present he was quite
obstreperous, would run along the wall, sit in the cockloft, and shout and
scream. But if anyone was in the room with him, he would sit drowsy at the
end of the table. He would eat as much as any four, and cared very little
about what was set before him, yet was never satisfied. After having long
thought how they should get rid of him, a shrewd female engaged to drive
him from the house. One day, when he was out in the fields, she killed a
pig, and made a pudding (sausage) of it, together with the skin and hair,
which, on his return, she placed before him. As was his custom, he began
slashing away at it, but as he ate he gradually became thoughtful, and at last
sat quite still with the knife in his hand and eyeing the pudding: he then
exclaimed, 'Pudding with hide, and pudding with hair, pudding with eyes
and pudding with bones in it. I have now seen thrice a young wood spring

1   Hibbert's *Shetland* quoted by Faye, pp. 60, 61; Thiele, op. cit., iii, p. 51.

up on Tiis lake, but never before did I see such a pudding! The fiend will stay here no longer!' Saying these words he ran off and never turned.

———

There dwelt in Christiansö a man and his wife who neglected to have their child christened in proper time, in consequence of which a subterranean woman exchanged it for her own babe, which was so miserable a being that it could neither eat nor drink, and must inevitably have perished, if the mother had not come every night to suckle it. Being greatly troubled and perplexed on account of this changeling, the woman at length hit on the following plan for getting rid of it. Having instructed her servant maid what she should ask and say, she heated the oven very hot, whereupon the girl, in a voice loud enough to be heard by the Troll-folk, said, 'Why do you heat the oven so hot, Mistress?' To which the woman answered, 'I am going to burn my child.' When the girl had asked this question three times, and received the same answer, she took the changeling and laid it on the peel, as if about to thrust it into the oven. At this moment the subterranean woman rushed in, took her child from the peel, and returned the woman her own, with these words, 'There is your child! I have done by it better than you have by mine.' And, in fact, the child was, as she said, both thriving and strong.

## How to Distinguish a Changeling

When a child is born, the lights in the lying-in chamber must not be extinguished; for otherwise the infant may easily be exchanged by the underground folk. At a place in North Jutland, it happened many years ago in a lying-in room that the mother could get no sleep while the lights were burning. So the husband resolved to take the child in his arm, in order to keep strict watch over it as long as it was dark in the room. But unfortunately he fell asleep without having noticed in which arm he held his child, and on being waked by a shake of the arm, he saw a tall woman standing by the bed, and found that he had an infant in each arm. The woman instantly vanished, but there he lay, without knowing which of the two children was his own. In this difficulty he went to the priest, who advised him to get a wild stallion colt, which would enable him to discover the right one. They accordingly procured such a wild colt, which was so unmanageable that three men could hardly lead it; then laid both infants wrapped up on the ground, and led the colt to smell to them. And it was curious to see how the colt each time that it smelt to the one, would lick it and was quite quiet, while every time that it smelt to the other it was restive and strove to kick the infant. By this method it was ascertained infallibly which was the changeling. While they were standing, there came suddenly a tall woman running, who snatched up the changeling and disappeared with it.

*The Scots too, had their changelings, though they appear to have been of a far more social character than those of Scandinavia; at least if we may judge from the jovial little fellow described in Chambers* (Pop. Rh. p. 55). *A gudewife, named Tibbie Dickson, having occasion to go to the town of Dunse, left her babe (a changeling) in the care of her neighbour, Wullie Grieve, the tailor. 'So Wullie sits doon at the fire, and awa' wi' her yarn gaes the wife; but scarce had she steekit the door, an' wan half-way down the closs, whan the bairn cocks up on its doup in the cradle, and rounds in Wullie's lug, "Wullie Tyler, an ye winna tell my mither whan she comes back, I'se play ye a bonnie spring on the bagpipes." . . . So he rounds again in the bairn's lug, "Play up, my duo (dove), an' I'se tell naebody." Wi' that, the fairy ripes amang the cradle strae, an' poos oot a pair o' pipes, sic as tyler Wullie ne'er had seen in a' his days – muntit wi' ivory, an' gold, an' silver, an' dymonts, an' what not . . . Wullie had nae great goo o' his performance; so he sits thinkin to himself – "This maun be a deil's get; an' I ken weel hoo to treat them; an' gin I while the time awa, Auld Waughorn himsel may come to rock his son's cradle, an' play me some foul prank;" so he catches the bairn by the cuff o' the neck, and whupt him into the fire, bagpipes and a'!' Surely this little fellow did not deserve so cruel a fate.*[1]

*Of another changeling it is related that, on seeing a huge fire kindled, with an eggshell boiling on it, having one end of a measuring rod set in it, he crept out of the cradle on his hands, while his legs still remained in the cradle, and thus, stretching himself out longer and longer, he at length reached quite across the floor up the chimney, when he exclaimed: 'Well! seven times have I seen the wood fall in Lessö forest, but never until now have seen so big a ladle in such a little pot!*[2]

*Methods nearly similar of getting rid of a changeling are, with some modifications, amazingly widespread throughout almost the whole of Europe. In the Irish tradition, the boy, on seeing the eggshells, exclaims, 'Fifteen hundred years have I been in the world, yet have never seen that before.' Walter Scott* (Minstrelsy, ii. p. 173), *quoting 'A Pleasant Treatise on Witchcraft', relates of a woman who, to ascertain whether her child were a changeling, was advised to break a dozen eggs, and place the twenty-four half shells before it, then to go out and listen at the door; for if the child spoke, it was a changeling. She did accordingly, and heard it say, 'Seven years old was I when I came to the nurse, and four years have I lived since, and never saw so many milk-pans before.' See also Waldron's Isle of Man, and Grimm,* Deutsche Mythologie, *p. 438, for other accounts. Similar stories are told of Highland-Scot and French changelings.*

*Various monstrous charms were resorted to in Scotland, for procuring the restoration of a child that had been so stolen; the most efficacious of which was supposed to be the roasting of the supposititious child upon the live embers, when, it was believed, it would vanish, and the true infant appear in the place whence it had been originally abstracted.*[3]

---

1    For other accounts, see Keightley, op, cit., p. 355.
2    Asbjörnsen, op. cit., ii, 165.
3    Scott's *Minstrelsy*, ii, 172.

# The Devil

## 1 – Friar Ruus

It is related that the devil once seeing how piously and virtuously the
monks lived in the convent of Esrom,[1] assumed a human form, and
knocked at the gate of the convent for admission, saying his name was
Ruus. He gave himself out for a scullion, and was received by the abbot as
such. Being one day alone with the head cook, he resisted his authority, for
which he received chastisement. At this he was sorely exasperated, and
having just then a kettle of boiling water on the fire, he seized the head
cook with all his might and set him on his head in the kettle; then ran out
crying and lamenting the calamity that had befallen his master. Thus by his
falsehood he deceived all the brethren in the convent, so that they
regarded him as free from all suspicion and appointed him their head
cook. Now this was precisely what Ruus had been aiming at, in order that
he might corrupt the whole of the monks together. He now prepared
viands so rich and delicate, that the monk forgot both prayer and fasting
and resigned himself to luxury. It is even said that he introduced women
into the convent, and thereby gained great favour with the abbot, who at
length prevailed on him to enter the fraternity, as he wished to have such
a cook constantly at hand. From that hour strife and wickedness so gained
the upper hand in the convent that it would inevitably have fallen into the
power of the evil one, if the brethren had not repented in time. For one day
Brother Ruus, being in the forest, saw there a beautiful fat cow, which he
slaughtered and took a quarter of it to the convent; the remainder he hung
up in a tree. When the owner of the cow missed it, and discovered three
quarters of it hanging in the tree, he determined to keep watch in another
tree, for the purpose of detecting the thief, when he came to fetch the rest.
By this means he discovered how the devils played their pranks in the
forest, and heard at the same time much talk about Friar Ruus, how he
would invite the abbot and monks to a banquet in hell. The peasant being
naturally exceedingly terrified at all this, went on the following day to the
abbot, to whom he related all he had heard and seen in the forest. On
hearing this, the abbot summoned all the monks to meet him in the
church, where they began to read and sing, so that Ruus, who could not
endure either, endeavoured to sneak away; but the abbot seized him by the
cowl and conjured him into a red horse, committing him to the power of
hell. For many years after this event, Friar Ruus's iron pot and gridiron
were shown in the convent of Esrom.

1    Formerly a celebrated monastery in the north of Seeland, not far from
Fredensborg.

*Before the conventual church was turned into a dwelling, the effigies of Friar Ruus and his epitaph, half Latin and half Danish, were to be seen there. His epitaph ran thus:*

> Hic jacet *John Praest, (John priest)*
> Qui dedit suum *graa Hest (grey horse)*
> Nec non de siligine *tue Laest, (two lasts)*
> Semper comedebat *det Baest, (the best)*
> Requiescit in pulvere *sud west. (south-west).*

To the foregoing, Molbech, in his *Ungdomsvandringer*, adds that 'the abbot afterwards constrained him to proceed to England, and without intermission to return, bringing with him, through the air, as much lead as amounted to 320,000 pounds weight, for the roof of the convent.'

## 2 – The Devil at Cards

Once on a Christmas Eve a set of profane gamesters were sitting in Lemvig playing at cards for large sums, and as they became more and more excited by loss and gain, they became at the same time more and more unrestrained in their abominable cursing and swearing. When the night was somewhat advanced, a knocking at the door was heard, and a well-dressed man entered, who begged permission to join the party. Having seated himself, he took the cards and began by losing a considerable sum. While they were thus sitting and playing, a card fell on the floor, and when one of the party, having taken a light, crept under the table to pick it up, he saw that claws protruded from the stranger's boots, whence it was evident that he was no other than the foul fiend, of whom it is well known that he can conceal everything except his claws. At this discovery, a messenger was instantly despatched to fetch the priest, who came and found the stranger still at the table, where he sat counting his money. The priest, who was a sagacious man, knew him instantly, and commanded him to depart; but the fiend answered, that the men by their gambling and swearing had called him, and that he would not go before he had tasted warm blood. The priest thereupon took a little dog, that was running about the room, and threw it to him, which he eagerly tore in pieces and devoured, excepting three hairs, which he was obliged to leave behind. The priest having thus satisfied him, bored a hole with an awl in the lead of one of the windows, and commanded him to make himself little and pass through it; because if he passed out by the door, he could quickly enter again by the same way. This cost the priest much trouble; but he pressed him so hard with reading and exorcisms, that he was at length compelled to obey, though he howled so loud that it was heard over the whole town.

## 3 – A Scholar Assigns Himself to the Devil

There was once a scholar in the school of Herlufsholm,[1] who through the devil's craft was seduced to give himself up to his power and will. He therefore wrote a contract on a strip of paper with his own blood, and stuck it in a hole in the church wall. But for the salvation of his sinful soul, which the fiend would else have seized, it happened that another scholar of the school found the paper and took it to the rector. Now nothing was to be done, but to have recourse to many prayers, whereby the devil's cunning was turned to naught; but it was long impossible to close up the hole in the wall so effectually that it was not immediately found open again.

## 4 – The Devil's Footstep

In a field near Sonneröd there is a row of stones, among which one has on it the mark of a footstep. Of this it is related, that the devil once rested his foot on it when he had carried a bride away from her bridegroom, and was obliged to wander far and wide with her before he could find a man, who for a hatfull of money would take the bridal wreath from her head; for as long as she had that on he had no power over her, the bridesmaids having placed it on her head in the name of Jesus.

## 5 – Jens Plovgaard

In Söndre-Nissum, near Ringkiöbing,[2] there dwelt a man named Jens Plovgaard, who was in league with the devil, and could therefore raise the dead and perform other feats of the kind, whereby he gained a considerable sum of money. But for this he was, on the other hand, after a certain number of years, to belong to the evil one. One day when he was absent from home, a fisherman from Thy came to ascertain what had become of a swine, but not meeting with Jens Plovgaard, and it being late, he slipped into the barn to sleep till the following morning, when he could accomplish his errand. In the middle of the night Jens returned home, who, on hearing that a man from Thy had been there to make inquiry of him concerning a lost swine, would immediately consult 'Eric',[3] and for that purpose went into the barn to raise him. The man, who was still awake, heard plainly how the devil was forced to obey. Jens asked him about the swine, but Eric would not utter a syllable, for he had observed that they were not alone;

---

1 Of Herlufsholm school see hereafter.
2 A small town on the west coast of Jutland.
3 The devil, like our 'old Harry', which is probably a corruption of the Danish term.

while Jens, on the other hand, ascribed his silence to sheer obstinacy, and therefore took his iron whip, with which he belaboured the fiend until he told him that the swine lay under an earth-slip, and described the place most accurately. When the fisherman heard this, he spared Jens Plovgaard all further trouble, and on his return dug in the slip, and found his swine.

The time at length arrived when the fiend, according to their compact, was to fetch Jens Plovgaard, who caused himself to be placed in a large cask together with an ample provision of meat and drink. This cask he caused to be buried in a field which was afterwards ploughed and sown. When the devil now came he could get no power over him, but ran backwards and forwards on the field every night for three weeks, and at last howled so terrifically that he might have been heard on the other side of the fiord as far as Ulfborg church. At the expiration of the three weeks Jens Plovgaard was free, and caused himself to be dug up; and from that time there was no man in the whole parish so pious as he; but his great cunning he possessed no longer.

## 6 – How the Devil Allowed Himself to be Outwitted

In Jutland there was once a priest who knew more than his Paternoster. One evening there came a message to him from the manor-house, requiring his attendance there with the least delay possible, his aid being quite indispensable. The fact was that the proprietor, in order to attain to his vast riches, had sold himself to the devil, who was already there to fetch him, his time being expired. The priest, who arrived at the house just at the moment when the fiend was about to depart with the master, endeavoured to prevail on him to grant a further delay, first a year, then a month – a week – a day, but not even an hour would the fiend grant him. There stood on the table a little stump of wax candle nearly burnt out, pointing to which the priest said, 'Thou wilt surely let him live as long as that stump lasts?' To this the fiend assented, but at the same moment the priest seizing the light, blew it out and put it into his pocket; so that for the present the fiend was obliged to leave the proprietor in peace, but who from that hour so amended his life that the devil got him not.

*A similar artifice with a wax candle occurs in* Norma Gest's Saga, *whereby Norma Gest attains to an age of many hundred years. In the* Popular Traditions and Tales of Poland, *we find the devil allowing himself to be tricked in the same manner. See also* 'The Devil outwitted' *in* Netherlandish Popular Traditions.

## 7 – The Lady of Kiölbygaard

On the road from Aalborg[1] to Thisted, through Östrel, there lies in a valley on the left a mansion called Kiölbygaard, in which there once dwelt a very rich lady, but who was as wicked as she was rich, and was, moreover, devoted to sorcery. One of her greatest delights was to hear that there were carousings and gaming at the inn on Sundays. Among the servants of the mansion there was one that stood high above others in her favour, to whom she frequently showed a large chest containing silver money, telling him that he might take as much of it as he would, but he was never able to raise a single piece from the chest. When he sometimes said that he wished he had so much money, because life must then be so joyous and pleasant, she always answered with a sigh, 'Yes, true! Were there no horrid death!'

One night one of her tenants came to the mansion to pay his rent, but found all in darkness, the family being in bed. He walked about the place until he came to a small apartment, in which he saw a light. On the middle of the floor he perceived a half-bushel measure, and immediately a dog of ferocious aspect entered the room, approached the measure and barked into it, and every time he barked there fell from his mouth several pieces of silver money into the measure, nor did he leave the place before it was quite full. A great desire now came over the man to take some of these silver coins, and he accordingly helped himself to thirty new pieces and put them into his purse. In the morning he went to the lady to pay his rent; but when she saw the new money, she declared that it had been taken from her. The man then told her what he had seen in the night, whereupon she was so terrified that she bestowed on him the farm which he had held on lease, in order to secure his silence as to what he had witnessed as long as he lived.

When this lady had for many years been leading so unrighteous a life, she one evening ordered her coachman to put the horses to, as she wished to take a drive. The man objected that it was so dark that he could not find the way, but she answered that the horses knew it well enough. She then for more than two hours rode over stock and stone, until the horses stopped before an illuminated mansion which the man had never observed before. They drove in, the lady alighted and went into the saloon which was illuminated. In the meanwhile, the man waited with the carriage. After a considerable time had elapsed he stole up to the window and peeped in, and saw his mistress sitting on the middle of the floor undressed; by her side a pile was burning, and a man stood combing her hair. Immediately after the man received orders to drive home, but from that hour no one ever saw the lady more, and the coachman's belief was that she was on that night conveyed to hell. Her family, it is true, gave out that she returned

1    A considerable town in Jutland.

home, and immediately after sickened and died; while others asserted that at her pompous funeral the coffin contained only a wisp of straw.

## 8 – A Feast with the Devil

In Östrel there once dwelt a man who entertained the suspicion that his wife was a witch, and one St John's eve resolved to remove his doubts by watching whether she went to the devil's banquet. At night therefore he kept an eye on her movements, and saw her take from a drawer a small phial of ointment which she rubbed over a peel, then setting herself astride on the peel, she said, 'Now in the devil's name!' and immediately at full speed flew up through the chimney. Hereupon the man did as he had seen his wife do, and flew after her on another peel, and at length descended in a mansion, in which there was a room brilliantly illuminated and full of people. On his entrance he saw the devil going round and the witches sitting at table, at the head of which sat his own wife. The devil then came to him and inquired his business, to which he answered that he had followed his wife. 'Old Eric' then handed him a book that he might inscribe his name in it, which he did, but adding the words 'in the name of God'. When the fiend saw what he had written he uttered a howl, and the whole mansion fell down. On the following morning the man found himself in a hole out in the fields, among a heap of human bones; but his wife he never saw again.

――――――

A girl once by chance saw her mistress take a pot from the cupboard in which there was an ointment, with which she had no sooner anointed a broomstick, than with the broomstick between her legs she flew away up the chimney. The girl, full of wonder at what she had seen, took the same pot out of the cupboard to see what it contained, and rubbed a little of the ointment on a brewing vat, when instantaneously she with the vat also flew up through the chimney straightways to the Blocksberg, where there was a numerous assemblage of old women with bass-viols and fiddles before them. The devil himself, whom they called Old Eric, when he had danced out a polonaise and paid the musicians, came to the girl with a book, in which he desired her to write her name; but she, instead of her name, first wrote the words with which it is usual to try the pen: 'Den, som mig föder', etc.; the devil, consequently, was unable to take the book back, and would not dance again the whole evening, although he had previously been never off the floor. Early on the following morning, which was St John's day, all the old dames rode back on their broomsticks, and the girl in her brewing vat, until they came to a brook, across which the old women sprang very nimbly; but the girl hesitated and thought within herself, 'It surely won't do to make such a jump with a brewing vat.' But at last she said, 'I can at any rate try.' So giving the vat a kick, it sprang as lightly as the broomsticks themselves; at which the girl laughing, exclaimed, 'That was a devil of a jump for a brewing vat!' But scarcely had she uttered the devil's name when the vat stopped, the book was away, and the good lass had to find her way back to Thisted on foot.

## The Book of Cyprianus

Cyprianus was a student, and by nature a gentle and orderly person, but he had passed through the Black School in Norway, and was therefore engaged to the devil to apply his learning and extraordinary faculties to the perpetration of evil. This grieved him in his latter years, his heart being good and pious; so to make the evil good again, he wrote a book, wherein he first shows how evil is to be done, and then how it may be remedied. The book begins by explaining what sorcery is, and with a warning against it. It is divided into three heads, viz. Cyprianus, Dr Faustus, and Jacob Ramel. The last two parts are written in characters which are said to be Persian or Arabic, and also in ordinary characters. In this book are taught exorcising, laying and raising of spirits, and all that of which mention is made in the 5th book of Moses, xviii. 10; 11, 12. Whether this book has been printed is uncertain, but manuscript copies of it are concealed here and there among the common people, who regard it as something sacred. Those who possess the book of Cyprianus need never want money, they can read the devil to them and from them, and no one can harm them, not even the devil himself. But whoever possesses the book cannot get rid of it; for whether he sells, burns or buries it, it will come back; and if a person cannot dispose of it before his death, it will go badly with him. The only method is to write his name in it in his own blood, and lay it in a secret place in the church, together with four shillings clerk's fee.

---

The following is the German tradition of Cyprianus:

In ancient times there lived in one of the Danish isles a man named Cyprianus, who was worse than the devil; consequently, after he was dead and gone to hell, he was again cast forth by the devil and replaced on his isle. There he wrote nine books, in the old Danish tongue, on witchcraft and magical spells. Whosoever has read all these nine books through becomes the property of the devil. From the original work three (or nine) copies are said to have been made by a monk, and mutilated copies of these to have been dispersed all over the world. A count, who resided in the castle of Ploen,[1] is said to have possessed a perfect copy, which he

---

1    The count here alluded to was, no doubt, Duke Hans Adolf of Holstein-Ploen, who was a great magician, and was finally carried off by the devil, through a window, though the matter was hushed up. He lived in the seventeenth century.

caused to be fastened with chains and buried under the castle; because in reading through eight books he was so troubled and terrified that he resolved on concealing it from the sight of the world. One of these books still exists in Flensborg,[1] Some spells from the nine books are still known among aged people. Whoever wishes to be initiated therein must first renounce his Christianity.

Two miles from Horsens[2] there dwelt a miller, who was a master in the black art and possessed the book of Cyprianus. A peasant having once stolen an axe from him, was obliged to bring it back at midnight, and was, moreover, borne so high in the air that his feet rattled among the tops of the trees in Bierre forest. This miller in fact performed so many wonderful things that all his neighbours were astonished at his feats. Impelled by curiosity, a journeyman miller once slipped into his master's private room, where having found an old quaint-looking volume, he began to read in it, when the horrible Satan appeared before him and asked his commands. The man, who was not aware that it was necessary to give the fiend some stiff job to execute, fell down in terror deprived of speech, and it would, no doubt, have been all over with him, had not his master entered at the moment and seen how matters stood. Snatching up the book, the miller instantly began to read in another place, in order, if possible, to drive the fiend away; but things had already gone too far, and nothing remained to be done but to give him something to do, so taking a sieve, he commanded him to bale water with it from the millpond; but being unable to do so, he was obliged to take his departure through the air, and left behind him a most loathsome stench.

*Cyprian's book is also known in Normandy, where a similar story is told under the title of* Le Grimoire du Curé. *Calderon has made Cyprian the hero of one of his dramas, in which he appears as a native of Antioch.*

## Of Witches

On St John's eve the witches, as it is generally known, have a meeting with 'Old Eric', though it rarely happens that others are witnesses of the spectacle.

In Giörding near Ribe[3] there was once a serving-man, who on that night

---

1   A considerable town in Sleswig.
2   A considerable town in Jutland.
3   A city on the west side of Jutland, with a fine old cathedral, said to be the first church in Denmark. The early kings frequently kept their court at Ribe.

placed a green turf on his head, that he might be invisible to the witches, and so slipped into the churchyard. While standing quite secure and looking at the wonderful witch-dance round Old Eric, who sat in the middle, it happened that one of the women came quite close to him, when, in springing aside, the turf fell from his head. In an instant he became visible to all the witches, who started off in pursuit of him, and had not the priest happened to be standing just without his gate, he would hardly have escaped falling into their clutches.

––––––––––

In a certain house everything went perversely; for which reason the inhabitants sent to a well-known wise woman. She came and went about the house both within and without. At last she stood still before a large stone, which lay just without the dwelling. 'This,' said she, 'should be rolled away.' But all that they could do with levers and other means was to no purpose: the stone would not move. At length the wise woman herself hobbled up to the stone, and scarcely had she touched it before it moved from its old station. Beneath was found a silken purse filled with the claws of cocks and eagles, human hair and nails. 'Put it into the fire together with a good bundle of pea-straw, that it may catch quickly,' said the old woman; and no sooner was this said than done. But the moment the fire began to take effect it began to howl and hiss as if the very house were ready to fall, and people who stood out in the fields hard by plainly saw a witch sally forth on her broomstick from the mouth of the oven. At the same moment the old woman died, who, it was supposed, had bewitched the house, and all the sorcery was at an end.

––––––––––

In the neighbourhood of Östrel a man served at a farm, the mistress of which unknown to him was a witch. Although she gave him good and wholesome food, he never thrived, but became thinner every day. At this being much troubled, he went to a wise man, to whom he communicated his case. From this man he learned that his mistress was a witch, and that at night, while he slept, she transformed him into a horse, and rode upon him to Troms church in Norway; so that it was not to be wondered at that his strength decreased. The wise man at the same time gave him an ointment with which to rub his head at night; then when he fell asleep he would have a violent itching on his head, when he would wake and see that he was standing outside of Troms church. The man did as he had been directed, and on waking the following night, he was standing by Troms church holding a bridle in his hand, which he had torn off in scratching his head; and behind him he saw many horses bound together by each other's tail. When he had for some time stood thus without the church door, his mistress came out and cast a friendly look at him; but he nodded for her to come nearer, and when she came he cast the bridle over her head, when instantly she was transformed into a handsome mare. He then mounted the mare and rode homewards. On his way he called at a farrier's and caused him to put four new shoes on the mare. On reaching home, he told his master that he had been out to buy a capital mare, which would go well with the one he already had. The master bought her of him for a good round sum; but when he took the bridle off, the mare disappeared and the mistress stood in her place with new horseshoes on her hands and feet. Then the man related all that had taken place; the wife was in consequence turned out of doors, and never got the horseshoes off her hands and feet.

*The North Germans have a story (The Witch with the bridle) very nearly resembling the foregoing. Müllenhoff, op. cit., No. 310.*

---

In Östrel there was at one time a vast number of witches. A huntsman, who was in the habit of passing by the farm of Baller, always observed in the neighbourhood either a hare or a wild duck; yet, notwithstanding that he shot (and was a sure shot), he never could hit either the one or the other. He once saw a duck lying in the water close by the farm, at which he shot many times, but the duck remained quite still and seemed not to notice the firing. As now neither shot nor slug would hit it, he cut a silver button from his jacket, said three *Aves* over it and put it into his piece. Now he hit the duck, which, however, flew out of the water into the farm, and hid itself in the poultry-house. The huntsman followed and told the people, who were sitting at supper, what he had done, and demanded the duck he had shot. The master told him he might go into the kitchen and speak to the servant maid, who would see to get him his duck. When he entered the kitchen there sat an ugly old beldam by the chimney, with only one shoe on, while the blood was running down her leg. She said she had fallen down and cut herself but the huntsman knew instantly that it was the witch that he had shot, and hurried out of the place with all possible speed.

---

At Bröndsted Mark, in the diocese of Ribe, there is shown a spot near the forest, where in former days a castle is said to have stood. In this castle dwelt a lady who was a witch, and one day when all the men of Bröndsted were at the chase, she, in the form of a hare, it is said, kept constantly teasing and tantalising them, until an old peasant, wiser than the others, took a silver button, loaded his piece with it, and shot the hare in the leg. The following day it was rumoured that the lady was sick. She never appeared again.

---

Two men from Svendstrup near Aalborg went out one night to shoot hares in the churchyard. For this purpose they stationed themselves in the church tower, expecting that game of some sort would appear, but in vain. At midnight, however, a swarm of hares burst forth from all the graves; but although the men at first ventured to shoot at them, not a single one fell, and their number so increased that the whole churchyard was completely hidden under their countless multitude. The men were then seized with a sudden terror, and with difficulty escaped unscathed.

*On Bornholm it is related that the witches make a kind of hare of old legs of stockings, with three harrow-prongs instead of legs. These hares, which they call 'smörbarrer', are sent by the witches to fetch milk from their neighbours' cattle. Hares used by the witches to milk cattle are also known in Sweden.*

---

In the parish of Vissenberg in Fyen there was once a woman who was generally regarded as a witch. When at the point of death, she could not divest herself of life; but another cunning woman, who was present, advised that straw should be placed under the chair in which the dying woman sat; for if she were a witch, she must die immediately afterwards, this means having never been known to fail. This advice was followed and the woman died shortly after.

## The Ship-master of Aarhuus[1] and the Finlap

A shipmaster from Aarhuus was once lying at Drontheim, where he formed an acquaintance with a Finlap, who often came on board to visit him. This Finlap, who could perform many sorceries, offered, among other things, to teach the shipmaster how to procure a wind. This, thought the skipper, might be very convenient, and the next day the Finlap brought a bag with him, which he placed outside the cabin, saying, that he needed only to take that with him, and he could make any wind. But the shipmaster on reflection would have no concern with it, suspecting that it came from the devil. The Finlap then asked him whether he wished to know how his wife and children were. On the skipper answering in the affirmative, the Finlap immediately fell down on the deck as if dead. After some time he rose, saying, 'I have been to Aarhuus. Thy wife was sitting drinking coffee; the others were also in good health, though one of the children had been ill. That thou mayest believe my words – dost thou know this?' at the same time handing him a silver spoon. 'This,' said the other, 'thou hast taken from my house in Aarhuus.' And so saying took the spoon and kept it.

---

1  A city on the east coast of Jutland, with a spacious old cathedral.

After they had been lying some time at Drontheim, the Finlap one morning said, 'Tomorrow we shall be under sail, and shall both have a good wind, although you are going southward and I northward. And I will further tell you that you will not go to Christiania fiord, to purchase a lading, as you think; but will get a better freight than you expect.' On the following morning both were under sail, and the wind changed so that the Jutlander had a fair wind for twelve hours, and afterwards the Fin for twelve hours. When off the isles of Öster-Riis the wind for the Jutlander was directly adverse, so that after having beaten about for nights and days, he was at last obliged to seek a port in the Öster-Riis islands. There one merchant outbid another in their offers of freight, but being eastward bound for a cargo, he declined their proposals, until a merchant at length offered him a freight to the Issefiord which almost equalled the value of a whole lading. This he could not withstand, but wrote to his owners, that for weighty considerations he had not followed their orders, an announcement which among the parties interested in Aarhuus excited the suspicion that he had lost his wits. On his arrival home after this trip, and when just stepping on shore, being questioned about his freight, he answered, 'I have it in my fob.' This proved highly satisfactory. On coming home to his wife, he inquired, 'How are all here?' 'Well,' was the answer. 'Has anyone been ill?' 'Yes, the young one.' 'Have you lost anything?' 'No – yes – no.' 'Think again.' 'Yes, a silver spoon.' 'There it is,' said the skipper, laying it on the table.

## Of Frit Skud

To acquire 'Frit Skud', that is, always to hit the mark aimed at, some lay certain prayers or secret words under the chamber of the piece. Others effect the same by letting the wind on a Thursday morning blow into the barrel. Such certain shooters are in league either with the evil one or with the wild huntsman, and whether they shoot to the east or to the west, their shot always brings them game of some kind.

On the manor of Thiele in Jutland there was once an old keeper, who often when out sporting, especially when he was rather drunk, would turn the piece backwards and fire it off; and he never did so without bringing down game.

## Traditions of Spectres

### 1 – The Flying Huntsman

All over the country a terrific apparition makes its appearance, of which everyone who has either seen or heard it speaks with shuddering. It occurs at various times that a rushing and buzzing, a shouting and uproar, a cracking and rattling are heard in the air, precisely as if a hunting party, with echoing horns, dogs with outstretched necks, and wild huntsmen, were galloping through the fields and forests. It is THE FLYING HUNTSMAN, says the peasant, laying himself on his face on the earth, or hiding himself behind a tree, until the hellish band has passed.

### 2 – Grön-jette

On the west side of Möen there is a forest called Grönvaeld, in which Grön-Jette (Green-giant[1]) hunts every night on horseback, with his head under his left arm, a spear in his hand, and many hounds around him. At harvest time the peasants leave a bundle of oats for his horse, that it may not trample down their grain in the night. Grönsund is named from him, as Phanefiörd is called after Phane, his betrothed. Near Frendrup a large stone is to be seen, which is said to have been Grön-Jette's sleeping place; and in the parish of Aastrup on Falster[2] are several mounds, in which those whom Grön-Jette has slain with his spear lie buried. But Grön-Jette and Phane lie buried on Harbölle Mark, in Stege parish, where a giant-grave is shown, a hundred and seventy ells long.

One night when Grön-Jette was hunting in Borre-Skov, he stopped his horse before Henrik Fyenboe's door, knocked, and ordered him to hold his dogs. He then rode away, Henrik Fyenboe standing in the meanwhile at his door holding the dogs for two hours. At length Grön-Jette returned with a mermaid lying across his horse, which he had shot, and said to the peasant, 'After her I have been hunting these seven years; but now I got her down by Falster.' He then asked for something to drink, having got which, he handed a gold coin to Henrik Fyenboe, which burnt a hole through his hand and disappeared on the earth. The huntsman then laughing said, 'Now thou canst say that Grön-Jette has held out his hand to thee. But that

---

1   The first component of this name Grimm (*Deutsche Mythologie*, op. cit., p. 896) considers to be the O. Nor. Grön (beard), and the entire name as identical with the O. Nor. Graniötunn, *the bearded giant,* without any allusion to the colour of his clothing.
2   One of the small Danish islands near Möen.

thou mayest not say that I have drunk at thy cost, take the band with which thou hast held the dogs.' He thereupon rode away, and Henrik took the band, which he long held under lock and key, and from that time increased in affluence; but at length, when he thought little of it, he became poorer than he had ever been, and died in great misery.

*In former times it was a superstition in Möen to leave a sheaf standing of the last stack that was housed; but at a later period, that the last sheaf of oats that was bound up should be thrown into the field with these words: 'This is for the Jöde of Upsala; this he shall have for his horse on Christmas Eve.' They believed that if they neglected this, their cattle would die. In Norway the custom prevailed of setting a sheaf on a pole for the birds, on Christmas Eve.*

## 3 – Palne-jaeger or Palne the Hunter

Like as King Valdemar hunts by night in Seeland does Palne the Hunter[1] hunt in Fyen; and it is related that a man, who, about a hundred years since, dwelt near Odense, once fell in with him. For when this man was one night gone with his people to bind barley, there came to him a tall and comely female, who asked, 'Have ye seen anything of Palne-Jaeger?' And on their answering that they had not seen him, she hastened through the wood. But an hour had scarcely elapsed when Palne-Jaeger came to the same people, with helmet and waving plume on his head, a bow on his left and a quiver on his right shoulder, and sandals on his feet. He inquired, 'Have ye seen anything of Langpatte?' And when they had given him the best intelligence they could, he hastened after her. He did not, however, catch her that night, as the same happened to the harvest people on the night following.

Every new year's night Palne-Jaeger fetches three horseshoes from one or other smithy in Fyen, and the smiths forget not to lay them ready for him on the anvil, as he always leaves three golden horseshoes in their stead. But if he comes to any smithy and does not find shoes, he removes the anvil, as it once happened to a smith in Korup, whose huge anvil Palne-Jaeger moved up into the tower of Seden church, whence the smith had great difficulty in getting it down again.

## 4 – Horns Jaeger

In the neighbourhood of Aarhuus Horns Jaeger hunts by night, to extirpate all the Elf-wives. Early one morning a man from Lyngen, who was out in the

1   Palnatoki, the founder of Jomsborg.

field to remove his horses, heard with terror a rustling in the air, and immediately saw a man on horseback coming towards him. It was Horns Jaeger, and he had with him three hounds bound with a silken cord. 'Hold my dogs,' cried he to the terrified peasant, and then again rode off; but returned shortly after, having two Elf-wives hanging across the horse's neck, who were bound together by their long hair. 'Give me my dogs now,' cried he to the peasant, 'and hold forth thy hand for drink-money.' The man did so, but the huntsman only put the end of three fingers into his hand, and having thus burnt him, rode away with the two howling Elf-wives.

## 5 – Jons Jaeger

In the neighbourhood of Aalborg Jons Jaeger often rides through the air, followed by a number of hounds that run on the earth. Whoever meets him must lie down flat, else he would be sick afterwards. Sometimes this huntsman may be heard calling his dogs with a horrid scream. If he happens to pass over a house in which two doors opposite each other stand open, his dogs pass through them; and if, at the same time, brewing or baking is going on in the house, it will all be spoiled.

## 6 – King Abel's Hunt

In Sleswig it is the Danish king Abel, the fratricide, that leads the Wild-hunt, who in an expedition against the Frieslanders (AD 1252) sank into a deep morass as he was fording the Eyder, where, being encumbered with the weight of his armour, he was slain. His body was buried in the cathedral, but his spirit found no rest. The canons dug up the corpse, and buried it in a morass near Gottorp, 'but in the place where he is buried and the neighbourhood, even within our own memory, horrid sounds and shrieks are heard, by which travellers by night are often terrified and rendered almost lifeless. Many persons worthy of credit relate and affirm that they have heard sounds so resembling a huntsman's horn, that anyone would say that a hunter was hunting there, and which the usual night-watch at Gottorp have frequently heard. It is, indeed, the general rumour that Abel has appeared to many in our time, black of aspect, riding on a small horse, and accompanied by three hounds, which appear to he burning like fire.'[1]

King Abel was buried in St Peter's church at Sleswig, but on account of his cruel fratricide he could find no rest in the grave. By night he haunted the church and disturbed the monks at their prayers, so that at length it

---

1   J. Cypraei, *Ann. Episcopor. Slesv.*, p. 267, quoted by Thiele, op. cit., i, p. 187

was found necessary to take up his body and sink it in a morass near Gottorp. To keep him in the grave, a sharp stake was driven down in the earth through him. The place is still known by the name of the king's grave. He nevertheless rides every night on a black horse, accompanied by a leash of dogs. Then is to he heard a slamming of gates, besides a terrific shouting and screaming, so that all who hear it are struck with fear.

Some ropemakers in Sönderborg once undertook to stop him, by stretching a rope across the street; but when he came, everything gave way before him.

*In Sweden, when a noise, like that of carriages and horses, is heard by night, the people say: 'Odin is passing by.'*[1]

## 7 – King Valdemar's Hunt

In Seeland it is King Valdemar[2] who rides, of whom a story is told similar to one related of Charlemagne. King Valdemar loved a lady from Rügen named Tovelille,[3] at whose death his sorrow was so great that he could not quit her corpse, but had it carried with him whithersoever he went. This being found inconvenient to those about the king, one of the courtiers seized a favourable moment to ascertain what it was that so attracted him to the dead body. He found on her finger an enchanted ring, which had been placed there by her mother, that even after death she might retain the love of Valdemar. The courtier took the ring from her finger, and the king's affection was instantly transferred from the dead lady to himself, who had retained the ring in his possession; so that whatever was to be done was to be done by or through him. This at length becoming exceedingly irksome to him, and as he knew that it was to the ring he was indebted for the king's favour, he threw it into a marsh as he was one day riding through Gurre wood. From that moment the king began to find more pleasure in the wood than in any other place. He caused the castle of Gurre to be built, and hunted in the wood day and night; at the same time it became a habit with him to utter the words which afterwards proved his curse: that God was welcome to keep heaven, if he might only hunt in Gurre.

He now rides every night from Burre to Gurre, and is known over all the

1   Geijer, *Sv. Rikes Häft.*, i, p. 268.
2   Valdemar IV of Denmark, surnamed Atterdag; he reigned from 1334 to 1375, and was the last male descendant of King Svend Estrithson, the nephew of Cnut the Great, by his sister Estrith, married to Ulf Jan.
3   Tovelille, i.e. the little dove. In like manner, Christian the Second's celebrated mistress was called Dyveke, signifying the same in Low German. She was of Dutch extraction.

country as the flying huntsman. In some places he is called the flying Marcolfus. When he approaches, great shouting and uproar and cracking of whips are heard in the air; the people then step aside and place themselves behind the trees. First come his coal-black hounds, which run on all sides snuffing the ground, with long red-hot tongues hanging out of their mouths. Then comes 'Wolmar' on his white horse, sometimes holding his own head under the left arm. When he meets anyone, especially an old person, he commands him to hold a couple of his hounds, and makes him either stand with them for several hours, or loose them immediately after a shot, on hearing which they break from all bonds and chains. When he is thus riding onwards, he is heard to slam the gates after him; and in many places where there is a passage through a farm, he rides in at one gate and out at the other, and no locks or bolts are so strong as not to fly open at his approach. In some places he takes his course even over the housetops, and in the neighbourhood of Herlufsholm there is said to be a house, the roof of which is considerably sunk in the middle, because he so often passes over it. In the north of Seeland he has another Gurre, where there are ruins, which are still called Valdemar's castle. It is a custom here for the old women, at St John's tide, to go out at night on the road, and open the gates for him. About two miles from Gurre is Valdemar's mount, surrounded by water. Here, according to the tradition, six priests in black walk every midnight, muttering over the islet. Between Sölleröd and Naerum, he hunts with black dogs and horses, on the road called Wolmar's way.

Having thus roamed about, he rests alternately at many places in the country. It is particularly related that he stops at Vallö castle, where he has a bedchamber, in which there stood two ready-made beds. Here he passes the night in the form of a black dog. In the same room stand two large chests, which, on being once opened, were found full of small round pieces of leather; 'for better money they had not in King Wolmar's time.' A subterraneous passage is said to connect Vallö castle with Töllösegaard, in the district (amt) of Holbek. Here he is also said to have had a chamber, and formerly even a maidservant was kept to wait on him. Sometimes he rests at Vordingborg, in 'Valdemar's Tower', or among the ruins of 'Valdemar's Castle', where young females and persons from his time are often seen to go and make beds. A peasant, who would not believe that the king thus came to his tower in the night, ventured once to pass the night there; but at midnight, in walked King Valdemar to him, greeted him in a friendly manner, and said, 'Thou hast my thanks for taking care of my tower,' at the same time holding out to him a gold coin, but which, when the peasant took it, burnt a round hole through his hand, and fell like a coal to the ground. From this dreadful money, an idea may be formed of what his sufferings must be. It sometimes happens, when an old man or woman has faithfully held his dogs for many hours, that he throws them something that appears like coal, and is, therefore, disregarded, but when examined, is found to be pure gold.

## Punishment for Removing Landmarks

Before the permanent allotment of lands, to every peasant, in sowing time, so much of the field or mark was assigned as was just and appropriate, and boundary-posts were driven between his and his neighbour's allotment. Whoever removed such marks, though he might escape punishment in this world, could find no rest in the grave, but by way of penalty must plough every night on the spot where his sin lay hidden. Of such ploughmen it is said, that when any person came near, they compelled him to drive their horses; and if anyone were so forced into their service, there was no other way to get free again than to take notice of the place where he began, and after the first turn to cast away the reins. He might then pursue his way unscathed.

---

Near Skive lies the manor of Krabbesholm, where there once dwelt a lady who wished to appropriate to herself an adjacent field, and therefore caused her overseer to put earth from the garden at Krabbesholm into his wooden shoes, with which he went to the field in dispute, and swore that he stood on the soil of Krabbesholm. The field was adjudged to the lady, but afterwards the overseer could not die before she had given it back; yet he, nevertheless, every night still goes round the field with earth in his wooden shoes.

---

Three men belonging to Spandet, in North Sleswig, swore away the beautiful meadow of Elkjaer from the village of Fjersted; in lieu of which the villagers got the inferior one of Sepkjaer. They had also put earth in their shoes. After their death they were long to be seen wandering about the meadow, wringing their hands and crying:

> Med Ret og Skjel,
> Det ved vi vel,
> Elkjaer ligger til Fjersted By,
> Sepkjaer ligger til Spandet.

> *By law and right,*
> *That know we well,*
> *Elkjaer belongs to Fjersted town,*
> *Sepkjaer belongs to Spandet,*

Near Ebeltoft dwelt a peasant who possessed land and cattle in superabundance, paid taxes both to church and state, brought his tithes at the right time, gave to the poor, and went every Sunday to church; yet, notwithstanding all this, there was not an individual in the whole neighbourhood that placed any real confidence in him. He died and was buried, but after having lain in the earth until harvest time, he was heard at night crying piteously over the field, 'Boundary here! Boundary there!' Now people discovered how in his lifetime he had acquired his wealth.

## A Sunday's Child

In Fyen there was a woman who was born on a Sunday, and, like other Sunday's children, had the faculty of seeing much that was hidden from others. But because, in consequence of this property, she could not pass by the church at night without seeing either a hearse or a spectre, the gift became a perfect burden to her. She therefore took the advice of a man skilled in such matters, who directed her, whenever she saw a spectre, to say, 'Go to heaven,' but when she met a hearse, 'Hang on.' Happening some time after to meet a hearse, she, through lapse of memory, cried out, 'Go to heaven!' and straightway the hearse rose up in the air and vanished. Afterwards meeting a spectre, she said to it, 'Hang on!' when the spectre clung round her neck, hung on her back, and drove her down into the earth before it. For three days her shrieks were heard, before the spectre could put an end to her wretched life.

## Spectres in St Knud's Church at Odense [1]

A man in Odense was once desirous of knowing what took place in the church in the night-time, and therefore one evening went into St Knud's, where he remained. At midnight he saw a spectre come forth from one of the graves holding a long wax taper, with which it went about and lighted all the candles in the church. Shortly after there came one spectre after another walking slowly from their graves, and placed themselves in the seats, among whom the man lying in concealment recognised many a good old friend. At length came a spectre in priestly attire, ascended the pulpit, and preached a sermon in an unknown tongue, until day began to dawn.

---

1  The chief town of the island of Fyen.

# Hans Naeb

In the village of Qvaerndrup in Fyen there was once a horrible spectre, which caused great fear and disquietude throughout the whole parish; as everyone that saw it died immediately after. This spectre had assumed the likeness of a dead man called Hans Naeb, and when it appeared to anyone, it was always with the cry, 'Look at Hans Naeb!' All the men in the place and then the women were already dead, and the turn now came to the young ones. In this impending danger a young fellow offered to encounter the apparition and endeavour to drive it away. For this purpose he went at midnight to the church path, through which the spectre was in the habit of passing, having previously provided himself with steel in various shapes. When the apparition approached, he fearlessly threw steel before its feet, so that it was obliged instantly to turn back, and appeared no more in the parish. But the young man being satisfied that it really was Hans Naeb, it was resolved to open his grave, to see if anything were amiss, when it was found that he was lying on his face in the coffin, whence it was evident to all that with his cry of 'Look at Hans Naeb' he had only wished to cause them to lay him on his back, it being well known that a corpse cannot have peace in the grave when it lies otherwise.

# A Sagacious Woman

Near Lille Vaerlöse in Seeland there once dwelt a farmer who associated with thieves and robbers, never went to church, and was in bad repute among all for his impiety. When he was dead and buried, and the funeral procession had returned from the church to drink 'grave beer' at the house of the deceased, they saw him sitting on the roof staring down on all who ventured to look up at him, so that scarcely one remained behind, all leaving the place as quickly as possible. At length came the priest, who began reading, and exorcised him down into Kalsmose hard by Farum lake; and that he might continue there till the world's end, a sharp stake was driven into the earth so that it just met his head. While all this was being done, an old crone chanced to be present who understood these matters better than the priest himself, and who taking a darning needle without an eye, stuck it into the stake. At this the spectre cried out from beneath: 'Thou shouldst not have done that, thou old witch! I should else have been at home before thee!' But now he is obliged to remain beneath, yet he flies about every night, and is a night-raven until cock-crowing.

## Master Mads and Herr Anders

Master Mads, the priest of Lumby, was full of shrewdness and cunning. He once said that the dead were liable to thirst, and caused a cask of beer to be brought to the funerals within the church, and when, somedays after, the beer was looked after, it was all drunk out. Many persons now conceived all sorts of opinions concerning him, and certain it is, that when Master Mads was dead he reappeared. His successor, Herr Anders, who was no less shrewd than Master Mads, undertook to exorcise his spirit, wheresoever it might chance to be. One night, therefore, he went out into the field which is now called the Pilelykke, taking with him three large books. There sure enough he met with Master Mads, with whom he had a hard struggle, and was hardly able to answer all the questions put to him by the learned sprite. So at length he had recourse to reading out of one of his books, which Master Mads, however, knocked out of his hand. In all haste Herr Anders then drew forth the second book, and again began to read; but the spectre struck this also out of his hand, saying, 'When thou wast a lad thou didst once steal a wheaten loaf in Elsinore.' But Herr Anders lost no time in throwing two skillings to him, answering, that with that it would be paid. At the same time he took forth the third book, from which he read so impressively that Master Mads found himself under the necessity of creeping into the earth at the spot where he was standing, and where a sharp stake of oak was driven to hold him down. Old folks say that they have seen the stake in its place, adding that on shaking it to and fro, a voice was always heard from beneath, crying, 'Pull it up! Pull it up!'

## Of Dragons

About a mile and a quarter from Sorö[1] stands Alsted church, in which there is still to be seen a picture representing a fight between a bull and a dragon, in commemoration, as people say, of an event which took place in the churchyard. According to the tradition, a dragon had taken up his abode near the church gate, and done great injury to the people, so that no one could enter the church, when an ancient wise man gave his advice, that a bull-calf should be reared with pure sweet milk, and after a certain time be set to fight with the serpent. At the end of the first year, the young bull was so strong, that everyone thought it might stand the encounter; but on seeing the serpent, it was so terrified, that it was found necessary to feed it in the same manner for another year. It was then less timid, but would not engage in combat until the end of the third year, when it proved so bold and vigorous that it instantly engaged in the conflict and killed the

1   A town in the west of Seeland, famed for its academy.

dragon. But the bull was so envenomed that it was found necessary to kill it also, and bury it together with the dragon.

*There is a tradition nearly similar of a dragon in the churchyard of Lyngby, a village near Copenhagen.*

———

Two miles from Aalborg are two mounts called Östbierg Bakker. Here many years since a dragon had his abode, and caused great affliction in the neighbourhood. At length there came a man skilled in the knowledge of serpents, who engaged to destroy the dragon. He caused a pile to be raised, and when it was kindled, mounted a courageous horse and rode up to the monster, which followed him whithersoever he rode, and thus came at length to the pile. The man then rode over the pile and the dragon crept after him through the midst of the fire. He then sprang a second time over the pile, and the serpent crept after him a second time. When he had thus ridden unscathed seven times over the fire, and the dragon had crept seven times through it, it was completely consumed.

## The Dam-horse

Once when some peasant children from Hirschholm[1] were playing by Agersö there sprang suddenly up from the water a large white 'adam-horse', and galloped about the field. The boys ran to look at it, and one of them ventured to set himself on its back; but in the same moment the horse darted off and was about to plunge into the lake, when the boy luckily exclaimed:

> 'Lord Jesus' cross!
> I never saw a larger horse!'

and it instantly vanished from under him.

———

To the north of Thisted[2] lies the village of Brund. From this village as three drunken peasants were crossing a field called Kronens Mark, one of them expressed a wish for a horse on which they could all ride home together, when suddenly an immensely large black horse stood before them, on whose back they thought they might all very well find room; but when two of them were mounted, the third in wonder cried out:

> 'Lord Jesus' cross
> Never saw I such a horse!'

1  A village about eight miles north of Copenhagen.
2  A little town on the Limfiord in the north of Jutland.

At the same moment the horse vanished, and there lay the three sprawling on the ground.

*In France the dam-horse is known by the name of the Lutin, and in the Shetland isles it is called the Shoopiltee. In both places it is said to appear as a little horse, which, when anyone has set himself on its back, rushes with him into the water.*

## The Hel-horse

In every churchyard in former days, before any human body was buried in it, a living horse was interred. This horse reappears and is known by the name of the 'Hel-horse'. It has only three legs, and if anyone meets it, it forebodes death. Hence is derived the saying when anyone has survived a dangerous illness: 'He gave death a peck of oats,' (as an offering or bribe).

In the cathedral yard at Aarhuus there is a Hel-horse, which sometimes makes its appearance. A man, whose windows looked into the cathedral yard, exclaimed one evening as he sat in his apartment, 'What horse is that outside?' 'It is perhaps the Hel-horse,' answered one sitting by him. 'Then I will see it!' said the man. While looking out of the window he grew as pale as a corpse; but he never mentioned afterwards what he had seen. Shortly after he fell sick and died.

*Hel is identical with Death, and in times of pestilence rides about on a three-legged horse, and strangles people; whence when a sickness rages it is said that 'Hel is going about'; or when in the night the dogs bark and howl, 'Hel is among the dogs'; when the sickness begins in a place, 'Hel is come'; or when it ceases, 'Hel is driven away'. Hel can be driven from one place to another; instances of this are related and persons named who have driven Hel from this or that town or village. When anyone lies sick to death, it is said: 'He has his Helsot' (mortal sickness); if he recovers it is said: 'He has settled matters with Hel'. When anyone stays out too long on an errand, people to this day say: 'You are a good one to send after Hel'.[1]*

## The Church-lamb

When anyone enters a church alone and when there is no service, it often happens that he sees the Church-lamb running about; for the church is built over a lamb, that it may not sink. Formerly, when a church was being built, it was customary to bury a living lamb under the altar, that the building might stand immoveable. This lamb's apparition is known by the

---

1   Müllenhoff, op. cit., p. 244..

name of the Church-lamb; and if a little child is to die, the Church-lamb is seen to dance on the threshold of the house.

*In all Fyen there is only one church that has its Church-lamb, while each of the others has its Church-sow. The custom of burying a living animal, that a church or a house may stand firm, extends itself to other animals besides a lamb, of which a swine and poultry are oftenest mentioned.[1]*

## The Grave-sow

In the streets of Aeröskiobing[2] there is often seen a Grave-sow, or, as it is also called, a Gray sow. This is said to be the apparition of a sow formerly buried alive, and when it appears, to forebode death and calamity.

## The Night-raven

Every exorcised spirit becomes, according to tradition, a night-raven. At the spot where a spirit has been exorcised, a sharp stake is driven into the earth, which passes through the left wing of the raven, causing a hole in it. It is only through the most frightful swamps and morasses that the Night-raven ascends. It first begins under the earth with the cry of 'Rok! Rok!' then 'Rok op! Rok op!' and when it has thus come forth, it flies away screaming, 'Hei! Hei! He! – i!' When it has flown up it resembles a cross, and at first hops on the ground like a magpie, and cries 'Bav! Bav! Bav!' It afterwards flies towards the east, to approach the holy sepulchre, because if it can come thither, it will get rest. When it flies overhead, care must be taken not to look up; for if anyone sees through the hole in its left wing, he himself becomes a night-raven, and the night-raven is released. In general the night-raven is harmless, and strives only to go farther and farther towards the east.

## The Jack o'Lantern

Jack o' lanterns are the spirits of unrighteous men[3] which by a false glimmer seek to mislead the traveller, and to decoy him into bogs and moors. The best safeguard against them, when they appear, is to turn one's cap inside out. When anyone sees a Jack o' lantern, let him take care not to point at him, for he will come if pointed at. It is also said that if anyone calls him, he will come and light him who called; but then let him be very cautious.

---

1   In building the new bridge at Halle, which was completed only in 1843, the people thought it would be requisite to immure a child in the foundation! Grimm, J., *Deutsche Mythologie*, op. cit., p. 1095.
2   A town on the north side of Aerö, a small island on the south of Fyen.
3   According to the Belgian tradition, they are the souls of unbaptised children.

Near Skovby on the isle of Falster[1] there are many Jack o' lanterns. The peasants say they are the souls of land-measurers who in their lifetime had perpetrated injustice in their measurements, and therefore run up Skovby bakke at midnight, which they measure with red-hot iron rods, crying, 'Here is the clear and right boundary! From here to there!'

## The Basilisk

When a cock is seven years old it lays an egg, from which when hatched there comes forth a basilisk, an ugly monster that kills people only by looking at them. It is said that the only method by which this creature can be destroyed is by holding a looking-glass before it; for it is so ugly that it cannot survive the sight of itself.

## The Jerusalem Shoemaker or Wandering Jew in Jutland

It is now very long since there was seen in Jutland a man mean and lowly in his garments, riding on a little white horse, with stirrups made of wood. When anyone asked him whence he came and whither he was directing his course, he was wont to answer, 'From Vendsyssel over Himmelsyssel southwards.' He foretold, and said of a stone in Mae, ' A thorn shall grow through the fissure in the stone, and in the thorn a magpie shall build her nest, hatch her young, and afterwards fly away with them.' And this came to pass as he had said. He further foretold that when the magpie was flown, there should be a great battle in Vendsyssel, and the greater part of the people perish. Afterwards the women should acquire the courage and heart of men and slay the enemy. But when he was asked what further should happen, he answered, 'Let the end follow.'

In Aalborg he foretold something to the town-magistrate, which did not particularly please him, and for which he caused him to be scourged. He then foretold again, that like as his blood was running down his back, so should the magistrate's blood run over the streets of Aalborg. And it happened as he had said; for in a quarrel which arose in the town, the townsmen slew the magistrate in the street.

Of Haseriisaa, which at that time did not flow through Aalborg, he foretold that a time should come when it should run through the town; which also took place as he had predicted. Coming one day to Bolstrup, and having according to his custom taken up his quarters in a kiln, he rode the next day to the public assembly (Ting), where the judge of the district asked him, 'How will it fare with me?' and got for answer, 'Thou shalt die

1   Lying near the south coast of Seeland.

in a kiln.' Nor did he fare better; for coming to poverty, he had at last no other place of shelter. Once when some boys scoffed at him, and one among them threw a cask-stave after him, he said, that a stave should be the boy's death; and the same boy, some time after, fell from a tree and struck a stave into his body. Of alms he accepted only so much as he required for the moment, and thus travelled from place to place.

*The story of the shoemaker of Jerusalem is generally known. When Jesus passed by his house, bending under the weight of the cross, he would rest an instant at his door; but the miscreant came out, and with imprecations drove the Saviour away, for the sake of gaining the favour of his enemies. The shoemaker, whose name was Ahasuerus, then drew on himself the curse ever to be a wanderer and never to find rest until doomsday.*[1]

1  Afzelius, op. cit., iii, p. 116.

## Of Lakes, Bottomless Pools, etc

### 1 – Tiis Lake

At Kundby, in the district of Holbek,[1] a Troll had his habitation in the high mount on which the church stands; but as the people in that neighbourhood were generally disposed to piety and went constantly to church, the Troll's greatest torment was the incessant ringing of hells in the church tower. At length he found himself compelled to take his departure; for nothing has contributed more to the migration of the Trolls than the increasing piety of the people and the more frequent ringing of bells. He crossed over to Fyen, where he lived for some time. It happened once that a man who had recently fixed his habitation in Kundby, came to Fyen and met this Troll on the road. 'Where hast thou thy home?' asked the Troll. There was nothing about the Troll unlike an ordinary person, therefore the man answered him truly, 'I am from Kundby.' 'From Kundby?' repeated the Troll, 'I don't know thee; though I think I know every man besides in Kundby. Wilt thou take a letter for me to Kundby?' The man expressed his willingness, and the Troll put the letter into the man's pocket, with the injunction not to take it thence until he came to Kundby church, where he would need merely to cast it over the wall of the churchyard, and the person would get it for whom it was intended. They then separated and the man thought no more of the letter; but when he had again crossed over to Seeland, and was sitting in the meadow where Tiis lake now is, the Troll's letter suddenly entered his thoughts. Taking it from his pocket, he sat a while with it in his hand, when on a sudden water began to bubble out from the seal, the letter expanded itself, and it was with difficulty that the man saved his life; for the Troll had enclosed a whole lake in the letter, intending by such a destruction to revenge himself on Kundby church. But God averted it, and the lake poured itself into the great hollow where it now is.

### 2 – The Sunken Mansion

In the neighbourhood of Lindenborg, near Aarhuus, there is a lake which no one has hitherto been able to fathom. Of this lake the following story is current in the neighbourhood. Many years ago there stood in the

1  A small town in Seeland on the Issefiord.

place where the lake now is, a proud, ancient castle or mansion, of which the only trace remaining is a road that led to the gate, but which is now lost under the waters of the lake. On one holy day-eve, when the family were from home, the servants of the place indulged in great revel and merriment, which at length proceeded so far, that in their state of drunkenness they wrapped a swine up in bed-linen, placed a cap on its head, and laid it in the master's bed. They then sent a message to the priest, summoning him to come without a moment's delay to administer to their master, who lay at the point of death. The priest was instantly there, and, observing no deception, read to the swine and did everything required by his vocation; but when he was about to administer the sacrament, all present burst into a fit of laughter, and the swine snapped the bread out of his hand. In terror he hurried from the place, but forgot to take his book with him. Just as he was hastening through the outer gate, the castle clock struck twelve, when a cracking and crashing began in every side and corner of the building. When he turned round the mansion had sunk and the lake rushed forth from the abyss. As he stood gazing, through fear and wonder unable to proceed, there came a little stool floating on the water to the border of the lake, on which lay the book that he had left in the mansion.

## Traditions of Wells

### 1 – Helen's Well

In Tisvilde Mark in Seeland, close on the coast, there is a spring, which beyond all others has acquired a celebrity on account of its miraculous virtues. On St John's day, pilgrimages are made to it by the sick and crippled, even from the most southern parts of the island; and many have there recovered their health down to the present day. This spring is called Helen's Well, and various are the traditions current respecting it.

---

There dwelt in Sweden a holy woman named Helen; she lived in a forest apart from human converse, and led a pure godly life. In her solitude she was assailed by some wicked men, who slew her and cast her body into the sea. There a large stone received her lifeless corpse and floated with it over to Seeland, where it was found under a high acclivity in Tibirke parish. But as, in consequence of the steepness, it was not practicable to bring it ashore, a miracle caused by her sanctity took place, the precipice burst asunder so that the body was borne through it into the plain. The cleft is still to be seen. At the spot where the body was first laid, a spring gushed forth, which is the celebrated well that still bears her name. When her body had been placed in a coffin, it was conveyed to Tisvilde church. When on its way, the bearers having used some indecent language, the bier became so heavy, that they could not move it from the spot, but it sank deep into the earth at the place which is still called Helen's grave. The stone on which she floated to Seeland yet lies on the strand, and bears evident traces of her body.

_____

Helen was a Scanian princess and much famed for her beauty. A king fell in love with her, and as he could not win her affection, he resolved on violence. In her distress Helen fled from place to place pursued by the king. When on reaching the seashore and the king was about to seize her, she plunged into the deep. But she did not perish. A large stone rose from the bottom of the ocean and received her, on which she floated over to Seeland. At the spot where she first set her foot on land there sprang forth a fountain which still bears her name, and she lived long in that neighbourhood, and was venerated and visited as a holy woman.

_____

Three pious sisters being on a voyage together, all perished, and the waves dispersed their bodies in three several directions. The first of these was named Helen. Her body came to Tisvilde, where a fountain sprang from her grave. The name of the second was Karen. Her body came to land at the spot in Odd's district, where St Karen's well is still shown. The third sister was in like manner cast on shore, and a well likewise sprang from her grave.

*On a cliff in Odd's district there is a spring called Thore's well, which may possibly have been so named from the third sister.*

## 2 – St Knud's Well

Near Harrested in Seeland, on the spot where Duke Knud Lavard was treacherously murdered by the king's son Magnus (AD 1129), a spring gushed forth, which is visited by persons suffering from bodily ailments. It bears the name of St Knud, and around it the grass is green both summer and winter.

## 3 – Snogskilde (Snake's-well)

Whoever is so fortunate as to catch a snake with a crown on its head, or, as it is also called, a royal snake, and eats a piece of its flesh, becomes 'fremsynet' (i.e. able to see into hidden things), understands the speech of animals, and can read any book whatsoever.

From such an event Snogskilde in Fyen derives its name and origin. As a man was going down the hills in Guldbierg parish he saw a royal snake putting its head forth from the earth, which he quickly seized and ran off with it, followed by a multitude of snakes, all bent on rescuing their king; but the man, casting off his wooden shoes, reached his little hut in safety, instantly ate a part of the snake, and thus acquired a vast insight into the secrets of this world. From the hole, through which the crowned snake had crept forth, there sprang a fountain, which for many years after was fenced in and visited, on account of the wonderful virtue of its water in the cure of all diseases. It has now fallen into neglect.

*On the isle of Mors[1] there are said to be white vipers, though they are found hut seldom. Whoever eats one acquires an extraordinary degree of understanding, together with the faculty of seeing things invisible to others.*

## The Sandhills at Nestved

At Fladsö there dwelt a Troll who bore a grudge against the inhabitants of Nestved.[2] He therefore one day took his leather bag, went to the beach, and filled it with sand. It was now his intention to do the people of Nestved a great injury, by burying their houses under the sand; but as he was on his way to the town, with the sack on his shoulders, the sand ran out through a hole, and caused the row of sandhills that lie between Fladsö and Nestved; nor until he reached the spot where the castle of Husvold formerly stood, was he aware that be had lost the greater part of the sand, at which he was so angry that he cast the remainder against Nestved, where it is still to be seen, a solitary sandhill.

## Of Trees

In Rugaard Forest there is a tree which has no leaves, of which it is related, that although it has the appearance of other trees, it is, nevertheless, an elf, who by night goes about the forest. To injure this tree would be dangerous, and would surely call forth vengeance.

## The Lonely Thorn

One often sees in a field a solitary thorn, which never grows larger. Such are always bewitched, and care should be taken not to approach them too near in the night-time, as there comes a fiery wheel forth from the bush, which, if a person cannot run away from it, will destroy him.

---

1  A small island in the Liimfiord, in the north of Jutland.
2  A town in the south of Seeland.

## Of the Pestilence in Jutland

On the east side of the churchyard of Fuur no one is buried, because when the Black Death raged in the country, a living child was buried there, in order to stay the contagion.

*Other instances are given of this method of staying the pestilence.*

## The Rat-hunter

On the Alhede the people were grievously annoyed with rats, mice and other vermin, when there came an itinerant rat-hunter who undertook to drive them all away. He first, however, inquired whether they had ever seen a dragon thereabouts, and on their answering in the negative, caused a pile to be raised on the middle of the heath, having kindled which he sat by it on a chair. While the fire was burning he took forth a book, out of which he read much, and while he read, rats and mice, serpents and various reptiles were seen to go into the fire. But at last there came a dragon, at the sight of which the man complained that he was betrayed and must now perish himself. The serpent then wound his tail round both the man and his chair, and thus entered the fire, where they both perished together.

# Historical

## 1 – Habor and Signelil

Near Ringsted[1] lies Sigersted, so called from King Sigar, who resided there. His daughter, Signelil, loved a noble warrior named Habor, and to this day is shown, near Alsted, the place where they usually met. It still bears the name of Signelil's walk.

One day, when chasing a hart, and pursuing it across the rivulet of Vrangstrup, her horse fell under her, so that she was exposed to much danger. At this instant Habor appeared, sprang into the stream and rescued her. Their love at length became so ardent, that Habor, disguised as a waiting-maid, secretly gained admission to Signelil, which Gunvare, Signelil's nurse, treacherously betrayed to King Sigar. The whole affair being now divulged, and Habor being seized by the king's men, the two lovers formed the resolution of dying together. Habor was conducted to Stanghöi, there to be hanged; but feeling desirous in his last moments of proving the fidelity of Signelil, he requested that, before he was hanged, his cloak might be suspended on the gibbet, that he might thence form an idea how he himself should hang. Signelil, in the meanwhile, cast all her jewels into a deep pit, which is still called Signelil's well; whence the saying derives its origin, that Sigersted has more gold and silver than it knows of. She then shut herself in her bower, anxiously watching the gibbet on which Habor was to suffer. On perceiving the cloak, she set fire to the bower, in the belief that Habor was already dead. When the bower together with Signelil was consumed, and Habor was convinced of her love, he resigned himself to his fate, and was buried in Hagehöi. But the accursed nurse had no great joy of her treachery, being afterwards cast into a well, which still bears the name of the Nurse's Well.

*This is one of the most ancient and celebrated of all the Scandinavian traditions. In Saxo the narrative at length is admirably given. See also W. Grimm, Altdänische Heldenlieder, p. 509, also Udvalgte Danske Viser, iii. pp. 403, sqq., where the several places in Denmark, Sweden and Norway are specified which claim to be the scene of the tragedy.*

---

1    Once a considerable, but now a small, town in Seeland. In its church (St Bent's), formerly belonging to the Benedictine convent, are deposited the remains of several of the early kings and royal personages.

## 2 – Feggeklit

There was once, in days of yore, a king in Mors named Fegge or Fengo. His castle was on the hill which after him is still called Feggeklit, from whence he could order his ships out to sea. He and his brother, Horvendil, ruled alternately on land and on sea, so that one, during three years, should be engaged in piratical expeditions abroad, while the other directed the government at home. But Fegge, growing jealous of Horvendil's good fortune and increasing power, slew him and married his widow, which murder was afterwards avenged by Horvendil's son, Amlet, who slew Fegge, whose grave is still to be seen on Feggeklit.

## 3 – Jellinge Barrows

About two miles to the north-west of Veile, near the village of Jellinge, lie King Gorm the Old and his queen, Thyra, each in a barrow by the side of the churchyard. On Thyra's barrow, it is said, there was formerly a fair fountain, which, as some relate, was conducted in copper pipes under the earth, from a hill near the village of Rugballe; while others say that it was derived from a spring that rises in Finnet field; others assure us that Thyra was suspected of infidelity towards her husband, but that three days after her interment, a fountain sprang from the earth in token of her innocence. A peasant once washed his horse in the water to cure it of the scab, in consequence of which profanation the well was dried up.

Near these barrows, just without the door of the church, stand two remarkable monuments of antiquity, namely, two very large stones with runic inscriptions, which tell of King Gorm and his queen Thyra. This writing can, however, be no longer read by anyone, unless he stands on his head and has been to the Black School. A cunning priest once read the writing, and thereby learned the existence of treasure lying sunk in a field on a large stone; but where it is now to be found, nobody knows.

## 4 – Holger the Dane under Kronborg[1]

Under the castle of Kronborg a clashing of arms was frequently to be heard, for which no one could assign a cause, and in the whole country not one could be found daring enough to descend into its nethermost passages. To a slave, who had forfeited his life, his pardon and freedom were promised, if, by descending as far as the passage admitted, he could bring information of what he there met with. He came at length to a large iron door, which, on his knocking, opened of itself, and he found himself in a deep

1 The castle at Elsinore, which guards the passage of the Sound.

vault. From the middle of the roof hung a lamp nearly burnt out, and beneath it was an immense stone table, around which sat steel-clad warriors bending down, and resting their heads on their crossed arms. He who sat at the end of the table then arose; it was Holger the Dane; but in lifting his head from his arm, the stone table burst asunder, for his beard had grown into it. 'Reach me thy hand!' said he to the slave; but the latter, not venturing to give his hand, held out an iron bar instead, which Holger so squeezed that the marks remained visible. At length letting it go, he exclaimed: 'It gladdens me that there are still men in Denmark!'

## 5 – Bishop William's Footmark

At the door on the south side of Roeskilde[1] cathedral, there is still to be seen on the threshold the place where Bishop William in his anger set his foot, when he prevented King Svend Estrithsen from entering the church, and excommunicated him, for having profaned the holy edifice with unjust bloodshed.

## 6 – Bishop William's Death and Burial

When the tidings reached Bishop William of Roeskilde that his king and master, Svend, surnamed Estrithsen, was dead, at an advanced age, in Jutland, he prepared to go and meet the king's body. Before he set out he went into the church of the Holy Trinity, called the grave-diggers to him, ordered them first to dig a grave for the king and then one for himself; as he felt certain that he should immediately follow his beloved master. He then entered a carriage and proceeded to meet the royal corpse. On reaching Topshöge forest he observed two remarkably high trees, which he ordered his attendants to fell and to form a coffin of them. Supposing that the bishop intended the coffin for the king's body, they executed his order and placed the coffin on a vehicle to be conveyed after them. But on emerging from the forest, Bishop William seeing the king's body drawing nigh, ordered the driver to stop; he then descended from the carriage, spread his cloak on the ground, fell on his knees, and prayed to God for peace and a happy departure. When the attendants, who were standing by, had long wondered that the bishop still continued prostrate, they raised his head and saw that he was no more. They then laid his body in the coffin and conveyed it back to Roeskilde. Thus was his corpse borne after the king's, and buried in the quire, in the place that he had himself selected.

---

1  Formerly the capital of Denmark and the residence of the Danish monarchs, whose burial-place is in its venerable cathedral.

Afterwards, when Bishop Svend Norbagge[1] was rebuilding the church of hewn stone, and all was completed as far as the quire, it being found that Bishop William's burial-place occupied too much room, he ordered it to be removed. In the night there came a man clad in priestly attire to the precentor, who lay asleep, and ordered him to greet Bishop Svend and say to him, that he ought to have been satisfied with the honour of completing the reconstruction of the church, and not to have separated his body from the king's; adding, that if Bishop Svend had led a less godly life, he would have taken revenge on himself, but now he would be revenged on the building only that he had raised. With these words he thrust at the wall with his staff so that a whole column came falling down in fragments. The precentor, on awaking from his dream, saw that the column was thrown down, and found himself lying amid the rubbish, but without having suffered any injury. When informed of this occurrence, Bishop Svend answered, that it was not to be wondered at that Bishop William was so hasty and unyielding after his death, seeing that he had been so during his whole life.

For a long time the grave remained untouched, until the death of Bishop Asker, when it was thought that the most honourable place for him was by the side of Bishop William, of which opinion were the precentor Herman, the schoolmaster Arnfast, and the provost Isaac. These three opened the grave, and found, on examining it, Bishop William's cope, which spread around so sweet and pleasant an odour, that they thence concluded he must be blessed in heaven. The odour was at the same time so powerful, that for three days those who had touched the cope could not wash it off their fingers. But when they threw his bones aside with no respect, each received his punishment. Herman the precentor got the St Anthony's fire in his nose, of which within three days he died. The schoolmaster, who, by way of remedy for an increasing debility of the limbs, took to drinking, became such a sufferer that he vomited up his liver, and confessed to Bishop Absalon, who visited him, that he suffered all because of that sin: he entered a cloister and died three months after. Provost Isaac, who saw

---

1    Of this prelate, a Norwegian by birth, Saxo (pp. 559, *sq.*) relates a story worth repeating: When raised to the episcopal dignity, Svend though well versed in his own native literature, was miserably deficient in Latin. The preference shown him by the king excited the envy of many, and by way of rendering him ridiculous, it was contrived, when he had to celebrate mass, to lay before him a book in which the first two letters of *famulum*, in the prayer for the king, were erased; so that in his ignorance he prayed God to protect his majesty, *mulum suum*. On inspecting the book, the king at once perceived the trick, and caused the bishop (whom he loved for his virtues) to apply himself to the study of the liberal arts, in which he afterwards excelled.

how the other two were punished, sold all that he owned and founded the convent of St Mary in Roeskilde, but nevertheless died of a wasting sickness.

## 7 – The Punishment of Inhumanity

When King Cnut the Saint was pursued to the church of St Alban in Odense, he knelt down before the high altar, prayed to God for forgiveness of his sins, and prepared himself for death. While there kneeling he suffered severely from thirst, and therefore besought a Jutlander, who peered in at a window, to be so compassionate as to give him a little drink of water. The man thereupon ran to a brook and brought some water in a jug; but when in the act of reaching it in to the king, another Jutlander, who was standing by, struck the vessel with his spear, so that all the water was spilt on the church floor. Then said the king to him who had broken the jug, 'Dost thou deny me a little drink of water?' And having said this, he was slain by a stone that was cast at him (AD 1086). But the pitiless Jute met with his reward. He became mad and suffered from burning thirst, and one day having laid himself down by a spring to draw up water, he slipped half way down into the well and remained hanging by the legs, with his head close to the water, though without touching it, and so perished.

## 8 – Svend Grathe's Military Chest

In Jutland, near the village of Kragelund, there is a large morass called Graa-Mose. It was formerly called Grathe Mose, it having been there that Svend Grathe was slain by King Valdemar (AD 1157). Connected with this place is the following tradition. When Svend Grathe saw that the battle was lost, he caused his large military chest to be cast into the slough (for such at that time it was), from which cause there is seen, as in every place where treasure is concealed, lights burning by night. Hitherto it has been sought for in vain; and a schoolteacher, who had one night stuck pegs where he saw the lights, found them all pulled up on the following morning.

## 9 – The Two Church Towers

Herr Asser Ryg resolved on building a church at Fienneslövlille; but before the same was finished, he was obliged to go to the wars with his kinsmen. When on the eve of departure, he desired his wife, who was at the time pregnant, that if she brought him a son, to place a tower on the church, but if a daughter, then to omit that ornament. When he returned some time after, lo, there stood the church with two towers! His wife had brought him two sons, and these were Absalon and Esbern Snare.

*The words of Saxo (see Dahlmann, Gesch. v. Dännem., I, p. 279, note) render this tradition rather doubtful: 'quanquam (Hesbernus) natu praestet.' Absalon was the celebrated archbishop of Lund and still more celebrated statesman and warrior under Valdemar I, surnamed the Great. His brother, Esbern (Asbiörn), was also a distinguished statesman and warrior.*

## 10 – Archbishop Absalon's Death

Absalon had wronged a peasant, who, when on his deathbed, cited the archbishop before the judgement-seat of God; and at the moment when the peasant died, Absalon was also called to his account. It befell at the same time in the monastery of Sorö, that the brethren, who had received no tidings of the archbishop's death, heard, on the evening of the same day, a mournful voice near the altar, saying, 'Sora! Sora! Pro me supplex ora!'

## 11 – Dannebrog

While King Valdemar the Victorious was fighting against the heathen Livonians, with the view of converting them to the Christian faith, Archbishop Andrew of Lund stood, like the Moses of his time, on a high hill, offering up prayers to God for the success of the Danish arms. And it is said, that as long as he was able to hold his arms aloft, the Danes were successful; but the instant he let them sink, through the weakness of age, the heathens gained the advantage. On which account, the other priests, who were present, supported his arms as long as the conflict lasted. It was in this battle the miracle took place, that, when the Danish principal banner was lost in the heat of the contest, there fell from heaven a banner bearing a white cross on a red field, and to this the Danes owed the victory. This precious banner was preserved for a long time after, and it was the general belief, that wherever it was, there was victory certain. They named it the Dannebrog. On the spot where this battle was fought, the town of Wolmar was afterwards built, and so named after King Valdemar.

## 12 – Dannebrog Ships

On Gienner Mark, about a mile from Apenrade,[1] there are still the remains of an ancient monument called the Dannebrog ships. It is said to have originally consisted of twenty greater or smaller stones, shaped into the

---

1   A town on the east coast of Sleswig.

figure of ships, and set up on a level spot in the form of an oval, so that the end of one stone is parted from the next only by another stone standing up between them.

Of these stones it is related, that when King Valdemar II had conquered the heathen Livonians, through the aid of the miracle of the Dannebrog, he, on his way back to Denmark, caused these stones to be set up near the bay formed by the Baltic on the east of the rural village of Gienner, as a lasting monument of his victory, on which account they were called the Dannebrog ships.

In the course of time some of these stones have been broken and placed in the fences of the peasants; there is, nevertheless, still a remnant of them left standing, and ancient people, who have seen more of them, declare that they had the form of ships.

## 13 – St Niels (Nicholas), the Patron of Aarhuus

When King Cnut the Sixth was on his way from North- to South-Jutland, and was in Haderslev,[1] where he intended to pass the night, there came a soothsayer to him, who had knowledge of the stars. This man declared he had read in the heavens that on the next night a child would be conceived, who in the course of time should acquire great renown and be in favour both with God and man. On hearing this, the king was instantly seized with a strong desire to be the father of so fortunate a babe, and forthwith gave orders that a noble young lady should be secretly conducted to him on the following night and share his bed. This took place as he had commanded, and the said young lady, at the expiration of nine months, brought a boy into the world, who cost his mother her life. This prince, who at his baptism received the name of Niels, was delivered to the king's sister, to be reared by her until he was sufficiently grown up to be conducted to the court, there to be instructed in martial exercises and knightly demeanour. When Prince Niels had been some time at court, it came to his knowledge that his existence had cost his mother her life, which circumstance had such an effect on his mind, that from that moment he entirely altered his course of life; so that it was said of him, that from that time he never laughed. The dissipations of the court were so distasteful to him, that he sought solitude, and devoted himself to praying and fasting to that degree, that every Friday he partook only of bread and water, renounced the use of linen, clothed himself in a garment of hair,

---

1   Or, Gem. Hadersleben, a town of Sleswig. South Jutland is another name for the duchy of Sleswig, which it bore till the close of the fourteenth century.

and passed the nights in devout prayer on his bare knees. At last he resolved wholly to forsake the turmoil of the world, and withdrew to Aarhuus, there to pass the remainder of his life. In that city he founded a monastery with a church, which was afterwards called by his name. To this cloister he retired, and chose a monk named Hugo to live with him, besides whom he associated with no one.

A short time before his death, which happened in the year 1180, a revelation took place. The before-mentioned Hugo, who slept in the same apartment with the prince, saw in the night a procession of young clergymen enter the chamber, clad in their robes of ceremony, with purple copes, and bearing lighted wax tapers in their hands. At the brilliancy of the light Hugo awoke, rose from his bed, fell on his knees before his young master, and related to him the vision he had seen, asking what it betokened. The prince answered that it was a message from heaven, to announce that he should die on the night following. The next day he summoned to him his friends in the city and all the monks of the convent, gave them kind exhortations, and bade them farewell. He then distributed liberal alms among the poor, and departed hence, as he had predicted, on the following night, after having directed to be buried in the church of St Oluf by the sea, which church he had, during his life, enriched with royal donations. After his death, it seemed to Bishop Svend of Aarhuus that the spot chosen by the prince was too mean for so exalted a personage; he would, therefore, have had his body borne to the conventual church of St Nicholas; but it happened that a star was seen to fall from heaven on the eastern side of St Oluf's church, which was interpreted to signify that the prince by that miracle repeated his wish and command; so that the bishop was forced to comply. After his burial in that church, divers miracles took place there from time to time. By the grave a wooden cross was erected, which in the course of time having become decayed, these words were heard thrice repeated, 'Make a new cross of oak from Skeibye forest, and set it on the mound where St Niels is buried!' This was done as ordered, and the trunk that was brought from the forest was so large and heavy, that five yoke of oxen could hardly draw it into Aarhuus.

Near to the grave there stood a large apple-tree. A person having once climbed up this tree for the purpose of stealing the fruit, became palsied both head and foot, so that he could neither descend nor even move, before he had prayed to the saint for forgiveness, and made a vow that he would never again be tempted to rob him of his apples.

There was a box placed by the grave, which day and night stood open to receive the pious gifts of everyone who had, through the intercession of the saint, recovered from blindness, deafness, or other corporal infirmity. From this box a thief was once tempted to carry off a pair of curiously wrought eyes of silver, which a man, who had been restored to sight at St Niels' grave, had placed in it. This thief came from Horsens, and desiring to hasten back with his booty, ran the whole night on the way, as he thought, to that town; but at daybreak met a priest just entering a churchyard, from whom he learned that he was still in St Oluf's church-yard, and that, notwithstanding all his running, he had not stirred from the spot. He then confessed his enormous sin, and having given back the silver eyes, without difficulty found the way back to Horsens.

A cow belonging to a poor woman having died, St Niels restored it to life. He did in like manner with a flock of sheep in Randlev; and a hawk, which had died on King Valdemar's hand, became again living on calling on St Niels.

He was once standing near some workmen, who were cutting timber in Viby forest for a church that was to be built. Hearing them complain of thirst, he forthwith caused a spring to gush out for their refreshment, which still bears his name, and is visited by the sick.

After St Niels had performed many such miracles, and his shrine been richly gifted, there arose in the time of King Eric Menved an apprehension, that the sweet and powerful odour, which issued from his grave, would tempt Marsk Stig and his band of robbers over from the isle of Hielm, not far from Aarhuus. In consequence of this apprehension, both St Niels and his shrine were removed to St Clement's church in Aarhuus; but from that time he performed no more miracles, and the pleasant odour from his bones entirely ceased and returned not again – not even after he had been made a saint by the pope.

## 14 – Little Kirsten's (Christine's) Grave

Just without the north door of Vestervig[1] church there is a remarkably long gravestone, with a cross engraved on it, and an illegible inscription. Beneath it lies Little Kirsten, the sister of King Valdemar the First. During the absence of the king she entered into an illicit connection with Buris, prince of the Wends, and brother to the queen, by whom she became pregnant. When the king on his return observed what had taken place, he called, as it is said, Little Kirsten out to dance, and danced her to death. Prince Buris he ordered to be blinded and cast into prison. After a time, when the king's anger was somewhat mitigated, he allowed the unhappy prince to choose another prison, and he chose the monastery of Vestervig, where he was kept confined until his death in a tower, which stood where

---

1   A town on the Liimfiord, on the west side of Jutland.

the churchyard now is; and it is related that he had, a chain round his body so long that he could go from his tower to Kirsten's grave, which he daily visited. The queen, his sister, on the other hand, who had always hated Little Kirsten, came one day riding that way, and to show her contempt, galloped over the grave; but the stone proved less hard than her heart, and received the dints of the horse's hoofs.

## 15 – Marsk Stig

After the death of Marsk Stig at Hielm,[1] his corpse was conveyed by night to the church of Hintzeholm, and there secretly buried by his followers, who would not have it known where he rested, lest his remains should suffer insult. But at the time they brought the body to the church, it happened that a servant girl saw a light in the building and men carrying in a corpse. This she told to the priest, and the grave was afterwards searched. But the priest not knowing who it was that had been so buried, made no mention of the circumstance, but took the velvet that was over the coffin, a part of which he gave to the girl. A considerable time after this event, the same girl became the wife of one of Marsk Stig's followers, who one day noticing the velvet on a cushion, inquired of her whence she got it? She thereupon recounted what had taken place; but as he was fearful that his master's resting-place might thereby be one day discovered, he killed her, although he entertained much affection for her.

## 16 – King Valdemar and Queen Helvig

Once when king Valdemar was in the act of mounting his horse, and had already set one foot in the stirrup, he fell into deep thought, and so continued standing, to the great astonishment of those present. At length one of his attendants ventured to ask him why he thus continued standing? The king answered, that if he could not inform him, nor procure him information whether that over which he was pondering would happen or not, he must never again appear before him. With this answer the man went away full of sorrow; he wandered about in the forest, and knew not to which side he should turn. At length he observed a woman in the forest sitting by a fire, who on his approach asked him why he appeared so sorrowful, and on his informing her, laughed at him, saying, 'Greet thy

---

1 Stig Andersen was Marsk (i.e. Marshal) of the kingdom. He was one of the assassins of King Erik Glipping, who, it is said, had dishonoured his wife. Under the reign of Erik Menved, son of the murdered king, the Marsk being outlawed, fortified himself on Hielm, a little island off the coast of Jutland in the Cattegat. See *Danske Viser*, ii, pp. 115–162.

master and tell him, that Sweden can easily fall to Denmark, if he will receive Queen Helvig into favour!' Queen Helvig was in disgrace, and had been repudiated by the king; for which reason, on hearing the man's answer, he was very angry, and said that such should never be the case.

It happened, however, as through a miracle, that as the king was once hunting in the forest near the castle of Söborg, where Queen Helvig was at the time residing, he saw a damsel, with whose beauty he was so smitten that he ordered his attendants to conduct her to him at midnight. But when the servants came to employ force against this young person, announcing to her at the same time the king's will, Queen Helvig, who had received information of the whole affair, resolved on putting on the young girl's clothes, and letting herself be conducted by the attendants to the king her consort. She became pregnant, and gave birth to a daughter, afterwards the celebrated Queen Margaret, who united Sweden with Denmark and Norway.

*This and the three following traditions refer to King Valdemar IV surnamed Atterdag (from atter, again, and dag, day), in consequence, it is supposed, of his frequent use of the expression 'Morgen er atter en Dag' (Tomorrow is again a day). His queen, Helvig, was confined in the castle of Söborg until her death, on account of the affair with Folker Lovmandsen.*

---

Once when king Volmar was about to mount on horseback, he continued standing with his left foot in the stirrup, and appeared lost in thought. At this moment a man was led by whom the king had condemned to death, who falling on his knees, prayed for his life. The king starting said, 'If thou canst enable me to know what the thought was that has just passed from my mind, and whether it will be accomplished, thou shalt be free.' Hereupon the man got permission to travel over the country to all those skilled in secret knowledge; but no one could answer his inquiry. One evening he came to Borbierg, a steep cliff lying out in the sea. Here he struck thrice with the white staff he had in his hand, and the dwarf of the cliff came out. He could, however, afford no information: 'But I have,' said he, 'a great-grandfather in Dagbierg Daas, who is an old and very sagacious man: try your luck with him.' The man took staff in hand and hied away to Dagbierg, but fared not a whit better there; the dwarf knew nothing whatever: 'But I have a great-great-grandfather in the Rödsteen (Red-stone) on Fuur; if he can't inform you, no one can.' The man then dragged on to the isle of Fuur, and it happened to be just midnight when he stood by the cave and knocked three times. A very little old man came tottering forth. 'Yes, I can help thee, sure enough; but first thou shalt tell me three truths.' The man bethought himself a moment, and said, 'Much have I travelled and far have I been,[1] yet never have seen so firm a house as thine.' 'Yes, that I can well believe, for it is a cave of one stone; – now again!' 'Much have I travelled and far have I been, yet never have seen so much gold and silver in one spot.' 'Yes, that is very possible; but now another.' 'Much have I travelled and far have I been, yet never have seen so little a man with so long a beard.' For it was so long that the little man almost trod on it. 'Yes,' said the mannikin, 'and now I will tell thee what the king was thinking about, and that is, whether he could get Denmark, Norway and Sweden hammered together; but that will only take place under his daughter.' The man was heartily rejoiced, appeared with his answer before the king, and got remission of his sentence according to promise.

## 17 – Queen Helvig and Falk Lohman

When King Valdemar Atterdag discovered that Queen Helvig was unfaithful to him, and held illicit intercourse with Falk Lohman, he caused the latter to be hanged without the Strand-gate at Nyborg,[2] and adjudged the queen to witness the execution from the ramparts. The prison in which he was confined was in the castle, and till within a few years was shown, under the name of Falk Lohman's chamber. But the queen yet appears mourning on the ramparts, and, it is said, sometimes speaks to the sentinels, one of whom so won her favour, that she promised him he should, every morning, in a certain place and under a particular stone find a dollar. For some time the soldier regularly found his dollar, but having fallen sick and sending one of his comrades to fetch it, there was no dollar there, nor has one been found under the stone from that time.

## 18 – Queen Margaret when a Child

Queen Helvig had forfeited the favour of the king her husband, and for several years been confined in Gurre castle, because she had caused Tovelille, the king's mistress, to be killed in a bath. It happened that the king, when once riding over the 'Copper-bridge', noticed a pretty little girl, in a peasant's dress, standing at the castle gate. Being much pleased with the child, he placed her before him on his horse. 'Now,' said the little one, 'we will ride to court.' 'What wilt thou do there?' asked the king. 'Beg forgiveness for my mother, Queen Helvig,' answered the child. This so softened the king's anger, that he took his queen again into favour. The little girl was named Margaret; she grew up and became queen of the three northern realms.

---

1  Almost the words of Odin in the Eddaic poem, Vafthrudnir's Mâl.
2  A fortified town on the island of Fyen, whence is the regular passage over to Seeland.

## 19 – Prophecy of King Frederic the First's Accession to the Throne

In the year 1515, when King Christian II was celebrating his marriage in the palace at Copenhagen, and the assembled nobles were sitting amid joy and festivity, Duke Frederic, the king's paternal uncle, entered the hall. Among the nobles present was Ditlef Rewentlow, who was reported to be well skilled in astronomy and the black art. When he saw the duke entering, he hastily rose, saying to those around him: 'Stand up, ye Danish nobles! And advance to meet your future king!' Which prophecy, after a lapse of eight years, was fulfilled, and Ditlef Rewentlow, on the accession of Frederic I, became his chancellor and privy counsellor.

## 20 – Spectacles Ducats

In the reign of King Christian IV a gold mine was discovered in Norway, from which the king caused some half-ducats to be coined. But some foreign traders having denied that it was Norwegian gold, it being quite unheard of to find gold in Norway, the king was indignant; and therefore, when more gold was afterwards found there, he ordered half- and quarter-ducats to be coined, bearing for device a pair of spectacles, thereby signifying that those who were still doubtful, might put on their spectacles to see the better.

## *Of Historical Persons, Family Traditions, etc*

### 1 – The Arms of the Bille Family

In the arms of the noble family of Bille there is a dwarf or little wild man, concerning whom there is the following tradition.

Many hundred years ago there was a great drought in the country, so that all the water mills were stopped, and the people could get no corn ground. During this calamity a land-proprietor of the above-mentioned family was walking in his courtyard, much perplexed and dejected, when a little dwarf came to him, whose body was all shaggy, and in his hand carrying a tree that had been torn up by the roots. Standing before the proprietor, he asked him why he was so sad. To which the other answered, 'What can it avail if I tell thee, for thou canst not help me?' The dwarf replied, 'Thou art sad because thou canst not get thy corn ground, and hast many children and people that require bread. But I will show thee a place on thy own grounds where thou canst build seven mills that shall never lack water.' And having pointed out to him the spot, Herr Bille built there the seven mills still existing by Ellebro Dam, which are never at a stand for want of water, winter or summer.

It is further related that the same dwarf gave him a little white horn, which, as long as it remained in his family, should preserve them in prosperity. This horn, it is said, was long preserved at Söholm in Seeland.

### 2 – Herr Eske Brok

Herr Eske Brok, who dwelt at Vemmeltoft, going one day into the fields, amused himself with striking the air with his stick, when suddenly a hat fell at his feet, which he ordered his servant to take up, and placed it on his own head; but had no sooner done so than he became invisible. He then tried it on his servant with the same result; so that whoever had the hat on became invisible to others. Greatly delighted with his prize, he took it home with him. Shortly after a bareheaded boy came to the gate, requesting to speak with Herr Eske Brok. When the latter appeared, the boy requested to have his hat back, which Herr Eske had struck from his head with a stick, offering a hundred ducats for it, and afterwards more, if he would let him have it. But all that the boy could say was to no purpose, for Herr Eske had taken a particular fancy to the hat. At length the boy promised him, that if he would give it back, his posterity should never come to want anything, and by this means got the hat from the 'junker', who thought that with such a promise it was well paid. But the boy, when going out at the door, said, 'Thou shalt leave no sons behind thee, but daughters only!' And so it proved in the sequel, for Herr Eske's wife brought forth several sons all dead-born, and he himself died the last of his race.

## 3 – The Half-full Bottle

When the Swedes above a hundred years since invaded Holstein, it happened that after a battle in which the Danes were victorious, a soldier, who had his post on the field, had with great difficulty obtained a bottle of beer to allay his burning thirst. When about to drink he heard a Swede, who had lost both his legs, calling to him in a faint voice, and begging a refreshing draught. The soldier thereupon went to him, and seeing his deplorable condition, bent forwards to reach him the bottle; but at the same moment the treacherous enemy fired his pistol at him, hoping even in death to have his revenge. But the ball missed, for our Lord held his hand over the compassionate soldier. Rising up he drank half the contents of the bottle, and then held it out to the traitor saying, 'Scoundrel! Now thou shalt have only the half.'

When this reached the ears of the king, he ordered the soldier to be called before him, and gave him a coat of arms, in which was a half-filled bottle; and this bearing has continued in his family, which yet lives in Flensborg.

## 4 – Heer Erland Limbek

The Limbeks were an eminent race in Denmark, but are now extinct; from, it is said, the following cause.

While Herr Erland Limbek was residing at Gravengaard in Jutland, there one day came a dwarf to him as he was walking in his fields, complaining that he was engaged in hostilities with another dwarf, and feared that he was hardly strong enough to withstand him, unless Herr Erland would come to his aid on a certain day. He at the same time promised the knight that if he would do so, his race should be powerful and prosperous as long as the world lasted. Herr Erland promised to assist the dwarf, and fixed both time and place; but being one night unable to sleep, and tossing himself about in the bed, his wife asked him why he was so restless. He then imparted to her the promise he had made to the dwarf, whereupon she exclaimed, 'God forbid, my dear husband, that you should have intercourse with such demons!' and persuaded him to break his word. Some time after, on a Christmas Eve, as Herr Erland was sitting merry with his family and friends, the door of the room was opened, and a little dwarf in a habit of gold embroidery entered, saying to the knight, 'Had you kept your word, I would have kept mine; but now your race shall from day to day degenerate and be despised, and at last be extinguished, and the last of your family shall be mad!' Hereupon Herr Erland became angry, and said, 'Dost thou threaten me?' and attempted to strike him, but the dwarf retired to the door. The knight then ordered a servant to seize him, but the dwarf slipped away in haste, yet was, nevertheless, jammed in the doorway, so that he lost one of his shoes, which proved to be of pure gold. From this event the knight acquired the name of Herr Erland Guldsko.

## 5 – The Family of Monrad

The family of Monrad is said to descend from a miller in Hungary, who in a war with the Turks raised a body of men and destroyed a large Turkish force, whereby he relieved a corps of Imperialists. As a reward for so important a service, the emperor made him a general and raised him to the rank of noble, giving him shield and helmet, and commanding him to bear in his shield a half-moon, in remembrance of the Turks, and a mill-wheel, that he might remember his former condition; whence he and his posterity acquired the name of Mondrad.[1]

## 6 – The Name and Arms of the Rosenkrandses

The first of the Rosenkrands family was Herr Eric. In company with Stie Hvide he made a journey to Rome, where the pope gave him a wreath (krands) of roses, which, as a remembrance, he caused to be represented on his helmet, whence his family acquired its name. This Herr Rosenkrands lies buried in Hiörringholms Mark.

---

In the year 663 the young Herr Styge, a son of the king of Denmark, made a journey to King Ekuin in England, for the purpose of helping him in war. There, on account of his valour, he became a great favourite, particularly of the ladies; but the one that loved him most was the daughter of Reduval, the prince royal, and he, on his part, also loved her. He therefore continued at court throughout the winter; but when summer came the princess was pregnant. After his departure from England, the princess was delivered of a son, which she laid in a golden coffer, with a consecrated candle and salt, because he had not been baptised, and placed the coffer out on the sea strand. One day her father, the prince royal, Reduval,

---

1 From Ger. Mond, *moon* and Rad, *wheel*.

happening to ride by, found the infant, and concluding from the golden coffer that he was of high parentage, he had him reared and gave him the name of Carl. After the king's death, the prince royal, Reduval, ascended the throne of England, of which he was the first Christian king. Carl in the meanwhile grew up and became distinguished for bravery, so that the king thought he could not do better than marry him to his daughter. When the wedding was just about to take place, the princess disclosed to the bridegroom that he was her own son by Prince Styge of Denmark. At this intelligence the king was so exasperated, that he declared at first she should perish on the pile; but the young Carl interceded for her and effected a marriage with her and Prince Styge, who had been separated from her for nineteen years.

In remembrance of these events, Prince Carl divided his shield into four parts by a white cross, whereby he betokened that he was a Christian; he next painted it transversely red and blue, thereby betokening that he was both a Danish and an English prince. In the first quarter he placed a white lion crowned, to denote Denmark; in the fourth another white lion for England. In the second and third quarters he placed a black and white chess-board, thereby signifying the separation that had so long existed between his father and mother. And these are the arms of Rosenkrands.

## 7 – The Arms of the Trolle Family

The Trolles were in their time, particularly in the fifteenth and sixteenth centuries, one of the first families in Denmark. In allusion to their name, they bore in their coat a Troll or demon, and wherever monuments of the family are to be seen, this demon is to be seen also. Even in the cathedral of Roeskilde, he is represented on the iron lattice which encloses the sepulchral chapel of the family. He there appears larger than life with a long tail and claws in a half-flying attitude, the effect of which, when viewed on a sudden, is somewhat startling. The Trolle family is now extinct. One of its most illustrious members was Admiral Herluf Trolle, the founder of the school of Herlufsholm in the seventeenth century, the Eton or Winchester of Denmark.[1]

## 8 – Major-general Svanwedel

About two hundred years ago, there dwelt at Nörre-Vosborg in Jutland a proprietor named Svanwedel. He had been a major-general in the Swedish war, and was, moreover, skilled in the black art. On one occasion, during

---

1  Kohl's *Reisen in Dänemark*, i, p. 283. See also p. 292.

the war in Scania, he was surrounded by the enemy, and had with him only a small body of troops. But he managed to help himself; for in the night he transformed a quantity of rushes, that were growing in the field, into soldiers, with whose aid he attacked and beat the enemy. Next morning these soldiers were all rushes again standing on the field as before.

When he died at Vosborg, his body was, according to usage, deposited in the castle chapel before being conveyed to the church. One evening, as his daughter entered the chapel, he rose up in his coffin and directed her to send for Magister Niels, the priest of Huusby. Although this Magister Niels, during the general's lifetime, had been constantly quarrelling with him, he nevertheless came without delay, having with him a sharp axe. He then shut himself in the chapel with the corpse, but what passed between them no one knows; only such a noise was heard within that the whole mansion shook with it. At length all was again silent, and Master Niels came out with his axe, looking deadly pale. From that time the general remained quiet in his coffin, and was buried with great pomp in Ulvborg church.

# Traditions of Towns and Other Places

## 1 – The Ramparts of Copenhagen

Many years ago, when the ramparts were being raised round Copenhagen, the earth always sank, so that it was not possible to get it to stand firm. They therefore took a little innocent girl, placed her on a chair by a table, and gave her playthings and sweetmeats. While she thus sat enjoying herself, twelve masons built an arch over her, which when completed they covered over with earth, to the sound of music with drums and trumpets. By this process they are, it is said, rendered immoveable.

*It is a universal tradition that every kind of building is strengthened when any living being is buried beneath it. For such sacrifices, a lamb, a swine, or poultry, are generally chosen. Heinrich Heine (Die romantische Schule, p. 270), says on this subject: 'In the middle age the opinion prevailed, that when any building was to be erected, something living must be killed, on the blood of which the foundation must he laid, by which process the building would continue firm and immoveable And in ballads and traditions the remembrance is still preserved how children or animals were slaughtered, for the purpose of strengthening large buildings with their blood.'*

## 2 – The Image of St Oluf

St Oluf had a chapel at Taasinge, in which his image was preserved. This it was the custom of the peasants to carry about their fields, after they had put their seed in the ground, that they might have a plentiful harvest. It once happened that a countryman, who had been carrying the image about his fields, and ought to have restored it to its place in the chapel, thought it advisable to wait till the following day, but having no better place wherein to deposit it, he laid it in the oven. Next morning the servant maid having to bake, and not knowing that St Oluf was there, put fire in the oven, and so the image was burnt. From that time it is said that the village has no good luck to expect.

## 3 – Secret Passages under Aalborg

Under the town of Aalborg there are many secret passages, which are relics of the monkish times. The largest of these is said to lead from the old convent, used at present partly as a hospital and partly as a school, and is supposed to extend, under the fiord, as far as Sundby, where there was formerly a convent of nuns. The descent to this passage was well secured;

for first it was closed with a brazen door, on which many beautiful figures were sculptured, and next with four doors of iron, one within another. One side passage led from this chief one to the church of St Mary, under the mansion in which King Hans died. The ascent into the church was through a tomb. Another branch led from the chief passage to St Budolf's church, and thence to the 'Murede Port's bridge'. A third branch led, in an opposite direction, from St Mary's church, or from the convent, to the old castle of Aalborghuus.

A student once undertook to explore these passages, which he entered with a cord bound fast round his body. In one hand he had a sword, in the other a light. At the outside of the entrance he had placed people, who at a given sign should draw him back by means of the cord. But after he had been in two hours without making any sign, they drew the cord, the end of which was burnt off. The student was never again heard of.

# Of Churches and Convents

## 1 – Of Churches

When King Cnut, surnamed the Saint, was building the first churches in the country, he wished them to be so strong that they might last until the end of the world. He therefore prayed to God for direction how he might build strong and masterly. He then went to the seashore, where there lay much froth (scum). This he ordered the masons to take and to build with it. Through his sanctity this froth became as hard as stone, and the churches that have such walls will never decay as long as the world endures.

*Of the so-called froth-walls many instances occur among the old country churches of Denmark. They consist of a porous mass which the peasants call fraa (froth), the production of which the master-masons declare is to them a perfect riddle. Notwithstanding its porosity, it is extremely durable. From the description it would seem to be of the nature of travertine or piperine, of which the ancient builders made use, and which is still much used in the South. As long as it lies in its natural bed it is so soft that it may be cut out with a spade, but by the influence of the atmosphere it increases in hardness from year to year.*

## 2 – The Tower of St Mary's in Copenhagen

In the year 1514, when a spire was being placed on the tower of St Mary's cathedral in Copenhagen, a carpenter's man had an altercation with his master, and in his anger boasted that he was as able a workman as himself.

To make an end of the dispute, the master laid a beam out from the top of the tower, took an axe in his hand, went out on the beam, and struck the axe fast in the end of it. Having done this, and being safely returned, he ordered his man to go and fetch him the axe. The man went without hesitation, but while standing on the end of the beam, and in the act of seizing the axe, it seemed to him that there were two, and he asked: 'Master! Which is it to be?' The master then knew how it was with him, and answered only, 'God be merciful to thy poor soul!' At the same instant the man reeled from the beam.

*A story nearly the same is related of the tower of St Cnut's church in Odense, but in which the man, when on the end of the beam, looked over the town, and in his trepidation cried, 'Master! Bulbro is coming nearer!' Bulbro is a small place near Odense.*

## 3 – The Chimes in the Tower of St Nicholas

During the great fire at Copenhagen, and while the church of St Nicholas was enveloped in flames, the tower long stood reeling from one side to another. People, too, relate who heard it, that the chimes in the meanwhile played of themselves the psalm, 'God knows how near me is mine end.'

## 4 – The Sea-troll in The Issefiord

In former days there dwelt in the Issefiord[1] a Troll, who was accustomed to stop every vessel that entered the fiord and demand a man from each. This calamity had been long endured, when it became known that the power of the Troll would last until the head of Pope Lucius should be shown him, who had been beheaded in Rome many centuries before. Some monks were accordingly forthwith sent to Rome to fetch the head. When the ship returned and was about to run into the fiord, the Troll made his appearance; but as soon as they held forth the head and the Troll got a sight of it, he with a horrid howl transformed himself into a rock. In Roeskilde cathedral many representations are to be seen which may be explained by this tradition.

---

1   The Issefiord or firth runs from the Cattegat in various directions into Seeland. The city of Roeskilde is built on the south end of one of its arms called the Roeskilde fiord.

## 5 – Roeskilde Cathedral

In the year 1084 Roeskilde cathedral was dedicated to Pope Lucius, who in the year 253 had suffered martyrdom, he having offered to be the patron saint of the church. For before the church was built, Bishop Svend Norbagge despatched two canons to Rome to fetch some relic of a saint to whom the church might be dedicated. The immense number of relics of all sorts which they found there caused them no small embarrassment, but in order to choose a fitting one, they sought to strengthen their judgement by prayer. While thus engaged in devotion, one of the canons fell asleep, when Pope Lucius appeared before him, proffered his patronage, and gave such an exact description of his skull, that they easily found it among all the others. This skull was accordingly chosen and conveyed to Denmark, where, set in gold, it was long preserved as the most precious possession of Roeskilde cathedral.

## 6 – Veiby Church

In Veiby church in Seeland there was formerly kept a man's dried-up hand. Of this it is related that it had belonged to a man, who many years before was burnt for having murdered his father, and therefore could not be consumed by the fire.

## 7 – Kallundborg Church

When Esbern Snare was building Kallundborg[1] church, the work at first did not succeed, but there came a Troll to him offering his service, and with him Esbern Snare made an agreement, that when the church was finished, he should either say what the Troll's name was, or should give him his heart and his eyes. The work now went on well, and was supported by stone pillars. But when it was nearly complete, one half-pillar only being wanting, Esbern Snare began to feel alarmed, because he was still ignorant how the Troll was called. He went wandering about the fields sorrowing, and one day, being weary and sad, he lay down on Ulshöi Banke to rest. He there heard a Troll-wife within the mound saying, 'Be still, my child, tomorrow Fin thy father will come and give thee Esbern Snare's eyes and heart to play with.' On hearing these words, Esbern

---

1    A town on the west coast of Seeland. Esbern Snare's church still exists, the five towers of which render it a conspicuous object for miles around. In the castle, not a vestige of which remains, Christian II died (1559), after a confinement of twenty-seven years, *viz*, seventeen at Sönderborg and ten at Kallundborg. King Albert of Sweden was also imprisoned in the castle of Kallundborg by Queen Margaret.

became himself again and returned to the church. At this moment the Troll entered, bringing the half-pillar that was wanting, when Esbern, on seeing him, saluted him by his name of Fin. Hearing this, the Troll was so angry, that he flew off through the air with the half-pillar; and therefore the church has only three pillars and a half.

Kallundborg church has five spires, built by Esbern Snare. The highest, which stands in the middle, is for his mother, and the four standing about it for his four daughters, one of whom was lame, and therefore one of the spires is less than the others.

## 8 – Rachlöv Church

To the north-east of Kallundborg lies the village of Rachlöv; but the church is a considerable distance from it in the open field. This circumstance is thus accounted for. While the village church was building, it was found that what had been built up during the day was constantly thrown down in the night. It was therefore determined, by the advice of some sagacious persons, to place two red bulls on the spot, for the purpose of driving away the evil spirits; and this was done accordingly. But on the following morning, one of the bulls was found killed outright, near to the town; the other was discovered standing out in the field on an eminence, wounded and misused. Hence the folks clearly enough saw that the evil spirits had no power in this place, and therefore resolved there to erect their church.

## 9 – The Altar-piece in Sorö Church

The altar-piece in Sorö church represents the Last Supper. It was at first determined that the twelve apostles should be painted after the twelve professors of Sorö Academy, but as they could not agree who should be Judas, twelve peasants were fetched from the village of Haverup, after whom the twelve apostles were painted. Of these, Andrew the shoemaker offered himself for Judas, but afterwards sank into all kinds of depravity, and things went extremely ill with him.

## 10 – Blood Spots on the Wall of Karise Church

A hunter in Stevnsherred was desirous of being an unerring shot. He therefore took the sacrament, but held the bread in his mouth until he came out of church. He then loaded his piece, put the bread into it, and fired it against the church wall. On the place where he struck the wall there is a hole, out of which blood flows, and which may still be seen.

Of another huntsman it is said that he stuck the wafer on the church wall and shot at it.

## 11 – The Church at Falster

There once dwelt on the island of Falster a lady of rank, who was extremely rich, but had neither son nor daughter to inherit her wealth. She therefore resolved to make a pious use of it, and caused a church to be built that was both spacious and magnificent. When the church was finished, she caused altar-candles to be lighted, and going through the quire to the altar, she cast herself on her knees and prayed to God that, in reward for her pious gift, he would add as many years to her life as the church should stand. Then from time to time her relations and servants died; but she who had preferred so foolish a prayer, continued to live. At length she had no longer a friend or relation to converse with, and saw children grow up, become aged and die, and their children again grow old, while she herself was wasting through extreme age, so that she gradually lost the use of all her senses. Sometimes, however, she recovered her voice, though for one hour only at midnight every Christmas. On one of these nights she desired to be laid in an oaken coffin and placed in the church, that she might there die; but that the priest should attend her every Christmas night to receive her commands. From that time her coffin has stood in the church, but she has not yet been permitted to die. Every Christmas night the priest comes to her, lifts the lid of the coffin, and as he gradually raises it, she rises slowly up. When sitting up, she asks, 'Is my church yet standing?' And when the priest answers 'Yes,' she sighs and says:

> 'Ak! give Gud, at min Kirke var braendt;
> Thi da er först al mill Jammer fuldendt!'
>
> *Ah! God grant that my church were burnt;*
> *For then only would my affliction be ended.*

She then sinks back again into the coffin, the priest lets the lid fall, and does not come again until the next Christmas night.

## 12 – Maribo Church

In Maribo church, by one of the pillars, there is set up the image of a monk pointing to another pillar, in which, the tradition tells us, a treasure was hidden by the monks when they were compelled to leave the place.[1]

## 13 – Aarhuus Cathedral

Aarhuus cathedral was, in the time of Catholicism, dedicated to St Clement; because that saint, after his martyrdom, was cast ashore, bound to an anchor, near Aarhuus, after having been tossed about on the ocean for eleven hundred years. He was there buried, and in memory of him his figure with the anchor is to be seen on the altar-piece.

Before the Reformation, it was a custom in the same cathedral, during the solemn service of Good Friday eve, to send forth a tremendous voice, through a hole in the vaulting of the church, saying, 'Ever accursed be Judas!' On this occasion a large hunting horn was used, which till our time was preserved in the church. During the malediction a hollow, trembling voice was sent forth from the upper gallery of the north transept, uttering the words of Judas, 'I have sinned in that I have betrayed the innocent blood.'

## 14 – Ribe Cathedral

In Ribe cathedral there is a door called Cat's-head door (Kathöved Dör), in memory of an old tradition, to wit, that once on a time a poor skipper belonging to Ribe came to an island where the inhabitants were plagued with an overwhelming number of mice. Luckily he had a cat on board, which he took on shore with him, and so destroyed or drove off a vast number of them. His cat he sold to the inhabitants, for which having received a considerable sum, he sailed home and returned to the island with a whole cargo of cats, by which traffic he became so rich, that he had whereon to live for the rest of his life. When the hour of death drew nigh, he resolved to employ his wealth in building a church in Ribe, as a memorial of which benefit there is, we are told, a representation in the said church of a cat and four mice.

*The above-mentioned skipper may be styled the Danish Whittington. There was also an Italian Whittington, of whom it is related, in a letter from Lorenzo Magalotti to Ottavio*

---

1  The learned antiquary Arndt is reported to have declared that he found in the Vatican library a memorandum stating that a treasure of manuscripts and documents was concealed in a pillar of Maribo church.

*Falconieri (Idelers Handb. der ital. Lit., I, p. 355), that he, Ansaldo degli Ormanni by name, having arrived at one of the Canary islands, was invited by the king to dinner. During the repast he observed that all the attendants went about with long sticks, for the purpose of driving away the rats, which made constant attacks on the viands. Seeing this, he hastened to his ship and returned with two cats, which in an incredibly short time made an appalling slaughter among the enemy. He made a present of these cats to the king, who in return bestowed on him immense riches. On his return to his native country he related how he had acquired his wealth; whereupon a certain Giocondo de' Fisanti resolved on trying his luck there. Having sold his house, he embarked with a quantity of pearls and other precious things, in the belief that the king would no doubt prize such gifts much more highly than two cats. On his arrival he accordingly presented his gifts to the king, who valued them much, but having nothing which he considered more precious than the two cats, he gave one of them to Giocondo, who by his speculation was reduced to a state of poverty.*

## 15 – The Church at Erritsö

Many years ago there lived at Erritsö, near Fredericia, a very poor man, who one day said, 'If I had a large sum of money, I would build a church for the parish.' The following night he dreamed that if he went to the south bridge at Veile, he would make his fortune. He followed the intimation, and strolled backwards and forwards on the bridge, until it grew late, but without seeing any sign of his good fortune. When just on the point of returning, he was accosted by an officer, who asked him why he had spent the whole day so on the bridge. He told him his dream, on hearing which the officer related to him in return, that he also, on the preceding night, had dreamed, that in a barn at Erritsö, belonging to a man whose name he mentioned, a treasure lay buried. But the name he mentioned was the man's own, who prudently kept his own counsel, hastened home, and found the treasure in his barn. The man was faithful to his word and built the church.

*There is a story nearly similar to the above related of a treasure at Tanslet on the isle of Alien. The reader will, no doubt, be agreeably surprised at meeting with a tradition of near kin to the foregoing, respecting the reputed founder of Dundonald castle, in Ayrshire:*

  *Donald Din, or Din Donald, was originally a poor man, but had the faculty of dreaming lucky dreams. Upon one occasion he dreamed, thrice in one night, that if he were to go to London Bridge, he would become a wealthy man. He went accordingly, saw a man looking over the parapet of the bridge, whom he accosted courteously, and, after a little conversation, entrusted with the secret of the occasion of his visiting London Bridge. The stranger told him that he had made a very foolish errand, for he himself had once had a similar vision, which directed him to go to a certain spot in Ayrshire, in Scotland, where he would find a vast treasure; and, for his part, he had never once thought of obeying the injunction. From his description of the spot, the sly Scotsman at once perceived that the treasure in question must be concealed in no other place than his own humble* kail-yard *at home, to which he immediately repaired, in full expectation of finding it. Nor was he disappointed; for, after destroying many good and promising cabbages, and completely cracking credit with his wife, who esteemed him mad, he found a large potful of gold coin, with the proceeds of which he built a stout cattle for himself, and became the founder of a flourishing family.*[1]

## 16 – The Altar-piece in Sleswig Cathedral

Master Hans Brüggemann, born in Husum, was a skilful artisan and able man. It was he who made the beautiful altar-piece for the monks of Bordesholm, which, in the year 1666, was removed to the cathedral of Sleswig, on which, it is said, he and his men laboured for seven years, and of which every figure was steeped in oil, to prevent injury from worms. When the work was finished, King Christian II and his queen Elizabeth came to see it; on which occasion, Brüggemann, availing himself of the opportunity, carved likenesses of them both in wood, which he placed on two pillars on each side of the altar.

When the Lübeckers saw this work, they wished Hans Brüggemann to execute an altar-piece for them equally beautiful. This he not only engaged to do, but also to make one still more beautiful. Hereat the monks of Bordesholm were stung by jealousy, and gave him something which caused a fluxion and weakness of his eyes, so that he could no longer work. He died in the town of Eiderstädt, near Bordesholm.

*Of the altar-piece of the church of Nörre-Broby in Fyen it is also said, that when the artist had completed it, he was asked whether he could execute another better or equally good, and on his answering in the affirmative, 'they' put out his eyes. See a similar story of a clock at Cambray in Wolf, Niederl. Sagen, p. 444.*

1    Chambers, *Pop. Rh.*, p. 12.

## Traditions Relating to Mansions

### 1 – Herlufsholm

When Fru Birgitte Giöe was dead and the council of the realm had the direction of the school of Herlufsholm, it reached the ears of some of the family that the deed of gift was lost, a circumstance from which they hoped to derive advantage. The rector and the clergyman of the place were consequently summoned to Copenhagen, and found themselves in no trifling embarrassment by their inability to find the document. But when the priest, full of anxiety, had lain down on his bed, the night previous to his departure for Copenhagen, Fru Birgitte Giöe appeared before him; for she was unwilling that after her death the school should come to nothing, through the avarice of her family. The priest saw her go to an old table, and strike several blows on one of its legs. At this he was greatly surprised, and the following morning, on examining the table, he found, in a secret drawer, the lost document, which, accompanied by the rector, he produced in Copenhagen, and thus saved the school of Herlufsholm.

### 2 – Vaargaard

Many years ago, there dwelt at Vaargaard a lady named Fru Ingeborg, the widow of one of the family of Scheel, a great oppressor of the peasantry, whom he deprived of a meadow called Agersted Enge. But if the lord had been unjust and cruel to his tenants, his widow was still more so. Once on the anniversary of her husband's death, being on her way to church, she said to her coachman, 'I would fain know how things go with my poor husband.' To which the coachman, whose name was Claus, and who was a sly knave, answered, 'Ay, gracious lady! But that is not easy to say, though he will certainly not be suffering from cold; for it is no doubt warm enough where he is.' At this the lady was highly exasperated and threatened to take his life, if on the third Sunday following he did not bring her intelligence how it fared with her late husband. Claus, who well knew that his lady mistress never failed to keep her word when she promised any evil, resolved in the first instance to consult with the priest at Albek, who was as stiff in his book as any bishop, and understood equally well both how to keep people in their graves and to call them forth. But this priest, on consulting with a relation, was apprehensive that the task would prove too hard for him. Fortunately, however, the coachman had a brother who was a priest in Norway; of him therefore it would be safest to seek counsel, seeing that the Norwegian priests are more cunning in such matters than any others. Claus consequently made a trip to Norway, and found his brother, who instantly addressed him with, 'Welcome, Claus! Things must, indeed, be desperate with you, since you come all the way to me!' From these words the coachman saw plainly that his brother was perfectly aware how matters stood. On the following day, Claus asked him for advice and help. After some consideration, he answered, 'I can, it is true, compel your dead master to reappear; but it will prove a dangerous business if you are afraid of him, for you must yourself tell him your message.' It was now resolved that on the following night at twelve o'clock they would go to a crossroad in a large forest, and summon him forth. At the hour and place appointed the priest began to read so that the coachman's hair stood on end. At once a dreadful uproar was heard, and a red-hot chariot, with horses spouting fire on every side, came dashing through the forest, and stopped at the place where they were standing. Claus instantly knew his master again, although he was red-hot. 'Who will speak with me?' roared the master from the chariot. Claus took off his hat and said, 'I have to greet my gracious master from my gracious mistress, and to inquire how he fares since his death.' 'Tell her,' answered his master, 'that I am in hell, where there is a seat making for her, which only wants the last step; when that is laid down she will be fetched, if she does not restore Agersted Enge! But as a proof that thou hast spoken with me, I will give thee my wedding ring, which thou canst show her.' The priest then whispered to the coachman that he should hold out his hat, and in the same moment the ring fell in to the hat, through which it burned a hole and fell on the ground, from which Claus took it up. In the next moment, both chariot and horses were away.

On the third Sunday, Claus was standing outside of Vaar churchyard when Fru Ingeborg was driven by. On seeing him the gracious lady instantly inquired what message he had brought, when the coachman related to her all that he had seen and heard, and gave her the ring, which she instantly recognised. 'It is well,' said she, 'thou hast saved thy life. If I am to be with my husband when I am dead, be it so, but Agersted Enge I will never give back!'

Shortly after there was a pompous spectacle in Vaar church. It was the gracious lady's funeral. But she soon reappeared by night, and committed so much mischief in the castle yard, that the miller and the mill-folks ran to the priest at Albek, who read over her, conjured her out of the yard, and laid her in a pond hard by called Pulsen. Beyond this he had no power over her, but is obliged to allow her every year to approach a cock's step nearer to Vaargaard; and it is, moreover, said that whenever in this manner she reaches the spot from whence she was driven by the priest, Vaargaard will sink in ruin. On the place where she was conjured into Pulsen not a blade of grass ever grows, and by the scorched-up streaks in the field it may be seen how many cock's steps she has already gone.

# Traditions of priest and Wise Men

## 1 – St Andrew of Slagelse

In the year 1205 there lived in Slagelse a priest of St Peter's church who was known by the name of Holy Anders. Of this holy man it is related, that with eleven others he sailed to the Holy Land; but that when on the eve of returning, and the wind being fair, he would not proceed on the voyage until he had heard mass at Joppa. When the mass was ended and his companions were already on their way back, he found himself in much tribulation on the seashore viewing the distant vessel, when a man rode up to him and desired him to mount before him. Anders did so; but as they rode along he fell asleep in the stranger's arms. On waking he looked about him with astonishment, for he found himself on a mound just outside of Slagelse, and had, nevertheless, been to St James of Compostella in Portugal,[1] to St Olaf's in Drontheim, and many other holy places. But a long time elapsed before his companions, who had left him at Joppa, returned to Denmark, whereat all people greatly marvelled.

He was so holy a man that when he performed his devotions in the open air, he was wont to hang his cap and gloves on the sunbeams,[2] and thereby acquired an extraordinary reputation, and at length became the patron saint of Slagelse. It once happened that when he would thus hang his gloves on a sunbeam, they fell to the ground, at which he was deeply afflicted and asked our Lord, in what respect he had sinned, seeing that the miracle no longer succeeded, and was then given to understand that one of the inmates of the monastery had stolen a hedge-stake, and so defiled the sacred community. The mound on which St Anders was awakened, acquired from that event the name of the Hvilehöi (mound of rest), which it retains until this day.

St Anders interested himself also in the welfare of the people of Slagelse, by going with their petition to King Valdemar, in consequence of which the king promised to add to the land belonging to Slagelse as much as St Anders could ride round on a colt a day old, during the time the king was in the bath. He took the king at his word, and rode with such speed that the courtiers were obliged, from time to time, to run to the king in the bath, saying that if he did not make haste, St Anders would ride round the

---

1   Sic.
2   The monks of Adewert also hung their caps and cowls on the sunbeams. See Wolf, *Niederländische Sagen*, Leipzig, 1843, p. 411.

whole country. To this act the town of Slagelse is indebted for its extensive town fields.

On the Hvilehöi there stands a cross with the inscription: 'In memoriam divi Andreae, quiescentis Joppae et heic loci expergefacti.' When this cross was once suffered to fall into decay, a general murrain among the cattle ensued, but which ceased the instant a new cross was set up.

## 2 – Master Laurids

In Hadsherred in Jutland there was once a priest by name Master Laurids. He could lay the dead and call them from their graves, and, consequently, it hardly need be said, had many contests with the devil, in all which, however, his Satanic Majesty invariably came off second best.

It once happened to Master Laurids, when returning from a short journey, that on passing Skandrup church, his horses stopped, and were unable to draw the carriage from the spot; but Master Laurids, who well understood how matters were, shook his head and ordered his man to take off the right hind-wheel and lay it in the basket behind; for he knew that it was the devil who had placed himself on it for the purpose of making the carriage heavy. This was more than the devil had bargained for, for he had now to get down, take his station under the carriage, and hold it up. In this fashion Master Laurids made him follow during the whole night. When at length he set him at liberty, the fiend cast the axletree from his shoulder with such force that it was broken by the fall, at which Master Laurids smiling, said, 'See! He can do that yet!'

*That the devil on such occasions must go under the carriage instead of the fourth wheel was a universal popular belief not only in Denmark, but in other countries. A Catholic legend relates a similar miracle of St Benedict, which has supplied the subject of a well-known composition by the painter Ditlef Lindau at Rome.*

## 3 – The Priest of Nörre-Vilstrup

At the close of the last century there lived in the village of Nörre-Vilstrup, near Veile,[1] a priest who knew more than his Paternoster, and who employed the extraordinary power, which he had acquired in the Black School,[2] for the profit and happiness of his parishioners; on which account he was much beloved and respected. For the sake of this power, he had, it was said, sworn to wear only one garter; and it was well known to all that he never did wear two.

---

1   A small town on the east side of Jutland.
2   See more about the Black School in *North German Popular Traditions*.

To the parsonage there was attached a little thicket, which lay at a short distance from the village, from which the priest's kindling wood and fire-wood were sometimes stolen. He one day asked his servants whether they had no firewood to fetch from thence. To which they answered that for some time past there was none. 'You may at all events,' said he, 'take a wagon and drive out.' They did so, and there found a man from the village who had piled up a large quantity of brushwood, which he was about to carry off, but which the priest's men took away and carted home.

*The provost Petrus Aegidii at Bröns was a magician. A youth, who wanted to go to Ribe, took the provost's horse from the meadow; but the animal would not go forwards, and the lad could not get off his back, even when a couple of millers' men endeavoured to assist him. He was therefore obliged to ride to the priest. 'Art thou there?' said the good man. 'Go and take the horse back to the field, and play me no more such pranks.'*[1]

## 4 – St Kield of Viborg[2]

He was a very holy man, performed many miracles, was on that account made bishop of Viborg, and after his death canonised by the pope.

Before his sanctity was known, he was once expelled by the monks from the convent, and driven away; but meeting one of the conventual servants, who had been sent out to fetch water, he besought him to let him drink out of his pitcher. He did so, when Kield turned the water to wine, which he ordered the servant to take to the convent with his greeting to the brothers, and the request that they would drink that wine to his health. He was then speedily recalled and received with great joy.

One morning early, when reading mass at the altar, the lights were suddenly extinguished, so that it was quite dark; but he, nevertheless, continued reading the mass.

After his death, the report of his sanctity reached the pope at Rome, who caused his name to be enrolled in the catalogue of saints. His body was laid in a costly shrine, and suspended by golden chains from the vaulted roof of the chapel. His richly gilded coffin, called St Kield's ark, was held in great veneration until the Reformation, when it was taken down and placed behind the altar in the cathedral, where it perished in the great fire.

---

1    Rhode, *Haderslev-Amt*, quoted by Müllenhoff, op. cit., p. 600.
2    The oldest and most remarkable town in Jutland. From the remotest times the Danish monarchs on their accession received homage at Viborg, and here were held the assemblies of the States of the kingdom. Its venerable cathedral perished by fire in 1726. In its crypt masses were sung for the soul of the murdered king, Eric Glipping (AD 1287), which were continued till long after the Reformation.

# Treasures and Treasure-diggers

## 1 – The Treasure in Hvirvel Bakke

Hvirvel Bakke is said to be quite full of gold, whence it is that on every Christmas Eve it appears to be on fire. If anyone would only venture to shoot over the bakke,[1] he might no doubt take the whole of it, but nowadays no one dares do such a thing.

## 2 – The Treasure in Daugbierg-daus

At Daugstrup, not far from Viborg, there is a barrow called Daugbierg-Daus. Of this barrow it is said that it is always enveloped in a blue mist, and that under it lies a large copper kettle full of money. One night, two peasants went to dig for this treasure, and had already proceeded so far as to get hold of the two handles of the kettle; when all sorts of wonderful things took place, for the purpose of diverting them from their undertaking. At one moment they saw a large black dog with a red-hot tongue, then came a cock drawing a load of hay, next came a chariot with four black horses; but in spite of all this the men did not allow themselves to speak, and went on with their digging. At length a clown passing by, stopped before them and said, 'See! Daugbierg is on fire!' and when they looked in that direction, it was precisely as if the whole village stood in a blaze.[2] At this moment one of the men forgot to keep silence, and at the instant he began to cry out the treasure sank, and although they have often since endeavoured to raise it, the Trolls have always prevented them by their sorcery.

1  Bakke is a small hill or rising ground.
2  A similar superstition prevailed in Scotland. About a century ago, we are told, that the laird of Craufurdland and his domestics, when on the point of drawing up a pot of gold from the bottom of a pool, heard a noise overhead, which caused them to let go their prize and look upwards. They perceived a terrific figure standing on the top of the hill, using violent gesticulations, and crying:

> Tip tow!
> Craufurdland's a' in a low!

Whereupon the laird, believing that the evil one had set fire to his house, in order to divert him from his researches, left the scene, followed by his servants, and ran home to save what he could. Of course there was no fire whatever at the house.

Chambers, *Popular Rhymes, etc.*, p. 13.

*In digging up a treasure the strictest silence is necessary; hence Oehlenschlaeger in his poem 'Skattegraveren' (the Treasure-digger) says:*

> Men hvis et Ord du taler,
> Forsvinder den igien.

> But if a word thou utter,
> It vanishes again

## 3 – The Treasure on Fuur

The little isle of Fuur in the Liimfiord rests on a vast stone, in the middle of which dwells a Troll. When the shepherds in the field place their ear to the ground, they sometimes hear him locking and unlocking his great money chests; and a peasant, who for three Christmas nights went thither at midnight, saw at the third time, the Troll sitting on the hillock displaying all his treasures. If anyone shoots over such things, he can freely take of them as much as he will, and so did this peasant. But when he was on his return home and very near his dwelling, it seemed to him to be in flames. In his alarm he cast from him all he had taken, and when he reached home all was safe, but the treasure was gone.

On the north side of the isle a small part of the stone may be clearly seen among high, heath-grown hills, and many names are there inscribed of persons who have visited the spot. On a level with the earth is a hole through which a person can enter the stone, but it is not known how far anyone can go, as the greater number do not venture beyond five steps.

## 4 – The Treasure in Lodal

In Sallingherred there is a valley called Lodal, where formerly a light was seen burning every night. But it happened that a Holsteiner came to the place, who desired to be shown the way to Lodal, it having been revealed to him in a dream, that on the spot where a light was to be seen burning he should dig and find a treasure. He dug accordingly and found in the earth a capacious copper kettle full of gold, but upon the gold there lay a large black poodle with a ring round its neck. This he carefully lifted from the kettle, laid it on his greatcoat, and so got possession of the treasure, of which he distributed a portion to the peasants who had assisted him, and then departed. From that time the light ceased to burn; but sometimes the dog may be seen running about in Lodal.

# *Traditions of Robbers*

## 1 – Thyre Bolöxe and Her Sons

Close along an arm of the Issefiord in Seeland, the road passes through Borreveile forest, where is yet to be seen the so-called Thyre's cave.

This Thyre, surnamed Bolöxe, with her twelve sons were notorious robbers, but being at length captured, were all executed at Roeskilde.[1] The following tradition concerning them is still current among the peasantry thereabouts.

It often happens, when anyone drives past the cave by night, that the horses suddenly begin to sweat violently, and are scarcely able to drag the carriage. A countryman, who on such an occasion descended from his vehicle and peeped through the left side of the headstall, saw that he had Thyre Bolöxe and her twelve sons sitting behind. His only resource was to take off the hind wheel and lay it in the vehicle; for by so doing all such spectres are compelled to run under the carriage, for the purpose of holding up the axle-tree.

## 2 – Stark Olger

In Ugilt krat (thicket), between Hiöring and Fladstrand, when the country thereabouts had much forest land, there was a robber who called himself Staerk (Strong) Olger or Ole. He robbed and murdered whenever he had an opportunity, but he was particularly notorious for murdering pregnant women. At length the men having armed themselves, surrounded the entire wood and captured him, when he thus confessed: 'It is well that you have caught me this time; for henceforth no bond would have bound or hand held me; for I had already eaten the hearts of six unborn children! Could I but have got the seventh!'

## Voldborg's Day

On Voldborg's day, that is the day preceding Whit-Sunday, there was in former times a great merrymaking throughout the country, or, as it was called, *the riding in of summer*. The youth of both sexes prepared themselves for the festival, and decorated themselves with their best for the

---

1    In the year 1716.

procession. The young men's procession, in which all were on horseback, was headed by two stewards, who rode forward to announce their approach. These were followed by two old men, each holding in his hand a long pole decorated with ribands, garlands, silk handkerchiefs, and whatever else might appear showy. After them came the Count of May (Maigreve) with his two attendants, and lastly the whole procession, two and two, all clad in blue or red frocks, with white napkins from the shoulder down under the opposite arm, and ribands fluttering in their hats. The May-count had two garlands, one over each shoulder, while every other had one only. In the middle of the procession rode the musicians, playing on violins, drums and fifes. When they came to a boundary, a garland was laid on the place of entrance; and when in the villages or at the mansions they met any young females, they threw garlands to them, which was an invitation to their guild or feast. When they entered a town or village, both stewards went to a house and begged that the procession might enter; and when permission was granted, they rode thrice round the court, and on passing the windows saluted the inmates. They then dismounted, and the leading singers began to sing, the rest, at the end of every verse, falling in with 'med Glaede' (with joy). On coming to a particular verse, two of the party went to the church, where they knelt on the threshold, and while in that position the others sang the rest of the song. They afterwards danced a while, and were regaled with beer and brandy, and sometimes received money also. They then re-mounted their horses, rode again round the court, and proceeded farther in the same order.

When the girls *ran summer in,* they assembled where the festival or guild was to be, clad in green with white napkins, and garlands on their heads and over their shoulders. Thence they proceeded to the fields and formed themselves in a circle, when the steward tried a garland on each, until he found one that it fitted: she was then Countess of May (Maigrevinde). The procession then went its round. Whoever would receive them raised a pole adorned with flowers and garlands, as a sign. According to other accounts, the Count of May, on their return, cast a garland on the girl he chose for Countess.

**Friar Ruus**[1] (*continued from p.* 353)

In consequence of his skill in the culinary art, and of certain secret services rendered by him to the abbot and monks of Esrom, Ruus was, by universal suffrage, elected a member of the brotherhood, in which character he sojourned among them during a period of seven years. Having much leisure on his hands, he was in the habit of sitting at the convent gate and amusing himself with cutting oaken cudgels. On being asked for what purpose he designed the cudgels, he answered, that it was well to be prepared in case of thieves coming by night. Shortly after, a dispute ensues among the brethren about a female, one party being headed by the abbot, the other by the prior. Both parties apply to Ruus for cudgels, and both receive a supply. A battle then takes place between them in the church, where they are assembled at matins, during which Ruus extinguishes the lights, and in the heat of the mêlée hurls a heavy bench in the midst of the combatants. After the limbs of many are broken, and others more or less maimed, Ruus, with a sanctified countenance, appears among them with a light, reproves them for their unseemly conduct, and exhorts them to peace and concord.

Sometime after this event, Ruus goes out to amuse himself, and forgets to prepare supper for the convent. As he is hurrying home he sees a cow grazing, which he kills, taking with him a hind quarter. In the preceding part we have seen that the owner of the cow lies in wait for the thief and, while concealed in a hollow tree, sees Lucifer with a company of devils assemble on its summit. These recount to their prince their several exploits, Ruus among the rest, who promises to bring with him all the brotherhood, but that they should previously murder each other. When the devils had taken flight, the peasant hastened to the convent, where he related to the abbot all he had heard while in the tree. At his recital the holy man was not a little terrified, and, having assembled the fraternity, related to them all that the man had told him. Thereupon they betake themselves to prayer, and ring for mass, when the abbot, taking Ruus with him, orders him to remain, without stirring from the spot during the whole mass. Upon Ruus saying he could no longer stay, during the administration of the sacrament, the abbot conjures him into the form of a horse. On promising to do no more harm, he is set free and passes over to England.

---

1    From *Die Deutschen Volksbücher* von Karl Simrock, Bd. 6. As a more detailed narrative of the doings of Friar Ruus, after he became head cook, may not be uninteresting to the reader, I add the sequel of his story, abridged from the metrical account of him in the above-named work, which I had not at hand when translating the portion of his history already given. In the German story, he is called Rausch, which is the same as the Danish Ruus, and signifies *drunkenness, debauchery.*

In England he enters the king's fair daughter, whereupon her father sends for all the wise and learned men from Paris and elsewhere; but not one of them is powerful enough to cast forth the evil spirit from the body of the princess. At length the demon himself exclaims, 'I am Brother Ruus. No one can expel me from this fair vessel, save the abbot of Esrom, to whom I have sworn obedience.' This dignitary had, it seems, in the meanwhile, become as holy again as ever. The abbot is, consequently, sent for, who casts out the evil spirit, commanding him to stand before him in a horse's form; when, to the great astonishment of the king and all present, the abbot binds him with a heavy chain.

Seeing a quantity of lead lying close by, the abbot requested, as his sole reward, to have as much of it, for the roof of his convent, as Ruus could carry on his back. Ruus carries accordingly the enormous weight of three hundred thousand pounds. The king and the abbot then sit down to dinner, but before they have finished their repast, Ruus appears before them, telling them he has carried the lead and waits for further orders, asking, at the same time, whether he should take the palace and set it by the side of the convent. The abbot desires him to let the palace stand, and merely conduct him safely back to Esrom. Then taking leave of the king, after giving him his blessing, the holy man gives his hand to the devil,[1] who forthwith sets him down safe and sound at his own gate. The fiend then asks where his future residence is to be, when the abbot assigns him a neighbouring hill, in which he is to sojourn till doomsday.

---

1   According to the Danish metrical version, Ruus takes the abbot on his back. Thiele, op. cit., ii, p. 148.

# Danish Popular Belief [1]

1 If a girl wishes to know what sort of a husband she is to have, she must on New Year's eve pour some melted lead into a glass of water, and the following morning observe what form it has assumed. If it resembles a pair of scissors, she will inevitably get a tailor; if a hammer, he will be a smith, etc. Another method, equally efficacious, is to break an egg into a glass of water, and judge from the figure it takes.

2 If girls are desirous of seeing their future husbands, let them on the eve of the Epiphany, before going to bed, repeat the following verses:

> Ye three holy kings, to you I pray,
> That ye tonight will let me see
> Whose cloth I shall spread,
> Whose bed I shall make,
> Whose name I shall bear,
> Whose bride I shall be.

3 Another formula, probably to be repeated on the anniversary of St Lucy (13th December), is the following:

> Lucy the gentle
> Shall give me to know
> Whose cloth I shall spread,
> Whose bed I shall make,
> Whose child I shall bear,
> Whose beloved I shall be,
> In whose arm I shall sleep.

4 It is a custom among the girls on St John's day to gather St John's wort (hypericum) and place it between the beams under the roof, in order to form from it a judgement as to the future. The usual mode is, to place one plant for themselves and another for their sweetheart: if these grow together, it is a presage of a wedding. Or they set the plants between the beams, that they may know from them which of their relations shall have a long life, and which a short one. If the plant grows up towards the roof, it is a good sign; but if downwards, it betokens sickness and death. [2]

---

1    Thiele, op. cit., iii, p. 95 *sqq.*
2    The heathen festival of the Summer Solstice, or Death of Baldur, was, it seems, by the Christian missionaries made to coincide with the anniversary of the Nativity of St

5 When lads and lasses wish to know who shall remove from, and who shall stay in, the house, they cast a shoe over their head towards the door. If it falls so that the heel is turned towards the door, the party will remain; if the toe lies towards the door, they will remove.

6 If a person sees the cuckoo for the first time in the year while he is yet fasting, it is said, 'The cuckoo befools us.' If it is a male person, he shall not find any cattle or anything else he may seek after. If it is a girl, she must be on her guard against young men, lest she be be-fooled by them. If it is old folks, they have good reason to fear sickness.

7 If servants see the stork, for the first time in the year, flying, it betokens that they will change their place during that year. If they see it standing, they will continue in their situation.

8 To discover a thief, particularly among the servants, it was formerly the custom to 'make the sieve move'. For this purpose, the master placed a sieve in equilibrium on the point of a pair of scissors, and then repeated the names of all the servants, at the same time watching the sieve, which would infallibly begin to move, when the thief was named.

9 When anything is stolen, recourse should be had to the 'cunning folks', who have the faculty of forcing the thief to bring back the stolen property.

10 From Christmas day till New Year's day nothing that runs round may be set in motion; there must, consequently, be neither spinning nor winding.[1]

11 On Christmas night at midnight the cattle rise in their stalls.

12 If, when sitting at table on Christmas Eve, you wish to know whether any of those present will die before the next Christmas, go out silently and peep through one of the window panes: the person who appears sitting at table without a head, will die in the following year.

---

John the Baptist. Instead of Baldur's brow (see p. 26, note 2), the plant appropriated to the Christian holyday was the hypericum (or androsaemum), which in England also was once 'considered as powerful for the expulsion of witches, and for the prognostication of the fates of young men and maidens. In Lower Saxony girls gather sprigs of it, and fasten them to the walls of their chamber. If the sprig, the next morning, remains fresh, a suitor may be expected; if it droops or withers, the maiden is destined to an early grave. Hyp. perforatum was the species used in this country.' Walker's *Flora of Oxfordshire*, p. 217. Finn Magnusen, *Den Aeldre Edda*, i, p. 17. The name androsaemum (ἀνδρὸς αἷμα) is probably an allusion to the decollation of the Baptist; the plant containing a reddish fluid.

1    In Anspach, when on Christmas or New Year's Eve the candles of a Christmas tree are lighted, a person has only to observe the shadows of those present, to discover who will die in the coming year: in the shadow they will appear without heads.

13 At a party it is not good for thirteen to sit down to table; for then one of them must die before a year is over.

14 To cut one's nails on a Friday brings luck.

15 When your nails or hair have been cut, the cuttings should either be burnt or buried; for if evil-disposed persons get possession of them, they may bewitch the person who had borne them.[1]

16 If a person finds a broken needle on the ground, before he has said his morning prayer, he will get either blows or bad words.[2]

17 If the eyes of a corpse stand open, it betokens that one of the same family will die shortly after.

18 Clothes and linen that have belonged to one dead, soon decay and fall in pieces, even as the corpse rots in the grave.

19 A corpse must not be buried in the clothes of a living person; because as the clothes rot in the grave, so will the person to whom the clothes had belonged consume and waste.

20 When the tallow round a burning candle curls itself like a shaving, it forebodes the death of someone, most commonly of the person towards whom it points.[3]

21 One must not weep over the dying, still less let tears fall on them; for then they cannot rest in the grave.

22 If in the morning blue spots appear on the body, they are the pinches of a spectre, and betoken the death of a relative or dear friend.

23 It was the custom formerly, when a person died, to cause the bells to toll immediately, while the departed soul was passing to heaven.[4]

24 When dogs howl they forebode death.

25 When a magpie perches on a house, it is a sign that strangers are coming.

---

1    In Swabia the superstition is universal, that cuttings of hair must he burnt, or cast into running water; for if a bird should get them and carry them away, either the person's hair will fall off or the witches may harm him. *Journal von und für Deutschl.*, 1788, p. 441.

2    Holberg's *Uden Hoved og Hale*, Act 1, Sc. 2.

3    In England, too, on the same occasion, we say, 'See! There is a winding-sheet in the candle.'

4    Our passing bell, still in use, though the belief in which it originated has long ceased to prevail.

26  If swallows or storks build their nests on the house, they must not be disturbed: they bring good luck.[1]

27  If you find a four-lobed clover, or a twin nut, or a skilling, you must keep it, as either of them brings luck.

28  On going out in the morning you should take notice whom you meet; it not being good to meet an old woman; nor is it a good sign if a hare runs across the way.[2]

29  If a person wishes to see the devil or have any communication with him, he must walk round the church thrice, and at the third time stop at the church door, and either cry 'Come out', or whistle through the keyhole.

30  If anyone wishes to know whether a deceased person has had intercourse with the devil during his life, let him peep through the harness of the horses that draw the hearse; when, if such has been the case, he will see a black dog sitting behind the carriage.

31  Whoever possesses the book of Cyprian, can by reading out of it perform all sorts of conjurations; but when in possession of the book, a person cannot easily get rid of it; for whether he sells, or burns, or buries it, it always returns to its owner.

32  If anyone has the book of Cyprian, he can read the devil to him; but he must be prepared to give him such work to do as will cause him annoyance. But it is a bad affair, if a person does not also know how to read him away again.

33  Only those children that are born on a Sunday or a holyday can see spirits.

34  If anyone is afraid of spectres, let him strew flax-seed before his door; then no spirit can cross the threshold. A preventive equally efficacious is, to place one's slippers by the bedside with the heels towards the bed.[3] Spectres may also be driven away by smoking the room with the

---

1   Olaf Tryggvason, although a Christian, observed whether the crow stood on its right or left foot, and predicted good or evil accordingly; whence his enemies nicknamed him *kråkabein* (crow-leg).

2   'The coal-miners in the north of England account it specially unlucky to cross a woman on their way to the pit, and many a miner, if he catches a glimpse, or fancies he does so, of the flutter of a female dress, will turn on his heel and go back to bed again.' – *Morning Chronicle*, 20th December 1849. This superstition was no doubt brought over by the Scandinavian settlers in the north of England.

3   Holberg's *Uden Hoved og Hale*, Act 1, Sc. 2.

snuff of a tallow candle; while wax lights attract them: hence it partly arises that churches are always haunted. Another preventive is, to place steel at the door.

35 If you nail a horseshoe fast to the step of the door, no spirit can enter.[1]

36 When the peasant women have prepared their dough, they are accustomed to make a cross either on the dough or on the bread made from it; that the trolls may not injure it.

37 If a person enters the church too early in the morning, he may happen to see the dead, how they sit in the pews.

38 Trolls dare not pronounce the word *cross*, but call it merely 'here and there'.

39 When out fishing, men must be careful not to quarrel about the draught; nor must one envy another; as the fish will then instantly disappear from the spot.

40 If a person dies who, it is feared, will reappear, as a preventive, let a basinful of water be thrown after the corpse, when it is carried out.

41 It is absurd to shoot at a spectre, as the bullet will return on him who shot it. But if the piece be loaded with a silver button, that will infallibly take effect.

42 The third night after burial the dead are wont to walk.

43 A pregnant woman must not walk over a place where a knife has been ground; as it causes a difficult delivery. But if she spits thrice on the spot, there is no danger.

44 If a child is weighed immediately after it is born, it will not thrive afterwards.

45 If a child be lifted out of one window and taken in through another, it will never grow bigger.

46 If a lying-in woman dies before delivery, she will give birth forty weeks after in the grave. For which reason, a needle, thread, scissors, &c. should be buried with her, that she may sew the baby-linen.

47 By the breastbone of a Martinmas goose it may be known how the winter will be. The white in it is a sign of snow; but the brown forebodes very severe cold. It is also to be observed that the foremost part by the neck foretells of winter before Christmas; but the hinder part of winter after Christmas.

---

1 A superstition equally common in England.

48 As the weather is on the day of the Seven Sleepers (27th July), so it will continue for seven weeks.

49 It often happens that mariners in the wide ocean see a ship – in all respects resembling a real one – sailing by, and at the same instant vanishing from their sight. It is the spectre-ship, and forebodes that a vessel will soon go to the bottom on that spot.

50 Every seventh year the cock lays an egg. When it is hatched, a basilisk comes forth, which kills people merely by lookabeling at them. It is also said, that this animal can be killed only by holding a mirror before it, it being so ugly that it cannot survive the sight of itself.

51 If you desire to know your future fortune at New Year's tide, take a loaf, a knife and a skilling, with which go out and look at the moon, when the new moon shines. If then you open a psalm-book, you will be able from what the place contains to judge of the most important things.

52 On the eve of Maundy Thursday the country folks cast axes and iron wedges on the sown fields, and fasten steel on all their doors, that the witches may not injure them.

53 A ringing in the left ear betokens that somebody is speaking ill of you; but good, if the ringing be in the right ear.

54 If anyone goes to church on Maundy Thursday, and has, without knowing it, a pullet's egg (i.e. the first egg a hen lays) with him, he will see all the women that are witches with sieves or milk-pails on their heads.

55 The following is recommended as a remedy for the toothache – Take an elder-twig, first put it into your mouth, then stick it in the wall, saying, 'Depart, thou evil spirit.'

56 As a cure for the ague, it is good to stick a twig of elder in the ground, but without uttering a word while so doing. The disease will then pass into the twig, and attach itself to the first person that unfortunately approaches the spot.

57 In Norway, it is thought unlucky to meet a hare, but lucky to meet a bear or a wolf.

NORTHERN MYTHOLOGY
VOLUME III

*Popular Traditions and Superstitions of
North Germany and the Netherlands*

# Popular Traditions of
# Schleswig, Holstein, Lauenburg[1]

### The Creation of Adam (from the Old Frisic)

God created the first man, which was Adam, from eight things, the bones from stone, the flesh from earth, the blood from water, the heart from wind, the thoughts from clouds, the sweat from dew, the hair from grass, the eyes from the sun, and then blew in the holy spirit; and then from his rib he created Eve, Adam's companion.

*See Wodana, p. xix. (from Richthofen, p. 211), and remarks of Grimm from Haupt's* Zeitschrift. *Compare also the account of man's creation in the 'Dialogue between Saturn and Solomon.'* Analecta Anglo-Saxonica, p. 110, *and 'Anglo-Saxon Dialogues' (Aelfric Soc. edit. by Kemble), p. 178.*

### The Ehrengang – Walk of Honour

In many places in the north of Germany, chiefly on eminences or elevated plains, there is found a species of monument, consisting of a large number of granite stones, placed in an oblong square. Four stones stand near to each other, one of which is always much larger than the rest. Such monuments are now known by the name of 'Ehrengang', or *Walk of honour,* because, in ancient times, princes and chieftains, after a victory, here, it is said, made their solemn processions, accompanied with many ceremonies. Near Nehmten, between Bornhöved and Stocksee, and on the Kremsfeld near Segeberg, these monuments are in the best preservation.

*Near Raubierg, in the bailiwick of Apenrade, there is a spot set round with stones, called Kongens Heststald (the King's stable), where there was once a great battle.*

---

1    From Müllenhoff, *Sagen, Märchen und Lieder der Herzogthümer Schleswig, Holstein und Lauenburg,* Kiel, 1845, unless otherwise expressed.

## The Lime-tree in Nortorf

On the south-west side of the churchyard in Nortorf[1] there stands a venerable three-branched lime-tree, beneath whose boughs courts of justice, festivals, marriages, contracts, etc. were anciently held and made. All contracts were there made orally, and were sealed, as it was called, with a 'doppen'. This doppen consisted in simply pressing the thumb against the trunk of the tree.

*Between Blumenthal and Sprenge, to the south of Kiel, there stood formerly the sacred Schwerk- or Dreieiche (triple oak). In its vicinity lay an enormously huge stone, of which a portion of from 30 to 40 feet long and 20 feet wide was to be seen in the last century. A hill hard by is called the Heiligenberg (sacred hill).* Westphal. Monum. Ined., iv, pref. 216, and the representation No. 21. Schröder Topographie von Holstein, i, 60.

## Our Lady on Horseback

When the church of Delve in North Ditmarschen was to be built, the people, being unable to decide on a site for it, caused an image of the Virgin to be tied on a pied mare, which they let run whithersoever it would, and wherever it was found on the following morning, there should their church be erected. Next morning the mare was found in a marshy spot thickly overgrown with thorns and underwood. After having cut down and cleared all this, they transferred their village thither, and named the church 'Unse leve Fru up dem Perde', or, *Our Lady on horseback*.

## The Dancer

At a splendid wedding in the old noble mansion of Hoierswort in Eiderstedt,[2] there was among the company a young girl who was the most enthusiastic dancer far and near; she was, in fact, during the evening constantly engaged in dancing. When her mother warned her against it, she said petulantly, 'If the devil himself were to call me out, I would not refuse him!' At the same instant a stranger entered and invited her to dance. It was the devil, to whom she had given her word. He whirled her about so long that the blood at length issued from her mouth, and she fell down dead. The traces are still visible in the saloon, and are indelible. But the girl herself has no rest. Every night as the clock strikes twelve she must rise from her grave and enter the saloon, an infernal music then strikes up, and the whole mansion is in an uproar. Every person, who may happen to pass a night in the saloon, she calls up to dance; but hitherto no one has

1 A town not far from Rendsburg.
2 A bailiwick on the west coast of Sleswig.

ventured to dance with her. Yet if any Christian man would venture, she would be released. She once so terrified a young dissipated fellow, that he lost all inclination for merrymaking, and whenever he heard a violin, fancied that the spectre had again broken loose.

---

Two young damsels went together to take the sacrament, having partaken of which, and while still by the altar, one said to the other, 'Do you go to the wedding this evening?' 'Don't speak of it,' said her companion; but she continued, 'I shall go, and dance till I am tired: I could dance myself dead today.' In the evening, while at the wedding-party and in the height of the dancing, a tall, comely young gentleman entered, whom no one knew, who invited her to dance. At first they danced quite soberly, but by degrees more and more madly, and even when the musicians made a pause they continued without intermission. To the rest of the company this seemed mysterious, and they caused a song to be struck up, in the hope of bringing them to a stand. But the stranger danced with the damsel out at the door and vanished. The girl was found in a dung-pit, into which she sank in the sight of all. It was believed that her mother had, while she was a child, sold her to the devil.

## The Devil and the Card-players

In the village of Hellewadt, close on the high road leading from Apenrade to Lügumkloster, there is an inn called the Klöveres (Ace of clubs), which name it derives from the following incident. At this house, which did not stand in the best repute, there was formerly much card-playing. One winter evening a company was assembled there, among whom there was no lack of cursing and swearing and unseemly conversation; the devil of course being repeatedly invoked; when quite unexpected and observed by no one, a journeyman mechanic entered the room and seated himself among the players. In a short time all the luck turned to the side of the stranger, whereby the others found themselves not in the best possible humour. A card fell under the table, it was the ace of clubs, and when one of the party stooped to pick it up, he observed that the stranger had a horse's foot. On this, laying down his cards, he left the room without uttering a syllable. His conduct attracted the notice of the others, and a second person now designedly let a card fall on the floor, when, stooping to pick it up, he saw what the other had seen, and like him silently left the place. Their example was followed by the rest of the company, so that at length the devil was left sitting by himself. The host was in the greatest embarrassment; in his perplexity he sent for the clergyman to exorcise the evil one. The holy man came with three books under his arm, two of which the devil immediately kicked out of his hand, but the third he luckily held fast. The clergyman then requested the people of the house to give him a needle, with which he made a hole in the lead of the casement, through which, by dint of reading out of his book, he forced the fiend to pass and seek the boundless space.

According to one version of the story, the priest, instead of a needle, used a stick.

## The Beacon-burning

On the day of St Peter in Cathedra (22nd February) a great festival was formerly held in North Friesland. It was a spring festival; for then the mariners left the shore and put out to sea. On the eve of the above-mentioned day, great fires (biiken) were lighted on certain hills, and all then, with their wives and sweethearts, danced round the flames, every dancer holding in his hand a wisp of burning straw, which he swung about, crying all the time, 'Wedke teare!' or 'Vike tare!' (Wedke, i.e. Woden, consume!)[1]

As late as the preceding century this festival was universally celebrated in North Friesland; on the second day there were great feastings. The clergy had long declaimed against it, though without effect; but one night, before St Peter's day, the people of Rantum, having according to custom called on 'Wede', the fires being extinguished, and all gone to rest, were awakened at midnight, and to their astonishment saw an immense fire again burning on the Biikenberg. On hurrying towards it for the purpose of quenching it, they perceived a black monster resembling a large poodle slinking down the hill. The dread was now general that they would for ever have to harbour the devil, or that at least he would be a frequent visitor among them; they consequently made a vow from that day never to repeat the beacon-burning. Nevertheless on Westerlandföhr and Osterlandsilt the children still kindle bonfires on the 22nd February.

*On the island of Silt the Spring or Petrithing (court) was anciently held on the Thing-hill on the 22nd February. The Summer- or Petri-Paulithing took place on the 29th June, and the Autumn-thing on the 26th October. In Ditmarschen, on Walpurgis eve (30th April) they kindle great fires on the hills and crossways, which they call 'baken' (beacons). The boys and young people bring straw and dry boughs from all parts, and the night is passed amid rejoicing and dancing about the flames. Some of the larger youths take bundles of burning straw on a fork, and run about swinging them until they are burnt out. On the island of Femern (which was peopled from Ditmarschen) they in like manner celebrate the 30th April with the lighting of beacons (bakenbrennen). In the*

1   That is, consume (accept) the offerings, as in the days of heathenism.

*Wilstermarsch the boys and youths, on Easter eve, carry large bundles of lighted straw about the fields; and in East Holstein, both on Easter eve and St John's eve, they light fires on the hills and roads.*

## No Spinning on Saturday Evening

That there should be no spinning on a Saturday evening is a widespread belief, as it brings only detriment and punishment. There were two old women, good friends, and the most indefatigable spinners in the village; so that in fact their wheels, even on a Saturday evening, never stood still. At length one of them died; but on the Saturday evening following she appeared to the other, who as usual was busy at her wheel, and showed her her burning hand, saying:

> Sieh, was ich in der Hölle gewann,
> Weil ich am Sonnabendabend spann!
>
> *See what I in hell have won,*
> *Because on Saturday eve I spun!*

## Nor in the twelve days of Christmas

In these twelve days there should be no spinning, nor any flax left on the distaff, else 'Wode' will gallop through it.

A woman, nevertheless, resolved on making the experiment, and sat down and spun, but immediately sank into a profound sleep, from which she woke only by someone opening the door and entering. The intruder demanded the spinning-wheel to be given him, and began to spin. The woman could do nothing but continually keep throwing to him what flax she had, but which was all immediately spun, wound and rolled up. The devil then demanded more, and the woman brought him all the tow she had in the house, and then all her wool; but he still called for more, and it was yet only four o'clock in the morning and the day far distant. In her tribulation the woman ran to a neighbour, a cunning old crone, who was already aware of what was going forward in the house; for she came out to meet her, and fortunately soon relieved her from her troublesome visitor. Had the devil spun up all, and the woman been unable to supply him till daybreak, it would have cost her her life.

## New Year's Eve

On New Year's eve the cows and horses speak with one another. A peasant who was sceptical on this point laid himself in the rack and listened. At midnight he heard one horse say to another, 'This year we shall get rid of our master.' This so terrified him that he fell sick and soon after died. The same horses drew him to the churchyard.

————

On the same night, or on the eve of some other festival, at twelve o'clock all water is turned into wine. A woman was so foolhardy as to go one night to a well. While bending over it for the purpose of drawing from it, there came one and said:

> All Water is Wyn,
> unn dyn beiden Ogen sünt myn;
>
> *All water is wine, and thy two eyes are mine;*

at the same time depriving her of both her eyes. Others relate of another woman that it was said to her,

> All Water is Wyn,
> unn wat dar by is myn,
>
> *All water is wine, and what thereby is mine,*

and instantly the woman disappeared.


## Divine Service of the Dead

One night an old woman in Kiel awoke and thought it was time to go to morning service; for it seemed to her that she heard the bells and the organ. She rose accordingly, took cloak and lantern – for it was winter – and went to the church of St Nicholas. But when there she could not find the psalms, as the whole congregation sang quite differently from what stood in her psalm-book; the people also appeared unknown to her, but among them she perceived one woman who exactly resembled a neighbour that had been dead for many years. A woman then approached her, who had also been long in her grave; it was her gossip. This woman told her that she must go out; for the church at that time was not for her; but that she must not look round, else evil might befall her. The woman went out as quickly as she could, and as the church door was slammed after her, her cloak was caught At this moment the clock struck twelve. She unclasped her cloak from her shoulders, with the intention of fetching it away in the morning; but when she returned for that purpose, she found it torn into little fragments, the dead having tripped over it.

## The Spectre at Gramm

The countess Anna Sophia Schack became a widow at an early age. At Gramm she passed a life of dissipation and licentiousness, and finally sold her soul to the devil. After a certain number of years the fiend was to fetch her away on an appointed evening, as soon as the wax light on the table should be burnt out. At Gramm things now went on more madly than ever. The appointed evening at length came, and the wax light was standing before the countess, who was now seized with unutterable anguish. She sent for the clergyman and to him communicated her secret. He advised her to extinguish the light and cause the little piece remaining to be enclosed within the east wall of the church. This was done, and the evil one had no power over her. Shortly after a fire broke out in the church. It was early in the morning, and the countess was still in bed when the intelligence reached her. On hearing it she instantly sprang up, and in her light morning attire and without shoes hurried to the church, which stood about a mile and a quarter distant from her dwelling. By her earnest entreaties and promises she encouraged the people to extinguish the fire, so that at least the east wall might be preserved. From that time the countess became an altered person; her cheerfulness and good humour had fled and given place to a gnawing sorrow which brought her to the grave. But at midnight a beautiful female form in snow-white attire is seen in the castle, wringing her hands, with downcast, anxious countenance, pacing incessantly from one apartment to another, and at last stopping in the upper saloon of the centre building, where, standing for some minutes before the fireplace, she gazes motionless on some blood-spots, and then vanishes.

A young countess, who in later times was on a visit to Gramm, was, while sitting at the harpsichord, so terrified by the apparition that she shortly after died. No one enters the old mansion without shuddering.

## The Gongers

In Keitum on the island of Silt a woman died before her delivery, and appeared several times to the servant of the clergyman, and had no rest in the grave, until her scissors, needle and thread were placed by her side. This is a common usage in North Friesland.

There are many apparitions there, or 'Gongers'; for whoever is unjustly slain, or has removed landmarks, or fraudulently ploughed off land, finds no rest in the grave. Blasphemers, and those that have cursed themselves, and suicides must in like manner appear again. To such a Gonger let no one hold out his hand; it will be burnt, become black, and fall off.

When anyone is drowned at sea, he announces it to his relations. Though

the Gonger does not announce himself to his nearest of kin, but to those in
the third or fourth degree. In the evening twilight or at night he appears in
the clothes in which he was drowned. He then looks in at the house door,
and leans with his arm against it, or else wanders about the house, but soon
disappears and returns on the following evening at the same hour. By night
– usually in heavy, drawn-up boots that are filled with water – he will open
the chamber door, extinguish the light, and lie down on the coverlet by the
side of the sleeper. In the morning there is a stream of seawater in the room,
that has trickled from his clothes. If the relations are not convinced by these
signs, the Gonger will continue to appear until they believe that he has
perished. He also gives other notices: it is related that

A mariner with his two sons once sailed from Amrum with seed bound
for Holland. The younger son had no inclination for the voyage, and
implored his mother to let him remain at home; but she told him it was his
father's will, and that go he must. When on their way to the harbour at
Bosk, in passing over the dam, he said to his mother and the others with
him, 'Think of me when you pass over these stones.' In the same night they
perished. The mariner's sister dwelt in the same house with him; at night
she had laid her white neck-kerchief by her bed, and in the morning found
on it three drops of blood. She then knew that her relations had perished
and had been with her during the night.

### The Staven-wüfke [1]

This is a spectre resembling a mourning woman, who appears on old
pasture grounds, hills and void places, where houses once had stood, but
which now, naked and desolate, are either washed by the sea or surrounded by the sand of the downs. Sometimes she wanders about these
melancholy places, and sometimes is seen sitting and weeping on the spot
where once had been the domestic hearth. [2]

### The Land-divider

At the time of the partition and fencing of the land, there arose between the
villages of Alversdorf and Röst, in South Ditmarschen, great disputes about
their boundaries. The partition could not be determined until a man of
Alversdorf declared that he knew it accurately and would settle it on oath.
For this purpose he went to the boundary of the Alversdorf land, by the ford

---

1    From Staven, *the place on which a house stands or has once stood,* and Wüfke, lit.
*wifekin,* Ger. Weibchen. She is likewise called the Stadem-Wüfke.
2    Kohl, *Marschen und Inseln,* ii, 289.

at Tensbüttel, where it passes through the Gieselau, filled his shoes with sand, then appeared near Röst, and made oath that he was standing on Alversdorf ground. By this fraud he believed he had avoided perjury. But after death he was doomed to wander on the boundary-line as a fire-sprite. A flame, the height of a man, was there long to be seen dancing about, until the moor was dried up. Whenever it flared up higher than usual, the people would cry out, 'Dat is de Scheelvaegt!' (That is the land-divider!) At the spot where he put the sand into his shoes, everyone, who passes at night and has not a pure conscience, must for a considerable distance bear the devil on his back like a burden of a hundred pounds weight.

Between the lordship of Röest and the village of Rabenkirchen in Angeln there was once a dispute about a wood. The lord one morning filled his shoes with earth from his garden, stuck twigs from the trees in his court-yard in his hat, and made oath in the wood, which lawfully belonged to the village of Rabenkirchen, that he was standing on his own ground, and that the boughs above his head were his.

## The Black School

Of the Black School there is much to tell both in North Friesland and in the Danish territories. The devil in person is the teacher, and preachers just entering on their career are there instructed. Almost every pastor knows something of the black art, while others are perfect adepts in it; but have therefore assigned their souls to the devil, though under certain conditions. One, for instance, must during his whole life wear one and the same woollen under-waistcoat; another may shave himself only on Saturdays; a third may wear only one garter; a fourth has bound himself never to enter a church, or never to stay in one longer than an hour or half an hour. If from inadvertence they once only transgress the condition, their soul is for ever lost. Everyone who has been in the Black School has power over spirits, and is specially skilled in exorcising the ghosts of the departed and other spectres. With one word they can *wish* themselves from one place to another, and know all that passes at home in their absence.

A certain Pastor Fabricius in Medelbye was particularly skilful. Once, while at a christening in Holt, he compelled a youngster, who was in the act of robbing an apple-tree in the parsonage garden, to sit in it till he returned home and released him. At another time, while in the middle of a sermon, he struck the cushion of the pulpit and cried, 'Stop!' and as the people were leaving the church, there stood a man, as fixed as a statue, with a sack full of fresh-cut grass that he had stolen from the churchyard during the service. He had many magical books. One day during church-time, his maidservant was cleaning his study, and through curiosity began to read in a little book she found there. On a sudden all seemed alive in the room, and a multitude of the most hideous forms and spectres made their appearance, approaching nearer and nearer to the girl, who was almost dead with fright. The priest, who in the church was instantly aware of what was going on at home, suddenly in the middle of his sermon said 'Amen,' hurried to his house, and laid the spirits, who would else have destroyed the girl.

But the devil is always laying traps for those that have made a contract with him, and if the above-mentioned Pastor Fabricius had put on more than one garter, the fiend would have carried him off. But the devil was no match for Pastor Fabricius, who was always on his guard, when in the morning he saw two garters lying by his bed. The devil would also frequently, in the shape of a flea, torment the maidservant while knitting stockings for her master, and cause her to err in the number of stitches. The stocking would then generally be too wide and hang loose about the parson's heels, though he cared but little for that. In fact, the devil could never get an advantage over him.

*Pastor Ziegler, the author of a Holstein Idiotikon, never wore more than one garter. People said that he had entered into a contract with the devil, and that when it was expired the devil came to fetch him. The pastor would first dress himself decently and was very dilatory, put on his stockings inside out, etc. When tying his second garter, the devil, bursting with vexation, said to him that he would wait only till he had finished tying his garter. 'In that case then,' said Ziegler, 'I will never tie it as long as I live'; and again laid himself down to sleep. The devil was obliged to depart.*

## Fast-reading

A man went one day into one of the churches of Hamburg, and found at the back of the altar a book, in which he began to read, and went on reading and reading, till he at length *read himself fast*. He strove to release himself and to give his thoughts another direction, but in vain; he was obliged to stand reading on and on, while a cold sweat stood on his forehead and he trembled in every limb; he would have died, had he not been observed by an old man, who, it is said, was a Catholic priest, who guessing what had befallen him, advised him to read the whole backwards; for that only by so doing he could release himself. The man did so and escaped without further inconvenience.

# Fast-writing

In Wilster many persons are masters of what is termed *fast-writing*. Two thieves having one night broken into the house of a rich man, and violently demanded his keys, he intimated to them that if they would only abstain from violence, he would deliver to them everything, which they might peaceably divide between them; he wished merely that all might be done quietly and regularly. When the thieves had got possession of the money, they sat down at the table and began to divide it; but when they had finished their work and were about to rise, they could neither move their hands from the money nor the money from the table. In the meanwhile, the household was assembled. 'Oho,' said the master, 'we may now go quietly to bed again, they can very comfortably remain sitting.' On the following morning, having sent for the police, he loosed the thieves.

Another, whose cabbages were constantly stolen from his garden, *wrote the thief fast* from Saturday night till Sunday, when he was just in the act of passing over the fence with a full load on his back. There he was compelled to sit riding on the fence while all the people were going to and returning from church, so that all might see him. He was then released and allowed to depart.

# Turning the Sieve

During a time of war, a butcher of Amrum, having more business than he could well manage alone, took the son of a neighbour to assist him. In this youth he placed so much confidence that he even showed him the place in which he had laid by a few hundred dollars. This the son communicated to his mother, and both were seized with an irresistible desire to get possession of the money; so that on the following morning, when the mother came for a pound or two of meat, the son contrived to place the bag containing the money in the bottom of her basket. When the butcher some days after discovered his loss, his suspicion immediately fell on his assistant; but the other protested his innocence, swearing by all that is holy.

There was at this time in Morsum on Silt a celebrated sorcerer, who could discover thieves and compel them to restore the stolen property. The butcher sent his wife thither, and the sorcerer immediately took his measures. He ordered a flour-sieve to be brought, placed in it a key and a pair of scissors, and set it on a large vessel filled with water. He then uttered some magical sentences, and the woman pronounced several times the names of all suspected persons. As often as she mentioned the name of her neighbour, the key and scissors danced about; and when the sorcerer desired her to look into the water, she plainly saw her husband's assistant in the act of handing the money to his mother. But the sorcerer informed her that it would not be possible to recover the money, because the thieves had already crossed the water with it.

*In Ditmarschen, for this process with the sieve, they use a family bible and family key. The latter is laid for a few minutes in the former, for the sake of sanctifying it; the cunning man then takes the key, causes the sieve to turn round upon it, pronouncing at the same time the several names, when that person is the thief at the mention of whose name the sieve falls.*

*In Mecklenburg the process is somewhat different. They there take a sieve, that has been inherited from relations, lay it on the rim, open a pair of inherited scissors, and stick the points so deep into the rim of the sieve that it may be supported by them. Two then, of opposite sexes, go with the sieve into a perfectly dark place, hold the middle finger of the right hand under the ring of the scissors, and so raise up the sieve. It is very clear that the ring 'will slide from the finger on the slightest motion, and the sieve fall down, it being hardly possible to hold it level in the dark. One then asks the other: 'In the name, etc. I ask of thee; tell me truly and lie not: who has stolen this or that? Has Hans, Fritz, Peter, done it?' On naming the guilty one, the ring slides off, the sieve falls to the ground, and the thief is detected.*

*According to other accounts the operation is performed in the light, and the sieve does not fall, but turns. Grimm, J., Deutsche Mythologie, op. cit., p. 1062.*

*In England, 'the vulgar, in many parts, have an abominable practice of using a riddle and a pair of scissors in divination. If they have had anything stolen from them, the riddle and shears are sure to be resorted to. A similar mode of discovering thieves or others suspected of any crime prevailed among the Greeks.' Vide Potter's Gr. Antiq., i, p. 352, Brocket, voce Riddle. Grimm, J., Deutsche Mythologie, op. cit., p. 1062, also vol. ii, p. 269, No. 8. Kuhn und Schwartz, Norddeutsche Sagen, p. 523.*

## A Murderer cited

In a public house in Tondern some profane persons were sitting at cards during divine service. The game became more and more exciting, and in the dispute which followed, one stabbed the other with his knife. The murderer fled. When the dead was to be buried, the coffin was borne to the marketplace and there set down; it was then struck on the lid with a hammer, and the murderer was cited. He was at the time in Riga, and afterwards discovered himself to a friend who came thither, to whom he told the hour in which those hammer strokes struck into his heart.

## The Magic Kettle

There was once in Oppendorp a young serving-man, who was a very strong, useful fellow. This was at the time when all the talk was about giving the serfs their freedom. The young fellows were overjoyed at the prospect, but could not await the day of their emancipation. Among the rest, to our serving-man also the time seemed too long, so one morning, when he ought to have been at the plough, he was far away over the hills. His master was vexed at thus losing his best man, and did all he could to get him back, but not a trace of him could be obtained.

After some time there came a Jew up to the farm, to whom they related the story. The Jew said, 'We can very well get him again.' This the people told to their master, who let the Jew come to him and asked him if what he had said were true? The Jew said, 'Yes,' provided he had what was requisite for the purpose and also good payment. The payment was soon agreed on, and the Jew undertook to get the man back, if he had a piece of any stuff that he had worn for a year. The master ordered search to be made, and an old under-jacket was found. The Jew then ordered a black cock and a black he-cat to be caught; these he killed, and then took some other things, but which he kept quite secret. At night he set a large kettle on the fire, into which, at midnight, he put the jacket, the black cat, the black cock, and the other things, and began boiling them. And he boiled and boiled all night and the following day, so that he boiled twice twenty-four hours. When it was evening there came a man running up the yard, covered with mud from head to foot and breathless, who on reaching the house door fell down senseless from exhaustion. It was the runaway servant. On coming to himself, his first words were, 'Heaven be praised that I am again in Oppendorp!' He said that he had been in Amsterdam, that he woke one night and was so excited as he had never been in his life. He felt obliged to dress himself, he knew not why; and then he was forced to run without cessation both by night and by day. How he crossed the water he knew not; tired and hungry as he was it mattered not, he was forced to run on and on, being unable to stand for a moment still.

## The Devil's Cat

A peasant had three beautiful, large cats. A neighbour begged to have one of them, and obtained it. To accustom it to the place, he shut it up in the loft. At night the cat, popping its head through the window, said, 'What shall I bring tonight?' 'Thou shalt bring mice,' answered the man. The cat then set to work, and cast all it caught on the floor. Next morning the place was so full of dead mice that it was hardly possible to open the door, and the man was employed the whole day in throwing them away by bushels. At night the cat again put its head through the aperture and asked, 'What shall I bring tonight?' 'Thou shalt bring rye,' answered the peasant. The cat was now busily employed in shooting down rye, so that in the morning the door could not be opened. The man then saw that the cat was a witch, and carried it back to his neighbour, in which he acted prudently; for had he given it work a third time, he could never have got rid of it. In one respect, however, he did not act prudently, to wit, in not saying the second time, 'Thou shalt bring gold'; for then he would have got as much gold as he did rye.

## Mönöloke

There was in former times a spirit known among the people under the name of Mönöloke; so that when anyone became unexpectedly rich, it was said of him: 'The Mönöloke peeps out of his pocket.' The Mönöloke was a puppet made in the devil's name of white wax, and was clad in a petticoat of blue taffety, with a vest of black velvet; the legs and feet were bare. Those who would derive aid from it must preserve it carefully and keep it clean.

## Witches in Friesland

The people of Donsum, in the island of Föhr, are accounted sorcerers; the women in particular are all said to be witches. On this account no one cares to hold any intercourse with them, and no one marries out of the village. On a Friday, no woman is to be found at home; because on that day they hold their meetings and have dances on a barren heath. In the evening they ride thither on horses, though usually they have wings on their shoulders and fly. In their flight they are often unable to stop at the right time, so that if a church steeple is in their way, they fly against it. From hurts received in their fall, on the following day they lie sick. Where their dances have been held, there may be found on the next day rags and tatters of all kinds and colours, pieces of riband, needles with which in bewitched wax they have pierced many a one's heart, blood and matter. They can transform themselves into cats and horses, swans and eagles. A young man once went to visit his betrothed; when about to enter the house, there lay a white horse in the doorway. This was just on a Friday evening. A man, who had been much annoyed by witches, going once out a shooting, saw a bird with a plumage of surprising beauty. He aimed at and shot it, when the bird became a woman. As a bridal pair were passing by a lake near Donsum, there were some swans sailing on the water, seeing which the bride said, 'I will just go to the swans for a moment.' She went, and the swans proved to be her sisters. She also became a swan, and they all fluttered and beat with their wings. The bridegroom had to go home alone. The witches often change themselves into seals, and follow the mariners and fishermen. They frequently enter houses in the shape of toads. Children are to be carefully protected from their look. If a riband or a small cord with a knot in it is found lying in the way, let no one touch it, for the witches have placed it there. No one may lend to the witches any sharp instrument, as scissors, a knife, and, least of all, needles. A man's cow died: he set the heart with the other entrails on the fire and boiled them, when the witch (who had killed the cow) was obliged to come. When no butter will come, it is usual to stick knives round the cover of the churn; the first woman that then enters is the witch. Houses and stables may be protected from witches by nailing a horse's foot over the door, or burying a lizard alive under the threshold. Asa-foetida is also used for the same purpose.[1]

*The foregoing holds good not only of the women in Donsum, but also of those of Silt, Amrum, and the other islands. On the 1st May they all ride to the Blocksberg.*

## Witches

Whoever desires to become a witch yields herself to the devil and abjures God in these words:

> Hier trete ich in dieses Nest,
> Und verlasse unsern Herrn Jesu Christ!

> *Here enter I in this one's nest,*
> *And forsake our Lord Jesus Christ!*

Then will the sorcery succeed, in which they instruct one another, and which they learn from the devil, who comes to them. On St John's eve and on the 1st May they have their meetings and dances. From these assemblies they return home sick almost to death. Of all witches it is related, that on Wolber's (Walburg's) eve they ride to the Blocksberg. On that evening no one may hinder them, and whoever makes a cross over the door through which they must pass, will afterwards feel their vengeance, and get a severe beating. They pass through chimneys and holes, and ride on brooms, he-goats, cats, cocks, old sows, asses and spotted dogs, which the devil frequently sends them.

Of their merrymaking on the Rugenberg it is related, that as soon as the witches, each in her own fashion, are all arrived, they prepare a repast, either of geese or fresh (i.e. unsalted, unsmoked) beef sprinkled with mustard, with which they eat bread baked in an iron pot, and drink beer out of wooden or tin cups. The devil brings the kettle with him from Lütjenbrode. Then the dancing begins, when each witch dances with a

1   See p. 281.

devil, while an old woman sings and two kettles are beaten. On the surrounding mountains fires shine forth. Whoever approaches is drawn into the circle and whirled about till he sinks down breathless. When day dawns they all vanish. On the following morning are to be seen on the mountain traces of fowls and of horses' and goats' feet, and in the middle lies a heap of ashes.

———

If an old woman is suspected of being a witch, it is the custom to throw a handful of salt after her, when, if she really is a witch, she will look round. When anyone who is thought to be a witch will enter a house, it is merely necessary to place a broom inverted in the doorway: if she is a witch, she cannot enter. Some young men once adopted the following plan. On St John's eve they went to a meadow, where they rolled themselves naked in the dew. On the Sunday following they went to the church, and saw that every woman who was a witch carried a milk-pail on her head[1] and the number of these was very great, both women and girls.

A couple of young peasants once resolved to watch the witches on St John's eve, and for this purpose put the horses to a pair of patrimonial harrows, with which they drove out on one side of the village, one going to the right, the other to the left. They went round the village till they met on the opposite side. The circle which they thus drew round the place the witches could not transgress. They left one small opening where they awaited the witches, and placed the two harrows aslant against each other, beneath which they laid themselves. At midnight all the witches flew out from their several chimneys on pitchforks and broomsticks. They all had to pass by the two, and among them one of them recognised his own wife, 'Are you there too, my old woman?' cried he, and thus betrayed himself; and the witches all rushing upon him, drove the sharp spikes of the harrow into his body; for he had been so thoughtless as to turn them inwards. He did not escape with life.

Whoever desires to see the witches dance, must take an old plank from a coffin lid, from which a knot has been thrust, and peep through the hole.

## The Witches' Present

Late one night as a musician was on the road from Todendorf to Puttgarden, he was met by a number of witches, who immediately surrounded him, and said, 'Play us some tune.' Fright prevented him from speaking, but at length he contrived to tell them that he had no violin.

———

1   See p. 426, No. 54.

'That makes no difference,' answered the witches, 'for we have one.' When he began playing, they danced wildly around him, springing as high as a house. At last they were tired, and gave the man for reward an apronful of 'kröbels' (a sort of apple-cake). On reaching home, he laid the violin and the kröbels on a shelf and went to bed. On the following morning, when he went to look at his presents, the violin proved to be an old cat, the bow a cat's tail, and the kröbels nothing but horse-dung.

## Wind-knots

At Siseby on the Slei there dwelt a woman who was a sorceress and could change the wind. The Sleswig herring-fishers used frequently to land there. Once when they would return to Sleswig, the wind being west, they requested the woman to change it. She agreed to do so for a dish of fish. She then gave them a cloth with three knots, telling them they might undo the first and the second, but not the third until they had reached land. The men spread their sails, although the wind was west; but no sooner had the oldest of the party undone the first knot, than there came a beautiful fair wind from the east. On undoing the second knot they had storm, and arrived at the city with the utmost speed. They were now curious to know what would follow if they undid the third knot; but no sooner had they done so than a violent hurricane assailed them from the west, so that they were obliged to leap into the water, in order to draw their vessel on shore.

## The St John's Blood

At Klostersand near Elmshorn there was formerly, between the Pilgerberg and the Kuppelberg, the so-called Hexenkuhle. Here on certain days, particularly on St John's day, between twelve and one o'clock, old women may be seen wandering about in search of a plant which grows only on the Pilgerberg. This plant has in its root grains containing a purple-red juice, which they call St John's blood. This the old women collect in tin boxes and carefully preserve it. But it is only when gathered at noon that it can perform miracles[1]; when the clock strikes one, its virtue is passed.

---

1  These flowers were cull'd at noon – Moore.

## The Waxen Image

A man in Amrum lay for a long time sick, and nothing afforded him relief. While he so lay, a miller observed from his mill that a woman was in the daily habit of going to the 'Dönk'am'. He one day followed her footsteps, dug, and found in the sand a little waxen image of a man with a pin stuck through the heart. He drew the pin out, took the image home, and burnt it. From that hour the man became well.

## The Witches stuff in Dissension

When a bridal bed is to be stuffed, great caution is necessary; for the witches can stuff into it either harmony or dissension, according as they may be affected to the bridal pair. For a young couple, who fondly loved each other, but against whom certain old women bore a grudge, they stuffed in dissension. Both bride and bridegroom had passed a happy wedding-day, but scarcely were they in bed when they began to quarrel, till at length they came to blows, The parents of the bridegroom, who lay in a bed near, heard the noise, but could not restore peace between them. They then advised the young couple to transfer themselves to their bed, which they did and passed the night amicably. But no sooner had the old folks laid themselves in the other bed than they began quarrelling, though they had never before had a difference between them; and this lasted till morning. They then examined the bed, when, on taking out the feathers, they found them all twisted together in wreaths and rings with silken threads of all colours. Now it was manifest that the old women who had stuffed the bed were witches, and had twisted dissension into it.

*In Amrum a man lay sick and bewitched to death. While placing him in the coffin one of his legs fell off. On opening his pillow, a bewitched wreath of feathers of all sorts, and colours was found in it.*

## Witches take Butter

There was a time when the witches were particularly mischievous. It was then indispensable for every housewife to have a handle made of the wood of the service (quicken) tree to her churn; else she could never be sure of getting butter. A man one morning early, on his way from Jägerup to Hadersleben, heard, as he passed by Woiensgaard, that they were churning in the yard; but at the same time he observed that a woman whom he knew was standing by the side of a running brook and churning with a stick in the water. On that same day he again saw her selling a large lump of butter in Hadersleben. In the evening as he again passed by Woiens, they were still churning; whereupon he went to the house and assured them that their labour was all in vain, for the butter was already sold at Hadersleben.

## The Severed Hand [1]

In Eiderstedt there was a miller who had the misfortune to have his mill burnt every Christmas eve. He had, however, a courageous servant who undertook to keep watch in the mill on that portentous night. He kindled a blazing fire and made himself a good kettleful of porridge, which he stirred about with a large ladle. He had an old sabre lying by him. Ere long, there came a whole regiment of cats into the mill, and he heard one say in a low tone to another, 'Mousekin! Go and sit by Hanskin!' and a beautiful milk-white cat came creeping softly to him and would place herself by his side. At this, taking a ladleful of the scalding porridge, he dashed it in her face, then seizing the sabre, he cut off one of her paws. The cats now all disappeared. On looking at the paw more attentively, he found, instead of a paw, that it was a woman's delicate hand, with a gold ring on one of the fingers, whereon was his master's cypher. Next morning the miller's wife lay in bed and would not rise. 'Give me thy hand, wife!' said the miller. At first she refused, but was obliged at length to hold out her mutilated limb. When the authorities got intelligence of this event, the woman was burnt for a witch.

## A Witch as a Hare

In Bödelsdorf there dwelt, and perhaps still dwells, a very old woman, in whose service no one would ever continue; for when the servants were employed in the fields she always knew exactly what they had done and said, as she was ever present among them. Sometimes she would be a duck and swim on the water; then, if the men and girls pelted her with stones, she would merely dive down and rise immediately afterwards. At other times she would be a hare and run through the corn when it was cut, and never received a hurt, however often the men shot at her. But once, when they were going out to mow, one of the men provided himself with a silver button, with which he loaded his piece and shot the hare. On his return in the evening he found the old woman with a wound in her arm which would never heal. With inherited silver a person may hit whatever has been rendered invulnerable by sorcery. Both muskets and rifles can be

1   See p. 250.

bewitched, and there are persons who can cause bullets to glide off from them in another direction. When a gun is bewitched, the best remedy is to put a living snake into the barrel and shoot it off; then will the sorcery be neutralised. Inherited silver is, moreover, useful in numerous other cases. If a little be scraped off and given to a sick person, the paroxysms will abate. If anyone has an inherited earring, and wears it, it will relieve the most violent toothache.

When a witch is wounded with such a silver button or bullet, she must resume her natural form.

## Werwolves

On a hot harvest day some reapers lay down in the field to take their noontide sleep, when one who could not sleep observed that the one next to him rose softly and girded himself with a strap, whereupon he became a wolf.

By addressing a werwolf thrice by his baptismal name, he resumes his human form.

––––––––––

A young man belonging to Jägerup returning late one night from Billund, was attacked, when near Jägerup, by three werwolves, and would probably have been torn to pieces, had he not saved himself by leaping into a rye-field; for then they had no more power over him.

## The Long Horse

Some young persons belonging to Kassöe, a village near Apenrade, being one Sunday evening on their way to a dance at Hüdewad, when they came to a brook that runs between the two villages, found themselves unable to cross it, in consequence of the recent rains that had greatly swelled it. While looking about them, they perceived an old horse standing close by, and resolved on mounting him and riding through the rivulet. But when one pair had mounted, they saw there was still room for another; and when another mounted, there was place for a fourth; till that at length the whole party seated themselves on his back. When in the middle of the rivulet, one who sat foremost happening to look round, and seeing so many persons sitting on the horse's back, cried out in astonishment, 'Cross of Jesus, what a long jade!' But scarcely had he uttered the words, when the goblin horse's back snapped asunder, the riders all fell into the water, and the horse vanished with an appalling howl.

## The Mannigfual or Giant Ship

The North Frisic mariners tell of a gigantic ship, the 'Mannigfual'. This ship is so vast that the captain always rides about the deck on horseback, for the purpose of giving his orders. The sailors, who climb up the rigging when young, come down again stricken in years with grey beards and hair. While so employed they keep themselves alive by frequent visits to the blocks of the cordage, which contain rooms for refection.

This monstrous vessel once steered its course from the Atlantic ocean into the British channel; but being unable, on account of the narrowness of the strait, to pass between Dover and Calais, the captain had the lucky thought of having the whole larboard side smeared over with white soap. This operation proved effectual; the Mannigfual passed through safely and entered the North sea. From that time the cliffs of Dover got their white, soapy appearance, from the soap that was rubbed off, and the foam raised by the motion of the vessel.

Once the giant ship (we are not told how) found itself in the Baltic; but the crew soon discovered that the water was too shallow. To get afloat again, they found it necessary to throw the ballast together with the dirt and ashes of the galley overboard. From the ballast the isle of Bornholm derives its origin, and from the rubbish the little neighbouring isle of Christiansö.

## The Basilisk

When a cock is seven (according to others twenty) years old, it lays an egg, out of which comes an animal, which is the basilisk. All living things, on which it directs its look, must instantly die, and even stones burst asunder. There have been people who have kept such an animal for many years in a dark cellar; but durst not open the cellar, lest the light should enter. If a mirror be held before a basilisk, and it thus gets a sight of itself, it must die like another being.[1]

## The Nightmare

When seven boys or seven girls are born in succession, one among them is a nightmare, that visits those sleeping, sets itself on their breast, oppresses and torments them.

A man had got such a nightmare for his wife without knowing it; but he was soon sensible that many nights she had disappeared from his bed. One night, therefore, he kept himself awake in order to watch her, and saw

1   See p. 376.

how she rose from the bed and, as the door was fast bolted, slipped through the hole for the strap by which the latch was lifted up. After some time she returned by the way she went. Next morning the man stopped up the opening in the door, and now always found his wife by his side.

When a considerable time had passed, the man thinking she had cast off and forgotten her bad habit, drew out the peg, in order to use the latch again; but in the following night, the woman was missing and never came back[1]; though every Sunday morning the man found clean linen laid out for him.

*The mistletoe is recommended as a remedy for the nightmare; it is, therefore, sometimes called marentakken (mare-branches), or alfranken (elf-tendrils). Thunder-stones are likewise considered a remedy.*

## The Hel-horse

At Jordkirch, in the neighbourhood of Apenrade, this creature frequented a lonely way called Langfort, making a noise like that of a horse, well shod on all its four hoofs, on a stone pavement.[2] He is said to be headless. In Tondern an old, three-legged, grey (or white), blind horse goes clattering through the streets every night. In every house before which he stands, or into which he looks, somebody must die. Old people have often witnessed this, and thus been enabled to foretell a death. This horse is called Hel, and is said to have no master, though some assert that an old woman in black rides on him.

## Flames in the Water

Fishermen relate that by a bridge in Rendsburg a whimpering is often heard in the water like that of a young child; sometimes, too, small flames dart up, which are always a sign that someone will perish. The Eyder is, generally speaking, a bad river; every year it requires a sacrifice. The same may be said of the bay of Kiel and the lake of Ploen.

## Of the Underground Folk

When our Lord was on earth, he came one day to the house of a woman who had five comely and five ugly children. On his entering the house she concealed the five ugly children in the cellar. The Lord then desired the children to be brought before him, and when he saw the five comely ones,

---

1   See p. 346.
2   The Danish Hel-horse has only three legs. See 374.

he inquired of the woman where her other children were. She answered, 'I have no other children.' The Lord then blessed the five comely children and cursed the ugly ones, saying, 'What is beneath shall remain beneath, and what is above shall remain above.' When the woman went again into the cellar, the five children had disappeared. From them spring the Underground Folk.[1]

_____

Under the earth, particularly in barrows of the dead, there dwell little people called by the Holsteiners Dwarge (Dwarfs) or Unnererske (Subterraneans).

They have been in the country from time immemorial. At Heinkenborstel, in the bailiwick of Rendsburg, there once dwelt such people. These asserted that they had lived there before the invention of beer-brewing.[2]

It is quite certain that there are such underground people. An old woman in Angeln had been told by her grandfather, that once when ploughing in his field, in which there was a giant's mount (Riesenberg), he saw a little underground woman in a white sark come out of it, but who, on seeing him, instantly fled.

In the district of Pinneberg, whenever there is a wedding feast, it may be observed that the underground people sit among the guests at table and help to eat the dinner; for on the side of the table at which they sit, double the quantity vanishes of what is consumed on the opposite side.[3]

They are said to wear many golden chains, and to have many golden vessels, which they hang out on the bushes, on which they also spread their linen to dry.

They can be very mischievous. From a man in Süderstapel they took a horse, and only returned it when it became lame.

When a child falls and cries, it is told that it could not help it; that the underground folk had caught it by the leg.

_____

A man and his wife passing one night by a mount near Krumesse in Lauenburg, saw a long procession of underground folk, none of them higher than the leg of a chair. One who rode foremost on a little horse, wore an enormously high peaked cap. At this sight both cried out, 'All good spirits praise God the Lord',[4] when instantly the foremost rider began

_____

1  See p. 309.
2  This is very characteristic. What an idea such people must entertain in remote antiquity!
3  See p. 321.
4  Alle guten Geister loben Gott den Herrn.

to grow higher and higher, and at last became a giant. The whole procession then turned about and entered the mount.

## The Önnerbänkissen in Fögedshoog

The Önnerbänkissen (Subterraneans) in Amrum live chiefly in the Fögedshoog by the Downs (Dünen). They have been seen at night dancing round it in the moonlight, and spreading their linen out on it by day. In the winter they have been known to skate on the water of Merum. A wanton fellow once resolved on destroying their habitation. He dug far into the hill, and fancied he had found the dwellings of the Önnerbänkissen, when to his astonishment and horror he saw his own dwelling standing in a blaze.[1] Throwing aside his spade and mattock, he ran with all speed to the village, on reaching which he found the fire was a delusion. The fright, however, taught him a lesson, and from that time no one has disturbed the Önnerbänkissen in Fögedshoog.

## The Subterranean Potters

On the Morsumkliff in Silt are found a great quantity of all kinds of smith's and potter's ware, in the shape of pipes, boxes, balls, pots, etc. On Silt they call them Önnererskpottjüg (subterranean crockery ware), on Amrum, Traaldaasker (Troll-boxes), because they are made by the Underground folk.

In Holstein it is believed that the corn found in the urns from the old graves, thrives, when sown in the fields and gardens, better than any other. Milk also becomes richer and yields more butter when it has stood in such pots. If the poultry drink out of them, they will not become ill.

## The Underground Smith

A man riding one morning past the Dreiberge, on the road between Apenrade and Jordkirch, heard smiths there at work, and cried out that he wished they would make him a chaff-knife. In the evening, when he was returning, he actually found lying on the hill a spick-span new knife. He laid down as much money as was equivalent to the usual cost of such a knife, and took it with him. It proved to be of excellent temper and keenness; but wounds caused by it were incurable.

1 See p. 312, 334, *et passim.*

## Kettles borrowed

Close to Geltorf near Sleswig there is a hill called the Hochberg, and hard by is another, the Brehochberg. These were inhabited by underground people. In former times the country folks were on quite friendly terms with the subterraneans. When there was to be a wedding in the village, and kettles, pans, pots and the like were wanted, they would go to the door and knock. 'What do you want?' the underground people would then ask. 'We want to borrow a kettle of you; for Hans and Trina are to be married tomorrow.' 'How big must the kettle be?' And the peasants could then get a kettle and pottery ware of just the size they required, which they must fetch away on the following morning before sunrise. In return for this accommodation, they needed only to give the fragments remaining of the viands that had been cooked in the vessels, which they left before the hill.

## The Dragedukke

As a man was once ploughing, he observed a broken bread-peel and a broken oven-rake lying on the ground. He took them home, mended them, and again laid them in the same place. For this service he was rewarded with a 'Dragedukke', which is a box, in which there is always only a little money, but out of which a person may take as much as he will.

## The Gossips

A man went to a mount and called to the dwarf that dwelt in it, praying him to give him a son, and then he would invite him to stand godfather. The dwarf promised to grant his request, if he would keep his word. But when the man's wife had given birth to a son, he was loth to invite the dwarf, yet was, nevertheless, obliged to go to him for that purpose. The dwarf considered himself highly honoured and promised to come; but as the man was going out, he called after him, 'What company are you to have besides?' 'Our Lord, Mary and St Peter are the other gossips,' answered the man. 'You must excuse me then,' said the dwarf, 'if I don't come.' He gave, however, a handsome christening present.

*In the Jutish version of the story (Molbech, Eventyr, p. 359), instead of Christ, etc. Tordenveir (Thunder-storm) is named; and in the Swedish, Thor himself.*

## Drum-music

In the field of Mellerup, on the high road to Apenrade, there is a barrow. As a man, who was to give a wedding entertainment on the following day, and had been to the town to buy all things necessary, was passing by, a little man sprang from the mount and invited himself to the wedding, promising to bring with him, for a present, a lump of gold as large as a man's head. 'Then you shall come,' said the man. The little man then asked what music they were to have? 'Drums and kettle-drums,' answered the man. The dwarf thereupon begged leave to recall his words, as he could not endure drum-music.[1]

## The Mill-stone suspended by a Silken Thread

One hot summer's day a lad and a lass were at work in a hayfield near the Stellerberg. They were betrothed to each other, and would have been married, but were wretchedly poor. While thus employed, they saw a large toad stealing by them. The young man was on the point of killing the ugly animal with his hayfork, but the girl seizing his arm prayed him to spare the poor creature's life. The young man, however, enjoyed his sport for a while, by appearing as if bent on killing the toad, until it had disappeared. On their return home in the evening, their employer told them they were invited to be gossips at a christening on the following day, a voice to that effect having been heard, though no person was visible at the time. The pair knew not what to think of the matter, but early on the following morning, when rising, the young man found grits or sawdust strewed by his bedside; at the entrance, too, and before the house he also found grains of corn, and, proceeding in their track, he came at last to the Stellerberg. There he heard a voice from the hill, desiring him to come again at noon and bring his betrothed with him; for they should stand gossips. The young man having given his lass due notice, they made themselves ready, and at twelve o'clock went together to the hill. They found it standing open, and were received by a little man in a grey coat, who conducted them in through a long passage. Within all was magnificent and costly: the walls, flooring and roof glittered with gold and precious stones; a sumptuous table, with gold and silver plate and the most delicious viands, stood in the centre; but the whole apartment swarmed with little grim-looking beings, all pressing round the bed of the lying-in woman. When the young man and his betrothed entered, they brought to the former the child he should hold at the font, and conducted him to the spot where the sacred ceremony was to take place. During the performance of the holy rite, happening to cast a look upwards, he saw exactly over him a millstone suspended from the roof by a silken thread. He endeavoured to move from the spot, but could not stir a step. In agony he awaited the end of the ceremony, and then drew back in

1  See p. 335.

haste. The little man in grey then approached and thanked him. With respect to the millstone, he told him that he might now perfectly well imagine what his wife must have suffered in mind, when on the preceding day he was about to stab her with his fork; for she was the toad. The pair were then well entertained by the little folks, and after they had eaten, the grey mannikin conducted them out of the hill, but previously gave the girl an apronful of shavings. These she was inclined to throw away instantly, but her sweetheart desired her to keep them, as they would serve to light the fire. On their way home the burden became so heavy that she threw away the half of it, and when they reached the house the remainder proved to be all bright ducats. Thereupon the young man ran back for the purpose of gathering up all that had been thrown away, but it had disappeared. They, however, got enough to enable them to build a farmhouse and be married, and lived happily together for many years.[1]

## Pingel is Dead!

In Jagel, near Sleswig, there was once a host who observed with vexation that his beer always ran out too fast, without his knowing how. But one day, when on his way from the city, where he had been to fetch a fresh supply, he heard, on passing the Jagelberg, where there is a giant-grave, a voice crying in a tone of lamentation: 'Pingel is dead! Pingel is dead!' On his return home he related what he had heard to his wife, and had scarcely uttered the words when a little underground man came rushing out of the cellar, and crying:

> Ach, is Pingel tot, is Pingel tot,
> So hab ich hier Bier genug geholt,

> *Ah, if Pingel's dead, if Pingel's dead,*
> *Then have I fetched beer enough,*

and then ran off. A jug was afterwards found in the cellar standing by the beer-cask, which the little man had left behind; for it was for the sick Pingel that he had stolen the beer.

One version of the story has the name of Pippe instead of Pingel; according to another the jug is of silver, and the dwarf runs away crying, 'Is King Pippe dead? Is King Pippe dead?' Another has: 'As Pilatje duad?'

---

1   The above version of the story is given in preference to one from Swinemünde (Kuhn and Schwartz, op. cit., p. 321), the latter containing some details more characteristic of the good old times than delicate and edifying. See also p. 320.

## The Builder Zi

A man had undertaken to build the church at Eckwadt by a certain day, but was soon sensible that it was not in his power to fulfill his contract. One night, while wandering about out of humour and pondering as to the course he should pursue, a little hill-man accosted him, and offered him his services. The builder at first listened contemptuously to the little man's magniloquent speech, but at length it was settled between them, that the dwarf should erect the church within the given space, and that the builder should by that time ascertain his name; if he failed in so doing, he should, body and soul, belong to the little man. Rejoiced at heart the builder went home; for he thought, 'If he himself will not tell me his name, I can, at all events, extract it from his work-people.' But it fell out quite contrary to his expectations; for the little man used neither workmen nor labourers, but finished everything himself with incredible rapidity; so that the builder clearly saw that all would be complete by the time agreed on. Sadder than the first time, he was again wandering about the fields, when, in passing by a mount, he heard a crying within it, and on listening more attentively, distinguished the following words:

> Vys! vaer still Baen mint,
> Maaen kommer Faer Zi
> Mae Christen Bloi te die.

> *Hush! be still, my child,*
> *Tomorrow comes thy father Zi*
> *With Christian blood for thee.*

Now was the builder overjoyed, for he well knew to whom the words alluded, and hastened home. It was just the morning of the day on which the church should be ready, and the dwarf was busied on placing the last stone – for he worked only during the night – when the builder called to him from a distance:

> God Maaen, Zi! God Maaen, Zi!
> Saetter du nu den sidste Steen i?

> *Good-morning, Zi! Good-morning, Zi!*
> *Are you now placing the last stone?*

When the goblin heard himself addressed by name he was furious, and hurling away the stone that he was in the act of placing, retired within his cave. The hole which was thus left could never be filled up. In the night everything was cast out. A mason, that once endeavoured to build it up, was attacked by a wasting malady. At a later period, a window was placed there, which the goblin suffered to remain.[1]

*The church at Munkbrarup, in Angeln, was built in like manner. The miserable builder hears a child crying under the earth, and the mother saying to it, ' Hush, thou little creature! This evening thy father Sipp will come, and give thee Christian blood to drink.'*

## Father Finn

In very old times the dwarfs had long wars with men, and also with one another. When they were absent in the wars, their wives at home sang by the cradle a particular kind of song. North of Braderup, on the heath, there is a giant-mount, from which was once heard the following:

> Heia, hei, alt Jungen es min.
> Mearen kumt din Vaader Finn
> Me di Man sin Haud.
>
> *Heigh ho, the child is mine.*
> *Tomorrow comes thy father Finn*
> *With a man's head.*

## The House with Ninety-nine Windows

The house of a peasant in Eiderstedt was burnt to the ground. The man sorely afflicted was walking about his field, when he was accosted by a little man in a grey coat and with a horse's foot, who inquired the cause of his sadness. The man told him of his misfortune and that he was without the means of rebuilding his house; whereupon the little man promised to build him one with a hundred windows, and to have it ready in one night, before the first cock-crowing, if the man would promise him his soul. The peasant agreed to the condition, and in the night the devil began to build. The house was soon all but finished, the windows alone remaining to be put in. While the devil was busy about the last window, the man began to crow and clap with his hands, at which the devil laughed. But the cock in the stable had heard the crowing, and answered it just as the devil was fitting in the last pane. Finding himself thus outwitted, the arch-fiend took his departure, though not till he had wrung the neck of the cock. No one has ever been able to put in the pane, nor will any furniture remain in the apartment where it is wanting; all flies out. The room requires no cleaning, being always as neat as broom could make it.

1  See pp. 254–5, 299–300, 404–5.

# Ekke Nekkepenn

The dwarfs are particularly fond of human females. One was once in love
with a young girl of Rantum, and was even betrothed to her. After some time,
however, she changed her mind and would break off the engagement. The
dwarf said to her, 'I will teach you to keep your word; and only if you can tell
me how I am called, shall you be free.' The girl now made inquiries in all
quarters after the name of the dwarf; but no one could inform her. Vexed and
sad she wandered about and sought the loneliest places, the nearer the time
drew nigh when the dwarf should fetch her away. But as she one day was
passing by a mount, she heard within it the following lines sung:

> Delling skell ik bruw,
> Mearen skell ik baak,
> Aurmearn skell ik Bröllep haa:
> Ik jit Ekke Nekkepenn,
> Min Brid es Inge fan Raantem;
> En dit weet nemmen üs ik alliining.

> *Today I shall brew,*
> *Tomorrow I shall bake,*
> *After tomorrow I shall be married:*
> *I am called Ekke Nekkepenn,*
> *My bride is Inge of Rantum;*
> *And this no one knows but I alone.*

When the dwarf came on the third day to fetch her and said, 'What am I
called?' she answered, 'You are called Ekke Nekkepenn.' He then disappeared, and never returned.

*So, in the story of the Dwarf in the Schweckhäuserberge (near Göttingen), he is
overheard repeating the lines:*

> *Hier sitz ich, Gold schnitz ich,*
> *Ich heisse Holzrührlein, Bonneführlein.*
> *Wenn das die Mutter wüsst,*
> *So behielt' sie ihr Mägdlein.*

> *Here I sit, gold I carve,*
> *I am call'd Holzrührlein, Bonneführlein.*
> *If the mother knew that,*
> *She would retain her daughter.*[1]

*Of the same class with the foregoing are the stories of Rumpelstilzchen (Grimm, K. and
H. M., p. 55) and Müllenhoff, Fru Rumpentrumpen, (Müllenhof, p. 409).*

1   From Harry, op. cit., i, p. 16.

## The Carved Image

A peasant, who a hundred years since dwelt on a plot of land at the foot of the Bügberg, near Felsted, on his way to the mill, while his wife was lying in childbed, heard, when not far from the mill, a voice from the hill, saying, 'Carve Liese with her long nose.' He thought: 'That can be no other than my wife; but their project shall not succeed.' So as soon as he returned home, he placed two women to watch by his wife, and went to bed, being extremely drowsy, yet, nevertheless, was by anxiety prevented from sleeping. At midnight the women, who ought to have watched, had fallen asleep; but the man heard a noise, and saw how the underground people came in at the window, lifted wife and child out of bed and laid a wooden figure in their place. He instantly started up, was just in time to catch his wife by the leg, and cried, 'Stop! leave me mine and take your own!' The subterraneans were then obliged to retreat with their wooden Liese, and the man retained his own.

## A Subterranean Child caught

Some young peasants once resolved on catching one of the subterraneans. These people never appear by day, and but seldom by night; to catch one was, therefore, no easy task. They waited till St John's eve, and then some of the boldest lay in wait, for the purpose of kidnapping one. But these creatures are nimble and their places of retreat small. They would all have escaped had not the most active of the young men caught a young girl by the apron. Full of joy he conveyed the little damsel home with him to his wife, who placed her in her lap, caressed her, gave her sugar and all sorts of nice things, asked her her name, age and so on. But the little creature neither cried nor laughed, nor ate nor drank. And thus she continued from day to day; neither by promises nor threats could a sound be extracted from her lips. At length there came an old woman who advised them to set about everything wrong; for that the underground folk could not endure, and she would immediately begin to speak. Thereupon the young woman took the little one with her into the kitchen and desired her to wash the turf nicely for soup, while she cut up the meat to light the fire. The little one did not move. The woman then took the turf herself and washed it three times. The little one stared, but did not move. But when the woman had cut up the meat, and appeared as if about to make a fire with it, she said, 'Woman, you surely will not sin against God?' 'No,' said the woman, 'if thou wilt speak, I will do right; but else, wrong.' From that time the little one spoke; but shortly after found means to escape. Sometime after, when the woman had given birth to a daughter, there lay one morning a changeling in the cradle.

## Changelings

Before the custom was introduced of having newborn children immediately blessed by the midwife, the dwarfs were in the constant practice of
changing them for their own, in doing which they showed much cunning.
When a child was born they would pinch the ear of a cow that was near,
and when the people, hearing the animal's bellowing, ran out to learn the
cause of it, the dwarf would slip in and change the child. It happened once
that a father saw how his infant was being dragged out of the apartment.
He grasped it just at the right moment and drew it to him. He, moreover,
kept possession of the changeling, which was found in the bed by the side
of the lying-in woman, in spite of all the attempts of the subterraneans at
least to recover their own child. By placing on his head the hat of the
subterranean infant, he could see the dwarfs sitting round the table among
the women, and regaling themselves with coffee.

The dwarf child continued long in the house, but would never speak.
But someone having advised the foster-parents to make a brewing in a
hen's egg, and then pour the beer into a goose's egg, the dwarf, after
making all sorts of manifestations of astonishment, at length cried out:

> Ik bün so oelt
> As de Behmer Woelt,
> Unn heff in myn Läebn
> So'n Bro nich seen.
>
> *I am as old*
> *As the Behmer wold,*
> *And have in my life*
> *Such a brewing not seen.*

The 'Wichtelmanner' had stolen a child out of its cradle, and left a
changeling, with a huge head and staring eyes, in its stead, which ate and
drank voraciously. In her distress the mother applied to a neighbour, who
advised her to carry the changeling into the kitchen, set it on the hearth,
kindle a fire, and boil water in two eggshells: that would cause the
changeling to laugh, and as soon as he laughed it would be all over with him.
The woman did as her neighbour advised. As she was placing the eggshells
on the fire, the clodpate exclaimed, 'I now am as old as the Westerwald, and
have never till this moment seen anything boiled in an eggshell!' and then
began to laugh. While he was laughing there came in a multitude of
Wichtelmannikins, bringing with them the woman's own child, which they
placed on the hearth, and took the changeling away with them.[1]

---

1  Grimm, J. & W., *Kinder- und Hausmärchen*, op. cit., No. 39. Wichtel
(Wichtelmann) is the Frankish name for *elf*.

A person once saw a female dwarf going across a field with a stolen child. The sight was a singular one; for she could not hold the babe sufficiently high, on account of its length, and therefore kept constantly calling to it:

> Baer op dyn Gewant,
> Dat du nich haekst
> In den gälen Orant.

> *Hold up thy robe,*
> *That thou be not hook'd*
> *In the bitter orant.*

*Orant or dorant (antirrhinum or marrubium) scares away Dwarfs (Wichtel) and Nikkers. See Grimm, J., Deutsche Mythologie, op. cit., p. 1164.*

---

In Eiderstedt a woman one night kindled a huge fire in the middle of the barn, and placed upon it an exceedingly diminutive pot. When a Kielkropf (changeling) that she had was fetched, it clapped its hands in full astonishment, and cried in a shrill voice, 'I am now fifty years old, and have never seen the like!' The woman would have thrown the Kielkropf into the fire, but it was snatched from her, and her own genuine child stood there before her.

*Similar stories are almost innumerable in Germany, but the foregoing, together with the two following, will amply suffice to show the resemblance between the German traditions of changelings and those of Scandinavia.*

---

Before going to bed, a pair of open scissors must be laid in the cradle of a newborn child, until it is baptised. If it sleeps by its mother, at the last swathing a cross must be made on its breast and forehead; else the subterraneans will change it.

There was once in Amrum a woman whose youngest son was stolen by these beings; but the child they left in place of the stolen one so closely resembled it, that the mother at first was not aware of the deception. But afterwards their own child came back, and the parents were wholly unable to determine which was theirs, until an accident settled the difficulty. It was in the harvest, and the woman going one day to the thrashing-floor, took up a shovel and began casting aside the thrashed-out corn; both boys being present. One of them fell a laughing, and in answer to the woman's question, why he laughed said, 'My father just came in and fetched half a ton of rye, and in going out fell and broke his leg.' Thereupon said the woman, 'Thou art the one; go therefore to the place thou camest from.' She then seized the boy and flung him through the window of the thrashing-house, and never again set eyes on him.

It is to be observed that a thrashing-floor should always be swept *with* the sun, and never in the opposite direction; otherwise the subterraneans will steal the corn. The woman, it evidently appeared, had taken this precaution.

## The Kielkropp

Not far from the town of Lauenburg there is a village called Böken, in which, many hundred years ago, there stood a chapel, where there was an image of the holy mother, made of wood. This image was at that time held in the highest veneration; for if any persons were sick, the people would carry them to the image and let them lie before it for some time, when they would be cured.

Not far from the above-mentioned village there lived a peasant, who, although he had been married for many years, was childless. This afflicted him sorely: he stormed and raved, maltreated and maledicted his wife the whole livelong day, until she at length unexpectedly said to him, 'You may cease your ill-usage, you will soon have your wish; for I feel that I shall be a mother.' At this intelligence the peasant was overjoyed; and thenceforward treated his wife more kindly. But that which gave him so much delight was to be his greatest affliction. When the child was born it was all right and proper as to its body and limbs, but its head was larger than that of the largest man. Such children the people at that time called *Kielkropps*, and believed that the devil himself, or one of his associates, was their father, and that they brought only misfortune into a house. But be all that as it may, our peasant had got his Kielkropp and must keep it. During a space of three years the child's head grew larger and larger, and looked like a great basket, while its other members continued as diminutive as they had been from the first, so that it could neither go nor stand; nor could it utter a word, but only moaned and screamed both by day and night.

One evening as the woman was sitting with the Kielkropp on her lap, and was lamenting over it, she said to her husband, 'A thought just strikes me which may probably be of good to us. Tomorrow is Sunday: put then the child into a basket and take it to the holy mother Mary of Böken, lay the basket before her, and rock the child in it for some time: that will, perhaps, be of service.' The peasant willingly followed her advice, on the following morning put his basket in order, laid fresh hay in it together with some bedding, placed his Kielkropp in it, and went his way. When on the bridge that crosses a water near Böken, he heard, just as he reached the middle, a voice behind him, crying, 'Where now, Kielkropp?' which the child in the panier answered by, 'I'm going to be rocked, that I may thrive.'[1] On

1   See p. 334.

hearing the child begin to speak the man was greatly terrified, but instantly recovering himself, he dashed the basket, Kielkropp amid all, into the water, saying, 'If thou canst speak, thou monster, then go to where thou hast learned.' At once a loud cry was heard from under the bridge, as when many people call out together, at which the man was not a little frightened, and made all possible haste home, without once looking behind him, where he told his wife in what manner he had got rid of the Kielkropp.

## The Underground Folk Emigrate

The grandfather of a watchmaker still living in Hohn, was when a boy one day tending cows in a neighbouring field, and to protect himself from the rain, had thrown his father's large coat over his shoulders. While standing under a tree, he found himself on a sudden surrounded by a multitude of underground folk, holding each other's hand, and thus forming a circle about him. They told him they were about leaving the neighbourhood, and that he should go with them. To his question why they were going, they answered, that they could not endure the ringing of the bells in the village.[1] But the young man not liking to be detained by them, broke through the circle, leaving the coat behind, which they stripped from his shoulders. On the following day, however, he found it in the same place hanging on a bush.

## The Wolterkens–Niss-puk–Büsemann–Niske

The Wolterkens appear to be identical with the Scandinavian Nisser. In Meldorf the schoolchildren have a festival, when the girls decorate the schoolroom with flowers. In the afternoon and evening they dance, and then say, 'We have Nesskuk,' or 'We celebrate Nesskuk.'

The Nisken always frequent dark, concealed places in the house or stable, and even in the pile of wood. They disappear before everyone that approaches them. At night the people of the house must clear the hearth, and place a kettle of pure water for the use of the little officious people. The Niss-Puk, moreover, always requires a mess of sweet porridge with butter to be set for him in a certain place.

Persons from the district of Stapelholm, who have seen the Niss-Puk, describe him as not larger than an infant of a year or a year and a half old. Others say that he is as large as one of three years. He has a large head and long arms, and small but bright, cunning eyes.[2] He wears red stockings

---

1   See p. 336.
2   The people of Silt say he has very large eyes; whence of inquisitive persons it is said: 'He stares like a Puk.'

and a long grey or green tick coat, on the head a red, peaked cap. He delights in a pair of soft, easy slippers, and when he gets such he may be heard at night slipping about the floor in them.

These beings sometimes appear in a hideous form, to the great terror of the inmates, at which they testify their delight by a loud laugh.

People frighten children with the Büsemann, who dwells in the stable; in Föhr they are kept in awe by the blind Jug; in Ditmarschen by Pulterklaes. And who knows not the formidable Roppert (Ruprecht)? The domestic goblin was formerly known under the name of Chimken.

*In some respects the Niss-Puk resembles the Galgenmännlein or Alraun of South Germany, who is enclosed in a bottle, can be sold by his owner, but always for a price less than the sum he paid for him. The soul of the last owner belongs to the Galgenmännlein. See the tale of 'Das Galgenmännlein' in Binder's Schwäbische Volkssagen.*

## The Subterraneans lick up Milk

About seventy years ago little underground beings were seen in many farms in the Wilstermarsch, who did little more than accompany the maids and men home in the morning after they had been milking, and sedulously lick up the drops of milk that had been spilt. But when in measuring out nothing was spilt, they would overturn all the vessels and run away. These people were about a foot and a half high, wore black clothes and a peaked, red cap. Wherever they came, people thought they brought a special blessing on the house.

In the Frisic islands the housewives have frequently observed, when brewing, that the little people usually came in the shape of toads, and licked from off the floor the new beer that had been spilt. No one does them any harm, and the beer so spilt must be left for them, as well as the crumbs of bread that fall from the table.

## The Klabautermann

The Klabautermann sits under the ship's capstan, and is a little fellow with yellow breeches, horseman's boots, a large, fiery-red head, green teeth, and a steeple-crowned hat. If a ship is doomed to perish, the Klabautermann may be heard running up and down the shrouds in a state of disquietude, and making a noise among the rigging and in the hold; so that the crew leave the ship, and the sooner the better.[1]

---

1   Kuhn and Schwartz, op. cit., p. 423.

When such a goblin is on board a ship, and on friendly terms with the crew, the vessel will not sink and every voyage will be prosperous; if he abandons it, things will go ill. Everything that is broken during the day in the ship he sets to rights in the night, and is therefore often called the Klütermann (joiner).[1] He also prepares many things for the sailors, and even performs them. If he is in a bad humour, he makes an awful noise, throws about the firewood, spars, and other things, knocks on the ship's sides, destroys many things, hinders those at work, and unseen gives the sailors violent cuffs on the head. From all this uproar it is supposed that he derives his name.[2]

## Of the Ranzaus

Of the very old and ducal Sleswig family of Ranzau it is recorded, that to an ancestress of their house there came one night, as she lay in bed by her husband's side, a little man bearing a lantern, who having waked her, prayed her to follow him. She did so (every door and gate opening spontaneously as they passed) and arrived at length in a hollow mount, in which there lay a little woman in the pains of labour. When the said noble dame Von Ranzau, at the earnest entreaty of the little woman, had laid her hand upon her head, she was instantly delivered. The lady, who had been standing in great fear, now hastened back, and was attended home by her said diminutive companion. At parting she received from the little man, in recompense for her service, a large piece of gold, of which, at his suggestion, she caused to be made fifty counters, a herring, and two spindles for her daughter. At the same time he gave her also this notice: That her posterity must carefully preserve those articles, if, from being affluent, they would not in time become needy persons; for that as long as none of them were lost, they would increase in honour and repute. I think that the person who related to me this remarkable anecdote, at the same time informed me, that either the herring or one of the golden counters had disappeared from among these treasures.

*According to an oral tradition in Thiele (i, p. 134), the little man conducts the countess into the cellar of the castle of Breitenburg. She receives from him a golden spinning-wheel for her daughter and a golden sabre for her son, together with the prediction, that as long as those things were preserved in the family, it should flourish in wealth and consideration. Both presents are, it is said, still preserved in the mansion.*

*According to another account, the gifts consisted in a tablecloth, a spool, and gold, of*

1 From klütern, to *make or mend small delicate works, particularly of wood.*
2 From klappen, *to make a noise, clabauder (clabauderie)?*

*which a chain was made, and some coined into money. Dame Sophia Ranzau of Seeholm related this of her grandfather Henry Ranzau's wife.*

*The tradition of a Frau von Hahn, who was fetched by a water-nix, agrees (as I have heard it related) with the Ranzau tradition. The countess is conducted into a cellar, receives a present of shavings, which turn to gold, a large beaker made from which is still shown at Neuhaus. Other things made from the same are lost.*

---

The newly married countess, who was of a Danish family, was sleeping by her husband's side, when a noise was heard, the bed-curtains were drawn aside, and she saw a little woman of extraordinary beauty, not more than a cubit high, standing before her holding a light. 'Fear not,' she said, 'I will do you no harm, but bring you good luck, if you afford the assistance which I require. Rise up and follow me; but take heed to eat nothing that may be offered you, nor accept any other gift than what I shall present to you, and which you may safely receive.'

The countess accompanied her, and the way led under the earth. They came into an apartment that was resplendent with gold and precious stones, and full of little men and women. Before long their king appeared, and conducted the countess to a bed, in which lay the queen in the pains of childbirth, beseeching her to give her assistance. The countess did her best, and the queen was safely delivered of a son. At this there was great rejoicing among the guests; the countess was led to a table covered with the choicest viands, and pressed to partake of them; but she touched nothing, neither would she accept any of the precious stones, which lay in golden dishes. At length she was led forth by her first conductress, and brought back to her bed.

The little woman then said, 'You have rendered a great service to our realm, for which you shall be rewarded. Here are three wooden staves; lay them under your pillow, and tomorrow morning they will be changed to gold. From the first of these let there be made a herring; from the second, counters; from the third, a spindle; and reveal this whole affair to no one in the world, except your husband. You will have three children, who will form the three branches of a house. The one that gets the herring will be very successful in war, both himself and his posterity; the one that gets the counters will, together with his children, fill high offices of state; the one that gets the spindle will be blessed with numerous offspring.'

After these words the little hill-woman departed, and the countess fell asleep. When she woke she related to her husband the events of the night. The count laughed at her, regarding the whole as a dream; but when she put her hand under the pillow, there lay three gold bars. Both were astonished, and employed them precisely in the manner prescribed.

The prediction was accurately fulfilled: those branches of the house which carefully preserved the treasures, still exist, while others, who were less careful, are extinct. Of the branch that got the coined money it is related, that a king of Denmark once desired to have one of the pieces; but at the moment the king received it, the individual who gave it to him was seized with a violent stomachache.

*In L'Amant oisif, Bruxelles, 1711, pp. 405–411, the foregoing tradition is told under the title of 'La Comtesse de Falinsperk'.*

---

A benevolent countess (Ranzau) at Breitenburg, who was frequently herself the bearer of her household medicines to the sick, was one stormy evening called to the house of an old woman, who dwelt at the other extremity of the village. She was in the act of going, but was prevented by her husband. While sitting alone in the twilight, she heard a noise, and before her stood the house-goblin with herbs and potions, who bade her take them and carry them to the sick, and rather to obey the voice of her own heart than the prohibition of her husband. The countess followed the goblin's bidding, and through her care and the medicaments the sick woman speedily recovered. On the following evening, as the countess was again sitting alone in the twilight, she saw the goblin standing by the hearth and stirring the fire. When the fire had blazed up, he threw into it an apronful of shavings, and said to the countess, 'When the fire is burnt out, look among the ashes, and what you find there preserve carefully. As long as those things continue in your family, so long will fortune favour the counts of Ranzau.' When the fire was out the countess made a search, and found a golden spindle, a golden beaker, and something besides. The last-mentioned fell to a younger branch, who lost it, and is now without property; but the spindle is still at Breitenburg, and the beaker at Rastorf.

*At Breitenburg fifty golden pennings are carefully preserved in a silver box, on which are the arms of John Ranzau and Dame Anna Walstorf, his wife. The inscription on these pennings is engraved and filled in with black.*

## Josias Ranzau's Magic Sword

As Anna Walstorf was one night in pious prayer making mention of her absent husband, she was humbly besought by a subterranean mount-man to give aid to his wife who was in the pains of childbirth. She followed the little man through many cellars and vaults of her castle of Breitenburg that were quite unknown to her, until she came to a bright crystal rock. On a touch from her companion it flew open, and in a spacious hall she saw an innumerable multitude of similarly little men collected round an elevated spot. She advanced and found the queen in the pangs of labour and at the point of death. Dame Anna, who was well skilled in the preparation of medicines, mixed a potion for the patient, through the virtue of which she was soon delivered of a son. Their joy was beyond expression, and the grateful husband presented their benefactress with some gold, which appeared like shavings, enjoining her to preserve it as the greatest treasure; that the fortunes of her house depended on it. At a subsequent period she caused to be made from it three things, viz, some small pieces of money, a distaff and a herring, which were afterwards divided among the several branches of the family.

The herring at a later period fell to the share of Josias Ranzau, who, full of military ardour, caused it to be made into a sword-hilt. He entered the French service, in which he shared in many battles, and at length attained to the rank of field-marshal. He was one of the most desperate duellists, and even when he had arrived at an advanced age, and was possessed of the highest dignity, he would go disguised among the soldiers and pick quarrels with them. He once fought with an esteemed friend, because he had written his name incorrectly. But so long as he carried his magic sword, he was never, in any battle, either struck by a bullet or wounded by a stroke. No one had for a long time placed any confidence in him, it being evident to everyone that there was some sorcery in the matter, so that when Caspar von Bockwold, a Holstein nobleman, had divulged the story of the goblin, in a company at Strasburg, many persons denied him the praise of valour, and ascribed all his feats to the herring. At this, maddened with rage, Josias, in the presence of all, cast his sword into the Rhine. Still victory did not forsake him, though he had to pay dear for it; so that at last, of all those members of which a man has two, he had lost one, and had besides sixty severe wounds on his body.

## We are Removing!

Cases have been known of houses in which whole families and swarms of Puks or Nisser have taken their abode, and have thereby been rendered uninhabitable. In Husum there once lived two families of these beings, one at a baker's, the other at a brewer's. At night they turned everything topsy-turvy, made the most horrible noises, ran up and down the stairs; sometimes they were in the cellar, sometimes in the chambers; from the baker they stole his flour, from the brewer his beer. They were so little, that when pursued, like spiders and worms, they would creep into the smallest crevices, where they would make an incessant outcry. The people at length could endure them no longer, and resolved to remove. Their moveables had all been carried out, and the maidservants from both houses came the last, carrying the brooms on their shoulders. They met together, when Ann inquired of Susan where they were going. But before she could answer, many little voices cried from one of the brooms, 'We are removing!' The girls at first were frightened, but soon recovered their presence of mind. There was a pond close at hand; into this both plunged their brooms, and left them in the water. They then betook themselves to their new habitations, and were no more annoyed by these noxious beings. But it was soon remarked that all the fish in the pond grew sick, and by degrees died; and women, who late in the evening fetched water from the pond, declared by all that was holy that they had repeatedly heard small voices in the water crying out, 'We have removed! We have gone away!'

---

In Neumünster a man had offended a Niss, because he had put no butter in his porridge. In revenge the Niss played such pranks and caused so much annoyance that the people were obliged to remove. When the last person with the broom was crossing the threshold, the Niss, who was sitting in the broom, called out, 'I too am here,' and removed with them.

---

At a place also in Angeln, some people left their house, on account of a Niss. When the last cartload was just ready to go, he was sitting behind, and laughing said, 'We move today'.

*The reader will have already seen in the* Danish Popular Traditions *stories nearly identical with the three foregoing, which are here selected from many others as striking examples of the close resemblance existing between the superstitions of North Germany and those of Scandinavia.*

## The Snake-king

A girl working in the field once found a bunch of fourteen or fifteen snakes, all hissing together; one of which had a golden crown. The girl untied her white apron and laid it on the ground near the group, when the largest of the snakes, the one that had the crown, came and laid his crown on the apron. It was of pure gold and set with many precious stones of a green colour. The girl instantly sprang forwards and snatched it up; seeing which the snake-king cried so horribly that the girl was deafened by the noise. She afterwards sold the crown for a considerable sum.[1]

---

In the ruins of the old Duborg, near Flensborg, there lives a bluish snake that wears on its head a small crown of the finest gold. It appears but once

---

1   See p. 380.

a day, at the hour of noon, and then for a moment only. Whoever can catch it, or get its crown, is fortunate. The king would instantly give twenty thousand dollars current for the crown; for whoever wears it is immortal.

## Thunder

In Silt, if anyone finds a thunderstone, he carefully preserves it; because thunder will never cause any injury in a house where there is such a stone.[1]

## The Stars

Old maids and bachelors, according to the North Frisians, are curiously employed after death. As soon as the sun is sunk below the horizon, the old maids must cut stars out of it, which the old bachelors, during the night, must blow up in the east, going all the time up or down a ladder.

## The Man in the Moon

At the time when wishing was of avail, a man, one Christmas Eve, stole cabbages from his neighbour's garden. When just in the act of walking off with his load, he was perceived by the people, who conjured (wished) him up in the moon. There he stands in the full moon to be seen by everybody, bearing his load of cabbages to all eternity. Every Christmas Eve he is said to turn round once. Others say that he stole willow boughs, which he must bear for ever.

In Silt the story goes that he was a sheep-stealer, that enticed sheep to him with a bundle of cabbages, until, as an everlasting warning to others, he was placed in the moon, where be constantly holds in his hand a bundle of cabbages.

The people of Rantum say that he is a giant, who at the time of the flow stands in a stooping posture, because he is then taking up water, which be pours out on the earth, and thereby causes the flow; but at the time of the ebb he stands erect and rests from his labour, when the water can subside again.

## Hans Dümkt

Of Charles's Wain, or, as it is more usually called, the Great Bear, it is said, that it is the wagon, in which Elias, our Lord, and other saints journeyed to heaven. But the very small star above the centre one in the pole is the wagoner, Hans Dümkt. He was in the service of our Lord, and had a very

1   See p. 48n.

comfortable place; but by degrees he did his work more and more negligently. Our Lord often warned and chided him; but Hans cared very little for that. He was particularly careless in cutting chaff; none that he cut could be used, being cut much too long. At this our Lord was at last so angry that he set him on the pole of the celestial wain, where he may be seen every evening, as a warning to all serving-men that cut chaff too long.

*According to one tradition, Hans Dümken (or Dümkt) was a carrier, who conveyed our Lord, who in remuneration promised him the kingdom of heaven; but the man said he would rather drive to all eternity, from sunset to sunrise. Grimm, J.,* Deutsche Mythologie, *op. cit., p. 688.*

## The Wandering Jew

For many years the Wandering Jew has been a wanderer from city to city. He is never hungry nor thirsty, and never grows old. He takes rest always out of doors, and may not sleep under a roof. It is said that he was some years ago in Lüneburg, where he slept on a stone just without the city.

A few years since he was seen in Sundewith, not far from Beuschau. He carried a basket, out of which there grew moss. He rests only on Christmas Eve, when he finds a plough in the field; for on that alone may he sit.

## The Wode

Many persons have, in the twelve nights of Christmas and particularly on Christmas Eve, seen the Wode on his progress. He rides a large white horse, a huntsman on foot and four-and-twenty fierce dogs follow him. In every place through which he passes, the hedges fall with a crash, and a road opens itself before him; but towards morning they are all erect again. Some assert that his horse has only three legs. He always rides on certain ways, past the doors of the houses, and with such speed that his dogs are not always able to keep pace with him: they may be heard panting and howling, and sometimes one has been left on the road. One of them was once found in a house at Wulfsdorf, another at Fuhlenhagen, lying on the hearth, incessantly howling and panting, until the next Christmas Eve, when the Wode again took it with him. At Christmas Eve no linen ought to be left out, as the dogs tear it to tatters. There should also be no baking, as it would cause a Wild-hunt. Everything in the house must be quiet. If the door is left open, the Wode and his dogs will pass through and consume all that is in the house, but particularly the dough, if baking be going forwards.[1]

---

1  Woden here appears as sadly fallen from his former high estate. This and the following story might not inaptly, in a twofold sense, be also titled 'The Descent of Odin'.

The Wode once entered the house of a poor peasant, and his dogs devoured everything. The poor man made great lamentation, and asked the Wode what compensation he was to have for the damage he had sustained. The Wode told him that he should be paid. Shortly after he came dragging along a dead dog, which he told the peasant to throw into his chimney; when he had done so, the skin burst, and there fell from it many bright gold pieces.

The Wode has a certain road, through which he rides every night during the twelve days of Christmas. At his approach the subterraneans must flee before him, as he is bent on extirpating them from the earth. An old peasant one night late saw the subterraneans running along; they did not appear terrified and cried out, 'He can't catch us today, he must let us go, he has not washed himself this morning.' On proceeding a little farther, he met the Wode, who asked him what they had been saying. 'They said,' answered the old man, ' that you have not washed yourself this morning, and must therefore let them go.' When the Wode heard this he stopped his horse, let it stale, dismounted and washed himself therewith; then remounted and continued his chase after the subterraneans. After a little while the peasant saw him returning, having with him many bound together by their yellow hair,[1] besides a number hanging down on each side of his horse. Thus did he pursue the subterraneans until they all have disappeared; he therefore hunts no longer on the earth, but only in the air above. The Wode is known throughout Lauenburg, and people everywhere close their doors against him át Christmas time.

––––––––––

A Mecklenburg tradition places the connection between Odin and the Wild Hunt beyond a doubt.

When, as it often happens, the dogs bark on the heaths, in the woods and crossways, the countryman knows it to be *Wod* that is leading them, and pities the wanderer that has not reached his home.

A drunken peasant passing one night through a forest on his way from the town, heard the Wild Hunt, and the noise of the dogs and the cry of the huntsmen in the air. 'In the middle of the road! In the middle of the road!'[2]

––––––––––

1 The subterranean folk have not yellow hair. Those alluded to above must be the *moss-folk* and *wood-wives*, who resemble children of three years, and are friendly to mankind. See Grimm, J., *Deutsche Mythologie*, op. cit., p. 881, *note*.

2 The reason of this warning appears from the same superstition as current in the isle of Usedom. When the Wild Hunt passes by, the cry is frequently heard of:

> Ho ho! blîw innen Middelwech,
> Denn bîten dî de Hunne nich.
>
> *Hallo hallo! keep in the middle way,*
> *Then will the dogs not bite thee.*

Kuhn und Schwartz, op. cit., p. 427

cried a voice, but to which he gave no heed. On a sudden a tall man on a white horse precipitated himself from the clouds before him. 'Art thou strong?' said he. 'Let us try which can pull the strongest. Here take hold of this chain.' The countryman took hold of the heavy chain, and the wild hunter soared aloft. The countryman wound the chain round an oak, and the huntsman tugged in vain. 'Thou hast surely wound the chain round the oak,' said Wod, descending from the clouds. 'No,' said the countryman, who had hastily loosed it, 'see I am holding it in my hands.' 'Then thou shalt be mine up in the clouds,' cried the huntsman, again mounting. The countryman now quickly fastened the chain again round the oak, and Wod was as unsuccessful as before. 'But hast thou not fastened the chain round the oak?' said Wod, again descending. 'No,' said the countryman, 'see I am holding it in my hands.' 'If thou wert heavier than lead, thou must up with me in the clouds, notwithstanding.' Saying this he darted up like lightning, but the countryman had recourse to his old process. The dogs barked, the carriages rolled, the horses neighed up aloft, the oak cracked at its roots and seemed to turn; the countryman felt far from easy, but the tree stood its ground. 'Thou hast pulled capitally,' said the huntsman. 'Many men have I made mine: thou art the first that has withstood me. I will reward thee.' Now loud was the uproar of the hunt, 'Hallo, holla! Wol, wol!' The countryman sneaked away towards home, when from an unseen height, a deer fell dying before him, and there stood Wod, who, springing from his white horse, cut up the game. 'The blood shalt thou have and a haunch besides,' said Wod. 'Sir,' said the countryman, 'thy servant has neither pail nor pitcher.' 'Take thy boot off,' cried Wod. He did so. 'Now march home with blood and flesh to wife and brat.' Fear at first caused his burden to seem light, but by degrees it grew heavier and heavier, so that he could scarcely walk under it. Bent almost double and dripping with sweat, he at length reached his hut, and behold! the boot was full of gold, and the haunch turned out to be a leather bag filled with silver.[1]

---

1  Lisch, *Meklenb. Jahrb.*, quoted by Grimm, J., *Deutsche Mythologie*, op. cit., pp. 876, 877.

# The Man without a Shadow

Many preachers and sacristans in former times visited (and still visit) the Black School, and are there instructed by the devil in the black art, by means of which they can exorcise spectres, spirits of the dead, and even the devil himself. The devil gives the instruction, though not gratis. The condition is, that whosoever, at the termination of the lecture, when the course is ended, of all the pupils that frequent the school, goes last out by the door, shall belong to him. By many, who proved more cunning than their master, he has been outwitted, among others, by the sacristan of Bröns, in the west part of the bailiwick of Hadersleben, He was the last of all that left the school, but he knew how to help himself, when the devil would lay hold on him. The school-door was to the south, and it happened that the lecture was finished in bright sunshine, exactly at noon; so the sacristan very justly said, that not he, but his shadow was the last to go out; that, if he liked, the devil was welcome to keep. The devil could object nothing to this reasoning, and let the man go, but detained his shadow. From that time the sacristan has been shadowless; and many who have seen and known him can testify, that even in the brightest sunshine not the faintest appearance of a shadow accompanies him.

*It hardly need be mentioned that Chamisso's 'Peter Schlemihl' is founded on a similar tradition. According to a Spanish tradition, there was a cave at Salamanca in which the devil always maintained seven pupils, under the condition that when they were fully instructed, the last must pay the reckoning. One day when he was dismissing his scholars, and had ordered the last to remain, the scholar pointed to his shadow, saying, 'That is the last'. The devil was obliged to be content with the shadow, and the pupil continued for the rest of his life shadowless.*

*Jamieson, speaking of the Scottish superstition, says: 'Losing one's shadow arrives to such as are studying the art of necromancy. When a class of students hare made a certain progress in their mystic studies, they are obliged to run through a subterraneous hall, where the devil literally catches the hindmost in the race, unless he crosses the hall so speedily, that the arch-enemy can only apprehend his shadow. In the latter case the person of the sage never after throws any shade, and those who have thus lost their shadow always prove the best magicians.' See Grimm, J., Deutsche Mythologie, op. cit., p. 976. Most readers will recollect Walter Scott's lines, in the 'Lay of the Last Minstrel', when speaking of the lady of Buccleuch's father, who had studied in 'Padua, far beyond the sea':*

> *For when in studious mood he paced*
> *St Andrew's cloister'd hall,*
> *His form no darkening shadow traced*
> *Upon the sunny wall.*

## Devil against Devil

A cross painted on the principal door of the house is a safeguard against witches; it is also good to have in the house a wafer that has been purloined at the communion. If cattle are bewitched and no butter can be produced, the cows, churns and pails must in the evening be silently smoked. The witch will then usually come and ask admission, but no one may be let in, however hard they may knock at the door.

---

At a house in Wilster a child was sick. A cunning woman said there was some sorcery in the case, and that the child must be smoked at twelve o'clock at night, every door being closed. The person that had bewitched it would then come, when blood must be drawn from him or her on a cloth, and the cloth burnt. At the hour specified every door was carefully closed; before the windows, and reaching almost to the top, sheets were hung, all precisely as the cunning woman had directed. But the house had window-shutters after the old fashion, made to turn up, so that under every window they hung like a sort of flap, on which, when not turned up, a person might contrive to stand and look through the window. And so it was here; for while they were smoking the child, and before it had struck twelve, the witch suddenly peeped over the sheet into the room. On seeing her, the man rushed out, struck her in the face, and received the blood on a cloth, which being burnt, the child recovered.

---

In the neighbourhood of Büsum there dwelt a wealthy peasant, who had an only daughter whom he tenderly loved. But his old mother-in-law was a witch. People knew that she had on several occasions transformed herself to a cat or other animal; in companies, too, she has caused the whole room to be filled with ravens, so that the guests were forced to withdraw. She did harm to both man and beast. If anyone passed a night in her house, and his slippers stood the wrong way, she would, when she thought that everyone was asleep, enter the chamber and turn the slippers.[1] This is a certain proof that she was a witch; for so they constantly do; otherwise they would have no power over the sleeper. But witches must always have one person in their family on whom to exercise their malice. The old mother-in-law grudged the peasant his good fortune, and at length bewitched his daughter most wickedly. She presented the young maiden with a beautiful new dress, which she, suspecting no guile, put on on the following Sunday, intending to appear in it at church. But it was hardly on her back before her hair stood on end, her eyes rolled wildly, and for internal

---

1 See *Sw. Pop. Belief*, p. 307, No. 50, and *Dan. Pop. Belief*, p. 424, No. 34.

burning she could not contain herself. She dashed herself against the windows and doors like a savage cat, raved and raged at everybody, but without knowing anyone, and it was not without much difficulty that she could be undressed and placed in bed. The raving fit then passed, but was succeeded by the greatest debility and exhaustion. And thus she lay for a length of time, and was daily dwindling away. No physician could afford her relief, for they all confessed that they were ignorant of her malady. Her parents were inconsolable. Some sagacious persons, to whom they had recourse, told them at last that an old woman had bewitched their daughter, but that they were powerless against her. Only in Hamburg there lived a man who could probably relieve her; if he failed, all attempts would be vain. Her father, resolved on leaving nothing untried, instantly set out for Hamburg, and spoke with the man, who, after he had heard a full state of the case, opened a large book, written in characters which nobody but himself understood. At the expiration of a quarter of an hour, the man told the peasant that his daughter was certainly under the influence of witchcraft, but that he would give him a pot of medicine, that would most probably afford her relief, if only he could carry it home whole; as the evil spirit would use every endeavour to break it. On the following day the peasant received the pot from the doctor, and soon arrived without impediment at Büsum. But now all must go wrong. The ship's boy was ordered to carry the basket containing the pot on shore and to the house of the peasant; but hardly had he set foot on dry land, when the sand rose like a waterspout, threw the youngster down, and dashed the basket out of his hand, so that the pot was broken in a thousand fragments. Thus was the journey in vain. After a very short delay, the man was again on his way to the wonderful doctor, when, having related his mishap, he was informed by the sage that the task was now much more difficult, but that he must come again in two days. The doctor had in the interim made everything ready, and packed up the pot, and now enjoined the peasant to keep the strictest watch over it; adding that there was still one other method of saving his daughter, but one that he should very reluctantly have recourse to, even if her father would consent. This time the peasant returned home by land, having the basket with the pot under the seat of his vehicle, and arrived within sight of his house in safety, and was even on his own ground, when, on the level earth, the vehicle was suddenly upset, and although the peasant himself sustained no injury, the pot was broken in pieces. The man, who had his daughter's recovery much at heart, allowed himself no rest, although his wife, and more especially his mother-in-law, would retain him, telling him he ought to take some repose after his great toil; but all was to no purpose; he mounted his horse, and in twelve hours was again in Hamburg. The doctor now informed him that one course alone remained, which was to boil the old witch in oil; but before commencing this process, he would show him the person who had bewitched his daughter. He then went into an adjacent apartment, muttered, with all kinds of hocus-pocus, some unintelligible spells, and in quarter of an hour came back with a large mirror under his arm. This he placed on the table, and desired the peasant to look into it. The man did so, and instantly recognised in it his old mother-in-law. He was deeply grieved at the sight, yet on calling to mind what his daughter had suffered, and that if her malady continued, it must soon terminate her existence, he formed his resolution, and said to the doctor that he might do what he thought proper, let whatever might come afterwards. The doctor appointed him to come again at noon on the following day. At the time fixed the peasant was in attendance, when the doctor led him into a detached apartment, and then withdrew. At the expiration of an hour he called him into the kitchen, where he had a large kettle on the fire, into which he poured oil and other things, under all sorts of spells and ceremonies, and then shut it close with a heavy lid. What was in the kettle now began to work and boil, the noise in it grew louder and louder, and the peasant thought he could distinguish the moans of a human being. Whatever it was, it seemed resolved to remain no longer, but to get air, and strove with all its might to raise the lid. 'Now is the time,' said the doctor, springing forwards and holding down the lid with all his strength; and shortly after called to the peasant for his assistance; and only with the utmost difficulty could they succeed in preventing it from running over. When the boiling ceased, all gradually grew more quiet, and was at length quite still. 'Now,' said the doctor, 'your daughter is saved, and the old woman is no more.' The peasant felt ill at ease, and although pleased at the intelligence, the doctor appeared to him as something unearthly. He instantly paid him his due, hastened back to his inn, and on the following day, as early as possible, mounted his horse and rode home. On entering his dwelling, his daughter, quite healthy and cheerful, came to meet him, and related to him that her old grandmother had died a horrible death on the previous day. At noon she was attacked by an internal burning, which from one minute to another became more intense. In bed she could not remain, had torn open the doors and windows, thrown off her clothes, rolled and writhed about the floor, crying and moaning the whole time so that she might be heard at a considerable distance. Not till the day was far advanced did she become gradually more calm, and at length uttered not a sound. Until then no one could remain with her, but now on entering, they found on the spot where she had lain a small heap of ashes and some burnt bones. From that hour the daughter recovered her health, and lived several years after.

## Witches take away Butter

When the dew falls on May morning it will be a good butter year. On such a morning a witch, before sunrise, went into her neighbours' fields, took up the dew with large linen cloths, then wrung them out, and so collected the dew in a vessel. Of this, every time she wished to make butter, she took a spoonful, and poured it into the churn, saying at the same time, 'From every house a spoonful'.[1] By this process she took every time so much butter from those neighbours to whom the fields belonged. On one occasion her man had to churn, but, not rightly understanding the matter, said when taking the dew, 'From every house a bushelful.'[2] He then began to churn, when there came so much butter, that it ran over the whole house, and the people were at a loss what to do with it.

*The appellation of Daustriker (Thaustreicher), dew-striker or scraper, for a witch, is no doubt derived from the above superstition. See more on the subject in Grimm,* Deutsche Mythologie, *op. cit., p. 1026.*

## Calves Bewitched

A farmer could never rear a calf; as often as he attempted it, the animal fell sick, and seemed unable either to live or to die, so that he was obliged to kill it. In his trouble he had recourse to a cunning man, who advised him, when the like happened again, to take the sick animal into his yard and shoot at it. 'You will not be able to kill it,' added he, 'but continue to load and fire; somebody will then soon come, and the matter will be settled.' After a time another calf fell ill, when he did as the man had recommended. After he had fired several shots without killing the calf, a female neighbour came in running and crying out, 'Stop your shooting; you will shoot all my oxen dead in the meadow.' Every shot had killed an ox. The man ceased from shooting, and from that day could rear his calves.

## Foreseeing

In Owschlag, near Sleswig, there were formerly some remarkable men. Among them there was one who could foresee and foretell funerals, weddings, etc. He must, when anything passed by his house in the night, rise from his bed and look at it; and if he lay too long and the thing was passed, be must run after it until he got sight of it. The cause of this was, that he had once trodden on the tail of a howling dog and looked between his ears. At first this wonderful faculty afforded him much amusement, and

1   Uet elk hues en Läpel vull.
2   Uet elk hues en Schäpel vull.

to many persons be foretold a variety of incidents most accurately; though as he grew old it became burdensome to him, But he could not get rid of it or sleep in quiet, until he had worn his shirt turned for a whole year.

## The Communion-cup at Viöl

As an inhabitant of Viöl was one night riding from Flensborg, he passed by a grave-mound where the underground folk were celebrating a great festival, and just in the act of sending round a large golden beaker, in which was a beverage in appearance resembling buttermilk. The peasant drew up his horse and knavishly entreated them to let him have a draught from the beaker. In the most cordial manner they handed it to him; but he, having got possession of it, cast the liquor behind him and galloped away. He soon heard a subterranean cry, 'Dreibein (Three-legs) come out!' and on looking back, saw a monster close behind him; but his horse was swifter than Dreibein. He then heard many voices at once crying, 'Zweibein (Two-legs) come out!' and saw another monster much more frightful and much swifter than Dreibein; yet was unable to overtake him. Then be heard them with one voice crying, 'Einbein (One-leg) come out!' On turning again, he saw a third monster far far more hideous and larger than the preceding one, which came after him with gigantic springs, head over heels; and would have caught him, had not the door of his house luckily stood open; for scarcely had he slammed it to, when there stood Einbein banging against it; but was, nevertheless, forced to remain outside. On the following morning the peasant found that the drink had singed off half of his horse's tail. The beaker he presented to the church, in fulfilment of a vow he made in his fright on seeing Einbein.[1]

## White Women

Beneath the village of Sahrensdorf, in Femern, there dwelt in former times White-women, who gladly stole unbaptised children. As a protection against them, a light was burnt immediately after the birth of a child, which must constantly burn in the chamber until the child was christened.

---

1   See pp. 325–6, 328, *sqq*.

# Popular Traditions of
## Mecklenburg, the Mark, Saxony, Thuringia, Brunswick, Hanover, Oldenburg, Westphalia [1]

## Fru Gode

In the twelve days of Christmas Fru Gode makes her tour, and has been met, by many a one. As a man was once busy with his horses in the stable, Fru Gode came, and handing him a stake, requested him to make a point to it. At first he refused, but, on her promising him a good reward, did what she required. When it was finished, she told him to gather up the chips that had fallen, which he did, and found them all pure gold.

Formerly much was related of Fru Gode, how she rode through the air with her dogs. When she had one day passed over a farmyard, the farmer happening to go out, found a little dog lying before his door. He took it in, and together with his wife fed and cherished it. But in the following year, and exactly at the same time, the dog suddenly disappeared, and in his bed there lay a large lump of gold. That must have been intended by Fru Gode for the farmer, who until then was a poor man, but now at once became rich.

*The name of Fru Gode, though applied in the middle age to a female being Grimm (Deutsche Mythologie, op. cit., p. 231) considers a corruption from Fro Woden (Dominus Woden). In her annual tour and transformation of the shavings into gold, she resembles Berhta. Fru Gauden was, as we are told (Deutsche Mythologie, op. cit., p. 877), a lady of consideration and wealth, who was so enthusiastically fond of the chase that she uttered the sinful words, 'If I might always hunt, I would never wish to enter heaven.' She had twenty-four daughters, all as mad as herself. One day, when mother and daughters were dashing in full gallop through field and forest, and in their wild joy uttered the profane words, 'The chase is better than heaven!' behold! before the*

1   From Kuhn and Schwartz, *Norddeutsche Sagen, Märchen und Gebräuche*, Leipsig, 1848, unless otherwise expressed.

*eyes of the mother the daughters' clothes are turned to hair, their arms to legs, and four-and-twenty hounds bark round the hunting car of the mother; four of which take the duty of the horses, the rest accompany the carriage, and away goes the wild group up into the clouds, there, between heaven and earth, to hunt, as they had wished, without cessation, from day to day, from year to year. Long have they been weary of their wild amusement, and deplore the sinful wish; but they must bear the consequences of their crime, until the hour comes for their release. Come it one day will, but when? No one can say. In the twelve days of Christmas (for at other times we mortals are not aware of her presence), Fru Gauden directs her course to the habitations of men; on Christmas night, or the last night of the year, she likes to traverse the streets of the village, and where she finds a house-door open, she sends in a little dog. In the morning a little dog comes wagging its tail to the inhabitant; it does no harm beyond disturbing the nocturnal quiet by its whining, it will be neither appeased nor driven away. If anyone kills it, it will by day be changed into a stone, which, if thrown away, will return to the house and again become a dog. This dog will whine and moan during the whole year, bring disease and death to man and beast, and peril of fire on the house; and not till the return of the twelve days will the house regain its quiet. Hence everyone takes especial care, both morning and evening, to keep the house-door well-closed. Some people were once foolish enough to kill the dog, but from that day they never prospered, and at length their house was burnt to the ground. More fortunate are they who render a service to Fru Gauden, who, in the darkness of the night, sometimes misses her road, and finds herself in a crossway. Now a crossway is a stumbling-block to the good lady, and whenever she finds herself in one, she contrives to break some part of her chariot which she is unable to repair. On such an occasion she once came, clad like a stately dame, to the bedside of a serving-man, waked and implored his aid. The man complied with her desire, followed her to the crossway, and found that one of the wheels of her vehicle had flown off. Having set her conveyance to rights, she desired him, by way of remuneration, to put into his pocket what appeared like ordure. The man was indignant at such a proposal, but allowed himself to be somewhat pacified on her assuring him that worthless as the present appeared, it would not prove so. On the strength of this assurance he was induced to take some with him, when lo! to his no small astonishment, by daybreak it began to glitter like burnished gold, and was in fact the purest gold!*

## The Klabautersmanneken or Pûkse

These beings take up their abode in houses, but particularly in mills and ships, where they live on the milk that is placed for them, in return for which they render all kinds of services: they milk the cows, curry the horses, work in the kitchen, wash the ship, help to weigh the anchor, and do a variety of other jobs. There is nothing to be more feared than the Klabautersmanneken leaving the ship. On which account great care must be taken not to leave a coat for them, or a pair of shoes, for then they would instantly leave the vessel. They wear a short red jacket, not in the best condition, and not always quite covering their nakedness, so that the heart sometimes melts at the sight of them. In houses they like to live in the timber-work, on which account, when pulling down a house, the beams ought not to be thrown away, but employed, as far as possible, in building the new house.

## The Horse-mare

In Usedom there once lived a man, who had a horse that had always been vigorous and in good condition, but at once became meagre and lost strength; and notwithstanding that it was well fed, never could recover. This appeared very singular to the owner, and he thought the matter over and over, but could not satisfy himself. At length he sent for a cunning man, who, on seeing the horse, said that he would soon find a remedy. He remained there that night, and at midnight went to the stable, stopped a knot-hole in the door, then fetched the owner of the horse, and they both entered the stable. To his great astonishment he there saw a woman of his acquaintance sitting on the horse, and, although she strove with all her might, unable to descend from it. It was the Horse-mare that was so caught. She besought them most earnestly to set her free, which they did, but only after she had promised never to repeat her visits.[1]

## A Woman-werwolf

At Caseburg, on the isle of Usedom, a man and his wife were busy in the field making hay, when after some time the woman said to the man that she had no more peace, she could no longer stay, and went away. But she had previously desired her husband to promise, that if perchance a wild beast should come, he would throw his hat at it and then run away, that it might not hurt him. She had been gone only a little while, when a wolf came swimming across the Swine, and ran directly towards the haymakers. The man threw his hat at it, which the animal instantly tore to rags. But in the meantime, a boy had run up with a pitchfork, and stabbed the wolf from behind, which in the same moment became changed; and all were not a little astonished, when they saw that it was the man's wife, whom the boy had killed.

1   See p. 346.

## The Heckethaler[2]

In Swinemünde there lived many years ago a man who had a 'Heckethaler', which he obtained in the following manner. On New Year's night he went to the church door, having with him in a bag an entirely black he-cat, without even a single white hair. Taking the cat on his back, he walked backwards from the church door round the church, and his round being completed, knocked thrice. A man then came forth and inquired whether he would sell the cat?

'Yes'

'For how much?'

'For a dollar.'

'That's too much; I'll give eight groschen'

'He is not to be had for that.'

Thereupon he went a second time in the same manner round the church, knocked again, the same man stepped out, he repeated his question, and the man now offered sixteen groschen

'He is not to be had for that.'

And now he went a third time backwards round the church, knocked again, the man again came forth; he demanded, and now received his dollar. Then throwing the bag with the cat in it on the ground, he ran as fast as he could back to his house. From that time let him pay out the dollar as often as he might, the moment the last groschen was spent, he had the entire dollar again in his pocket.

*According to another account from Cottbus, we are informed that, if anyone desires to have a Heckethaler, he must in the longest night put a black he-cat into a bag, which must be bound fast with ninety-nine knots. He must then go thrice round the church, and every time he comes to the door, call to the sacristan through the keyhole. At the third time the sacristan (and he is the devil) comes, when the man asks him whether he will buy a hare, and for the cat in the bag receives a dollar; he must then hasten to get into a house; for if the devil looses the knots and overtakes the seller, he is a lost man. The dollar so obtained is the Heckethaler, and is to be got rid of only by placing it in salt. From this superstition is evidently derived the proverb to buy a cat in a bag. The act of walking thrice round the church, in religious and superstitious ceremonies, is of remote antiquity.*

2   From hecken, *to produce, hatch.*

## Milk Abstracted

In Caseburg there was once a peasant whose cows would yield no milk, however well he might feed them, so that he at last saw that they must be bewitched, and sent for a cunning man to aid him. The man came, went into the cowhouse, looked at the animals, and saw at once how matters stood – they were bewitched. He then took a walk about the village, in order to discover the witch, and in a neighbour's cowhouse, saw his wife standing close by the wall, which joined the aforesaid peasant's outhouses. Into the wall she had driven a broomstick, on which a pail was hung, and was milking the broomstick, which yielded milk like a natural udder. Thus was the witch discovered. He threatened to have her punished; and from that day the peasant's cows yielded milk.

*Notwithstanding the burlesque character of the above, a superstition very near akin to it was known in Scotland, where witches were supposed to have it in their power to supply themselves with milk, by pulling at a hair-rope, as dairymaids tug the teats of cattle, and using the following conjuration:*

> *Mear's milk, and deer's milk,*
> *And every beast that bears milk,*
> *Atween St Johnston and Dundee,*
> *Come a' to me, come a' to me.*[1]

## Witches Discovered

At Neppermin, in Usedom, there lived two peasants, one of whom had been sick for three years and unable to rise from his bed; for on placing his foot on the ground, he suffered the most excruciating pain. The servants of the two peasants had strong suspicions that the wives of their masters were witches. To ascertain the point, they hid themselves on Walburgis night in the stove of the woman whose husband was sick. They had not been long there when six witches came, one as a swine, another as a cat, another as a hare with three legs, and the others under various forms; among whom were the two peasants' wives. When they were all assembled, one said, 'I am so hungry today, and know not how to satisfy my craving.' Whereupon another answered, 'Our neighbour opposite lies in childbed, let us fetch her infant and kill it'; and at the instant one hurried away, and soon returned with the babe. But now a knife was wanting. The sick man's wife then said, 'For these three years past I have had a knife inserted in my husband's thigh, which I draw out every Walburgis night: I'll fetch that. If

1 . Chambers, *Pop. Rh.*, p. 34.

he but knew it, he could rise up.' She then went into an adjoining room, and immediately returned with a knife not much less than a foot long. This they were just in the act of applying to the breast of the infant, when one of the men in the stove exclaimed, ' Lord Jesus!' at which the witches were scattered in all directions; but the man hastened to his master and related to him all that had passed. At first he was incredulous, but on rising he found he could walk without pain. On entering the room, they there found both the child and the knife, which the witches had left behind. The man then went and denounced his own wife, who confessed who the other witches were, and they were all condemned to the flames.

## Hünensteine (Giant-stones)

All over the Ukermark are these gigantic stones to be found; but the neighbourhood of Prenzlau more particularly abounds in them; for it is there that the first church (the Marienkirche) was built in the country, for which reason the Hünen[1] hurled immense blocks of stone in that direction. Such a block lies in the vicinity of Sternhagen and Buchholz, on the heath, in which there is the impression of the five fingers of a giant, who would cast it from the Rhine to the above-named church. Many other similar stones lie about the fields of Wichmannsdorf and Berkholz, all of which are fragments of a huge block that had been hurled at Prenzlau by a giant, but burst in shivers on its passage.

## A Horse Comes out of the Water

In the neighbourhood of Jagow, as a peasant was ploughing late one Saturday, when the sun was already gone down, there came suddenly, out of a lake that lay close by his field, a horse with traces complete, which harnessed himself to the other horses, and then trotted off at such a rapid pace that one furrow after another was cut in the twinkling of an eye. The peasant followed breathless, the sweat running from his hair and face, and his horses were white with foam. In this way the horse continued for a full half hour, without a moment's rest, until he vanished by the same way that he came. The peasant then hastened home, and never again ploughed on a Saturday.

*The above-mentioned being is evidently a German Nök. See pp. 241–3.*

1    In these traditions a Hüne is identical with a Riese, Dan. Jaette, all signifying *giant*. The tradition of giants casting stones at churches is universal over all the North. See pp. 338.

## Old Frick

Old Frick, or Fuik, is the devil's grandmother, and has frequently been heard making a great noise in the night. Many also have seen, and at once recognised her by the large dogs, which she always has with her; for when they barked, pure fire has issued from their mouths and nostrils.

In former times, when the Mill-laws[1] were in force, the people of Naugarten were obliged to send their corn to be ground to the mill at Boitzenburg. A peasant had once driven his corn thither, but having stayed till it was rather late, did not reach home with his wagon-load of flour before dark. On his way he heard on a sudden a tremendous uproar, and immediately after, Old Frick with her dogs came thundering along. In his fright, the only way to save himself that occurred to him was to pour out the contents of his flour-sacks to the dogs, which instantly set to work, and in a twinkling most ravenously devoured every atom of flour. Had he not so done, it would have gone hard with him. Frightened and sad he hastened home, with his empty sacks, and said to his wife, 'Mother, it has gone ill with me; I have met with Old Frick, and as quickly as I could have thrown out all the flour to her dogs, in order to get clear of them.' 'As the sacks are empty,' said the wife, 'they may be thrown aside.' The man did accordingly, but what was his surprise, when, on coming to the same place on the following morning, there stood his sacks well-filled, just as when, on the preceding evening, he brought them from Boitzenburg!

## The Witches' Ride

There was once a peasant that had an old wife, who had a great partiality for her man Hans. One night, when the peasant was gone to bed, but the wife was alone in the kitchen, in came Hans, as usual, and saw how she was anointing first her grey he-cat and then her own feet with some ointment or salve. 'What art thou doing there?' said he (for in his master's absence he always *thoued* her). 'I am going to the Blocksberg,' answered she, 'and if thou canst keep from babbling, thou mayest go with me, and be my servant.' Thereupon she desired him to fetch the black cock, and when both animals had been smeared with the ointment, there in one instant stood before them a grey horse and a black stallion. The woman then seating herself on the grey, said:

> 'Up und davon, nirgends an!'

> *Up and away, nowhere run foul!*

---

1 The *thirlage* of the Scottish law, by which every tenant was forced to take his grain to be ground at the lord's mill.

and away it went with her through the chimney. Hans now mounted his steed, and as she had told him he must do exactly as she did, he would also repeat her words, but had not well remembered them, and said:

'Up und davon, alle weg an!'

*Up and away, all the way run foul!*

then away went he also through the chimney, but during the journey bounced now against a tree, then against a rock, till he was bruised and excoriated from head to foot; but at length arrived at the Blocksberg. On their arrival the woman dismounted, and ordered Hans to hold the horses and remain with the other servants, of whom there was a considerable number. Hans did as he had been ordered, and after some time, was with all the others admittted to the feast, where he ate and drank to his heart's content; but when their orgies were about to commence, he and the rest were obliged to quit the place. At last, when all was over, Hans and his mistress again mounted their horses and returned home.

Some time after, Hans quarrelled with his mistress and went to live with another master. When the time came round again for visiting the Blocksberg, he thought he would play the old woman a trick, and said to his companions, 'If you would like to see how my old dame rides to the Blocksberg with the old alehouse-keeper, come with me.' And saying this he led them to a crossway, where a couple of harrows were standing, which they placed aslant against each other, and sat down under them.[1] They had not been there long when a tramp of horses approached them. 'See, see!' cried Hans, 'that's the old woman on the grey, and the one behind on the black horse is the old alehouse-man.' All now saw her, as they sat under the harrows, and at the same time remarked that she rode at first directly to the crossway, but then took a direction along one of the ways, as she could not pass across them. On the following day Hans was in the field, and on a sudden remarked that the old woman was on the point of making an attack upon him. In vain did he look around for a place of refuge, but there was no escape for him. Just in time, however, a way occurred to him: he took a cord, which he had at hand, wound it round his body, drew it between his legs and up over his back and shoulders to his front, and then tied both ends in a strong cross-knot; so that, both before and behind, he was *cross-bound,* and the old woman could do him no harm. When she drew near, and saw how he was secured, she gave him fair words: that he might again enter her service, and all should be forgotten. Hans, however, manifested no desire to return; and then she begged him at least to tell his

1    See p. 444.

companions that she did not ride on the grey horse the preceding night, and if he promised to do so, he should have twenty dollars. To this Hans consented, and received his money, and at night, while sitting with his companions over a jug of beer, he said, 'Hear! I told you yesterday that the old woman rode on a grey horse; but that a not true; she rode only on her grey cat.'

## Kobolds or Goblins

The Krampenbude, a fisher-house, about a German mile from Köpenick, on the Wendish Spree, is also called the Kobold's house, because a Kobold formerly played his pranks there. His chief amusement was, when the fishermen at night were lying asleep, to lay them even. For this purpose, he would first draw them up till their heads all lay in a straight line; but then their legs would be out of the line, and he had to go to their feet, and pull them till the tips of their toes were all in a row. This game he would continue till broad daylight.[1]

In the neighbourhood of Köpenick a man had a Kobold that had become troublesome to him. To get rid of him, he had resolved on changing his abode and leaving his unwelcome guest behind. On the evening previous to his removal, in passing along by the gutter, he saw the Kobold sitting by it, and asked him what he was doing? 'Why,' answered the Kobold, 'I am washing out my rags, as we move tomorrow.' The man then seeing that he must still keep the Kobold, took him along with him.

Of the Kobolds it is related that they take their abode in the unfrequented parts of a building, or in wood-houses. Their method of communicating to the master of the house their wish to live in his family, and to serve him, is somewhat remarkable. At night they bring shavings into the house, and put dung of every kind of cattle into the vessels filled with milk. If, on seeing all this, the master of the house neither sweeps away the shavings nor casts the dung out of the milk-vessels, but, together with his family, partakes of the foul milk, then will the Kobolds appear to him and abide with him. The grateful, modest, well-fed Kobolds bring to those that feed and harbour them, corn, which they steal from the barns of their neighbours.[2]

1   See p. 342.
2   Dobeneck, vol. i, pp. 125 *sqq.*

## Jack o' Lanterns with Long Legs

As a peasant of Hermsdorf was returning home one evening late, he saw a Jack o' lantern, and being of a courageous nature went up to it. The Jack o' lantern without much deliberation, took to his heels with the peasant close after him, who observed that he had most wonderfully long legs, and from top to toe consisted of glowing fire; but in the same instant he vanished, and the man could hardly find his path again in the thick darkness.

## Jack o' Lanterns Driven away by Cursing

In the neighbourhood of Storkow, as a clergyman with his servant was driving home one night late, they saw, on reaching a certain spot, a Jack o' lantern coming towards them, which merrily danced along before the horses. Sometimes there were several of them, and at last there came so many, that the horses became quite shy and fearful, and would not stir from the spot. The clergyman also felt uneasy, and began to pray aloud; but the more he prayed the more Jack o' lanterns came, so that the servant at length said, 'Just leave that off; so they will never go; but I'll send them packing'; at the same time roaring out, 'Will ye be off in the devil's name!' In a moment not a Jack o' lantern was to be seen.

## A Jack o' Lantern Caught

A cowherd near Rathenow, who had been all day on the heath with his cattle, on his return home at dark was not aware that one of his cows was missing. On discovering his loss, he immediately went in search of her; but after seeking her here and there and all over the forest, without finding her, he sat down, overcome with fatigue, on the stump of an old tree, and prepared to smoke his pipe. While he was thus sitting there came all at once a countless multitude of Jack o' lanterns dancing wildly around him, so that he would have been not a little terrified, had he not been a courageous fellow. He remained, however, sitting quietly and filling his pipe, but just as he was about to light it, they began to fly about his head, so that he expected every moment they would singe his hair. He therefore seized his stick and began to strike about him; but the more he struck the more Jack o' lanterns came. At last he made a grasp at one of them, and found that he held in his hand a bone. This seemed to have scared the others, as they instantly disappeared; but the man put the bone into his pocket, lighted his pipe, and returned home. On the following morning, he again drove out his herd, and also found the missing cow; but on his return in the evening, when it was already dark, he saw a couple of lights before his window, and supposing that a neighbour with a lantern was come to consult him about a sick cow, he opened the window and saw the entire village street full of Jack o' lanterns, which came in large bodies dancing and whirling about, and crying, 'If you don't give us our comrade, we will burn your house!' He now first recollected the bone, and said, 'Don't make such a stupid hubbub; surely the bone cannot be your comrade.' But they cried yet more loudly, 'If you don't give us our comrade, we will burn your house!' Thinking then the matter serious, he took the bone, laid it on the palm of his hand, and held it out of the window, when it instantly became a bright, flickering Jack o' lantern, and danced away, all the others surrounding it as in joy, and then merrily hopping and springing out of the village.

## Frau Harke

In former times Frau Harke had her abode on one of the highest of the Camern hills, which after her bears the name of the Frau Harkenberg, from whence she often descended, through the Frau Harkengrund (also named after her), to the lake of Schönfeld, for the purpose of fetching water. She was of immense stature and strength, and once took a ploughman, who was ploughing in a field near the mountain, together with his oxen and plough, up in her apron, to play with them. But when she showed them to her father, he ordered her to carry them all back to the place where she found them, 'Because,' said he, 'if the little ones below yonder do not plough, the big ones up here cannot bake.'

Once when carrying an apronful of earth, her apron-string gave way, and the earth fell on the ground, and that is now the Collenburg, the highest mountain in the neighbourhood, on which lay the huge block of granite, which she hurled at the church of Havelberg.

*When the old oaks disappeared from the mountains, Frau Harke migrated to Thuringia. She is known also in Lower Saxony.*

## The Nickelmann or Nick

Children should not go too near the water, because under its surface the black Nickelmann sits, who snaps at them. Above he is formed like a man, but below like a fish, and has very sharp teeth. His usual food is fishes, though he not infrequently drags down human beings. In Thale they were formerly obliged annually to throw a black cock into the Bode; for if they omitted to do so, someone would certainly die within the year. The little black figures, in wooden boxes, which spring up when the box is opened, are in Ilseburg called Nickelmännlein (Nickelmannikins).

As the midwife in Westerhausen was sitting one evening in her room, someone tapped at her window, and requested her to come out. She went out, and there stood a Nick, who desired her to follow him. They both proceeded to the rivulet, where the Nick taking a rod, beat on the water, which immediately separated into two parts, and they went down dry-footed. Here she assisted the Nickel-wife in her hour of difficulty, who in gratitude told her, that if the Nick should ask her what remuneration she wished, she must not ask for money, but for some of the sweepings. She then went and took the infant to the bath, and heard the Nickelmann's children, five of whom were running about, ask their father, 'Shall we break her neck?'[1] but their father forbade them. When the midwife had finished, the Nick asked her what remuneration she required, when she requested, as the wife had enjoined her, a little of the sweepings behind the door. 'God has counselled thee to speak thus,' said the Nickelmann, and gave her what she asked. He then conducted her home. When in her own house, she looked at the sweepings, and they had all become pure gold.[2]

## The Princess Ilse

On the Ilsenstein there lived in ancient times a knight, who had a daughter of surpassing beauty named Ilse. She loved the knight that dwelt in the castle on the Westerberg opposite to them; but at that time the two mountains were not separated from each other by the present intervening valley. The father of the princess Ilse would not consent to her union with the knight, and as they saw each other daily, in spite of his prohibition, he, who was a mighty giant, struck the rock through the middle, and thereby caused the valley. In her despair Ilse cast herself down into the raging flood beneath, and gave it its name, and from that time she often appears in a long white robe, with a broad black hat, and is usually now known by the simple appellation of 'the Jungfer'. Formerly she was to be seen daily descending to a stone by the second Ilse-bridge, in which there was a deep hollow containing water, even in the driest seasons, in which she bathed. But the stone is no longer there, and she appears no more in the valley. Her last appearance is said to have been three hundred years ago, on Ascension day, in commemoration of which a festival was long held there on that day, to which people from all the neighbourhood flocked together, when a great fair was also held. There were also two bands of music, one on the Ilsenstein, the other on the Westerberg, in which the enchanted prince is confined; but the festival has fallen more and more into desuetude, and there is now only

---

1  See Grimm, J., *Deutsche Mythologie*, op. cit., p. 463.
2  See pp. 317–18.

a little music on that day in the hostel called 'The Trouts' (Zu den Forellen). But the general belief is, that the princess will mount to heaven on an Ascension day, and it is only a few'years since that the peasants awaited the event from hour to hour. In Ilseburg, Ascension day is held so sacred, that it is thought whoever sews or mends on it will be struck by lightning.

---

As a shepherd was once driving his flock over the Ilsenstein, and had stopped to rest for a while by a spring, leaning on his staff, the mountain suddenly opened – for in his staff, though without his knowledge, there was a *Springwurzel* – and the princess stood before him. She commanded him to follow her, and when he was within, said to him that he might take as much gold as he desired. The shepherd crammed his pockets full, and when he had taken enough, was about to depart, when the princess called to him, 'Do not forget the best!' But he, thinking she meant that he had not taken gold enough, filled his hat, while she alluded to his staff with the Springwurzel, which on entering he had placed against the wall. So that when he was going out, the rock suddenly closing, severed him in two.

---

A horse-boy lost a couple of his horses, and while he was out seeking them, and was sitting on the Ilsenstein crying, because he could not find them, the mountain suddenly opened, and before him stood the princess, who asked him why he was crying. He told her of his loss, and she ordered him to follow her. They then entered the mountain, and came into a vast stable, containing many horses, among others his own two. He was overjoyed at seeing them, and was leading them out, but the princess told him that he could not have them again, though she would give him for them gold enough to buy a hundred others, Saying this she filled his wallet, at the same time enjoining him not to open it before he had passed over the third Ilse-bridge. But being an inquisitive fellow, he was impatient to see how much she had given him, and on reaching the second bridge, could no longer withstand the temptation, opened the knapsack and – found in it nothing but horse-dung. 'What,' thought he, 'canst thou do with that?' at the same time throwing it into the Ilse; but hearing it go kling kling as it fell, he quickly looked into his knapsack, to see if any remained behind, and found some genuine pistoles.

Goethe, in Faust, makes one of the witches, on her way to the Blocksberg, pass over the Ilsenstein:

> 1st W.    Welchen Weg kommst du her?
> 2nd W.                                 Uebern Ilsenstein!
> Da guckt' ich der Eule ins Nest hinein.
> Die macht' em Paar Augen!

> *Which way comest thou hither?*
> *Over the Ilsenstein!*
> *There I peep'd into the owl's nest.*
> *She made a pair of eyes!*

'The Springwurzel is a plant, that may be procured in the following manner: The nest of a green or black woodpecker, when it has young, must be stopt with a wooden plug. The bird on seeing it flies away, knowing where to find a wonderful root, which men would seek for in vain. This the bird bears in its bill, and holds it against the plug, which, as if driven by the most violent blow, instantly springs out. If the party has concealed himself, and at the bird's approach makes a great noise, it will be frightened and let the root fall. Some spread a white or red cloth under the nest, on which the bird will cast the root, after having made use of it.' This superstition was known to Pliny – See H. N. x. 18.[1]

## Hans Von Hackelnberg

Hans von Hackelnberg was chief huntsman in Brunswick, and loved the chase above all other worldly things. He rode a grey horse, the wildest animal that was anywhere to be found. From the Harz he went to the Hakel, and while there dreamt that he would come to his death through a wild boar. On the following day there was to be a great hunt, when he related his dream to his companions, adding scornfully, that it would, indeed, be something strange, if he were to perish through a wild boar. He then proceeded to the hunt and found a boar exactly resembling the one he had seen in his dream. He eagerly pursued it, and at length slew it, and shortly after returned home. While the boar was being cut up, Hackelnberg held the head aloft to contemplate that which was to occasion his death; but the head slipped out of his hand, and one of the tusks wounded him so severely in the leg that it eventually cost him his life. From that time he hunts, with the cry of 'Hallo,' and followed by his associates, up and down the Hakel.

*According to another version of the story, the hunt was in the Harz, and Hackelnberg, yielding to the persuasions of his friends, stayed at home. On receiving the wound, Hackelnberg is made to say, 'If I am to die from such a scratch, I would rather hunt for ever.' But the wound became worse and worse, and he hastened back to Brunswick, but came only as far as the inn called the Klipperkrug, near Wülperode, where he laid himself down and died. His steel cap and the iron headpiece of his mule are still to be seen there. In the garden of the inn, which was formerly a churchyard, lies his*

---

1    Grimm, J., *Deutsche Mythologie*, op. cit., p. 925.

*gravestone, having on it the representation of a knight on a mule, with a short flowing mantle and high ruff, holding a riding-whip in his hand; near him two little dogs appear in the act of running. On the edge of the long quadrangular stone is an inscription only partially legible, viz. – Domini 1581 den 13 Martii. From that time Hackelnberg hunts, followed by a number of little dogs, up and down the Harz. Some say he is seen with two large bloodhounds galloping away; and it is further related that his love of the chase was so great, that he prayed that his portion of bliss might consist in being permitted to hunt for ever.*

A man once mocked Hackelnberg, as he heard him riding through the air with his 'Hoho!' and was pursued by him to his own door, which he entered, and went rattling after him even into the hayloft, to which he had fled for security. There Hackelnberg threw a horse's leg to him. On the following morning the man died.

Another time some horse-boys, watching on the common by night, called after him as he came rushing by with his dogs; when rending a horse in pieces, he took one piece for himself, threw another to his dogs, and also gave a part to each of the horse-boys, saying:

> Hast du helfen jagen,
> sollst auch helfen knagen!
>
> If thou hast help'd to hunt,
> Thou shalt also help to gnaw!

and then rode away. The boys who ate of the roast continued alive, but those who did not died shortly after.

Some others lying by a fire in the field one night as Hackelnberg passed by, called to him, 'Half a horse!' whereat he threw a horse's leg down into the fire. They then called to him to bring them some salt, which he was unable to do, and the horse's leg vanished.

At Rocklum, not far from Wolfenbüttel, there are several earth-mounds on an eminence, of one of which it is related, that Hackelnberg with the Wild Hunt once passing by, felt a grain of sand in his shoe, which he shook out, and thus formed the hillock. According to one tradition, Hackelnberg returns every seventh year, and makes his tour.

The following are the Westphalian traditions of Hackelnberg:[1]

Hackelbärend (as he is called) was a huntsman who hunted on Sundays, on account of which profanation he was, after his death, banished to the

---

1 Grimm, J., *Deutsche Mythologie*, op. cit., p. 873, from Weddigen's *Westfäl. Mag.*, Redeker's *Westfäl. Sagen*, etc.

air, where, with his dogs, he must hunt both by day and night without any rest. According to some, he hunts only in the twelve nights of Christmas; according to others, always when the storm-wind howls; for which reason some call him the *Joljäger* (from *jolen*, *to howl*, or Yuletide?). On one of his progresses, Hackelnberg left one of his dogs behind in a barn at Isenstädt (bishopric of Minden). There the animal lay a 'whole year, every attempt to remove him proving fruitless; but when, in the following year, Hackelnberg with his Wild Hunt again passed by, the dog suddenly sprang up, and ran barking and yelling after the troop.

Two young fellows going one night from Bergkirchen, through the forest, to visit their sweethearts, heard in the air above them wild noise of dogs and a voice at intervals crying, 'Hoto, hoto!' This was Hackelblock, the wild huntsman, with his company. One of the young men was so rash as to call out, mocking him, 'Hoto, hoto!' at which Hackelblock approached, and with his whole pack rode over him. Of the unfortunate young man not a trace could be found.

Hackelnberg rides in rain and storm through the Thuringian forest, but in preference through the Hackel (a forest between Halberstadt, Gröningen and Derenburg). On his deathbed he would hear nothing about heaven, and to the priest's exhortation said, that our Lord God might keep his heaven, provided only that he might continue to hunt. At which the priest exclaimed, 'Then hunt until the last day!' A malediction now in the course of fulfilment. A faint barking or yelping in the air announces his approach; a screech owl flies before him, called by the people the *tutosel*. Wanderers, who fall in his way, throw themselves on their faces, and let him ride over them. Tutosel, it is said, was a nun, who after her death associated herself with Hackelnberg, and mingled her 'Uhu!' with his 'Huhu!'

Hackelnberg (according to another tradition) hunted on Sundays, and compelled all the peasants dependent on him to accompany him. One day there came two horsemen galloping up beside him, who commanded him to go with them. One of them, on his right, was fierce and wild of aspect, and from his horse's mouth and nostrils there sprang forth fire; while the rider on his left was of gentler and milder mien; but Hackelnberg turned to the wild one, who galloped off with him, and in whose company he must hunt until the last day. Others say that Hackelnberg lived in Sölling, not far from Uslar; that he led a pious life, but was so devoted to the chase, that on his deathbed he prayed to God that he would allow him, for his share of heaven, to hunt in Sölling till the day of judgement. His prayer was granted, and often in the forest is to be heard at night the baying of dogs and an appalling blast of horns. His grave is in Sölling; near him lie two black dogs.

*The inconsistent diversity of place evidently shows that Hackelnberg is a mythic being; a name occurring in so many parts must be more than historic. The Westphalian form of the name, Hackelberend, I consider the oldest and most genuine. Hakolberand is unquestionably an Old Saxon denomination of Wôdan, which has been gradually corrupted into Hakkelberg, Hakkenberg, Hakkelblok, etc. The Mecklenburg tradition of 'Wod' (see p. 61) places this connection of the Wild Huntsman with Woden beyond a doubt.[1]*

## Witches in Gittelde

In Gittelde there were formerly many witches, and the houses which they inhabited might be known by fire often to be seen over the chimneys; for then Urian was sitting above, and brought them whatever they required.

There was once a witch there, who had a serving-man named Hans, who was always driving in great loads of wood, but yet never observed that any was ever burnt, and that, nevertheless, eatables were always at hand. He resolved on knowing how this came to pass; so while the others were gone to church, he feigned to go with them, but returned and entered the house by a back door and then hid himself under a tub in the kitchen. He had not been there long, when one came, and called, 'Hei kucket, hei kucket.' 'They are all at church,' said the mistress; but the call was repeated, 'Hei kucket, hei kucket, shall I wring his neck?' 'Ah, what is it you want I'' said the woman, 'I tell you they are all in church.' The voice now asked, 'What will you eat?' 'Baked pears,' answered the woman, and instantly they were hissing in the dish which she held out. She next requested to have dumplings, then sauerkraut, both of which were immediately given to her. Hans was a witness of all this, but kept quite still, and at length stole out. When they were all at table he said, 'I am so unwell, I am so unwell,' and would eat nothing, but was afterwards forced to take something. When they had eaten, the woman drew him aside and asked him why he had refused to eat, when he told her he had witnessed all that had passed, and would go and inform against her. Bat she prayed him not to do so, promised to give him a good sum of money, and also to instruct him in witchcraft. Hans accepted the money, and yielded to her persuasions. The woman then ordered him to go and buy a new pot. He did so, and on his return she told him to sit on it and say: 'I believe in this pot,' etc. But Hans, placing himself upon it, said, 'I believe in God,' etc. At which the pot burst into shivers and a large frog appeared sitting beneath it. Hans thereupon went instantly and informed against the woman. An immense pile was then raised, whereon to burn the old witch, who, when placed upon it,

---

1    Grimm, J., *Deutsche Mythologie*, op. cit., p. 875.

cried out to Hans, 'Thou hast eaten mice instead of baked pears, thou hast eaten spiders instead of dumplings, thou has eaten worms instead of sauerkraut!' The flames then closed upon her.

## The Monk of the Mines

In the mines about Clausthal and Andreasberg a spectre was formerly seen, who was denominated the Bergmönch. He was clad as a monk, but was of gigantic stature, and always carried in his hand a large tallow candle, which never went out. When the miners entered in the morning, he would stand at the aperture with his light, letting them pass under it; in the shafts, too, they often met him.

*The Bergmönch was formerly a bergmaster or director, who took such delight in mining, that, when at the point of death, he prayed that, instead of happy rest in heaven, he might wander about till the last day, over hill and dale, in pits and shafts, and superintend the mining. He appears to the men in the dress of a bergmaster, with a silver mining lamp. To those towards whom he is well-disposed he renders many kind services, and appears to them in a human form and of ordinary stature; while to others he appears in his true form. His eyes sprout forth flames, and are like coach-wheels; his legs are like spiders' webs.[1]*

## The Demons of the Mine

As a miner was one day working in a shaft, there came to him a little man clad in white, with a light in his hand, who beckoned to him to follow him. He did so, and they came into a spacious hall, where a number of persons were sitting, all attired like the little man, and eating and drinking. A cup of wine was also handed to the miner, to whom, when he had been hospitably treated, the little man gave a gold pin, telling him, that if anyone should take it from him, he had only to let him know, and he would wring the neck of him who had taken it, and get the pin for him again. He then conducted him out of the mountain and vanished. When the miner returned home, all appeared strange to him, he knew no one that he met, and no one knew him; he then went to the clergyman, who looked through the church book, when it proved that he had been three ages of man down in the bowels of the earth with the spirits, though to him it seemed but a few hours. But the chief officer of the mines, when he heard the man's narrative, was seized with a longing after the gold pin, and when the man refused to give it him, had it taken from him by force. The miner then returned to the mine and made his complaint to the little white man, who

1    Harrys, op. cit., ii, No. 2.

went immediately, wrung the officer's neck, and restored to the man his pin, by which he became so wealthy, that he had enough for his whole life.

## The Night-raven or Eternal Wagoner

In the night the 'hor, hor', or 'hrok, hrok' of the night-raven is frequently to be heard. This bird is much larger than the common raven, and almost as large as a full-grown hen. By some he is called the Eternal Wagoner, who also say that he wished, for his share of heaven, to drive to all eternity; and he accordingly drives without cessation, sitting on the middle horse of the celestial wain, of which the four large stars behind are the four wheels, but the three foremost stars, which stand in a crooked line, the three horses; and the little star over the middle-most is the eternal wagoner. He guides the horses, and as the wagon always goes in a circle, they do not stand in a right line with one another, but in a curve, being always on the turn. Before midnight the wagon is said to be going out, when the pole inclines upwards; and after midnight it goes home, and then the pole inclines downwards.[1]

## Frau Hulle (Holda, Hulde)

In the popular traditions of Germany, Holda (Hulda, Holle) appears as a superior being, favourably disposed towards mankind, and angry only when she perceives any disorder or neglect in housewifery. The German traditions relative to Holda are current chiefly in Hesse and Thuringia. She is believed to influence the atmospheric phenomena. When the sun shines, Holda is said to be combing her hair; when it snows, she is making her bed.[2] She likes to dwell in lakes and fountains. At noon she is to be seen as a beautiful, fair woman, bathing in the stream and then vanishing. Mortals arrive at her dwelling through a fountain. She rides in a chariot, which she once caused a countryman to repair for her, the chips from which, when collected, proved to be solid gold. Her annual visit, which takes place during the twelve days of Christmas, when spirits are said to wander, and animals, such as the wolf, are not to be mentioned by name,[3] brings fruitfulness to the land. Like Woden, Holda also traverses the air, and, like him, belongs to the Wild Hunt. Hence the notion that the witches ride in company with Holda. According to the popular belief, the souls of unbaptised children are received into the Wild Hunt, and fall to the share of the heathen deities, Woden or Holda.

1 See p. 471.
2 Grimm, J. & W., *Kinder- und Hausmärchen*, op. cit., p. 24.
3 See p. 287.

To this idea of Holda it is, no doubt, to be attributed, that, instead of a divine form, she is made to assume that of an ugly, long-nosed, long-toothed crone, with matted, shaggy hair. 'He has been riding with Holle' is said of a person whose hair is uncombed and bristling.

Holda is also described as an encourager of spinning. To industrious lasses she gives spindles, and in the night spins their spool full; while she burns or dirties the wheels of idle spinners. An industrious, good girl, whose spool fell into her fountain, she rewarded with a shower of gold. When she goes her round at Christmas all the spinning-wheels are plentifully furnished, and left standing for her; but by Shrovetide, when she returns home, all must be spun off: at which season the spinning-wheels are put out of sight; because flax spun at Shrovetide turns out ill, it being a holy time of rest. If she finds everything as it should be, she gives her blessing: 'So many hairs so many good years'; in the opposite case, her malediction: 'So many hairs so many bad years.'

According to another German tradition, no flax should remain on the distaff during the twelve days of Christmas, lest Frau Holla should come. This is akin to the Danish superstition, that, from Yule-day to New year's day, nothing that runs round may be put in motion, consequently neither reel nor spindle.[1]

Out of her fountain children come, and women who go down into it become healthy and fruitful. She appropriates to herself those that are drowned.

On account of these multifarious attributes, Holda was generally considered a divinity of much importance. Burchard, bishop of Worms, mentions it as the popular belief that on certain nights women rode with her on all kinds of animals, and were supposed to belong to her train.[2]

---

As a woman was once going up the Kyffhäuser, in Thuringia, for the purpose of gathering brushwood, she saw, although it was only April, an old woman sitting and collecting cotton capsules, of which she had a large heap lying by her. But it being usual to collect these only in the height of summer, the woman was surprised, and asked the crone what she intended to do with them, as they were not yet fit for use. The old woman told her she might take with her as many as she wished, and that she would soon find a use for them; but the other would not believe her. She then gave the woman a whole apronful, and also put some into her basket. The woman then went to gather hazel-twigs, but on opening her apron,

---

1   See p. 422, No. 10.
2   Grimm, J., *Deutsche Mythologie*, op. cit., p. 245. Müller, *Gesch. der Altd. Relig.*, p. 122.

found she had pure gold pieces in it, as well as in the basket. Thereupon she ran back to the spot where the old woman had been sitting, but both she and the heap of capsules had disappeared.

———————

As a man was going over a mountain late in the evening, he saw Frau Hulle sitting, busily occupied in stripping flax capsules, of which she had a large heap lying before her. The man wished her a good evening; she thanked him courteously and said, he might put some of the capsules into his pocket and take them home. The man thanked her for her goodwill, but said he had plenty already, and therefore would not encumber himself. He had proceeded only a little way farther, when something in his shoe began to give him pain, and on examination, he found in it some large particles of gold. These were the capsules, a few of which had fallen into his shoe.

## Traditions of the Kyffhäuser

In the Kyffhäuser the emperor Frederic Barbarossa exists in a state of enchantment. There he sits, with all his knights and squires, at a large table, through which his beard has grown. Beneath the mountain all is splendid and radiant with gold and precious stones; and although it is a subterranean cavern, it is as light as in the sunniest day. There are the most magnificent trees and shrubs, and through the middle of this paradise there flows a brook, from which if a handful of mud be taken, it will instantly become pure gold. Here a horseman constantly rides up and down; but others say he sits on a cock, and is very probably the evil one himself, who has effected all this enchantment. A shepherd one St John's day entered the mountain when it was standing open, and beheld all its splendour with amazement. The horseman before-mentioned then made a sign to him to take some of the horsemeal, which he did, and which proved to be all gold.

———————

Some musicians returning from a wedding, had to pass over the Kyffhäuser, when one among them, a mad-brained fellow, said, 'Listen, friends – as we have played so much, we will play up something to the old emperor Frederic.' The others at first refused, saying they were tired, but he talked them over so humorously, that they at length all struck up. When they ceased a young damsel stepped out from the Erfurt gate, who brought them the old emperor's thanks, and gave to each, as a remembrance, a horse's head. All stared with astonishment as the young damsel disappeared, and began to reproach their mad companion for having stopped them for the sake of such a paltry reward, and threw their horses' heads far away from them. But their companion was as merry as ever, and kept his head, saying, 'If it's good for nothing else, it will serve as a joke with my old dame.' They then went home, and the merry one clandestinely laid the head under the bolster. On waking in the morning he said to his wife: 'Just look what a handsome present I have brought you from old Redbeard.' She raised the bolster, and the man thought, now she will be finely frightened, but to his unutterable astonishment she drew forth a lump of gold, so heavy that she could hardly lift it.

Some say that the emperor Otto sits in the Kyffhäuser, and that a musician having one day met him near the mountain, the emperor ordered him to strike up a march, and gave him, when he had played it, three bones as a reward, which he was not to look at before he reached home, and then he found them turned to pure gold.

––––––––––

In the Kifhäuser, in Thuringia, sleeps Frederic Redbeard. He sits at a round stone table, supporting his head on his hand and nodding. His beard grows round the table, and has already made the circuit twice; when it shall have grown round a third time, the king will wake. On issuing from the mountain he will hang his shield on a withered tree, which will then become green, and a better time will ensue. Some have, however, seen him awake. Of a shepherd, who had played him a pleasing tune, he inquired, 'Do the ravens still fly round the mountain?' and on the shepherd answering in the affirmative, he said, 'Then must I sleep a hundred years longer.' This shepherd was taken into the king's armoury, and was presented with the foot of a hand-basin of pure gold.[1]

## The Smith of Jüterbogk[2]

In the little town of Jüterbogk there once dwelt a smith, of whom both young and old relate a wonderful story. This smith when a youth had a very strict father and faithfully observed God's commandments. He had travelled much and passed through many adventures, and was, moreover, skilful and active in his art beyond all belief. He possessed a chalybeate tincture that made every harness or mail coat impenetrable that was washed with it. He had been with the army of the emperor Frederic II, in which he had borne the office of imperial armourer, and had made the campaign of Milan and Apulia. There he had captured the standard of the

1   Grimm, J., *Deutsche Mythologie*, op. cit., p. 907. The original sleeper both here and in the Odenberg was, no doubt, Odin (Wuotan), as appears from the inquiry about the ravens, which could hardly be objects of interest to the emperor Frederic Barbarossa – Ibid. Vorrede. p. xvi,
2   From Bechstein's *Deutsches Märchenbuch*, Leipzig, 1848, p. 44, and his *Kiffhäusersagen*.

city; and, after the death of the emperor, had returned home with a considerable treasure. He had seen good days, and afterwards evil ones, and was more than a hundred years old. Once, when sitting in his garden under an old pear tree, there came a little grey man riding on an ass, who had previously often proved himself the smith's guardian spirit. The little man took up his quarters with the smith, and had his ass shod, which the smith willingly did without requiring any remuneration. The little man then said to Peter (for so the smith was named) that he should wish three wishes, but in so doing *not forget the best*. So – because his pears had often been stolen by thieves – he wished that whoever climbed up into his pear-tree might not be able to come down without his permission; and – because thefts had often been perpetrated in his apartment – he wished that no one might enter it without his permission, unless it were through the keyhole. At each of these foolish wishes, the little man reminded him *not to forget the best*; whereupon the smith uttered his third wish, saying: 'The best is a good *schnapps* (dram), and therefore I will wish that this flask may never be empty.' 'Thy wishes are granted,' said the old man, then drew his hand over some bars of iron that were lying in the smithy, mounted his ass and rode away. The iron was found changed to bright silver. The smith, who had been so poor, was now rich again, and lived on and on in considerable comfort; for the never-failing cordial drops in the flask were, unknown to the smith, an elixir of life. At length, however, Death, who seemed to have forgotten him, knocked at his door. The smith, according to all appearance, was perfectly ready to go with him, and begged him to allow him a little refreshment, and to have the goodness to get him a few pears from the tree, which he could no longer climb on account of the weakness of age. Death then mounted the tree, but no sooner was he up than the smith cried out, 'There stay!' for he felt a wish to live a little longer. Death now devoured every pear on the tree, and then began his fasts, until from hunger he consumed himself, even to his skin and hair, whence it is that he is now such a horrible dry skeleton. In the world no more beings died, neither men nor beasts, whereby no slight inconvenience was occasioned. But at length the smith went to Death, who was rattling in the tree, and agreed with him for a further respite. He then let Death loose. Urged by all the furies, Death now flew away and began to make a clearance in the world. Being unable to wreak his vengeance on the smith, he set the devil upon him, that he might fetch him. The fiend instantly commenced his journey, but the cunning smith smelt the brimstone at a distance, closed his door, held with his workmen a leather bag to the keyhole, and as Master Urian passed through – for by no other way could he enter the smithy – tied up the mouth of the bag, laid it on the anvil, and then with the heaviest hammers began beating so unmercifully on the poor devil that he lost all sense of hearing and seeing, was become quite tender, and swore never to come again.

The smith now lived long in peace, until, when all his friends and acquaintance were dead, he became weary of living on earth. He therefore set out on his journey and proceeded to heaven, where he humbly knocked at the gate. St Peter looked out, in whom Peter the smith recognised his patron and guardian spirit, who had often visibly rescued him from danger and difficulty, and had lastly granted him the three wishes. But now said St Peter, 'Take thyself hence; to thee is heaven closed: thou didst forget to wish for *the* best – for eternal happiness!' At this answer Peter turned away and resolved on trying his luck in the opposite realm, and returning downwards, soon found himself on the straight, broad and well-frequented road. But when the devil was informed that the smith of Jüterbogk was approaching, he slammed the door in his face, and placed his kingdom in a state of defence. So when the smith of Jüterbogk could not find an asylum either in heaven or hell, and had no inclination to return to the world, he went down into the Kiffhaüser, to his old master, the emperor Frederic. The old kaiser was delighted at seeing his armourer Peter, and immediately asked him whether the ravens still continued to fly about the tower of the ruined castle of Kiffhaüsen. And when Peter answered in the affirmative, old Redbeard heaved a sigh. But the smith remained in the mountain, and shoes the emperor's palfrey, and those of the noble damsels of his court, until the hour of the emperor's deliverance strikes, which will also be that of his own. And that will happen – the tradition tells us – when the ravens no longer fly round the mountain, and on the Rüthsfeld, near the Kiffhaüser, an old withered worn-out pear-tree again sends out shoots, bears foliage and blossoms. Then will the emperor come forth with all his armed followers, will fight the great fight of deliverance, and hang his shield on the renovated tree; after which he will go with his companions into everlasting rest.

## The Wunderblume (Miracle-flower)

In the old castle of Questenberg there are still inestimable treasures, and many a one has thereby become rich. In Sangerhausen there was once a man, who, as he was passing across a field on his way to Questenberg, saw a beautiful flower, which he plucked, and proceeded on his way. When arrived in the village, he thought to himself, 'So often as I have been in Questenberg, I have never yet been up to the old castle: I'll go now.' He did so, and when he reached it he observed a large iron door, on stepping towards which, it flew open, and he entered into a spacious vault. There he saw gold and silver lying in vast heaps, of which he first crammed his pockets full, and when they would hold no more, filled his hat. At this moment a voice was heard, saying, 'Forget not the best!' But he went out, and as he was passing through the entrance, the door slammed to and crushed his heel, so that he was lame ever after. He had left the Wunderblume in the vault.[1]

Another, who had also found the Wunderblume and likewise the iron door, fetched every day a silver coin of a quadrangular form, which he took to Nordhausen, and there disposed of for five dollars. But he soon thought: Why should I go so often? And then took two, and shortly after, three pieces, till at length he came with a wagon, but found no more.

*In another account it is said, that the Wunderblume grows in the Johannisthal in Clausthal. Whoever is perfectly innocent, and to whom it is, moreover, granted to find it by accident – for those that seek for it never find it – acquires the faculty, as long as he carries it about him, of making himself invisible, and of understanding the speech of animals.*

*A story, in most of its essential parts agreeing with the above, is related of King Abel's palace in Sleswig. See 'Die gelbe Blume' in Müllenhoff, No. 468. See also Grimm, J., Deutsche Mythologie, op. cit., p. 923.*

## The Werwolf's Girdle

Formerly there were persons who, by putting on a certain girdle, could change themselves into werwolves. A man in the neighbourhood of Steina, who had such a girdle, forgot once, when he was going out, to lock it up, as it was his custom to do. In his absence his little son chanced to find it, and buckled it round him, and was in an instant turned into such an animal, which to outward appearance resembled a bundle of pea-straw, and went rolling out like an unwieldy bear. When those who were in the room perceived this, they hurried forth and fetched the father, who came just in time to unbuckle the belt, before the child had done any mischief. The boy afterwards said, that when he had put on the girdle, he was seized with such a raging hunger, that he was ready to tear in pieces and devour all that came in his way.

## Traditions of Dwarfs

Once upon a time, at a marriage feast, there was an abundance of all sorts of viands, but no sooner were they served up than they disappeared, so that the bride and bridegroom looked on each other in amazement, and laid their heads together, but finally resolved to go on serving the guests as long

1   See p. 493.

as anything remained to serve, and not let them depart with hungry stomachs. But when the company came to offer their presents, the dwarfs – for it was they who had helped to eat the dinner – took off their hats, when it appeared very evidently how the eatables had vanished with such rapidity; for the whole room swarmed with those beings.[1] But if they had helped to eat, they helped also in bestowing presents, everyone placing a piece of gold in the basket, which proved scarcely large enough to hold them all.

———————

A farmer had a beautiful field of peas, but when he came to gather them, the pods were almost all empty, and when he set himself to watch, he heard a rustling, but saw no one. So one day he and his man went to the field together, having with them a rope, of which each taking an end, they ran up and down the field, and thus swept off their mist-caps (nebelkappen) from the heads of the dwarfs. Being thus captured, they had to pay the farmer dearly for his peas, before they could get their caps back; but no sooner had they got them than they were off with a 'Hui!'

———————

A dwarf came one day to a farmer and requested him to cut for him an ear of barley every day, telling him it should not be to his detriment. The farmer did so, going himself daily to cut the ear; and the dwarf came as regularly, took the ear on his back, and went away panting under his burden. In the meanwhile, the farmer's cattle became larger and fatter from day to day, though he gave them hardly any fodder. But one day the farmer having no time to spare, sent his man to cut the ear, who seeing the dwarf go panting away under it, laughed at him, and said that it was but an ear of barley, and that he had no occasion to pant so. This the dwarf took amiss, and never returned, while the farmer's cattle visibly grew leaner and leaner, and all the food that was given them was of no avail; the number of their ribs might have been counted.

———————

A dwarf came one day to a girl and gave her a distaff full of flax, on which there was enough for her whole life, provided she never spun it quite off. She spun from one year to another, and yet the distaff was always full, and she got so much yarn that she was constantly adding one piece of fine linen to another. At last she thought she might as well know what was beneath the flax, and why she might never spin it all off; and so she spun quicker and quicker, and had at length the end of it between her fingers. But under the flax there was nothing on the distaff, and the everlasting supply was irrecoverably gone.

See pp. 321–2.

## Traditions of the Hübichenstein[1]

### 1 The Dwarf King

In days of yore the Gübich was in the habit of making his appearance in the neighbourhood about the Hübichenstein, near Grund[2] for deep under the Hübichenstein the dwarfs had their dwelling, and the Gübich was their king. He had shaggy hair like a bear, and a very ancient visage. So he formerly appeared to the people. On those to whom he was well-disposed he bestowed great riches; but to those who offended him, or otherwise excited his wrath, he caused much annoyance. He knew all the salutary plants in the Harz, and thereby restored many a one to health; but he never would allow anyone to ascend the Hübichenstein.[3]

The Gübich was of short stature, but could stretch himself out to a considerable length. Formerly he might appear in the upper world once in every hundred years; but now he may no longer do so.

*Some say the Hübichenstein floated to its present site at the time of the Deluge; others that a giant found it in his shoe and shook it out there.*

### 2 The Ascent of the Hübichenstein

In the forest-house at Grund there dwelt in former times a forester, who lost his wife at a very early period, and had only one son. The youth was said to be both good and clever, only somewhat too inquisitive, as youths nowadays are wont to be. This lad one day went out with some of his companions to take a walk in the wood, and on reaching the Hübichenstein their discourse turned upon its height, when one of them said, *that* could easily be ascertained by anyone who would ascend it. Whereupon the forester's son remarked, that to ascend it was a trifling matter, and he would undertake the adventure, although the others strongly endeavoured to dissuade him; for whenever anyone has ascended it, he has not been able to come down again, and on the following morning has been found lying at the foot dashed to atoms. To this story the

---

1   This and the following traditions are from Harry, op. cit., *Sagen, Märchen und Legenden Niedersachsens.*
2   A small town at the western extremity of the Harz, remarkable for its vast subterranean works for the draining of the mines.
3   Those that went up were unable to descend; for having reached the summit, they were unable to move a foot, and on the following morning were found dashed to pieces beneath.

forester's son gave no credit, but, laughing, said that he would be the first to do the deed, and would not allow himself to be held back. His task must have been hard enough, for what is now called the Little Hübichenstein was formerly much higher than that which is now called the Great Hübichenstein, and, was therefore then named the Great Hübichenstein.

When standing on the summit he laughed at and jeered his friends, saying they appeared as diminutive as dwarfs. When he had stood thus for some time the wind began to blow and he thought it advisable to descend, but could not, being unable to move a foot; while those below were unable to afford him the slightest aid. At length he besought his friends to grant him a last favour and shoot him down, that he might not fall alive. But this no one would do. Intelligence of the incident had now reached his father, who going to the spot saw with his own eyes his son standing on the Great Hübichenstein and without the means of helping him. He wept, tore his hair, and was almost frantic with grief, but all this availed nothing. When evening came on the sky was cloudy, the wind began to rage, and the rain fell in such torrents that no one could stand against it, and the people bore the old forester back to his house by force. When again at home he thought, 'Thou wilt only do a benefit to thy child, and the merciful God will forgive thee.' He then took his best rifle and again went forth to the Hübichenstein. When he was out of Grund the rain suddenly ceased, while over Grund it fell in torrents, all around being clear and the moon bright. On his way to the Hübichenstein he began to weep and to pray, and was quite overcome by anguish of heart and sorrow; when on a sudden a little man appeared close by him with a snow-white beard and leaning on a fir-branch. 'Good luck to you,' said the little man, and at the same time asked him why he was going so late into the wood. The forester felt somewhat terrified, but had no inclination to say whither he was going or for what purpose. The little man then asked him why he sighed so repeatedly, and what afflicted him so that the tears were constantly running down his cheeks; adding that he should impart the cause of his sorrow, and that all might yet be well. The forester was now more communicative, and informed him, if perchance he did not know it already, that he was the man whose son was standing fixed on the Hübichenstein; that the devil had tempted him to make the ascent; that the young man had implored everyone for God's sake to shoot him down; but that no one had been so compassionate; so that the task devolved on him; for he trusted that God would not regard it as a sin. For how could he wait until his own child should fall down alive and perish so miserably? He then began again to lament, and said that he had not merited such a calamity on his son, whom he had reared up with all care, kept him strictly to church and to school; that he was, moreover, so pious, and would not have vexed a child or trodden on a worm. He would rather have died with his beloved wife than lived to experience such an affliction, and be thus forsaken and have no child to close his eyes. This lament went to the old man's heart; but while the forester was yet speaking the little man suddenly vanished. The father now looked up to the peak of the Hübichenstein, placed himself at its foot and levelled his piece at his son, who called to him, beseeching him only to fire, and saying he feared not to leave the world at that moment. The forester was about to fire, when in one instant thousands of little men came springing forth from all the hedges and bushes. They hurried towards him, pelted him with fir-cones, made all sorts of faces at him, and beat him about the legs with thorns and briars. The more he strove to defend himself the worse it was, and they were so nimble that he could not catch a single one. In the midst of them stood the little man with the snow-white beard, egging the others on. At length the forester, seeing that he could do nothing, returned to his dwelling.

No sooner was he gone than all was uproar on the Hübichenstein, little men without number coming from all directions up the rock, all on iron ladders, that reached from the foot to the summit, and everyone holding a brazen mining lamp in his hand; of these some were young, others old and with shaggy heads like a bear. The first that ascended was an old man with a snow-white beard which reached to his breast, and holding a silver mining lamp that shone like the bright sun; on his head was a golden crown. He commanded the others and was their king – This was the Gübich.

When on the summit, he said to the forester's son, 'Who has ordered thee to ascend my stone? In strictness I ought to have thee thrown to the bottom, and never shall another so escape; but I have compassion on thy father, because he is a most worthy man.'

The Gübich thereupon released him, and desired him to descend on one of the ladders; but his knees seemed almost broken. The Gübich then called one of his little men to him, who placing the youth on his shoulders, carried him down with the utmost ease. When they were descended, and the dwarf had set down his burden, the Gübich, taking the young man's hand, conducted him into his palace under the Hübichenstein. They entered an apartment, the walls of which glittered with galena;[1] the roof consisted of a single piece of heavy spar, as white as snow, from which there hung a great crown light, composed wholly of crystal and precious stones of great magnitude; the floor was strewed with green fir-branches, and the panels were resplendent with gold and gems. In the middle of the apartment stood a table of brown haematite,[1] before which was a silver chair, sitting down on

---

1 Sulphuret of lead.

which the dwarf king desired the forester's son also to seat himself. With a silver hammer he then struck on the table, which gave forth so sweet a sound that the like was never heard on earth. In an instant a thousand little females entered, bearing in strawberries and raspberries, of which the Gübich invited the forester's son to partake. They then conversed together, while the little men and women performed some music. When the repast was over, the Gübich again struck the table with the silver hammer, and before the sweet tones had died away, the little women brought in vessels of solid silver; and the Gübich invited the young man to drink. He did so, but anything so excellent he had never before drunk.

When the forester's son was thus refreshed, the Gübich conducted him into another apartment, in which stood a large brewing copper full of guilders, as bright as if just issued from the mint.

The Gübich informed him that that was his treasure, which his subjects had to provide for him; that from it he had assisted many a poor person, and was not the enemy of man; but that people must leave him in peace. 'If now thou wilt render me a service,' added he, 'thou shalt not repent it. Know that so long as the Great Hübichenstein continues to be *the Great,* I have authority on it, and may go about on the earth; but when the Great Hübichenstein becomes *the Little,* it will cost me my crown, and then I may rule only under the earth. Now the people are always shooting at hawks and buzzards up on the Hübichenstein, and that I cannot suffer; for if they strike the stone, a part crumbles off. If therefore thou wilt take care that no one injures the stone, thou shalt become a rich man, and mayest take from the brewing copper as much as thou wilt.' The forester's son promised accordingly, and gave him his hand; then taking from the copper as much as he would, filled his pockets and his cap. The Gübich then conducted him into another apartment, in which there was a bed of moss prepared with the greatest care. The Gübich told him that he would wake him early in the morning, and wished him good-night. He had not slept long when he awoke, and, on opening his eyes, saw that the morning was already grey. On looking about him, he found he was lying at the foot of the Hübichenstein, with his cap full of guilders by his side, and his pockets also full of guilders.

His adventure he related to the authorities, and bestowed a portion of his riches on the poor, and built a church in Grund, where there had not previously been one. And the authorities made a law that no one should ascend the Hübichenstein, and no one there shoot at hawks or buzzards or ravens. And as long as the Great Hübichenstein continued unimpaired the Gübich resided there, and did much good and punished evil, and was seen by many.

1    Fibrous brown iron ore, 'brauner Glaskopf'.

But in the Thirty Years' War, the imperialists, through wantonness, battered down the peak of the Great Hübichenstein with their artillery, from which time no one has ever seen the Gübich.

## 3 The Silver Fir-cone

Very very long ago there dwelt in Grund a miner, who in the cupboard of his room had a fir-cone of pure silver, as natural as if it had grown on a tree. Now anyone may well ask how a miner could get such a treasure? His story, as he has told it to many, was as follows.

His great-grandfather, who was also a miner, was once sick for many weeks together, and it was a time of dearth, and the miners in those days had no allowance during sickness as at present; that custom having been introduced at a later period. He had seven children living, so that it may easily be imagined there was no superabundance of bread for them, or, indeed, of anything else. The miner and his wife were now quite disheartened. The wife, as she was one day standing before the door, thinking on what was to be done, resolved on going to the forest and gathering a basketful of fir-cones, in the hope of selling them, as they would at all events fetch something. She set out accordingly, and, when on her way to the forest, thinking of her sad fate, tears came into her eyes, and she sat down and wept, holding her hands before her face. Having thus sat a while, on looking up she saw standing before her a little old man with a snow-white beard and clad in a singular garb, who had apparently been long gazing on her. He inquired the cause of her sorrow; she answered that he could not help her. But the little man, in a friendly tone, said, people were wont not to give credit to others for what they can do, and that she might confidently tell him the cause of her grief. Being thus encouraged, she related to him how her husband had been long sick, that they had seven children, and not a morsel of bread in the house, that they had pledged or sold everything, and that the owner would no longer suffer them to remain in the house; that she was then come out for the purpose of gathering a load of fir-cones, to enable them to buy some bread. The little man then strove to console her, bidding her be of good cheer, and saying that all would yet go well, and that if she wished for good fir-cones, she had only to go to the Hübichenstein, and not be afraid. He then bade her good-morning and went into the thicket.

But the woman went to the Hübichenstein, where, having placed her basket on the ground, she began looking for fir-cones. No sooner had she begun her search than fir-cones fell about her on every side, and in such abundance that she at first thought that boys had concealed themselves in the Hübichenstein and were making sport with her, at the instigation of the little man. She therefore snatched up her basket and hurried away, not feeling desirous of having her eyes beaten out of her head. Though her fear was quite groundless; for all the cones had fallen into the basket; but persons in such affliction are heedless of what passes around them; so she left the Hübichenstein and went to another spot, where she filled her basket, though she had no need to gather many more. On her way home, the basket, at every instant, grew heavier and heavier, so that she was obliged to rest many times before she reached her dwelling. Though this seemed to her very extraordinary, she entertained no suspicions, and, on reaching her home, went to empty her basket in the shed, with the intention of returning to the forest for more cones. But, to her unutterable astonishment, cones of pure silver fell from her basket. She resolved at once not to keep them, thinking they came there by no righteous means; 'And who knows,' thought she, 'whether the little fellow is not Satan himself?' She then related to her husband all that had taken place, describing the little man, and asked him whether it could all be by fair means, and whether she might keep the cones? Her husband answered that she might keep them all, and that the little man was no doubt the Gübich, who had helped many a poor person.

On the following morning he would allow her no rest; she must go again to the forest; perhaps she might again meet with the Gübich, and have an opportunity of thanking him. And so it happened, for no sooner had she reached the spot than she saw the little man with the snow-white beard, who asked her whether on the preceding day she had not found beautiful fir-cones? When she began to thank him, and to tell him how she was now free from all her difficulties, the Gübich laughed and gave her a bunch of plants, of which she should make her husband a drink, by the virtue of which he would soon be well again. He then went again into the thicket. But the woman returned home, prepared the drink, and from that hour her husband became well, and they lived long and happy together. The silver they took to the mint and became immensely rich, and did much good to many poor people. One of the cones they preserved as a remembrance, and that is the one which the miner had standing in his cupboard.

## The Bell-pond

In the village of Moringen, near Göttingen, there is a garden, in which is a pond called the Opferteich. In ancient times public meetings were held in its vicinity, under a large oak, from the sacrifices at which the pond is said to have derived its name of the Opferteich, or sacrificial pond. It is very deep, has no visible afflux, but plentiful subterranean springs.

It is related that every year at Christmas, from the hour of twelve till one, a bell is heard tolling from its depth.

The knights of the Temple, who formerly had a house there, once had a new bell cast and hung in the church tower still in existence; but they forgot, before using it, to have it consecrated to divine service, and baptised according to ancient custom. It was their intention to use the bell, for the first time, for mass on Christmas Eve; but hardly had it struck the first stroke, when it was torn away by a miraculous power, and projected, through the sound-hole of the tower, into the Opferteich. There it lies to this day; but every Christmas Eve it rises to the surface, tolls, and sinks again. No fish can live in that water.

## The Bell at Coenhausen

In the church of Coenhausen, in the county of Dassel, there is a bell, on which is the following inscription: 'I call the living, bewail the dead, and drive away thunder.' The people of the place have, from time immemorial, placed great confidence in this bell, and believe that in a storm, as soon as the bell sounds, the thunder must cease.

## The Children of Hameln

In the year 1284, the town of Hameln was intolerably infested with rats. One day there came a man to the town, most singularly clad, and no one knew from whence, who gave himself out for a rat-catcher, and offered, for a certain sum of money, to rid them of those noxious animals. The townsmen agreed to his proposal, and promised him the remuneration required. Thereupon the man drew forth a pipe, and piped, and in an instant the rats came hurrying forth from every house, cellar and corner, and in such numbers that the streets were over and over covered with them. The man then proceeded to the gate leading to Lachem and Aerzen, and, on reaching the Weser, tucked up his dress and walked into the river; and the rats, following his example, plunged into the water and were drowned. But no sooner were the townsmen relieved from their torment, than they repented of their promise, and on the plea that the man was a sorcerer, refused to pay him the stipulated remuneration. At this he was furious, and vowed vengeance.

On the 26th June, the day of St John and St Paul, when almost every Christian soul was in church, the sorcerer again entered the town, but this time in a different guise. He was clad as a huntsman, with a fire-red hat, and had a most terrific countenance. He struck up a tune, at which all the children were so fascinated, that they must needs follow him at every step. Slowly he marched up the narrow street leading to the east gate, with the children in great number after him; then, passing through the gate, proceeded to a mountain called the Koppelberg, in which they all disappeared.

This was witnessed by a nursery-maid, who related that the mountain opened, and as soon as the man with the children (to the number of a hundred and thirty) had entered, closed again. Two little boys, it is said, remained behind, one of whom was blind, and could, therefore, only recount what he had heard, and the other dumb, who could only point out the spot where the calamity had taken place. Fathers and mothers now rushed out at the east gate, but when they came to the mountain, nothing was there observable but a small hollow, where the sorcerer had entered.

The street through which the sorcerer led the children is called the Bungenstrasse, because no music, no drum (Bunge) may be played in it. If a bridal procession passes through it, the music must cease until it is out of it. It is not many years since, that on the Koppelberg – now overgrown with thorns – two stone crosses were to be seen, which, it is said, were in remembrance of this event; the history of it is also sculptured on the wall of a house in the Bungengasse, as well as in many other places in the town, both in wood and stone. For a long time the town dated its public documents from this calamity.

*Many are the relations of this event. Grimm, J. & W., Deutsche Sagen, i, p. 330.*


## The White Ghosts in the Lüningsberg

Many years ago the White Ghosts in the Lüningsberg, near Aerzen, where the beautiful, level grass-plot lies amid verdant copses, were in the habit of playing by night at skittles, with golden skittles and golden bowls. It must have been a wondrous sight, when in the nocturnal darkness the glittering bowls were rolling swift as an arrow along the smooth, green turf, and the skittles fell with a clear, musical sound. It must have been a beauteous spectacle, when the moon, bright and full, stood over the forest, in the blue heaven, and illumined the oaks, beeches and firs, which encircled the mysterious skittle-ground. When the sounding skittles fell, the little party-coloured birds in the trees have oftentimes been waked, and looked with inquisitive eyes from the branches; hares, roes, foxes and badgers have approached to look on, and all conducted themselves becomingly. The ghosts in the Lüningsberg had for a long time carried on their play, in which no one was willing to disturb them. The people in Aerzen had much to tell about the golden bowls and skittles; but no living soul had ever ventured into the forest by night; the terror was too great.

But there was a journeyman weaver, who had travelled and wandered much in foreign lands. On his return home, the miller's fair daughter,

Anna, gave greater delight to his heart than all that he had seen in the world besides. Both were, however, wretchedly poor, and, therefore, unable to marry; but Henry, for such was his name, who was a daring young fellow, soon hit upon a project. 'I will go to the Lüningsberg,' said he, 'when the ghosts are bowling at their golden skittles, and get hold of one of them.' So one fine, mild night, he stole timidly and softly through the shrubs and fields, but on reaching the forest his heart beat violently. He approached the grass-plot, and now witnessed all that had been related to him. He saw how the little white spectres hurled with an arrow's speed their bright bowls along the verdant turf, which instantly came rolling back to them spontaneously; how the golden skittles fell with a tuneful clang. The fox also, and the badger, and the roe, and the hare, he saw sitting peaceably together, and the little birds merrily hopping to the sound among the branches. He crouched down as low as possible among the underwood on the heath, fearful of being discovered by the ghosts; but at the same time creeping nearer and nearer to the glittering skittles, till at length he could almost reach one with his hand. At this moment a vigorous bowl sent one of the skittles into the underwood in which Henry was concealed; he seized it, crying, 'Anna! Anna!' and, with the precious booty, hurried breathless to the outlet of the forest. But the ghosts had heard his exclamation, their skittle is stolen, they lament its loss for a moment, and then, urged on by rage, pursue the audacious mortal, to inflict on him some terrible chastisement. Henry had, however, reached the meadow which lies beneath the Lüningsberg, and hastened towards the old, brittle trunk, which is laid across the Humme by way of bridge. The ghosts were close behind him, he could hear them breathe, an icy chill ran through his whole frame; he missed the narrow path, yet not dismayed, sprang into the Humme – to his salvation! 'Lucky art thou,' cried the ghosts, 'in water we have no power; we could have seized thee on the tree-trunk, and would have wrung thy neck.'

Breathless he reached the opposite bank, from which he saw the ghosts, like forms of mist, flitting to and fro; but they could find no crossing.

Henry and Anna soon had a merry wedding. Henry bought an old house, demolished it and built a new one on its site. The ghosts on the Lüningsberg from that time disappeared. At the present day the spot on the mountain is shown, where they played with golden skittles; and when the boys and girls of the place pass by the house on the Mühlbach, before which stands the large lime-tree, they whisper to each other, 'That is the house that was built from the golden skittle of the ghosts in the Lüningsberg.'

# The Rose of Hildesheim

As the emperor Lewis the Pious[1] was one day hunting, he lost a cross that was filled with relics. On discovering his loss, he sent his attendants in all directions to search for the holy treasure, and at the same time made a vow to build a church on the spot where it should be found. The men followed the trace of the hunt, and found, far in the forest, and in the midst of the snow, the cross hanging on a blooming wild rose-bush. They reported the miracle to the emperor, who immediately commanded a chapel to be erected there, with the altar on the spot where the cross was found on the bush. The rose flourished admirably on the sacred spot, and now, with its leafy shoots and branches, like a vine, covers the arches of the cathedral up to its very roof.

# The Smith in the Hüggel

Not far from Osnabrück is the Hüggel, which is said to have formerly abounded in gold and silver. The inhabitants of the neighbourhood tell of many wonders connected with the spacious cave contained in the mountain.

Where, on the rugged declivity of the hill, the road leads through the defile to the village of Hagen, there lived, in days of yore, a smith, who was not like other men, but nevertheless supplied his employers with the best workmanship. He was a faithful husband, a provident father to his children and servants, beneficent to strangers, and, never suffered a poor wanderer to pass his door without relief. But one Sunday, as his wife was just coming from church, she was struck dead by lightning. At this the smith fell into despair, murmured against God, would not hear of comfort, nor even see his children again. At the expiration of a year he was attacked by a fatal malady, and when in his last moments, there came a stranger to him of venerable aspect, with a long, white beard, who conveyed him into the hollow cleft of the Hüggel, where, in atonement for his crime, and for the purifying of his soul, he should wander, and be the Metal-king, until the mountain yielded no more produce: he should, moreover, rest by day, and by night continue to do good to his earthly brethren.

In the cool mine his kindly, beneficent disposition resumed its activity. Gold and silver, he well knew, did not contribute to make men happy, and he therefore toiled to extract from the poorest veins the more useful iron, and is said, in his earlier time, to have made many implements both

---

1    Or 'le Débonnaire' as he is called by the French chroniclers.

domestic and agricultural. At a later period, he limited his labour to the shoeing of horses. Before the cave a post was fixed, to which the country people tied their horses to be shod; not omitting, however, at the same time, to leave the regular price on a large stone that lay close by. But the smith was never seen, and remained undisturbed in his cave.[1]

A rash young fellow, instigated by avarice, once ventured to enter into the cavern. He lighted his mining-lamp, took a bundle of twigs under his arm, and proceeded along under the cavern's lofty, blackened roof. He had now to choose between two ways, one right, the other left, and fortunately chose the right-hand one; but his provision of twigs, which he had taken to mark his way, was now exhausted; yet return and procure a new one he would not. At the end of the passage he came to an iron door, which, however, gave him but little trouble; for at a couple of vigorous strokes with his hammer it flew open; but the current that rushed forth extinguished his lamp. 'Come in,' cried a shrill, clear voice, that pierced his very soul. Half stupefied, he stepped forwards. From the arching of the roof and the side walls there shone a wondrous light; on the massive pillars and smooth walls there flitted curiously quivering figures backwards and forwards. The Metal-king, among a number of misshapen spirits of the mine, with attendants on each side, sat on a long block of pure silver, with a considerable heap of shining gold before them. 'Come in, friend,' exclaimed the same shrill voice. 'Sit down by side of me.' There was a vacant seat there, but which did not seem to please the intruder. 'But why so timid? Be bold, no harm shall befall thee; as thou hast come, so will we send thee back, and will, moreover, give thee a good lesson with thee on the way; if thou canst act according to which, thou mayest save something; if otherwise, all may be lost. Step up to this table.' Pale as a corpse and with tottering steps he advanced to the table. 'Discontent at the loss of thy goods and chattels,' continued the Metal-king, 'has misled thee to become dissolute, to neglect thy work, and to seek after forbidden treasures. Change thy stubborn disposition, and thou wilt turn stones into gold; cease from arrogance, and thou wilt have in thy coffers gold and silver in abundance. Thou desirest to have immense treasures at once, without any cooperation of thine; think only how perilous that is, and how often it is fruitless. Dig well thy field and garden, cultivate thy meadows and hills, and thou wilt gain to thyself mines of gold and silver.'

When the Metal-king had thus spoken, there was heard a screaming as of ravens, and a hissing and crying as of night-owls, and a storm-wind

---

1 English readers will be here again reminded of Wayland Smith, traditionally said to work in this way at his smithy, a Megalithic tomb on the Berkshire Downs. See p. 311.

came rushing against the man, and drove him forcibly and irresistibly forth, through the dark, damp passages. When he again found himself in the open air, he vowed to follow the old Hüggelman's counsel, but never again to visit him in his cave.

Some say that the Hüggelman's evil inclinations again returned, that he was no longer kindly disposed to the country people, but often threw up in the air red-hot ploughshares, thereby wantonly causing great terror among the peasantry; whence they concluded that the silver-mine was nearly exhausted.

## The Deer-stealer

In the Harz there was once an incorrigible deer-stealer. Whenever he knew that a head of game was anywhere to be had, it was no longer safe. He had heard that in Little Clausthal, at the hour of midnight, on Good Friday, a roe with her fawn appeared, which no one dared to shoot; but he only laughed at the superstitious tale; and one day, just before Easter, being in a jovial company, and the conversation turning on the roe of Little Clausthal, he declared his disbelief of the whole story, and turned it into ridicule, saying, 'Who will wager that I don't shoot both the roe and her fawn, and have them for dinner on the first Easter-holiday?' The company strove to dissuade him from the attempt, but in vain; so on the Good Friday night he took his way to Little Clausthal. On reaching the pond he observed a thick mist hanging over it, which reached to the sky, and completely concealed the pond. In the mist he heard sounds like the voices of many persons whispering together, and strange forms seemed, from time to time, to issue from it. Along the road also many forms glided like insubstantial shadows, all of which vanished in the mist that hovered over the pond; but he augured no evil. He crossed over and stationed himself at the end of the valley, behind a bush. Exactly at the time there came the roe with her fawn, and he shot the fawn. On seeing it fall, he sprang forwards, bound its feet together, slung it across his shoulder, and returned. When he reached the spot where the pond now is again, there stood, where the pond had been, a church, brilliantly lighted; a loud singing was heard from within, with the organ pealing forth at intervals. 'This,' thought he, 'is most extraordinary; I will, however, just step in. On entering, he found the church full of people, but all of whom appeared as if they had been lying in the grave for ages; their garb, too, was of a fashion he had never seen. He greeted the congregation, but no one thanked him, though some nodded, while others shook their heads, made signs to each other, and pointed with their fingers at him. The lights at the altar and in the chandeliers burned with a blue flame, and from the chalice on the altar a blue light trembled forth. The priest then appeared before the altar, but his speech was not that of earthly men; it was as if wind and thunder filled the whole edifice: from his mouth likewise there issued a blue flame. At once a crash was heard in the church, as if the very earth had split into shivers. The priest then pointed at him and cried, 'Accursed Sabbath-breaker!' and the sprites placing themselves before him, howled forth the same words. He rushed headlong out of the church, stupefied with fear and horror; and as he hurried forth, the door was slammed after him, so that his heels were stricken off. He reached the road, and there continued lying till morning. When he came to himself, there was the pond as it had ever been, but the fawn was away. He was sick to death, and could hardly drag himself home. After lying nine days, he was just able to relate his adventure, and then died.

## The Freischütz

In former times there lived in Zellerfeld a gamekeeper, who was a Freischütz. During his apprenticeship he never had any luck in shooting, and on that account was very sad and disheartened. One day as he was walking quite inconsolable about his district, and almost resolved to throw up his calling, he met a man clad in green, who asked him why he appeared so disconsolate. When the young man had told him, he replied, 'If that's all, it may easily be remedied, it only requires a little courage. I will put you in the way, comrade. Go to the communion, and keep the real body in your mouth, and when you come out of church, take your piece, go into the wood, nail the real body to a tree, and fire at it thrice in the name of the devil. When you have so done, you may fire away into the blue sky, and bring down whatever you will.'[1] The young man allowed himself to be seduced, and in this manner became a Freischütz. In his character of gamekeeper he would frequently show his dexterity by way of sport, and sometimes when in the long winter evenings he had company with him, he would ask them what they would eat – a roasted hare, or fawn, or a partridge. He would then take his gun, shoot out of the window and say, 'Go into the garden,' or, 'Go into the yard,' or, 'The street; there it lies.' And when they went where he had said, there they found it. Not infrequently, too, he would ask, 'Where shall it lie?' and every time it would be found lying where they had said.

A person once requested him to teach him the art; but he would not until the other had sworn never to teach anyone besides, or to reveal how

1   See p. 363.

he himself had become a Freischütz. He continued his course for many years. At last, when lying on his deathbed, he started suddenly up, rushed through the chamber like a maniac, crying, 'No, devil! Not yet! Thou shalt not have me yet!' But to what purpose? In the midst of his crying he fell down dead; and on examination it appeared that his neck had been wrung, and around it there was a blue stripe like a blue string. It was now that the man above-mentioned related what had taken place between him and the gamekeeper.

## The Oldenburg Horn[1]

In the year 990 after the birth of Christ, Count Otto[2] ruled over the county of Oldenburg. Having, as a good sportsman, a great love for the chase, he set out, on the 20th July of the above-mentioned year, with many of his nobles and servants, on a hunting party, and would, in the first instance, seek for game in the forest of Bernefeuer. The count himself being in chase of a roe, and following it alone from the wood of Bernefeuer to the Osenberg, lost both sight and hearing of his attendants. On his white horse he stopped on the middle of the hill, and looked around him for his greyhounds, but could neither see nor hear a single one. He now said to himself (for the weather was excessively hot), 'Oh God! If someone had but a draught of cool water to give me!' Scarcely had the count uttered the words when the Osenberg opened, and out of the cleft there came a beautiful damsel, well adorned, attired in goodly clothing, with fine tresses parted on her shoulders, a wreath of flowers on her head, and holding in her hand a costly silver-gilt vessel in the form of a hunting horn, of beautiful and cunning workmanship, granulated and exquisitely finished, and soldered together, and ornamented with many armorial bearings, that are now but little known, and with strange, unintelligible writing in the manner of the old antiques, and was altogether beautifully and curiously wrought. This, which was filled with some liquor, she presented to the count, praying him to drink from it to refresh himself.

The count having received the silver-gilded horn from the damsel, raised the cover and looked into it, but, on shaking it, was not pleased with the beverage, or whatever it might be, contained in it, and therefore declined the damsel's proffered drink. Whereupon she said, 'My dear lord, drink only on my faith; for it will do you no harm, but will tend to your benefit';

---

1  Dobeneck's *Volksglauben*, I, p. 83, from Hamelmann's *Oldenburger Chronik*, 1599, folio, where an engraving of the horn is given. See also Grimm, J. & W., *Deutsche Sagen*, p. 541.
2  In Kuhn and Schwartz, op. cit., p. 280, the story is told of Count Anthony Günther.

assuring him, moreover, that if he would drink of it, it would go well with him and his, and thenceforth with the whole house of Oldenburg, and the whole country would thrive and prosper. But, if the count would not believe her and would not drink out of it, that there would in future be no unity in the succeeding Oldenburg family. But as the count placed no faith in her words, and, not without good reason, had a great objection to drink, he swung the horn, which he was holding in his hand, behind him and poured out its contents, whereof a portion was splashed over the white horse, the hair of which, where it was sprinkled and wetted, fell off. On seeing this the maiden desired to have back her horn, but the count, still holding it in his hand, hastened down the hill, and on looking round, observed that the damsel had again entered the cleft; then feeling a terror from what had befallen him, he clapped spurs to his horse and galloped at full speed to his followers, to whom he related his adventure, showing them the horn, which he took with him to Oldenburg. And this horn, because it was obtained in so wonderful a manner, was regarded as a precious jewel both by him and all succeeding princes of the house of Oldenburg, and is even at this day preserved at Oldenburg, where I myself have often seen it. By many it is praised on account both of its workmanship and antiquity. So far the Oldenburg Chronicler.

*In 'Notes and Queries,' No. 61, there is the following communication from Sir Walter C. Trevelyan respecting this celebrated horn –*

> *The Oldenburg Horn is preserved among the antiquities in the gallery of the king of Denmark at Copenhagen. It is of silver gilt, and ornamented in paste with enamel. It is considered by the Danish antiquaries to be of the time of Christian I, in the latter half of the fifteenth century. There are engraved on it coats of arms and inscriptions, which show that it was made for King Christian I in honour of the three kings or wise men, on whose festival he used it at Cologne.*
>
> *An inscription containing the names of the three 'kings of Cologne' seems not to have been unusual on horns of this description. (See p. 15 of this volume) The so-called Oldenburg Horn is now, as No. 1, preserved, among other objects of interest at Copenhagen, in the little palace of Rosenborg, a structure of Christian IV, after the designs of Inigo Jones.*

## The Cuckoo – the Pleiades

According to an old tradition, the cuckoo was once a baker's man, and therefore bears a dun-coloured plumage, appearing as if sprinkled with flour. In a time of dearth, he had stolen from the dough brought by the poor people to bake, and on drawing it thus diminished from the oven, was wont to cry out, 'Gukuk!' (see, see!). For this our Lord, as a punishment, transformed him into a bird that ever repeats that cry. Hence the rimes,

> Kukuk, beckenknecht,[1]
> sag mir recht
> wie viel jahr ich leben soll?
>
> *Cuckoo, bakerman, tell me right*
> *how many years I shall live?*[2]

In Ditmarschen the question *how long shall I live?* is asked of the cuckoo in the following terms,

> Kukuk in Häwen,
> Wo lang' schal ik läwen?
> Sett dy in de gröne Grastyt
> Un tell myn Jaerstyt.
>
> *Cuckoo in heaven,*
> *How long shall I live?*
> *Set thee in the green grass-tide,*
> *And tell my years' tide.*

In Lauenburg,

| | |
|---|---|
| Kukuk | *Cuckoo,* |
| Spekbuk, | *Fat-paunch,* |
| Ik bir dy: | *I pray thee:* |
| Seg my doch, | *Tell me now,* |
| Wo väel Joe | *How many years* |
| Law' ik noch? | *I yet shall live?*[3] |

Of the origin of the Pleiades the following is related. Jesus one day passing by a baker's shop, whence the fumes of new bread issued, sent one of his disciples in to beg a loaf. The baker himself refused; but his wife, who with her six daughters was standing at a little distance, gave him a loaf secretly; for which good deed they were placed in heaven as seven stars; but the baker was transformed to a cuckoo, which proclaims the spring from St Tiburtius (14th April) till St John (24th June), that is, as long as the seven stars are visible.[4] Traditions of the cuckoo are numerous throughout Europe.

---

1 Beckerknecht?       2 Grimm, J., *Deutsche Mythologie*, op. cit., p. 641.
3 Müllenhoff, op cit., p. 509. See also pp. 287, 304, 419–20.
4 Grimm, J., *Deutsche Mythologie*, op. cit., p. 691

# North German Customs and Superstitions[1]

## Shrovetide

In the neighbourhood of Mellin, in the Altmark, they flog each other out of bed with rods. The party flogged must treat the flogger; hence everyone rises as early as possible.[2]

At Ilseburg in the Harz, on New Year's eve and Shrovetide, the youths go about the streets disguised and making a noise. Cakes are also baked there, on the eve of Ash Wednesday, of a triangular form. In some parts of Thuringia, in the neighbourhood of Wallhausen, these cakes are square, and are called kröppels. Throughout the whole Mark pancakes are baked at Shrovetide.

About Altenburg and some places in the Harz, there is no spinning on the eve of Ash Wednesday, lest Frau Holle should come. Some also say, lest they should have crooked cattle. In some places they say that if they spin on Shrove Tuesday night, between twelve and one o'clock, Frau Holle will come and sit on the hatchel. On the distaff of those that will spin, they set a little doll.

In some places in the neighbourhood of the Kyffhäuser, they make – particularly the thrashers – a little figure, carrying a flail, a rake, a bushel measure and a half-peck measure. This they place on a table, and collect gifts for it. The custom is now on the decline, the gens d'armes! having pronounced it idolatry.

At Shrovetide sauerkraut and smoked sausage (Knackwurst) are to be eaten. *Stendal.*

At Basum, near Osnabrück, there is throwing at cocks at Shrovetide.

---

1   From Kuhn and Schwartz, *Norddeutsche Sagen, Märchen und Gebräuche*, Leipzig, 1848, unless otherwise expressed
2   This custom prevails over all Denmark, where the children use a particular kind of rod ornamented with gilt paper and ribands, and called a Fastelavnsriis (Shrovetide rod).

## Candlemas

When the sun shines on the altar on Candlemas day, there will be a second winter.

Many think it not right to spin at Candlemas. *Altmark*.


## Easter[1]

Almost everywhere in the north of Germany there is ball-play at Easter. At Landsberg on the Wartha, the 'Osterball' is celebrated. The holiday begins with leading an ass, dressed out for the occasion, about the town, with great rejoicings, having a rider on his back; all then proceed to the meadow, where the play takes place. Dancing and other amusements conclude the holiday.

At Camern on the Elbe the young men alone and the girls alone go the two Sundays preceding Easter, before the houses of those who were married during the foregoing year, the former demanding the 'Kliese', a wooden ball, and the latter the 'Brautball', or Bride-ball, which is of considerable size and made of leather. On the second day of Easter they appear again before the door to receive the balls, and repeat some doggrel verses. The ball-play is played with the 'Kliese', at which each one endeavours to drive the ball from his hole. The bride-ball is struck backwards and forwards until it is beaten to pieces.

At Warthe in the Ukermark the boys go about flogging the girls on the first day of Easter, in return for which they must give them fish and potatoes on the second feast-day; the boys providing the music for a dance.

In many places coloured Easter eggs are given away, particularly by their sponsors to the children. In some places they are rolled down a declivity, when there is a race after them.

Easter fires are lighted in many places, particularly in the North Harz (and sometimes in the South Harz), in the Altmark, Brunswick, Hanover and Westphalia. They are usually kindled on certain eminences and hills, which thence bear the name of 'Osterberge'. The manner of proceeding varies according to circumstances; where there are declivities, burning tar-barrels are rolled down. In the mining towns of the Harz the fire is usually kindled on Eastereve, when a tree is commonly set up, surrounded with brushwood and burnt. In Grund they run about with torches.

---

1   So called from the goddess Eastre, according to the testimony of Beda *De Temp. Rat.*, ch. xiii, who says: 'apud eos (Anglorum populos) Aprilis *Esturmonath,* qui nunc paschalis mensis interpretatur, quondam a *dea* illorum, quae Eostra vocabatur, et cui in illo festa celebratur, nomen habuit; a cujus nomine nunc paschale tempus cognominant, consueto *antiquæ observationis* vocabulo gaudia novæ solennitatis vocantes.'

If Easter water is to be fetched, it must be only from a running stream, and against the current, and between midnight and sunrise. In Swinemünde they take it *with* the stream, repeating certain lines. In the neighbourhood of Woldegk in Mecklenburg the maidservants fetch Easter water on Easter morning, or on the preceding evening spread out linen cloths in the garden, and in the morning wash themselves with the dew, rain, or snow that has fallen on them. This preserves them from illness for the whole year. In Sachsenburg on the Unstrut they ride the horses into the water; then they will not be ill during all the year. The Easter water has virtue only when, while drawing it, the wind is due east.

If it rains on Good Friday, the turf will be parched up three times during the year.

On Good Friday, after sunset, wreaths of elder should be twined and hung up in the houses: they will then not be struck by lightning. *Neukirchen near Chemnitz.*

On Good Friday one should not go into the garden, lest it cause caterpillars. *Stendal.*

On Maundy Thursday green kale should be eaten.

In the neighbourhood of Cammin the village boys hunt squirrels at Easter. They go into the forest, and when they have found one, they drive it with sticks and stones from tree to tree, until it falls down dead.

## The First of April

Among children it is everywhere the custom to make April fools. In Berlin the little ones are sent to the apothecary's to fetch crabs' blood or gnats' fat. This custom is prolonged to the end of the month.

## May-day

As soon as the first heralds of spring appear, the youth of Berlin issue from the gates to fetch mayflies and buttercups, both of which they exchange for pins. The mayflies they let fly again, singing:

| | |
|---|---|
| Maikäferchen fliege, | *May-chaferkin fly,* |
| Dein Vater ist im Kriege | *Thy father's in the war,* |
| Deine Mutter ist in Pommerland | *Thy mother's in Pomerania* |
| Pommerland ist abgebrannt! | *Pomerania is all burnt!* |
| Maikäferchen fliege. | *May-chaferkin fly.* |

In the North Harz they say that the witches must dance away the snow on the Blocksberg on the 1st May. Also, that on 'Wolpern' eve the great giant dances on the Blocksberg with the little dwarfs, that is, the devil with the witches. In many places it is a saying, that if the witches return in the twelve days, then must the snow be away.

When the girls on the 1st May have not yet turned up their land, they get 'Walburgs'; that is, they make for them a scarecrow with a spade in its hand, and set it in the garden. *Ukermark and Mittelmark*.

If a man desires to know what sort of a wife he shall have, he must ride on Walpurg's Night on a broomstick to the stable, and knock thrice, then go to the pigsty and hear what pig grunts, whether an old or a young one. His wife will be old or young accordingly. *Hassleben*.

On Christmas night, New Year's night, and Walpurg's Night, no persons should go to bed, lest the witches should come and bewitch them. *Rauen*.

On Walpurg's eve no cat may be teased nor admitted into a house: it may be a witch.[1]

If a woman puts her petticoat on the hind part before, she will be secure against witchcraft.

If anyone goes out unwashed on a Friday, the witches have power over him.

If anyone wishes to see the witches, he must take an egg with him that was laid on Maundy Thursday and place himself in a crossway. Or he must go into the church on a Good Friday, but hasten out before the blessing. In Bergkirchen a man did so once, and saw three witches, one with a water-pot, one with a spinning-wheel, and the third with a corn-sieve, who all carried on their work during the sermon.[2]

At Christmas, New Year and Michaelmas, a scythe or something sharp should be laid in the fodder; the witches can then do no harm to the cattle. *Mellin*.

In the night of the 1st May and on Michaelmas day the witches ride to the Blocksberg, and on the two following Sundays they go to church, where anyone may see them, if he has with him rye from three fields; he will then see some with butter-tubs, some with milk-pails on their heads. But he must hasten out of the church before the blessing, else they will bewitch him in one way or other. *Güssefeld in the Altmark*.

On the night before the 1st May the witches ride on the tails of magpies to the Blocksberg; for which reason no magpies are seen on the 1st May, as they are not yet returned. *Güssefeld*.

If anyone wishes to see the witches, he must place himself in a crossway on May-night, cut a piece of turf, and lay it on his head; they can then do him no harm.[3] *Scharzfeld*.

When lumps of feathers are found in the bed, it is said that the witches are sitting in it. They come on May-day before sunrise, and have often been seen in the Herring-market at Emden. When a witch issues forth, her body lies in bed as stiff as a flint-stone. *Moorhausen near Aurich.*

In Saterland a certain fungus is called witches' butter.[1]

## Whitsuntide

In Sannen they cut down willow branches a fortnight before Easter, and then a wrestling-match takes place; the victor is proclaimed king, and receives from the little ones, that are unable to mount a horse without help, bridle money and mounting money.

In Stapel the Whitsuntide-willow is to be cut on the third Easter day. At Whitsuntide there is a foot-race; the conqueror is declared king; the last in the race must carry the tarred rags with which the whips are smeared. Afterwards there is a horse-race, at which the king in the foot-race is first in the row, as the place of honour. Whoever falls from his horse must carry the tarred rags.

In Blumenhagen, near Vierraden, the stableboys smack their whips in cadence on Whitsun eve. On the first festival day the so-called 'Kantenreiten' takes place. A little loaf (Weck) of white bread is set on a pole, and the one who first reaches it is king. The last must carry the tarred rags. The smacking of whips on Whitsun eve is usual in many other places. In some villages the race is for a hat, handkerchief, etc.

In Saterland shooting at a bird is practised. He who shoots down the last is declared king, and receives a decorated hat, which he wears at the dance in the evening, and preserves till the next year. A similar shooting takes place in many other parts. In Hanover and Brunswick they shoot at a target; the best shooter is king, and nails the target to the gable of his roof.

In the villages of Brunswick everything at Whitsuntide is decorated with may (birch); sometimes also a May-bride adorned with flowers is to be seen, and in some places they make a May-king, who is completely concealed in sprigs of May. What they have collected they take to the Whitsuntide-field and there eat it. A May-king is usual in many other places.

2   See p. 303.

## St John's or Midsummer Day

In the South Harz and in Thuringia the so-called St John's fires are common. In Edersleben, near Sangerhausen, the proceeding is as follows: A high pole is set up, on which a tar-barrel is placed, having a chain drawn through it that reaches to the ground. When it is on fire they swing the barrel round the pole amid great rejoicing. In the neighbourhood of Baruth, down to recent times, St John's fires were lighted, as well as in the Catholic parts of Westphalia.

In Gandersheim a tall fir is set up, which is completely stripped to its summit; on this they hang handkerchiefs and the like, to be climbed for.

In Sachsenburg, on St John's day, the children make a 'Rosenstock'. At night they barricade the street with a rope, on which they hang wreaths of birch and flowers. They also set birch branches before the house and raise a large tree, round which they dance. Whoever will pass through the street must pay something, out of which the music and the birch are paid for. In the parts south of the Fürstenwald, there is, about the same time, a shooting for a hat, or a 'Rosenbaum'. A pole is raised, on which are streamers, a wreath and a crown, also handkerchiefs and the like, to be climbed for. The best climber up the 'Rosenbaum' is rewarded with a bouquet in his hat.

In the neighbourhood of the Kyffhäuser the girls throw at cocks.

In the 'Jantjenacht' (St John's eve) the witches hold their meeting, at which they eat the berries of the mountain-ash. *Moorhausen and Nordmoor in E. Friesland.*

Treasures burn especially on St John's night, and those who know how can raise them. *Ukermark.*

On St John's day there should be fetched nothing green, it will cause cancer. Vegetables should be gathered the evening before. *Mellin in the Altmark.*

On St John's day, between twelve and one o'clock, there grows in many places a hand out of the ground, which they call St John's hand. Whoever possesses such a hand is lucky, as its stroke is good against all kinds of fluxions and other maladies. It is not to be confounded with the so-called bear's-foot, a plant which also grows on St John's day, and the roots of which have likewise the form of a hand. *Brodewin in the Ukermark.*

The Divining rod (Wünschelruthe) must be cut from a hazel backwards on St John's day, and must then be bound on a child that has been baptised, and so receive the name of John. *Gramzow in the Ukermark.*

On St John's day, between eleven and twelve o'clock, the beech-nuts open. If it then rains in them, the mast will fail; if the weather is fine, the mast will be good. The nuts then close up again. *Neighbourhood of Hessen-Oldendorf.*

If anyone wishes to have a goblin (Kobold), he must go, on St John's day, between twelve and one at noon, into the forest, to an anthill, on which he will find a bird sitting, to which he must speak certain words, when it will transform itself into a little fellow and jump into a bag held ready for the purpose, and in which he must carry him home, where he will perform all the work committed to him, with the utmost speed. *Perleberg.*

On St John's day children should be weaned; then they will have good luck. *Stendal.*

On St John's day, between eleven and twelve at noon, a burdock root should be dug up. Under it will be found a coal, which is good for many things. *Stendal.*

## Harvest Customs

Formerly it was the custom at harvest to leave a bunch standing on the field, round which the reapers danced, throwing up their caps and crying, 'Waul, Waul, Waul,' or 'Wôl, Wôl, Wôl.' *Hageburg and environs of the Steinhudersee.*[1]

Throughout the whole Ukermark, and in many of the parts adjacent, the custom prevails at the end of the rye-harvest, and, in some places, at the carrying in of every kind of grain, to make a puppet out of the last sheaf, and either to carry it home rejoicing with the last load, or let it be borne to the village by the girl who is the last ready with her binding. In accordance with the one or the other of these usages, the custom is called *bringing the old man* (den ollen brengen), or it is said of the girl, *she has the old man* (dei het den ollen). Customs nearly akin to the above-mentioned prevail in several other places.[2]

At Grochwitz, near Torgau, it is a saying at Bartholomew tide, 'Now Herke is abroad, now we must get in our winter corn, else it will be spoiled.'

At Heteborn, when the flax was not housed at Bartholomew tide, it was formerly the saying, 'Frau Harke will come.'

About Halberstadt they say that in the dog days the crows do not drink.

When the rye is housed the storks depart, and all assemble on the Blocksberg, where they bite one of their number to death. *Brill near Aurich.*

## St Michael's Day

On St Michael's day no work is done in the field. *Rauen.*

Nor is there any spinning. *Altmark*

---

1  See Grimm, J., *Deutsche Mythologie*, op. cit., pp. 142, 143. Wôl is no doubt a corruption of Wôd (Woden).
2  For old harvest customs in England, see Brockett's *Gloss. of N. Country Words*, voce Melldoll, and Halliwell's *Archaic Dict.*, voce Mare.

## St Martin's Day

In many places a roasted goose is the orthodox fare on St Martin's day.

## St Andrew's Eve[1]

On St Andrew's eve the girls can cause their future sweethearts or husbands to appear to them in a dream. For this purpose, before going to sleep, they repeat the following rimes:

> Andreas-Abend ist heute,
> Schlafen alle Leute,
> Schlafen alle Menschenkind,
> Die zwischen Himmel und Erde sind,
> Bis auf diesen einzigen Mann,
> Der mir zur Ehe werden kann.

> *St Andrew's eve is today,*
> *Sleep all people,*
> *Sleep all children of men,*
> *Who are between heaven and earth,*
> *Except this only man,*
> *Who may be mine in marriage.*

If a girl desires to know in what neighbourhood the man dwells, who is one day to be her husband, she must go, between eleven and twelve o'clock at night, in perfect silence, into the garden, shake the hedge, and repeat these words:

> Erbzaun ich schüttel Dich,
> Ich rüttel Dich.
> Wo mein fein Liebchen wohnt, da regt sichs.
> Kann er sich nicht selber melden,
> So lass nur ein Hündchen bellen.

> Old hedge, I shake thee,
> I jog thee.
> Where my gentle lover dwells, there let there be stirring.
> If he cannot announce himself,
> Then only let a little dog bark.

Then will a dog be heard to bark in the neighbourhood where the future lover dwells.

---

1    This title is from Harrys, op. cit., ii, p. 25. The matter is from the Upper Harz, and oral.

The future husband may be also made to appear on St Andrew's eve by the following process. At nightfall let a girl shut herself up naked in her sleeping room, take two beakers, and into one pour clear water, into the other wine. These let her place on the table, which is to be covered with white, and repeat the following words,

> Dresmes
> Mein lieber Sankt Andrea!
> Lass doch vor mir erscheinen
> Den Herzallerliebsten meinen.
> Soil er mir werdeu reich,
> Schenkt er mir eine Kanne Wein;
> Soll er mir werden arm,
> So schenke win eine Kanne Wasser.

> *My dear Saint Andrew!*
> *Let now appear before me*
> *My heart's most dearly beloved.*
> *If he shall be rich,*
> *He will pour a cup of wine;*
> *If he is to be poor,*
> *Let him pour a cup of water.*

or,
> Bettspond, ich trete Dich,
> Sankt Andres, ich bitt Dich:
> Lass doch erscheinen
> Den Herzallerliebsten meinen.
> Soll ich mit ihm werden reich,
> Kommt er mit dem grünen Zweig;
> Soll ich mit ihm werden arm,
> Kommt er mit dem Knaust Brod im Arm.

> *Bedstead, I tread thee,*
> *Saint Andrew, I pray thee:*
> *Let now appear*
> *My heart's most dearly beloved.*
> *If I shall be rich with him,*
> *He will come with a green bough;*
> *If I shall be poor with him,*
> *He will come with a crust of bread in his arm.*

When that is done, the form of the future husband will enter at the door and drink out of one of the cups. If he is poor, he will drink of the water; if rich, he will take the wine.

An over-curious girl once summoned her future husband in the above manner. Precisely as the clock struck twelve he appeared, drank of the wine, laid a three-edged dagger on the table and vanished. The girl put the dagger into her trunk. Some years after there came a man from a distant part to the town where the girl dwelt, bought property there, and married her. He was in fact the identical person whose form had already appeared to her. Some time after their marriage, the husband chanced to open the trunk, and there found the dagger, at the sight of which he became furious. 'Thou art then the girl,' cried he, 'who years ago forced me to come hither from afar in the night; and it was no dream. Die therefore!' and with these words he thrust the dagger into her heart.

Hence if the future husband, when he appears, lays such a thing on the table, it must be destroyed; for if he again sees what he then brought with him, he will at least bear a grudge towards his wife, for having by her spell caused him so much anxiety and pain.

If anyone wishes to know whether he (or she) will die in the following year, let him (or her) on St Andrew's eve, before going to bed, make on the table a little pointed heap of flour. If on the following morning the heap has fallen asunder, the party will die.

On St Andrew's eve it may also be learned which of the persons present love one another, or will one day be united. For this purpose a vessel with pure water is placed on a table, and on the water are laid little cups of silver foil inscribed with the names of the persons whose future is to be ascertained. These little cups are called 'nappelpfäng' (cup-pennies). If a young man's cup comes so near to that of a girl, that they both seem to cleave together, they will make a match. By the nappelpfängs it may also be seen, whether a loving pair will one day be legally united; in which experiment one of the cups represents the bride, one the bridegroom, and a third the priest. If the three come together so that the priest stands before the other two, the lovers may cherish the hope of being wedded.

On St Andrew's eve young girls may ascertain what coloured hair their future husbands have. For this object there formerly prevailed, and probably still prevails, the so-called *hair-snatching*. If a girl wishes to know the colour of her future husband's hair, she must take hold of the latch of the door and thrice call out, 'Gentle love, if thou lovest me, show thyself.' She must then quickly open the door a little way, and make a rapid grasp out in the dark, and she will find in her hand a lock of her future mate's hair. But she must be quite alone in the house, and make the trial at night between the hours of eleven and twelve, and unknown to anyone.

# Christmas

The custom is widespread among the country people throughout the whole north of Germany of having a man on Christmas Eve to enter the apartment, disguised with a long beard, and enveloped either in fur or in pea-straw, who asks the children whether they can pray, and, if they stand the trial, rewards them with apples, nuts and gingerbread (pepper-cakes); and, on the other hand, punishes those that have learned nothing. In the Middle Mark the name most generally given to this personage is De hêle Christ (the Holy Christ), or Knecht Ruprecht. In other parts he is called Hans Ruprecht, which is sometimes corrupted into Rumpknecht; in Mecklenburg he is known as Rû Clås (Rough Nicholas); in the Altmark and as far as East Friesland, as Bûr and Bullerclås He sometimes carries a long staff and a bag of ashes, and has little bells on his clothes. With the bag he beats those children who have not learned to pray, and is for that reason called also Aschenclås. Sometimes he rides about on a white horse, and not infrequently has with him a sort of Jack Pudding, as an attendant. Accompanied by fairies, as they call them, or men dressed as old women, with blackened faces, he appears in some places, and is occasionally attended by one enveloped in pea-straw, who is called the bear, and led by a long chain. In many places the 'Holy Christ' – usually a young girl clad in white – who causes the youngsters to pray, and the rider on the white horse, appear as distinct persons. In some towns in Westphalia the white horse makes its appearance at Christmas or New Year's day. In Osnabrück it is called the Spanish horse.

On the isle of Usedom, Ruprecht goes about at Christmas, making the children pray; but under this denomination three persons are comprised, one of whom bears a rod and a bag of ashes, another bears the 'Klapperbock', which is a pole on which a goatskin is hung, surmounted by a goat's head of wood, to the under-jaw of which a line is fastened, which passing through the upper one runs through the throat, so that when pulled by the bearer, the two jaws make a rattling together. With this Klapperbock those children that do not know how to pray are beaten. Last of all the third person appears riding on a white horse. In all these places Christmas presents, wrapped in almost countless coverings, are thrown at the door of the party to be gifted, the giver crying out, 'Jûlklapp'.

In the neighbourhood of Boitzenburg in the Ukermark, Winter and Summer formerly went about at Christmas, contending with each other for precedence. It was usually two old women by whom the contest was represented. Summer carried a scythe and a rake, Winter a flail, with which each indicated the labours to be performed in those two seasons. A peasant of Hardenbeck still retained in his memory the following fragment of their respective speeches:

#### Winter

Ich bin den Winter stolz,
Ich baue Brücken ohne Holz.

*I am the winter proud,*
*I build bridges without wood.*

#### Summer

Ich bin der Summer fein,
Ich mähe mein Korn,
Und harke es wohl auf,
Und fahr es in die Scheun.

*I am the summer fine,*
*I mow my corn,*
*And rake it well together,*
*And carry it into the barn.*

#### Winter

Ich dresche das Korn und fahr es zur Stadt,
Dass jeder seine Nahrung davon hat.

*I thrash the corn and carry it to the city,*
*That everyone may have his sustenance therefrom.*

Whoever is desirous of knowing how the weather will be in the coming year, must on Christmas Eve take an onion, cut it through, and out of it make twelve cups, put salt into every one, and then place them in a row. The months corresponding to those cups in which the salt on the following morning is found wet, will be wet, and the contrary.   *Querfurt*

If a girl desires to know of what condition her future lover will be, she must on Christmas night listen at the large kettle walled into the stove (Ofenblase). If the water in it makes a roaring noise, he will be a smith; and so, according to the various tones of the water, the several trades may be determined.   *Edersleben near Sangerhausen*

If straw be drawn at Christmas from the roof of an inherited dwelling, and taken to the barn and thrashed, and grains of corn be found in it, it betokens good luck for the coming year.   *Ibid.*

At Elliehausen, near Göttingen, they lay the fodder for the cattle at Christmas out in the open air: then will the cattle thrive well.

In the whole country between Adelepsen and Minden it is believed that the hop becomes green on Christmas night, and comes forth even from under the deepest snow, but that afterwards nothing more of it is to be seen. The same belief prevails in other places.

In the territory of Münster[1] the custom of *windowing* still exists. At Christmas the young men enter through the window to their sweethearts, and continue with them all night. The parents do not disturb them, knowing it will be a match. If the girl is averse to the suitor, she drives him out of the window with a broom.  *From Delmenhorst*

In Berlin, the boys go about on the 'Weinachtsmarkt' selling what they call Waldteufel. These. are cylinders of pasteboard open beneath, but above fastened with horsehair to a wooden handle, which when swung round, send forth a humming sound. Wooden rattles and paper flags are sold at the same time.

At Christmas green kale should be fetched from the garden of the neighbour three doors off, and some of it given to every beast in the stalls. It protects them against witchcraft.  *Camern*

If at the Christmas festival a woman boils green kale, takes the ladle with which it was stirred, and goes with it, concealed under her apron, to the church door, just as the priest is saying the Pater noster, she will discover who are the witches of the place, and that by their extraordinary, but otherwise invisible, headgear. But she must stay for a moment only, else she runs the risk of being threatened and persecuted by the evil one.

*Camern*

All domestic utensils must at this time be kept in safe custody: not one of them should be lent out, though they are occasionally asked for by those who would injure the owner.[2]  *Camern*

If anyone, with moderate fodder, will have sound and fat horses, let him take a bundle of hay, go with it on Christmas night at midnight thrice round the church, and give it to the horses.  *Camern*

## The New Year

In many places, particularly in the Harz, and westward as far as the Weser, it is the custom on New Year's eve to fire guns, which they call shooting the new year.[3]

In some parts of East Friesland they bake at the new year Nüjårskaukjes, a sort of thin cake pressed into a mould of iron, in which the figures of a horse and other animals are represented.

---

1   Also in Holstein and Danish Friesland, though not limited to any particular season of the year.
2   By witchcraft?
3   This custom is universal also in Denmark.

In the Saterland it is the custom for the young men to bring into the house of the girls they wish to court, and also for neighbours to each other's houses, a 'Wêpelrôt' (called also a 'Tûnskêr') with these words:

> Hier brang wi jô êne wêpelrôt;
> woi jü mi wet rêke,
> so moije jô nit lang bedonkje.

> *Here bring we you a wêpelrôt;*
> *if you will give me something,*
> *you must not long consider.*

Saying these words they usually fire off a pistol, and throw the Wêpelrôt into the house, and then run off with all speed. The people of the house then run after the thrower and endeavour to catch him. If they overtake him, he is brought back, and must either ride on the kettle-hook or drink water mixed with soot (rôtwasser). Afterwards they entertain him. The Wêpelrôt is made of a willow staff, on the top of which a garland in the form of a wheel is fastened, the spokes of which protrude through the circumference, and on their points have apples stuck. In the middle of the wheel there is a broad ornament of gold foil, from which issue over the whole garland thick, white, ray-like bunches of willow shavings.

In the neighbourhood of Görlitz and in the Ukermark, on New Year's Eve, they lay straw-bands at mealtime under the table, on which they place their feet. When the meal is over, one of the party creeps on all-fours under the table, and another sits upon him and draws forth the straw-bands. These he takes into the garden and binds them round the trees; they will then bear well.

On New Year's Eve quite fresh flax must be put on the distaff, and on New Year's morning a brand-new shirt of newly-spun linen should be put on. On New Year's Eve also there must be no winding, else the reel would turn incessantly the whole year through.    *Kirchboitzen near Hudemühlen*

On New Year's day one must eat millet or herring; then one will have money throughout the year. Others eat of nine (or seven) different dishes, but among which there must be Mohnstriezel'.[1]    *Stendal*

Whoever sees his shadow without a head on the eve of St Silvester, will die in the next year.

---

1    A food made of pounded poppy seeds mixed with white bread and milk.

# Twelfthtide

In many places it is said there may be no spinning at this season, but that feathers must be plucked. At Pechüle, near Luckenwalde, they say the tubes of the plucked feathers should be preserved, as they are good against moths, bugs and other vermin.

In the country between Hameln and Minden, and in other places, it is said that no dung should be carried out during the twelve days of Christmas (or Twelfths); else the cattle will be sick in the following year, or wolves will be drawn to the stall.

In some parts of Oldenburg it was formerly said that no wheel should turn during the twelve days; consequently there was neither spinning nor any carting out of dung. In some few houses all this is observed even at the present day. In such houses no sewing goes forward; but if it is indispensable, they go to a neighbour's.

In some places on the left bank of the Weser they say, that whoever spins or winds on Twelfth-day eve, or during the Twelfths, will get, instead of yarn, black-puddings or sausages. In other places they say, that those who spin during the Twelfths spin toads into the house.

Brooms bound during the Twelfths protect against witchcraft. When the cattle are first driven out in spring, such a broom should be laid on the threshold over which they have to pass; then nothing evil can harm them throughout the year. If a weasel has caused the udder of a cow to swell, it must be stroked thrice crosswise with such a broom, which must then in silence be laid under the crib; and so the cow will get well.   *Prignitz*

In the Twelfths thread should be spun, and broken arms or legs be bound five or six times round with it, then they will speedily become sound.   *Grochwitz*

In the Twelfths a piece of yarn should be spun and wound the contrary way, through which if a child that is unquiet be put thrice it will be quiet. Or it may be put as many times through the steps of a ladder, or through its mother's wedding-dress.   *Usedom*

Into yarn spun during the Twelfths no moths will come.

*Liepe near Rathenow*

In the Twelfths neither baking utensils nor wood may lie before the oven.   *Wredenhagen in Mecklenburg*

In the Twelfths no peas should be eaten.

*Ukermark, Mecklenburg, Thuringia*

In the Twelfths, but especially on Christmas Day, green kale, pig's head and pudding (sausage) of lights should be eaten.   *Ukermark*

At Quatzow in Mecklenburg the prohibitions during the Twelfths are still rigidly observed. Many animals may not be called by their right name, and, instead of *fox,* one must say *long-tail;* instead of *mouse, floor-runner* (Bönlöper), etc.[1] Whoever neglects so to do pays a fine, which is afterwards spent in drinking.

In the Havelland it is a saying, that in the Twelfths they have a calendar for the whole year; i.e. as the weather is during the twelve days, so it will be the whole year.

Those who wear linen made from yarn spun during the Twelfths will be devoured by the wolf.  *Usedom and Wollin*

Whatever is dreamed during the Twelfths will come to pass in the twelve months of the year.  *Arnstadt*

If hens are fattened with peas during the Twelfths, they will lay many eggs.  *Camern*

Animals, unless known to you, are not to be trusted during the Twelfths, as the witches often assume their forms, particularly those of cats, dogs, three-legged hares, etc., in order to steal unobserved into houses and seek out their booty. If a person makes three crosses with his hand against them, he is safe from them.  *Camern*

To protect cattle against harm in the Twelfths, something of steel should be concealed in their provender, a scythe or the like; they should also be fed with stolen kale.  *Grabow in Mecklenburg*

In the Twelfths magpies should be shot and burnt to powder, which is good for the ague.  *Lausitz*


## Supernatural Beings of Twelfthtide

In the greater part of the north of Germany the belief is not yet wholly defunct, particularly among the peasantry, of the wandering of certain supernatural beings during the twelve days of Christmas; although, in place of the old heathenish idea with regard to such beings, we have now usually the harmless threat only of certain punishments for those who, by working, especially by spinning, violate the injunction to keep this time holily. The name, however, of these beings is, although often in mere joke, still combined with the threatened punishment, but the belief in them is now almost everywhere regarded as superstition; and not infrequently, instead of the old prohibitory formula, a facetious one is used, like the following: 'Those who do not spin in the Twelfth may not wind on the thirteenth.'

In Usedom and Wollin they say, 'The Waud will come', when all is not spun off.

---

1   See p. 287.

In the Twelfths Frû Gode makes her tour and befouls the distaffs of those who have not spun all off on Twelfth day. *Neighbourhood of Neu-Strelitz as far as Röbel.* In the territory of Schwerin the same is said of Frû Wôd in Thymen and Godendorf, of Frû Wås, or Frû Wåsen.[1]

In the Twelfths Frû Gaue makes her tour at the head of the Wild Hunt; on which account people keep their doors shut, and avoid going out at night, from the fear of meeting her.[2] *Grabow in Mecklenburg.*

Frû Wågen (in some places Frû Gôden, Gôëd, Gôïk, Gôdke, Gôdsche) comes in the night and befouls the flax, if it be left on the distaff at night during the Twelfths. *Mechow, on the frontier of Mecklenburg, etc.*

In some parts she is called the Fuik, the Fui, or the Fricke, in others, Frû Herken.

In some villages on the Huy they say that when between the old and the new year anything is left on the distaff, the 'Märtche' or 'Märtchen' will come.

## The Mârt – Mârte – Mârten – Nachtmârt (The Nightmare)

Under all these denominations is designated that spectral being which places itself on the breast of the sleeping, depriving them of the powers of motion and utterance. Its approach is heard like the gnawing of a mouse, or the soft tread of a cat. If anyone puts on inherited gloves and seizes it, he can hold it fast; or if every aperture in the room be stopped, as soon as the sighing and groaning of the sleeper begin, the Mârt will be caught.

A powerful remedy against the pressure of the nightmare is to cross the arms and legs before going to sleep.

In the pines, branches are often found quite curled together, having almost the appearance of nests. When it rains, persons should be careful not to pass under such branches; for whoever is touched with a raindrop from one of these nests will in the night be oppressed with the 'Murraue'.[3]

Of persons whose eyebrows grow together they say he (or she) is a Murraue.[4]

Murraues are both male and female, and are always Sunday's children.[5] If a Murraue presses anyone, he must say he will give it something; it will then come on the following day and fetch the present. *Braunsdorf near Fürstenwald.*

1 See pp. 481–2; p. 307, No. 46; p. 422, No. 10.
2 See p. 482.
3 The Wendish name for the nightmare.
4 See p. 346.
5 See pp. 370; pp. 424, No. 33.

The Murraue creeps up the body of the sleeper. Its weight is first felt on the feet, then on the belly, and lastly on the breast, when the sufferer can no longer move a limb. If the patient by chance surmises who it is, he must instantly address it by name; it must then make its retreat.   *Teupitz*

If the sufferer supposes it to be an acquaintance, he needs only to call it by name, and it will appear bodily.

It is good against the nightmare, when going to bed, to turn one's shoes with the toes outward from the bed.[1]

When there are seven boys or seven girls in a family, one is a nightmare, unknown to him or herself.[2]

## Dråk – Kobold – Fire-drake

The Dråk appears as a fiery stripe passing through the air, as large as the pole that is placed across a cartload of hay. If a person on seeing him does not get under shelter, he will be befouled by him, and not get rid of the stench till long after. *Swinemünde*. He brings those persons something that have made a compact with him.   *Barsinghausen on the Deister*

The Drake (Trâch) is as large as a cauldron, and a person can very well sit in him, and fly with him to any desired spot.   *Bockswiesen near Grund*

The Kobold appears also as a fiery stripe with a broad head, which he usually shakes from one side to the other. If he enters a house and the serving-man takes a wheel off the wagon, he must burn himself out of the house. On the earth the Kobold appears like a black cat.   *Altmark*

The Drake carries treasures through the air. If a person sees him, he must cry, 'Halb part!' He will then bring him something. But he must take care to stand under a roof, or the Drake will cover him with filth, which he will not again get rid of.   *Hassleben near Prenzlau*

The Drake or Kobold traverses the air as a blue stripe, and brings corn. If a knife or a fire-steel be cast at him, he will burst, and must let fall that which he is carrying.   *Pechüle near Luckenwald*

The Drake has a head as large as a milk-pail, and a long tail.   *Mürow*

The Drake carries treasures through the air like a bird; whoever possesses him, he will lie with them in a cask like a calf. But the Kobold curries the horses, helps to draw when the cart is heavy, and takes care in general of everything belonging to the stable and carts.   *W. Buchholz*

The Kobold brings luck to those that possess him. The Drake brings all kinds of things, as cream, cheese, etc. A person must consign himself to him with his own blood.   *Sachsenburg near Oldisleben*

---

1   See p. 424, No. 34.
2   See p. 449.

The Puks, Kobold, or Drake is a little fellow with red jacket and cap, who may be seen passing through the air as a fiery stripe.  *Westliche Ukermark*

The Fürdråk (Fire-drake) or Lütche Ole is the evil one. The Stepke, Fürdråk or Mertche are one.  *Dalle on the Lüneburg Heath*

If you desire to secure the Drake and compel him to yield up a part of that which he is carrying with him, two persons must place their legs across each other's, in silence, or draw off the fourth wheel of a wagon, and then hasten to get under a roof, else it will go badly.

In the Saterland they call the Kobold Alrûn,[1] a denomination which occurs also in East Friesland. According to the account of a woman in Nordmohr, he is a little fellow scarcely a foot high, whom they enclose in a 'spind'[2] and feed with biscuit and milk, whereby he becomes so strong that he can carry a whole load of rye in his mouth to his master. In Neustadt-Gödens it is a saying, when one has luck at play, that he has an Alrûn in his pocket.

The Bier-esel inhabits the cellar. He gets the beer into the house, rinses the bottles and glasses, washes down the tables and the like; for all which a can of beer must be set for him at night; else he would be angry and break everything.  *Grochwitz near Torgau*

## Dwarfs

The most usual name for these in the north of Germany is 'Unnerêrdschke' (Subterraneans). In the Harz they call them 'Querje', 'Querxe' (Dwarfs). In Scharrel, in the Saterland, they are called 'Olkers', and are said to be buried in the old grave-mounds, for which reason the vessels found in these are called 'Olkerspött' (Olker's pottery). They are also called 'Bargmänkes' (Hill-mannikins), or 'Erdmänkes' (Earth-mannikins).

When the dwarfs have stolen a child and left a changeling in its stead, this must not be touched with the hands, but the cradle must be overturned, so that it falls out, then with an old broom it should be swept out at the door, when the dwarfs will come and bring back the stolen child. Changelings are not more than twenty years old.[3]  *Görlitz*

In Bergkirchen the matting of the horses' manes is ascribed to the Subterraneans.

1  See Grimm, J., *Deutsche Mythologie*, op. cit., p. 1153.
2  A measure in Lüneburg equal to an eighth of a scheffel or bushel.
3  Quite at variance with the preceding accounts. See pp. 460–2 and pp. 349–50..

# Jack o' Lanterns

In the south Altmark they call the Jack o' lanterns 'Dickepôten'. If a person prays as soon as he sees one, he draws it to him; if he curses, it retires.[1] In some parts they are called Huckepôten, and Tückbolde, and are said to have been persons that removed landmarks.[2] In the neighbourhood of Magdeburg they call them Lüchtemännekens. To cause them to appear, it is sufficient to call out, 'Ninove, Ninove.'

Jack o' lanterns mislead persons, though they are sometimes serviceable. In many places they call them land-measurers,[3] and are seen like figures of fire, or running to and fro with a red-hot measuring-rod. These are persons who have falsely sworn away land, or fraudulently measured it, or removed landmarks. They are frequently said to be the souls of unbaptised children, that have no rest in the grave, and must hover between heaven and earth.[4] They are also called running fires, and wild fires.

# The Nix

The Nickelmann or Håkelmann sits in the water with a long well-hook, with which he drags children down, when they approach too near the water's edge. *Thale*

When the water-fowl is heard to pipe in the Bode, someone must be drowned; the millers in Thale, therefore, as soon as they hear it, throw in a black hen.

When the tranquillity of the water is disturbed, either by angling or with nets, the Nix may frequently be heard to laugh and clap his hands; for somebody will be drowned. *Teupitz, Görlitz*

# The Wild Huntsman

Many assert that the Wild Huntsman and his train consist of the ghosts of deceased huntsmen.

The nocturnal huntsman carries his head under his arm, has many dogs with him, and as he goes takes the people along with him. If anyone calls to him to bring him a piece of meat, he will find it at his door in the morning; but he can never rid himself of it again, unless by desiring the huntsman to bring salt,[5] when the meat will disappear, and the hunter himself will not return. *Görlitz*

---

1 See p. 490.
2 See pp. 296–7.
3 See pp. 436 and 375.
4 See p. 375 and note 3.
5 See p. 495.

In the Twelfths the Helljäger hunts on the earth, at other times he rides through the air. All doors should therefore be shut early, else three dogs will run into the house and stay in it till the next Twelfths[1]      *Moor-hausmoor*

## The Devil

Never to miss one's aim in shooting, one must repeat

> Komm teufel und halte mir das thier,
> Ich gebe dir meine seele dafür.
>
> *Come, devil, and hold for me the game,*
> *I'll give thee my soul in return.*

Or the communion-bread should be taken out of the mouth, and a gun loaded with it.[2]      *Swinemünde*

'The devil has thrashed peas upon him,' is said of one whose face is pock-marked.

## Marriage

When a bridal pair is going to church, it is the custom, before they leave the house, to throw a firebrand on the threshold over which they must pass. The mother of the bride strews dill in her shoes, saying:

> Dille lass nicht Wille,
> Salz lass nicht nach.
>
> *Dill cease not from will,*
> *Salt relax not.*

The bride and bridegroom also strew dill and salt in their shoes, as a protection against witchcraft. When before the altar, they must stand as near together as possible, so that no one can see between them.[3]      *Rauen.*

Marriages should take place in the full of the moon; then everything afterwards will be in full. Tuesdays and Fridays are particularly dedicated to marriages.      *Stendal*

At Marthe, near Templin, on a wedding-day, it was formerly the custom for three men, disguised as women, but with blackened faces, to come at midnight and play all sorts of pranks, and at last make the bride dance with them. A nearly similar custom existed also in other places.

On the wedding-night all the old pottery is to be thrown out before the door of the bride: the more shards the more luck.      *Rauen*

---

1   See pp. 471, *sq.*      2   See p. 519.
3   See p. 305, No. 10.

In the Saterland it was formerly a custom to put a ladle into the hands of a bride, as soon as she entered her husband's house, and to lead her thrice round the fire.

## Birth and Baptism

When there is a newborn child in the house, nothing ought to be lent out; else the child will have nothing hereafter.  *Mellin*

In some towns it is a common practice on the birthday of a child to give it a cake with a *life's light* placed on it, which must not be extinguished, but allowed to burn to the end.

In the cradle of a newborn child there should be laid orant,[1] blue marjoram, black cumin, a right shirt-sleeve and a left stocking; the 'Nickert' then cannot harm it.  *Pechüle*

If a child is born with a mole, it must be stroked with the hand of a dead person of the other sex: as the dead decays, so will the mole pass away. Or go in the moon increase to a crossway, look at the moon, at the same time stroking the mole with the hand, and say,

> Alles was ich sehe nimmt zu,
> alles was ich streiche nimmt ab.  *Swinemünde*

> All that I see increases,
> all that I stroke decreases.

One ought not to go with an unbaptised child to anyone: it brings misfortune to the house.  *Stendal*

## Death and Burial

If the master of the house dies, one must go into the garden and shake the trees, saying, 'The master is dead, the master is dead,' else they will decay. In like manner a person must go to the beehive, knock, and repeat the same words, else the bees will fly away.  *Rauen*

When a person dies, the window must be opened, that the soul may fly out. If it is a man, a comb, a razor, and soap should be laid in the coffin.

*Rauen*

If a person dies in a house, there should be no baking in it on that day.

*Rauen*

If new-baked bread has a crack, one of the family will die soon.  *Rauen*

If a person is sick, it should be noticed, after supper, what direction the smoke of the candle, when blown out, takes: if towards the church, the person will die.  *Swinemünde*

---

1   Antirrhinum (snapdragon), or, according to others, marrubium (horehound).

The soul of a person that dies on shipboard passes into a bird: when it appears, it is to predict the death of another.

If it be wished to know whether an absent person is alive or dead, lay a piece of bread and a coal on the table, and exactly between both hold a darning needle suspended by a thread. If it moves more towards the bread, the person is well; if towards the coal, he is dead. In a similar manner it may be ascertained whether a sick person will recover or die.

*Rohrberg in the Altmark*

## Wounds, Diseases, etc.

If a person has wounded himself, let him cut in an upward direction a piece off from a branch of a fruit-tree, and apply it to the recent wound, so that the blood may adhere to it, and then lay it in some part of the house where it is quite dark, when the bleeding will cease.    *Mellin.*

*A charm against pain from a wound.*

> Christus lag und schlief,
> seine Wunden waren tief,
> sie kellten nicht,
> sie schwellten nicht,
> also sollen diese Wunden auch sein.
> I. N. G. d. V. u. s. w.                    *Swinemünde*

> *Christ lay and slept,*
> *his wounds were deep,*
> *they pained not,*
> *they swelled not,*
> *so shall these wounds also be.*
> *In the name, etc.*

*Another:*
> Heil sind die Wunden,
> heil sind die Stunden,
> heilig ist der Tag,
> da Wunden und Wehtag schach.
> I. N. G. u. s. w.

> *Whole are the wounds,*
> *whole are the hours,*
> *holy is the day,*
> *when the wounds and illness befell.*
> *In the name, etc.*

*When a limb has been amputated*, the charmer takes a twig from a broom, presses the wound together with it, wraps it in the bloody linen, and lays it in a dry place, saying:

> Unserm Herrn Christus seine Wunden,
> die werden nicht verbunden,
> aber diese Wunden, die warden verbunden.
> I. N. G. u. s. w.                              *Swinemünde*

> *The wounds of our Lord Christ,*
> *they are not bound,*
> *but these wounds, they are bound.*
> *In the name, etc.*

*If anyone has a cut-wound*, let it be bound with adhesive plaster, cooled with vinegar and water, and the following words be uttered:

> Du Blut des Lebens halte an,
> wie Christus stand am Kreuzesstamm,
> halt an du Blut die Ader dein,
> weil Christus stand am Kreuzesstamm.
> I. N. G. u. s. w.                              *Swinemünde*

> *Thou blood of life, stop!*
> *as Christ stood at the cross's stem,*
> *stop, thou blood, thy vein,*
> *because Christ stood at the cross's stem.*
> *In the name, etc.*

To staunch blood

> Ich ging über eine Brücke,
> worunter drei Ströme liefen,
> der erste hiess Gut,
> der zweite hiess Blut,
> der dritte hiess Eipipperjahn;
> Blut du sollst stille stain.
> I. N. G. u. s. w. (dreimal)                    *Swinemünde*

> *I went over a bridge under which*
> *three streams ran,*
> *the first was called Gut,*
> *the second was called Blut (blood),*
> *the third was called 'Eipipperjahn';*
> *blood, thou shalt stand still.*
> *In the name, etc. (thrice)*

*Another:*　Es gingen drei Jungfern en hohlen Weg,
die erste nahm das runde,
die zweite nahm das trull,
die dritte drückt es nieder,
dass es nicht komme wieder.
I. N. G. u. s. w.　　　　　　　　　　　　*Mellin*

*There went three maidens the hollow way,*
*the first took the round,*
*the second took the 'trull',*
*the third pressed it down,*
*that it may not come again.*
*In the name, etc.*

*A Latin spell for bad eyes, quoted by Grimm (p.1196), closely resembles this and also some of the following ones: 'Juvat subnectere incantationis formulam, qua in Marchia Brandenburgensi atque adjacentibus regionibus in ophthalmia curanda uti solent anus decrepitae, insanos ritus deperientes, quam quidem factis variis gesticulationibus ac digitis ante dolentes oculos ter decussatim motis, rauco susurramine semel atque iterum emutire consuescunt, ita autem habent: "Ibant aliquando tres puellae in via virente, prima noverat remedium aliquod contra suffusionem oculorum, altera noverat aliquid contra albuginem, et tertia profecto contra inflammationem, eaeque sanabant una ratione omnia."' In nomine Patris, etc.*

**When a person has an ague,** he must go to the churchyard, and there take a bone from a grave. This, between eleven and twelve o'clock at night, when all is quiet, he must burn in silence, and drink the coal in water: he will then get rid of the fever.　　*Nahmitz*

**When a person has an ague,** he must go into the forest, walk round an oak, and say:

Goden abend du gode olle,
Ick brenge dî dat warme un dat kolle.

Good-evening, thou good one old,
I bring thee the warm and the cold.

The fever will then depart.　　　　　　　　　　*Mittelmark*

*Or* he may go to a river, dip the right foot in, and say:

> In dies Wasser tret ich,
> Christi Blut anbet ich,
> dies Wasser mid Christi Blut
> ist für das sieben und siebenzigsterlei Fieber gut.[1]

> *In this water step I,*
> *Christ's blood adore I,*
> *this water and Christ's blood*
> *is for the seventy-seventh fever[1] good.*

This must be spoken thrice in the name of God, and water at the same time taken from the river and drunk: the fever will then go away.     *Swinemünde*

*To write away an ague.* Write the following on a leaf:

> Des Fuchs ohne Lungen,
> der Storch ohne Zungen,
> die Taube ohne Gall
> hilft für das sieben mid siebenzigsterlei Fieber all.

> *The fox without lungs,*
> *the stork without tongue,*
> *the dove without gall*
> *help for the seven and seventieth fever all.*

If this leaf be worn round the neck, the fever will keep away.

*For the 'Zahnrose'* (Erysipelas in the teeth)     *Rauen*

> Es kam eine Jungfer aus Engelland,[2]
> eine Rose trug sie in ihrer Hand,
> bis die Sonne untergang,
> die sieben und siebsigsterlei Zahnrose verschwand.

> *There came a maiden from Engelland,*
> *a rose she carried in her hand,*
> *when the sun went down,*
> *the seven and seventieth zahnrose disappeared.*

---

1    A fever probably that was to be allowed to continue for seventy-seven days before it was checked by the spell.
2    Angeln?

*For the 'Hilge'* (eruption) *and the Rose* (erysipelas) it is good to stroke them downwards, blow thrice on the cross, and say:

> Es gingen drei Jungfern auf grünen Wegen,
> die eine pflückt die Blumen ab,
> die zweite pflückt die Liljen ab,
> die dritte trieb das Hilge unde die Rose ab.     *Swinemünde*

> *There went three maidens on the green ways,*
> *the first gathered flowers,*
> *the second gathered lilies,*
> *the third drove away the 'hilge' and the rose.*

*To cure the Rose.* Silently, and as well if after sunset, the wise man enters and examines the Rose, whether it is a running, 'brand',[1] or white Rose, and says accordingly:

> Brand (laufende, weisse) Rose
> ick böte[2] dî,
> Im namen Gottes verstrikst du dî
> I. N. G. u. s. w.

> *'Brand' (running, white), Rose, I expel thee,*
> *in God's name betake thee hence.*
> *In the name, etc.*

At the same time making the sign of the cross three times over the diseased part. This he must repeat on three several days. It is particularly good to do it on Fridays.     *Camern*

*To allay the 'Hilg'*

> Es gingen drei Jungfern an einen Berg,
> Des eine hat es schmal, der andre hat es platt.
> I. N. G. u. s. w.            *MS. from Swinemünde*

> *There went three maidens to a hill,*
> *the one had it narrow, the other had it flat.*
> *In the name, etc.*

---

1   Inflammatory.
2   Mhg. büefsen = wegschaffen, stillen.

*To allay the toothache*

> Du sollst nicht weh thun,
> du sollst nicht schellen,
> du sollst nicht schwellen,
> du sollst nicht ritten,
> du sollst nicht splitten,
> du sollst nicht weh thun.
> I. N. G. u. s. w.                    *MS. from Swinemünde*

> *Thou shalt not ache,*
> *thou shalt not break (scale, shell off),*
> *thou shalt not swell,*
> *thou shalt not torture (tear, rend),*
> *thou shalt not split,*
> *thou shalt not ache.*
> *In the name, etc.*

**When a person has toothache**, let him go and complain to a tree, by preference to a pear tree. This is to be done by taking hold of the tree, going thrice round it, and saying:

> Birnbaum, ich klage dir,
> drei Würmer die stechen mir;
> der einer ist grau,
> der andre ist blaue,
> der dritte ist roth,
> ich wollte wünschen sie wären alle drei todt.
> I. N. G. u. s. w.

> *Pear tree, I complain to thee,*
> *three worms sting me;*
> *the one is grey,*
> *the second is blue,*
> *the third is red,*
> *I would wish they were all three dead.*
> *In the name, etc.*

*For the ringworm or tetter.* Go to a yellow willow, stroke the tetter thrice with one of its branches, and say:

> Die Zeter und die Weide,
> die wollten beide streiten,
> die Weide, die gewann,
> die Zeter, die verschwand.
> I. N. G. u. s. w.                                            *Paretz*

> *The tetter and the willow,*
> *they would both contend,*
> *the willow, it won,*
> *the tetter it vanish'd.*
> *In the name, etc.*

*Or:*        Die Flechte und die Weide
> gingen beid' im Streite,
> die Weide, die verging,
> die Flechte, die verschwindt[1]            *Swinemünde*

> *The ringworm and the willow*
> *both enter'd into strife,*
> *the willow it decay'd,*
> *the tetter disappear'd.*

*Or:*        Der Mond und die Flecht
> die liegen beid' im Recht,
> die Flechte und der Mond
> fingen beide an zu gehn,
> der Mond, der gewann,
> die Flecht, die verschwand.

> The moon and the ringworm,
> they were both at strife,
> the ringworm and the moon
> began both to go,
> the moon he[2] won,
> the ringworm disappear'd.

1  verschwand?
2  See p. 14, note 2.

*For a fire*

> Es gingen drei Heiligen wohl über das Land,
> da begegnet ihnen des höllische Feuerbrand.
> Er sprach: Du sollst weichen,
> und der Schaden soll schleichen.
> I. N. G. u. s. w. (dreimal)          *MS. from Swinemünde*

> *There went three holy men over the land,*
> *there they met with a hellish fire.*
> *He said, Thou shalt withdraw,*
> *and the harm shall slink away.*
> *In the name, etc. (thrice)*

*To allay the pain of a burn*

> Es gingen drei heiligen Wehtag[1]
> auf einen schmalen Weg,
> der eine pflückt das Laub vom Baum,
> der andre pflückt das Gras vom Weg,
> der dritte nahm die Wehtag weg.
> I. N. G. u. s. w.          *MS. from Swinemünde*

> *There went three holy men*
> *upon a narrow way,*
> *the one pluck'd the leaves from the tree,*
> *the second pluck'd the grass from the way,*
> *the third took the malady away.*
> *In the name, etc.*

**When a person has burnt himself**, he must stroke the part upwards thrice, and say:

> Wie hoch ist der Häben,
> wie roth ist der Krebs,
> wie kalt is die Todtenhand,
> damit stille ich den Brand.
> I. N. G. u. s. w.          *Swinemünde*

> *As the heaven is high,*
> *as the crayfish is red,*
> *as the dead hand is cold,*
> *therewith still I the burn.*
> *In the name, etc.*

---

1  Wehtag is, no doubt, an error of the scribe or press.

*For the Stôt* (disorder of the eye, sty?). Take in silence a little stone from the field, press it on the eye, and lay it afterwards in the place whence it was taken. During the operation say thrice:

> Es gingen drei Jungfern auf grünen Wegen,
> die eine hob die Steine aus den Wegen,
> die zweite hob das Laub vom Baum,
> die dritte hob das Stôt aus dem Auge.
> I. N. G. u. s. w.                                    *Swinemünde*

> *There went three maidens on the green ways,*
> *one lifted the stones out of the ways,*
> *the second gather'd the leaves from the tree,*
> *the third removed the 'stôt' from the eye.*
> *In the name, etc.*

*To charm away the gout.* Let the patient completely strip himself before sunrise or after sunset, and say:

> Die[1] reissende, laufende Gicht,
> ich beschwöre dich bei dem höchsten Gericht,
> ich beschwöre dich bei dem höchsten Mann,
> der dir die reissende, laufende
> Gicht stillen kann.

> *Thou tearing, running (flying) gout,*
> *I conjure thee by the highest tribunal,*
> *I conjure thee by the highest man,*
> *who the tearing, running gout can allay.*

*For dizziness*

> Der Himmel ist hoch,✠
> die Wolken sind hell,✠
> so wie sich der Himmel✠ zertheilt✠
> zertheilt sich der Schwindel im augenblick und schnell.✠
> I. N. G. u. s. w.                          *MS. from Swinemünde*

> The heaven is high,
> the clouds are clear,
> so as the heaven dissolves,
> shall the dizziness dissolve in a moment and quickly.
> In the name, etc.

1   Du?

*To staunch blood.*[1]

> Auf unserm Herrn Gott sein Haupt,
> da blühen drei Rosen,
> die erste ist seine Tugend,
> die zweite ist seine Jugend,
> die dritte ist sein Will,
> Blut, steh du in des Wunde still,
> dass du weder Geschwüre
> noch Eitesbeulen gebest.
> I. N. G. u. s. w.

> *On the head of our Lord God*
> *there bloom three roses,*
> *the first is his virtue,*
> *the second is his youth,*
> *the third is his will.*
> *Blood, stand thou in the wound still,*
> *so that thou neither sore*
> *nor abscess givest.*
> *In the name, etc.*

*Or:*

> Bloet sta still!
> na uns Herr Christus syn Will,
> Im namen Gottes des Vaters und Sohn:
> nu steit dat Bloet schon.

> *Blood, stand still!*
> *after our Lord Christ's will.*
> *In the name of God the Father and Son:*
> *now the blood already stops.*

*Or:*

> Ich sage dir, Blut, stehe still,
> es ist Maria ihr Will, es ist Maria ihr Begehr,
> steh du mir nun und immermehr.
> I. N. G. u. s. w.

> *I say to thee, blood, stand still,*
> *it is Mary's will, it is Mary's desire,*
> *stand thou now and evermore.*
> *In the name, etc.*

---

1   The following rimes are from Müllenhoff, op. cit., pp. 511, *sqq.*

*For apoplexy (Mord)*

> Mord, du hest äer daelschlaen:
> unse Herr Christus segt,
> du schast wedder upstaen.
>
> *Apoplexy, thou hast struck her down:*
> *our Lord Christ sayeth,*
> *thou again shalt rise.*

*Or:*

> Uns Herr Christus un de Moert,
> de güngen tosamen daer en enge Poert.
> Uns Herr Christus de gewann,
> de Schlag und de Moert verschwand.
>
> *Our Lord Christ and the apoplexy*
> *went together through a narrow gate.*
> *Our Lord Christ won,*
> *the stroke[1] and apoplexy disappear'd.*

*For the gout.* Take hold of an oak, or a young shoot of one already felled (Ekenhessen), and say:

> Ekenhessen, ik klag dy,
> all de ryten Gicht de plagt my.
> Ik kann dar nich faer gaen,
> du kannst damit bestaen.
> Den eersten Vagel, de aewer dy flügt,
> den gif dat mit in de Flucht,
> de näem dat mit in de Lucht.
> I. N. G. u. s. w.
>
> *Oak-shoot, I to thee complain,*
> *all the torturing gout plagues me.*
> *I cannot for it go,*
> *thou canst stand it.*
> *The first bird that flies above thee,*
> *to him give it in his flight,*
> *let him take it with him in the air.*
> *In the name, etc.*

---

1    Paralytic.

*For the rickets*

> Engelsche Krankheit verswinn,
> wie de Dau an de Sünn,
> wie de Kukuk vör den Saevenstern,
>
> *English malady disappear,*
> *like the dew in the sun,*
> *like the cuckoo before the seven stars.*[1]

*For tetters*

> De Hechel un de Flechel,
> de gingen all beid aewer en Stechel.[2]
> De Hechel de gewunn,
> un de Flechel verswunn.
> I. N. G. u. s. w.
>
> *The hatchel and the ringworm,*
> *they both went over a stile.*
> *The hatchel won,*
> *and the ringworm disappear'd.*
> *In the name, etc.*

*For the tinea or scald head (Barmgrund).* Fetch water in silence, wash the head with it lukewarm, saying,

> So standen drei Mädchen wohl vor dem Brunn,
> de ene de wusch, de ander de wrung'.
> Darin ist verdrunken en Katt un en Hunt
> damit verdryw ik dy den Barmgrunt.
>
> *So stood three maidens before the well,*
> *the one, she wash'd, the second, she wrung.*
> *Therein were drown'd a cat and a dog,*
> *therewith I drive away thee, the barmgrund.*

Or, more intelligibly. To eradicate this eruption, let a person wash himself in a puddle, in which it is usual to drown dogs and cats, and repeat the formula: 'In this water, in which many a cat and dog has been drowned, do I mitigate the "barmgrund".'[3]

---

1   The ursa major, or Charles's wain.
2   Anglo-Saxon, stipel.
3   Grimm, J., *Deutsche Mythologie*, op. cit., p. cxlv.

*For the erysipelas (Helldink)*

>Ik segg: Helldink, Helldink,
>du schast ni stäken,
>du schast ni bräken.
>  Helldink, Helldink,
>du schast ni kellen,
>du schast ni schwellen.
>Dat schast du ny doen,
>Dat schast du ny doen.

>*I say: Helldink, Helldink,*
>*thou shalt not prick,*
>*thou shalt not break.*
>  *Helldink, Helldink,*
>*thou shalt not torment,*
>*thou shalt not swell.*
>*That shalt thou never do,*
>*That shalt thou never do.*

*Or:*

>Peter un Paul gingen aewert Moer.
>Wat begegen äer daer?
>  Helldink, Helldink –
>'Helldink, wo wullt du hin?'
>  'Na'n Dörp.'
>'Wat wullt du daer?'
>  'Kellen un schwellen un wee doen.'
>'Dat schast du ny doen.
>'Dat befäel ik dy in Gottes Namen.'

>*Peter and Paul went over a moor.*
>*What met them there?*
>*Helldink, Helldink.*
>*'Helldink, whither wilt thou?'*
>  *'To the village.'*
>*'What wilt thou there?'*
>  *'Torment and swell and cause pain.'*
>*'That thou shalt not do.*
>*'That I command thee in God's name.'*

Or:
        Hildink, ik ra' dy.
        Ra' ik dy nich seer,
        so jag' ik dy noch väel meer.
        I. N. G. u. s. w.

        *Helldink, I counsel thee.*
        *If I counsel thee not much,*
        *yet I drive thee away much more.*
        *In the name, etc.*

This is to be said thrice, after a pause thrice again, and after a second pause thrice again. At each time the diseased part is to be blown on crosswise.

Or:
Instead of blowing crosswise, fire may be struck with flint and steel in a cross direction:

        Hier schrief ik enen Rink
        mit en stalern Messer,
        De Rink is sunt,
        dat Hildink verschwund.

        *Here mark I a ring*
        *with a steel knife.*
        *The ring is whole,*
        *the heldink has disappeare'd.*

Or:
        Rode Ros' un witte Ros',
        dunkle Ros' un helle Ros', verswinn,
        wie de Dau vör de Sünn.

        *Red rose and white rose,*
        *dark rose and light rose, vanish,*
        *like the dew before the sun.*

*For the 'Bellrose':*

> Petrus und Paulus
> gingen uet Kruet te söken;
> daer wollen se de Ros' mit verteen,[1]
> de Kelleros', de Schwelleros',
> de Stäkeros', de Bräkeros', de Blätteros';
> awer allens wollen se damit verteen.
> I. N. G. u. s. w.

> *Peter and Paul*
> *went out plants to seek;*
> *there they would take the rose away with them,*
> *the paining-rose, the swelling rose,*
> *the pricking-rose, the breaking-rose, the leafy rose;*
> *but they would take away all with them.*
> *In the name, etc.*

*For an excrescence.* Lay the finger on it but without looking at it, and say:

> Was ich seh, das wächst,
> was ich [nicht] seh, das vergeht.
> I. N. G. u. s. w.

> *What I see, that waxes,*
> *what I see not, that decays.*
> *In the name, etc.*

*For warts* there is but one remedy; they are to be got rid of only in moonshine. During the moon's increase go into the open air, look steadfastly at the moon, and stroke with the hand over the warts, saying these words:

> Was ich ansehe, nimmt zu,
> was ich überstreiche, nimmt ab.

> *What I look on increases,*
> *what I stroke over decreases.*

---

1    For verziehen?

*For a whitlow*. Not to be uttered too rapidly, and only once each time.

> De Adel un de Stoel,
> de gungen beid an enen Poel,
> De Adel de verswunn,
> de Stoel de gewunn.
> I. N. G. u. s. w.

> *The whitlow and the stool,*[1]
> *they went both to a pool.*
> *The whitlow it disappear'd,*
> *the stool it won.*
> *In the name, etc.*

*For a pain in the finger*

> Ik rad' en Bäten
> mit Heisterknaken,
> mit Kreienföten,
> semi dy de Weedag' uten Finger staken.

> *I advise a cure*
> *with magpies' bones,*
> *with feet of crows,*
> *Finger that shall drive the pain out of thy finger.*

*For a sprained foot*

> Ik hol' rnyn Foet in'n Kattengang',[2]
> so stil ik wol den Gnirrband.[3]

> *I hold my foot in the cat's way,*
> *and so I still the sprain.*

---

1  Purgatio alvi?
2  Through which the cats can leap.
3  Correctly *Knirrband*.

*For a speck on the eye*

> Daer seten dre Jüngfern an den Weg,
> de een de puest dat Sant uten Weg,
> de ander de puest dat Lov vannen Boem,
> tie drürr de puest dat Mael von Oeg,
> I. N. G. u. s. w.

> *There sat three maidens in the way,*
> *one blew the sand out of the way,*
> *the second blew the leaves from the tree,*
> *the third blew the speck from the eye.*
> *In the name, etc.*

*For a sprained wrist.* At sunrise lay the arm, from the elbow to the point of the finger, flat on the threshold, and remain within the house. Let the charmer then take an axe, and place himself before the door, saying, 'I chop, I chop, I chop!' The patient is then to ask, 'What dost thou chop?' The operator will answer, 'The sprain.' Let the patient then take the axe, and stroke the arm with it crosswise thrice, in the name of God. The axe is then to be restored to its place in silence, and the affliction will subside.

*Swinemünde*

At Rauen, near Fürstenwalde, it is said, when a person has a violent headache, he has *the perverse,* or *black, elves.* The remedy is, to bind a cloth round his head at night, with which he is to sleep, and on the following morning to go with it to a wise man, who will charm the cloth; the elves will then depart. Besides the black elves, which are the worst, there are also red elves and white elves; but whatever their colour may be, the malady shows itself chiefly in causing a loss of memory.

If a child by much crying had got a rupture, take it to a young oak – split in two lengthwise, and draw the child through the split. Then bind the parts thus rent asunder together, and plaster the rent over with loam. If the oak continues growing and the wound heals up, the rupture will also be healed.   *Rauen – Delmenhorst*

*This method of curing a ruptured child was also known in England. White, in his History of Selborne, informs us that, 'in a farm-yard, near the middle of the village, stands at this day (an. 1789) a row of pollard ashes, which, by the seams and long cicatrices down their sides, manifestly show that, in former times, they have been cleft asunder. These trees, when young and flexible, were severed and held open by wedges, while ruptured children, stripped naked, were pushed through the apertures, under a persuasion that, by such a process, the poor babes would be cured of their infirmity. As soon as the operation was over, the tree, in the suffering part, was plastered with loam, and carefully swathed up. If the part coalesced and soldered together, as usually fell out, where the feat was performed with any adroitness at all, the party was cured; but where the cleft continued to gape, the operation, it was supposed, would prove ineffectual. We have several persons now living in the village, who, in their childhood, were supposed to be healed by this superstitious ceremony, derived down, perhaps, from our Saxon ancestors, who practised it before their conversion to Christianity.'*

Tetters and warts disappear if touched with the hand of a corpse.   *Stendal*
When you have eaten eggs, the shells are to be broken, else you will get the ague.   *Mark*

*This is also done in England, and for the sound reason, that the witches may not use them as boats. The same injunction is current likewise in Belgium, but whether from the same prudential motive is not stated.*

## House, Field, Etc

On entering a new dwelling the first thing to be provided is bread; you will then always have your bread there.

If you bring cornflowers with you into the house, the bread will grow mouldy.   *Mellin*

What a person dreams the first night in a house will come to pass.

On Saturday night there should be no spinning after sunset.

*Altmark and Mecklenburg*

Else the mice will nestle in it.   *Near Wolfenbüttel*

On Thursday evening there should be no spinning, nor any dung carried out on that day.   *Altmark*

In planting trees the planter should grasp them with both hands, and somebody should stand by: they will then bear well. *Stendal*

The first fruit of a tree should be gathered into a large sack, and some left on the tree; then it will always bear well.   *Stendal.*

Peas should be sown only on Wednesdays and Saturdays; else the birds will carry them off.   *Stendal*

Millet sown after sunset will not be eaten by the birds.   *Camern*

When the cattle go for the first time to the pasture, a piece of turf should be laid before the door; they will then not get the grass distemper.   *Mellin*

That the witches may have no power over a newly bought beast, it must be dragged into the stall backwards; and in order that it may thrive, the first time it goes to pasture, earth should be put into its mouth, which it should be made to swallow.   *Mellin*

When unruly beasts will not be driven to market or elsewhere, pluck at three several times some hairs from their eyelashes and put them in your pocket; they will then go tamely.   *Camern*

When beasts are driven to pasture for the first time, strew sand or straw before the stall-door, so that the animals must tread on it. The traces made by them, if thrown back into the stall, will cause them to find yard and stall again without help. An axe and a broom laid crosswise on the threshold of the yard-gate will have the same effect, and moreover protect them against witchcraft.   *Camern*

A person, on entering into service, should immediately get a piece of wood in the new abode, wrap it in a rag or morsel of paper, and wear it for three days under the arm: the party will then have a kind master and mistress throughout the year.   *Camern*

If anything is stolen from a person, to discover the thief, take a family psalm-book, open it and place on it a family key, saying, 'N. N. has stolen it' (naming the thing); the other (N. N.?) will answer: 'No, he has not stolen it.' If such is the case, the key will remain motionless; but if he has really stolen it, the key will move from its place.   *Rauen*

If anything is stolen from a person, he must take an inherited book, and in it bind an inherited key, then hold it on two fingers and say, 'Inherited book (Erwbôk) I ask thee, has A. B. stolen my linen (or whatever else it may be)? or C. D.?' At whichever person's name the book turns, that is the thief.   *Havelland*


## To fix a thief

Unser Heiland Christus Jesus, der ging in den Garten,
der heiligen Engel und der Jungfrau Maria zu warten;
da kamen die Diebe und wollten das Kindlein stehlen,
das konnten vier und zwanzig Legionen Engel nicht verhehlen.
'Binde, Petrus, binde, eilend und geschwinde,
dass der Dieb uns stehe stille wie ein Stock, und schreie wie ein Bock.
Binde, Petrus, binde, dass der Dieb uns stehe stille
und alle Sterne zähle, die an dem Himmel stehen.
Binde, Petrus, binde, dass der Dieb uns stehe stille,
dass meine leiblichen Augen ihn sehen,
und meine leibliche Zunge ihn spreche.
Das gebiet' ich dir Dieb im Namen des heiligen Bartus,
Der aller Körnlein Meister ist.'                    *MS. from Swinemünde*


*Our Saviour Christ Jesus, he went into the garden,*
*to await the holy angel and the Virgin Mary;*
*there came the thieves and would steal the little child,*
*whom four and twenty legions of angels could not conceal.*

'Bind, Peter, bind, hastily and quick,
that the thief may stand still as a stock, and cry like a goat.
Bind, Peter, bind, that the thief may stand still
and count all the stars, that stand in heaven.
Bind, Peter, bind, that the thief may stand still,
that my bodily eyes may see him,
and my bodily tongue speak to him.
That I command for thee, thief, in the name of St Bart,
who is of every grain the master.'

This spell is to be uttered after sunset, the utterer, at the same time, going three times round the place to which he supposes the thief will come. While so doing he must not look about, and must stop exactly at the point from which he started, and then say thrice, 'In the name of,' etc. On the following morning the thief will be found fast bound to the spot. He must then loose him with these words, 'Hear, thief, I hereby release thee. In the name of,' etc. But this must be done before sunrise, else the thief will turn black, and die within a year.

## To fix a thief

Unsre Mutter Gottes, die ging wohl über Land,  sie nahm ihr liebes
Kind bei der Hand;
da kamen drei, drei, drei Diebe,
die wollten ihr das Kind stehlen, sie schrie:
'Sanct Peter bind', Sanct Peter bind', Sanct Peter binde.'
'Ich habe gebunden mit Gottes Hand, mit meinen eignen Händen,
mit Todeshänden, mit eisernen Bänden,
dass Dieb und Diebin sollen stehn, und nicht von der Stelle gehn.
Sie sollen stehen wie ein Stock, und sehen wie ein Bock,
zählen alle Sterne, die am Himmel stehn,
und alle Tropfen, die in das frunde Meer gehn.'

*Oral from Swinemünde*

*Our Mother of God was going over the land,*
*she took her dear child by the hand;*
*then came three, three, three thieves,*
*who would steal the child from her, she cried:*
*'Saint Peter bind, Saint Peter bind, Saint Peter bind.'*
*'I have bound with God's hand, with my own hands,*
*with death's hands, with iron bands,*
*that male and female thief shall stand, and not go from the place.*

> *They shall stand as a stock, and look like a goat,*
> *count all the stars that stand in heaven,*
> *and all the drops which go into the deep sea.'*

The release is in the following words:

> Stehst du hier in Teufelsband,
> so gehe hin in Gottes Hand;
> ich stosse dich von mir mit meiner linken Hand,
> I. N. G. u. s. w.

> *As thou standest here in the devil's band,*
> *so go hence into the hand of God;*
> *I thrust thee from me with my left hand.*
> *In the name, etc.*

*Another form:*[1]

> Mutter Maria reiste wohl über das Land,
> sie hat ihr liebes Kind bei der Hand.
> Da kamen die Diebe und wollten stehlen.
> Da sprach sie zu St Peter:'Binde!'
> St Peter sprach: 'Ich habe gebunden
> mit eisernen Banden, mit Gottes Handen.
> Du, Dieb (und Diebin), sollst[2] gebunden sein.
> Wiederum sollst du stille stehen und nirgends hingehen.
> Du sollt[2] stehen als ein Stock und starr sehen als ein Bock, und
> zählen all das Gras, das auf der Erde wachst.
> Wiederum sollt du stille stehen und nirgends hingehen,
> sollt stehen als ein Stock und starr sehen als ein Bock,
> und zählen die Sterne, die am Himmel stehen.
> Wiederum sollst du stille stehen und nirgends hingehen;
> du sollt stehen als ein Stock und starr sehen als ein Bock,
> and zählen den Sand, der liegt am Meeresgrund.
> Wiederum sollst du stille stehen and nirgends hingehen;
> du sollt stehen als ein Stock und starr sehen als ein Bock,
> bis ich dir mit meiner Zunge Urlaub gebe.
> Den Himmel gebe ich dir zu deiner Hütte,
> und die Erde zu Schuhen deiner Füsse.
> Amen! in des Teufels Namen.

---

1   From Müllenhoff, op. cit., p. 517.
2   *Sic.*

Mother Mary was journeying over the land,
she had her beloved child by the hand.
Then came the thieves and would steal.
Then spake she to St Peter: 'Bind!'
St Peter said: 'I have bound with iron bands, with God's hands.
Thou, thief (and thiefess), shalt be bound.
Again thou shalt stand still and nowhere go hence.
Thou shalt stand as a stock, and look staring as a goat,
and count all the grass that grows on the earth.
Again thou shalt stand still and nowhere go hence,
Thou shalt stand as a stock, and look staring as a goat,
and count the stars which stand in heaven.
Again thou shalt stand still and nowhere go hence;
thou shalt stand as a stock, and look staring as a goat,
and count the sand that lies on the sea's ground.
Again thou shalt stand still and nowhere go hence;
Thou shalt stand as a stock, and look staring as a goat,
until I with my tongue give thee leave.
The heaven I give thee for thy hut,
and the earth for shoes to thy feet.
Amen! in the devil's name.'

*Against fire:*[1]

Brant, Brant, du geist aewer Moor un Lant.
Mit myn gesegnete Hant rade ik düssen Brant.
I. N. G. u. s. w.

Fire, fire, thou goest over moor and land.
With my hallowed hand I control this fire.
In the name, etc.

*Or:*　　　Petrus und Johannes giengen beide wandeln.
Petrus nahm den Stab in die Hand,
damit still ik dy den Brand.

Peter and John went both wandering.
Peter took the staff in his hand,
therewith quench I thee, the fire.

---

1　The following rimes are from Müllenhoff, op. cit., pp. 516, *sqq.*

*Or:*        Hoch is de Häwen,
roet is de Kräwen
koelt is de Dodenhant, damit still ik düssen Brant.
I. N. G. a. s. w.

*High is the heaven, red is the crayfish,*
*cold is the dead-hand, wherewith I quench this fire.*
*In the name, etc.*

*Or:*        Gott und Petrus gehen übers Land,
sie sehen brennen einen Brand,
'Brand, du sollst nicht brennen,
Brand, du sollst nicht sengen,
Brand, du sollst nicht hitzen,
Brand, du sollst nicht schwitzen,
bis die liebe Mutter Gottes
ihren andern Sohn sollte gebären.'
I. N. G. u. s. w.

*God and Peter go over the land,*
*they see a fire burning.*
*'Fire, thou shalt not burn,*
*Fire, thou shalt not singe,*
*Fire, thou shalt not heat,*
*Fire, thou shalt not cause to sweat,*
*until the dear mother of God*
*shall have borne her second son.'*
      *In The name, etc.*

*Against rain*:

Rägen, Rägen, rush'! de König faert to Busch.
Laet den Rägen aewergaen, laet tie Sünn wedderkamen.
Lewe Sünn, kam' wedder mit dyn golden Fedder;
mit dyn golden Stralen beschyn uns altomalen.
(Beschyn dat ganze Engelland, da hangt de Klocken an de Wand,
wo Maria baven sitt mit dat lütje Kind in Schoet.
Haelt en Stutenbotterbrot,[1] my wat, dy wat,
unse lütje Mueschkatt wat; denn hewt wy altomael wat.)

---

1    Stutenbrod is a kind of pastry or cake in the form of a lozenge, common in Hamburg.

*Rain, rain, patter! the king is going to the bush.*
*Let the rain pass over, let the sun come again.*
*Dear sun, come again with thy golden plumage;*
*with thy golden beams illumine us altogether.*
*(Illumine the whole Engelland,[1] where the bells hang on the wall,*
*where Mary sits above with the little child in her lap.*
*Go get a 'Stutenbotterbrot', a bit for me, a bit for thee,*
*a bit for our little mouse-cat; then have we all of us a bit.)*

## Birds, Etc

If a girl hears the stork chattering on its first coming, she will break something; if she sees one flying, she will ride in a bridal carriage; if she sees one standing, she will be asked to stand gossip.    *Mellin*

If storks fly in a circle above a company of people, one of those persons will soon die.    *Stendal*

If ravens fly over a house making a great croaking, a person will soon die in it.    *Rauen*

If a dog howls before a house, it forebodes death or fire in it.

Magpies may not be shot, it is unlucky.    *Neighbourhood of Crossen*

If the klewitt (a species of owl) screams at night, someone will soon die.

*Steina in the Harz*

*Verses to the snail:*

Schneckhûs, Peckhûs, stäk du dîn vêr Hörner rût,
süst schmît ick dî in'n Gråven, då frêten dî tie Råven.

*Stendal*

*Schneckhûs, Peckhûs, stick thou thy four horns out,*
*else I will smite thee into the ditch, there the ravens*

*will devour thee.*

*Or:*    Taekeltuet, kruep net dyn Hues,
dyn Hues dat brennt, dyn Kinder de flennt,[2]
dyn Fru de ligt in Wäken: kann'k dy nich mael spräken?
Taekeltuet, u. s. w.

*Taekeltuet, creep out of thy house,*
*thy house is on fire, thy children, they cry,*
*thy wife, she lies in childbed: can I not once speak with thee?*
*Taekeltuet, etc.*

---

1    Qu. Angeln?
2    Flennen, *to cry or laugh with a distorted mouth.*

Or:        Snaek, Snaek, komm heruet,
                sunst tobräk ik dy dyn Hues.

                *Snail, snail, come out,*
                *else I will break thy house to pieces.*

Or:        Slingemues, kruep uet dyn Hues,
                stick all dyn veer (fief) Höern uet.
                Wullt du's nech uetstäken,
                will ik dyn Hues tobräken.
                Slingemues, u. s. w.[1]

                *Slingemues, creep out of thy house,*
                *stick all thy four (five) horns out.*
                *If thou wilt not stick them out,*
                *I'll break thy house to pieces.*
                *Slingemues, etc.*

'In England the snail scoops out hollows, little rotund chambers, in limestone, for its residence... The following is a boy's invocation to the snail to come out of such holes, and other places of retreat resorted to by it –

                *Snail, snail, come out of your hole,*
                *Or else I will beat you as black as a coal.'*

In Scotland they say:

                '*Snail, snail, shoot out your horn,*
                *And tell us if it will be a bonnie day the morn.'*[2]

In the South of Italy the snail is thus addressed:

                '*Snail, snail, put out your horn,*
                *Your mother is laughing you to scorn,*
                *For she has a little son just born.'*[3]

---

1   This and the two preceding addresses to the snail are from Müllenhoff, op. cit., p. 509.
2   Chambers, *Pop. Rh.*, p. 43.
3   Taylor's translation of Basile's *Pentamerone*, p. 183.

*To the ladybird* (from the marsh of the Elbe)

> Maikatt, flügg weg, stüff weg,
> bring' my morgen goet Wedder med.

> May-cat, fly away, hasten away,
> bring me good weather with you tomorrow.

*Another* (from Ploen)

> Marspäert (Markpäert), fleeg in Himmel!
> Bring' my' a Sack voll Kringeln, my een, dy een,
> alle lütten Engeln een.

> Marspäert, fly to heaven!
> Bring me a sack full of biscuits, one for me, one for thee,
> for all the little angels one.[1]

## The Elder

An undoubted relic of old times, connected with this tree, existed till a comparatively recent period among the peasants of Lower Saxony, who, when about to lop an elder, were accustomed to utter this prayer:

> Frau Ellhorn, gib mir was von deinem Holz;
> dann will ich dir von meinem auch was geben,
> wann es wächst im Walde.

> Lady Elder, give me some of thy wood;
> then will I also give thee some of mine,
> when it grows in the forest.

This they repeated three times, with bended knees and folded hands.[2]

*Puschkait, the ancient Prussian god of the earth, is said to dwell under the elder.*

*In England, magical practices with elders were forbidden at a very early period. In the 'Canones editi sub Eadgaro Rege' it is enacted thaet preosta gehwilc forbeod tha gemearr, de man drifd on ellenum, and eac on odrum mislícum treowum – that is, that every priest forbid the vain practices, that are carried on with elders, and also with various other trees.[3]*

---

1   This and the preceding are from Müllenhoff, op. cit., pp. 508, 509. See also p. 104, Grimm, J., *Deutsche Mythologie*, op. cit., p. 658 and Chambers, *Pop. Rh.*, p. 43.
2   Arnkiel, cited by Grimm, *Deutsche Mythologie*, op. cit. p. 618; Müllenhoff, op. cit., p. 510; Thiele, op. cit., i, p. 196, edn. 1820.
3   *Anc. Laws and Inst. of England*, p. 396, folio edition.

## The Elements and Natural Phenomena

When there is a calm, scratch with an old nail on the foremast; then wind will rise. *Hamburg*

When the wind has been long contrary, and you meet with another ship, throw an old broom before it; the wind will then change, you will get a fair, the other ship a contrary wind. *Hamburg*

When a storm rises, a fire should be kindled; it will not then strike the house. *Bergkirchen*

When it thunders, they say in the Mark: 'Peter is playing at bowls,' or, 'The angels are playing at bowls.'

The lightning does not strike a house in which there is a thunderbolt[1], or fire burning on the hearth, or a bird has built its nest. *Lautenthal*

After sunset there is frequently formed what is called a *weather tree* (Wetterbaum), a form of cloud resembling a tree, according to which the weather will be regulated; to whatever quarter the points are directed the wind will blow. *Tilleda. Bartelfelde in the Harz.* In the Ukermark, they say in some places: 'Abraham's tree is flowering, it will rain.' In other places: 'If Abraham's tree flowers in the afternoon, the weather will be fair; if after midnight, there will be rain.'

According as the breastbone of a goose is white or red, the winter will be cold or mild.[2] *Mark*

When it snows, they say in Nordalbingia and in the Harz : 'Peter is shaking his bed'; in the Ukermark: 'Peter rules,' or: 'The angels are plucking feathers and down.' In the autumn mornings, when the fine white threads are hanging on the shrubs and bushes, they say: 'The Metten (Fates)[3] have been spinning.' In summer, if the weather has been long dry: 'It's God's hay-days.' If it rains while the sun shines: 'The old witch is frying pancakes'; 'They have a holiday in hell'; 'The devil is bleaching his grandmother'; or, 'A tailor is gone to heaven.'[4]

Whatever is undertaken during the moon's increase succeeds, and the full moon brings all things to fullness, while that which is begun during the wane fails. But for maladies all potions and the like should be taken during the wane, for then the malady will also wane. *Stendal*

No one should remove on a Monday, because then the house affairs will not thrive. If a servant enters a new service on a Monday, he will not long continue in it. *Stendal*

When the stars shoot, the weather is about to change.

---

1 See p. 48n.
2 See p. 425, No. 47.
3 Anglo-Saxon, Metten, *parca*.
4 Müllenhoff, op. cit., p. 583.

Every person has his light in heaven, which when he dies goes out; and in its place a new one makes its appearance, as men are constantly being born.[1] *Brodewin.*

Names of constellations. Heaven's chariot (the Great Bear), St Peter's staff (Orion), the Silver Stars (Pleiades).[2] *Brodewin.* Another constellation is called the Plough and Harrow, another the Crooked Rake. *Baltrum.*

## Miscellaneous

1 Whoever carries about him a four-lobed clover leaf, cannot be fascinated, i.e. he can see through all magical delusions.[3]   *Mellin*

2 On St Lucy's day (13th December)[4] nothing should be lent.   *Rauen*

3 White spots on the nails denote luck.   *Berlin*

4 Yarn spun by a child of seven years makes a person bullet-proof.   *Liepe*

5 To obtain what you wish from another, lay a swallow's tongue under your own, and then kiss the party.   *MS. from Swinemünde*

6 To obtain the love of women, carry about you a bat's blood, or a swallow's heart.   *MS. from Swinemünde*

7 To cause a person to reveal a secret, lay a daw's heart under his left side, and he will impart whatever you desire to know.

*MS. from Swinemünde*

8 A malefactor's arm-bone carried in the pocket is a security against vermin. If a thief carries such a bone about him, the party whom he designs to rob cannot wake.[5]   *Stendal*

9 A found horseshoe, if nailed on the threshold with the points turned outwards, brings luck; but if they are turned inwards, it brings misfortune.   *Berlin and other places*

10 To be beloved by everybody carry about you the heart either of a pewet or a green frog. The eyes of a pewet, if carried about a person, make him witty and agreeable; and if worn on the breast, when before a judge, the party will be acquitted; and whoever carries with him in a bag the heart of a pewet, cannot be defrauded by traders; and if the heart be dried and reduced to powder, and laid under the head at night, the party will dream where there is treasure hidden.   *Stendal*

---

1 See Grimm, J. & W., *Kinder- und Hausmärchen*, op. cit., No. 44
2 See Grimm, J., *Deutsche Mythologie*, op. cit., p. 690 *sq.*
3 See p. 424, No. 27.
4 See Grimm, J., *Deutsche Mythologie*, op. cit., pp. 250, 1212.
5 See in *Netherl. Tradit.* the 'Thief's Foot', etc.

11 Unlucky days. In January: 1st, 3rd, 6th, 17th and18th. In February: 8th, 16th and 17th. In March: 1st, 12th, 13th and 15th. In April: 3rd, 15th, 17th and 18th. In May: 8th, 10th, 17th and 30th. In June: 1st and 7th. In July: 1st, 5th and 6th. In August: 1st, 3rd, 18th and 20th. In September: 15th, 18th and 30th. In October: 15th and 17th. In November: 11 and 17th. In December: 1st, 7th and 11th. A child born on any of these days will seldom be long-lived; or if it lives, will be poor and miserable. On any of these days no marriage is desirable, and whoever travels on one of them, is sure to come home out of health. The most unlucky of them, on which no one should travel, are: 13th March, 18th August, 1st, 3rd and 30th September. But there are three days which are unlucky above all others, and whoever is bled on one of them will surely die in seven or eight days after, viz. 1st April, on which the traitor Judas was born; 1st August, on which the devil was cast down from heaven; 1st December, on which Sodom and Gomorrha were destroyed by fire from heaven.  *Stendal*

12 If a child be lifted out through a window, it must be taken in by the same, else it will grow no more.[1]  *Ibid.*

13 If a person who has a wen lets it be struck with a pea-ladle, or a pregnant woman tread on it, it will disappear.  *Ibid.*

14 If a person takes water from his neighbour's well after sunset, he takes with him his neighbour's luck and prosperity.  *Ibid.*

15 If a hare runs across one's path, it is unlucky.  *Ibid.*

16 If your nose itches, you will hear news.  *Ibid.*

17 If you dream of losing a cheek-tooth, one of the family will soon die.  *Ibid.*

18 To dream of fish betokens money; of a bright-burning fire, luck; of falling into water, illness.

19 To carry a purse of moleskin is lucky.  *Mark*

1   See p. 306, No. 30.

# Netherlandish Popular Traditions[1]

## Kaboutermannekens

The inhabitants of the village of Herselt. relate that, on the occasion of a war, a great multitude of Kaboutermannekens came into their neighbourhood. They took up their abode near to the village, in the middle of a large forest, in which there were several caverns. They frequently came to the village, to fetch one thing or other, but without doing harm to anyone. When their women grew old they caused them to descend into a pit, with a milk-loaf in their hand, and then carefully closed up the pit's mouth. The peasants say that the women were very contented with this kind of death, and were by no means forced to it.

---

In the village of Gelrode there is a small hill called the Kabouterberg, in which there are many caverns dug, which in former days were the habitations of the Kaboutermannekens. If the miller of the place's millstone was worn, he had only to lay it before his mill, together with a slice of bread and butter and a glass of beer, and he was sure of finding it the next morning beautifully sharpened. He did in like manner when he wanted his linen washed.

---

The Redcaps or Klabbers, called also Kaboutermannekens, often increase the wood. In the night, when the moon does not shine, they enter a house through the chimney, make themselves a fire on the hearth, and set themselves quietly before, it. But no one sees the fire except the Redcaps, though it warms more than an ordinary fire. In the morning the housewife often finds of a large bundle of brushwood only a few little twigs lying on the dogs; but these she readily kindles, because she knows that they burn as long as a great bundle, and give double the warmth. If while the wood is burning the housewife should curse the Redcap or cross herself, the twigs would flare out in an instant.

---

1    From Wolf, *Niederländische Sagen*, Leipsig, 1843.

A poor peasant, whose wife was suddenly taken ill, rose in the night to churn. He had already in the evening placed everything in readiness, and set the milk in large pots near the fire, that the work might proceed the more speedily. On entering the place he saw to his great astonishment that the fire was still burning, and that a little man half asleep was sitting before it. The noise of the man's wooden shoes waked the mannikin, who started up, looked hard at the man, but without uttering a word. The peasant was equally silent, but cast a stolen side-glance at the intruder, and saw that he was clad in red from head to foot, and had a green face and green hands. Then looking straight before him, he took from a corner a bundle of firewood, cast it down by the hearth, and went quietly to sleep. Next morning the butter was all set and ready, so that he had only to take it to market; there was, moreover, a larger quantity than he had ever got from the milk. His wife soon recovered, Redcap continued to churn for them, and the man gradually became so rich that he kept many cows, and could lay by a whole stockingful of shining dollars. And no wonder, for by degrees Redcap did all the work; he ploughed the fields, took care of the cattle, and in short performed more than the work of three men.

But prosperity corrupted the peasant. He now went every evening to the pothouse, played away his money, and regularly returned home drunk. This did not please Redcap, and he reproached him accordingly. At first he gave ear to him, but soon disregarded him, and at length went so far, that, returning home one night late and drunk, he grossly abused Redcap, and threw the bundle of firewood into the well, which his wife had carefully made ready.

In the same moment Redcap disappeared. On the following morning the wife was sick, the stocking, instead of dollars, was filled with coals, the cows died, the house and stalls fell to ruin, and the fields lay waste. The peasant then came to his senses, but it was too late, and let him pray and wail as he might that Redcap would restore him to prosperity, it was of no avail; on the contrary, the following night Redcap was heard laughing round the house and jeering him.

Shortly after, the man died poor and miserable.

———

Near Turnhout a young man was deeply in love with a maiden. The courtship had long continued without any suspicion of its existence on the part of their respective parents. The youth at length growing impatient, went one day to the damsel's father, and requested his consent to their union. But the old man being proud and overbearing, considered the young man too poor, and said to him, 'I cannot imagine how you can think of demanding the hand of my daughter: if you cannot lay down a thousand guilders, you need not let such a thing enter your mind.'

This was a heavy blow to the young man, and he slunk home full of trouble, not knowing what he should do. At home he found no comfort; for the counting of his little stock of money was no longer a pleasure to him, as it fell far short of a thousand guilders; but which he must, nevertheless, obtain. He then went into the fields, and meditated self-destruction; for life had no longer any pleasure for him. As he was now going he knew not whither, on a sudden a Kaboutermanneken stood at his side, who asked him the cause of his affliction. With tearful eyes the young man recounted to him what had taken place. When he had finished his story the Kaboutermanneken laughed and said, 'So, only a thousand guilders; that's not worth letting a single hair grow grey for.' 'True,' said the youth, 'but if one has it not?' 'Well,' replied the Kaboutermanneken, 'one can then always get it. Thou hast ever been a brave youth, and therefore the matter may easily be managed. Just go home and count thy money, and come back and let me know how much it falls short.' 'How much it falls short?' sighed the young man, 'that I know but too well – eight hundred guilders.' 'Thou hast not well counted it,' said the Kaboutermanneken, laughing, 'go and count it once again.'

Full of joy the young man now ran back to the house and again counted his money, when lo! there were a thousand gold guilders. Instantly he returned, considering it his first duty to thank his benefactor, but he was not to be seen, and often as he cried, 'Kaboutermanneken! Kaboutermanneken!' he came no more. He then ran home again, packed up the money, put on his Sunday clothes, and went to the father of the damsel, to whom he counted out a thousand guilders. Within a week the marriage took place, and they both lived long in peace and content.

---

Between Turnhout and Casterle there is a hill, which is to this day called the Kaboutermannekensberg. The Kabouternannekens that once dwelt in it were very numerous, but withal of a very evil nature, their greatest delight being to inflict all possible injury on the inhabitants of the neighbourhood. When night had begun, no one was longer secure. They then went round and carried off with them everything they fancied, fowls, ducks, geese, oxen, cows and calves, money, in short everything, even household utensils. This lasted a considerable length of time, but now we hear no more of it.

---

A miller in Kempnerland found often in the morning his work in the mill performed, let it have been ever so much; though only when he left some bread and butter, which on these occasions disappeared. This surprised the man; so one evening he concealed himself behind some flour-sacks, and saw a naked Kaboutermanneken come, eat the bread and butter, and begin to work in the mill. The miller being grieved to see the little fellow naked, went to a tailor and ordered a pair of breeches and a jacket to be made for him, which on the following evening he laid along with the bread and butter. The Kaboutermanneken came and danced for joy, on seeing the handsome garments, quickly ate up the bread and butter, put on the clothes, proudly strutted about, and disappeared without the miller seeing which way he went. He never returned.

Now thought the miller, 'Wait a little, I'll soon catch thee'; and with that intention went and sat on a little bridge that was over a brook, which the Kaboutermannekens were in the habit of crossing every evening. He did not wait long before they appeared. When the first stepped on the bridge, he said to the miller, 'Who art thou, man?' but the miller made no answer; for he was looking out for the Kaboutermanneken with the clothes on, and those that he saw were naked. The second also said, 'Who art thou, man?' but he still kept silence; and so it went on till the last came, and he had on the clothes that the miller had placed in the mill. 'Haha,' cried the miller, 'have I got thee?' and was about to seize the manneken, when suddenly a voice, like that of his wife, was heard from the rivulet, crying for help, when the miller turning round in a hurry, plumped into the water; but the Kaboutermannekens were all away.

---

An old man from the hamlet of Landorp, which lies not far from Aerschot on the little river Demer, has often related the following:

A certain Heer Percy, who dwelt on the opposite side of the Demer, was in the habit of being ferried over every evening, for the purpose of visiting the inn at Landorp. He usually stayed till it was very late, and when he wished to return, the ferryman was gone to bed. But Heer Percy cared little for that, for he was on good terms with the Kaboutermannekens, who, as soon as the ferryman was asleep, hastened to the bank, and when Heer Percy came out of the inn, called aloud, 'Heer Percy! Heer Percy! come quickly; we will ferry you over. Come, Heer Percy!' Then would Heer Percy proceed to the bank, and the mannekens convey him across, when he gave them a large jug of beer for their trouble.

He usually also engaged them for the next day, to make coffee early in the morning, milk the cows, clean the house, etc.; and all this they did most punctually; nor did they drink a drop of the coffee or milk, but left it untouched until Heer Percy gave them some. Thus they acted, and were so faithful because he was so kind to them. On the other hand, however, the neighbours had to suffer a thousand annoyances from them. They drank the milk of their cows, spoiled their butter, and played pranks innumerable; for all which the neighbours were highly incensed against Heer Percy; but they could do him no harm, for the Kaboutermannekens protected and watched over him that no injury might befall him.

# Kludde

Kludde or Kleure is the name of an evil spirit which plays its pranks in a great part of Brabant and Flanders. With respect to its form it is a perfect Proteus; for which reason the peasants are so fearful of him, that they will not for any consideration venture into a forest, a field, or a road, which, according to common report, is haunted by Kludde.

This spirit often transforms himself into a tree, which at first appears quite small and delicate, but soon raises itself to an immeasurable height, and is lost in the clouds, while everything around it on earth is thrown into confusion. Another time he will clothe himself with the skin of a great black dog, and so run on his hind legs, at the same time rattling a chain that is round his neck, and will spring suddenly on the neck of the first person he meets; and when he has thrown him on the ground, entirely vanish. But Kludde oftenest appears as an old, half-starved horse, and as such is a bugbear to all grooms and horse-boys, who relate that when they leave their horses in the field at night, it frequently happens that, instead of their well-known horse or mare, they set themselves on Kludde, who instantly runs off with them at full speed, until he comes to some water, into which he pitches his terrified rider. While the poor fellow is struggling to save himself, Kludde lays himself with his belly flat on the ground and sets up a fiendish laugh, until his victim, sullen and angry, shall have worked himself out of his bath.

Occasionally Kludde assumes the form of a cat, a frog, a bat, or any other animal. His approach may be known by two little blue flames, which fluttering and dancing go before him. These flames are, as far as can be ascertained, the eyes of the spectre. It is difficult to escape from Kludde, even by running from him at the utmost speed in a zigzag; for, like a snake, he will wind in all directions with equal rapidity.

When this spectre takes his flight, he cries, 'Kludde, Kludde!' whence comes his name.

In the neighbourhood of Ostend Kludde is known as a Water-necker (Water-nix), and in the flat country about that town as a Werwolf.

---

As two young men and a girl were going along in the country, one of them, who was the lover of the girl, said to his comrade, 'Stop for a moment, I see something yonder.' 'What dost thou see?' asked the other. 'Kludde,' was the answer. 'See, now he is a dog – now he is growing up high – now he is little again – a sheep – no, a cat . . .' and thus he went on talking, while neither his companion nor the girl could perceive anything. His friend at length said, 'If thou seest Kludde again, let me know, and I will go up to him.' 'Then go now,' said the other, 'he is just running before me.' His friend went accordingly, but could see nothing of Kludde.

So it lasted until they came to the house of the young man who had all along seen the spectre running before him. Before the house there lay a flat stone, under which the young man's father was in the habit of placing the key of the house, that he might not be under the necessity of rising from his bed, when his son happened to stay late at the public house. 'Don't you now see him?' cried the young man. 'He is sitting on the stone, to prevent me from getting the key.' Saying these words, he took his lass by the arm, adding, 'Come, Mieken, we will accompany you home, for you are frightened.' On his return he still saw Kludde sitting on the stone. The other then took courage and went to the stone, when Kludde sprang aside, so that he could take the key, with which he opened the door for his comrade, who hurried in, lest Kludde should be at his heels, while the other quietly went his way, without having seen a trace of the spectre.

## Osschaert

Formerly the town of Hamme, near Dendermonde, was infested by an evil spirit named Osschaert, of whom it can hardly be said that he was altogether a scourge to the peaceable inhabitants of the neighbourhood, for to the good Christians of the middle age he was at the same time very beneficial, in being a terror to the wicked, and in having forced many a one to turn into the path of righteousness.

His usual abode was the spot where the chapel of Twee Bruggen now stands, and the immediate neighbourhood the scene of his exploits. If anyone towards midnight were foolhardy enough to cry out, or even to mutter the rimes,

> Grypke, grypke grauw,
> Wilt gy my grypen, Grypt my nou.
>
> *Grypke, grypke grey,*
> *If thou wilt gripe me, Gripe me now.*

Then would Osschaert leap on his back, with outspread claws clamber up to his shoulders, and force him groaning and panting to carry him, until good fortune brings him to a crossway, over which the evil spirit being unable to pass, casts away his half-dead bearer.

It would seem that Osschaert had been repeatedly irritated by the above rimes, for the longer he infested the place the worse he grew, until at length it was not only the drunken and the foolhardy who teased him that were the objects of his malice, but everyone that he found abroad at unseasonable hours of the night. The husbandman consequently left the field with hasty steps before sunset, the benighted traveller anxiously sought a shelter before nightfall, and not a few of the country people trembled even at their firesides, sending up fervent prayers that the spectre might have no power over them.

But most painful was Osschaert's riding to those who had some heavy burden on their conscience. On such he pressed with an intolerable weight, struck his claws deep into their flesh, burned their necks with his hellish fiery breath, and thereby infected with a most insufferable stench every respiration of the sinner. Even when anyone thus tormented sank down from pain and weariness, he got no respite; he must rise again and continue his course until he reached either a crossway or an image of the Virgin in the vicinity of one.

But at Hamme there lived a pious priest, who, deeply affected by the misery inflicted on his flock by Osschaert, resolved to drive him away, and by exorcism s banished him, for ninety-nine years, to the seashore, where he still wanders.

––––––––––

An old man from the neighbourhood of Doel related many of Osschaert's tricks, among which was the following.

His grandfather, when a young man, had gone one evening on a courting expedition. On his return he had to cross a field, when on a sudden an enormous monster of a horse stood before him. Then thought my grandfather, 'Halt, this is Osschaert; thou must get out of the way'; and so he did, with the intention of passing through the churchyard; but he had hardly got again into the main road, when a huge dog as big as a horse met him; whereupon he turned his back, crossed himself, and struck into another path leading to the churchyard; but scarcely had he reached it before a rabbit sprang backwards and forwards before him. 'Osschaert has some design upon me this evening,' said he to himself, and turned for the purpose of going round the churchyard, when, at the corner of the gate, there stands a gigantic ass, with fiery eyes as large as plates

This perplexed him so prodigiously, that although he was not the most timid of mortals, he sprang over the wall and ran home with all speed, where he arrived bathed in sweat.

––––––––––

There was once a fisherman named Blommaert, who dwelt at Kieldrecht and had no wife, but only a little boat, a net and a hut. When he brought his fish home in the evening, he was in the habit of throwing them into a tub of water, which stood by the window near the hearth.

On rising in the morning he always remarked that some fish were missing, and that somebody had been scattering the ashes on the hearth, no doubt for the purpose of broiling the fish on the still glowing embers.

The fisher examined his hut, but finding no opening, felt fully convinced that it was Osschaert who had played him the trick. He soon forgot the affair but to his no small vexation found on the following morning that his fish had again been taken and broiled on the embers. 'Now,' thought he, 'I will cure Master Osschaert of that trick,' and so covered the whole hearth with horse-dung, over which he scattered a few ashes.

Osschaert came as usual to get and roast his fish, saying as he entered, 'Blommeken, vischkens braeyen'; but when he came to the hearth he spoiled the beautiful trout with the horse-dung, and went away doubling and shaking his fists; while the fisherman, who was awake, burst into a loud laugh. So far so good; but Osschaert knew how to be revenged. On the following morning, to wit, the fisherman went out and cast his net, and soon after attempted to haul it up, but found it inconceivably heavy. At length, when after much toil and trouble he had pulled it to the surface of the water, he saw that there were no fish in it, but only an immense heap of horse-dung. Osschaert now gave a hearty laugh, and the fisherman full of vexation returned home.[1]

## The Necker

In the rivers and springs spirits have often been seen, which the German Belgians call Neckers. These spirits sometimes sang most beautiful melodies in chorus; sometimes, like women, they were seen arranging their hair in the river. They have also been known to converse with men, and to play all sorts of games.

———

Near Ghent a little old man has often been seen on the water of the Scheldt. He was a Necker (Nix), and was constantly sighing and moaning. Two children once, who were playing on the river's bank, saw him coming towards them, and ran away, at which the Necker cried piteously. He did harm to no one. If any person asked him the cause of his sorrow, he would fetch a deep sigh and disappear.

———

Throughout Brabant the tradition is current that the Necker sucks the blood of the drowned. From rivulets the mournful cry of a child is often

———

1    Osschaert and the Yorkshire *Barguest* seem nearly identical. There was a Barguest named the Picktree Brag, whose usual form was that of a little galloway, 'in which shape a farmer, still or lately living thereabouts, reported that it had come to him one night as he was going home; that he got upon it and rode very quietly till it came to a great pond, to which it ran and threw him in, and *went laughing away.*' Keightley, op, cit., p. 310; Scott's *Minstrelsy*, i, p. cx.

heard; but to this no great attention need be paid, as it is often only a deception of the Necker.

Those drowned of the name of Jan have the singular property of remaining upright in the water, and under no circumstances are they ever found lying on the side.

## The Three Nixen of Jupille

One autumn evening as the joyful inhabitants of Jupille, at the end of the vintage, were springing about and dancing on the verdant turf, three damsels suddenly approached them from the banks of the Meuse, and joined the mirthful assemblage. They were attired in garments of dazzling whiteness, and on their fair locks wore garlands of fresh-blown water-lilies. Whether they walked or only glided on the earth no one could say. The young lads of Jupille had never met with such light dancers.

When the dancing was over, all sat down in a circle, and the three damsels began to sing, and that with such sweet voices that the eyes of all were fixed on them, and no one thought how far the night was already advanced. To their surprise the clock struck the hour of midnight, when the damsels, after whispering a few words together, greeted the company round, and soon disappeared.

On the following evening, just as the moon was risen, they returned, when the young men instantly hastened up to them, requesting them to dance. As the night was sultry, one of them drew off her gloves, which her partner took charge of. This time the clock struck twelve while they were still engaged in the dance. Terrified at the sound the damsels started and were hastening away, when one exclaimed, 'Where are my gloves?' But the youth would not restore them, retaining them as a pledge of love; and. the damsel, with her companions, hurried away without them. Her partner followed with equal speed; being but too desirous of discovering where the beauteous maiden dwelt. They proceeded on and on, when, on reaching the Meuse, the damsels sprang into the water and vanished.

When on the following morning the love-sick youth revisited the spot, the water there was blood-red. The maidens never appeared again.[1]

---

1   In connection with the foregoing tradition, see the epitome of German Mythology below.

# Flerus

In a farmhouse near Ostend everything went on satisfactorily and prosperously, so that in a short time the owner became one of the wealthiest persons in the neighbourhood. This was ascribed to a domestic sprite named Flerus, who had his abode there, and appeared sometimes under a human form, sometimes in that of an animal. If a horse was sick, Flerus was called, who appeared at the instant as a strong and lively horse, willingly suffered himself to be harnessed, and performed thrice the quantity of work of any other horse. He never flinched from a service: even if the maidservants foresaw that they would not have time to sweep the house thoroughly, Flerus would come at their call, would draw water and carry it to them The only remuneration he looked for was a little fresh milk with sugar.

But once a couple of young and thoughtless servant-girls, who had been made rather wanton by the good nature of Flerus, resolved on playing him a trick. They called him and he instantly came; but when he had performed the work required of him, they set before him, instead of his usual meal, fresh milk with garlic. Scarcely, however, had he tasted it when he vanished, saying:

> Melk en look!
> Flerus verhuist, En't geluk ook.

> Milk and garlic!
> Flerus decamps, and good luck eke.

From that hour no more was heard or seen of Flerus in the place, and everything went crab-fashion. From him the place acquired the name of Flerushof.

# The Werwolf

A man had once gone out with his bow to attend a shooting match at Ronsse, but when about halfway to the place, he saw on a sudden a large wolf spring from a thicket and rush towards a young girl, that was sitting in a meadow by the roadside watching cows. The man did not long hesitate, but quickly drawing forth an arrow, took aim, and luckily hit the wolf in the right side, so that the arrow remained sticking in the wound, and the animal ran back howling into the wood.

On the following day he heard that a serving-man of the burgomaster's lay at the point of death, in consequence of having been shot in the right side on the preceding day. This so excited the man's curiosity, that he went to the wounded man and requested to see the arrow, which he instantly recognised as one of his own. Then having desired all those present to withdraw, when he was alone with the man, he persuaded him to confess how he had received the wound, when he acknowledged that he was the Werwolf. He died on the following day.

## The Maere

In the village of Alveringen a cunning man was once called to see a woman who was mare-ridden. He took a handful of dry sand, uttered certain words, and cast the sand in the air, and all about, under the tables, chairs and cupboards, in short, in every corner. Hardly had he done this, when at once there stood a woman in the chamber, of whom no one knew whence she came, and whom no one had ever before seen. She did not long deliberate, but quickly opened the door and escaped. 'There was your Mare,' said the man, 'she will not return in a hurry, for she is now marked.' On the persons present inquiring how or with what she was marked, he answered, 'Simply with a grain of sand; but her power is now at an end.'

—————

As some reapers were one day at work in a field near Vilvorde, they found a naked woman lying apparently asleep; yet it was no natural sleep, for it did not appear to the men that she breathed. Curious to know what might be the matter with the woman, they went and called a shepherd, who had the reputation of being skilled in hidden things. On seeing the woman, he at once said, 'She is not asleep, but is a Mare, who has just stripped herself for the purpose of riding someone.' The reapers laughed at this, and said the shepherd was befooling them; but he said, 'Wait only an instant, and you shall see something extraordinary.' He then bent down to the woman and whispered a word or two in her ear, when they immediately saw a little animal, the length of a finger and of singular form, come running and creep into the woman's mouth. The shepherd then gave her a smart push so that she rolled over thrice, and which caused her to wake, when after looking about her with astonishment, she got up and fled with all possible speed, to the great surprise of the reapers, who enjoyed the thing amazingly.

—————

Two young men in the neighbourhood of Vilvorde loved the same damsel; but one of them, the comelier of the two, had an affliction, for which he had tried a number of remedies, yet all to no purpose – he suffered every night from the Mare. Complaining one day to his rival how he was tormented the instant he got into bed, and how every remedy had proved vain, the other laughed at him, and said, 'O, there is nothing more easy; I will give thee advice, which, if thou wilt follow it, will secure thee from all such visitations in future. Hold a sharp and well pointed knife with the *point* towards thy breast, when thou liest down in bed, and do not go to sleep; then will the Mare have visited thee for the last time.'

The poor lad, overjoyed at the thought of getting rid of the spectre on such easy terms, forgot in his delight half of the counsel, and held the knife with the *handle* towards his breast, so that the point stood upright; and lucky was it that he did so; for when the Mare came as usual, she wounded herself on the point of the knife, and returned no more. In the other case she would have driven the knife into his breast.

———

In Liege there was at one time a number of persons who by wishing could afflict anyone with the mare; to be again free from which people gave them money, and in return received from them a bottle. Into this they had to void their urine, which they placed a while in the sun, and then brought it to the person to whom they had given the money. This person then led the patient to some water, by which he stood with his back towards it, and then threw the bottle over his head into it.

———

A nobleman dwelling at his castle in the neighbourhood of Sittard, was every night plagued with a Mare. He sent for his physician, and at length for the clergyman, but neither could supply him with a remedy for the evil. This reached the ears of a shepherd, who came to the nobleman and told him that he had a certain remedy for the Mare. On the nobleman asking him in what it consisted, he said, 'If the Mare comes again, let her remain quiet; but when she is gone, make water, put it in a bottle, and keep it carefully; you will then see something wonderful.' The nobleman did so, and shut the bottle up in his cupboard, keeping the key in his pocket.

Next day about noon there came an old woman to the gate, asking whether they had any old broken glass to sell. The maidservant gave her all the broken glass, but she again inquired whether they had no entire bottles, and requested her to ask her master whether he had any. The master, who instantly knew what she was driving at, answered that he had none. She then asked whether she could not speak with the master herself. On seeing him she besought him to give her the bottle that he had in his cupboard, and at his refusal, fell at his feet and wept bitterly, promising that she would do him no further injury. He thereupon took the bottle, and broke it,[1] and drove the old woman with blows from the door. He was thus relieved from the Mare, who never again returned.

———

1 The original adds: 'und zur Stunde lief das Wasser also von dem alten Weibe weg, dass das ganze Zimmer voll wurde'.

My aunt's grandmother, says Mynh. Van Swygenhoven, had once a horse that was mare-ridden. This coming to the knowledge of a neighbour, he brought two bricks, which he laid crosswise, bound them fast with a cord, and hung them on the horse. The animal instantly ceased from sweating and feeling uneasiness, and the Mare no more tormented it.

## Dwarf-smithies

In the Walloon provinces there is not a village nor a hamlet that has not its dwarf-cave or dwarf-hole. In the forests the vestiges of former smithies are often met with, which the people call dwarf-smithies. Whole pigs of iron or lead are also frequently found, which date from the time of the goblins.

To those that are kind to them these dwarfs are very serviceable; only care must be taken to place food for them every night.

## Lodder

One warm summer night three reapers went to the field for the purpose of completing their labour, which, in consequence of the great heat, they had been obliged to intermit. The moon not having yet risen, they could scarcely see, and therefore resolved, after laying aside their clothes, to sit down for a short time, until it grew lighter. Scarcely, however, had they deposited their garments, when they heard a distant rattling as of chains, but which constantly came nearer and nearer, and at length reached the spot where the clothes were lying. One of the men then stood up to look after their clothes, but there they lay undisturbed, and he saw nothing, though the rattling still continued.

In the meanwhile, it gradually became darker, and thunder was heard at a distance, so the reapers resolved to return home; for they saw that it would be impossible for them to work. They had but just put on their clothes when the rattling suddenly and quickly came quite close to them, and something passed between the legs of one of them which carried him off with it. He cried as loud as he could, 'Lodder! Lodder! Strike! Strike! I am sitting on him.' But the others laughed at him, for although they saw him riding away, they could not see Lodder, for he had made himself invisible. So the more they laughed, the more vexed was the man, and the more lustily he cried out; for he well knew on whose back he was sitting. In short, he was carried on and on till he came to a large pond, into which Lodder threw himself and left the terrified reaper lying half dead on the grass.

When the others came up, they saw plainly that it was earnest, and from that time have never laughed when anything extraordinary happened to them in the night.

A wild young fellow coming home late one night, heard, while he was putting the key into the lock, something on the ground that continually went ticktack, ticktack, ticktack. Stooping down he found it was a silver watch, which he joyfully placed in his pocket. On entering his room he drew it out, for the purpose of seeing at what hour it stood. At that moment the church clock struck twelve, and the watch became cold and icy in his hand, and on looking at it, it was a large, fat toad. In his fright he dashed it on the ground, when suddenly there stood a huge dog before him, with eyes like lanterns, which after having stared at him till he fell on his bed in a fright, darted through the window, which at that moment sprang open, when from without hahaha! long resounded in his ears. He then knew that it was Lodder.

---

On a Saturday evening the country lads usually go to the window of their sweethearts and settle with them where they shall meet on the Sunday. A young fellow from Tissel, who was on the same errand, had, in order to reach the house in which his sweetheart dwelt, to cross over a brook; but when he came to the spot where the bridge should be, it was no longer there, but there was Lodder sitting in the grass. 'What dost thou want?' said Lodder. 'I want to go to my sweetheart,' answered the young man, 'but I don't see the bridge.' 'Then I can help thee,' said Lodder, at the same time stretching himself at full length across the water, so that his paws reached the opposite bank; and the youth taking courage, passed over Lodder's back and neck and arms, and when he found himself on the opposite bank he courteously thanked Lodder. After having conversed a while with his lass, he took his way home. In passing through a cornfield he heard an infant piteously crying, and on proceeding to the spot whence the voice seemed to come, he found a boy of about eight years old, whom he took on his back and continued his way to the brook, where Lodder was still sitting. 'What hast thou there?' asked Lodder. 'A poor child,' answered the young man, 'whom I will keep with me till tomorrow, when he will perhaps find his parents.' 'It is well,' said Lodder, stretching out his paws, and again placing himself across the brook. But as he was passing over Lodder's legs, the boy on his shoulders grew uncommonly heavy, so that Lodder cried out, 'Thou art getting too heavy for me, I shall let thee fall.' 'Just stay a little while, dear Lodder,' said the young man, 'I shall be over in a second.' But the boy grew heavier and heavier, and when they were on Lodder's back, he blew hot into the young man's neck, and struck his long nails into his shoulders: at the same moment Lodder vanished, and the young man fell into the water, where he instantly crossed himself, and so released himself from the boy. He then scrambled out of the brook and ran home as fast as he could, while behind him resounded hahaha!

# Witchery

In the village of Oostbrouck, near Utrecht, there lived a widow, who kept a manservant, that performed both domestic and field labour. This servant, such persons being generally curious, had through his window frequently remarked that his mistress, when she thought that all were asleep, went to a particular place in the stable, and there took hay from the crib. This surprised him, and he wondered within himself why his mistress did so, and resolved to try what would be the effect, if he did the same. So once, after she had been in the stable, he went in, looked carefully around, and took some hay. But scarcely had he taken it in his hand before he was hurried through the air, and borne away to the little town of Wyck, and into a large underground cellar, where he found a numerous assemblage of men and women. When his mistress and the others perceived him, they were at first frightened, and asked him how he came among them, and he then related to them the whole affair. His mistress on hearing it fell into a violent rage, and began to deliberate with her associates on the steps it were most advisable to take; but all were of opinion that the best course would be to receive the man amicably, and engage him not to blab. Now came the hour of parting, and it was again a subject of discussion, whether they should kill him or let him go free, but they resolved on the latter course; and after he had promised not to divulge what he had witnessed, his mistress took him on her shoulders, and they both flew off through the air. But when they came to a lake the woman thought within herself it were better to throw him into the water, for then there would be an end to all tattling, and she did accordingly, giving him a smart shake, so that the poor fellow fell into the lake.

But his guardian angel would not allow him so to die, and he escaped with his life, yet lay in great pain among the rushes, groaning and wailing most piteously. Some persons, who were passing by, hearing him, dragged him out, and inquired how he came there, when he related to them all that had befallen him. They then laid him on a wagon and conveyed him to Utrecht, where he related his story to the burgomaster, John Culemburg, at which that magistrate greatly marvelled. The widow being afterwards seized, made a full confession and received the punishment she merited.

# The Long Wapper of Antwerp [1]

My late father, says the veracious narrator, as well as my ancient aunt and all my acquaintances, have in my younger days talked to me a thousand times about the Long Wapper, and of the numerous tricks which that extraordinary being played to the inhabitants of the good city of Antwerp.

His tricks were not always malicious, but consisted frequently in rogueries and the like; yet something always lay at the bottom of them that was not altogether right, and regarding which one might entertain unfavourable thoughts. It is, too, a well-known fact that he has carried many a one off with him, but whither the Lord alone knows. It would seem that people were afraid to speak ill of him, for who could say that he was not listening? Who or what he was I cannot say, for no one knew anything of the matter. As long as he abode in the city, his name was scarcely ever pronounced; and it was only when all traces of him had disappeared, that persons ventured to communicate to each other their thoughts concerning him. My schoolmistress, who was very religious, often spoke of him, and told us he was a spirit from the other world; but I for my part believe that he was a rich man belonging to the city, who had made a compact with the devil. Indeed, at a later period I heard that several noble and high city families were in league with him, and were by family connected with him, and therefore had good reason to keep the truth secret.

In former days the Wappersrui, which is now arched over, lay quite open, and the place now called the Wappersbrücke was a real, true bridge. There it was that the Long Wapper chiefly made his haunt, and from him both the above names are derived. He usually made his first appearance from under the bridge, strode with his long legs out of the water to the rampart, there in an instant shrank to a diminutive size, and then appeared as one of the street boys. He would then mingle with the other boys, and no one ever recognised him, for he always assumed the form of one of them that did not happen to be present. This took place usually in the hours between light and dark, for then the boys came from school or from their meals, and began their play. One of their favourite games was 'shove-hat', at which one of them, on whom it fell by lot, gave his hat, which the others shoved with their feet backwards and forwards, until he to whom it belonged was fortunate enough to overtake and seize it. All went on well till it fell to the lot of the Long Wapper to give his hat; but then woe to him who gave the first push to the hat! He broke his wooden shoes in pieces and fractured his toes; for the supposed hat was a heavy iron pot. Then was

1  Partly from 'Wodana', p. ii,

to be heard the loud hahaha! of the jeering sprite, whom all now sought after, but no one found.

At night, when he could find no more boys to plague and irritate in their games, there was not a single street in the whole city that was wholly secure from his pranks. Not an old woman nor a young girl could be out at a late hour, without experiencing his artifice. In the neighbourhood of the Flesh-market in particular he perpetrated a number of shameful acts; though what they exactly were I no longer remember. Two cases are, however, still fresh in my recollection, and that just because they happened to a person of my acquaintance. This person was returning home from her work about eleven o'clock one night, when she heard the cry of a little infant proceeding from the Flesh-market. On approaching the spot, she found there, on a stone bench, a poor little creature that appeared not many hours old, in neat, white swaddling clothes. She took up the little being and pressed it to her bosom, thinking it was a forsaken babe that had been exposed by its parents, in the expectation that someone would keep and nourish the poor foundling. As it continued crying and would not be pacified, the good woman resolved to give it the breast, for she had at the time a suckling at home. Having so done she proceeded on her way, but with every step she took the child grew larger and larger, and heavier and heavier, so that when she was within a few steps of her own door she could no longer carry her burden, but was obliged to let go the wonderful suckling, which did not, however, fall on the ground, but glided away under her arm, and at the same moment hahaha! resounded behind her. On her turning round, a voice addressed her with, 'Thanks, good woman, thanks! I have nicely quenched my thirst.' Wondering hereat, she looked to see who spoke, and there stood the Long Wapper close to her, with his head towering far above the houses.

From that time she was very cautious, and whenever, on returning home late at night, she met with anything that appeared in the least degree suspicious, she instantly either crossed herself, or called for aid to the mother of God, or one of the saints or holy angels, and then naturally all went right; and by following this course she continued free from all annoyance for a considerable time. Once, however, as she was on her way home about midnight, she all at once observed a white handkerchief or napkin lying on the ground before her. Thinking she was in luck's way, she was carrying it off, when it stretched itself out more and more, slipped away from her, and at length became so long that she saw it was the Long Wapper again, who now leisurely strode over the houses, at the same time laughing aloud. Of such pranks I could have told you God knows how many; for every night something new occurred, and that not in one place only, but in many at the same time; so that it was evident he could multiply himself.

And then if I were to speak of the various forms under which he appeared! Sometimes he was a cat, sometimes a dog, sometimes a clergyman, sometimes a richly clad personage, who with sweetmeats and the like enticed children to go with him, the Lord alone knows whither. Often would he stand of an incredible height at the lofty church windows, and disturb the late devotions with cursing and blasphemy. At another time he would knock at the windows of the second and even the third stories of the houses, striking the greatest terror into the inhabitants. If he saw any lace-makers or other women or men working late at night, he would cry out to them, 'The night is for me, the day for you!'[1] In wealthy houses he would appear in the form of an acquaintance and sit with the family at table; and when all were enjoying themselves in peace and contentment, would suddenly vanish, laughing at his host. He would frequently mingle with card-players, lose much money, and refuse to pay. If then a quarrel ensued, he would call his fellow-gamesters out, to settle the dispute out of doors, when generally one would lose one's life.

What chiefly made my late father believe that the destruction of souls was one of the Long Wapper's principal objects, was the following occurrence: A man, whose wife was in labour, going out late one night to fetch a midwife, encountered so many difficulties in his way that it would be no easy task to recount them. In the meantime, the poor woman was left alone in her sufferings, and the child would inevitably have died without baptism, had the man – who was my own uncle – not extricated himself by timely recourse to prayer.

But the best preservative against the Long Wapper was an image of the Virgin, for that he could never pass. Since that time such images have been set up at the corners of all the streets, which is the principal reason why he left Antwerp. He now haunts the seacoast.                                        •

---

In the foregoing account of the Long Wapper we have mentioned that no one ever ventured to speak ill of him, or even to whisper the most innocent suppositions concerning him; for no one could be certain that he was not speaking with him himself. In general it did not turn out well for those who said anything about him; for when they went out at night they might be sure of being, in one place or other, obliged to pass between his legs; for he would place himself across the street, with his feet against the opposite sides, and make himself so tall that his whole body rose above the houses, and thus break the neck of many a one that passed under him.

When playing with children he often allowed them to win a great deal,

---

1   The cry of the Wild Huntsman.

particularly at marbles; but when the poor things returned home, and full of joy would exhibit their winnings, the marbles were changed to filthy horse-dung.

He one day played at thieves against the church of the Friars Preachers, and the lot fell on him to be the hangman, an office he willingly undertook. When it came to the hanging, he really hanged him who played the thief, so that the poor boy died; and then at one bounce away he sprang into the water, leaving the others with the dead body, and laughing at them into the bargain.

A few days after this villainous act, a cooper in St Pietersvliet took a journeyman into his service, who at first was very handy and attentive to his business. But one day the master ordered him to throw a handful of shavings into a cask and set them on fire, as coopers are in the habit of doing; but before the master was aware of it, the journeyman had kindled the fire in the workshop, and chopped all the hoops in pieces. When the cooper saw this he was exasperated, and was about seizing his rascally man by the hair, to revenge himself for the damage; but he fled, pursued by his angry master, and sprang, bursting into his usual scoffing laugh, into the water. The cooper now saw pretty clearly with whom he had had to do, and instantly hastened back to his workshop, where he found everything in flames, and not till after much exertion, with the help of his neighbours, could the fire be extinguished.

Shortly after this he hired himself to a brewer. After having been a whole day industrious and attentive, he was ordered in the evening to roll away a full tun of beer. This he contrived to roll over one of his fellow-journeymen, and the poor man was killed. Wapper was pursued by all the brewer's men, who would avenge their mate, but he leaped in the Brouwersvliet and vanished. Some who did not know him sprang after him to catch him, but they were piteously drowned.

Another time he appeared in broad day selling mussels, and passing by a house where four women were sitting before the door at work, he strongly recommended his mussels to them, at the same time opening one, which he very courteously offered to one of the women. She took it, but when in her mouth it was nothing but dirt. He apologised and opened a second. This time all four saw that it was a fine, sound mussel. Another of the women was about to swallow it, but felt something crawling about in her mouth, which on spitting it out proved to be a large, black spider. The women fell upon him, but he defended himself, left two of them for dead and vanished.

Equally atrocious was his conduct towards three youths. They were sitting together in the Ridder-straet, wishing to play at cards, but wanted a fourth. The Long Wapper comes by, offers to play with them, and the game begins. Shortly after a quarrel arises, and from words they soon proceed to fighting; the Long Wapper strikes them dead, one after another, and then was away no one knew how or whither. Often, too, when he mingled with card-players, which frequently happened, he would suffer himself to be pursued by his fellow-gamesters, and so entice them into the water, and there cause them to perish. He once went into an inn, the sign of the Horn, and there made such a disturbance that the night-watch were on the point of seizing him, but he escaped from them and sprang into the water. Those who leaped in after him, with the intention of capturing him, paid for their temerity with their lives.

Sometimes he appeared as a little child. Once in the Beddenstraet some persons found a newborn child lying in the middle of the road on a dunghill. They instantly took the little creature into a house, warmed and fed it with pap, and for ten days took all possible care of it. Then all at once it grew large, ran out of the house, and laughed at the good folks who had been so kind to it. The same happened to a washerwoman, who returning from church found a child in the street, which she took home and fed, and which, when it was warm and satisfied, said, laughing aloud, 'Thanks, mammy; I was very cold and hungry'; with which words it disappeared up the chimney. Something similar also befell three lads. They had gone out to cut osiers; and on the esplanade of the citadel found a child lying in the path. After considering what to do with it, they agreed that one of them should take it with him and give it to his mother. The lad then taking it in his arms, proceeded with it homewards, followed by the others. He had not, however, gone far before he began to complain of fatigue, and begged one of his companions to carry the child. In his arms, too, it grew so heavy, that he fell down with it, and then they resolved that two together should carry it. This lasted for a while, when it became too heavy for them, and the third was obliged to aid them. When they had proceeded a few steps further, the three being unable longer to bear their burden, laid it on the grass and sat down by the side of it. Then all of a sudden the child began to increase, and became larger and larger, and they saw clearly that it was the Long Wapper.

One poor man he struck with deadly terror. This man was so poor that he had not even a handful of straw for his children to sleep on; when one evening returning from his work he found a large bundle of straw lying in the street. This he gladly took home with him, saying to himself, 'Now my poor children can for once have a soft bed.' But hardly had he thrown down the straw in his hut, before it moved and stood erect. The wife seeing this, instantly ran to get holy water, with which having sprinkled it, it instantly flew out through the chimney.

But ten times worse is that which befell a rich woman in Antwerp. This woman led a very licentious life, and had four lovers, all of whom visited her in the evenings, but at different hours, so that no one knew anything of the others. The Long Wapper one night assumed the form of this lady. At ten o'clock came the first lover, and the Long Wapper said to him, 'What dost thou desire?' 'I desire you for a wife,' said the spark. 'Thou shalt have me,' replied Wapper, 'if thou wilt go instantly to the churchyard of our Lady, and there sit for two hours on the transverse of the great cross.' 'Good,' said he, 'that shall be done'; and he went and did accordingly.

At half-past ten came the second. 'What dost thou desire?' asked the Long Wapper. 'I wish to marry you,' answered the suitor. 'Thou shalt have me,' replied Wapper, 'if thou wilt go previously to the churchyard of our Lady, there take a coffin, drag it to the foot of the great cross, and lay thyself in it till midnight.' 'Good,' said the lover, 'that shall be done at once'; and he went and did so.

About eleven o'clock came the third. Him the Long Wapper commissioned to go to the coffin at the foot of the cross in our Lady's churchyard, to knock thrice on the lid, and to wait there till midnight.

At half-past eleven came the fourth, and Wapper asked him what his wishes were. 'To wed you,' answered he. 'Thou shalt do so,' replied Wapper, 'if thou wilt take the iron chain in the kitchen, and dragging it after thee, run three times round the cross in the churchyard of our Lady.' 'Good,' said the spark, 'that I will do.'

The first had set himself on the cross, but had fallen dead with fright to the earth, on seeing the second place the coffin at his feet. The second died with fright when the third struck thrice on the coffin; the third fell down dead when the fourth came rattling his chain, and the fourth knew not what to think, when be found his three rivals lying stiff and cold around the cross. With all speed he ran from the churchyard to the lady, to tell her what had happened, and to hold her to her word. But she of course knew nothing of the matter; when, however, on the following day, she was informed of the miserable death of her three lovers, she put an end to her own life.

## The Wild Hunt

The concubine of an ecclesiastic having died, the night after her decease, as a soldier and his comrades were riding through a forest, they were surprised at hearing a woman's voice crying for help. Shortly after they saw the woman running towards them. One of the soldiers then descending from his horse, made a circle round himself on the earth with his sword, into which he drew the woman. Immediately after they heard a fearful noise in the air, like that of many huntsmen and dogs, at which the woman trembled violently. But the soldier, giving his horse to one of his comrades, took hold of the woman's long tresses and wound them round his left arm, while in his right hand he held his sword stretched out before him.

When the Wild Hunt drew nigh, the woman whispered to the soldier, 'Ride without me, ride without me, there he comes.' The soldier, however, continued holding her fast by the hair, but she tore herself away and fled, leaving her long tresses in his hand. But the huntsman soon caught her and threw her across his saddle, so that her head and arms hung down on one side, and her legs on the other.

Next morning, when he entered the town, the soldier related his adventure and showed the hair on his arm. The people at first would not believe him, but went and opened the coffin, and there found the body lying without hair.

## The Wild Huntsman's Present

As two countrymen were coming late one night through the Sonienbusch, one of them quite drunk, the other being a pious, sober man, they suddenly heard at a distance a cracking of whips, barking of dogs, and tramp of horses. 'God preserve us, here's the Wild Huntsman!' said the sober countryman; but the drunkard laughed and said, 'I would fain know what the foul fiend catches,' and then in a loud voice cried, 'Holla Sir Hunter, pray give me part of your game.' At this the other crossed himself, and they pursued their way home. On the following morning, when the drunkard's wife would go out to fetch water, she found, on opening the door, the hind quarter of an ox that had died in the village about a month before, and had been thrown on the common laystall, and which stank horribly, and was full of worms and maggots.

## The Eternal Huntsman of Wynendael

In the neighbourhood of the castle of Wynendael, the former palace of the Counts of Flanders, there dwelt a long time ago an aged peasant, who had a son that was entirely devoted to the chase, and instead of ploughing and cultivating the fields, was always roaming about the woods and forests. His father had often reproached him for this propensity, but he continued in his old course.

When the old peasant at length lay on his deathbed, he had his son called to him, for the purpose of giving him a last Christian exhortation. He came not, but whistling to his dogs, went out into the thicket. At this the old man was struck with terrific despair, and he cursed his son with the appalling words, 'Hunt then for ever! Aye for ever!' He then turned his head and expired.

From that time the unhappy son has wandered restless about the woods. At night he is frequently heard crying, 'Jacko! Jacko! Jacko!' and then the whole neighbourhood re-echoes with the noise of the huntsman and the baying of dogs.

Others say that the huntsman was, by his father's malediction, transformed to a bird of prey, and flies about in that form, following and attacking both men and beasts, and constantly crying, 'Jacko! Jacko! Jacko!'

In these latter years the old woods about Wynendael have been grubbed up, since which time the huntsman has gone farther up.

## Jack o' Lanterns Baptised

Jack o' Lanterns are, as tradition tells us, the souls of unbaptised children. Because these souls cannot enter heaven, they take their abode in forests, and in dark and desert places, where they mourn over their hard lot. If at night they get sight of any person, they run up to him, and then hasten on before him, to show him the way to some water, that he may baptise them therewith. And that no one should neglect to do, because the poor beings must remain without the gates of paradise until someone takes pity on them.

## Malegy's Palfrey

On the Monday following the little Tuindag (or fair), in the year 1521, three young damsels, Magdalena Ghyselin, Lucia Larmeson and Maxima Vanden Driessche, who dwelt near each other in the street of the Recollets at Ypres, tempted by the coolness of the evening, were walking slowly through the city, when, in the Temple street, they were surprised by the sight of a little horse, which seemed to be wandering about without a master. The animal was of such extraordinary beauty, that the three maidens stood still to admire it. Its skin was white, without hair, and exceedingly smooth; on each haunch there appeared, as if embroidered, a green parrot, and round its body hung many garlands of flowers; its legs were as round as turned pillars, its mane was of gold fringe, and its tail composed of many-coloured ribands; on its back was a saddle of rose-coloured damask.

While the three maidens were thus standing lost in wonder at the uncommon beauty of the horse, a man came running, who appeared to be the master of the strayed animal, who turning to the delighted females, asked them if they had ever seen so handsome a palfrey? 'No,' answered they in ecstasy. 'That I can easily believe,' continued he in a courteous tone, 'for this horse comes from Japan. I have only today arrived in Ypres: its qualities render it even more worthy of admiration than its beautiful form. It will not suffer any male to ride it, and instantly throws anyone that ventures to make the experiment; but it is particularly adapted to carry young damsels, as you may perceive by its splendid saddle. Whenever such wish to mount it, it instantly sinks down on its knees, to receive them on its back. And if you are inclined, ladies, to make a little tour with it, let all three mount, and say where you live, or whither you would like to go; it will convey you thither with all comfort, as if it felt itself flattered at being employed in the service of the fair.'

'What say you?' said Magdalena, who was the boldest of the three, to her two friends; 'I have already been on horseback once, and if you will venture, I will sit foremost and hold the rein; you can sit behind and take fast hold of me.' 'We are willing,' said the two others. 'So, courage, nag,' said the man, at the same time patting the animal; 'bend your knees before the young ladies, that they may mount.' In an instant the horse fell on its knees, and the damsels mounted. 'Now,' said Magdalena Vanden Driessche to the man, 'you must not let the horse run or leap, for I am afraid of falling off.' 'Fear not,' answered the man, 'it shall not leap ; say only where you wish to go.' 'Home,' answered the three at once, 'we live near each other in the street of the Recollets.' 'So, my nag, you have heard: be gentle and ride on with the young ladies,' said the man to the wonderful animal.

Magdalena held fast by the rein, which was a plaited silken cord, to guide the horse, and the proud animal stepped on so gently that its tread could scarcely be beard; but by degrees its pace became quicker and quicker, till at length it seemed to fly along the road like an arrow. It was already without the city gate before the three maidens were aware that they were deceived.

It was now night, and it would not be possible to conjecture the distance that the horse had travelled; but all at once it stopped before a magnificent palace of vast dimensions, the innumerable windows of which appeared like so many furnaces, so intense was the light within the place. The melodious tones of a thousand musical instruments charmed the ears of the listening damsels; it seemed also that they were dancing merrily within.

At once the gate flew open, the palfrey bearing the three maidens entered, followed by its master, and the gate closed of itself after them. A moment after a side-door opened, and a numerous and richly-clad party of ladies presented themselves to the eyes of the young damsels from Ypres. In the middle of the apartment stood a well-furnished table, at the head of which sat a stately personage, who seemed to be the master of the mansion.

Some of the young damsels then stood up, approached the three maidens, and assisted them to dismount from Malegy's palfrey, which again bent its knees; after which they invited them to enter. But the three maidens, who had not recovered from their surprise, craved pardon for their unseasonable appearance at the palace, and were about to begin the recital of what had befallen them. But their excuses found no hearers, and they were obliged to yield to the request of the young ladies. They entered accordingly. Scarcely had they sufficiently feasted their eyes on the splendid attire of the ladies, when their attention was attracted to the lord of the mansion. His dress consisted of an ample robe of damask, which covered his whole person; on his head he had a kind of turban, in the front of which projected a small mirror, and on both sides of which were attached diamonds and other precious stones. This personage was not less courteous than the young ladies, and by his flattering discourse so seduced them, that from sheer politeness they sat down to table and partook of the good cheer.

The three maidens had waited till the supper was over to give an explanation of their adventure; but when they began to inquire for a guide to conduct, them back to their parents, who would be distressed on account of their long absence, the master of the palace arose from his seat and said, 'Dear friends! Now that Malegy's palfrey has procured us the pleasure of receiving in our mansion these noble damsels from Ypres, we must not neglect anything that may contribute to their passing the evening cheerfully and pleasantly – Let us play at forfeits.'

And as if all the ladies had divined the thought of their lord, they had already ranged themselves in a circle when he uttered the last words, leaving places vacant for the damsels from Ypres, whom they pressed to join the party. But Magdalena Ghyselin said, 'I cannot play with you, for my parents will be alarmed if I stay longer.' 'Nor can I,' said Lucia Larmeson. 'I must positively be at home tonight,' said Maxima Vanden Driessche, who was the youngest, and feared being chidden. At this refusal the eyes of the master assumed such a diabolic expression, and his countenance was overspread with such an angry gloom, that they quickly sat down in the circle, to withdraw themselves from the terrific fascination of that visage. They immediately thought that their refusal was an incivility, and charged themselves with causing the unfavourable change which they remarked in the manner of the lord of the mansion. They then played at forfeits.

When it came to the turn of the three maidens to repeat after the master the words he had spoken, their usual quickness at forfeits deserted them, for they were so disconcerted by his looks, that they lost every time, and had to forfeit. This course of bad luck lasted so long that all the three were obliged to give everything they had, so that at last they parted with all their ornaments, as earrings, chains, rings and bracelets, and even their clothes. With beating hearts they awaited the end of the game.

'Now,' said the great man, 'before we proceed to the redeeming of the forfeits, let us drink to the health of Malegy's palfrey, which has so wondrously brought the young ladies to our dwelling.' At these words the eyes of the ladies of the palace grew brighter and shot forth little flames, which almost blinded our three maidens. The master of the palfrey then entered, filled the glasses, and the salver went formally round. It seemed that the lips of the great man muttered some mysterious words, and anyone who could have been an indifferent spectator of what was passing, would have seen that his turban stood higher than before, as if something were growing on his head that lifted it up.

They raised their glasses to their mouths, but no sooner had the first drop of liquid passed over the lips of the three maidens, than they seemed at once to wake from a dream, and found themselves under the blue sky, in the dewy grass that grew in the bottom of a great hollow. The sorcery was at an end. The three maidens were sitting in a deep cavity on the Kemmelberg, two hours distant from the city, yet totally ignorant of the place they were in. It may easily be imagined with what dejection they looked on one another, in the middle of the night, half-naked, and in an unknown place thrown into a pit, from which nothing could be seen but the stars glittering in the heavens. Mute astonishment soon, however, gave place to a general lamentation over their miserable plight. At length, having found means to escape from the pit, they wandered bareheaded and barefooted for some time round the mountain, till at length they perceived a peasant's cottage, towards which they directed their steps.

They knocked at the door: the cottager rose and asked what they wanted. They told him their adventure, and inquired the name of the place where they were. 'On the Kemmelberg,' was the answer, 'and as I hear, you have been in the clutches of the sorceresses, who on the mountain here make such a hideous noise every night. Only an hour ago I got up and put my head out of the window, yet saw nothing but a great light, although I heard playing, singing and dancing without cessation.

The three girls begged for the loan of clothes, and for assistance, but the cottager's wife, who in her bed had heard all that passed, cried out, 'No, Klaes, give them no assistance: persons who dare to appear so naked at our door can be no other than sorceresses, that come to deceive us and to bewitch our child, for I hear it crying already: let us rather seize and burn them.' 'I believe thou art right, wife,' said the man, 'for it is impossible that three young damsels from Ypres, daughters of respectable persons, should come to the Kemmelberg at such an improper hour, and without clothes.' Saying this he seized Magdalena, who stood nearest to him, by her blue under-petticoat. Lucia and Maxima ran down the mountain and escaped. Magdalena screamed and struggled, but with little chance of effecting her escape, when luckily the hook of her petticoat broke, by which accident she was enabled to run off, leaving her garment in the hands of the peasant.

After having wandered through many unknown ways, our scantily-clad damsels, with tearful eyes, cheeks red with shame, and beating hearts, came at length to a hostel, at the door of which they knocked. They did not venture to tell the master, who instantly rose, how they had fallen into so miserable a plight, lest they should receive no better treatment than they had already experienced, and therefore devised a falsehood, making the host believe that they had been attacked and stripped by robbers. Their story inspired pity, they were taken in and provided with clothes.

'But who are you?' inquired the host. 'I,' said Magdalena, 'am the daughter of Baldwin Ghyselin, and these are my near neighbours.' 'What, the daughter of my friend Ghyselin in the street of the Recollets at Ypres!' exclaimed the host. 'That being the case I will instantly put the horses to my wagon, in which I last week carried a load of wood to his house, and will this night conduct you home.' 'Oh do so, do so, good man,' cried the three at once. 'Our parents will handsomely reward you for the trouble.' In less than half an hour the wagon with two horses stood ready before the door of the inn, and the three maidens, dressed in the hostess's clothes, sprang into it, and the party drove off. When they had ridden about an hour, it appeared to the host that he had deviated from the right road. 'That is admirable,' said he. 'I know the way from Kemmel to Ypres as well as my Paternoster, and yet I have taken a wrong road.' The anxiety of the damsels may be easily conceived, when they thought of Malegy's palfrey, that had carried them so supernaturally over hedge and ditch. 'It is wonderful,' said the host again, 'I cannot govern my horses. Here we are now in the middle of a field; and I cannot imagine how the horses could possibly have dragged the wagon into it.' And the wagon went on more and more rapidly, and was dragged with violence across dikes, through thickets, over ploughed land, and through rivulets. A shadow floated constantly before the horses. 'It's the shadow of Malegy's horse,' whispered the three girls with alarm. They at length entered a broad road, and the wagon stopped; the horses reeked with the sweat that ran from them; the shadow had vanished, and day was beginning to dawn. 'The witches, of the Kemmelberg have misled us,' said the host, looking as pale as a corpse, 'but their influence is at an end; for the dawn already appears yonder in the east.' At this moment a countryman passed by on his way to the field. 'Friend, what road is this we are in?' asked the host. 'What road?' repeated the man. 'Yes, I must inquire, though it seems laughable; for I ought to drive the way from Kemmel to Ypres blindfold, so well do I know it; and yet I don't exactly see whereabouts I am at this moment.' The countryman smiled. 'I believe you, friend,' said he. 'You talk about Ypres, and you are more than ten hours distant from it; for you are now on the road from Steenvoorde to Cassel. Don't you see the town in the distance yonder?' 'Oh heavens,' cried the damsels with a sigh, 'how could we be so silly as to ride on Malegy's horse?' Who knows where their wandering would have ended, if Malegy's palfrey had not been surprised by the daylight?

It was with great difficulty that they reached the city of Ypres on that day. What passed in their parental home on their return may easily be imagined; there sadness and anxiety gave place to joy and astonishment at the relation of what they had undergone.

Three years after, Magdalena Ghyselin was married, and the marvellous adventure of herself and two friends was represented on the wall of the best apartment, together with the date. Magdalena explained the subject of the pictures to her children, which they, at a later period, interpreted to their offspring; and thus the story has been handed down to us, with the conviction that in days of yore envious witches held their meetings on the Kemmelberg, around a pit, which in perpetual remembrance of this event, has ever since been named the Kinderput, or Children's pit.

## The Fiddlestick

An old fiddler on his way came one night to the neighbourhood of Hesdin, during a raging storm. He had to pass through the forest, but in the darkness missed his path, and wandered about for a long time without being able to find it. Angry hereat, he struck his stick violently on the ground and let such an impious malediction escape from him as had never before passed his lips. At the same instant he descried a bright light at a distance, the sight of which inspiring him with new courage, he hastened through thick and thin towards it. On arriving close to it, he saw that it issued from the windows of a splendid palace, which he never before had seen, and of which he had never heard a syllable spoken.

Overjoyed, however, at the thought of finding a shelter, he passed through the gate, hastened across the forecourt, and soon found himself standing before the open door of a brilliantly lighted saloon, in which were many persons of both sexes. Some were sitting at long tables around a sumptuous banquet, others were engaged in play at smaller tables; but the greater number were, amid shouts of revelry, whirling about in a merry dance. After the old man had looked on for some time, he approached one who seemed to he the master of the palace, and begged he might be allowed to pass the night in a corner of the mansion. A benignant smile and friendly nod were the sole answer; but a servant richly clad came and relieved him of his violin, which he hung on a golden nail. The old man could now go about the saloon to his heart's content; but his first steps were to the stage on which the musicians were placed, where to his great delight he perceived a violoncello more beautiful than any he had ever seen, and immediately thought he would try the tone of it. But while he was casting his eyes around, for the purpose of discovering the steps that led up to the stage – for he considered himself fully capable of performing with the best of the players – he observed there a face quite familiar to him; it was that of his teacher in the art, who had been dead above thirty years. 'Holy mother, what do I see!' exclaimed the old man astounded. At the same instant the whole company, with servants – tables, musicians and palace, all vanished.

On the following morning some persons from Auffin found the old fiddler lying senseless at the foot of the gallows. In his hand was a white fiddlestick; but his own violin and bow were hanging on the toe of one of the malefactors there suspended, round whose shoulders the artist's cloak was carefully wrapped.

When recovered from his swoon, the old man hastened home, where on more closely examining the white fiddlestick, he saw that it was a human bone, and that on it, inlaid in silver, was the name of a person in Hesdin, who bore a very indifferent character among his neighbours.

When the artist took the bow to him, the man turned pale, and offered him a purse that should never be empty, but always contain six pounds Parisian, provided he would keep the affair secret. This the other readily promised, took the purse, and soon became a rich man.

## The Fiddler Tricked

An old fiddler, who had been playing at the fair at Opbrakel, and was returning with well-filled pockets and contented mind to his home, had, in order to arrive at Nederbraekel, to pass through a wood. It was already midnight, and Kartof (such was the name of the old man) was proceeding through the wood, when by chance putting his hand in his pocket, he felt his pipe. 'Ah,' said he to himself, 'if I had only a spark of fire, how comfortably I could smoke my pipe!' Scarcely were the words out of his mouth, when in the middle of the wood, at about a hundred paces distant, he perceived a light. On proceeding towards it, he saw as he drew near that there was a large wood fire, around which a number of men and women hand in hand were dancing and merrymaking. 'Good ladies and gentlemen, I wish you a pleasant evening,' said Kartof. 'Will you kindly allow me to take a spark of your fire?' 'Readily, readily,' answered the dancers, everyone at the same time springing forward to give him a light; so that he soon blew forth clouds of balmy smoke. Perceiving Kartof's fiddle, the dancers asked whether he would not strike up a quadrille. 'Ah, why not?' answered the old man simpering; and in an instant all left the spot and conducted him to a spacious saloon in a large palace. Here the fiddler tuned his instrument, a glass of costly wine was presented to him, and now the dancing began right merrily. To rouse the player, every time that his fiddlestick flagged, the dancers dropped a piece of gold into his instrument, which the old man saw with devouring eyes. His glass also was filled the moment it was empty. But the two operations were so often repeated, that both the fiddle and the eyes of the player became all the duller, and the latter at length closed through drunkenness; so that Kartof fell asleep and the dancing ceased.

The sun had risen high when Kartof woke, who just raised his heavy head to see where he had been so long sleeping, and gradually to collect his thoughts a little together. He lay in the middle of the wood by a heap of ashes, among which some charcoal was still glimmering. He then stood up and felt for his fiddle; for drunk as he had been, he had not forgotten the events of the night. He turned his instrument about, for the purpose of shaking out the gold pieces that had appeared so attractive to him, but, O horrible deception! They proved to be only beech leaves that fell on the ground. On further consideration he was convinced that the trick had been played him by phantoms; for in the whole neighbourhood he had never seen any palace, save that which the sprites had that night caused to appear and vanish.

## The Fiddler in the Gallows-field at Antwerp

Near Antwerp there is a large field where formerly the gallows stood, whence its name of the Gallows-field. Beyond this field there dwelt many years ago a fiddler, a pleasant, jovial man, who was a sort of necessary appendage at every wedding and christening in the city; for he was everywhere a welcome guest.

Returning late one night from the city, where he had been engaged at a wedding party, he took his way across the Gallows-field. Here to his no small surprise he found a large assembly of women dancing and making merry; and a little farther he lighted on another company of many hundreds sitting and feasting at sumptuously covered tables. He rubbed his eyes, not knowing whether he were awake or dreaming, and stood lost for a while in wonder. One of the women stepping up to him, said, 'Pray, good musician, oblige us with a tune.' He required no second asking, but sat down, adjusted his instrument, and struck up a merry tune, at which the feasters rose from table, took each other's hand and danced. When the dance was ended, one of the women came and presented to him a silver cup filled with wine, which he took with thanks, saying: 'Now, my honoured ladies, to your health! May God bless you!' But scarcely had the last words passed his lips, before all had vanished, and he found himself alone, with the cup and his fiddle, sitting – on the gallows! from which, not without difficulty and danger, he contrived to descend only on the following dawn. The cup he of course retained, and long preserved, and showed it to many persons, to whom he related the adventure.

## The Wedding-feast at Carron-Saint-Martin

The bridegroom was the wealthiest man, the bride the fairest maid in all the country about. The wedding was splendid, and all went on merrily till the hour for dancing drew nigh. It was then suddenly announced to the young bridegroom that a little man, a stranger, was at the door craving admission, and ere he could answer, the extraordinary guest was already standing in the saloon. Scarcely had the bridegroom cast eyes on him when his cheeks grew deadly pale, and he but coldly returned the stranger's greeting. This, however, gave the latter not the slightest concern, but seating himself at the table, he emptied the most capacious beer jug at one draught, and devoured the largest ham clean to the bone, so that all the guests were seized with a cold shuddering; for they could not imagine that any man in the world could eat and drink such a quantity.

When the table was cleared the stranger said to the bridegroom, who sat still as pale as a corpse, 'Now this I call a gay wedding, at which there is not a solitary fiddle.' Whereupon one of the company told him, that the musician was prevented from coming by the bad weather. 'Oh, if that's all,' replied the newcomer, 'I'll soon set the matter right: I have my violin standing just by the door.' Having said this, he stepped out and instantly returned with his instrument, seated himself in a chair placed on the table, and began playing the merriest tunes imaginable.

All now arranged themselves for dancing with the exception of the bridegroom, who stood in a corner buried in thought. No sooner, however, did the stranger get a glimpse of him than, springing from the table, he hastened towards him, saying, 'How now, Hans? This is the happiest day of your life, and you stand there as if you could not count three.' But the bridegroom continued as it were in a dream. The stranger then laid his hand familiarly on his shoulder, and at the same instant the stings of hell seemed to penetrate him; he rushed forward in the most frantic joy, danced, leapt, cried, raved and laughed so horribly that he might have been pronounced a maniac rather than a rational being, who was looking forward to the realisation, within a short time, of his long-cherished wishes. The other guests were seized with a similar drunken frenzy, and persisted in their wild mirth until the clock announced the hour of midnight. The stranger then putting the violin into his pocket, descended from the table, approached the bridegroom and in a cold, calm tone said, 'It's now time I think?'

'One night, only one night longer,' said the person addressed, trembling as with the most desperate ague.

'No!' was the answer.

'Then give me yet one hour, one short hour.'

'No!' was repeated in an inexorable tone.

'A quarter of an hour then,' said the bridegroom imploringly.

'No!'

'Yet will I have compassion on thee,' continued the stranger, after having for a moment enjoyed the despair of the poor wretch. 'If thy wife will undersign this, I will grant thee eight days more.'

The bridegroom snatched from the hand of the stranger a sheet of vellum with characters written in gold, cast on it a protracted look, and then with horror dashed it on the ground.

'Then I must take leave of the company,' said the stranger, 'and you will perhaps accompany me a step or two?'

With these words the little man politely greeted all present, threw his arm familiarly round the neck of the bridegroom, and with him quitted the apartment, after having whispered to the bride, 'Adieu, child; don't be angry with me for taking away your husband; you shall soon see him again.'

The poor bride did indeed see him again, but not until the following day, and then as a blackened half-consumed corpse. When he was conveyed to the church all the consecrated lights went out, and the grave, in which the coffin was deposited, was on the following morning found empty.

## Riding on Calves

In the village of Capelle, three hours distant from Antwerp, there lived a respectable farmer, whose wife was a witch and attended every sabbath.

One night she asked her husband whether he would not accompany her, to which, being of a curious disposition, he consented. The woman then fetched two calves, on which they mounted: she also enjoined him not to utter a syllable, and then said,

> Over haeg en over heg,
> Tot Keulen in den wynkelder,
>
> *Over hedge and over haw,*
> *To Cologne in the wine-cellar,*

and away they went through the air on and on, till they came to a great water. There the calves making a spring, were instantly on the opposite side. At this the man was so surprised that he cried aloud, 'God bless us all, what a jump for a calf!'[1] But in the same moment the calf vanished, and the farmer stood alone and in a strange country. Next morning, on inquiring of a passer-by in what direction the village of Capelle lay, the man had never heard of such a place; but on asking how far distant the famous city of Antwerp was, he was answered: 'Ah, you must travel a long way before you reach that, for it is sixty hours distant from this place.'

## The Woman transformed to a Horse

At a large farm at Bollebeck there dwelt a serving-man, who although he always got nutritious food from the farmer's wife, yet daily grew thinner and thinner. His fellow-servants frequently asked him the cause of this, but he constantly answered that he knew not, until at length the shepherd, who was his most intimate friend, fished the matter out of him. To him he confessed that every night the farmer's wife came to his bedside and threw a bridle over his head, by virtue of which he became instantly turned to a horse; she would then set herself upon him, and ride on him throughout the night. 'That seems to me incredible,' said the shepherd, 'but let me lie in thy bed tonight; I should like to try the thing for once.' The man agreed, and the shepherd laid himself in his bed.

About ten o'clock the farmer's wife came in softly, and was about to cast the bridle over him, but he was too quick for her, snatched it out of her hand and cast it over her own head; when in one second there she stood before him as a horse! He rode her about the fields the whole night, and

1　See p. 358.

when the day began to dawn he took her back and led her to the farmer, saying, 'Master, there is a horsedealer in the village, who wishes to dispose of this mare, for which he asks five hundred francs.' 'She is sold,' said the farmer, 'come in and I will give thee the money.' 'But it's without the bridle,' said the shepherd, 'which he requires to have back.' The farmer laughing said, 'Be it so, the bargain stands,' at the same time counting out the money, which the shepherd speedily pocketed, and took the bridle off the mare, when lo, there stood the wife bodily before them! Shedding bitter tears she fell at her husband's feet, promising never again to do the like. The shepherd kept the money, but made a promise never to divulge what had taken place, which he kept till his dying day.[1]

## The Cats of Stockhem

There was a man in Stockhem, whose wife was in childbed, and who, when the child was safely brought into the world, put on his Sunday clothes and hastened to acquaint his mother-in-law with the auspicious event. 'O,' said the mother-in-law, 'I know that already; I have just been told it.' At this the man was greatly surprised, for no one in Stockhem knew anything of the matter, and the wife's mother lived a good half-hour from the village. When the man was returning and quietly going along by the brook that runs by the roadside, a cat suddenly darted after him, and passed between his legs: a second followed, a third, a fourth, and so on to the number at least of thirty. All these surrounded the man and so annoyed him that he struck into the midst of them with his stick. But his striking was to little purpose, they evaded his blows, and in reward for his good intention, cast him into the brook, after having torn from him his silver shoe buckles.

Wet and fatigued the poor man reached his home, and instantly sent for the priest, to whom he related the adventure. 'Ah,' said the priest, 'I see what's in the wind, and all that I can say and advise is this: give nothing to anybody that begs of you at the door, if you desire your wife and child to continue well.' The man promised to follow the advice, and observed it faithfully, at least for a while.

On the following morning there came a poor old woman to the door, begging for a morsel of bread; but the man said, 'Go your way, I give nothing.' In the afternoon there came two very aged women, one leading the other: they were dismissed in a similar manner. Greybeards, cripples, children came begging, but no one got anything, and this went on for more than three weeks.

1    See p. 360–1.

The woman had in the meantime become quite well again, and the child grew every day stronger and stronger. One forenoon, when she was sitting at home with the babe on her lap, an old woman came, who begged in a most piteous tone, imploring with tears that a morsel of bread might be given her; for that for two days she had not tasted food. The man was prudent and said, 'No; go away, I'll give you nothing.' But the wife, who had a tender heart, entreated her husband so long, that at last he gave the crone a piece of bread.

Scarcely had the wife with her child re-entered the apartment, when the infant was snatched from her by invisible hands, and dashed against the ceiling. On falling to the ground, no one thought it had escaped with its life. The woman at the same instant received a shock, which threw her into a corner. All cried and screamed. The man ran to the priest, beseeching him to aid them speedily. The good pastor came instantly, but pronounced both mother and child beyond all help; and so it proved, as both died within a week.

## A Witch Burnt

The castle of Erendegen was so awfully haunted, that it would not have been possible, with all the gold in the world, to prevail on anyone of the peasants of the village to pass a single night in it. At last, however, a man came to the place who was known by the name of bold Jan, who offered to go to the castle, and stay any length of time, requiring only to be furnished with everything necessary for the frying of pancakes. This was promised, and Jan in the evening proceeded to the castle.

In one of the best rooms he made a fire and began busily to fry, when the door opened, and in walked a black cat, and sat down before the fire, as if for the purpose of warming herself. She then asked Jan what he was doing. 'I am frying pancakes, my little friend,' said Jan, and the words were hardly out of his mouth, when seven cats entered at the same time, one of which appeared to be the superior. These likewise asked Jan what he was doing, and Jan again answered, 'I am frying pancakes.' The cats then taking each other's paw began to dance round and round. Jan now filled the pan with butter, which when melted and scalding hot, he threw over the cats, and in one instant they all vanished.

On the following day it was said in the village, that the shoemaker's wife was burnt over her whole body, of which the soldier knew something, and assured the inhabitants that thenceforth the castle would be no more haunted. And so it proved, for the cats never ventured to return.[1]

1   See p. 250.

## The Red Cloth

In former times peasant-women were often observed to bring butter to the market of Turnhout in such quantities as to excite everyone's astonishment, it being known that they did not own a cow, or, at the most, had only a single one. The general belief was that this butter came from the Kaboutermannekens, and by the aid of a red cloth.

One of these women, who was suspected of having such a red cloth, often brought butter to a certain house, which butter was as sweet as a nut and as yellow as gold. When she came, a cup of coffee was usually given to her, and sometimes a slice of bread and butter; for she was a pleasant, lively woman. The master of the house, however, not feeling quite satisfied respecting her, went to a priest, to whom he communicated his doubts. The priest gave him a little box, directing him to hang it under the chair in which the woman might be sitting.

On the next market-day the woman as usual brought her butter, and having received payment for it, a cup of coffee was given to her. While she was sitting, the man came clandestinely and hung the box on her chair, then seated himself opposite to her, to observe what she would do. She appeared in nowise disconcerted, but sat unusually long, talking incessantly till the clock struck twelve. Then said the man, 'Good woman, we are now going to dine, and you are probably going to do the same; it is therefore time for you to go home.' The woman answered, 'Yes, you are right,' and would rise from her seat, but could not, for the chair clung to her. On seeing this, the man full of rage exclaimed, 'Stand up and pack yourself off.' The woman was terrified, and said trembling, 'I will readily do so, but you must first take away the thing that you have hung to the chair; for it holds me fast.' The man then removed the box, struck the woman, and thrust her out of doors.

## The Tormented Witch

The children of two pious persons in Amsterdam being bewitched, a neighbour advised them to boil oak chips in water which had been drawn from below a cross-bridge; then would the devil's journeywoman make her appearance, and the children be well again. At first the parents gave no heed to this advice, but afterwards, from compassion to the children, adopted it, though with closed doors, and without the knowledge of anyone. At the first boiling of the water, a female neighbour came in running and crying out, 'Ye devil-casters! Ye devil-casters!' and continued thus crying and running about the house as long as the pot was on the fire; whence it evidently appeared whom the poor infants had to thank for their sufferings.

## The Ace of Hearts Pierced

An officer in Antwerp had seduced a maiden and deserted her. In her resentment she consulted a sorceress, who gave her an ace of hearts with the following directions: the next night, when the clock struck twelve, to take a full glass of white wine, lay the card upon it, and pierce the heart exactly through the middle with a needle. She would then be revenged. She did so, but when she pierced the card, three drops of blood fell into the glass.

On that evening the officer was sitting with his comrades in a tavern. Just as the clock struck twelve, while he was in the act of raising his glass, he suddenly grew pale and fell down dead. The others, not aware that he was no more, carried him out and laid him on a bed, when on examination it was found that he had a deep wound in the region of the heart.

## The Lost Chain

A citizen's daughter in Antwerp had received a gold chain from her mother as a present. It was on a Sunday that it was given to her, she wore it the whole day, and at night placed it, carefully wrapped in cotton, in her drawer. Next morning wishing to feast her eyes on it, she found, on opening the drawer, that it had disappeared. She now went to a sorceress, in the hope of discovering who had stolen the chain. The woman told her that the chain was already in third hands, but that she would recover it, if she conducted herself discreetly. She then fetched a crucifix, a wax candle, a candlestick, and a paper of needles. The cross she placed before her with the back of the image towards her, the candle she set in the candlestick, and then stuck every needle into it. 'This is a cruel process,' said she, 'for everyone of these needles will wound the thief.' 'That matters little,' answered the girl, 'provided only I get my chain again.' The sorceress assured her she would recover it, and that she might return home quite easy.

On the evening of the same day, as the girl was sitting by the fire with her mother, talking over the loss of the chain, her eldest brother, breathless and pale, rushed into the apartment. In answer to the questions put to him, he could only answer, 'The dog, the dog with the fiery eyes has gone upstairs, oh the dog!' 'What means all this?' said the mother, opening the door, when a large dog darted down the stairs, passed by her and sprang out of the house. 'Lord preserve us, the devil!' cried the woman; but the girl exclaimed with delight, 'He has brought me my chain back!' All crossed themselves, and went upstairs, and searched, but found nothing; every chest, every closet, even the beds were rummaged, but no chain appeared. At length said the woman, 'Stop: in the garret there are the sacks of apples, which we had carried up yesterday from the garden; it may be in one of them.' 'You are certainly very silly,' said the daughter laughing; but the mother replied, 'Who can know? Nothing is lost by seeking.' And the woman was right; for at the bottom of one of the sacks the chain was found folded up in paper.

## The Landmark Removed

Near the village of Vierzel there dwelt in former times a peasant, who was so impelled by the desire of increasing his land that he removed the boundary-posts that separated his fields from those of his neighbour, and thereby stole a considerable piece of land. The neighbour was a heartily good man, who suspected no one of evil, and therefore never was sensible of the other's dishonesty. Thus the peasant enjoyed the fruits of his robbery as long as he lived. But now came his hour of death, and so unexpectedly that be had no opportunity to confess his sins. After his decease, the peasants of the neighbourhood saw him every night, between the hours of twelve and one, running through the field, bearing a heavy stake on his back, and crying incessantly, 'Where shall I set it? Where shall I leave it?'

He had long been running about in this manner, when it chanced that a drunken peasant, who was passing through the field, finding himself unable to proceed farther, laid himself down and fell asleep. On the stroke of twelve the ghost appeared with the landmark, and cried as usual, 'Where shall I set it? Where shall I leave it?' The drunkard waked by the cry, raised his head, and looking on the ghost, said, 'Thou ragamuffin, set it again where thou stolest it from, thou blockhead!' 'The Lord be thanked! Now I am released!' cried the ghost joyfully, and went and set the stake again in its old place; and from that time never returned.

*A precisely similar story is told of a spectre near Tondern, in Sleswig. See Müllenhoff, p. 189. The superstition is one of the most widespread.*

## The Bold Soldier of Antwerp[1]

There was in former days a house in the Little Market at Antwerp that had four storeys, and was as beautiful as a royal palace; but no one would live in it because it was haunted. At the stroke of twelve there came a spectre, that ran up and down the stairs; and when it struck one, it would place itself behind the street-door, and begin to howl so horribly that everyone

---

1   See Grimm, J. & W., *Kinder- und Hausmärchen*, op. cit., No. 4.

felt pity for it. But no one had courage enough to enter the house, which thus continued empty, although the ghost every night cried, 'Release my soul! Release my soul!'

This had continued a long while, when an old soldier from the wars came to the city, who, on hearing people speak of the house, said he would sleep a night in it, if a hundred guilders were given him beforehand. The landlord wondered at this, but the soldier said, he feared neither devil nor goblin; for what God protects is well protected. The landlord then said, 'Give me thy hand as a pledge, and tell me with what I must provide thee.' 'Give me,' said the soldier, 'a good supply of wood cut small, a dozen bottles of wine, a bottle of brandy, and a pot full of dough, together with a good pan, that I may bake my cakes.' 'That thou shalt have,' answered the landlord; and when the soldier had all he required, he went with it at nightfall into the house.

Having struck a light, he carried all his gear into an apartment on the first storey, in which there still remained a table and two chairs, and then made a large fire on the hearth, by which he placed his dough, that it might rise a little. He next broke the necks off his bottles, and so did not long continue altogether sober, though he well knew what he said and did. Thirst being now succeeded by hunger, he took his pan, set it on the fire, and threw into it a good ladleful of dough. The cake promised well, smelt most temptingly, was already brown on one side, and the soldier was in the act of turning it, when something suddenly fell down the chimney into the pan, and the cake was in the ashes!

The soldier was not a little angry at this disaster, but reconciled himself to his fate and filled the pan anew. While the cake was baking, he looked at what had fallen down the chimney and found it was an arm-bone. At this the brave warrior began to laugh, and said, 'You want to frighten me, but you won't do it with your horse's bone.' He then seized the pan, to take out the cake, preferring to eat it half baked rather than undergo a second disappointment; but in the same instant a rattling was heard in the chimney, a number of bones fell into the pan, and the cake into the ashes.

'Now, by Jove,' said he, 'that is too bad. They ought to let me be quiet, for I am hungry. To pitch the whole backbone of a colt into my pan!' But he was grievously mistaken, for it was the backbone of a human being. Highly enraged he seized the bones and dashed them with such violence against the wall that they flew in pieces. Out of humour he again sat down by the pan and made several attempts to bake his cake, but every time down fell one or other bone, and, by way of conclusion, a skull, which the soldier hurled as far as he could send it.

'Now the sport will be at an end,' said he, and began again to bake, and this time without interruption, so that he had a good dishful of cakes on the table, and had already sat down and was eating comfortably, when the clock struck. He counted; it was twelve. In the same instant he looked up, and saw that in the corner facing him the bones had united and stood there as a hideous skeleton with a white linen over its shoulders. The soldier rubbed his eyes, thinking it a dream, but seeing that it was a real skeleton, he called to it merrily, ' Ha Mr Death! How goes it? You are uncommonly thin. But come and eat and drink with me, provided cake and wine will not fall through your body.' The skeleton made no answer, but merely pointed with its finger. 'Well, speak then, if you are from God,' said he laughing; 'but if from the devil, make yourself scarce.' The skeleton continued pointing, but said nothing, and the soldier growing tired of this, ate on leisurely, taking no further notice of its movements. It now struck half-past twelve, and the skeleton striding out of its corner, approached the table. 'Ah,' cried the soldier, 'say what you want, but keep at a distance, else we are no longer friends.' The skeleton then stretching forth its hands, touched that of the soldier and burned a hole in it. 'Hui, the devil!' cried he. 'What's this?' at the same time snatching up an empty bottle and hurling it at the skeleton; but it flew in vacant space. He was now in a towering passion, and would thrust the spectre out, but he grasped the empty air, the skeleton constantly making signs and pointing towards the door.

The soldier at length growing weary of this dumb show, took up the light and said: 'Well, I'll go with you, do you only go first.'

The skeleton went first as far as the stairs, and made a sign to the soldier that he should go down; but he was prudent enough not to do so, saying, 'Go you first, always first; you shall not break my neck.' They thus descended into a passage, in which lay a heavy stone, having an iron ring in it. The ghost made a sign to him to raise the stone, but he laughed and said: 'If you want to lift up the stone, you must do it yourself.' The ghost did so, and the soldier then saw that there was a great hole beneath it, in which stood three iron pots. 'Do you see that money?' said the skeleton. 'Aha, countryman, you speak Flemish,' cried the soldier, highly delighted, 'that's capital. Yes, I see something that looks like a ten-guilder piece.'

The ghost now drew up the three pots and said, 'This is money which I concealed before my death.' 'So,' said the soldier, 'you are dead then?' The ghost continued without answering, 'I had to burn in hell as long as the money was not found. You have released me from hell.' 'A pretty fellow you!' said the soldier; 'In gratitude for the service, you have burnt my hand.' 'I shall burn no more,' said the ghost laughing; 'just feel my hand now, it's quite cold.' But the other drawing back his hand, cried, 'Much obliged all the same, no ceremony; I know you birds.' 'Now I beseech you to bestow one of the pots on the poor, to give one to the church that masses may be said for my soul, and –' 'This is an awkward business,' exclaimed the soldier, 'I am not your lackey. But what were you going to say?' 'The third pot is for you,' whispered the ghost. And the soldier leaped and danced and fell into the hole and his light with him, so that he sat in the dark. 'Ho spritekin,' cried he, 'give me a lift out!' But the ghost had vanished, and he had to scramble out as well as he could. When he again found himself safe on the ground, he felt for his candle and for the stairs, went up, and lay down to sleep.

On the following day he did as the ghost had directed, gave one pot to the poor, another to the church, and found so much in the third, that he became a very rich man, rode every day in a coach, and went every day to the tavern.

## Mariken of Nymwegen

At the time when Duke Arent of Gelderland was taken prisoner by his son, Duke Adolf and his confederates (AD 1465), there dwelt about three miles from Nymwegen a pious priest, named Gysbrecht, who had with him a beautiful young girl, named Mariken, the daughter of his sister, her mother being dead. This maiden superintended the good man's household, and was exceedingly active and vigilant.

Now it once happened that the priest had occasion for various articles that could only be got in Nymwegen, as candles, oil, vinegar and matches; so he gave Mariken eight stivers and sent her to the city, at the same time enjoining her, if her purchases were not made in time for her to return by daylight, to go and pass the night at her aunt's; for she was a lively, handsome girl, and a mischance might but too easily befall her. Mariken promised so to do, and went to Nymwegen. But scarcely had her uncle lost sight of her when he repented of having suffered her to go, and said to himself, 'Would that I had kept her at home; it is too dangerous to send young damsels and women alone about the country; for the villainy of the world is very manifold.' Yet what was he to do? He must have a light when it was dark, and he must also eat; besides which, it was now too late; for Mariken was already far far away.

The aunt, to whom he had recommended his niece, busied herself much with politics, and was an enthusiastic partisan of Duke Adolf. She had just been conversing with several other women concerning him, and had in the course of her haranguing become so excited, that she appeared more like a furious female devil than a respectable Christian woman, when Mariken entered the room. It was grown too late for the good lass to think of returning home, she had therefore followed her uncle's injunction, and now greeted her aunt in these gentle and courteous terms, 'Dear aunt! May our Lord sweeten all your suffering, and protect those whom you love against every evil.' But the aunt turning her head, assailed her with these unchristianlike words, 'Ha ha! Welcome devil, how goes it in hell?' Mariken, though horrified at the dreadful expressions, quietly deposited her purchases in a corner, and modestly requested a night's lodging. But for her petition the aunt had no ears; for she was sunk too deep in politics. The poor girl again and more earnestly besought her, but to as little purpose as before: she went on raving, 'What! Thou drivest the devil into my head; but I will bind him, I will swathe and lace him on a pillow like a child: I hardly know whether I am standing on my head or my feet,' – and much more in the same strain. Vexed and saddened, Mariken packed her purchases together, resolving to pass the night under the blue vault of heaven rather than at her aunt's, and said, 'I will now ask nothing more from any living soul, even should the real devil himself come to me.' She then left the house of her aunt and the city of Nymwegen, and walked on and on, in the hope of reaching home.

But when alone in the open country, and overpowered by fatigue and hunger, she could proceed no further, she abandoned herself to despair, and weeping bitterly exclaimed, 'Oh help me, help me, me unhappy maiden, God or devil; it is the same to me'; and she held her hands before her face, and dried her humid eyes with her apron. While so doing, she was startled by suddenly seeing an elegant personage stand before her, who in a friendly voice said to her, 'Tell me, pretty damsel, why you are so afflicted.' Mariken was not a little terrified at hearing herself addressed by one, of whom the instant before she had not seen a trace; but the stranger continued, 'You must not be terrified, my fair maiden; for I love you most heartily, and if you are content, I will make you a lady of ladies.' This somewhat tranquillised Mariken, who said, 'But tell me then, dear friend, truly who you are?' The stranger answered, 'A master of all arts am I, and if you will love me, I will teach you instantly the seven liberal arts, to wit, Music, Rhetoric, Logic, Grammar, Geometry, Arithmetic and Alchemy.' Mariken stared on hearing all these erudite names repeated, and felt quite pleased at the idea of learning so much; but she insisted beforehand on knowing the stranger's name. 'That I can tell you,' said he. 'I am called Monen with one eye; but that is not all that you have to expect from me: of gold and jewels, for instance, and money, you shall never be in want, if you only grant me your love.' 'Is that true?' said Mariken with astonishment, 'then I really have nothing to object; there is, however, another thing besides, that I would gladly learn, and that is the art of necromancy. My uncle has a beautiful book about it, with which he could do wonders, and drive the devil through a pinhole. That art I must also learn.'

This was a hard blow for the stranger, for at no price would he willingly have taught that art; and therefore said, 'Desist from that wish, my love, the art of necromancy is a very dangerous one, and many a one has lost his life by it. Think only that in the conjuring of spirits, if you fail but in one word, or even in a single syllable, it is all over with you, and then I can no more call you my heart's delight. But in compensation I will instruct you in the great art of understanding every language in the world; and that I would fain believe will be more pleasing to my beloved.' Mariken agreed to the proposal, and requested the stranger to begin his instruction forthwith. But he said, 'I have previously one request to make, dear girl, and that is that from henceforth you change your name; for I cannot endure it: Mariken! Ah!' To this the damsel would not consent; so when Monen saw that for the moment his object was not attainable, he contented himself with the promise she made him, never to make the sign of the holy cross. He then spoke on indifferent subjects, but by degrees returned to that of changing her name, and proposed that, instead of the odd, ill-sounding Mariken, she should assume the more usual and more euphonic appellation of Emmeken. With this proposal she complied, and immediately after they both set out for Bois-le-Duc and Antwerp. Before they reached the first-mentioned place Mariken was already in possession of all that had been promised by Monen, without being conscious how it came to pass.

Master Gysbrecht in the meanwhile knew not what to think about his niece. Two, three, four days had passed, and she was still absent. The house became more and more melancholy to the good man. At length, unable to endure suspense any longer, he took his stick, and proceeded to his sister in Nymwegen; for he expected as a certainty to find Mariken there. But the impious woman scoffed at his anxiety, and when Gysbrecht earnestly implored her to tell him where Mariken could be found, she answered, 'How should I know? She was here a week ago, and I sent her to the devil, with whom she is most probably rambling about.'

The good man was now inconsolable, but strove gradually to collect himself, addressed a fervent prayer to our Lady of Aix-la-Chapelle and St Servatius of Maestricht, and with tottering steps returned to his lonely dwelling.

But the aunt's barbarous malediction did not go unpunished; for a few days after, the castellain to whose safe custody Duke Arent had been entrusted, set his captive at liberty, who was received with loud demonstrations of joy in Bois-le-Duc. At this the wicked woman was so bitterly enraged that she no longer knew what she did, and in her fury laid violent hands on herself.

Of all this Mariken knew nothing. She was quietly staying with Monen at the Tree Tavern in the great marketplace at Antwerp. This was a notorious house, where all kinds of rabble were in the habit of assembling: prostitutes, thieves, sharpers, swindling tradesfolk, and the Lord knows what besides, all of whom raved and rioted so that it was horrible to hear. Some of these light gentry soon introduced themselves to Mariken and Monen, being strongly attracted by the beauty of the former. But Mariken turning to her companion, said, 'Tell me, my love, is not that geometry, when I count the drops of wind in the can yonder?' Monen answered, 'Quite right, child, you have well retained the art I taught you yesterday.' The guests were astounded at the young woman's erudition, but their wonder increased when Monen informed them she was mistress of all the seven arts, and among the rest of rhetoric, which was the oldest of all. They wished to have a specimen, and this flattered the damsel, who rising repeated a poetical piece, which was so ingenious that the verses at the end, and in the middle, and everywhere, rimed together; so that a number of persons soon gathered round her, listening to her with open mouths. Monen had in the meantime slipped away from her, and mingled with the listeners, whereby giving a push to one and a push to another, he soon set them all at loggerheads together. This so delighted Monen, who, as everyone will see, was no other than the incarnate Satan himself, that he resolved to make a longer stay at The Tree; 'For,' said he to himself, 'if he above yonder puts no stop to me, I shall in a year's time get more than a thousand souls into my clutches.'

Emmeken was not pleased with this spectacle, and often thought within herself that Monen was not one of the best of persons; and this thought was the more lively within her, when she called to mind the promise she had made, never to make the sign of the cross. But while she was thus standing and pondering, a pair of jovial companions approached her, and all the good suggestions of her conscience were away, and she amused herself with the two frivolous sparks.

Thus did Emmeken, or Mariken, live during a period of six years, and Monen took more and more delight in her. But now a longing rose in her heart to see once again her uncle Gysbrecht and her other friends and acquaintances, to whom she would gladly have shown how learned she had become. At this wish Monen was far from feeling pleased, and strove to dissuade Mariken from harbouring it; but she said, 'I am resolved on going,' and he was compelled to comply; so they set out for Nymwegen, and arrived there on the day of the fair. On that day a play in a booth was annually performed there, and Emmeken was desirous of seeing it, for she had often heard her uncle say how delightful it was. But Monen expressed anger at her intention, and wondered how so learned a person could feel an interest in such trifles; for he feared that from the pious drama, which usually had more useful influence on the people than preaching and teaching, she might contract other thoughts, and become unfaithful to him. But Emmeken persisted in her resolution, and he was forced to accompany her to the place.

On their arrival Mascheroen, who had just entered, was saying, 'I am Breherio Mascheroen, the advocate of Lucifer, and will call God to account for being more clement to men, who are perpetually sinning, than to us devils, who have sinned but once, and for that once must burn eternally and without hope in the abyss of hell.' Having said this, he turned to the Lord and called him to account. Whereupon God said, 'I have declared and promised that whosoever repents in time shall find grace to eternity.' Mascheroen replied, 'But that was not in our time in the Old Testament, and therefore I maintain that we suffer unjustly.' Christ now rose and said, 'Why then did I die, unless to change all that, and bring all men to grace? You prefer an unjust complaint, Mascheroen, and my father is quite right.' 'If that is the case,' rejoined the advocate, 'then God ought now to be much more rigorous towards man than formerly in the Old Testament, and that it cannot be said he is, Sir Christ.' Then God the Father spoke, 'Yes, that is true, and if mankind do not mend their ways, I will cause my sharp sword of justice to fall upon them.'

Then our Lady, who also was present, took this greatly to heart, and besought her son at least to send forewarnings to mankind, such as comets, double suns, earthquakes and the like. But Jesus was inexorable and persisted in his anger, because man only grew worse and worse the oftener he was warned.

'Come, my dear Emmeken,' cried Monen impatiently, 'what good can you derive from such babble? Come, let us talk on more rational subjects.' But Emmeken would not stir a foot's breadth from the spot, and the less so, as Mascheroen having just asked whether God would not allow him to torment mankind, Mary in most beautiful and touching expressions implored him to forgive them. Then did bitter repentance cut through the very heart of Mariken, and notwithstanding Monen's reiterated proposals to drink a can of wine with him in the finest hostelry in the city, she would not leave the place. Monen now waxed wroth, and vociferated, 'By the lungs and spleen of Lucifer, come away from here, or I will carry thee with shoes and stockings to hell!' And with these words he darted with Emmeken, like an arrow, up into the air.[1]

Poor Mariken would inevitably have been lost, had the wicked fiend after his falling again been able to grasp her; but he was prevented by her uncle, Master Gysbrecht, who being come to Nymwegen, as a spectator of the dramatic representation, was fortunately close at hand. He recognised her

---

1   Here some lines seem wanting, the narrative being evidently imperfect.

instantly, sprang quickly towards her, and by his powerful prayer scared the furious Monen away from her. When Emmeken recovered and perceived her uncle, she was overjoyed, confessed to him her course of life, during the last seven years, and implored his forgiveness, being, as she said, already sufficiently miserable in being condemned to eternity. This, however, Master Gysbrecht would not admit, but with edifying words exhorted her to repentance and amendment, through which she might be sure of eternal happiness.

Monen in the meantime continued standing by her side; for he would gladly have taken his Emmeken with him. But on his once venturing to dart upon her, Gysbrecht put his arm round her, and in a threatening voice said, 'Take care of thyself, accursed sprite; for if thou attemptest any violence, I will read to thee something from my breviary that shall soon drive thee hence.' Then seeing that all was lost, Monen roared and howled terrifically, 'Oh me, wretched sprite! What will become of me! How they will torture me with red-hot tongs, if I lose her! What will become of me!' at the same time emitting red, raging flames from his nose, mouth and ears, so that it was appalling to behold. This, however, did not disturb Master Gysbrecht, who calmly taking Mariken by the hand, led her to the dean, who was a very learned and holy priest.

When the dean had heard the recital of Mariken's sins, he said that he could not forgive them, for that they were too great and manifold. At this Gysbrecht was troubled, and proceeded with her to the church, and thence took with him the holy Eucharist, being resolved on going to the bishop of Cologne, but fearing violence from Monen on his journey thither. And it was soon manifest that the prudent priest had done well; for Monen was constantly at hand, and from time to time tore down huge branches of oak and hurled at them, though of course without effect, as God protected the pious travellers.

When Magister Gysbrecht had laid the affair before the bishop of Cologne, and related to him every particular, the prelate said, 'My dear son! This is a sin of which it is not in my power to grant forgiveness, that can only be obtained from the pope at Rome.' Still Gysbrecht despaired not, but full of confidence went with Mariken over hill and dale until they reached the holy city. No sooner was the pope apprised of the affair than he caused Mariken to appear before him, and heard her confession. But on learning that she had been the devil's mistress, and that, on her account and through her, more than two hundred persons had lost their lives, the holy father was horror-stricken, and exclaimed, 'O God and Father, how can such things be possible! Great, exceedingly great are the mercy and grace of the Lord, but so deeply I hardly dare dive into the treasure.' He then sank in profound meditation, and commanded Gysbrecht to come to him and thus spoke, 'My good and faithful son! Although I am the holy father, I know not whether I can remit such frightful sins: but let three rings of iron be made, and close them round your niece's neck and arms. When these shall either be worn out, or fall off spontaneously, then are her sins forgiven.'

Gysbrecht did so, and travelled back with Mariken to Nymwegen, where she entered the convent of the Converted Sisters. He there bade her an affectionate farewell, and enjoined her to persevere in her penance, as heaven would then without doubt forgive her her sins.

There Mariken lived for very many years, in the most rigid austerity and retirement, the rings constantly remaining on her neck and arms. But when she was very old and felt that her end was nigh, an angel suddenly appeared by her bed and touched the rings, which instantly fell off. She then piously slept in the Lord.

Her grave was long after to be seen in the conventual church, on the stone of which her whole history was inscribed; and the three rings were hung on the adjacent wall, as memorials and proofs of its veracity.

## The Devil of Nederbraekel

The servant of a rich farmer having spent all his money, came towards home one evening reeling with drunkenness. Dark thoughts passed through the brain of the miserable being, who dreaded both the cudgel of his master and the consequences of an empty pocket. In his weak but excited state of mind, he resolved to sell his soul to the devil, in the hope of escape from so dreary a prospect; and on reaching a crossway, he summoned all the devils, and swore that his soul was for sale. A devil came, but told him that he could not attain his object unless he previously offered a black hen to the prince of the infernal realms, which he promised to do. For this purpose, when the clock struck twelve at night was the time appointed. When the awful hour approached, the man stood ready with the black hen, which he had stolen from his master, under his frock, and hardly had the clock struck the first stroke, before all the devils made their appearance. Their chief stepping forwards, took the hen, which the man drew forth trembling. The bargain was now concluded, and as an acknowledgement of the agreement, the man was required to set his signature in blood in a little book that the devil had brought with him.

The man on his return was not reprimanded by his master, and his pockets were never empty. Whenever he put his hand in he drew forth a piece of seventy-five cents, with which he paid his reckoning, when he had been drinking in an alehouse. Once when he was watching his master's sheep, they, through his heedlessness, ran into a neighbour's field, where they did serious injury to the corn. This the peasant, to whom the land belonged, had witnessed, and came running with the intention of inflicting chastisement on the shepherd for the damage done. The latter was too well aware of the bodily strength of the peasant not to feel terrified; but the craft of the devil came to help him out of his peril. Both shepherd and sheep were transformed into dung-heaps before the peasant could reach the spot, where he stood staring about him in the utmost astonishment.

Thus did he continue to live; but the five years, at the expiration of which the devil was to become possessor of his soul, were nearly ended, and the seller dreaded nothing more than that moment. What does he do? He goes to the priest of Nederbraekel, to whom he makes a full confession. The, priest, naturally well-disposed to rescue an erring Christian soul from the fire of hell, causes him first to perform an act of penitence, and then tells him to come to him on the following day, being the dreaded day of settlement. The man had hardly been an hour in the house of the holy pastor, before a great noise of chains and devilry was heard in the chimney. The man, who was sitting close beneath, was seized with unutterable terror, and not without cause; for he was lifted on high, and seemed for ever lost; but the priest, who had founded his hope on the efficacy of his prayers cast himself promptly on his knees and repeated the gospel of St John. The man in the meanwhile being incessantly cast up and down, fell at length, half dead with fright, miserably bruised and bloody, to the ground with the little book by his side; and the devil was away and continued away.

## The Devil Outwitted

There once lived in Louvain a rich merchant, who had gained all his money and possessions by selling himself body and soul to the devil. With his riches the man possessed also much craft, and could help himself when others could neither advise nor aid; and so it proved, when at the expiration of seven years, the devil came for the purpose of fetching him.

He took the devil in a friendly manner by the hand and, as it was just evening, said, 'Wife, bring a light quickly for the gentleman.' 'That is not at all necessary,' said the devil, 'I am merely come to fetch you.' 'Yes, yes, that I know very well,' said the merchant, 'only just grant me the time till this little candle-end is burnt out, as I have a few letters to sign and to put on my coat.' 'Very well,' said the devil, 'but only till the candle is burnt out.' 'Good,' said the merchant, and going into the next room, ordered the maidservant to place a large cask full of water close to a very deep pit that was dug in the garden. The menservants also carried, each of them, a cask to the spot; and when all was done, they were ordered each to take a shovel, and stand round the pit. The merchant then returned to the devil, who seeing that not more than about an inch of candle remained, said laughing, 'Now get yourself ready, it will soon be burnt out.' 'That I see, and am content; but I shall hold you to your word, and stay till it is burnt.' 'Of course,' answered the devil, 'I stick to my word.' 'It is dark in the next room,' continued the merchant, 'but I must find the great book with clasps, so let me just take the light for one moment.' ' Certainly,' said the devil, 'but I'll go with you.' He did so, and the merchant's trepidation was now on the increase. When in the next room, he said on a sudden, 'Ah, now I know, the key is in the garden door.' And with these words he ran out with the light into the garden, and before the devil could overtake him, threw it into the pit, and the man and the maids poured water upon it, and then filled up the hole with earth. Now came the devil into the garden and asked, 'Well, did you get the key? And how is it with the candle? Where is it?' 'The candle?' said the merchant. 'Yes, the candle.' 'Ha, ha, ha! It is not yet burnt out,' answered the merchant laughing, 'and will not be burnt out for the next fifty years; it lies there a hundred fathom deep in the earth.' When the devil heard this he screamed awfully, and went off with a most intolerable stench.[1]

## The Freischütz

There was once a fowler who for a long time could never bring down a bird. One day, when wandering about the woods in despair, his employer having threatened to dismiss him, there suddenly stood a well-clad man before him, who asked him the cause of his sorrow. The fowler told him the reason, at which the other laughed heartily. 'Why do you laugh at and ridicule me?' asked the fowler. 'Do so again, and you will get a bullet in your carcase.' At this the man laughed yet more and said, 'A bullet from you? One must be a pretty good shot to hit me at three paces, and you are but a bungler.' 'You'll not say that twice,' cried the fowler, choking with anger, then levelled his piece and fired. The stranger continued laughing, and said, offering him the bullet, 'There, take your bullet back, it's of no use.' The fowler now felt somewhat alarmed, but was soon relieved by the other saying, 'Let me have a shot. Do you see that sparrow sitting on the church steeple yonder? I'll bring it down for you.' 'Do if you can,' said the fowler laughing, and at the same instant the report was heard and the sparrow fell. 'You shall shoot so, too,' continued the stranger, 'and hit whatever you wish, without even seeing it; and if you see it, let it be as far off as it will, you shall hit it, if you will only give me your signature and

1   See p. 355.

make an engagement with me for seven years. I merely require your soul.' 'Done,' said the fowler, 'I agree; but on condition that you always tell me what I shoot at.' 'Granted,' said the stranger. The man then signed his name on a paper with his blood, and the devil disappeared.

For seven years the fowler shot so that it was wonderful to see, and received from his master a stipend such as no fowler in the whole world had ever received. But when the last day but one had arrived, he was very sad, knowing that the devil would come for him on the following morning. His wife observing his affliction, inquired the cause, and, after some hesitation, he told her how he had entered into a compact with the devil, under the condition that the fiend should always tell him what he was shooting at, when the game was somewhat distant. 'Then I can help you, my dear man,' said the wife laughing, 'only go out boldly with your gun, but be careful to shoot at nothing without first asking what it is.' The fowler went out, and no sooner was he away than the wife stripped herself naked, smeared her whole body with syrup, and then rolled herself in a feather bed, which she had cut open for the purpose, so that she more resembled a bird than a human being. She then went and sprang about the field. Shortly after came her husband with the devil, when the latter seeing this singular feathered animal, cried out to the fowler, 'There, fire!' 'But what is it?' asked the fowler. The devil looked and looked, but could not make out what it was, and at last reluctantly said, I really cannot exactly say.' 'Ha ha ha! Then is our covenant at an end,' said the fowler, laughing heartily; and the devil vanished with an intolerable stench. The wife laughed still more, and joyfully embraced her thus rescued husband.

## The Barn of Montecouvez

After an abundant harvest, a young farmer, who had neglected to repair his barn, knew not how to shelter his corn. As he was walking about the fields, in a melancholy mood, and looking at his beautiful grain, a gentleman stepped up to him and inquired the way to the castle of Catelet. The farmer undertook to guide him thither. On their way the stranger asked his companion why he appeared so sad, and the latter related to him the unfortunate plight in which he found himself. On hearing it, the stranger offered to assist him, if he would enter into a compact with him to be his vassal after a year, and attend him in his possessions as a serf. With this proposal the poor farmer complied, but with the condition that he should have a home for his wife and children, to which the stranger with a grisly laugh agreed. The farmer then subscribed the contract, according to which the barn must be ready before the first cock-crowing: having no ink, he signed it with his blood. They then separated; the stranger went towards the castle, and soon disappeared from the sight of the farmer, who returned to his dwelling.

The nearer he approached his house, the more suspicious did the contract appear into which he had entered, and still more so when he saw, by the side of the house, the workmen sent by the stranger busily engaged in laying beam on beam and brick on brick, though at the same time not a sound of hammer or plane, saw or axe was to he heard; and yet towering oaks were brought and sawed into pieces, huge piles of stone were hewn and shaped.

Thus amazed and troubled he entered his dwelling, where his wife was sitting in no less trepidation and astonishment; for dog and cat, cocks and hens, ducks and geese were thronging about her and crying, while the horses in the stable were kicking and foaming.

But most terrified of all was a large cock, the finest of the whole neighbourhood, and of all the animals of the place the greatest favourite of his mistress. This bird, when he could find no other refuge from fear and danger, flew into his mistress's lap, but who in her fright pushed him from her, and, crossing herself, cried out for help. No sooner, however, had the cock recovered himself from his fall than he sent forth a loud cock-a-doodle-doo. At the same instant there resounded from the barn a tremendous noise, so that the earth trembled, all the workmen vanished in an instant, and the barn remained unfinished. On the following morning the villagers were not a little surprised at seeing the beautiful barn full of sheaves of every kind; for they could not conceive how they had all come there, and the farmer took good care not to let a syllable transpire of his adventure.

The hole, which remained unclosed in the gable, could not be filled up by any means whatever, and continues open unto this day; from which time also a cock on the farm always crows earlier than every other in the village.

## The Devil's Barn at Gallemaerde

Some hundred years ago, the occupier of the farm to which the above-named barn belonged was so unfortunate as to suffer the loss of it, whether by wind or fire I cannot say; but so much is certain, that it was in August, and that on the following day he was to carry his corn. In his despair the farmer was wandering about his fields, when suddenly a person appeared before him who asked him the cause of his sadness, whereupon the farmer related to him the whole matter. 'O, is that all?' said the stranger, when the man had ended his story, 'that I can easily remedy. If you will just write your name in your blood on this parchment, your barn shall be fixed and ready tomorrow before the cock crows; if not, our contract is void.' While saying these words the stranger drew from his pocket a slip of parchment, and having pricked the hand of the farmer with a needle, the latter signed his name on it with the trickling blood. The poor man, however, soon repented of having so thoughtlessly sold his soul to the devil, and from sheer anxiety could not sleep; and his wife, when informed of the bargain he had made, could also get no sleep, but was as troubled and terrified as himself,

But woman's craft excels all other craft, says an old proverb, the truth of which was here manifested. For long before the time of cock-crowing, the wife jumped out of bed and ran before the house, where she saw an endless multitude of workmen employed on the barn. But observing that there was still a portion of the side-wall to be completed, she quickly clapped her mouth between her hands, and cried with all her might 'Cock-a-doodle-doo! Cock-a-doodle-doo!' and was followed by all the cocks in the neighbourhood, each of which sent forth a hearty cock-a-doodle-doo. At the same instant every workman vanished, and the barn remained unfinished.

Since that time repeated attempts have been made to close up the hole, but the devil always comes in the night and breaks it open again, out of pure spite for having been so tricked by a farmer's wife.


## How to Become Invisible

Formerly there were many persons here (in Bierbeck) who could make themselves invisible, by means of a little bone, which they carried about them. This bone they obtained in the following manner. They went at night, between the hours of twelve and one, to a crossway, having on one side a hedge or only a bush. On this they laid a black cat, tied up in a sack, as an offering to the devil. On the following morning the cat would be gone, but a small bone would be found at the bottom of the sack, which possessed the virtue required.


## The Travelling Mother

When a whirlwind rages on the earth, and carries everything along with it, many persons regard it as a natural phenomenon; but it is nothing else than the Travelling Mother, who is making her circuit.

## The Lying-in Woman

In the neighbourhood of towns there is often to be seen a whirlwind suddenly descending or rising. One may then be quite certain that in that very moment a woman hard by has died in childbed without having by confession previously purified herself from a deadly sin. Into heaven she may not come, and therefore passes down to hell; but there they dare not receive her, because, through the pains she has suffered, she has already made ample atonement; and thus she again ascends, seeking a permanent place.

## Wanne Thekla

Wanne Thekla is the queen of the elves and witches, as well as of the spirits in general that fly through the air. When the weather is dark and stormy, she plays her part. At night she descends on earth followed by a long train of her companions, and dances, and springs, and drinks on the Pottelberg, where a gibbet formerly stood. On the Leije, which flows through the city, she has a beautiful ship, in which, after the revels of the night, she and her companions sail away at the command of 'Wind mit vieren.'[1]

## The Everlasting Jew

In the year 1640, two citizens, who dwelt in the Tanners' street at Brussels, met in the Forest of Soignies an old man, whose clothes appeared much the worse for wear, and were besides extremely old-fashioned. They invited him to accompany them to the hostelry, which he did, but refused to sit down, and drank standing. As he walked with the two citizens towards the gate, he told them many things, most of which were relations of events that had taken place several hundred years before; whence the citizens soon discovered that their companion must he Isaac Laquedem the Jew, who refused to let our Lord rest at his door; and they left him filled with horror.[2]

## Elves

Eggshells may often be observed floating on the water; in these the Elves swim about. It is likewise said that the bubbles, which are frequently to be

---

1 Literally *Wind with four;* probably an allusion to the expression fahren mit vieren (Pferden), *to go or drive with four (horses);* in other words: *Sail away with all speed;* thus comparing their course by water to a land journey with horses.
2 See pp. 471 and 376.

seen on ponds where there are no fish, are inhabited by them. The Elf-leaf, or Sorceresses' plant, is particularly grateful to them, and therefore ought not to be plucked.

There are also wicked Elves, that prepare the poison in certain plants. Experienced shepherds are careful not to let their flocks feed after sunset. 'Nightwort,' say they, 'belongs to the Elves, and whoever takes it must die.' Nor does any man dare to sleep in a meadow or pasture after sunset, for he would have everything to fear.

In Brabant there are many little hills, called by the people Elfin-bergs, in which these Elves dwell.

## Flabbaert

As some young men were returning home from the fair at Kerselaere, one of them, a brother of the priest, and a notorious swearer, began to curse and swear most awfully, and particularly against Flabbaert, a red sprite that haunts that neighbourhood. This went on smoothly for a while, but at length Flabbaert grew tired of it, so seizing the youth by the crag, he dipped him a few times in the water, and then dashed him on shore so that every rib in his body cracked.

When the priest heard of it on the following day, he did not pity his brother, but said he was rightly served; he, however, banished the sprite for a hundred years to the shores of the Red Sea.

## Why the Jews do not eat Swine's Flesh

When our Lord was living on earth, he once journeyed through Flanders, and there were some dozens of Jews standing together, who laughed at and ridiculed him, when they saw him at a distance. 'Wait,' said one of them, 'we'll make a trial of his miraculous power, and see whether he can guess well.' And thereupon they placed one of the set under a tub, and when Jesus came up, they asked him to tell them what was under the tub. 'That I will tell you instantly,' said Jesus, 'it's a swine.' At this the Jews laughed, thinking they had tricked him, and lifted up the tub. But what great eyes did they not make, when their quondam comrade, in the form of a swine, and uttering a most furious grunt, slipped from under the tub, and ran to a herd of swine that happened to be just passing! Then all the Jews ran after it, in the hope of catching their companion, but were unable to distinguish one pig from another, so alike were they all. And to this day the Jews eat no pork, because they are afraid of killing and devouring a descendant of that swine.

## The Spectres' Mass

A woman of Hofstade was going to the city one morning early: her way lay by an old chapel, which within the last ten years has been demolished, in which she perceived a light. On entering, she found the place full of forms with white kerchiefs round their heads; and as she stood gazing, three priests came from the sacristy and approached the high altar; they were followed by the sacristan and choristers, and the mass commenced. But they did not move about like living beings, but seemed to float lightly on the earth; their robes also appeared quite faded. At this spectacle the woman was struck with a shuddering horror, and was quitting the chapel, but the door was closed and she was compelled to remain. When the mass was over, the priests melted into air, the lights went out, and all the white forms vanished. At the same moment the chapel clock struck one.

When the sacristan opened the door in the morning, he found the woman lying on the pavement half dead with fear.[1]

## Alvina

When the wind loudly howls and whistles, they say in West Flanders, 'Hark! Alvina weeps.' Alvina was the beautiful daughter of a king, who, in consequence of her marriage, was cursed by her parents to wander about to all eternity. On this tradition there is an old popular ballad, of which I have been unable to obtain more than a few lines; among others, the following:

> Ik voel dat ik moet gaen
> Vliegen in de winden, zoo lang de wereld staet,
> En nooit geen troost meer vinden.
> Adieu Kinders, lieve vruchten!
> Adieu Man, die de oorzaek zijt.
> Unmoeden moet voor eeuwig zuchten!

> I feel that I must go flying in the winds,
> As long as the world stands,
> And never more comfort find
> Adieu, children, dear fruits!
> Adieu, husband, who art the cause.
> Incessantly must for ever sigh!
> Incessantly must for ever sigh!

1   See pp. 434 and 370.

## Roodselken

In the great flax fields of Flanders there grows a plant the bright green leaves of which are sprinkled, as it were, with red spots: whence its name of Roodselken. According to the tradition, this plant stood under the cross, and was sprinkled with the Saviour's blood, which was never after washed off, neither by rain nor snow.

## The Burning Land-measurer

A land-measurer near Farsum had in his lifetime acted dishonestly. When he had a piece of land to measure, he suffered himself to be bribed by one or other, and then allotted to the party more than was just. For which cause he was condemned after his death to wander as a burning man with a burning measuring-staff; and so he yet measures every night.[1]

## Cowls Hung on Sunbeams

In the time of Wigbold, fourth abbot of Adewert, monastic discipline was there in full flower. There is even a tradition that all the monks of that house lived in such holy simplicity, that they frequently hung their caps and cowls on the rays of the sun, not knowing better than that they were long poles. The fame of their holy life was widely spread, and many persons renounced the world, for the sake of serving the Lord in their society.[2]

## White Maidens (Witte Juffers) and White Women (Witte Wijven) in Friesland

At the time of the emperor Lothair there were many ghosts and spectres in Friesland. They dwelt on the summits of small hills, in artificial caverns, but which were the work of no human hands. They were usually called Witte Wijven. Of their figure nothing certain is known. Nightly wanderers, shepherds, watchmen in the cornfields, pregnant women and children they frequently carried off to their caverns and subterraneous places, from which sighs, crying of children and sobs were often heard to issue. On this account a careful watch was held over pregnant women and young children, that the White Women might not carry them away. One of them still haunts near Bierum, others near Golinse, Eenum, Farsum, etc.[3]

---

1   See pp. 296, 369, 375, 436 and 542.
2   See p. 412.
3   See p. 479.

At the present day they are called Witte Juffers, and are distinguished from the Witte Wijven, who are said to be of a quite opposite character. They give aid to women in labour, lead wanderers back to the right road, and in every respect show themselves kind and friendly towards mankind. Their habitations, too, are less repulsive, and are often in the vicinity of towns and villages. They are for the most part hills, or caves overgrown with trees, as that near Lochern in Holland, where three Witte Wijven dwell together. In Friesland and Drenthe every child knows them. Whoever approaches such caves or hills, or enters them, will see wonderful things.

## The Three Sisters

Near Louvain are three graves, in which the bodies of three pious sisters are buried. Before the graves three clear springs gush forth, and thither Christian folks frequently go on pilgrimage, particularly to obtain a cure for women who are suffering under disease. But in order to know whether a woman will recover or die of the malady, the custom is to take a hood belonging to her and lay it on the water. If it sinks, no recovery is to be looked for; if it swims, the disease is curable. It is, however, necessary to pray fervently and to bring an offering, which must consist of a needle, a thread of yarn and some corn, all obtained by begging.

## St Gertrud's Minne (Memory)

St Gertrud had withdrawn from the world, in order to devote her days to the service of God. But a knight, who had previously been in love with her, did not on that account relinquish his hopes, but continued in the neighbourhood of the convent, notwithstanding Gertrud's repeated declaration never to swerve from her vow. Seeing that all his endeavours were vain, he summoned the devil to his aid, and assigned his soul to him at the expiration of seven years, for which Satan promised to help him to attain his object. But the seven years passed, and the aid of the evil one had effected nothing. Nevertheless he insisted on having the soul of the knight, who was compelled to submit to his fate.

Now appeared St John to Gertrud in a dream, and announced to her the danger in which the knight was placed; whereupon Gertrud, who had in the in meantime become abbess of her cloister, immediately on rising assembled all her nuns, accompanied by whom she proceeded to the convent gate, just as the devil was passing with his prey. Approaching the knight she presented to him a cup of wine, which she exhorted him to empty to the protection of St John. The knight did so, and had scarcely swallowed the last drop, when the covenant, torn in pieces, fell at his feet, accompanied by a hideous howl of the foul fiend.

Hence St Gertrud is represented holding in one hand a crosier, and in the other a cup, and from this event originates the custom of drinking to *Sinte Geerteminne*.

## The Lily

There was once in days of yore a conjurer who cut people's heads off and set them on again. One day, when he was practising his art, a travelling journeyman entered the room as a spectator. On the table before the conjurer there stood a large glass filled with distilled water, out of which grew a white lily every time the conjurer cut a head off, which he called the lily of life. When the conjurer had cut a head off, the traveller quickly stepped up to the table, and with a sharp knife severed the stalk of the lily, without being observed by anyone; so that when the conjurer would replace the head, the operation failed, whereupon he was seized and burnt for a murderer.

This took place, as I have often heard my father relate, in the year 1528, and that anterior to the French Revolution the judicial acts concerning it were still to be seen.

## The Feather Heart

In a family of my acquaintance the following story has often been related to me.

A young maiden lay sick, and to all appearance incurable. All the physicians had employed their skill on her, but all was in vain. At length the mother went to an old Capuchin friar, to whom she related her case, and who spoke to her thus, 'My dear woman, your daughter's malady is not to be cured by physicians, that is impossible, for she is bewitched; but cut open the paillasse and the featherbed, on which she lies, and in one of the two you will find a heart of feathers, which must instantly be cast into the fire.'

The woman followed the friar's advice, and in fact a heart of feathers was found in the featherbed. No sooner was it burnt than her daughter recovered.

## Love Magic

Take a host, or holy wafer, but which has not yet been consecrated, write on it certain words with blood from the ring-finger, and then let a priest say five masses over it. Divide the wafer in two equal parts, of which keep one, and give the other to the person whose love you desire to gain.

_____

Some persons make images of earth, wax, precious stones, or mixtures of certain things. These they baptise with the name of the person whom they wish to inspire with love, and with the same ceremonies that the priests employ in real baptisms; excepting that they call on and conjure the devil, and add scandalous, blasphemous words. They then melt the image, when at the same time the heart of the person, whose name the image bears, will be inspired with love, though it had previously been insensible to that passion.

_____

In a mansion in the town of N— there sat three young damsels, on the eve of a festival, at a covered table, on which were three plates, and at which so many vacant places were left for the coming bridegrooms. These they expected after the performance of the prescribed ceremonies. But there appeared only two young nobles, who attached themselves to two of the young ladies at the table. The third came not. At this the third damsel, after long expectation, growing impatient, looked out of the window, when exactly opposite to her she saw a coffin, in which lay a young person exactly resembling herself. This apparition so shocked her, that she fell sick and died soon after.

_____

Three maidens were sitting stark naked at a table, each having a glass before her, one containing water, another beer, and the third wine. They were awaiting their bridegrooms. First appeared a serving-man, who took the glass of water and departed. Then came a cooper, who took the glass of beer and went his way. Next entered a village schoolmaster, who snatched up the glass of wine and carried it off.

The result of the process proves its efficacy. The lass, who had a glass of water before her, married a serving-man, with whom she had little bread and plenty of water. The second got a cooper for her husband, with whom she suffered no want, though her life was a miserable one, for she had nothing but pain and suffering. How it fared with the third I never heard, for she went to another country with her husband, who was a schoolmaster.[1]

_____

1   See p. 531.

When the girls in Belgium desire to see their lovers in a dream, they lay their garters crosswise at the foot of the bed, and a little looking-glass under the pillow. They then in a dream see the image of their future husband appearing in the glass.

On the first Friday of every month, they also repeat the following:

> Lune, lune, belle lune,
> Faites me voir en mon dormant
> Le mari que j'aurai en mon vivant.

If a girl finds an entire corn in her bread and butter, she can see her future husband. For this purpose she must stick the corn in a crack of the door, and then keep watch. The third person that passes is the future one.

Others say that the future one will merely be of the same trade with the third person that passes by the house.

---

If a girl desires to be sure whether her sweetheart still loves her, she must fold her garter three times, over every fold pronounce certain words, then lay it under her pillow, and without uttering a syllable, go to bed. If at midnight she sees her lover looking fresh and well, then all is right, and she will soon be married; but if in his stead a corpse appears, she may give up all hope, for she will never get her lover. In either case the lover has much to suffer during the night.

## Thief's Foot – Thief's Hand – Thief's Finger

In West Flanders, not far from Bailleul, a thief was taken, on whom was found the foot of one that had been hanged, which he used for the purpose of putting people to sleep.

---

Two fellows once came to Huy, who pretended to be exceedingly fatigued, and when they had supped would not retire to a sleeping room, but begged their host would allow them to take a nap on the hearth. But the maidservant, who did not like the looks of the two guests, remained by the kitchen door and peeped through a chink, when she saw that one of them drew a thief's hand from his pocket, the fingers of which, after having rubbed them with an ointment, he lighted, and they all burned except one. Again they held this finger to the fire, but still it would not burn, at which they appeared much surprised, and one said, 'There must surely be someone in the house who is not yet asleep.' They then hung the hand with its four burning fingers by the chimney, and went out to call their associates. But the maid followed them instantly and made the door fast, then ran upstairs, where the landlord slept, that she might wake him, but was unable, notwithstanding all her shaking and calling.

In the meantime, the thieves had returned and were endeavouring to enter the house by a window, but the maid cast them down from the ladder. They then took a different course, and would have forced an entrance, had it not occurred to the maid that the burning fingers might probably be the cause of her master's profound sleep. Impressed with this idea she ran to the kitchen, and blew them out, when the master and his menservants instantly awoke, and soon drove away the robbers.

---

In the village of Alveringen there formerly lived a sorceress, who had a thief's finger, over which nine masses had been read. For being acquainted with the sacristan, she had wrapped it in a cloth and laid it on the altar, telling him it was a relic. With this finger she performed wonderful things. When she had lighted it – for such fingers burn like a candle – everyone in the house where she might be was put to sleep. She would then steal money and everything else that she fancied, until she was at last detected, and the stolen property found in her possession.

## The Magic Sword

Mynheer Hincke Van Wurben had a magic sword that had been given to him by a monk. It had been bought at the hour in which Mars ruled; the cross was forged on a Tuesday, and on that day was finished; in the hilt a piece of wood was enclosed that had been struck by thunder. All this was performed in the hour of Mars. A sword so prepared causes the swords of all opponents to fly in pieces.

If a man desires not to be wounded by anyone, let him bind on his right arm a serpent's skin covered over with a tanned eel-skin. Then let an iron token be forged from a piece of an executioner's sword, but in the hour of Mars, and set it in a ring. Then if the person be about to fight, let him press the ring against his forehead, and place it on the finger next to the little finger of his right hand. Round the ring let there be engraven the words, 'O Castres, prince of arms, through the God of Abraham, Isaac and Jacob.'

## Witches' Ointment

Sorceresses destroy with their ceremonies both baptised and unbaptised children (especially the former, when a cross has not been made or a prayer said over them), as well in the cradle as by the side of their parents, whence the latter often think that they have smothered the child. When the infant is buried, the witches steal the corpse out of the coffin, put it into a kettle, and boil it until the flesh falls from the bones. From the more solid parts of this decoction they make an ointment, by means of which they exercise their arts, transform themselves, etc. The fluid they pour into bottles, and whoever drinks of it and lets certain ceremonies be performed over him by the sorceresses, becomes initiated in their arts and a master thereof.

## Milk-taking – Milk Beaten

An old sorceress would from envy take the milk from a neighbour's cow, and for this purpose went with a knife before the place in which the cow was, placed herself towards the moonlight, and repeated these words:

> Hier snyd ick een spaen
> In mollekens ghewaen,
> Ende een ander daer toe,
> So neem ick bet melck van deser koe.

> *Here cut I a chip*
> *In the dairy's wall,*
> *And another thereto,*
> *So take I the milk from this cow.*

The owner of the cow hearing this, took a thick cord and ran to the sorceress, whom he beat unmercifully, at the same time saying:

> Hier slaen ick eenen slach,
> Ende eenen andern als ick mach,
> Ende den derden daer toe,
> So behoud ick d' melck metter koe.

> *Here strike I a stroke,*
> *And another as I may,*
> *And a third thereto,*
> *So keep I the milk with the cow.*

This was the best method he could adopt.

----

When a sorceress steals milk, there is no better way to punish her than the one I am about to communicate. When such a woman has by her arts milked all the milk from a cow, the cow must soon after be milked again. Let the milk thus obtained be set on the fire and made warm, and when it is sufficiently warm, beat it with a stick until not a drop is left in the vessel. The milk that is flowing on the ground may also be beaten, for the more the beating the better, as every stroke given to the milk the sorceress gets on her back from the devil. It has often happened here (Laeken) that sorceresses have been confined to their bed for a week and more, from having been so beaten.[1]

## Corn-stealing

A sorceress walked round a field that was full of ripe corn, repeating the verse 'Super aspidem', etc. On her return home she instantly went up into the loft, took a tube, and repeated the same verse, when all the corn fell through the tube down before her, not a grain being left in the field.

## A Sorceress Caught

About the end of the sixteenth century, the following event took place in West Flanders. A peasant was sitting with his son drinking in an alehouse, and, as was the custom, made a mark on his dung-fork with chalk for every jug of beer he drank. When about leaving the house he called for the hostess, and asked her how much he had drunk; but the hostess asked him in her turn, how many marks he had on his fork. The peasant refused to tell her, and the woman grew angry, and said in her rage, 'For this thou shalt not reach home tonight, be assured of that, or I'll never come back.' The peasant laughed at this, threw the money on the table for what he had really consumed, and went away.

But when he came to the water and entered the boat, he could not move it from the shore, and therefore called to three soldiers who happened to be passing, 'Halloo, comrades, will you help me to push my boat off? I will gladly give you a drink of beer.' The soldiers came to his aid, but all was in vain, for the boat was and continued fixed. 'Wait a moment,' said one of the soldiers, panting and sweating with exertion, 'let us throw the things out of the boat that are lying there in the middle; then it will no doubt go better.' They did so, and scarcely had they thrown out the last piece when they discovered an enormous toad in the bottom of the boat, with eyes like glowing coals. One of the soldiers, drawing his sword, stabbed the monster through the body and cast it into the water, where the others gave it many wounds in the belly; for it swam in the water on its back.

They now again applied themselves to move the boat, when it went without any trouble, at which the peasant was so pleased, that taking the soldiers by the arm, he returned with them to the alehouse. After he had

1    See p. 77, and Grimm, J., *Deutsche Mythologie*, op. cit., p. 1025.

ordered some beer, he inquired of the maid where her mistress was. 'Ah,' said she, 'my mistress is in bed at the point of death.' 'Haha,' said the peasant, laughing, 'dost thou think I am not sober? Why I saw her not a quarter of an hour ago, and she was then quite lively and well, and gave me a precious scolding.' 'It is so, nevertheless,' answered the maid, 'you may see her yourself, if you like.'

Thereupon the peasant and the three soldiers went into the room where the woman was lying and piteously moaning with pain; for she had many wounds precisely corresponding to those that had been inflicted on the toad. The peasant asked the maid how it had all happened, but she answered she knew not, as her mistress had not been out of the house.

The peasant then hastened to the magistrate, to whom he related the affair, whence it appeared evident that the toad was no other than the hostess, who had assumed the form of that reptile, for the purpose of preventing the man from returning home.

## Witchery Expelled

Sorceresses melt lead and pour it into cold water, where it immediately assumes a human form. They then ask the person bewitched, into what part of his or her body, who has caused the evil, they wish it to be sent. When the patient has told them this, they make a cut or prick with a knife in that part of the leaden image, at the same time saying where the party is that has inflicted the evil, but without mentioning their name. The perpetrator then gets the evil.[1]

## The Gravedigger

It was on All-Saints' day, and the gravedigger was ill with a fever, and his gossip came to see him. 'Is it not unlucky,' said the gravedigger, 'that I am ill, and must go tonight in the cold and snow to dig a grave?' 'O, I'll do that for you,' said the gossip, 'that's but a little service.' The gravedigger gladly accepted it.

The gossip having provided himself with a spade and pickaxe, and warmed his inward man a little at the ale-house, went about ten o'clock to the churchyard, and had finished his job by half-past eleven. But just as he was about to return home there came a long procession of white friars, each bearing a taper in his hand, who made the round of the churchyard, and as they passed by the gossip let their tapers fall before him, and the last threw him a large ball with two wicks.

1   See p. 260–1.

The gossip thought within himself, 'Haha, the grave-digger said nothing about the monks. The wax will pay me for my labour. In a month or two I will sell it and get a pretty bit of money out of it, which my wife need know nothing about.' He then gathered up all the pieces, wrapped them in a cloth, and hid them under his bed.

The next day was the festival of All-Souls. The gossip had gone early to bed, but could not sleep. As the clock was striking twelve, three knocks were heard at his door. The man instantly jumped up, opened the door, and behold, there stood the white monks of the preceding night, only that they had no lights. They marched into the house two and two, then into the chamber, walked round it, and ranged themselves round the bed, on which the gossip had fallen backwards through terror. On a sudden their white mantles fell from their shoulders, and the gossip saw from under the bedclothes in which he had wrapped himself up to the ears, that they were all skeletons, but to each of which one or other part was wanting, to one an arm, to another a leg, to another the backbone, and to the last the head. At the same time there was a movement under the bed; the cloth came forth spontaneously, and unfolded itself in the middle of the room, when the gossip saw that the supposed wax lights were all bones, and the large ball with two wicks a grinning skull. The skeletons now cried out all together: 'Give me my leg-bone,' 'Give me my arm-bone,' 'Give me my backbone,' 'Give me my rib': all of which the gossip was obliged to give back even to the last piece, which was the head, and which he replaced on the last one; but who had no sooner got it on his shoulders, than seeing a violin hanging on the wall, he took it down and handed it to the gossip, that he might play on it, at the same time placing himself behind him with extended arms, as if he would beat time. The other skeletons then, taking each other's hand, began a dance, and made a most appalling clatter. As to the poor gossip, he lost all sense of hearing and seeing, but durst not leave off playing; for every time he slackened he got a box on the ear from the skeleton behind him. And all this lasted till morning, when the skeletons put on their cloaks and went away.

The gossip and his wife never uttered a syllable in their lives about this adventure until their last confession, when they related the whole to their spiritual father.

## The Coffin

Dr Abraham Van der Meer, an upright and zealous Reformer, relates in his *Memorabilia*, that his grandmother, while residing at the Hague, being one summer night unable to sleep, placed herself, about four o'clock in the morning, at the window, and there saw a coffin coming up the Spui Straat, but without anyone else seeming to notice it. It moved on until it stood up erect before a house, where it vanished in an open window. Before six weeks had expired every inmate of that house had died of the plague.

## Zevenbergen

Before arriving at Dort, there is to be seen by the high road a large body of water, in the middle of which a lonely church tower raises its head.

There stood formerly the rich and populous city of Zevenbergen, the inhabitants of which made use of gold and silver as if they had been copper. All the latches of their doors, all the hasps of their windows were of pure gold; all the nails in their houses, all their kitchen utensils were of silver. In short their riches are not to be described, and were attended with an arrogance still less susceptible of description.

At one time it happened that every night a mermaid came flying, and seated herself on the top of the tower of the church, which was dedicated to St Lobbetjen, and there sang:

> Zevenbergen sol vergaen,
> En Lobbetjens toren blyven staen.
>
> *Zevenbergen shall perish,*
> *And Lobbetjen's tower remain standing.*

This song everyone heard, but no one heeded it, or, in consequence of it, turned from his arrogance. At length God grew weary, and in one night there arose so frightful a storm of wind and rain, accompanied by thunder, over the city, that it perished in one instant, all except the church, which remained standing and yet remains, as the mermaid had sung. Over the site of the city an expanse of water spread itself.

Fishermen who navigate the lake assert that they have frequently seen the glittering gilded roofs of Zevenbergen; but no one has ever ventured to descend into its mysterious depths.

## How Count Baldwin of Flanders Married a Devil

When Count Baldwin the Ninth of Flanders had disdainfully refused to marry the beautiful princess Beatrix, daughter of the king of France, the emperor of Constantinople came and sought her hand and obtained her from her father. At this Baldwin being much discontented, took leave of the most potent and noble king of France, and returned to his town of Noyon, where he remained three days. On the fourth day, having a great desire to hunt in the forest of Noyon, he assembled his huntsmen and followers, and went out with staff in hand accompanied by his hounds. In the forest they lighted on a wild boar of extraordinary size and power, and quite black. On hearing the dogs it fled, with the hunters close after it, but it killed four of the best hounds that were at the chase. At this the count was bitterly vexed, and swore that he would never return until he had slain the boar, which then ran out of the forest of Noyon and fled into that of Mormay, and hastened to reach a spot where it could rest in peace. But the count pursued it with his staff, leaving his attendants far behind, and now springing from his horse and grasping his staff with both hands, said, 'Boar, turn hitherwards, for it must gratify thee to encounter the count of Flanders.' The boar instantly rose and rushed on the count, who struck it with such force that it fell stunned to the earth. He then killed it, and placing himself upon it, fell into deep reflection, emerging from which he was greatly surprised that none of his followers had joined him. After sitting thus a while, he looked round and saw a young damsel coming towards him, quite alone and mounted on a jet-black palfrey. The count instantly rose to meet her, and taking hold of the rein of her palfrey, said, 'Lady, you are right welcome to me.' And the lady in a soft voice returned his greeting. The count then asked her why she rode so entirely unattended, and she gently answered, 'Sir, such is the will of the Almighty Father. I am the daughter of an Eastern king, who would bestow me in marriage against my will; but I swore and made an oath to God that I would never take a husband, unless it were the richest count in Christendom. I therefore left my home, attended by a numerous suite, but have now no one with me, having parted from them, as I feared they might conduct me back to my father; for I had made a vow that I would never return until I had met with the count of Flanders, whom I had heard so highly praised.'

While the count looked on the lady, he thought much of what she had said, and she pleased him beyond measure, so that he felt an ardent passion for her, and said, 'Fair damsel, I am the count of Flanders whom you seek, and I am the richest count under heaven, having fourteen counties subject to me; and as you have been seeking me, I will, if it be agreeable to you, take you to wife.' At this the lady expressed her satisfaction and willingness, provided he were what he represented himself. The count then asked the lady her name, also that of her father, and over what realm he reigned. She answered him that her baptismal name was Helius, 'But,' continued she, 'the name of my father you shall never know; such is the will of God, and you must not inquire further, for it may not be otherwise.' The count then, who was possessed by the evil spirit, setting his horn to his mouth, blew a loud blast, for his people to come to him; and there came Henry count of Valenciennes, Walter of St Omer's, and many others. They asked him whether he had taken nothing, and he answered, 'Yes, I have taken the noblest boar in the world, and God has also sent me this fair damsel whom you here see, and whom, as she is willing, I mean to make my wife.' At this the count of Valenciennes gazed on the lady, who was very elegantly attired, and rode on a palfrey than which none could be more beautiful. Notwithstanding all this, the count greatly blamed the count of Flanders for his intention of making her his lawful wife, and said, 'Sir, how do you know who she is? She is perhaps a young damsel who might be yours for money. If she pleases you, retain her as long as it may be agreeable to you, and then let her go; for so great a prince as you must act wisely.' Then said the count of Flanders to the count of Valenciennes, 'Speak more discreetly, for my heart bids me to marry this damsel.' At this his followers were much afflicted. The count then went away, taking with him the head of the boar, and proceeded to Cambray, accompanied by the lady, whom he married, and celebrated their nuptials with great feastings. She soon became pregnant, and at the end of nine months gave birth to a daughter, who at her baptism received the name of Jane, and had afterwards a second daughter, who was named Margaret. In the thirteen years, during which this woman lived with Baldwin, she laid heavy burdens on the people and did much evil in the country, for which the count was severely blamed. She went, indeed, to church and heard divine service, and also partook of the holy sacrament, until the elevation of the host in the mass; but then she would leave the church, at which the people greatly wondered and expressed themselves very mysteriously.

At this time the emperor of Constantinople was in great trepidation, because Acquillan, Sultan of Sura, had laid siege to Constantinople with a hundred thousand Saracens, and laid waste all the surrounding country. The emperor therefore summoned all his friends, and assembled an army of forty thousand Christians. But one day, making a sally and engaging with the Saracens, he was slain in the conflict; whereupon his army returned, bearing the body of their emperor, whom they honourably buried, and then proceeded to adopt measures for the further defence of the city; for the Sultan Acquillan had sworn not to depart before he had taken Constantinople; but the Christians, nevertheless, still found means to defend it.

During this time, Baldwin with his wife Helius was in the county of

Flanders. There it befell that, on Easter day in the year of grace 1188, the count of Flanders and the countess Helius with a noble train were at their palace of Wynandael, and thither many counts and barons, vassals of the count, were summoned and came accordingly. On this day the count held a splendid court, and when the hour of repast arrived, he placed himself with his guests at table. While thus sitting, there appeared before him an aged hermit leaning on a staff, and apparently a hundred years old, who prayed the count, in the name of God, to give him a dinner. The count graciously granted his request, and bade one of the attendants take care of the old man, and a place was assigned him at a table opposite to the count, but apart from the rest. The countess had not then entered the hall, but she came shortly after, and seated herself by the count, as was her wont. When the hermit saw her he was struck with fear, and instantly began to tremble, and repeatedly crossed himself, and could neither eat nor drink. And when the lady saw the hermit, she was sorely disquieted, for she feared he would cause her some great calamity, and therefore prayed the count to send him away, saying, 'Sir, he knows more artifices than anyone besides, and I cannot look upon him; I therefore beseech you to order his departure.'

At this the count said, 'Wife, it is good to bestow alms on those that ask them; but he who receives and needs them not is foolish; therefore it is my pleasure that the hermit be served and recruit his strength.' The count then turning towards the hermit, who sat apparently lost in thought, and neither ate nor drank, said to him, 'My good man, why eat you not? Conceal it not from me, if you desire aught else; ask for it, and it shall be given you.' The hermit then rose, and addressing the count and all the nobles presents exhorted them to cease from eating and drinking, for that they were in great peril, and then continued, 'But dread not before it is time to dread, for that which ye will soon see will inspire you with great dread. Nevertheless, put your trust in God and it cannot harm you.' At this address all were wonderstruck, and everyone sat silent and still, and ceased from eating and drinking. The hermit then conjured the countess in the name of the Almighty, and said to her, 'Thou devil, who sojournest in the body of this woman, I conjure thee, in the name of the Lord, who for us suffered a painful death on the cross, who drove thee from his holy paradises with all the evil spirits who had sinned through their pride; and by the holy sacraments, which God hath appointed; and by his great powers which will endure for ever, that thou depart from this company, and that ere thou goest, thou confess before all these lords why the count of Flanders hath been seduced by thee, that all may know it; and that thou go to the place whence thou camest, without touching aught with harmful hand, whatsoever it may be.'

When the lady heard herself thus exorcised, without the power of resistance, or of doing further injury to the count, or of remaining longer in Flanders, she began to speak and confess before all, saying, 'I am one of the angels that God cast from paradise, from which circumstance we suffer more misery than anyone can conceive and would gladly see everyone treading in our path, that God might, together with all others, also forgive us. Nor for thus seeking help can anyone justly blame us. The count in this case could but ill guard against us when he yielded to the sin of pride, and refused to marry the daughter of the king of France. God then permitted that I should enter the body of a royal maiden of the East who had died, and was one of the fairest on earth. I entered her corpse in the night and raised it up, and it had no other soul than me; for her soul was where it was destined to be. And the count could not withstand the temptation to make her his wife, and I left him but little enjoyment of life for thirteen years, and have inflicted much evil on the land of Flanders; and yet more dearly would he have paid, had he not been ever mindful of his Creator, and crossed himself on rising and on lying down to rest. His two daughters I have lost, in consequence of their having been baptised. I have nothing more to say, but now return to the East country, to give this body back to its grave.' Having thus spoken she vanished without doing injury to anyone, only carrying along with her a little pillar from one of the windows of the hall. At this the count and all present were struck with amazement, and rose from table, and the count bending his head to the good hermit, prayed him to say what it were best for him to do; when the hermit counselled him to go to the pope and from him obtain pardon for his sins; and then took his departure.

For three days the count continued lost in reflection within his palace; on the fourth he proceeded to Bruges. While there he was much ridiculed and insulted; the people pointed at him in the streets, and the children cried out, 'Come and see, there is the count that married the devil.' The like took place also in Ghent and Arras. Seeing this, he made a vow to go to Jerusalem, and provided for the administration of his dominions; but be first went to Rome, where the pope received him with great honour, and took him into his private chamber, where the count confessed to him his sins. At his confession the holy father was much astonished, and imposed on him, as an atonement, to journey to Constantinople and aid the noble empress, the daughter of the king of France, who was besieged by the Sultan Acquillan. The pope then remitted all his sins, and Baldwin proceeded on his way to Constantinople.

*The count of Flanders, to whom the foregoing legend relates, was the same who was raised to the dignity of emperor of the East, and who perished so miserably, having been taken prisoner by the Bulgarians in the Battle of Adrianople (c.1206), and after the mutilation of his limbs, left a prey to the beasts of the forest. His wife was not a devil, but*

*Mary of Champagne, a daughter of the sister of the French king, Philip Augustus. The story of his escape from prison, return to Flanders, and execution, as an impostor, at Lisle, is well known. Tieck's tale, 'Der Griechische Kaiser', is founded on this tradition.*

## The Poacher of Wetteren-Overbeke

At Wetteren-Overbeke there was a poacher who had been out the whole day but shot nothing. His ill-luck made him obstinate, so that he stayed in the field, in the hope of meeting with some game, and not being obliged to return home without having taken something. It was just midnight, when by the moonlight he saw a hare frisking about among the clover. He aimed at the animal and fired, but the recoil of his piece against his shoulder was so strong that it felled him to the ground. On rising and examining the piece, he found that the barrel was become quite crooked. This seemed very unaccountable to him, as he had not loaded it with a heavier charge than usual. At the same instant, the animal, that he thought dead, started up, and, instead of running away, came towards him. What sees he next? The hare was transformed to a black ball slowly rolling along! The poor poacher took to his heels in terror, fully convinced it was no other than the devil himself that was in chase of him. The ball in the meanwhile continued rolling after him, and grew bigger and bigger. At length, with the sweat pouring from him through fear and running, he succeeded in climbing up a tall tree, where he hoped to be in safety; but the black ball came rolling on to the tree, and was now become so great that it darkened all before the eyes of the poacher. Deadly terror now seized him; 'This monster,' thought he, 'can be no other than a warning from heaven, because I have transgressed the laws of my superiors.' Then falling on his knees, he made a vow never to poach again, when the black ball instantly disappeared.

## The Bloody Coach at Antwerp

This is a wonderfully beautiful carriage with four horses. In it sits a lady richly clad, who carries with her many sweetmeats and dainties, for the purpose of enticing such children as are out playing late in the streets; to whom she also promises that she will give them at her castle her little daughter for a playmate. If her artifice fails, she will drag them into the carriage by force, and stop their mouths, to prevent their crying out. She then conveys the poor little creatures far away to a great castle, where their great toes are cut off and they are suffered to bleed to death. Their blood is used as a bath for a great king, who is suffering from a grievous malady. It is observed that the children, whose blood can cure him, must all be under seven years of age.

## The Sand-gate at Mechlin

In the sixteenth century the Sand-gate at Mechlin was used as a powder-magazine. In the night of the 7th August, 1546, a terrific storm burst over the city, and the lightning struck the Sand-gate. A tremendous stroke shook the whole earth around, the tower flew in a thousand fragments in all directions, a shower of hot stones fell on the city, and several hundred houses were either shattered to pieces or greatly damaged. The city ditches were dried up, and the fishes were found lying about boiled or roasted. Above four hundred persons were instantly struck dead, many others died afterwards of the injuries they had suffered; while others, as cripples, bore to the end of their lives the marks of this calamity.

Shortly after this event some merchants from Friesland arrived at Mechlin, who anxiously desired to see the spot where the Sand-gate had stood. Having been conducted thither, they related that at the very hour when the Sand-gate was shivered to atoms, they were near a mill in Fries-land, where they saw many devils in the air directing their flight towards Mechlin. Of these one was heard to call to his companion in a horrible voice, 'Ha, Krombeen (Crooked leg) take the mill along with you.' To which Krombeen answered, 'I can't, I can't, I must hasten to Mechlin; Kortstaert (Short-tail) is behind us; the mill is left for him.' And in fact, the mill was struck down on the same night.

During this storm, which did injury not only in Mechlin, but in the whole country around, the sacristans of the village churches ran to sound the alarm bells. The sacristan of Putte would also do the like; yet notwithstanding all his efforts, the good man could not get into the church, but was twice held back. In his vexation he exclaimed, 'Surely here must be more than one devil at work.' A devil, who was sitting in a tree close by, hearing the words, answered, 'No, there you are wrong, I am here quite alone, the others are all off to Mechlin'

## Chess with the Devil

In the forest of Clairmarais, near Cambray, are to be seen the ruins of a convent of the same name, concerning the origin of which there is the following tradition. On the spot where it stood, a magnificent castle once raised its lofty towers, but that was long, very long ago, more than seven hundred years having passed since that time. In this castle dwelt a powerful knight, who had a beautiful wife, but who was exceedingly haughty, and too proud to associate with any person that was not, like herself, noble. The knight had once ridden out, and when evening came had not returned. In the meantime, another knight begged for admission into the castle, which the lady readily granted, and let him come into her bedchamber. There the stranger soon began with flattering words to gain the lady's favour, and at length told her, that out in the forest he had met with an old man, who loudly swore he would be revenged on her for having driven him from the castle. He had also declared that he was father to the lady of the castle, and that she was not of noble blood, but that he had exchanged her for a dead child with her supposed father, while she was yet in the cradle. With such and other discourses the stranger, who called himself Brudemer, so instigated the woman, that she hurried with him to the gate, and there stabbed her father. They then hurried back into the castle, and sat down to a game of chess.

After some time the door flew open, and the lord of Clairmarais entered the apartment with looks of fury. At the sight of him Brudemer burst into a loud laugh, while the noble lady was ready to sink into the earth, and grew deadly pale. But the knight approaching her, cried out, at the same time raising his sword, 'Let the devil fetch thee, thou parricide, thou adulteress!' But before he could strike, Brudemer seized her by the head, saying, 'I accept her,' and vanished with her accompanied by an appalling clap of thunder.

Not until late on the following day did the knight wake out of the state of stupefaction, into which these dreadful occurrences had thrown him, and then he resolved on having no more intercourse with the world. He afterwards entered into the monastery of the holy St Bertin, where he died a happy death.

The castle was then forsaken, no one being willing to dwell in it; for every night an awful tumult was heard there, nor did anyone return who ventured to enter it.

At length a pious Benedictine had the courage one evening to explore the castle. After having passed through many apartments, he sat down to rest in a small cabinet. Shortly after his entrance the door flew open, and a tall personage, on whose breast hung an escutcheon bearing the name of Brudemer, and with a deadly pale lady on his arm, stepped in. Behind them came a brilliant train of servants, and these were followed by eight young men, bearing heavy chests on their shoulders. The knight pointed to a table, on which there was a chessboard, and then to a chair standing by the table, in which the monk immediately placed himself. The knight sat down in one opposite, and both began to play. The monk played with the utmost caution, and calculated every move most carefully, and soon felt confident that he should overcome his adversary, when the lady pointed to a pawn, which the knight immediately moved. This changed the entire face of the game, and placed the monk in the greatest jeopardy; for he well knew that his soul would belong to the evil one, if he lost. At this move, too, the whole company gave a loud laugh. The monk now began to repent of his temerity, but resolved on making a virtue of necessity, so after a fervent prayer, pushed a pawn against that of his opponent. The knight seeing this became thoughtful, for the game was now again in favour of the monk, and every move improved the position of the latter, let him do whatever he might. When both had now made some further moves, and the game was manifestly in the hands of the pious ecclesiastic, there came at once a violent shock, the monk was thrown down, and everything vanished.

On the following morning the fortunate player found a female skeleton in rags and tatters lying by the side of the overthrown chess-table, and at the door eight chests full of gold and silver. He buried the dry bones in the castle yard, and then transformed the castle into a cloister, attached to which he erected a beautiful church, and became the first prior.

## Falkenberg

At the old castle of Falkenberg, in the province of Limburg, a spectre walks by night, and a voice from the ruins is heard to cry, 'Murder! Murder!' and it cries towards the north and the south, and the east and the west; and before the crier there go two small flames, which accompany him whithersoever he turns. And this voice has cried for six hundred years, and so long have also the two flames wandered.

Six hundred years ago the beautiful castle stood in its full glory, and was inhabited by two brothers of the noble race of Falkenberg. Their names were Waleram and Reginald, and they both loved Alix, the daughter of the count of Cleves. But Waleram was the favoured lover. His mother and the father of Alix readily consented to their union, and shortly after, the ceremony was performed with a splendour becoming their rank.

But Reginald meditated dark vengeance both on his brother and Alix; and when the feast was over and the young pair were about to be led to the bridal chamber, he hastened before them and concealed himself behind the bed. Lost in sweet dreams of love and happiness, the youthful couple thought not on their cruel brother, and hardly had they ascended the nuptial couch, when Reginald rushed forth and planted his dagger first in the breast of Waleram, and then in that of Alix. Waleram's first impulse was to clap his hand on his flowing wound, his next to grasp the murderer, with whose face his bloody hand came in contact; but his strength failed him, and he sank back lifeless. Reginald fled, after having cut a lock from the head of the unfortunate Alix.

On the following day there was loud lament and deep sorrow in the castle of Falkenberg; for everyone loved Waleram on account of his kind and benevolent heart, and Alix, whose soul was as beautiful as her body. No one doubted that Reginald was the assassin, and men were sent in every direction to seize him, but he was nowhere to be found.

At this time there dwelt in a forest near Falkenberg a holy hermit, who day and night lay in prayer before the altar of a little chapel that stood near his hermitage. It was near midnight, when someone knocked at the door of the chapel, and in the name of heaven prayed for admission. The recluse rose from prayer, opened the door, and recognised Reginald, who, shedding bitter tears, instantly fell at his feet, and besought him to hear his confession. The hermit raised him and led him to a seat, and Reginald confessed all, and as a proof, showed him the form of a hand stamped with blood on his countenance, and which he could not with any water wash away. When the man of God had heard all, he said, shuddering, 'It is not granted to me to absolve from sin so enormous; but pass the night with me in prayer; it may be that God will then give me to know what you shall do in order to obtain his forgiveness.' With these words he knelt before the altar, and Reginald knelt by his side: they both prayed.

When day began to dawn, the hermit rose and said, 'This is the behest of heaven. You shall go hence a humble and pious pilgrim, and ever journey towards the north, until you find no more earth on which to tread: a sign will then announce to you the rest.' Reginald answered, 'Amen,' craved the holy man's blessing, stepped to the lamp at the altar, where he burned the lock he had taken of Alix's hair, as he had been commanded by the hermit, then left the chapel and journeyed as a pilgrim on and on, and ever towards the north. And with him went two forms, one white on his right hand, one black on his left; and the black figure whispered in his ear much about his youth and the joys of the world, while his white attendant exhorted him to repentance, and to continue his journey, and set before his soul the everlasting joy of the blessed.

Thus had he journeyed for many a day, and many a week, and many a month, when one morning he found no more earth under his feet, and saw the wide ocean before him. At the same moment a boat approached the shore, and a man that sat in it made a sign to him, and said, 'We were expecting thee.' Then Reginald knew that this was the sign, and stepped into the boat, still attended by the two forms; and they rowed to a large ship with all her sails set; and when they were in the ship, the boatman disappeared and the ship sailed away. Reginald with his two attendants descended into a room below, where stood a table and chairs. Each of the two forms then taking a seat at the table, the black one drew forth a pair of dice, and they began playing for the soul of Reginald.

Six hundred years has that ship been sailing without either helm or helmsman, and so long have the two been playing for Reginald's soul. Their game will last till the last day. Mariners that sail on the North Sea often meet with the infernal vessel.

## The Monk of Afflighem

Towards the close of the eleventh century a most extraordinary event took place at the abbey of Afflighem.

It was one day announced to the pious Fulgentius, who at that time was abbot, that a stranger monk of venerable aspect had knocked at the gate and been admitted, who said he was one of the brethren of the cloister. The abbot caused him to be brought before him, and asked him who he was and whence he came? Whereunto the monk answered, that he had that morning sung matins with the rest of the brotherhood; that when they came to the verse of the 89th Psalm, where it is said, 'A thousand years in thy sight are but as yesterday', he had fallen into deep meditation, and continued sitting in the quire when all the others had departed. A little bird had then appeared to him, which sang most sweetly, and which, because it had so delighted him, he had followed into the forest, from whence, after a short stay, he was now returned, but found the abbey so changed that he no longer knew it. On Fulgentius asking him about his abbot, and also the name of the king that reigned at the time, it was found, to their great astonishment, that both had been dead three hundred years before.

The monk was startled, and said, 'Verily I now see that a thousand years are as yesterday in the sight of the Lord.' He then prayed the abbot to impart to him the holy sacraments, and, after partaking of them, died a holy and edifying death.

*A similar legend is related of the abbey of Heisterbach, opposite Bonn, and of some other abbeys. The story has been well paraphrased in German verse by E. Wegener. See* Nordischer Telegraph, *No. 31.*

## St Julian The Ferryman

Many hundred years ago there lived in the province of Saintonge a young and rich nobleman, whose name was Julian. His chief delight was in the chase, and he found little pleasure in prayer and exercises of piety.

One day, when following a hart, he penetrated far into the deep forest; but when he seemed to be on the point of capturing it, the animal suddenly stood still, turned its head, and in an audible voice said to Julian, 'Stop, Julian, and cease from pursuing me. Think rather of averting thy appalling destiny; for I announce unto thee, that with thy own hand thou wilt slay both father and mother.'

Julian was horror-struck at this dreadful prediction, and turning his horse, rode home, firmly resolved to flee from his native country and never to return, that he might avoid the fate which, according to the words of the hart, hung over him. Without saying a word to his parents, without considering how he was to support himself, he let his horse go whithersoever it would, until from fatigue it could proceed no further. Having no money, he sold it and bought a lute, with which he continued his journey, ever straight forwards; for his sole remaining wish was to withdraw himself from his paternal abode as far as possible.

A year had passed, when one evening, faint and ill, he reached a castle in the Ardennes. The lord of the castle, a man of kind disposition, received him hospitably, and desired his daughter, whose name was Basilissa, to take charge of the poor minstrel; for he was an enthusiastic lover of music, both instrumental and vocal. But when the beautiful maiden brought him the cup to drink, and manifested such tender solicitude for him, his heart was seized with a glowing passion, and he seemed at the same moment to be perfectly recovered. When, however, he called to mind that now, without name or rank, he could never aspire to the hand of Basilissa, his heart was ready to break. For a long time he knew not what course to follow, but at length resolved on parting from her and again setting out on his lonely wandering. On the third day, therefore, after his arrival he went to the lord of the castle, for the purpose of taking leave; but the good knight would not allow him to depart, pressing him to prolong his stay, a request in which Basilissa joined, and which Julian found himself quite unable to withstand.

Some days after, there was a great feast at the castle, and Julian sang at the table and played such sweet melodies that all were enraptured. On the following morning a splendid joust was to be held, of which, when Julian was apprised, his old passion rose within him, and he prayed the lord of the castle to be allowed to break a lance. The permission was granted, and he bore himself so gallantly that the prize was awarded to him in preference to every other. With equal bravery he conducted himself in a feud, in which his host was shortly afterwards engaged, and who at length conceived such a regard for him that he gave him his only daughter, the beautiful Basilissa, in marriage. Shortly after these events his father-in-law died, and Julian became lord of the castle and surrounding country.

The remembrance of the dreadful prediction was, however, never absent from his mind, and fervent as were his longings to see his parents again, he never ventured even to ask tidings of them, fearing always that the words of the hart might prove true. To free himself from this depressing thought, he had recourse to his former pastime, the chase.

To Julian's parents the loss of their son was a severe blow. Their happiness was at an end, and they finally resolved to seek him, and not to return till they had found him. Clad as pilgrims, they set out on their wanderings; they went from province to province, from city to city, from village to village, everywhere inquiring after their lost son, but no one could give them any tidings. At length they arrived in Belgium. When straying in the forest of Ardennes, they inquired of a rustic whether he could inform them of a shelter, and he directed them to the neighbouring castle, where they arrived faint and helpless in the morning. The castle was their son's. They knocked and were admitted by the porter. Julian had been out in the forest since sunrise; the servants therefore waked Basilissa, who soon came forth and gave the aged couple a friendly reception. When they had recruited their strength they related their history to the lady of the castle, and how they had been wandering for four years in search of their son. Basilissa immediately knew them for the parents of her consort; for he had frequently spoken to her of his departure from home, though without divulging the cause. Overjoyed at the thought of bearing such glad tidings to her husband, and at the same time of so agreeably surprising the venerable pair, she kept silence, and caused them to lie down in her own bed, that they might rest their weary limbs. Awaiting Julian's return, she then went to church, there to render thanks for the happy event.

Julian's horse had in the meantime wounded itself by stumbling over a stone, through which accident he was compelled to return. On arriving at the castle, he instantly proceeded to his bedchamber, where he expected still to find his wife, when seeing in his bed a man with a woman dressed in Basilissa's clothes, he instantly thought that she was faithless, and grasping his sword, in his blind fury he stabbed both the sleepers.

Could he have a presentiment how terribly he had fulfilled the prediction? For scarcely had he done the deed when he was seized with bitter repentance. Pursued by the wail and last groans of his victims, he was rushing from the castle, when the pious Basilissa returning from church stepped up to him. Julian started as one who trusted not his own eyesight. She wished to draw him into their bedchamber, that he might enjoy the pleasure of again seeing his parents; but he held her back, requesting only an answer to the question, who the sleepers were that he had found there? When Basilissa had informed him what they had related to her, he fell to the earth as if struck by lightning. Trembling with a dreadful presentiment, she hurried to the chamber; she shook them both, but she shook two corpses, and with a cry of horror she threw herself on the bloodstained bed.

It was long before Julian recovered his recollection. He then with tearful eyes confessed all, and communicated to her the hart's prediction. 'And now,' said he, 'farewell, beloved of my heart, and pray for me and forgive me; for I go from this place to atone for my sins.' Basilissa then falling on his neck answered, 'No, that you shall not do, my beloved husband; but if you persist in doing so, I will be your companion whithersoever you go.' And she was so, and on the following morning left the castle with Julian, and they continued their journey till they came to a little river called the Dender, and to the spot on which the town of Ath now stands. At that time pilgrims, on their way to the image of our blessed Lady of Hal, had, at the risk of their lives, to ford the river, there being no bridge there. For which reason Julian formed the resolution to build a hut on the bank and buy a boat, in which to ferry the pilgrims across, by which pious work he hoped to obtain forgiveness of his great sin.

For seven years he had ferried from one bank to the other, when one dark, rainy night, after he had retired fatigued with Basilissa to their bed of straw, they heard from the opposite bank a person in a mournful voice begging to be ferried over. Julian instantly rose, dressed himself, and, in spite of wind and weather, turned his boat towards the left bank of the river. Basilissa knelt by his side in the frail skiff and prayed; for the water raged so wildly that they expected to sink at every instant. On reaching the other shore they found an old pilgrim with dripping garments, lying on the earth and groaning piteously. They immediately threw their cloaks over him and bore him into the bark, which now appeared to push itself off, and rapidly yet tranquilly to steer towards the hut; though the waves were angrily dashing around it, and the winds awfully raging. When they reached the bank, Julian fastened the boat, while Basilissa prepared their straw bed for the pilgrim, they themselves lying by him on the hard, cold earth, having previously kindled a fire and refreshed the aged man with some warm milk.

But suddenly a brilliant light diffused itself in the hut, the pilgrim rose, his wet garments fell off, and he stood in divine majesty and splendour. It was the Lord Jesus himself. Julian and Basilissa fell on their knees trembling; but Jesus said, 'Thou hast made sufficient atonement, Julian; thy sin is forgiven thee, and I await thee and thy faithful wife.' With these words he vanished.

On the following day, as some persons were fishing in the neighbourhood, they heard melodies of heavenly sweetness issuing from the hut. On approaching and opening it, they found husband and wife kneeling, dead, encircled with a heavenly light. They buried them honourably. At a later period many miracles have taken place at their grave, and on the spot where the hut had stood was erected the beautiful church still existing of the hospitable, holy Julian.

## Lohengrin and Elsa – Lohengrin and Belaye

Many hundred years ago there was a duke of Brabant and Limburg, who had a beautiful daughter named Elsa. When this duke lay on his death-bed, he commended his daughter to one of his vassals, whose name was

Frederic of Telramonde and who was everywhere known and honoured as a valiant warrior, but was particularly esteemed, because at Stockholm in Sweden he had overcome a fierce dragon, and thereby acquired a hero's fame. But Frederic soon became proud and presumptuous, and would make Elsa his wife, and even falsely asserted that she had engaged her word to be faithful to him. But Elsa charged him with falsehood, and gave no ear to his suit. At this Frederic was bitterly exasperated, and more resolved than ever to compel her to give him her hand. With this object he laid a complaint before the emperor Henry, surnamed the Fowler,[1] and obtained from him a decree that Elsa should choose a champion, who in honourable combat should engage with Frederic, that the voice of God might decide either for or against him. But Elsa would select no champion, placing her sole hope in fervent prayer to the Lord, from whom alone she expected help and support.

One day at Montsalva on the Graal the bells were rung which are always a token that someone is in need of immediate aid, and Lohengrin, the son of Parcival, was chosen as deliverer of the oppressed. While his horse was standing ready for its rider, who was in the act of setting his foot in the stirrup, behold, a swan appeared on the water, drawing a little boat after it. Lohengrin regarded this as a sign from heaven, and ordered his horse to be led back to its stable, for he would enter the boat and follow the swan. And he did so, and commended himself to God, and in firm reliance on him, took no food with him. After the swan had conducted him for five days, it plunged its bill into the water and drew out a small fish, which it shared with Lohengrin, and then continued its course. But let us now return to Elsa, the daughter of the duke of Brabant and Limburg.

Elsa had in the meanwhile called all her vassals together; for one day passed after another, and no one came forward in her cause. But when these had assembled, there came the swan with the boat swimming up the Scheldt, having Lohengrin on board, sleeping on his shield. When the swan reached the bank, Lohengrin woke, sprang on shore, and was received by Elsa with unutterable joy and gratification. His helmet, shield and sword were then brought from the boat, when the swan disappeared, returning by the way it came.

When the first demonstrations of joy were over, Lohengrin asked the duchess under what evil she was suffering, and learned from her how Frederic was striving to ensnare her, and had falsely accused her to the emperor, and that now her cause was to be decided by the judgement of God. Lohengrin then assured her that he would be her champion, when

1   He reigned from 919 to 936.

Elsa immediately assembled all her kindred and subjects, who came to Saarbrücken, whence in a body they proceeded to Mentz. The emperor, who was keeping his court at Frankfurt, came also thither, and the day for the combat was fixed, and the lists erected. After both champions had asserted the justness of their cause, the conflict began; but Lohengrin proved victorious, and Frederic of Telramonde fell, and confessed that he had falsely accused the duchess Elsa, in punishment for which, according to the usage of the time, he suffered death by the axe. In reward, Lohengrin obtained the hand of the fair Elsa of Brabant, and their nuptials were celebrated with suitable magnificence. But Lohengrin at the same time besought his wife never to ask his name nor whence he came; for if she did either the one or the other, he could no longer continue with her.

Lohengrin and Elsa had long lived together in peace and happiness, and he proved a wise and just prince in the territories of Brabant and Limburg; but it chanced that in a tournament he dangerously wounded the duke of Cleves in the arm, at which the duchess being exasperated, and at the same time envious of Elsa, said to her, 'Your Lohengrin may be a doughty hero, and possibly a Christian also; but no one knows either whence he springs or who he is, so strangely did he make his appearance here.'

At these words the fair Elsa was sorely troubled, and at night, when lying in bed with her husband, she wept bitterly. Lohengrin observing this, said to her, 'My dear wife, why do you weep?' To which Elsa answered: 'The duchess of Cleves has caused me bitter affliction.' Hearing this, Lohengrin was silent and inquired no further. The following night the same question was asked and the same answer given, but Lohengrin still preserved silence, refraining from all further inquiry. But the third night the fair Elsa, quite unable longer to preserve her compliance with her husband's injunction, thus addressed him, 'My beloved lord and husband, I beseech you to tell me where you were born and from whom you spring; for my heart assures me that you must be of a very noble race.'

At daybreak Lohengrin rose and disclosed to her where he was born and from whom he sprang, and that Parcival was his father, that God had sent him to her from the Graal, and also that he could no longer live with her. Causing then his two children to be brought to him, he kissed them affectionately, gave them his horn and his sword, exhorting them to make a good use of it. To Elsa he gave a ring which he had formerly received from his mother. When all this was done, the swan came again with the boat; into which Lohengrin stepped and glided away down the Scheldt. Elsa had sunk in a swoon; when she recovered, she was afflicted and wept bitterly for the loss of her beloved consort, which she never ceased to deplore.

But Lohengrin arrived in the land of Lyzaboria, where he espoused the beautiful Belaye, who loved him beyond measure, and was particularly cautious not to make any inquiry respecting his descent, and was always sad when he was not with her, being in constant fear of his proving inconstant. But Lohengrin could not always sit at home, and therefore went frequently to the chase; at which time the fair Belaye would utter no word, but would sit as if life had taken its flight, and she was under the influence of some evil spell.

One of her women then advised her, that, in order to attach Lohengrin more closely to her, she should cut a piece of flesh from his side and eat it. But Belaye was indignant at the suggestion, and declared she would sooner suffer herself to be buried alive than hurt even a finger of her husband: she at the same time withdrew from her woman all her favour and confidence. Hereupon this treacherous woman went and uttered her base falsehoods to the friends of the beautiful Belaye, who immediately resolved to cut off from Lohengrin a piece of his flesh, in order that Belaye might recover. Therefore, when the hero had one day returned fatigued from the chase and had fallen asleep, they proceeded to their nefarious work. But Lohengrin at the same time had a dream, in which he saw thousands of swords directed against him, when starting from his sleep, he darted such fierce looks on those base men that they all trembled; then raising his hand, he laid about him and slew more than a hundred of them. But they, recovering courage and helping one another, succeeded in inflicting an incurable wound in his left arm. On seeing this, they felt in their hearts overcome by the valour he had displayed, and fell at his feet.

When Belaye was informed of this, she died of grief and horror, and was embalmed with Lohengrin, placed in a coffin, and buried with great solemnity. At a later period a convent was erected over their grave, and the bodies of both are there still shown to pilgrims. And all this happened five hundred years after the birth of our beloved Lord,[1] and from that time the country of Lyzaboria has, after Lohengrin, been called Lothringia.

## The Knight and the Swan

Duke Godfrey of Brabant died leaving no male heirs; but had in his testament provided that his territories should devolve on his duchess and his daughter. To this, however, his brother, the powerful duke of Saxony, paid little regard, but, in defiance of the complaints of the widow and orphan, took possession of the country, which according to the German law could not be inherited by a female.

The duchess hereupon resolved to lay her case before the king, and as

---

1   A singular anachronism. See note on p. 653.

Charles came shortly after into Belgium, and purposed holding a diet at Nymwegen, she appeared there with her daughter, and demanded justice. The duke of Saxony was there also, for the purpose of answering the complaint.

It happened as the king was looking through a window of the court, that he observed a white swan swimming towards him on the Rhine, drawing after it, by a silver chain, a little boat, in which lay a sleeping knight; his shield was his pillow, and near him lay his helm and hauberk. The swan navigated like a skilful seaman, and brought the boat to land. At this spectacle Charles and his court were greatly surprised; everyone forgot the complaint of the two princesses, and ran down to the river. In the meanwhile the knight had woke and quitted the bark. The king received him courteously, took him by the hand, and led him towards the castle. On leaving the boat the young hero said to the bird, 'Proceed prosperously on thy way back, dear swan! When I again require thee I will call thee.' The swan instantly began its course, and with the boat was soon out of sight. Everyone regarded the strange guest with eager curiosity; Charles returned to his tribunal, and assigned a seat to the young knight among the other princes.

The duchess of Brabant, in the presence of her beautiful daughter, now gave a full statement of her complaint, after which the duke of Saxony made his defence, finally offering to do battle for his rights, and calling on the duchess to name a champion to oppose him in defence of her cause. At this she was overcome with fear, for the duke was a renowned warrior, against whom no one would venture to contend. In vain did she cast her eyes round the hall, no one appeared ready to offer himself. At length the knight, who had been brought thither by the swan, arose and offered to be her champion; whereupon both sides armed for the conflict, when after a long and obstinate strife, victory declared herself on the side of the knight of the swan. The duke of Saxony lost his life, and the inheritance of the duchess was again free.

Then the duchess and her daughter made obeisance to the hero who had so gallantly fought in their behalf, and who accepted the offered hand of the daughter, though under the condition, that she should never ask whence he came, nor from what race he sprang; for if she did, he must forsake her.

The duke and the young duchess had two children, who were both amiable and well-nurtured; but their mother was ever more and more weighed down by the reflection that she knew not who was their father; till at length she ventured on the forbidden inquiry. The knight was fearfully affected and said, 'Now hast thou destroyed our happiness and seen me for the last time.' The duchess repented, but it was too late; all the people fell at his feet and implored him to remain. But the warrior armed himself, and the swan came swimming with the same little boat. He then kissed both his children, bade his wife farewell, and gave his benediction to all the people; after which he entered the boat, went his way and never returned. The duchess was sorely afflicted at her loss, but, nevertheless, educated her children with great care. From these children many noble races derive their descent – the houses of Gelderland and Cleves, also the counts of Rheineck, all of whom bear the swan in their coat-armour.

## Godfrey of Bouillon and the Swan

While the valiant duke Godfrey of Bouillon lay with his army of crusaders before the holy city of Jerusalem, he one day looked towards heaven and perceived a flying swan. Four times it flew round his head, and having so flown, it rose a little, then flew towards Jerusalem, to a tower, where it descended: and that was the tower through which Godfrey, in storming the city, forced an entrance.

## The Knight with the Swan

In the kingdom of Lillefort, which lay in Flanders, there lived in days of yore a king whose name was Pirion, and who had a wicked woman for his wife, named Matabruna. By this woman he had a son, named Oriant, who, on the death of his father, was crowned king of Lillefort.

It happened that King Oriant with his nobles rode out to the chase, and saw a hart, which they pursued for a considerable time. At length it sprang into a brook and thus escaped from the hunters. Oriant on seeing this turned his horse and came to a fountain where he dismounted, and sat down under a tree to rest. While thus sitting there came a beautiful and noble maiden with four female attendants, a knight and two man-servants. Addressing Oriant, who was sitting with his dogs by his side, she said, 'Sir, why do you hunt in my domain, and who has given you permission so to do? I saw how the hart you were in chase of escaped from you and leapt into the water; but had you taken it, it would not have been yours. I desire that you will withdraw from hence.'

When King Oriant heard the fair Beatrix speaking so wisely, he formed the design of making her his wife, and said in a soft voice, 'Beautiful damsel, I would not willingly act in opposition to your will, but here I may lawfully hunt, for I am Oriant, king of Lillefort, and all things hereabout are at my disposal.' When the knight, who was named Samari, heard this, he sprang from his horse; fell on his knees, greeted the king and said, 'Sir king, forgive my lady for that wherein she has erred towards you; for she knew you not, and is now fully sensible of her fault.' 'It is already forgiven,' answered the king, 'but she must, nevertheless, atone for it.' Then addressing himself to the lady, he said, 'Fair maiden, if you will be my bride, I will crown you as queen of Lillefort.' And having made this promise and confirmed it by oaths, he conducted the beautiful Beatrix to his palace, where the marriage should be solemnised with great pomp and rejoicings.

When Matabruna heard that Oriant was about to marry the damsel that he had met while hunting, she went to him boiling with anger. But Oriant laughed when he saw her, and said, 'Rejoice, for I have found the most beautiful female that lives on the earth.' Matabruna filled with rage answered, 'My dear son, it causes me unutterable grief, that you, who could have to wife the greatest lady in the world, should marry a simple individual.' But Oriant persisted, and the wicked mother also appeared content, though in her heart there rankled the bitterest malice against Beatrix.

When Oriant had for a time enjoyed the love of the fair Beatrix, she became pregnant. At this time an enemy having invaded the territory of Lillefort, the king with his chivalry prepared to take the field; but previous to his departure, he commended his wife to the tender care of his mother, which she promised to bestow, and then with many tears bade them farewell.

But scarcely had the king departed when Matabruna began to carry her wicked designs into effect. She summoned the midwife to her presence, and caused her to swear never to divulge that which she was about to impart to her. When the midwife had so sworn, Matabruna said, 'You are well aware what a detriment my son's marriage has been to the country; for which reason I would fain estrange him from his wife, which it will be easy to effect, as she is pregnant.' To this the woman answered, 'If it seem good to you, I will destroy the child.' 'That is not enough,' replied Matabruna. 'Beatrix is very large, and will, therefore, most probably bear twins: these you shall put aside, and in their stead show her two young dogs. I will then give the children to one who will carry them away, so that they shall no more be heard of.' To this plan the midwife agreed and promised to carry it out.

When the time for Beatrix's delivery drew near, these wicked women held two puppies in readiness. Instead, however, of two children, as they had expected, Beatrix bore seven, six sons and a daughter, all of whom had silver chains round their necks, as a proof of their mother's nobility. But this in nowise deranged Matabruna's plan: she took seven puppies, and caused them to be laid in the place of the children, when the midwife exclaimed, 'O queen, what is this? You have brought forth seven young dogs!' Then in haste came Matabruna, feigning to be greatly horrified, and said, 'Make away with the animals and bury them, that the king may preserve his honour and the affair be no more spoken of.' Beatrix in the meanwhile lay weak and senseless, and when she recovered, Matabruna came, and with cruel words reproached her for having given birth to seven dogs; and when Beatrix desired to see them, they were brought to her. At the sight of them she was horror-struck, and conscious that the king would now withdraw his love from her and put her to death. The midwife with her hypocritical words pretended to console her, saying that the king should know nothing of the matter; but Beatrix was not to be comforted, and saw in death alone the end of her sufferings.

Matabruna in the meantime called to her a servant named Marcus, and said, 'Friend, thou must do me a service, but must keep it a secret. The queen has given birth to six sons and a daughter, all of whom bear silver chains round their necks, a sign that they will all one day be great thieves and murderers. Therefore must they be destroyed, lest they bring disgrace on the king. This office thou shalt execute; for the queen believes she has brought forth seven puppies.' Marcus promised to perform her will, took the seven babes in his cloak and rode with them into the forest. But when be saw how beautiful they were, he was struck with compassion, and resolved to let them live; therefore having kissed them and shed many tears over them, he rode back to Lillefort, where he told Matabruna that he had destroyed them, who was overjoyed at the intelligence, and now resolved to accomplish the death of Beatrix.

While the children lay piteously moaning in the forest, they were heard by an old man who dwelt hard by, and who on coming to them and seeing them so forsaken, burst into tears, and having wrapped them in his cloak, carried them to his hut. There he purposed warming, and, as far as it was in his power, feeding them; but that was rendered needless, God having sent a white goat to the hut, which offered her teats to the babes and allowed them to suck; and this continued until they grew large and ran with the goat into the thicket. Then the old man, who was named Helias, made them clothing of leaves, to cover their nakedness.

King Oriant had in the meantime overcome all his enemies, and was on his way home; for he longed greatly to know how it had gone with his beloved wife. But when Matabruna heard that he was coming, she hastened to meet him, and no sooner were they together than she began to weep, and said, 'Ah my dear son, I rejoice that you are here again, although my heart is oppressed on account of your wife.' On hearing this the king was overwhelmed with surprise and apprehension, and asked what had taken place, whether Beatrix were dead or alive? To which Matabruna replied, 'No, she is not dead, but what has occurred relating to her is so shocking that I cannot express it.' The king then urged her, and insisted on knowing what had happened, when Matabruna informed him that Beatrix had been delivered of seven puppies, and called the midwife as a witness. This news afflicted Oriant beyond measure, and he went with one confidential knight into a chamber and wept bitterly, until overcome with the weight of his sorrow, he fell, asleep; while the noble lady Beatrix was in another apartment no less afflicted than her consort.

On the following day King Oriant assembled his council, ecclesiastic and secular, and said, 'I have caused you to meet here that we may deliberate on what is to be done with my queen.' He then laid the whole case before them. A wise man thereupon rose, and turning towards the king said, 'Sir king, at your desire I will answer you in the name of all these lords, and say what seems good to us. You shall not put the queen to death, but keep her in honourable custody, and leave the rest to God, who will make the truth manifest.' This counsel greatly comforted the king, for he ardently loved Beatrix, and he therefore adopted it, although a wicked knight arose and proposed that she should be burnt. So Beatrix was conducted to an apartment by two knights and honourably served.

The old man in the meantime took the most affectionate care of the children; in one of the boys he took especial delight, and named him after himself Helias. It once happened that one of Matabruna's huntsmen, named Savari, came into the forest and found the children with silver chains round their necks, just as they were eating apples with their bread. The huntsman found great pleasure in them and followed them into the hut, that he might learn who they were. On seeing the huntsman, the old man was alarmed lest some harm might befall the children; but the huntsman having dispelled his fears, he related to him how he had found and reared them.

At this recital the huntsman was astonished, and on his return related the whole to Matabruna, who instantly felt convinced that these were Oriant's children, and therefore ordered him to destroy them, threatening him that, in the event of his non-compliance, she would have him put to death. Surprised and terror-struck the man promised to execute her command, at which Matabruna was tranquillised, and going to those who had conveyed the children to the forest, she caused their eyes to be put out.

The huntsman Savari, taking seven men with him, went out for the purpose of destroying the children. On their way they came to a village where a great number of persons were assembled, in consequence, as they were informed, of a woman having just been burnt for the murder of her child. This touched the heart of Savari, who said to his associates, 'Behold a mirror for us: this woman has been burnt for having killed one infant, and we are to destroy seven.' On which the others said, 'No, we will not destroy them, but only take their chains from them and carry them to Matabruna, as a token of their death.' They then entered the forest and came to the hut, where they found only six of the children, the old man having taken the seventh with him to the village, to fetch bread. Seeing the strangers, the children cried piteously from terror and surprise; but Savari. said, 'Be still, dear children, we will not harm you,' and took the chains from their necks, when at the instant all the six were transformed into white swans, which flew up in the air, and mournfully wailed and screamed. At this Savari and his companions were so terrified that they fell in a swoon, and on recovering trembled with fright and said, 'Let us quickly leave this place, we have already been here too long: we will take the six chains to Matabruna, and say we have lost the seventh.'

But when they brought only six chains to Matabruna, she was bitterly enraged, and would not be pacified until they offered to pay her the value of the seventh, which they accordingly did. This wicked woman then sent the chains to a goldsmith that he might make a cup of them. When the goldsmith had placed one of the chains in the fire, to prove whether it were good silver, it became so heavy that it outweighed all the other chains together. He therefore gave the others to the custody of his wife, and made of the one two silver beakers, one of which he took to Matabruna, and kept the other for himself.

In the meanwhile the old man with Helias had returned home, and sought for the six children without finding them. On the following morning Helias came to the pond in which the swans were swimming, and was not a little surprised when they came to him. He gave them bread which they ate, and allowed him to caress them. And this he repeated from day to day, and never entered the thicket without first going to the pond.

But God heard the prayer of the unhappy mother, Beatrix, and let it be announced to the old man, that the six boys and the girl were the offspring of king Oriant, and also that six of them had been transformed. Whereupon calling Helias to him, the old man told him all, and Helias then took leave of him, recommending the swans to his tender care. He then went to the king, clad in leaves, barefooted and bareheaded, with a club in his hand, for the purpose of asserting his mother's rights and innocence.

The foes of the hapless Beatrix had in the meanwhile prevailed on the king to pronounce judgement on her and cause her to suffer death. She was, consequently, one day brought from her prison and conducted before Oriant, that she might in his presence defend herself; for a false knight, suborned by Matabruna, had preferred new charges against her. On entering the hall, Beatrix made humble obeisance to the king, fell on her knees, and prayed so fervently for grace, that everyone, and the king above all, felt profound pity for her. Oriant then asked the false knight of what he accused her, and the knight answered, that she had wished to give him poison, for the purpose of destroying both the king and Matabruna. Thereupon the king rose and said, 'Wife, you are heavily accused; what say you? Tell the truth, and if you are guilty, you shall die a shameful death, if no one will defend your cause.' But Beatrix again falling on her knees said, 'My dear lord, I know that I shall find no one who will do so; nevertheless, I swear to you and all these lords, that I have never harboured such a thought, so true as God is almighty, to whom I leave all vengeance on my enemies.'

When sentence of death was about to be pronounced, the young Helias with his club just reached the royal court, when a man stepping towards him, inquired his business. 'I seek the false knight, Marcus,' said Helias. 'I am he,' answered the man in jest, whereupon Helias, raising his club, struck him dead to the earth. At this another attendant came up and attempted to seize him, but Helias defended himself and said, 'Away from me, for I will not rest until I have slain that false knight, Marcus, who has unjustly accused my mother.' When one of the attendants heard this, he whispered to Helias that Marcus was then in the hall, that he had accused Beatrix of much, but that no one gave credit to the charges, as the queen was greatly beloved. When Helias heard the man speak thus, he embraced him, and the man conducted him to the hall, where many a heavy heart sighed for Beatrix. And Helias entered the hall, and appeared before the king, who immediately asked him whom he sought. 'I seek Marcus,' said he. The false knight, Marcus, being pointed out to him, he sprang to him, crying aloud, 'Thou false traitor! I challenge thee to battle, and thou shalt engage with me,' at the same time striking him such a blow with his fist that Marcus fell to the earth, and would have been slain outright, had not the other knights stepped forth and parted them. On seeing this, the king said to Helias, 'What makes thee so daring in my presence?' The youth answered, 'Sir, I am come hither to tell you truly all that has taken place.' 'Do so,' said the king, and Helias proceeded, 'My dear mother, cease now to weep and mourn, for I will restore you to happiness.' When the king heard these words, he was greatly astonished; but Helias, turning towards him, said, 'Sir, be it known to you that it is your mother, Matabruna alone who has caused so much evil to my mother.' And thereupon he related to the king everything, from beginning to end, and offered to remain as a prisoner at the court, until the truth of his account should have been confirmed by witnesses. At this the king was still more astonished, and demanded of Beatrix what she knew of the matter, who answered, 'Sir, I know nothing; for when I was in travail, I was overcome with pain, and knew not what took place. Whether your mother has done good or evil will be made to appear. Into the hands of God and this stripling I give the defence of my honour, and pray you to supply him with whatever he may require for the conflict.'

The queen was then led to a fair apartment, and the king proceeded to his mother, Matabruna, to whom he related all that had passed. She changed colour on hearing it, but hoped by smooth words to conceal her treachery. The king, however, gave no heed to them, but went and ordered Marcus to be committed to prison. He then caused beautiful armour to be prepared for Helias, and afterwards went, as if going to the chase, to visit the old man in the forest, that from him he might hear a confirmation of what the youth had related. The old man's narrative tallied in every particular with what he had heard from Helias, and the king was bitterly grieved on account of the injustice Beatrix had suffered at his hands.

On his return he instantly set the queen at liberty, and ordered Matabruna to be cast into prison and to be guarded by four attendants. He then ordered Marcus before him, that he might do battle with Helias Marcus, on entering the lists, felt weighed down with apprehension, though he would not let it appear, but with a loud voice called to Helias: 'Come, thou foolish stripling; it shall soon be seen what thou canst do against me.' Helias answered, 'O, thou false traitor, I rejoice in having to contend with thee, to avenge my mother, and defend her honour!'

They then rushed to the encounter, and Helias struck the false knight together with his horse to the earth, whereat Marcus enraged and astounded, exclaimed, 'Stripling! though such be thy prowess, thou shalt, nevertheless, soon feel the strength of my arm.' To which Helias replied, 'Come boldly on, I fear thee not.' Helias having now somewhat lowered his lance, Marcus took advantage of the circumstance, and treacherously wounded him in a place that was unprotected, so that the blood flowed. The people were struck with apprehension at this mishap, but God did not forsake Helias. On seeing his blood flow, he became yet more embittered, and cried to Marcus, 'O, thou false traitor, was it not enough for thee to attempt the destruction of my mother, but thou must deal treacherously by me? But with God's aid I will requite thee!' Then rushing a second time against each other, Helias struck his adversary's helmet from his head, and grasping his sword, so assailed him that he could not move a limb, and smote off his right arm. When the traitor found himself overcome, he yielded himself to the mercy of Helias, and said, 'Youth, thou hast conquered me, I yield, tell me who thou art.' Helias answered, 'I am a son of King Oriant and his faithful queen, Beatrix, and must see thee dead before I quit these lists.' 'Grant me my life and make me thy captive,' said Marcus, 'that I may confess all; and send for the goldsmith who had the chains.' While he was thus speaking, the judges of the field approached, and adjudged the victory to Helias, who desired them instantly to summon

King Oriant, his queen and all the lords; and when this was done, Marcus related all that had taken place, and when he had finished his confession, the king, clasping his beloved wife in his arms, with tearful eyes implored her forgiveness. They afterwards all proceeded to the palace, and rendered thanks to God for the victory of Helias; but the false knight was hung by the legs on a gibbet.

After these events had taken place, and great feastings and tournaments had been held, the king summoned Matabruna's goldsmith before him, that he might ascertain the truth respecting the silver chains. The goldsmith brought with him the five chains and the beaker, and related to the king the story of the sixth. When he had finished, the king said, 'You speak like an honest man, and therefore all is forgiven.' The king and the queen then took the chains, kissed them and wept for their children, who had been turned into swans. Then came the other Marcus, whose eyes Matabruna had caused to be put out, and Oriant asked him how he came by his blindness, when Marcus gave him a full account of his having, by the order of Matabruna, conveyed the children away and left them in the forest. When this was told to Matabruna, she gave the men that had been placed over her as a guard so much to drink that they fell asleep, and then fled to a strong castle, where she believed herself secure against all. The attendants were severely punished.

Helias having been informed that the king had five of the chains, went to him and prayed to have them, and swore that he would enjoy no rest until he had found his brothers and sisters. Scarcely had he uttered these words, than it was announced that six beautiful swans had come out of the forest and settled in the castle moat. At this intelligence Helias with the king and queen hurried forth. When the swans saw Helias they flapped their wings for joy and he stroked their plumage. He then showed them the chains, at the sight of which they pressed round him, and he hung a chain round the necks of five of them, when they were instantly turned to a human form, and ran to their dear parents to kiss and embrace them. When the last swan saw there was no chain for him, he was much afflicted, and strove to pluck every feather from his wing; but Helias mourned with him, and sought to comfort him, and the swan, as in gratitude, bowed down his head. There was now great rejoicing at the court, and King Oriant summoned all his knights and nobles together, and bestowed his kingdom on his son Helias, and left him at liberty to take what vengeance he thought proper on Matabruna. Helias then stormed and took the castle to which she had fled, took her prisoner, and ordered her to be burnt alive.

When Helias had long ruled over the realm of Lillefort in peace and tranquillity, he saw one morning, when looking through the window, the swan, his brother, drawing after him a little boat. Helias in this recognised a sign from God, and ordering his armour and silver shield to be brought, took leave of his parents and friends, and entered the boat. Hereat the swan was overjoyed, and beat with its wings, and departed with the boat, which in a short tinne was far far away from Lillefort.

At this time the emperor, Otto the First,[1] was holding an imperial diet in the city of Nymwegen, at which the count of Ardennes preferred a complaint against the duchess of Billoen, whose inheritance he would unjustly seize, and uttered gross calumnies against her, that she had poisoned her husband, and during his absence of three years beyond sea, had given birth to an illegitimate daughter, whereby the territory of Billoen now fell to him, the count of Ardennes. The emperor said, 'Woman, these are heavy charges, and if you cannot prove your innocence, you must die.' The count of Ardennes proceeded, and said, 'Sir emperor, in proof of the truth, I cast down my glove, and will engage in combat with anyone, be he who he may.' On hearing this, the emperor commanded the duchess to seek a champion to fight for her. The good woman looked on all sides, but found none.

Then on a sudden the clear notes of a horn were heard from the Rhine, and the emperor with all who were there assembled hastened to the windows, from whence they saw the swan with the boat, in which Helias stood completely armed, as was befitting a gentle knight. The emperor was greatly astonished at seeing the swan depart with the boat, after Helias had landed, and caused the knight to appear before him; while the duchess, who had observed the whole, felt her heart comforted, and said to her daughter, 'I this night dreamed that I was contending against the count, and that I was condemned to be burnt; but that there came a swan which brought water to quench the fire, and that from the water there sprang a fish, at the sight of which everyone trembled. Therefore do I believe that this knight will deliver me.'

When Helias appeared before the emperor, he greeted him courteously, and the emperor did the like to him, and inquired of him who he was and whence he came. Helias answered, 'I am a poor knight, and go out seeking adventures, and will faithfully serve you, if you require me.' The emperor replied, 'If you are a knight in search of adventures, you have found one here, and can fight for the honour of the duchess of Billoen, who is accused of a heinous crime.' Helias then turning, cast a glance on the duchess, who appeared to him an honourable lady; but when he looked on her daughter, his heart was smitten with love. He then requested permission of the emperor to speak alone with the duchess, which was readily granted. He

---

1   He reigned from 936 to 973.

asked her whether she were innocent or guilty, and the duchess answered in a firm tone, 'I am innocent.' Helias answered, 'Lady, you have then found a champion; I will defend your honour.'

Thereupon Helias, again approaching the emperor, said, 'Sir emperor, let him now enter the lists who accuses this lady, for the purpose of compassing her death; for I am ready to engage with him.' When he had so spoken, the count came forwards and said, 'Friend, what is it you desire? You appear very bold in a cause which in no wise concerns you.' To which Helias answered, 'There lies my glove, which I cast down for the honour of God, of these noble ladies, and of myself, and you shall this day see what a knight of adventure can perform.' The count then took up the glove, and the emperor inquired when they would fight, which Helias was desirous of doing on that day. The lists were therefore quickly made ready, and Helias appeared in armour with his silver shield, and the count in arms no less excellent. The emperor with his nobles, the duchess with her daughter, and an innumerable body of people, were spectators.

The knights encountered each other with such impetuosity that their lances were shivered, and then had recourse to their good swords, when Helias plied his weapon so vigorously that the count with difficulty could defend himself, and addressed his adversary thus, 'O, noble knight of the swan, make peace with me, so that I may attain my object, and I will bestow on you my daughter with the fertile land of Ardennes.' This address exasperated Helias, who answered, 'Do you imagine that I will imitate you in your treachery? Rather would I allow myself to be hewed limb by limb; therefore say no more; for I swear to you that I will grant you no grace, and in your despite will marry the duchess's daughter.' At this the count was filled with rage, and struck Helias with such force on the arm that the sword fell from his hand; but instantly springing from his horse, he seized the count, tore the shield from his neck, and wrenched his sword from him. The count prayed for grace, but Helias heeded not his prayer, and with his sword struck off his head.

Having thus overcome his adversary, Helias presented himself before the emperor, who received him nobly. The duchess also came with her daughter, and thanked him, and said, 'Sir, you have restored to me my lands; I give them back to you together with my daughter.' At this Helias was highly gratified, and on the following day the marriage was solemnised with great pomp and splendour. When the feastings had lasted for a fortnight, the new duke took leave of the emperor, after having sworn fealty to him, and departed with his consort for Billoen, where he soon arrived and was received with great joy; after having gallantly defended himself on the road against the friends and kindred of the count. Shortly after his wife became pregnant, and when the time came, she gave birth to a daughter, who was named Ida, who grew up in virtue, and was mother of the noble prince Godfrey, and his brothers, Baldwin and Eustace.

One day when the duchess was riding out with her husband, she asked him of what country he was, and what friends and kindred he had. But he would not answer her, and desired her never to repeat the questions for that if she did he must part from her. She said no more on the subject, and both lived in great harmony for six years.

But gradually the duchess lost all remembrance of the prohibition, and one day, when alone with Helias, she said to him, 'My beloved husband, I would fain know of what descent you are.' Helias was much troubled hereat and sorrowfully answered, 'I have told you that you should never know, and therefore should never inquire. I must now leave you, and shall go tomorrow to Nymwegen and take leave of the emperor.' The duchess wept bitterly and called her daughter, that she might add her entreaties to her own, and thus divert him from his purpose. But Helias told them that it might not be; and having assembled his nobles, he commended to them the mother and daughter, together with the territory of Billoen. He was yet speaking when the swan appeared, making a great noise with its wings, as if calling Helias, who now took a sad leave of all, and followed by the tears of the inhabitants, entered the boat, and was instantly drawn away by the swan.

But the duchess and her daughter hastened to Nymwegen, at which place they arrived before the knight of the swan. There they related to the emperor all that had taken place, and prayed for his intercession and aid. While they were thus speaking, the sound of Helias's horn was heard from the Rhine, and shortly after he himself appeared before the emperor. But earnestly as the emperor besought him not to forsake the duchess and her beautiful daughter, it was all in vain. Helias now prayed the emperor to aid and protect the two ladies, and having received that prince's assurance that his prayer was granted, again entered his boat. The swan beat with its wings on seeing him, and soon both found themselves in Lillefort.

King Oriant was sitting at table with his queen and their five children when the boat arrived. At the lively notes of Helias's horn, they all rushed to the windows of the palace, and on seeing the two brothers, they hastened down to embrace and kiss them. Their mother's first question was, 'My son, where hast thou been so long?' To which Helias answered, 'My mother, that I will tell you at another time.' She then asked what was become of the swan, and Helias informed her that it had remained in the water; upon which the mother said, 'I this night dreamed that the swan would recover its human form, if the two beakers were shown to it.' This seemed good to all, and when the swan saw the two beakers which the goldsmith had made of its chain, it was instantly restored to its human figure, and received the name of Esmeri; and there was consequently great rejoicing in the whole court.

Some time after Helias assembled all his friends and relations, and recounted to them his adventures, and when he had finished, said, 'I now bid all of you farewell; for I am about to leave the world, that I may expiate my sins and pray for all of you.' At this the whole court wept, though no one ventured to utter a word against his resolve. Helias then went, with a staff in his hand, to a monastery which his father had founded, and was received by the monks with much gladness. He afterwards caused a beautiful and spacious castle to be built in the Ardennes, exactly resembling that of Billoen, and to which he gave the same name. On the monastery he bestowed great franchises, and placed in it thirty monks, to pray day and night, and lived himself according to the rules of the monastery.

The duchess of Billoen and her daughter lived in the meanwhile in constant grief and affliction for the loss of Helias; for all the messengers that she had sent out, to get tidings of him, had returned without success. She at length despatched a servant, named Pucius, to Jerusalem, in search of Helias, who, finding no trace of him there, resolved on wandering to Rome. On this journey, however, he and his companions lost their way, and came to the Ardennes, and to the very castle that Helias had caused to be erected. At the sight of it Pucius said, 'Behold, here we are in my country, for this castle appears to me exactly like that of Billoen.' They then went to an inn in the village that was adjacent to the castle, and inquired where they were, and received answers to all their questions, and were, moreover, informed that King Oriant and Beatrix had left Lillefort and taken their abode at Billoen, that they might be near their beloved son Helias. When Pucius heard this he was overjoyed and thanked God.

On the following morning he went to the castle of Billoen, and the king and queen with their children came to meet him, when Esmeri, recognising his clothes, asked him whence he came. Pucius answered, that he was in search of the knight of the swan, by whose wife he had been sent out. At this intelligence Esmeri was rejoiced, and announced it to the king and queen, to whom Pucius must then relate all concerning the duchess: he, moreover, told them that her grand-daughter, Ida, was married to the count of Bonen.[1] Pucius was now conducted into the castle and nobly entertained. On the following morning he accompanied Esmeri to Helias, whom they found on his knees at prayer. On recognising Pucius, the knight of the swan fell on his neck and kissed him, and inquired after the duchess and his daughter. Pucius informed him of everything, and

1 Boulogne.

received from him his wedding ring to take to the duchess as a token, and also many costly presents for Ida.

Pucius immediately set out on his way home, after having taken leave of King Oriant and Beatrix, from whom he likewise received precious gifts for his mistress, and shortly after arrived in Billoen, just as the duchess with her daughter and son-in-law were sitting at table. Having presented the ring to the duchess, together with the other presents he recounted all his adventures. At his narrative the duchess was highly gratified, and with her daughter immediately made preparations for their journey; but the count of Bonen remained at home with his three sons, Godfrey, Baldwin and Eustace.

When the two ladies arrived at the castle of Billoen, they learned that Helias was lying in his bed sick, and were sadly grieved thereat. But Helias called them to him, and they all wept for joy at seeing each other again so unexpectedly. A few days afterwards Helias became worse, and his malady at length so increased that he died. This event caused such affliction to the duchess that she fell sick and soon followed her consort to the grave. Ida then, reluctant to remain where she had suffered such heavy losses, returned to her husband, and the people mourned bitterly for a long time.

## Popular Belief[1]

1 If a bride tears her bridal dress, it is not good: she will undergo much trouble.

2 A person should never give away the rings of dead friends or relatives: it is a sure sign that the giver will also soon die.

3 If a loaf lies topsy-turvy, it is not good.

4 If a knife lies the wrong way (verkeerd), it forebodes quarrelling.

5 If fire springs out on the hearth, you may be sure of soon receiving a visit.

6 To see ladybirds forebodes good luck.

7 Those who do not like cats will not get handsome wives.

8 Monday's haste is seldom good.

9 If the skeleton of a horse's foot be placed in the stable, the horses cannot be bewitched.

10 To recover from an ague, let a person tie his garter round the gallows.

---

1   From Wolf's *Wodana*, Gent, 1843, pp. 110–114, and pp. 221–225.

11 Between Easter and Whitsuntide the unfortunate make love.

12 The eggs of Maundy Thursday (Witten Donderdag) are good against thunder and lightning.[1]

13 St John's wort gathered before sunrise is good against lightning.

14 To be lucky at play, a person should carry about him a clover leaf of four lobes.

15 It is not good to comb the hair or cut the nails on a Friday.

16 A spider seen in the morning forebodes good luck; in the afternoon bad luck.

17 For an ague it is good to enclose a spider between the two halves of a nutshell, and wear it about the neck.[2]

18 To cure the toothache, rub the teeth with a bone from the churchyard: it is an infallible remedy.

19 If the bed of a dying person stands in a cross direction with the rafters, he will have a long and painful death.

20 Two forks across forebode strife or enmity.

21 To overthrow a saltcellar is not good: strife will follow.

22 When an egg is eaten the shell should be broken.

23 To be secure against ague, eat on Easter-day two eggs that were weighed on Good Friday.

24 To eat no flesh on Easter-day is good for the toothache.

25 If a person feels a tickling in the palm of the hand, he will receive money.

26 The howling of a dog forebodes the death of a person in the neighbourhood.

27 If on Christmas Eve you take a piece of fir and stick it in the fire, but let it not be quite burnt out, and put what remains under the bed, thunder will never fall on the house.

28 Three candles burning in one room forebode a marriage.[3]

29 Rain on Friday rain on Sunday.

30 It is not good to be married on a Friday.

31 To get out of bed with the right foot first forebodes good luck for the whole day.

---

1   In Denmark on this day (Hvid-torsdag) the peasants put nine kinds of herbs in their soup. The Germans have a similar superstition.
2   See Ashmole's *Diary*.
3   In such case the Danes say, 'O there is a bride in the room.'

32 Eggs laid on Whit-Sunday should be carefully preserved. If there be a fire, let one of them be cast into the flames, and the fire will have no more power.

33 If a bride desires to have good luck and prosperity in her wedded state, she must, on coming out of the church from her wedding, enter her house under two sabres laid crosswise over the door.

34 Eggs laid during the twelve days of Christmas should be carefully preserved; and if a hen is about to sit, place them under her, when all the other eggs under her will produce beautiful, large chickens.

35 On Christmas night, at twelve o'clock, all the cattle rise up and continue standing for some time, and then again lie down.

36 Nothing that is sown on Christmas Eve perishes, although it should be sown on the snow.

37 If the sun shines on Candlemas day (2nd February), the flax will prosper.

38 That which is sown on Shrove Tuesday will always continue green.

39 As many fogs as there are in March, so many bad fogs will come also after Easter, and in August.

40 On St Andrew's day, place a glass full of water on a table: if it runs over spontaneously, a wet year may be looked for; but if it continues full, that indicates a dry year.

41 To wash the hands well in the morning is a powerful means against witches and sorceresses.

42 If the sun shines while it rains, the witches are baking cakes.

43 Mistletoe hung over the bed is good against the nightmare.

44 If a woman desires to have a compliant husband, let her take old iron nails, of which let a ring be made on a Friday during mass, and afterwards lay the gospels upon it, and say a Paternoster daily. Then if she wears that ring on her finger, she will have a husband ready to grant her wishes for a year.

45 If a woman wishes her husband to love her, let her take a portion of her hair and offer it on the altar thrice with a lighted wax taper. As long as she carries that on her head, he will cherish a fervent love for her.

46 When a cold trembling creeps over the limbs, it is usual for a person to say: 'They are riding over my grave.'

47 When it rains while the sun shines there is a fair in hell.

48 Two knives laid across forebode misfortune.

49 When a child falls into the fire, you must, before taking it out, turn the

loaf, if it lies topsy-turvy. In Dendermonde and thereabouts they make a cross on the loaf with a knife.

50 Unlucky at play, lucky in marriage.

51 He has a mole's foot in his bag, is said of one that wins at play.

52 When the cats sit with their backs turned to the fire, it will rain.

53 If a person has long had the ague, to get rid of it he should tie a wisp of straw to a tree at the moment when the fit is coming on, and then run till the fit is past.

54 To turn a chair round forebodes fighting.

55 Mariners promise to eat no flesh on Easter-day, that they may be safe from storms at sea.

56 A tickling in the palm of the hand betokens the getting of blows.

57 In Furnes nobody will hire a maidservant on a Friday, nor will a maid enter her service on that day.

58 The person towards whom at dinner the point of a knife, that lies with the edge up, is directed, will be married within that year.

59 If two persons in a company, at the same moment, begin telling the same piece of news, they will be married at the same time.

60 Boiling dishwater betokens that the person who has to wash the dishes will not be married within seven years.

61 For thirteen to sit at table it is ill-boding. The person that then sits under the beam is a traitor. Of the thirteen one will die in that year.

62 To see lambs when out walking is good; pigs and crows bad. To see a crow flying over the paternal roof signifies bad news – misfortune.

63 Dandelion. Children blow off the feathery seeds and ask: 'How old shall I be?' As often as they blow before the last are blown off, so many years will they live. The girls ask on the same occasion: 'Does he love me? Yes – a little – much – no.' The word that is uttered when the last seeds fly off is the sentiment which they imagine to be in the breast of their lover. The same operation is performed with the dandelion, in order to know what o'clock it is.

64 Many persons, when their leg, their arm, their hand or their foot is *asleep,* make a cross on it with the thumb, to make the tingling cease. Others, when they gape, make a cross before the mouth.

65 When a drowned person is touched by a near kinsman, he begins to bleed at the nose.

66 When the ducks dive, bad weather may be expected. The rain will soon cease when the chickens take shelter.

67 A sorceress cannot rise from sitting if a woman clandestinely places her wedding ring under her chair.[1]

68 When after cutting the hair you throw the cuttings into a fire of green wood, the hair will never grow afterwards.

69 Hair that is cut off should never be thrown into the street: it may be taken up by a witch, who by its means can bewitch the person to whom it belonged.

70 When a person sneezes and no one says, 'God bless you,' a witch has power to bewitch the sneezer.

71 If a woman loses her wedding ring, she will soon be separated from her husband by death or otherwise.

72 Neither a knife nor scissors may be given to a friend: they cut love.

73 Let no one take a bone home with him from the churchyard: the dead will torment him till he returns it.[2]

74 If a knife be thrown off the table and fall on the back, it betokens an approaching wedding.

75 When the priest during mass turns and says *orate fratres*, he closes his eyes, that he may not see the witches, who then stand all with their backs towards the altar.

76 If a little spark shines on the wick of a candle, it betokens unexpected news. When many such sparks shine round the flame, forming a circle, then will a person triumph over his enemies.

77 In conjuring the devil it is necessary to have a light; words spoken in the dark having no power.

78 If a damsel cannot endure a dog, she will never get a good husband.

79 If a person is troubled with ague, he should stand naked opposite to the rising sun, and at the same time repeat a certain number of Paternosters and angelical salutations.

80 St Lupus's Cake. They bake a triangular cake in honour of the Holy Trinity, making in it five holes, in remembrance of the five wounds of Christ. This they give as alms, in honour of St Lupus, to the first beggar that presents himself by chance, not intentionally; in the belief that their flocks and herds are thereby rendered secure from wolves (lupi). This custom is common about Tirlemont and Louvain.

---

1 See a similar superstition at p. 609.
2 See p. 637–8.

81 It is a custom to immerse the images of saints in water, in order to obtain rain.

82 If a person has an ague, let him go, early in the morning (in der uchte), to an old willow, make three knots in a branch, and say: 'Good-morning, old one; I give thee the cold; good-morning, old one!'[1]

---

1   Westendorp, *N. Myth.*, p. 518. See also p. 547.

# Index

# The Folklore Society

**What is folklore?**   Folklore has been defined as 'traditional culture', but no one phrase can do justice to the subject. It embraces music, song, dance, drama, narrative, language, foods, medicine, arts and crafts, religion, magic and belief. Folklore is the way that people fill their lives with meaning, through the stories they share, the daily rituals they perform. Folklore can be both the expression of our individuality and the source of a sense of community. From standing stones to biker gangs, from ancient riddles to the latest joke craze, from King Arthur to the playground, from birth to death, folklore is the stuff of life.

**The Folklore Society: who we are.**   Since 1878 The Folklore Society has provided a meeting-ground for both academics and enthusiasts eager to learn about popular culture and traditional life. The Society promotes awareness of folklore within universities, museums, festivals, in fact wherever traditional culture is discussed and researched.

The Society has an elected committee which aims to be responsive to its members' needs. It therefore embraces a number of specialist groups, such as the East Anglia Folklore Group, to make the Society accessible to all.

**The Folklore Society: what we do.**   In order to encourage awareness of folklore the Society organises events, prizes and research projects. It runs at least one conference a year, and hosts the annual Katharine Briggs memorial lecture.

The Society publishes its own academic journal, *Folklore*, in association with Routledge. It also produces numerous monographs and pamphlets, either under its own imprint, *FLS Books*, or in conjunction with other publishers.

In addition to the journal *Folklore*, members receive a regular newsletter, *FLS News*, through which they can call on the expertise of the entire Society. They also have access to a specialist library with both reference and lending facilities and a substantial archive. The library constitutes a unique resource for the study of folklore, old and new.

**The Folklore Society: how to contact us.**   For details about how to join The Folklore Society and about our forthcoming activities and publications, contact: The Folklore Society, University College London, Gower Street, London WC1E 6BT

Telephone: 020 7862 8564 (with voice mail)
E-mail: folklore.society@talk21.com
Website: www.folklore–society.com

The Folklore Society is a Registered Charity No.1074552